Skiing
in
the USA &
Canada

ISBN 0–679–02093–4

Fodor's Skiing in the USA & Canada

Editor: Staci Capobianco
Writers: Craig Altschul, Rosemary Freskos, Peggi Simmons, Guy Thibaudeau
Contributors: Don Bilodeau, John Colebourne, Diana Hunt, Sara Widness
Illustrations: Alida Beck
Cover Photograph: Devore/Photographers, Aspen

Cover Design: Vignelli Associates

Special Sales

CONTENTS

FOREWORD

In North America, we are blessed with some of the best skiing in the world. Some of our peaks are up to 12,000 feet high with as much as 4,000 vertical feet of skiable terrain. The powder in Utah and the Bugaboos of British Columbia are legendary. Skiers come from all over the world to experience "champagne powder" and "white smoke," the epitome of snow quality.

The diversity of skiing on this continent is also unmatched elsewhere. There are nearly 1,000 ski areas in the United States and Canada, many offering cross country in addition to alpine skiing. There's something for everyone, and there's skiing almost everywhere. Only nine American states do not have alpine skiing. Even Hawaii has skiing on Mauna Kea in January and February. And in Canada, all provinces have a good choice of alpine centers.

Skiing in North America also comes with flair, from skiing *à la Française* in Quebec to cowboy skiing in the American West. Après-ski runs the gamut from guitar pickin' in New England to big-time stage productions and international entertainment in the Lake Tahoe region.

Fodor's Skiing in the USA & Canada is designed to help you plan your own ski trip based on your time, your budget, your energy, and your idea of what the trip should be. Perhaps after having read this guide, you'll have some new ideas.

This guide does not claim to list all ski areas in the United States and Canada. Rather, we have tried to select those areas we feel offer the most attractions for a skiing vacation. The areas were chosen for being among the best destinations or for their importance as day-trip areas near major metropolises. The choices were not easy, and you may not find your favorite local ski area included.

While every care has been taken to ensure the accuracy of the information in this guide, the passage of time will always bring change, and consequently the publisher cannot accept responsibility for errors that may occur.

All prices and opening times quoted in this guide are based on information supplied to us at press time. Hours and admission fees may change, however, and the prudent traveler will avoid inconvenience by calling ahead.

Fodor's wants to hear about your travel experiences, both pleasant and unpleasant. When a hotel or restaurant fails to live up to its billing, let us know and we will investigate the complaint and revise our entries where the facts warrant it.

Send your letters to the editors of Fodor's Travel Publications, 201 E. 50th Street, New York, NY 10022.

FACTS AT YOUR FINGERTIPS

by

GUY THIBAUDEAU

PLANNING YOUR SKI VACATION. One of the wisest precautions in preparing a ski vacation is to take the time to plan it well. We all know that if you throw enough money at something, it will correct itself, but most of us are not that fortunate and planning is important. Here are some considerations to bear in mind as you make your plans.

Who's Going. Your companions will have a major impact on just about every aspect of your ski vacation. If you go alone or with your friend or mate, you'll probably be happier in a full service hotel where you will spend the minimum amount of time housekeeping and the most time skiing and having a good time. However, if you are planning for a family or if you'll be traveling with children, some additional considerations come into play.

Traveling. Traveling may be half the fun of a vacation. However, carrying skis, boots, paraphernalia, and luggage from car to plane to bus while keeping track of young children can make traveling an ordeal if the trip is too long or not properly planned. Selecting an area that will require the fewest transfers en route is an important consideration.

Areas relatively close to major airports should be considered first, especially those within a few hours' flying time of your home. The larger the group, the simpler your travel arrangements should be. Check for direct flights from your home airport to the gateway city. Excellent ski gateways are Denver; Salt Lake City; Seattle; Portland, Oregon; and Montreal. From each airport you can reach a number of large destination resorts within 2 hours. Resorts such as Aspen, Sun Valley, and the Lake Tahoe areas may be great but entail longer traveling time, more transfers, and greater frustrations if you have a group in tow. Several major resorts have become more accessible of late with direct connections and major airline service to smaller airports right at or near the ski resort. Steamboat, Colorado, and Jackson Hole, Wyoming, are but two resorts that have added big-league air service from major U.S. airports. The same considerations of traveling time apply to automobile travel. While the logistics are less complex, you should try to avoid those 8–10 hour drives with children. Careful planning and proper mountain selection will avoid the children's version of the Chinese water torture: "When are we going to get there?"

Choice of Mountain. One of the biggest misconceptions is that "the larger the mountain, the greater the fun." Nothing could be farther from the truth, particularly with children. Small children like small things, and while you may think that junior will have the thrill of a lifetime riding the tram at a large mountain, he or she would quite likely be as happy—probably happier—on the T-bar and the bunny slope at a smaller area. The tremendous success of 620-foot Gray Rocks as a destination resort in the Laurentians north of Montreal is proof that big is not always better.

You may find it as much fun simply driving to Okemo from New York City, to Cannon Mountain from Boston, to Mont Ste-Anne from Montreal, or to Alta from Salt Lake City, rather than going through the tribulations of organizing everyone for a long, sometimes complicated flight to a big-name resort.

Consider the skiing skills of those in your party. Beginners will do better at a smaller area where they will not be overwhelmed by the mountain's size. The largest areas do cater to beginners, but the more accomplished skier will make better use of the mountain, while the novice will be limited to a certain area, often the lower slopes. And since beginners are almost always in ski school, learning on a smaller mountain can be just as rewarding as doing it on a larger and often colder and windier peak.

As you choose your mountain, be weary of a ski area's pamphlets that claim "something for everyone." There is no question that all areas have easy and difficult trails, but many areas have more of one than the other. For example, you won't want to initiate your paranoid in-law at Snowbird, Jackson Hole, or even Squaw Valley or Stowe. These mountains have reputations for macho skiing and will eat up unwary skiers. They overwhelm the first-time skier and do not help build the novice's confidence. If the first thing you must tell your group on arrival at the area is that slopes on the other side are easier, you've probably chosen the wrong area.

On the other hand, ski areas such as Winter Park, Park City, Alpine Meadows, Mount Snow, Mont Ste-Anne, and others, while they do have difficult runs for the advanced skier, are better suited to the beginner if only for the fact that easier runs are easily accessible from the base area.

Choice of Accommodations. Your choice of accommodations will depend on who's going. Singles or couples will have more leeway; families must be more selective. The larger the group, the more advantageous it is to look at the seemingly pricier condo and slopeside accommodations. Condominiums usually have room for anywhere from 4 to 10 people, and when the cost is split, it usually works out quite reasonably. You'll also save a bundle on meals for children in a fully equipped condo. Getting the family organized in the morning is another consideration. Ski-in, ski-out lodging lets you come and go as you please. Depending on buses and shuttles compounds the problem of getting to the slopes and requires better planning on your part. Of course it's no secret that the closer the accommodations are to the hill, the higher the price.

Budget. This is not necessarily the final consideration. For most of us, it's a part of every aspect of planning. Your budget and availability will affect almost every move you make.

You'll pay more, of course, in high season—Christmas to New Year's, as well as mid-February to mid-March, George Washington's Birthday, and in some cases Easter.

Ski packages are always your best bet if you're on a tight budget. The more included in your package price, the fewer the surprises when you get there. Find out if the tour package includes air fare (including your skis), transfer between airport and resort, accommodations, taxes and gratuities, lift tickets, meals, transport from your hotel to the slopes, and lessons.

The farther from the area, generally, the cheaper the accommodations. However, seemingly expensive on-mountain condos shared by several people can actually be a bargain. Good deals can often be had at smaller inns, where the overhead is smaller and the smiles often larger.

Length of stay is a direct factor in budgeting, although the longer the stay, the cheaper the per diem cost of your vacation. Most resorts now offer a choice of either two-day weekends, three- or four-day mini-ski weeks, or full-week packages. Excellent deals are often available at the large destination resorts for the weekend—staying over Saturday night—since ski-weekers usually leave Saturday with the new guests arriving on Sunday, so there are vacancies on Saturday night.

PACKAGE DEALS

Airlines and Travel Agents. All major airlines that fly to major ski gateway airports can offer you various package options when you fly with them. Packages are available for just about anywhere in North America. Many airlines offer fly-drive options where a rental car is thrown in; this is something to consider when traveling as a group, and particularly with a family. Other ski vacations are available as ground packages that you can combine with the flight option of your choice. These are not always the cheapest, but are often the most convenient. Continental Airlines, for example, whose hub airport is Denver's Stapleton, has a series of packages to over 19 top ski resorts in the Rockies. The deal includes lodging, lift tickets, and airfare, and trips start as low as $420 for a seven-day package. Continental can also arrange for rentals, lessons, and ground transportation from the airport, all with one phone call. Other airlines offer similar deals.

Ski Shows. One of the best places for ski travel information is your local ski show, usually held in most major markets between late September and early December. These are well advertised through the local media and are always listed in the "Coming Events" columns of magazines such as *Ski, Skiing, Snow Country, Powder,* and *Ski Canada* as well as in regional publications. Represented at ski shows are most of the main destination resorts accessible from your area as well as the smaller local areas where you will likely do most of your skiing. This is a great opportunity for you to talk to area representatives, people who live and ski there and know the area inside out. It's the best way to get the inside track and find out what the brochures don't say.

Airlines and tour operators are there as well, along with independent lodges. You can shop around for the best package deal or see if you can do better by making your own arrangements with the independent lodge and using a super-saver fare of some sort. Pick up literature for the areas that might interest you and take it home for further analysis.

Ski Clubs. In areas far away from the mountains, ski clubs are often an excellent source of ski travel information and travel deals. Oddly enough, it seems that the farther from the snow or the mountains, the more and better the ski clubs. Some of the best are found in Miami, Chicago, Atlanta, and London. Here you'll meet skiers who have experienced many different resorts, and their advice should help you decide on a package and an area.

You can get in touch with local ski clubs at a ski show by looking in the Yellow Pages of your telephone book, by contacting your local ski association, through a ski shop in your region, or by asking other skiers.

Ski Books and Magazines. Ski travel books such as this one will provide you with a wealth of information on preparing your vacation as well as on the major ski areas. They can be quite enlightening and helpful. Ski magazines such as *Ski, Skiing, Snow Country, Powder,* and *Ski Canada* will feature many destination resorts as well as some smaller, local areas. They can help convey the particular excitement and attraction of the resort with color photographs and the most current developments. They also carry travel guides and advertising with telephone numbers and addresses, so you can write for more details. Local ski publications can do the same while adding information on travel opportunities in your region.

Ski resort brochures can give you an excellent idea of what an area is all about, but remember that sales brochures are made to sell and will always make any area look like Shangri-La. If you read between the lines, however, you'll get a good idea of what the area has to offer. A well-produced brochure with color photographs showing the most recent improvements to the area is a sure sign of a first-class resort. However, if pictures are out of focus and skiers are depicted in baggie pants, you can probably surmise that the rope tow hasn't been greased in a while and that "quaint" and "rustic" are likely to be the best adjectives to describe the area.

Color trail maps in advertising brochures sometimes project a distorted picture of the area's size and slope difficulty. The use of shadows to accentuate steepness can often make trails seem much more difficult and the mountain higher than they are in reality. Check out the area's vertical rise, number of trails, and number of trails of your skiing ability. Look for a good proportion of top-to-bottom runs of your ability. There's no sense going to a 3,000-foot mountain if your type of skiing is limited only to part of the top or part of the bottom.

Regional, state, or provincial material on skiing vacations in different parts of the world is also available from state, provincial, or national tourist offices or the local chambers of commerce.

Finally, make sure your brochures and price lists are up to date. This is especially important when it comes to foreign destinations where prices are subject to fluctuations in exchange rates. What might have been a bargain two years ago could be out of your range today.

ACCOMMODATIONS. Lodging can run anywhere from dormitories and bed-and-breakfasts all the way to expensive hotel suites and luxurious condominiums, and the price range is just as wide. Getting a fix on value is not always easy, since per-day charges will vary with what's included and with the proximity to the lifts. There are essentially three package options:

European Plan (EP): no meals (except possibly for Continental breakfast) included.

American Plan (AP): all meals included.

Modified American Plan (MAP): breakfast and dinner included as part of the price. (This is the most common and practical option since it is not always possible or desirable to come back from the mountain to the hotel or lodge to grab lunch.)

In some instances, a ski-week package will include your lift ticket, so it's important to weigh that cost in the overall price of your stay. Some lodges also have free transportation in the way of a resort bus or hotel shuttle to the lifts and back. This is also a cost saver since it eliminates the need for a rental car. Some places also provide free accommodations and sometimes free skiing for children under 12 when they stay in the same room as their parents.

Small inns and lodges are what ski holidays were meant for in the first place, and it's a treat to be able to enjoy them. Don't expect color TV or exercise and video rooms here (although many inns and lodges are integrating these facilities). What these places lack in modern amenities they more than make up for in homey comfort, charm, and warmth. Your dealings are often directly with the owners, who are more sensitive to your needs and to your comfort. They usually serve breakfast and dinner, and in most cases you can have seconds without additional charge, a good thing after a rugged day on the mountain. They're usually quite reasonably priced and are more suited for couples or smaller families. They're not that popular with the singles crowd. However, you must beware—nowadays many so-called inns can turn out to be concrete towers.

There are now a wider variety of **hotels** popping up at ski resorts, including Hiltons, Sheratons, and Holiday Inns. There is probably a need for these or they wouldn't be there in the first place, but those flashy blocks of concrete and glass always look out of place in a mountain setting. For convenience, however, they can't be beat: color TV and phone in every room, built-in minibar, elevators, dining rooms and coffee shops, pools, saunas, Jacuzzis, exercise and game rooms—the works.

But there are other, more alpine hotels, usually wooden structures with fewer than 50 rooms, that will give you the feeling of being away from it all. Hotels that have the conveniences of the larger places but not their impersonal traits are good for almost everyone, especially when rooms are equipped with kitchenettes.

Condominiums are offered almost everywhere now, and there are so many different versions of condos these days—apartment-hotels, condominiums, condo hotels, time-share units, etc.—that it has become in many resorts the principal form of accommodation. The condo offers you the comforts of home, and while the initial cost may seem high, it can be shared because most condos will accommodate from 4 to 10 people. Condominiums are also ideal for families and large groups. You'll save on food because you can inexpensively cook your own meals instead of having to pay restaurant prices. In fact, with a condo you can more or less discount your cost of eating; you'd be eating the same amount if you were home.

Reservations and Deposits. Reservations are necessary most of the time, the only exceptions being before December 15 or after the beginning of April. Remember that high-season reservations are often booked long in advance and the Christmas and New Year's weeks are sometimes booked a full year or more ahead at the most popular resorts.

When booking your stay with a lodge, inn, or condo hotel, you'll be expected to send a deposit that will guarantee your reservation. Deposit policy varies with the establishments, but you'll be required to send 25–50 percent of the total cost of your stay when you reserve. The remainder will be payable on arrival. Be sure to find out about the hotel's payment policy: Which credit cards are accepted? Will they take your personal check?

FACTS ABOUT THE REGIONS. You will find descriptions of each region and its ski areas in the pages that follow, but as an overview, here is some general information to help you understand the differences between them.

Eastern United States

There are well over 100 alpine ski areas in Maine, New Hampshire, Vermont, and New York alone. They range anywhere from a couple of hundred feet vertical to as much as 3,200 feet at Whiteface, 3,060 feet at Killington, 2,600 feet at Sugarloaf and Sugarbush, and 2,350 feet at Stowe. Ski season has been stretched considerably in the East, thanks to snowmaking systems that allow most areas to open at least a few trails by Thanksgiving. Some centers are out for records; Killington prides itself on being the first to open and the last to close, with skiing from October to June (albeit extremely limited at either end). Snowfall, like the weather, is irregular in the East, and temperature is subject to considerable fluctuation. The biggest snowfalls in the East tend to come in February and March, so snowmaking has become a critical element in guaranteeing good skiing, and the number of trails covered with machine-made snow at an area is an important factor to consider.

Early-season skiing in the East is marginal at best despite claims otherwise, but late-season skiing is usually the best, partly because the ski slopes are often deserted.

Eastern snow is hard snow, but with sophisticated machine grooming, trails are resurfaced daily at the major areas. While the "hard stuff" is not yet a thing of the past, you are now less likely to encounter "boiler plate" conditions.

Eastern skiing is trail skiing except for the "snowfields" at the top of Sugarloaf. Trail selection is excellent, ranging from easy, unintimidating beginners' slopes found virtually everywhere to the icy chutes of Stowe's "Front Four" and the Volkswagen-sized moguls of Killington's Bear Mountain.

Access to all Eastern U.S. resorts is mainly by automobile, since there are few resorts of any size near major metropolitan areas. You should keep in mind, however, that some northern resorts are closer to Montreal than they are to major U.S. cities. Jay Peak and Smugglers' Notch are 2 hours from Montreal, Whiteface, 90 minutes; Stowe and Sugarbush, about 2½ hours.

The size of the ski area becomes more important in the East if you plan on being there for a full week. If you can ski all the trails on your first day, you may get bored by midweek. But anything with over 2,000 vertical feet is pretty respectable.

The Midwest

This is the training ground for ski vacationers to either the West or East. One might be tempted to neglect these 400–500-foot vertical mountains, but they play a major role in initiating new skiers. As Bill Hibbard, *Ski Magazine's* Midwest editor, puts it, "It's not the size that counts, it's the punch." What ski areas here lack in size, they make up for in quality: excellent ski schools and lots of lifts like at Boyne, Michigan, which has 10 lifts including three quadruple chairs and snowmaking on 90 percent of its slopes, all on less than a 500-foot vertical. However, unless you live in the region and have a limited budget, these mountains are not your ultimate ski destination. But as for any of the larger resorts, they'll do fine for anyone learning to ski and they'll cost you less!

The Rockies

This is the region skiers dream of: Colorado, Utah, Wyoming, New Mexico, and Idaho. Here are the country's oldest destination ski resorts and the ones with reputations as big as their mountains. Skiing here is done mostly between 5,000 feet and 11,000 feet, with plenty of above-tree-line skiing.

With almost 40 different resorts, Colorado is the most popular destination state. Snow is usually abundant, although snowmaking has appeared at several areas since the drought of the early 1980s. But snowmaking is not the staple it is in the East. It is usually used to start up areas should natural snow not be sufficient by Thanksgiving.

Two of the country's premiere resorts, Vail/Beaver Creek and Aspen, spearhead Colorado's reputation. But rising stars such as the Winter Park/Mary Jane complex, a favorite of Denverites; the Summit County areas of Keystone/Arapahoe Basin, Breckenridge, and Copper Mountain; and the isolated but high-spirited Steamboat and Crested Butte are solid backups for the leaders and are quickly developing strong reputations of their own.

Utah, although less frequented, has some of the world's best powder skiing, particularly at Alta and Snowbird and, to some extent, at Park City and Deer Valley (which is certainly the most luxurious area in the U.S.). And with the developing Utah Interconnect—linking Park City to Snowbird via Brighton and Solitude—the state is tops for skiing. Unusual state liquor and entertainment laws, however, limit the attraction for those looking for more than great skiing.

Difficult to get to but worth every mile is Sun Valley, Idaho, the nation's first world-class ski resort, which was opened in 1936 by Averell Harriman. The Sun Valley Lodge has been host to the best, the richest, the most powerful, and the most beautiful. And you can add your name to the list.

For challenge it's hard to beat Jackson Hole, Wyoming, where a 66-passenger aerial tram will take you to some of the country's most devastatingly steep chutes. Skiers entering Corbett's Couloir, for example, must lower themselves from a rope anchored on the cornice or jump in with a Hail Mary!

The Rockies are unquestionably American skiing at its best, and your only problem here is choosing among the wide variety of excellent resorts.

The West Coast

This region is fast emerging as a force in the destination area market. It has, in fact, some of the largest ski areas in the country. Mammoth, California, although a solid 6 hours from Los Angeles by car, is America's busiest resort, with somewhere in the vicinity of 1.5 million skier visits annually. Nestled around magnificent Lake Tahoe are half a dozen of the United States' most beautiful areas, led by Squaw Valley, the site of the 1960 Winter Olympics; its neighbor Alpine Meadows; and Heavenly Valley, where a 4,000-foot vertical makes it the area with the highest vertical drop in the country.

This is skiing in the High Sierra where the sun shines more than 80 percent of the time and they measure snowfalls in feet, not inches. If God's a skier, this is where He hangs out! It is one of the few regions in the United States where snowmaking firms have not made any major forays. With 400–500 inches of annual snowfall in some areas, the prospects for big sales are dim.

The snow is not, however, the same "champagne powder" as that found in Utah. Because of the milder climate, Sierra snow can often be moist and heavy; some call it "Sierra Cement," but it quickly develops a good, powdery consistency. Snow comes early and leaves late, and ski areas consistently run out of skiers before they run out of snow. If you want to ski late—into June at some areas—you can't go wrong with the West Coast and the Pacific Northwest.

Entertainment around Lake Tahoe is unmatched elsewhere in the skiing world. Nightclubs in nearby Reno and Stateline on the Nevada–California border at Heavenly Valley feature top entertainment and nightclub acts, along with gambling around every corner. All the big Las Vegas clubs are represented here as well: Harrah's, Caesars Palace, Circus Circus, and the MGM Grand Hotel with its fabulous stage shows.

Eastern Canada

Although there is some alpine skiing in Ontario, much of it is "club" skiing and resembles the U.S. Midwest. Eastern Canada destination skiing is basically found in Quebec. Skiing and the weather here compare quite well with the American East Coast and New England. But the big difference lies in the culture; this is French Canada, an area unlike anywhere else on this continent. Quebecers call it "Skiing à la Française," and that's 75 percent of the reason skiers are drawn here. The province's highest mountains, Mont Tremblant and Mont Ste-Anne, are just slightly over 2,000 vertical feet and, like other eastern centers, depend heavily on snowmaking.

Ski season runs from late November to mid-April with Gray Rocks, the dean of Canadian snowmaking, always the last to shut down in early May. The best part of the season is February to the end of March.

Here again, a favorable exchange rate for American visitors can weigh heavily in a decision of where to go for a skiing holiday.

Western Canada

In British Columbia, the mountains and climate are similar to the U.S. West Coast, with high mountains on the coast and somewhat smaller mountains at higher elevations in the interior. Ninety minutes north of Vancouver is Whistler-Blackcomb, a twin-peak resort that offers the highest vertical drop in North America, 5,280 feet. It is the home of summer racing camps and of Nancy Greene, who with Jean Claude Killy in 1966 and 1967 won the first two World Cup championships.

In the interior are several smaller but excellent areas where the snow is dry and regular and the crowds nonexistent. Ski areas like Fernie Snow Valley and Kimberley exceed 2,000 vertical feet, while Panorama at Invermere fetches 3,200 feet. These are more or less "local" areas, partly because they haven't been discovered yet and partly because their winter tourist industry is not yet sufficiently developed.

On the border between British Columbia and Alberta is every skier's dream—the best helicopter skiing in the world. This is a costly proposition, but one every serious skier must at least wish for. Across the Continental Divide lie the Alberta ski centers with the largest, Lake Louise, in a class by itself for all-around fine skiing. Sunshine Village near Banff is the one with the most above-tree-line skiing and the most dependable conditions. It is the last one to close, and only for lack of skiers. The newest resort in Alberta is Nakiska at Mount Allan, the Olympic mountain, site of the 1988 Winter Games. With over 3,000 vertical feet, it sits on the Eastern slope of the Canadian Rockies. Canadian Rockies skiing, while less developed than in the United States, can certainly match it slope for slope. And for Americans coming here, the favorable exchange rate makes the trip that much sweeter.

ENTERING CANADA. Customs regulations between the United States and Canada are among the most liberal in the world. Passing from one country to the other is usually a simple matter of presenting some valid and acceptable form of identification and answering a few simple questions about where you were born, where you live, why you are visiting Canada, and how long you will stay.

The identification need not be a passport, although this is certainly acceptable. You can also use a birth certificate, draft card, social security card, certificate of naturalization, or resident alien ("green") card. The entry procedure for citizens of Great Britain, Australia, and New Zealand is similarly simple.

Canada allows British and American guests to bring their cars (for less than 6 months), boats or canoes, rifles and shotguns (but not handguns or automatic weapons) and 200 rounds of ammunition, cameras, radios, sports equipment, and laptop computers into the country without paying any duty. Sometimes they will require a deposit for trailers and household equipment, but these are refundable when you cross back over the border. (This is to guarantee that you do not sell these items in Canada for a profit.) Needless to say, you may bring clothing, personal items, and any professional tools or equipment you need (if you work in Canada) without charge or restriction. It is also a good idea to carry your medical insurance and insurance for boats, vehicles, and personal luggage.

Some items are restricted, however. You need the contract for a rented car. And, if you are going to return home and leave behind a car you rented in the States, you have to fill out an E29B customs form. Tobacco is limited. Dogs, for hunting or pets, are duty-free, but you must bring a certificate from a veterinary inspector to prove that the dog has no communicable diseases. (Cats may enter without restriction.) All plants must be examined at the customs station to preclude the entry of destructive insects. Most important, Canadian officials are diligent in pursuing smugglers of narcotics and other illegal items.

MONEY. In the **Canadian chapters** of this guide, **all prices are listed in Canadian dollars.** The Canadian dollar, like the U.S. dollar, is divided into 100 cents, and coins and bills exist in the same denominations as in the U.S.—i.e., 1¢, 5¢, 10¢, etc.; $2, $5, $10, etc. A $1 coin was introduced in 1987. It is nicknamed the "looney," a reference to the loon that dominates one side of it.

Actual exchange rates fluctuate from day to day, but the Canadian dollar is usually worth about 88 U.S. cents and about 48 British pence. In order to get the most for your money, convert it before you leave home. Failing that, all Canadian banks can exchange U.S. funds at current market rates. Canadian banks are generally open 10 A.M. to 3 P.M., and some larger outlets are open longer hours Thursdays and Fridays. Most hotels, stores, and restaurants can change American dollars, but they may offer something less than the best rate. The best policy is to find the nearest

Thomas Cook foreign exchange office. There are Thomas Cook bureaus in Vancouver (617 Granville); Toronto (10 King St. E. and 55 Bloor St. W.); and Montreal (1155 Sherbrooke St. W.).

There are no restrictions on the amount of money you may bring into or take out of Canada. Both Canadians and foreign visitors may convert money from Canadian tender to another currency or from a foreign currency to Canadian dollars as often as they want, in amounts as great as they want, either inside or outside Canada.

TIPS FOR BRITISH VISITORS. Passports. You will need a valid passport and a U.S. Visitor's Visa (which can only be put in a passport of the 10-year kind) to enter the United States. You can obtain the visa either through your travel agent or airline or directly from the *United States Embassy,* Visa and Immigration Department, 5 Upper Grosvenor Square, London W1A 2JB (071–499–3443). You must apply by mail; allow six weeks.

Insurance. We recommend that you insure yourself to cover any possible health and motoring mishaps. *Europ Assistance,* 252 High Street, Croydon CR0 1NF (081–680–1234), is one such insurance provider.

Tour operators. From the United Kingdom, the main tour operators who offer ski packages to the United States and Canada are *American Dream,* 4 Station Parade, High St. North, London E6 1JD (081–470–1181), which offers packages to a wide range of resorts, including Aspen, Heavenly Valley, Jackson Hole, and Vail. *Canada Air Holidays,* 50 Sauchiehall St., Glasgow 623 AD (041–332–1511). *Continental Airlines Ski Vacations,* Beulah Court, Albert Rd., Horley, Surrey RH6 7HZ (0293–776979). *Hickie Borman Holidays,* 73 High St., Ewell, Surrey KT17 1RX (081–393–0127) offers packages to Breckenridge, Crested Butte, and resorts in Canada. *Intasun Skiscene,* Intersun House, 2 Cromwell Ave., Bromley, Kent BR2 9AQ (081–851–3321). *Skiscope,* Grosvenor Hall, Bolnore Rd., Haywards Heath, West Sussex RH16 4BX (0444 – 441000), offers packages to Aspen.

WHEN TO SKI. All brochures and ski area literature claim ideal skiing and weather conditions extend from November to late April or early May. However, there are definitely periods that are better than others. They wouldn't charge a premium price otherwise, would they?

It is difficult to understand the rush to get out on the boards by mid-November when snow cover is marginal, but in the East enthusiasm brings skiers out early, enticed by the first snowflakes and the cold that makes snowmaking possible. Ski areas searching for added revenues are now into promoting skiing at Thanksgiving, but a ski-week that early, unless it is to learn to ski, will only get you out in the worst part of the season. The snow is thin, machine-made snow only covers a few trails, and days are short and often gray. Doesn't seem like much fun, does it? On the other hand, in late March and early April, when snow depths are at their highest, ski areas are in full operation, and the days are longer with the sun warm and inviting, ski areas can't give their ski packages away. But anticipation is half the fun, it is said, and that's why people will pay $30 to ski a few trails at Vail in November but won't take the $5 offer to ski the whole wonderful area in late April.

Short of exceptionally favorable ski weather—meaning lots of early snow—skiing in the East before December 15 is usually dependent on the amount of machine-made snow produced. And while there may have been a good dump or two, the natural snow base is thin and you'll tear the bottom of your skis on all but the easiest runs and those with machine-made snow. By Christmas week, ski areas normally have more than 50 percent of their runs open and can be considered to offer good skiing.

In the West, early skiing is touch-and-go as well and depends on the timing of the first major storms that can come anytime from October to early December. However, most areas aim to open Thanksgiving on natural snow, or like everyone else, on machine-made.

January is usually a slow month for ski resorts and a good time to catch the best ski areas when they're not too busy. The snow by then is usually quite dry and powdery although temperatures are at their coldest. This is the best time to enjoy the legendary western powder, particularly in the Canadian and American Rockies and more specifically at powder heavens like Alta and Snowbird in Utah and in British Columbia's heli-skiing country.

February to mid-March is the most popular time everywhere and for obvious reasons: days are getting longer, the sun's a little higher, and the snow is usually quite dependable almost everywhere. The East gets its largest snowfalls during these months and, by then, the West has several feet of snow covering the trails. These are the busy times at all resorts and, along with Christmas, the periods for which you need to make your reservations far in advance.

But from mid-March on, when skiing and weather are often at their best, bookings start dropping off and by early April you can enjoy off-season rates at most resorts. This, in the opinion of many skiers, is the best time of the year unless you're a powderhound. And it will outclass by far any of the early-season skiing that is so anticipated.

The Late Season. Finally a word on very late-season skiing. While several areas are always trying to push the limits of winter further and further, there is a point of diminishing returns for both ski areas and skiers. After April 15 in the East, skiing becomes more of a freak show than real skiing and the areas that remain open do so more for the publicity they generate than for the great skiing they offer. Late-season skiing is only good when the nights are cold enough to freeze the snow. When the nights remain well above freezing, you ski in heavy corn snow and slush. Turning is difficult; if the same conditions were offered in January, they would be called dangerous. So while there is a certain kick out of skiing in May or June, it's far from being good skiing.

The only exceptions to this, of course, are high-altitude areas such as Arapahoe Basin, Colorado, with a summit elevation of 12,450 feet; Snowbird at 11,000 feet; Sunshine Village, Alberta, at 9,000 feet; Mount Bachelor and Timberline in Oregon, with more than 8,500 feet elevation; and Blackcomb Mountain in British Columbia, where there is year-round skiing on the summit glaciers.

ABOUT SNOWMAKING. Many still refer to machine-made snow as "artificial snow," as it was called in the early days. This conjures images of pulverized Styrofoam, crushed ice, and chemically generated snowflakes engineered in some laboratory. Nothing could be further from reality. In fact, the only thing artificial about it is the way it is made—not by nature but by men and machine. A more apt term would be natural snow made artificially, somewhat like a test-tube baby. It's real in every way.

Machine-made snow is produced simply by blowing water through a gun at a below-freezing temperature. The air pulverizes the water into tiny droplets that freeze on contact with the air. There are no chemicals added or needed to make snow, although areas will sometimes inject a bit of methanol to prevent freeze-up in the air pipes. High-tech snowmaking systems make use of computers to keep track of temperature swings, automatically controlling the amount of air needed to produce either the maximum amount of snow or the type of snow wanted.

Machine-made snow has done wonders for ski areas, particularly in the East and Midwest, where snow has lately been inadequate. It has created a new standard of quality in terms of coverage. Gone are the rocks, roots, and bare and thin spots that were accepted as part of the game as late as 1980. And while snowmaking does not cover 100 percent of all mountains, the new expectations prevent ski areas from opening trails that are inadequately covered. When one or a few trails are well covered, skiers don't want to ski the rougher, thinly covered natural snow runs.

In the East and Midwest, it bears repeating, snowmaking is a must. It is used to guarantee early-season skiing usually around mid- to late November, in time for Thanksgiving. Just as important, it is used extensively through the end of February or early March to build up and maintain a solid base, unaffected by the wild fluctuations of Eastern weather. It is also used to touch up areas that wear down from excess skier traffic and the continued grooming that also affects the snow. Among the greatest users of machine-made snow in the East are Killington, Vermont, where skiing starts in late October and extends into June, and Gray Rocks, in the Laurentians north of Montreal, certainly the only 600-foot mountain with a worldwide reputation and skiing every year into May.

Snowmaking, lo and behold, has even made forays into the Rockies where we have always been told that "snow is up to here . . . even up to there!" Well, as competitive and businesslike as skiing has become, it only took a couple of lean years in the early 1980s for the tenders to go out for pipes and compressors. But snowmaking here is not used in the same way and is not as critical as it is in the East.

Snowmaking in the Rockies is usually at the lower elevations and is used to start areas up in late November, should there be a shortage from the clouds. It is also used to prevent having to close down and refund deposits mid-winter in the event of a disastrous year, as happened in the early 1980s. This way, with a few trails covered and open, ski resorts are protected.

The only areas where snowmaking is really not needed is in Utah, where Alta and Snowbird sometimes wish they had a little less snow and a bit more sun, and in the High Sierras, where annual snowfalls of 300–500 inches have proved to be quite satisfactory.

Even European resorts are looking to snowmaking, since recent weather patterns in the Alps have played havoc with vacation and World Cup ski race schedules. The dependability of snowmaking has, in fact, been the saving grace for recent World Cup events, which were made up at North American snowmaking resorts after having been canceled for lack of snow in Europe.

One last note about snowmaking: It is more resistant to warm temperatures than natural snow since it has a higher density. Natural snowflakes are star shaped while machine-made snow is more like a solid pellet. It tends to make surfaces a bit harder than natural snow, but that's a small price to pay for good snow cover.

ABOUT GROOMING. Next to snowmaking, grooming is one of the areas where ski resorts have made their biggest strides. In the 1950s and 1960s, skiers were still pretty much left to themselves to pack the snow. As pleasant as this may be when the snow is light and powdery, it's no fun having to move "Sierra cement" or trying to edge on solid ice.

Grooming is one of the most important components of skiing and is something ski publications should do a better job of explaining. Weather being such an important element, saying a slope is "groomed" often projects the wrong idea of what snow conditions are like to the skier who is unaware of the marvels of modern-day technology.

Grooming tractors, "Sno-Cats" as they are called, cost $200,000, and more, and anything costing that much must do everything but climb trees. Attachments such as front-end U-blades for pushing the snow and leveling bumps, compacter bars for packing it, powder makers for softening hard surfaces, and hydrostatically driven snow tillers to break up the hardest crust all help make snow surfaces more often than not surprisingly good. Thanks to this equipment, a mogul-covered run one day can be as flat as a pancake the next, or an icy surface in the morning can be turned into a loose granular surface by afternoon.

Grooming and snowmaking are transforming the way people ski. While ungroomed runs in the past caused formidable obstacles to many, they forced skiers to ski more cautiously. You just couldn't go all-out when the moguls were as big as you were. But with today's meticulously manicured slopes, skiers have literally grown wings and are negotiating even advanced runs at speeds never possible before grooming.

The nation's top areas often proudly parade in formation their fleet of Piston Bullies, Thiokols, and BR–400 Ski-Dozers—a happy mix of farm machinery and military equipment. The latest machine to join ski areas' grooming arsenals is the "winch cat," a winch-equipped groomer that brings the snow *back up* a steep slope, grooming areas that were completely inaccessible in the past.

Next time you visit a ski area, take a look at its grooming equipment, observe it at work and you'll have an even better grasp of one of the key elements that make skiing a more enjoyable experience.

ABOUT SAFE SKIING. Skiing, like any other sport, has its risks. Yet overall, when ski areas take their responsibilities and skiers respect the Skier's Responsibility Code, the sport of skiing is not a dangerous activity.

The days of broken ankles and legs are far behind us now, with important technological advances in skiing equipment and teaching. Sure, people still break a bone from a fall now and then, but these injuries are more and more infrequent. Nowadays injuries and skiing accidents are more often caused by the behavior of skiers.

Grooming removes moguls on on all but the steepest of runs. This reduces the impact and many of the twisting injuries that skiers often experienced when skiing under difficult conditions. But leveling runs has turned them into literal speedways.

Inconsiderateness, ignorance of skiing rules, and uncontrolled speed have now become the major culprits in skiing injuries, many of which have become quite serious and sometimes fatal.

In planning your skiing vacation, it's important for you to know and apply the rules of safe skiing endorsed by the National Ski Areas Association, Ski Industries America, and the Canadian Ski Council: the Skier's Responsibility Code.

Safety Tips. Here are more common sense suggestions endorsed by the United Ski Industry Association.

• If you overtake another skier on the slope, call "on your right" or "on your left" so that he or she will know where to anticipate you.

• Remember that you too were once a beginner. Don't ski too fast or too close to novice skiers.

• If you ski into another skier or cause one to fall, you are legally responsible for stopping and providing assistance.

• Avoid skiing through ski classes. The same goes for race courses unless you are a participant.

• Do not attempt to stop a runaway ski. Instead, shout the warning "runaway ski" to people below.

• Don't take friends down trails they are not ready for.

• Be especially careful when there are small children on the trail. Even though they may be excellent skiers, they are very light and can be knocked over easily.

• After falling, get up promptly to avoid becoming an obstacle for another skier.

• Ski cautiously through a snowmaking area. Machine snow can be sticky when being made and you can fall if you are not prepared for it.

• Never tamper with ropes, signs, barriers, or markers. They are put up for a good reason.

• Don't cut lift lines, and try to keep off other people's skis while moving through the lift maze.

• Have your lift ticket or season's pass visible for checking so you do not hold up the line.

• Keep out of the way of snow-grooming vehicles. Stop and let them pass before proceeding.

• Ski defensively—expect the unexpected. Look ahead. Plan ahead. Be aware of what's around you. Be prepared to stop anytime.

• It is always wise to warm up for any strenuous activity. Skiing is no exception. Do your warm-up exercises at the top of the lift just before your first descent.

• Refrain from littering. Littering on the ski trails not only detracts from the beauty of the mountain but can cause someone to fall.

• Be careful when carrying equipment in crowded areas. Remember when you turn around, your long skis turn also, sweeping in a wide arc.

• To prevent theft when leaving equipment unattended, lock your skis and poles to one of the ski racks at the area. Use a coin-operated ski lock available at the area or carry a lightweight cable lock with you. If you don't have a lock, separating your skis may help.

Selecting the right trail. Suffice it to say that skiing an "expert" slope doesn't necessarily make **you** an expert! On the contrary, it can make a fool out of you, and, worse, you can cause injury to yourself and others.

Don't overestimate your capabilities. There's nothing wrong with a bit of extra challenge now and then but skiing over your head is not much fun. You wouldn't have much fun playing tennis against Ivan Lendl; it's no more pleasant to ski down "Suicide Pipeline" when you can barely handle "Easy Street." Particularly at large areas, don't ski without a trail map in your pocket. Know and understand the meaning of trail markings.

TRAIL-MARKING SYMBOLS. The symbols shown here constitute the standard international trail-marking system.

Remember, these symbols do not tell the whole story. They describe only the relative degree of challenge of a particular trail **compared to all other trails at that area.** Also, gradients and difficulty vary along each trail. Therefore, it is always a good idea to start off on the "easier" trails when visiting a new area. Then as you progress toward the area's "more difficult" and "most difficult" terrain, you will have a better grasp of the area's level of difficulty. That is why terrain rated

Green Circle. *Easier* trails and slopes.

Black Diamond. *Most difficult* trails and slopes.

Blue Square. *More difficult* trails and slopes which fall somewhere between easier and most difficult designations.

Triangle. Red Border and exclamation point on yellow background.
This symbol warns of an obstacle ahead. Ski with caution.

"more difficult" at Vail, Snowbird, Squaw Valley, and Jackson Hole may be tougher than the "most difficult" trails at an eastern area.

Some areas also have "double black diamond" trails, which are either extremely steep or unusually long, mogully, and difficult runs only for very strong or very calm skiers.

If you know and follow the rules and ski with common sense, you'll be safe on skis, as will everyone else.

NIGHT SKIING. For most nondestination ski areas—day ski areas—the feasibility of maintaining expensive facilities 12 months a year while only operating 4 or 5 months has always been a problem. Nowadays, however, many areas are coming to a fuller realization of their potential by developing summer programs and activities. They are also trying to maximize their winter utilization by operating longer hours and simultaneously offering skiers a more flexible skiing schedule. Enter night skiing.

Originally a ski area that was open at night would throw up a few bulbs here and there and charge 50 percent of the day rate to ski "under the stars." In those early days, skiers did better skiing under the full moon without lights. Night skiing could rightfully be called an experience, an adventure of sorts.

But the challenge of night skiing has all but been removed with the installation of high-powered mercury vapor and metalarc 1,000-watt lamps that in some cases generate over a million watts of lighting power and render the ski slopes bright as day.

As there is no problem playing baseball or football at night, so it is now with night skiing. In fact, visibility under modern lighting systems is always constant and often better than by day when "flat light" sometimes enters into the picture. Some areas even counter flat daylight by turning on the lights.

In North America, the most sophisticated and extensive night-skiing region lies 45 minutes north of Montreal, in the St-Sauveur Valley of the Laurentians. Here, within a radius of 5 miles, there are more than 70 night skiing trails at 7 resorts generating more than 4.5 million watts of brightness for the after-work crowd of skiers. One ski area alone, Mont St-Sauveur, has 1.1 million watts of power. At night the region radiates as much as a small city and draws a tremendous number of skiers. In fact, Mont St-Sauveur's night skiers are almost as numerous as its day skiers. This and other areas operate until 10:30 P.M. weekdays and midnight on weekends. Night tickets are sold from 3 P.M.

The only drawback for night skiing is that it tends to be colder at night, so dress warmly and check temperature forecasts. Remember, though, that the overnight low is usually reached in the early hours of the morning just before sunrise. So while temperatures drop steadily during the night, they'll normally still be far from the lowest when you finish skiing.

ABOUT SKI LESSONS. Ski lessons are not just for beginning skiers. Most people underestimate the importance of lessons and overestimate their capabilities.

If you've never skied before, lessons are paramount. Enjoying skiing the first time out can mean a lifetime of fun and enjoyment. Avoid making that first experience a bad one by borrowing a friend's equipment and taking a lesson from your neighbor who skis "pretty good." No matter how good a skier your friend might be, if he or she can't teach, your first experience might be disastrous. By renting equipment the first time out, you'll be fitted properly and you'll also avoid purchasing expensive equipment before you know if you'll enjoy the sport.

Instructors are used to beginners; they understand your apprehensions and are trained to analyze your skiing potential. They know which slope is the easiest at their area; which slope teaches best. What may seem like an easy slope to your friend might be too much for your first run.

Learning to ski is no longer the long process it once was. Improvements in teaching progression and the use of shorter skis have made it possible to make parallel turns and ski most intermediate trails within a ski week of lessons. In addition to teaching you to ski, instructors will introduce and familiarize you with your ski equipment, how it works, and how to take care of it for better performance. They'll talk to you about skiing safety, rules of the road and courtesy on the slopes, show you how to ride the lifts, and present the importance of exercising *before* your first run.

When planning a ski vacation, consider booking lessons as well. Resorts offer lessons for all abilities, including racing and touring groups, where advanced skiers go with an instructor to explore off-the-track mountain areas you wouldn't normally know about. This is particularly interesting at the larger areas, where there is a lot of tree or open skiing, such as Alta, Snowbird, Park City, Jackson Hole, Vail, Aspen, Sun Valley, Whistler-Blackcomb, Lake Louise, Mt. Bachelor, and others.

Race training camps are available from the best, including World Cup champions Phil and Steve Mahre. Their training sessions run different weeks at Keystone in Colorado, Heavenly Valley in California, and Stowe in Vermont, every winter. Check with the area for schedules and rates.

Refreshers. It's the wise skier who takes a lesson now and again to correct and strengthen technique. Technique evolves and although you might be skiing well, a lesson might help you master those big bumps that give you trouble or help you carve those turns a bit better.

ABOUT SNOW REPORTS. Once you've decided on a skiing vacation, snow reports take on a new meaning and their analysis most often is not that easy. Snow reports come from various sources.

Ski areas or their regional association almost always provide reports. Although some can be reliable they are usually given in such a way as to maximize the desirability of skiing at their area. They are prepared by the public relations or marketing department instead of the mountain manager or the ski patrol, who are the ones who really know what's happening on the mountains. Most ski areas have recorded snow phones where you can get the latest information. A good snow report will give the date and time of recording. Snowfall in the past 24 hours and up to 7 days can be meaningful, but accumulation "in the past 17 days" doesn't mean much if yesterday there were 2 inches of rain followed by subfreezing temperatures. Listen for temperatures as well. If it's 40° and the area claims to be making snow, you can hang up right away.

Snow quality is next. It is either powder, granular, frozen granular, corn, or icy.

Base depths are deceiving unless you know the area and the kind of snow cover it requires to be good. Two feet of base may be nothing in the Sierras, but in the East and Midwest, it's more than plenty. And with snowmaking in the picture, where are these base depths really taken? We've skied more than our share of ski areas where base depths averaged 20–40 inches and there were still bare patches on many runs. So don't go by the area that has the biggest base. It may just have the best PR department.

Number of trails open is an important factor to consider. But, here again, make sure you get complete information. Saying that 25 trails are open does not indicate the same situation at Killington and Jay Peak—Killington has 107 trails and Jay has 34. Thus, there is a better situation at Jay, because Killington would only have 23 percent of its runs open. Ski areas are into little games here, though. Early in the season, you'll often discover that the three trails open for skiing are "Upper this," "Lower that," and the "Arrival Plaza." Multiply that by three and you have nine runs open but only three ways down. Other centers will also play the percentage game where one wide trail represents 30 percent of the area's skiing acreage. So as soon as that one run opens up—30 percent of the mountain is open, but it's still only one run. You can't really knock areas for doing this, though. Giving a snow report for an area is about the same as a parent answering the question, "Do your children look good?" Of course they do!

Some areas do call a spade a spade, however, and you'll need to find that out for yourself in the region that interests you. In the East, for example, several state or provincially run areas, such as Whiteface and Gore in upstate New York; Cannon Mountain, New Hampshire; and Quebec City's Mont Ste-Anne, give straight, descriptive reports of conditions. And they usually don't open trails before they're sufficiently covered.

Newspapers should be able to provide some of the best information, but few devote enough space to do the job adequately. There's a lot of tedious repetition in ski reports, and newspapers are perfect for the job as readers can select without being subjected to the whole thing. Unfortunately, until they allow enough space, newspaper reports will be dated, incomplete, and often edited.

Radio and television are the best sources. They are the most immediate and are likely to have more professional reporters. The best reports will be those prepared by a specialist and not read by the staff announcer. In the latter case, you know the report is simply a compilation of what the areas themselves have phoned in. You can trust the person who calls it bad from time to time, because when he or she says it's good, you'll know it's truly good. Also follow weather reports. When you hear that the interstate is closed because of a major snowstorm, you'll know that the foot and a half of snow reported at the ski area is not wishful thinking by the PR department. Conversely, if television news show residents of Aspen planting rice, you can bet that skiing will be less than ideal unless it's done from behind a boat.

Here are some definitions to help you better understand snow reports. (See *Glossary of Ski Terms,* below, for additional definitions.)

• **Corn snow.** Spring condition. Large icelike granules sometimes the size of corn kernels caused by the melting of frozen granular.

• **Frozen Granular.** Granular snow that was once wet then frozen together forming a solid mass. This condition can also develop from extreme compacting by skiers. Frozen granular will support a ski pole planted in it, while ice will make chips and will not support your pole. **Caution:** Some skiers will call this condition ice and many areas will use the term instead of ice.

• **Granular Snow.** Old snow that is no longer powdery and soft. Cross-country skiers call it hard, grainy snow. It is abrasive. The snowflake is no longer star-shaped and has become more like a pellet because of aging, wear and tear, or grooming. This condition, contrary to common belief, is not a spring condition. It can happen anytime and it's no deterrent to the quality of skiing.

• **Ice.** Caused by rain followed by a freeze-up, freezing rain, or extreme skier traffic on wet snow.

• **Limited skiing.** Used when skiing at an area or on a certain level of trails is limited to less than 50 percent of the normally available terrain.

• **Packed powder.** Powder snow that has been packed mechanically or by skier traffic.

• **Powder snow.** Snow that is fresh and dry and in its original state. It is not always light but can be, as found in the higher elevations. Powder snow can have a variable consistency and will eventually become granular when it becomes more like a pellet than star-shaped. Powder snow, simply said, is dry, soft snow.

• **Sugar snow** is a breakdown of frozen granular snow in cold temperatures.

• **Variable conditions.** Used to describe a wide variety of surface conditions. No one surface type dominates. Often found in springtime, particularly at the bigger mountains where surfaces may be powder at the top and springlike at the bottom or varied from more northerly to more southerly exposed facings.

• **Wet snow.** A deep snowfall of wet snow, while advertised as great by the areas, is often very difficult to handle by skiers and dangerous for beginners or weak skiers. Packed and harder surfaces are often the safest conditions.

• **Windswept or windblown.** Irregular surfaces affected by winds that have formed drifts in some spots and exposed the base in others. Can cause icing.

Beware of adjectives such as **good** to **excellent** that some areas, particularly in the West, still use to describe conditions. They say nothing about skiing, and even when there is limited or even bad skiing, the minimum rating is often good.

These conditions are, of course, affected and often altered by grooming. You can read about grooming earlier in this section.

GLOSSARY OF SKI TERMS

Aerial tramway. A large lift, composed of two cabins holding up to 120 people, suspended by a moving cable traveling high above ground. Used mostly where topography requires very long spans.

Après-ski. Social activities at ski resorts after skiing.

Avalanche control. Evaluation of high-altitude steep terrain with a heavy accumulation of unstable snow and necessary prevention measures, such as blasting, to release avalanches.

Base. The plastic or polyethylene running surface on the bottom of your skis; also, the amount of packed snow reported by ski areas.

Boiler plate. Solid ice created by rain followed by a freeze-up.

Breakable crust. Crusty snow that can be broken easily by skiers. Usually caused by freezing rain immediately after a snowfall.

Bunny hill. A gentle slope for beginners.

Carved turn. A long, arc turn made with little or no side-slipping.

Catwalk. A narrow road for vehicular traffic or narrow trail linking two peaks or two trails on a traverse.

Certified. Used by the U.S. and Canadian Ski Instructors' Alliance to indicate that a skier has been tested and has passed examinations to become a ski instructor who is qualified to teach the technique approved by the governing body.

Chairlift. A method of uphill transportation in which chairs suspended from a moving cable bring skiers uphill two, three, and even four at a time.

Chatter. Vibration of skis on hard surfaces that prevents the edges from setting properly.

Christie. Short for Christiania, a turn invented in the latter part of the nineteenth century by the skiers of Christiania, now Oslo. Turn where skis are parallel when the turn is completed.

Chute. A steep, narrow trail.

Corn snow. A type of snow found in the springtime, when large icelike granules, the size of corn kernels, are formed by the melting of frozen granular by the sun.

Cornice. An overhanging ledge of snow or ice.

Crevasse. Deep, dangerous crack found in glaciers.

Crud. Heavy or crusty snow. Occasionally called "death crud" in the Rockies.

CSIA. Canadian Ski Instructors' Alliance. The association of Canadian ski instructors.

CSPS. Canadian Ski Patrol System. The Canadian body of ski safety and first aid volunteers who promote safety on the slopes and administer first aid when needed.

Damping. The ability of a ski to absorb vibration.

Downhill ski. The lower ski, the one normally on the outside of the turn.

Drop-off. An abrupt change from flat to steep.

Edges. Strips of metal on the edge of the ski's running surface to improve grip on the snow.

Edging. A method of controlling side-slippage in a turn. Also used to control speed.

Edgeset. Application of edging just before starting a turn.

Face. The steepest part of a mountain.

Fall line. The line a ball would follow if it rolled freely down the mountain.

Fanny pack. Small pack carried around the waist in which skiers carry their odds and ends.

Flat light. Poor visual condition, usually in haze or cloudy weather, when terrain contours cannot be properly delineated.

Free skiing. Skiing without restrictions; not in competition.

Frozen granular. A type of snow often mistaken for ice. It is granular snow that became wet and froze, forming a solid mass. It can usually be groomed quite easily.

Giant slalom. A form of alpine ski racing in which a skier must negotiate a series of gates connected by relatively long traverses. It combines elements of both slalom and downhill.

Glade. Ski slope where skiers ski beneath the trees.

GLM. Graduated Length Method of teaching skiing. It is based on the use of shorter skis to make turning easier at first, then progressing to longer ones.

Gondola. A ski lift composed of a series of small enclosed bubbles shaped like eggs and carrying anywhere from 3 to 6 passengers. They are loaded from a stationary position and then clamped onto the driving cable.

Grooming. What ski areas do with machinery to improve snow conditions.

Half-pipe. A hollowed-out half circle in the snow used by snowboarders for various maneuvers. A standard-size "pipe" is 400 feet long by 75 feet deep; with a slope between 19 and 23 degrees. It can be straight or curved.

Hardpack. Powder snow that has been packed hard by heavy skier traffic.

Herringbone. A method of climbing hills in which skis are edged and placed in a reverse-V position to prevent backslip. Frequently used by cross-country skiers.

High season. A time of year when resorts are busiest. In skiing, normally the Christmas–New Year's weeks, early February to mid-March, and Easter if it comes early. This is a period of higher rates.

High-speed gondola. A detachable gondola that can carry anywhere from 4 to 24 passengers at relatively high speed. In North America the highest capacity is 12 passengers, while in Europe there are several 24-passenger gondolas in service.

High-speed quad. A 4-passenger detachable grip chairlift (*see* quad).

Inside ski. The ski that is on the inside of the turn. The ski that becomes the uphill ski when the turn is terminated.

J-bar. Ski surface lift in the shape of a J carrying one skier at a time.

Lift line. The area where a lift runs, the straight cut through the trees. Also the area where skiers wait to get onto the lift.

Low season. Part of the season that is the least busy. In skiing, usually before Christmas, January, and from late March on.

Mashed potatoes. A snow condition encountered in very warm weather when the snow becomes very heavy and difficult to move around.

Meadow. Large, open slope usually with a moderate grade.

Mogul. A bump in the snow formed by the turning action of skiers. Moguls are quite common on steep slopes.

NASTAR. National Standard Race. Giant slalom-type of ski competition offered at many U.S. ski centers and open to anyone. Skiers can compare themselves to a national standard.

NSPS. National Ski Patrol System. The American body of ski safety and first aid volunteers who promote safety on the slopes and administer first aid when needed.

Package tour. A travel arrangement for which a skier pays for a number of services all at once. Package tours can include such things as airfare, transfers, accommodations, meals, and lift tickets. Packages can be more or less comprehensive.

Pomalift. A surface ski lift, also known as a "platterpull," consisting of a series of bars at the end of which each has a disk. The skier straddles the bar.

Powder. Fresh, dry snow; snow in its original shape—star shaped.

Powderhound. Skier who loves powder and will look for it in the most remote parts of a ski area.

Prejump. A method by which a skier jumps before the edge of a bump to avoid being projected too high.

Quad. Short for quadruple chair, a four-passenger chairlift that comes in two versions: fixed quad where each chair is permanently attached to the drive cable, and high-speed quad (sometimes referred to as detachable) where each chair releases temporarily from the drive cable and slows down allowing for easier loading and unloading. The high-speed quad travels at high speeds between loading and unloading terminals.

Release binding. The piece of equipment that keeps your boots secured to your skis. Usually includes a toe and a heel piece, both of which can release when forces are applied.

Rock garden. Expression used to illustrate a condition in which many rocks are exposed.

Rope tow. A form of surface lift consisting of a moving rope that skiers grasp to be pulled uphill. It was one of the earliest forms of uphill transport.

Ruts. Deep tracks in the snow caused by constant turning of skiers in the same area. Most frequently seen on racing courses.

Safety binding. A misnomer for release binding.

Schuss. Skiing straight down without controlling speed.

Schussboomer. Skier who skis rapidly and indiscriminately. Also known as a "bomber."

Shovel. The front part of the ski, including the upward turning part of the ski near the tip.

Sideslip. A sideways sliding of the skis, releasing the edges.

Sidewall. Side of a ski.

Sitzmark. A hole made when a skier falls in soft snow.

Skating. Skiing on one ski while pushing with the other. A method of traveling on flats or slight grades much like ice skating. A commonly practiced cross-country skiing technique.

Ski brake. A spring-loaded device included with all modern release bindings to prevent a runaway ski.

Slalom. Old Norwegian word meaning "zigzag" tracks downhill. Also a form of alpine ski racing in which a skier must negotiate a number of closely spaced gates in the fastest possible time.

Snowboarding. The snowboard is a wide monoski akin to a surfboard. With its own language and style this most recent phenomenon to hit the slopes has attracted primarily younger athletes who can easily master the balance skills needed to control the board. Most major ski resorts accept snowboarders and even cater to them with rental equipment and lessons. Trail maps now show special areas (see half-pipe, above) prepared for the maneuvers and competitions that are held. Next time you're on the slopes watch out for those "gnarly dudes," or maybe try joining them and get gnarly yourself.

Sno-Cat. The nickname given to a grooming tractor. It is actually the trade name for Tucker grooming machines.

Snow bunny. A novice or beginning skier. Usually reserved for females.

Snowplow. A basic ski maneuver whereby skis are placed in a V-position much like a snow plow. It is a means of controlling speed and initiating a turn.

Spring condition. A catch-all phrase used to describe the variety of conditions found in the springtime from frozen granular to mashed potatoes, including the possibility of bare patches.

Step-in binding. Ski binding for which the skier need not bend over to connect it with one's boot; one merely needs to step into it.

Super chair. An often-used marketing term for a high-speed quad chair.

T-bar. A surface lift in the form of a reversed-T pulled by a moving cable and hauling 2 skiers side-by-side.

Tail. Back end of a ski.

Telemark. A turn originating in the Telemark region of Norway in the late 1800s. It is performed on cross-country or special "telemark" skis by pushing one ski in front and ahead at an angle to the other ski. The leading ski carries much of the weight while the other leg, in kneeling position, helps to maintain balance. It is a turn best performed in deep snow. The technique is quite commonly practiced by skiers in the West and is becoming more popular in the East.

Terrain. The skiing surface of a ski area.

Transition. The change in ski terrain going from a flat section to a steeper one or vice-versa.

Traverse. Skiing across a slope at a certain angle with the fall line.

USSA. United States Ski Association. The national federation of American skiers and the sport's governing body.

Wind slab. Snow packed by the wind.

World Cup. A series of events run in several skiing disciplines to determine an overall champion every year. The World Cup Circuits regroup the top skiers in alpine, cross-country, freestyle, biathlon, and ski jumping.

Skiing—Where It All Began

A Short History

by
GUY THIBAUDEAU

Guy Thibaudeau has been a ski broadcaster and writer for more than 23 years. He lives in the Laurentians north of Montreal, from where he operates the MRG Ski Network, broadcasting daily ski and snow reports to more than 100 different media. He is a correspondent for several U.S. ski publications and for Le Ski, *Canada's leading French-language ski magazine.*

Skiing originated in the northern part of Europe and Asia several thousands of years ago. Skis thought to be more than 5,000 years old—the oldest known pair in the world—were found in Hoting, Sweden, and are displayed in the Djugarden Museum in Stockholm. The "Hoting Ski," as it is called, was short and wide, measuring 110 cm by 20 cm (approximately 43 inches by 8 inches). In 1931, a famous rock carving depicting a ski scene dating back over 4,000 years was found at Rodoy in Norway; it shows longer skis on two men hunting elk. Another positive proof of the early beginnings of skiing is the discovery of a ski tip found in northern Norway

19

that dates back over 2,500 years. It can be viewed today at the Holmenkollen Ski Museum in Oslo.

Skiing that far back, of course, was not a sport; it was merely a more practical way of getting around in the snow. The evolution of the skis themselves is quite interesting, going from relatively short skis at first to skis measuring as much as 12 feet, 2½ inches, in the seventeenth and eighteenth centuries.

There was also an era when a short and a long ski were used simultaneously—the long one for gliding and the short one, which had elk skin on the bottom for grip, for pushing. These were used by the Lapps about 250 years ago.

Skis were used through the ages by northern peoples and their armies to defend their territory. Sixteenth-century records document two major points in Norwegian and Swedish history when skiers played a major role. In 1200 A.D., during the battle of Oslo, King Sverre of Norway equipped his reconnaissance troups with skis to track the Swedish army's position. In 1206, during the Norwegian Civil War, two skiers—called "birch legs" because they wrapped their legs with birch bark for protection—carried the two-year-old royal Haakon Haakonsson to safety over the snow-covered mountains of Norway in the middle of winter. Haakon was to become Norway's greatest formative leader. A similar story surrounds the founding of Sweden and Gustav Vasa's rescue by skiing woodsmen who took the man who was to become their king from Salen to Mora, a distance of 85 km.

Both events are commemorated yearly by two ski races tracing the historic ski journeys that helped create Norway and Sweden: Norway's Birkebeiner-Rennet, a 55-km race from Lillehammer to Rena, and vice versa, in alternate years; and Sweden's famed Vasaloppet, in which over 12,000 skiers attempt to ski the 85-km distance from Salen to Mora.

But where did skiing as a sport actually begin?

In 1850 Sondre Norheim, a Norwegian farmhand from Morgedal in the southern Norwegian region of Telemark, found a way of fastening the foot to the ski with a heel binding. Before then, skiers wore only toestraps and were unable to turn because their feet would slip out immediately. With the foot properly fastened to the ski, modern skiing could begin—with the slalom.

At about the same period, Norheim had observed that it would be easier to land a jump on the steep part of a slope rather than on the flat. And jumping was on its way to becoming a sport and competitive activity.

In 1870, the same Norheim developed a ski with a sidecut—that is, narrower at the waist than at the tip and tail. This made turning a lot easier, and all ski manufacturers have been making skis with sidecuts ever since.

With his bindings and skis, Norheim developed a way of turning that he called the "Telemark" turn, after the district in which he lived.

As the popularity of skiing grew in Norway in the 1870s, the boys from Telemark were the hottest skiers around with their elegant Telemark turn. Their biggest rivals at ski meets were the fellows from Christiania (the old name for Oslo), who in time developed their own technique, skidding their skis wide apart but more or less parallel. They called it the "Christiania" turn (nowadays still referred to as the Christie).

The first skiing competitions were held in 1843 in northern Norway in the town of Tromso, north of the Arctic Circle. They were basically straight running events; the first cross-country races. Jumping came next with competitions in Telemark and Christiania in 1866, and then slalom in 1885.

Among the most famous Norwegian emigrants who spread skiing around the world were John A. "Snowshow" Thompson, who in 1856 began carrying the U.S. mail, sometimes 120 pounds of it, across the Sierra Nevada on skis. He did this for 13 years, until 1869, when the first transcontinental railroad was built. And then there was Herman "Jackrabbit" Johannsen. From the 1920s through the 1950s, Jackrabbit—so named by Canada's Cree Indians for his agility on skis—was instrumental in the development of cross-country and alpine skiing in both the Canadian and American East. Jackrabbit died in January 1987 at 111 years of age; he had skied until he was 110.

While the sport of skiing originated in Norway, the first signs of an organized technique came out of Austria in 1896, when an army officer, Mathias Zdarsky, set up a military ski school at Lilienfeld and published the first ski instruction manual. He is commonly acknowledged as "the father of alpine skiing." Around 1907, another Austrian, Hannes Schneider, studied and refined Zdarsky's method and developed the Arlberg technique, which made skiing a lot easier, and eclipsed the Telemark method for several decades.

After World War I, Schneider returned home more determined than ever to spread his skiing technique worldwide. Much like St. Peter and the Apostles, Schneider's disciples were sent around the skiing world promoting the philosophy that "skiing is a way of life." Hannes Schneider himself took the Arlberg technique to North Conway, New Hampshire; Herman Gadner, to Gray Rocks in the Laurentians; Fritz Loosli, to Lac Beauport north of Quebec City; Sepp Ruschp, to Stowe, Vermont; Luggi Foeger, to Yosemite; Otto Lang, to Mt. Rainier; and Friedl Pfeiffer, to Sun Valley, Idaho.

From there, ski resorts around the world began to develop along the European alpine model through the 1970s, when a more modern North American concept began to develop.

The first T-bars were installed in Switzerland in 1935 and the first aerial lift, the Parsenn funicular, erected in Davos in 1932. In the same year, Alec Foster built the first rope tow on the "Big Hill" at Shawbridge, north of Montreal. Sun Valley built the first chairlift in North America in 1936, when it became the U.S.'s first world-class ski resort. From there ski lifts of all sorts have developed, from T-bars to jet T-bars to platterpulls, J-bars, and double and triple chairs. The first quadruple detachable chair was installed at Breckenridge, Colorado, in 1982, and now the state of the art in uphill transportation is the "Vista Bahn," a detachable quad with a wind-protective bubble first installed at Vail, Colorado, for the winter of 1986. These are becoming more popular at resorts where cold or wind can be a factor.

Skiing has now spread around the world wherever there is snow. From Scandinavia, where it was born, to the alpine countries of Europe, where skiing technique evolved, to North and South America, Australia, Asia, Eastern Europe, and such unlikely areas as North Africa, Hawaii, India, Pakistan, and Iran, more than 30 million people throughout the world ski every year.

EASTERN
UNITED STATES

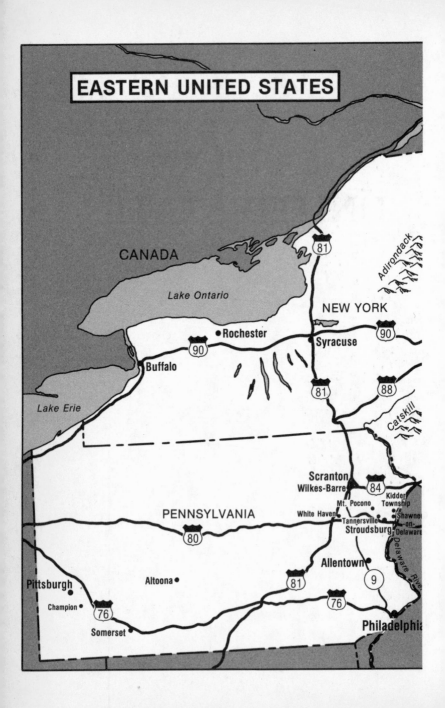

EASTERN UNITED STATES

CANADA

Lake Ontario

NEW YORK

81

90

●Rochester

Syracuse

90

Buffalo

81

88

Lake Erie

Catskill

Adirondack

Scranton

Wilkes-Barre

84

Kidder
Township

Mt. Pocono

White Haven

Shawnee
-on-
Delaware

PENNSYLVANIA

Tannersville

Stroudsburg

80

Allentown

Delaware River

9

Altoona ●

81

Pittsburgh

76

Champion ●

76

Philadelphia

Somerset ●

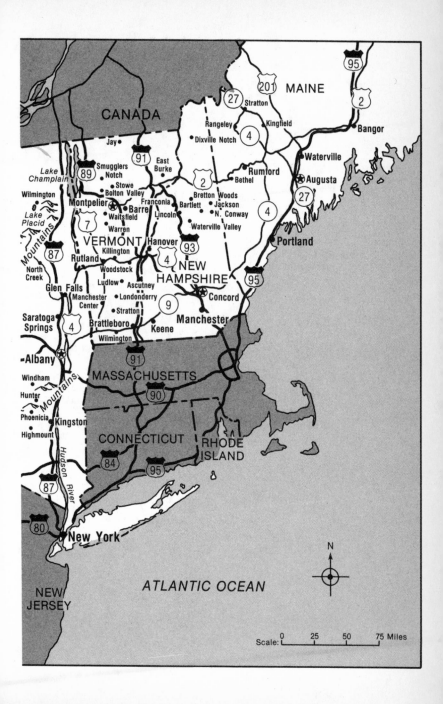

EASTERN UNITED STATES

revised and updated by
CRAIG ALTSCHUL
and
PEGGI SIMMONS

Eastern skiing and bottomless powder are not synonymous. But, as a friend once advised: "Don't trust any snow you can't hear."

Take a quick glance at the U.S. Ski Team rosters over the years. The best racers have always come from the east. The best skiers—period—come from this part of the globe. The reason: Eastern skiers know the meaning of edging. Carving a turn on good, hard, demanding snow calls for one to be on top of the skis. No cruise control here.

The Eastern United States is where skiers are made. It is the place to learn to ski and to perfect what you learn.

Eastern skiers in the know are convinced: Barring only the most bizarre weather patterns, there will be skiable—generally quite good—conditions at any eastern ski area any day between Thanksgiving and late March. Consider that as fact, regardless of what you see out your window or what your city-bound weather reporter says.

Snowmaking has become the stock-in-trade for eastern ski areas, the raison d'être. Some areas are better at it than others. Hunter Mountain in the Catskills, Killington and Okemo in Vermont, and Sunday River in Maine, to name a few, have taken it to an art form.

It is snowmaking that brings a great degree of parity to a decision on whether to head west to Colorado, Utah, or California, or whether to jump in the car and scoot off to the Green Mountains of Vermont, the Whites of New Hampshire, the Poconos of Pennsylvania, or the Adirondacks of New York State.

Of those who compare the apples and oranges of regional skiing in the United States, many believe that to enjoy skiing at its zenith is to float the back bowls of Vail under the Colorado bluebird skies. If the truth be known, there are only a few days when floating is possible *anywhere*—and you'd better get up before the locals.

Eastern skiing has something no other region can hope to have: tiny, historic mountain villages that were warm and homey long before skiing became fashionable. Old New England inns have walls that depict tales of generations gone by. Chefs prepare meals for serious country dining, and the people who greet you truly want you as their guests. Smoke swirls up from wood-burning stoves and the shops aren't cut from the mall mode like back home.

There are areas where you come for a day; others where you spend the weekend. A delightful way to enjoy a ski vacation is to come midweek. Many resorts (and towns) have Sunday-through-Thursday packages. And you'll find nary a lift line.

Today, generation gaps are diminished as families are playing in the snow together longer and longer. Why? Because the kids and teens are back, this time on snowboards. No longer a fad, but part of the tapestry, snowboarding really took off in the mid-eighties at Stratton Mountain, Vermont, and riders (earrings, funny hairdos, and avant-garde clothing aside) are now welcome most everywhere in the east.

When you ski in the east you should investigate trade associations like Ski 93 in New Hampshire, Ski New England, Vermont Ski Areas Association, Ski Areas of New York, Ski Maine Association, Pennsylvania Ski Area Operators, and others. They offer reduced rates and packages with tickets valid for several areas.

Finally, you should check for special events. Call the resort area you plan to visit and find out what's on deck. See the world's best racers compete head-to-head when the U.S. Pro Ski Tour is in town, or when members of the U.S. Ski Team come through for a North American Trophy Series or World Cup race. There are Winter Carnivals (the "granddaddy" is at Stowe, Vermont), recreational races, romantic (if cool) moonlit cross-country ski tours, dog sled races, and more.

There are mega resorts in the east, if glitz and a touch of glamor are your thing. But there are many more medium and small areas that offer intimacy, quality skiing, and fun.

Eastern skiing is unlike any other in the world. Bless it.

Maine

Some say that Maine most closely resembles the Pacific Northwest. Certainly the two boast a similarity in that their most important coastal cities are named Portland, and that both are interesting and historic in their own rights.

But it is the Western Mountains of Maine that attract skiers from Portland south to Boston and destination guests from throughout the east. While the choice of resorts is hardly unlimited, two can compete with the best the east—perhaps the nation—has to offer.

Sugarloaf/USA in the Carrabassett Valley has become a "mega-resort" in the sense that it is sophisticated and completely self-contained, catering to those who want dramatic skiing laced with every possible amenity.

While Sugarloaf continues to survive the financial realities of a "distant" resort, Sunday River has emerged as one of the nation's powerhouses in every good sense of the description. Sunday River never stops expanding, and few ski areas have the snowmaking results achieved here above the little Maine village of Bethel.

Emerging Saddleback—not far from Sugarloaf—has the promise of becoming a major player in Maine, while smaller areas dot the craggy landscape up and down the state.

Good skiing, L. L. Bean, and lobsters, too.

SADDLEBACK SKI AREA
AND SUMMER LAKE PRESERVE

Box 490
Rangeley ME 04970
Tel: 207–864–5671

Snow Report: 207–864–3380
Area Vertical: 1,830 ft.
Number of Trails: 40 on 100 acres
Lifts: 2 double chairs, 3 T-bars
Snowmaking: 50 percent of skiable terrain
Season: mid-November–mid-April

Saddleback Ski Area is one of two skiing mountains in Maine to top the 4,000-foot mark. (Saddleback is 4,116 feet and Sugarloaf 4,237 feet.) Saddleback overlooks much of the Rangeley Lakes Region and, from the summit, there are also views of Canada and New Hampshire. This is an area that since the early 1900s has lured visitors with its scenic and wilder-

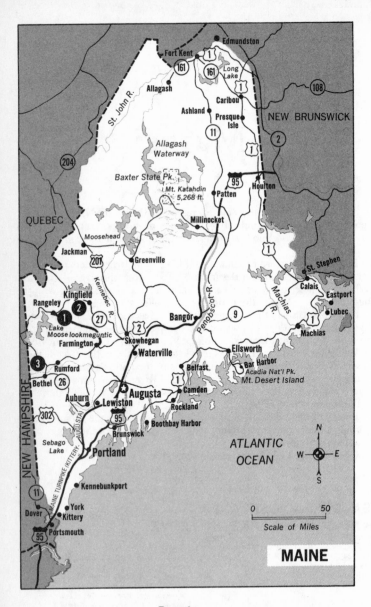

Resorts

Saddleback, 1
Sugarloaf/USA, 2
Sunday River, 3

ness charms. In the era of the grand hotels, steam locomotives whisked families away from the heat of summer cities to steamships that ferried guests to and fro across the lakes.

In the late 1950s, the recreation focus expanded from just warm weather activities to skiing. Saddleback Ski Area emerged in this decade and, by 1968, led the Maine ski industry by being the first major area to install snowmaking equipment. Today, Saddleback snowmaking covers more than 50 percent of the terrain and ensures top-to-bottom skiing on machine-made snow.

The mood here is laid back and uncrowded; the locals call it "elbowroom." Forty trails are about equally divided among "easiest," "more difficult," and "most difficult" designations. Part of the fun of Saddleback is its fixation on Western lore. Remember, these are the Western Mountains. So it's no surprise that Bronco Buster, a 3,000-foot-long black-diamond run from the summit, lures experts to the top. The summit is also accessible to intermediates on Cliffhanger, while the meandering 2.5-mile Lazy River is a favorite of beginners. Youngsters like the snow on White Stallion, while teens prefer Rough Rider and El Hombre, mainly for the moguls.

Saddleback and Rangeley have a family focus, and the region is one of the few places where you can escape the advantages of civilization without giving up creature comforts.

A 1984 acquisition of 12,000 acres of land is allowing Saddleback to become a four-season destination with lakes and big-mountain skiing. This purchase makes Saddleback one of the largest privately held ski areas in the United States with a skiing potential that lies in a semicircle of five mountains, only one of which now sports trails. Saddleback received approval to re-zone the mountain in 1989. The new "planned development district" has set in motion a multi-development plan for more lifts, trails, trailside lodging, and expanded snowmaking.

Practical Information for Saddleback

HOW TO GET THERE. Saddleback is located in the heart of Maine's Western Mountains, 125 miles from Portland and 220 from Boston. A crow could fly to Sugarloaf/USA 12 miles southwest. For the wingless, it's a 35-mile drive of about 45 minutes.

By air. *Continental, Delta, United,* and *USAir* fly to the Portland International Jetport. All major and regional airlines serve Boston's Logan Airport. Charter flights on *Bean's Flying Service,* 207–864–3722, are available from both Portland and Boston to nearby Rangeley Airport. Call Saddleback's reservation number, 207–864–5366, to arrange for a shuttle from the Rangeley Airport. *Mountain Air Services* can make rental cars available.

Avis (800–331–1212), *Budget* (800–527–0700), *Hertz* (800–654–3131), *National* (800–328–4567), and *Thrifty* (800–367–2277) **rent cars** out of the Portland International Jetport; all major rental car agencies are available at Boston's Logan Airport.

By car. From points south, take the Maine Turnpike north to Exit 12, then Rte. 4 north through Farmington to Rangeley, then drive 7 miles east on the Saddleback Mountain Road to the resort.

TELEPHONES. The area code for all Maine is 207.

ACCOMMODATIONS. While in the process of becoming a full-fledged, four-season destination whose primary focus is on summer lakes and big-mountain skiing, Saddleback draws on a decades-old collection of inns with a smattering of new inns and lodges primarily in nearby Rangeley. The *Saddleback/Rangeley Reservation Center,* Box 317 K, Rangeley ME 04970 (207–864–5364), provides information and reservation services for more than 25 establishments, including inns, housekeeping cottages, motels, condominiums, and private homes. Trendy pricing hasn't caught on here yet, so expect to find Down East hospitality at bargain prices. A three-day weekend, including lodging and skiing, ranges from $141 per person, double occupancy, in a comfortable motel to $171 per person in a trailside mountain home sleeping six people. Categories below are *Moderate,* $150 and up, and *Inexpensive,* under $150 for three-day lodging/skiing packages.

Moderate

Country Club Inn. Box 68, Rangeley 04970; 864–3831. This small inn is situated on a point overlooking Rangeley Lake and the Saddleback Mountain Range. It is a favorite of those who prefer country inn ambience. Located 7 miles from the slopes.

Rangeley Inn. Box 398, Rangeley 04970; 864–3341. Located in the heart of Rangeley, 7 miles from the slopes, this turn-of-the-century inn has been fully restored with brass beds, antiques, and private baths.

Rock Pond Mountain Homes. Box 490, Rangeley 04970; 864–5671. Saddleback's new trailside, 4-season planned community overlooks Saddleback Lake. These 36 3- to 5-bedroom homes are designed for family living and come fully equipped, some with their own indoor spa or sauna.

Town Park Condominiums. Box 680, Rangeley 04970; 864–5179. These 2-bedroom, 2-bath condos on Rangeley Lake offer a convenient in-town location about 7 miles from the slopes.

White Birch Condominiums. Box 490, Rangeley 04970; 864–5671. At the base of Saddleback, these comfortable 3–4 bedroom condominiums come fully equipped.

Inexpensive

Farmhouse Inn. Box 496, Rangeley 04970; 864–5805. This country inn nestled on a hillside overlooking Rangeley Lake offers private suites with their own kitchens and baths.

Hunter Cove. Box 2800, Rangeley 04970; 864–3383. Eight fully renovated lakeside cabins clustered on 6 wooded acres on Rangeley Lake, fully equipped, some with hot tubs; 8 miles from the slopes.

Town and Lake Motel. Box 47, Rangeley 04970; 864–3755. Located right on Rangeley Lake with motel rooms, kitchenettes, and 2-bedroom cottages with fireplaces.

RESTAURANTS. Just as Saddleback accommodations have staved off trendy pricing, so have the region's restaurants. Down East hospitality reigns at the dining places as well as at the lodges and inns. In this selection, the *Expensive* category has been eliminated. Average prices for a full meal for one person are as follows: *Moderate,* $10–$18 and *Inexpensive,* less than $10. Most restaurants accept the major credit cards, but it's always wise to check before you go. Many have special menus for children.

Moderate

Country Club Inn. Country Club Dr., Rangeley; 864–3831. The inn's restaurant is noted for its roast duck, veal, filet mignon, and extensive wine list. Reservations are a must.

Porter House Restaurant. Rte. 27, Eustis; 246–7932. A restored 1908 farmhouse featuring high-quality meats and fresh seafood, plus homemade breads and desserts.

Rangeley Inn. Main St., Rangeley; 864–3341. Specializes in seafood, chicken, veal, and beef dishes with a hint of French cuisine. The pub offers weekend entertainment and roaring fires. Reservations are a must.

Inexpensive

People's Choice. Rte. 4, Rangeley; 864–5220. Features a full selection of steaks, fish, and fowl with live entertainment on weekends.

Red Onion. Main St., Rangeley; 864–5022. Family-oriented place with pizza, daily specials, and other light fare. Take-out available.

HOW TO GET AROUND. Access to a **car** is imperative here, since there is no public transportation to speak of. Some lodges, however, may supply shuttle service to the slopes; check when making your reservations.

SEASONAL EVENTS. Black-diamond enthusiasts can ski free for 3 days by skiing Bronco Buster nonstop, top to bottom, during the annual *Bronco Buster Challenge* held in late **March** or early **April.** Over the years, more than 5,000 skiers have tried the challenge. Dog-sled racing is big in this neck of the woods, with New England competitions and local Rangeley meets scheduled in **January** and **March.**

OTHER SPORTS AND ACTIVITIES. The *Saddleback Ski Nordic Cross Country Center* (864–5671) offers terrain for all ability levels, with 40 km of groomed trails skirting lakes and mountains on the 12,000-acre preserve. The truly adventurous can trek to the summit and telemark to the base. Guide service for extended tours is available with advance notice. Saddleback's cross-country trail network claims to be the highest elevation trail network in New England, which translates, theoretically, into more natural snow.

Other ski touring facilities in the region include the *Carrabassett Valley Touring Center* (237–2205) with 85 km of trail loops; the *Winter's Inn* in Kingfield (265–5421) with 35 km of trails; *Akers Ski Center* in Andover (392–4582), with 25 km. In Farmington: *Holley Farm* (778–4869), 10 km (plus an indoor pool and sauna); and *Troll Valley* (778–2830), 25 km.

Over 100 miles of **snowmobile** trails are maintained regularly in the Rangeley region with rentals available. **Ice skating, sledding,** and **tobogganing** are also available.

NIGHTLIFE. On weekends and holidays, there's mellow folk music in the *Painted Pony Tavern* upstairs in the Saddleback base lodge (864–5921), or wander down to *Mike's Sports Pub & Grub* on Main Street in Rangeley (864–5616) for conversation and big-screen TV. A three-piece combo is often on board at the *Country Club Inn* on Mingo Loop Road in Rangeley (864–3831), and weekends at the *Rangeley Inn* on Main Street (864–3341). Catch rock 'n' roll and country rock at the *People's Choice* in Rangeley (864–5220).

SUGARLOAF/USA

Kingfield ME 04947
Tel: 207–237–2000

Snow Report: 207–237–2000
Area Vertical: 2,637 ft.
Number of Trails: 71 runs on 400 acres
Lifts: 1 triple chair, 2 quad chairs, 8 double
  chairs, 1 T-bar
Snowmaking: 80 percent of skiable terrain
Season: early November–early May

Down East, surrounded by the lumberjack lore of the deep Maine woods, sits an enigma called Sugarloaf/USA, or "The Loaf," to the locals. How else to describe a ski resort that pays annual tribute to an endangered species by hosting Yellow-Nosed Vole Day, boasts an $8 million hotel/conference center, has staged the Sugarloaf Schuss annually since 1951, and is surrounded by tongue-twisting geography like Mooselookmeguntic and Matawamkeag?

Sugarloaf/USA also has a sizable peak, at 4,237 feet, third among New England ski areas after Whiteface in New York and Killington in Vermont. Look for powder conditions here come spring, especially in a skiable snowfield, unusual to Eastern skiing, above the treeline of this giant in the Longfellow Mountains. In fact, it was discovering this snowfield 35 years ago that warmed the cockles of a few intrepid Maine skiing hearts of money and influence. They formed the Sugarloaf Ski Club in 1950. Donations and volunteer labor by the likes of Robert Bass of Bass Shoe Co. led to the first of what are now 70 trails.

Three decades ago, the nearby hunting lodges and camps, likely as not without electricity and running water, provided overnight accommodations for skiers. A bus parked at the base of Sugarloaf Mountain was equipped with a gas heater, toilets, and six bunk beds—a far cry from the 700 condominiums, some going for as high as $500,000, that now add sizzle to Sugarloaf's resort village, which, by the way, includes a seven-story conference center, Laundromat, bank, video rental store, 14 shops, and 13 restaurants.

The people of Maine themselves constitute over 50 percent of the resort's annual visitors, who sort themselves out by skiing abilities on expert trails such as the 9,000-foot Gondola Line that fan from the summit snowfield, on intermediate trails including the 3.5-mile Tote Road that goes from summit to base, and on novice trails that funnel into the village.

Some of the expert trails are left ungroomed for mogul buffs, and brand-new skiers are encouraged to ski—at no charge—on two easy trails served by ski lifts.

On-mountain hosts called Friends of Sugarloaf provide complimentary mountain tours. Every Sunday, guests are invited to join a 2-hour guided tour conducted by the resort's officers, winding up with a Continental breakfast in the base lodge. Seniors over age 70 ski free, as do youngsters 6 years and under.

Sugarloaf has found itself in and out of financial difficulties, but it somehow continues to reign as a superb all-around ski resort. Though well covered in the newspapers, the dollar problems are seldom, if ever, visible to the skier-guest.

Practical Information for Sugarloaf/USA

HOW TO GET THERE. Sugarloaf/USA is located 110 miles from Portland in Maine's Carrabassett Valley. It is just over 200 miles from Boston. **By air.** *Continental, Delta, United,* and *USAir* fly to the Portland International Jetport. All major and regional airlines service Boston's Logan Airport. Service by *Morgan Aviation,* Norridgewock (207–634–2039), is available between Portland and the Sugarloaf Regional Airport 8 miles away in Carrabassett. Contact Sugarloaf Area Reservations (800–THE–LOAF) to arrange for a pickup if you are staying in on-mountain lodging. *Mountain Express* runs luxury shuttle vans to and from the Portland International Jetport five times a day (207–237–2747 or 800–628–2821). *Ajax* (207–761–5955), *Avis* (800–331–1212), *Budget* (800–527–0700), *Hertz* (800–654–3131), and *National* (800–328–4567) rental car systems are located at the Portland International Jetport.

By car. Take the Maine Turnpike to Exit 12 to Rte. 4, north through Farmington to Rte. 27, and then north to Sugarloaf/USA.

TELEPHONES. The area code for all Maine is 207.

ACCOMMODATIONS. For on-mountain lodging call 800–THE–LOAF. The *Sugarloaf Area Chamber of Commerce,* Rte. 27, Valley Crossing, Box 2151, Carrabassett Valley, ME 04947 (800–THE–AREA), provides information on lodging in nearby towns as well as walk-to-the-slopes accommodations in the resort village that include nearly 250 studio–5-bedroom condominiums, the 120-room *Sugarloaf Hotel,* and the 42-room *Sugarloaf Inn.* Condominiums range per unit per night from $100 for a 1-bedroom that sleeps four to $250 for 5 bedrooms that sleeps 12. Inn and hotel categories in this section are *Expensive,* over $60; *Moderate,* $40–$60;

and *Inexpensive,* under $40 per night, double occupancy. American Express, MasterCard, and Visa are generally accepted.

Moderate to Expensive

Sugarloaf Inn. In Sugarloaf Village; 237–2000 or 800–THE–LOAF. Liftside lodging in a 40-room inn that features a cozy living room with fireplace, and a dining room overlooking the slopes.

Sugarloaf Mountain Condominiums. In village; 237–2000 or 800–THE–LOAF. Fully furnished condos, 700 units, offer a range of bedrooms, most with fireplaces.

Sugarloaf Mountain Hotel. In village; 237–2222. A full-service hotel reflecting the bounty of Maine's north woods in a comfortable and attractive wood-finished building. Has 120 rooms, lounge with light meals.

Moderate

Cathy's Place. Rte. 27, Stratton 04982; 246–2922. Motel with restaurant and lounge 7 miles from the mountain.

Hotel Herbert. Rte. 27, Kingfield 04947; 265–2000. The rooms are comfortably decorated with the owner's touch in each bathroom: a little yellow rubber ducky! Worth the 16-mile drive to the slopes.

Inn on Winter's Hill. Winter's Hill, Kingfield 04947; 265–5421. Classic hilltop mansion listed with National Register of Historic Places. Now a Clarion/Comfort Inn. MAP available.

Mountain View Motel. Rte. 27, Stratton 04982; 246–2033. Motel rooms and 2-bedroom apartments.

Spillover Motel. Rte. 27, Stratton 04982; 246–6571. Located 7 miles from the slopes, has 10 units.

Three Stanley Avenue Guest House. 3 Stanley Ave., Kingfield 04947; 265–5541. An old Victorian home with 7 rooms, some shared baths, breakfast served. Located 16 miles from the slopes.

The Widow's Walk. Rte. 27, Stratton 04982; 246–6901. Informal 6-room guest house in a Victorian home listed with the National Register of Historic Places and located about 7 miles from the lifts. Breakfast served.

Inexpensive

Judson's Sugarloaf Motel. Rte. 27, Carrabassett Valley 04947; 235–2641. A small motel with restaurant, across the street from the airport.

Lumberjack Lodge. Rte. 27, Carrabassett 04947; 237–2141. Chalet-style apartments at base of mountain sleep up to 8; sauna and game room on premises.

Stratton Motel. Rte. 27, Stratton 04982; 246–4171. Five units, with the Stratton Diner conveniently located across the street for coffee and breakfast.

Stratton Plaza. Rte. 27, Stratton 04982; 246–2000. An old hotel in the process of renovation.

Sugarloafer's Ski Dorm. Tufts Pond Rd., Kingfield 04947; 265–2041. A log fort turned dormitory with optional linen service about 15 miles from the lifts. MAP available.

Valley Motel. Rte. 27, Carrabassett Valley 04947; 235–2731. A motel with some dorm rooms, restaurant, and sauna. Located 7 miles from the slopes.

RESTAURANTS. Maine lobster isn't the only food served at restaurants in and around Sugarloaf. Continental and ethnic cuisines long ago made inroads to complement Down East specialties. Restaurants listed here are based on price. *Expensive,* $15 and above; *Moderate,* $10–$15; *Inexpensive,* $10 and less. The cost represents the price of a meal for one person, exclusive of drinks, tax, and tip. Unless otherwise noted, restaurants accept major credit cards.

Expensive

The Gladstone. In village; 237–2262. Menus change weekly but might include veal Dijon or chicken Kiev.

Julia's at Inn on Winter's Hill. Kingfield; 265–5421. Priciest restaurant in the area, with dessert specialties and monthly concerts served up in a Victorian mansion.

One Stanley Avenue. 1 Stanley Ave., Kingfield; 265–5541. A lumber baron's mansion that now serves French fare meriting its statewide rave reviews.

The Porter House. Rte. 27, Eustis; 246–7932. A restored 1908 farmhouse offers an American menu.

Truffle Hound. In village; 237–2355. Features an extensive menu that includes rack of lamb.

Moderate

Cathy's Place. Main St., Stratton; 246–2922. A favorite of locals, offering a prime ribs special on weekends.

The Carrabassett Yacht Club. Rte. 27, Carrabassett Valley; 235–2731. A local hangout. Pizzas, burgers, salads, friendly bar service. Entertainment.

Hotel Herbert. Main St., Kingfield; 265–2000. French and Yankee influences both reflected on the menu.

Longfellow's. Main St., Kingfield; 265–4394. A big menu includes such diverse types as Yankee, Italian, and Mexican.

The Seasons. In village; 237–2000. A greenhouse environment surrounded by ski slopes. Salad bar and children's menu.

Other moderately priced restaurants in the region include *Judson's Sugarloaf Motel,* Rte. 27, Carrabassett Valley, 235–2641; the *Stratton Diner,* Rte. 27, Stratton, 246–3111; and *Trail's Inn,* off Rte. 27, Eustis, 246–7511.

Inexpensive

The Bag & Kettle. In village; 237–2451. Favorite lunch and après-ski eatery offers sandwiches, soups, and entertainment.

D'Ellies. In village; 237–2490. Deli lunch and dinner menu, take-out orders. No credit cards.

Gepetto's. In village; 237–2191. Deli menu includes pizza.

HOW TO GET AROUND. A free **shuttle** makes the rounds of the base village. In fact, the shuttle, in operation since 1972, is a Sugarloaf/USA tradition. The village itself includes a video rental store, bank, Laundromat, shops, and restaurants. The valley is served by a fleet of green buses. Service is free.

SEASONAL EVENTS. *Yellow-Nosed Vole Day* kicks off events in early **December.** Skiers are invited to come in costume to help protect this endangered species. The *White White World Week Winter Carnival* is a **January** happening that includes minigolf around the village; a chili cook-off; a waiter/bartender race; and the *Canadian Club Celebrity,* a fundraiser for cancer research.

OTHER SPORTS AND ACTIVITIES. The *Carrabassett Valley Ski Touring Center* (237–2205) is only a mile away from Sugarloaf/USA and offers more than 85 km of **ski touring** loops. In fact, guests of some of the village condominiums can join this trail system right outside their doors. The center also maintains an Olympic-size **ice-skating** rink. (See Saddleback Ski Area for additional cross-country facilities nearby.)

The *Sugartree Health Club* at the Sugarloaf Inn Resort (237–2000) offers indoor **swimming,** hot tubs, saunas, steam rooms, **racquetball** courts, and exercise facilities.

Maine's Western Mountains can be explored by **snowmobile** on a series of trails maintained by the Maine Snowmobile Association. Maps are available; call 235–2100.

CHILDREN'S ACTIVITIES. The nursery is $18 for a half day, $30 for a full day for ages 2½ and up. A pre-ski program for ages 4–6 and a "Mountain Adventure" for ages 7–9 are offered: These programs cost $42 for a full day, $27 for a half day. For information on all programs, contact the Ski School, 237–2000.

NIGHTLIFE. You can stay right at Sugarloaf/USA and catch a little night music at *The Bag* (237–2451) and *Gepetto's* (237–2192). *The Widowmaker Lounge* in the base lodge (237–2000) offers nightly live entertainment, with reggae every Thursday night. And you may be able to carry on a conversation at *The Seasons Lounge* at the Sugarloaf Inn (237–2000), where a piano bar sets the pace. For teens, there's *Rascal's* on the mountain (237–2000).

Off the mountain, the *Carrabassett Yacht Club* (235–2731) and *Judson's* (235–2641), both on Route 27, Carrabassett Valley, feature rock, reggae, and country-western music. The *Herbert*, Route 27, Kingfield (265–2000), can be just about anything when it comes to music, with barber shop, Dixieland, and piano among the possibilities. You can find soft country and rock at *Longfellow's* on Route 27 in Kingfield (265–4394).

SUNDAY RIVER SKI RESORT

Box 450
Bethel ME 04217
Tel: 207–824–3000

Snow Report: 207–824–6400
Area Vertical: 1,865 ft.
Number of Trails: 60 trails on 420 acres, on 5 mountains
Lifts: 4 quad chairs, 4 triple chairs, 2 double chairs
Snowmaking: 93 percent of acreage
Season: early November–May

A good deal of the charm of Sunday River comes from its proximity—only 6 miles down the road—to the town of Bethel. The name Bethel means "House of God," a label that's stuck since the town was incorporated in 1796, just a few years after it hosted one of the last Indian raids in New England. Originally a Canadian holding, the town was founded in 1774 as Sudbury, Canada.

Perhaps the fact that Bethel is on a major river, the Androscoggin, and an east–west rail line ensured that the town would not be just another obscure village in the Maine woods. Situated near the foothills of New Hampshire's White Mountains, Bethel thrived as a summer resort.

In 1959 some folks from Bethel saw the potential of developing skiing in their already popular community. Sunday River was thus created, serving a primarily local and Maine clientele until 1972, when an infusion of professional ski area management and new dollars turned what was known as one of Maine's best-kept secrets into the third-largest ski area in New England and certainly the leader in New Hampshire and Maine. The resort will likely continue to expand well into the future, with more lifts and accommodations.

But this growth hasn't touched the character of the surrounding area. There's a notable absence of fast-food outlets and a choice of pre-twentieth century inns in and around Bethel compete with Sunday River's new condominiums and the large new mountain-top lodge, with a restaurant and skiing center, which opened at the summit of North Peak in 1990.

Sunday River skis from five distinct mountain peaks: North and Spruce peaks, Barker and Locke mountains, and White Cap. White Cap is the newest area, offering intermediate cruising terrain and challenging expert fare. Take the double-black-diamond warning seriously on White Heat. It's a wake-up call. The gentle South Ridge Slope is a novice's paradise.

The bulk of the skiing takes place on Barker Mountain, where wide-open intermediate terrain makes the average skier smile, especially after enjoying the 2½-mile Lazy River Trail. It's the half-mile Agony Trail, a double-black-diamond challenge, that attracts the teens, along with the moguls on Cascades and Monday Mourning. Novice skiers can get to the top of Barker Mountain for the views and meander back on the 3-Mile Trail, the longest run on the mountain.

Sunday River claims to be the only place in the country that offers a money-back guarantee if you don't learn to ski in a day. Called the Guaranteed Learn-To-Ski Program, it's open to anyone over 12. The Sunday River program has varied the normal ski school concept into what it calls "Perfect Turn," 75-minute clinics at various locations on the mountain. Groups are limited to six skiers.

Practical Information for Sunday River

HOW TO GET THERE. Sunday River is 73 miles northwest of Portland in Maine's White Mountains.

By air. The Portland International Jetport is the nearest gateway, served by *Continental, Delta, United,* and *USAir.* From the airport, van service is available with advance reservations through *Maine Tour & Travel* (800–456–2463).

Avis (800–331–1212), *Budget* (800–527–0700), and *Hertz* (800–654–3131) rental car systems are located at the Portland International Jetport.

By car. Take the Maine Turnpike to Exit 11, then Rte. 26 and north through Bethel; follow signs to Sunday River.

TELEPHONES. The area code for all Maine is 207.

ACCOMMODATIONS. *Sunday River Reservations,* Box 450, Bethel 04217 (824–2187), or the *Bethel Area Chamber of Commerce,* Box 121, Bethel 04217 (824–3585), can provide information on lodging and dining establishments that range from modern on-mountain condominiums to restored country inns and bed-and-breakfast homes. The on-mountain condominiums offer access to health-spa facilities including indoor swimming, whirlpool, and sauna. The *Snow Cap Lodge Ski Dorm,* within walking distance to the lifts (800–543–2SKI), is designed primarily for groups, although sometimes families and couples can get in. Hotel rates are based on double occupancy. Categories determined by price range are *Expensive,* $150–$280 per night; *Moderate,* $75–$150; *Inexpensive,* under $75. Many include breakfast or MAP plan for two. Most hotels are within 6 miles of the slopes unless noted otherwise.

Expensive

Bethel Inn & Country Club. Broad St., Bethel; 824–2175. Classic New England inn with swimming and health-spa amenities. Rate includes MAP.

Bethel Opera House. The Common, Bethel; 824–2312. An 1884 Victorian theater has been revamped to create 10 contemporary condominiums.

The Madison. Rte. 2, Rumford; 364–7973. A modern motel with health-spa facilities 15 miles from the slopes. Rate includes MAP.

Westways. Rte. 5, Lovell 04051; 928–2663. A New England inn 22 miles from the mountain. Rate includes MAP.

Moderate

Brookside Condominiums. At the slopes; 824–2187. Studio, 1–2 bedroom units.

Cascades Condominium Hotel. At the slopes; 824–2187. Studio and 1-bedroom units with indoor pool, health spa, and common room with fireplace.

The Chapman Inn. The Common, Bethel; 824–2657. Historic home on the common has whirlpool, sauna; breakfast included.

Four Seasons Inn. Main St., Bethel; 824–2755. Inn famous for serving dramatic flaming fruit compotes for breakfast. No children.

Kedarburn Inn. Rte. 35–37, Waterford 04088; 583–6182. Tastefully appointed with game room, lounge with entertainment; breakfast included. Located 25 miles from the area.

L'Auberge. Mill Hill, Bethel; 824–2774. A traditional inn except for the constellation painted on the ceiling. MAP available.

Merrill Brook Village Condominiums. At the slopes; 824–2187. One-bedroom deluxe units with fireplace and hot tub.

Norseman Inn. Rte. 2, Mayville Rd., Bethel; 824–2002. A country farmhouse with a Scandinavian flair. MAP available.

North Peak Condominiums. At the slopes; 824–2187. Two-bedroom units.

Olde Rowley Inn. Rte. 35–37, North Waterford 04264; 583–4143. An old stagecoach stop 20 miles from Sunday River. Breakfast available.

Philbrook Inn. North West Bethel Rd., Shelburne, NH 03581; 603–466–3831. One of the oldest Colonial inns in the area, in same family for generations. MAP available. Located 15 miles from the slopes.

South Ridge Townhouse Condominiums. At the slopes; 824–2187. One–three-bedroom units with fireplace or woodstove.

Sudbury Inn. Main St., Bethel; 824–2174. A Victorian dwelling with tin ceilings. Breakfast available.

Sunday River Inn. Bethel; 824–2410. A modern inn with on-premises cross-country center about 1 mile from the alpine trails. MAP available.

Sunrise and Fall Line Condominium Hotels. At the slopes; 284–2187. One-bedroom, split-level condominiums housing pool and health-spa facilities. Sunrise has large common room with fireplace. Fall Line has restaurant overlooking pool.

Inexpensive

The following establishments may be considered for the budget minded: **Bethel Spa Motel,** Main St., Bethel, 824–2989; **Lake Christopher Condos,** Rte. 26, Bryant Pond, 665–2500; **Snow Cap Lodge Ski Dorm,** trailside, Sunday River, 800–543–2754.

Inexpensive inns serving breakfast include: **Douglass Place,** Rte. 2, Bethel, 824–2229; **Lake House,** Rte. 35–37, Waterford, 583–4182, and **Rostay Motor Inn,** Rte. 2, Bethel, 824–3111.

RESTAURANTS. As in other parts of Maine, the cost of dining out in the vicinity of the Sunday River Ski Area can be easy on the pocketbook. Categories, determined by price, are: *Expensive,* $15 and above; *Moderate,* $10–$15; *Inexpensive,* less than $10. The price represents the cost of a meal for one person; drinks, tax, and tip extra. Unless specified, restaurants accept most major credit cards.

Expensive

The Lake House. Rt. 35–37, Waterford; 583–4182. Intimate dining in formal atmosphere. Menu includes duck à l'orange.

Moderate

The Bethel Inn. Broad St., Bethel; 824–2175. Classic New England inn with formal dining room overlooking golf course, cross-country skiing. Specialties include chicken pot pie at lunch and lobster at dinner.

Fall Line Restaurant. Sunday River Ski Resort; 824–2187. Seafood and steak dinners.

The Olde Rowley Inn. Rte. 35–37, North Waterford; 583–4143. Country dining by candlelight, including steak and seafood.

Rosetto's Ristorante. White Cap Lodge, Sunday River; 824–6224. Italian specialties.

Sudbury Inn. Main St., Bethel; 824–2174. Barbecued ribs are the specialty in this restored nineteenth-century inn. Reservations recommended.

Inexpensive

Charlie's Place. Main St., Bethel; 824–2732. A local pizza parlor with take-out service. No credit cards.

Mother's. Main St., Bethel; 824–2589. Old gingerbread house serves a casserole with Maine shrimp, plus tavern sandwiches.

The Only Place. Rte. 2, West Bethel; 836–3663. Claims to have the finest pizza north of Boston. No credit cards.

Saturday's Cantina. South Ridge Center, Sunday River; 824–3000. Mexican food.

HOW TO GET AROUND. Access to a **car** is imperative here, unless you are staying right at or near the mountain. A free on-mountain trolley runs from morning to late evening.

SEASONAL EVENTS. NASTAR is run daily. *Bust 'n Burn* and *Legends of Freestyle* on White Heat in early **April** feature top mogul skiers and former freestyle stars.

OTHER SPORTS AND ACTIVITIES. Two nearby inns offer **cross-country** ski facilities; the *Sunday River Inn & Ski Touring Center,* Bethel (824–2410), 25 miles of trails; the *Bethel Inn & Country Club,* Bethel (824–2175), 18 miles of trails. **Sleigh** and **dog-sled** rides are available at the ski area (824–3000). The on-mountain condominiums make available to guests, free of charge, indoor and outdoor swimming pools, saunas, and Jacuzzis.

HINTS TO THE HANDICAPPED. A Portland orthopedic surgeon lends his support to the Maine Handicapped Skiing that began in 1983 at Sunday River. Modeled after the Handicapped Skiers Program in Winter Park, Colorado, it focuses on skiers affected by various neuromuscular disorders as well as on amputees, the blind, and the deaf. Specialized equipment and a fully trained volunteer staff support the program. For more information write *Maine Handicapped Skiing,* RR2, Box 1971, Bethel, ME 04217, or call 207-824-3018.

DAY-CARE FACILITIES. A state-licensed nursery (824–3000) is available for children 6 weeks to 2 years old. A state-licensed day-care facility (824–3000) is available for children 2–6 years. *SKIwee* is for children 4–6 years and *Mogul Meisters* programs are for 7–12 years. Both are open 9 A.M. to 4:30 P.M. weekdays, with extended weekend hours. Full and half-day options, with rental equipment, are available. Children 5 and under ski free with parents.

NIGHTLIFE. There's daily après-ski entertainment 4–6 P.M. at *Bumps! Pub* in the White Cap Lodge at Sunday River (824–3000). Bumps! also offers weekend bands and dancing. For the less energetic, *Barker Mountain Lodge* at Sunday River (824–2187) offers mellow entertainment. Most nights there's live entertainment at the *Sudbury Inn,* Main Street in Bethel (824–2174); country bands at the *Backstage,* Summer Street in Bethel (824–3003); and a piano bar at the *Millbrook Tavern,* on Broad Street in the Bethel Inn (824–2175).

New Hampshire

The White Mountain National Forest takes up a sizable chunk (730,000 acres) of New Hampshire while encompassing the most dramatic mountains in the eastern United States, the Presidential Range. The granite peaks and outcroppings cut a bold northeast-to-southwest swath through the state, creating imaginary characters such as The Old Man of the Mountain who presides high above the valley near Franconia.

New Hampshire's Mt. Washington is the highest mountain in New England (6,288 feet) and is legendary for once having recorded a wind speed of 231 miles per hour. Even the imaginary "Old Man of the Mountain" winced that day. As a result of the severe weather, Mt. Washington can be skied only briefly each year. In the spring, the kind of skiers who carve notches in their dreams make the annual two-mile trek up Mt. Washington to ski the infamous Tuckerman's Ravine. That's the stuff tavern tales are made of.

New Hampshire's *real* ski areas are as diverse as they are bountiful. They are made for every type of skier. So close to the Boston metropolitan area—which is loaded with serious skiers—the White Mountains have become snowy magnets.

American skiing came into its own here when the famed Skimeister Hannes Schneider came from his native Austria to teach generations of skiers at Mount Cranmore. Now, 53 years later, Schneider's famous comment to his son Herbert remains descriptive: "It's not the Alps, but we're going to like it here."

Skiing history abounds here. The nation's first ski club was formed in Berlin by immigrant Scandinavian mill workers. The Dartmouth Outing Club hosted the nation's first winter carnival. Skiing at Cannon dates back to the twenties. Three New Hampshire ski areas had cable lifts as early as 1938: the famed Skimobile at Cranmore, an aerial tram at Cannon, and a chair at what is now Gunstock.

The Mount Washington Valley boasts a ski area variety pack. There's modern Attitash, traditional Wildcat, family-based Cranmore and Black Mountain, and the extensive, silent nordic wonders of the quaint village of Jackson. Name your outlet store and you'll find it—along with more than a share of weekend traffic—in North Conway. The main highway of I–93 on the western side of the range offers Bretton Woods, Cannon, Loon, and Waterville Valley.

With more than 100 lifts at 27 ski areas, skiing in New Hampshire, says the punster, should not be taken for granite.

41

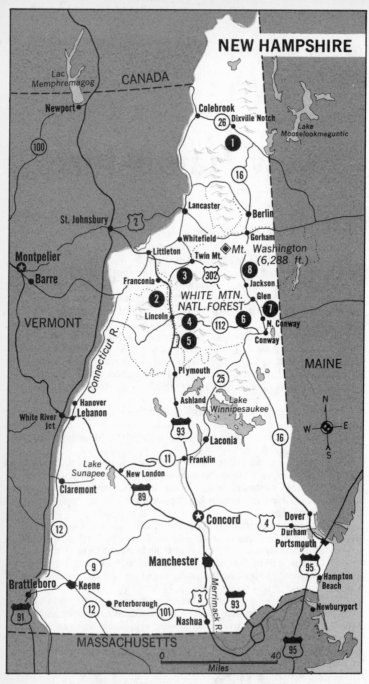

NEW HAMPSHIRE

Resorts

Attitash, 6
Balsams/Wilderness, 1
Bretton Woods, 3

Cannon Mountain, 2
Loon Mountain, 4
Mt. Cranmore, 7
Waterville Valley, 5
Wildcat Mountain, 8

BALSAMS/WILDERNESS

Dixville Notch NH 03576
Tel: 603–255–3400 or 800–255–0600,
800–255–0800 in NH

Snow Report: 603–255–3951
Area Vertical: 1,000 ft.
Number of Trails: 12 on 95 acres
Lifts: 1 double chair, 2 T-bars
Snowmaking: 80 percent of terrain
Season: mid-December–April

Like many of its New England counterparts, Balsams/Wilderness turned to luring winter guests after having been established for well over a century as a warm-weather mecca. In 1873, the Dix House opened to serve up to 50 guests. This was the precursor to today's 232-room The Balsams Grand Resort Hotel.

In 1954, Neil Tillotson purchased the hotel and surrounding 15,000 acres at an auction and moved a division of his company, Tillotson Manufacturing, to the sparsely populated area (Dixville Notch has about 30 residents), 13 miles from the Canadian border. The Tillotson Rubber Company found a home here where it still produces examination gloves.

In 1966, the Balsams/Wilderness Downhill and Cross-Country Ski Area was opened, adding a year-round focus to the region. Today, there are only two other grand resort hotels operating, summer only, in addition to The Balsams. They are the Mount Washington Hotel in Bretton Woods and the Mountain View House in Whitefield, NH.

There's not a wealth of alpine skiing here, and it wasn't until Tillotson purchased the estate that winter recreation became part of the four-season offering. Mt. Wilderness has an altitude of 2,650 feet, and its 12 trails provide skiing that ranges from easy to moderately difficult.

The ski lodge is built around a huge central stone fireplace and includes a cafeteria, nursery, and ski and rental shops. Hotel guests can also ski at any of the neighboring White Mountain ski areas free of charge, Monday through Thursday.

If you can pronounce them, the trail names on Dixville Peak are fun, drawing on natural landmarks such as Magalloway, Sanguinary, and Monadnock. Seven trails are marked with black diamonds. The Wind Whistle Ski School provides personalized instruction for children ages 3–6.

Cross-country skiers can enjoy more than 60 km of trails, most of which are groomed and tracked regularly. Novice terrain is mostly flat with more advanced skiing on runs offering a 1,000-foot vertical change. There is telemark skiing on alpine trails where guided tours are offered.

Practical Information for Balsams/Wilderness

HOW TO GET THERE. By car. *From Boston* take I-93 north to Exit 35, then take Rte. 3 to Colebrook, NH, and Rte. 26 to Dixville Notch. *From Hartford* take I-91 north to St. Johnsbury, VT, then Rte. 2 to Lancaster, NH, and Rte. 3 to Colebrook to Rte. 26 to Dixville Notch. *From Portland, ME,* take Rte. 302 west to Twin Mountain and Rte. 3. Continue as above.

By bus. From Boston take *Concord Trailways* (800–258–3722) to Colebrook, NH. Call the hotel (603–255–3400) to arrange to be picked up.

By air. Fly to Boston, Portland, or Hartford. Rent a car or call the hotel to arrange for a pickup.

TELEPHONES. The area code for all New Hampshire is 603.

ACCOMMODATIONS. The **Balsams Grand Resort Hotel** has 232 guest rooms, each with private bath. Rooms are available with twin, double, king- and queen-size beds. Each is individually decorated with Ethan Allen custom-finished furniture and wall paper. The "tower suite" is a luxuriously decorated, multilevel apartment with breathtaking views. It is appointed to provide its occupants with all the amenities they could desire on a honeymoon or special-occasion getaway. For reservations, call 800–255–0600 (in the U.S. and Canada); 800–255–0800 (NH only).

Room rates average $100–$140 per person, per night, double occupancy, on weekends. These rates include the room, skiing, breakfast, and dinner. Ski weeks range from $71 to $130 per person, per night, double occupancy.

RESTAURANTS. The award-winning cuisine offered by Certified Executive Chef Phil Learned and his staff is legendary. Guests choose from a wide range of selections that change daily on the table d'hôte menu. Entrees include prime rib, fresh seafood, duckling, veal, chicken, and various vegetarian dishes. Presentation of each entree includes a selection of vegetables and starches that complement the main course and its sauce. The desserts boggle the mind. An excellent selection of wines is available. Buffet dinners are served as an alternative on Wednesday and Saturday evenings. Gentlemen are requested to wear jackets for dinner.

Room service is available at all times. Coffee is served early each morning in the sun room. A coffee shop serves a selection of lighter foods during the day. Sandwiches are available in the Wilderness Lounge at noon for those not eating at the cafeteria in the ski-area base lodge.

HOW TO GET AROUND. There is a free **shuttle bus** between the hotel and the base lodge, located less than a mile away. Some guests prefer to use the cross-country ski trail from the hotel to the ski area.

OTHER SPORTS AND ACTIVITIES. Days here begin with *aerobic exercise classes.* A professional recreation staff organizes a full range of indoor and outdoor activities daily, with lectures, concerts, movies, and live music in two rooms—nightclub entertainment and disco dancing. An outdoor *ice-skating* rink is lit at night. *Hayrides* and *snowshoeing* outings are held afternoons and evenings. All these activities are included in the room rate.

DAY-CARE FACILITIES. A supervised nursery is operated in the base lodge daily from 9 A.M. to 4 P.M. for children "out of diapers" and older. Parents must pick up their children for lunch. Baby-sitters are arranged through the front desk. The nursery is free to hotel guests.

NIGHTLIFE. There are two rooms of dancing, nightclub shows, and feature-length movies nightly. Scheduled lectures and concerts are held during the season.

BRETTON WOODS SKI AREA

Rte. 302
Bretton Woods NH 03580
Tel: 603-278-5000

Snow Report: 603–278–5051
Area Vertical: 1,500 ft.
Number of Trails: 26 on 180 acres
Lifts: 1 quad chair, 1 triple chair, 2 double
* chairs, 1 T-bar*
Snowmaking: 98 percent
Season: end November–early April

Bretton Woods Ski Area looks east across the Ammonoosuc Valley straight up to Mt. Washington's 6,288-foot mass. On late afternoons, the vivid pinks and purples of alpenglow off Mt. Washington are a visual feast. The area is subject to a local phenomenon known as the Bretton Woods flurries—sunshine not very far away in North Conway or Twin Mountain with snow at Bretton Woods. (The 180-inch annual average snowfall is the greatest in New Hampshire.)

Located on a 2,600-acre private preserve in the White Mountain National Forest, Bretton Woods is an anomaly among eastern ski areas. It's one of the newest, having opened for alpine skiing in 1973; yet it is surrounded by the century-old tradition of a true grande dame among grande dame hotels, the Mt. Washington Hotel, whose massive size puts it in the same kind of scale, relatively speaking, as Mt. Washington. The 235-room Mt. Washington Hotel unfortunately is off-limits to skiers until it's winterized.

The ski area's setting is dramatic, and the preponderance of easy-to-intermediate trails, with only a sprinkling of steep and very short black-diamond terrain, allows skiers to focus as much on the beauty as on the skis.

In addition to creating one of the most esthetically pleasing base lodges in the country—a spacious, timbered structure—Bretton Woods has developed a solid base of slopeside beds and offers a free shuttle service.

There are only a few ski areas in this neck of the woods that offer night skiing. Bretton Woods is among them, opening two lifts from 4 to 10 P.M. Friday and Saturday nights.

A bonus—even though lift capacity is now more than 7,000 skiers per hour, Bretton Woods has a limited lift-ticket policy.

Practical Information for Bretton Woods

HOW TO GET THERE. Bretton Woods is one of four major New Hampshire ski resorts referred to as the Ski 93 Group. The others are Cannon Mountain, Loon Mountain, and Waterville Valley. All are easily accessible **by car** from southern corridors via I-93.

By air. Boston's Logan Airport is the gateway to Bretton Woods and other resorts in the Ski 93 Group. The airport is served by all major and regional carriers. *Delta, United,* and *USAir* fly directly to Manchester, NH. *Precision* also makes daily commuter flights from Boston to Manchester and Laconia, NH.

Car rental agencies available in Manchester are *Avis* (603–624–4000 or 800–331–1212), *Budget* (603–668–3166 or 800–527–0700), and *Hertz* (603–669–6320 or 800–654–3131). Avis also serves the Laconia Airport and *Merchant's Rent A Car* (603–528–1400) will pick up there.

By bus. *Concord Trailways* makes 2 round trips daily from downtown Boston and Logan Airport. For information and schedules, call 800–258–3722. Stops in towns near the Ski 93 Group areas include Campton (Waterville Valley), Lincoln (Loon Mountain), Franconia (Cannon Mountain), and Littleton (Cannon Mountain and Bretton Woods).

TELEPHONES. The area code for all New Hampshire is 603.

ACCOMMODATIONS. The *Bretton Woods Lodging Reservations and Information Service,* Rte. 302, Bretton Woods 03580, 603–278–4000 or 800–334–3910 in the northeast, can assist in finding lodging right at the mountain, or contact the *Twin Mountain Chamber of Commerce,* Box 194, Twin Mountain 03595, 603–846–5407. *Expensive* here is more than $100 per night; *Moderate,* $60–$100; and *Inexpensive,* under $60. All lodging is less than 10 miles from the slopes unless indicated otherwise.

Expensive

The Bretton Arms. Rte. 302, Bretton Woods 03575; 278–1000. A historic 32-room Victorian inn offering first-class accommodations and amenities.

Moderate

Après Jour Townhouses. Rte. 302, Bretton Woods 03575; 278–1711. Luxury accommodations with fireplaces, in-house cable TV.

Carroll Motel & Cottages. Rte. 3, Twin Mountain 03575; 846–5553. Motor inn with adjacent cottages, 2 and 3 bedrooms.

Condominiums at Bretton Woods. Rte. 302, Bretton Woods 03575; 278–4000 or 800–334–3910. One–four-bedroom condos, some with slopeside access, and most with special features, such as laundries, fireplaces, and decks. Located on the mountain.

The Lodge at Bretton Woods. Rte. 302, Bretton Woods 03574; 278–4000 or 800–334–3910. A contemporary 50-unit inn with indoor pool and sauna, restaurant.

Rosebrook Townhouses. Rte. 302, Bretton Woods 03575; 278–4000 or 800–334–3910. One- to four-bedroom fully furnished condominiums with fireplaces, optional maid service. Sleep up to 8.

The Wayside Inn & Motel. Rte. 302, Bethlehem 03574; 869–3364. A 19-room inn with 13 motel units and 180 miles of groomed snowmobile trails adjacent, 11 miles from the alpine slopes. On-premises dining, lounge, private or connecting baths.

Inexpensive

Boulder Motor Court. Rte. 302 E, Box 2063, Twin Mountain 03525; 846–5437. Ten cottages with mountain views, separate bedrooms, TVs, kitchenettes, some fireplaces.

Carlson's Motor Lodge. Rte. 302, Twin Mountain 03575; 846–5501. A 16-unit motor lodge with color TV, breakfast room, recreation room with Ping-Pong and pool table.

Four Seasons Motor Inn. Rte. 3, Twin Mountain 03525; 846–5708. Thirty rooms in a scenic location.

Grand View Lodge. Rte. N, Twin Mountain 03575; 846–5731. A New England inn with on-premises dining, lounge.

Lyons Motel. Rte. 3, Twin Mountain 03575; 846–5575. Motel and cottages, some with kitchenettes, on-premises restaurant, salad bar.

Mooney's Mountain Inn. Rte. 302, Twin Mountain 03575; 845–5013. Country inn with private or shared bath. Nightly wine and cheese hospitality, movies. In the morning, you'll get a hearty breakfast.

Northern Zermatt Inn & Motel. Rte. 3, Twin Mountain 03575; 846–5533. Has 15 rooms with private baths, color TV, some kitchenettes, public dining.

Paquette's Motor Inn. Rte. 3, Twin Mountain 03575; 846–5562. A 29-unit motel with color TV, dining room, fireplace, lounge with large-screen TV.

Thimbleberry Bed & Breakfast. Parker Rd., Twin Mountain 03575; 846–2211. Antique-decorated rooms, fresh home-baked breads and muffins for breakfast. No smoking.

RESTAURANTS. The clear mountain air can make a ski traveler hungrier than usual. Luckily, New Hampshire can provide the food to satisfy the inner self. Beef and fowl, seafood and freshwater fish, all are complemented by homemade soups, breads, and pastries. In this region, an *Expensive* meal would cost $20–$30; *Moderate,* $12–$20; *Inexpensive,* less than $12. Most restaurants accept the major credit cards, but it would be wise to check first before going.

Darby's Restaurant and Lounge. *Moderate.* Rte. 302, Bretton Woods; 278–1500. Specialties include prime rib and seafood.

Fabyan's Station. *Moderate.* Rte. 302, Bretton Woods; 846–2222. Italian specialties, seafood, and light fare served in remodeled turn-of-century railroad station.

The Grandview Lodge. *Moderate.* Rte. 3, Twin Mountain; 846–5731. The menu ranges from pizza to lobster.

Paquette's Motor Inn. *Moderate.* Rte. 3, Twin Mountain; 846–5562. Unique soup bar complements New England fare.

Rosa Flamingo's. *Moderate.* Rte. 302, Bethlehem; 869–3111. Italian specialties from pizza on up. Dining upstairs, lounge downstairs.

The Wayside Inn & Motel. *Moderate.* Rte. 302, Bethlehem; 869–3364. Continental fare.

Slopeside Restaurant & Lounge. *Inexpensive.* Bretton Woods Base Lodge; 278–5000. Menu includes sandwiches, soups, and light fare.

Our Place. *Inexpensive.* Rte. 3, Twin Mountain; 846–5578. A truck stop serving basic diner food.

HOW TO GET AROUND. If you are staying right at the mountain, free **shuttle** service is available. If not, a **car** is a necessity.

SEASONAL EVENTS. On **New Year's Eve,** there's a gala celebration that includes night skiing, a buffet, and torchlight parade, plus entertainment. And come **spring,** after a season of on-slope activities, there's the annual *Beach Party,* held traditionally on the last day of the ski season, and including bands, outdoor barbecue, and all kinds of contests—plus spring skiing.

OTHER SPORTS AND ACTIVITIES. NASTAR **races** are held here Saturday, Sundays, and daily during holiday periods. The *Bretton Woods Ski Touring Center* (278–5181) is ranked among the majors in the East, with 86 km of groomed and tracked trails on 3 major systems. Cross-country headquarters is the riding stable at the Mt. Washington Hotel.

DAY-CARE FACILITIES. Infants aged 2 months to 3 years are accommodated from 8:30 A.M. to 5 P.M. in a nursery. Older children can enroll in the *Hobbit Ski School,* which specializes in progressive instructional techniques for ages 4–12. This all-day program includes lift tickets, lessons, equipment, lunch, and supervised play/skiing.

NIGHTLIFE. Nightlife revolves around the ski area, with entertainment from 8 to closing Friday and Saturday, and daily from 2:30 to 6 P.M. during holiday periods.

CANNON MOUNTAIN

Franconia NH 03580
Tel: 603-823-5563

Snow Report: 800–552–1234
Area Vertical: 2,146 ft.
Number of Trails: 28 on 110 acres
Lifts: 1 quad chair, 2 doubles, 1 triple
  chair, 1 80-passenger tram, 1 pony lift
Snowmaking: 80 percent of terrain
Season: late November–mid-April

One of the oldest ski areas in the country, Cannon is geared to skiers looking for challenges, a reputation due, in part, to its size—4,180 feet—and a 2,146-foot vertical. Cannon's biggest fans are 24- to 34-year-old Bostonians, who delight in the challenges of the mountain's steep terrain.

This is a mountain of American skiing firsts: the first race trail, ski school, aerial tram, World Cup competition, and paid ski patrol. Local artifacts and lore and ski-related miscellany and history from all over the United States are collected at the New England Ski Museum at the base of the mountain.

Cannon Mountain, as part of the Franconia Notch State Park, is a state-operated ski area. When the legislature reorganized management and operation of the mountain, it replaced the two summit chairs with a quad and effectively doubled the snowmaking capacity, thus bringing the area into the modern era of competitiveness.

Practical Information for Cannon Mountain

HOW TO GET THERE. By car. From Concord, NH, which is 75 miles away, take I-93 to Franconia Notch, Exit 2 or 3. Cannon is 4 miles south of Franconia.

By bus. Both Franconia and Littleton (12 miles from Cannon) are served regularly by *Concord Trailways.* Call (603) 823–5661 for information and schedules. (For details on how to get to the region, see Bretton Woods section above.)

TELEPHONES. The area code for all of New Hampshire is 603.

ACCOMMODATIONS. This popular year-round recreation region offers a variety of lodgings. A selection is presented here. For additional information, contact the *Franconia-Easton-Sugar Hill Chamber of Commerce,* Box D, Rte. 18, Franconia 03580; 823–5661. Rates at these lodgings are per person based on double occupancy for three nights. Categories, determined by price, are *Expensive,* $75–$100 and up, depending on the meal plan offered; *Moderate,* $50–$75; *Inexpensive,* under $50. All lodging is within 10 miles of the mountain.

Expensive

Franconia Inn. Rte. 116, Franconia 03580; 823–5542. A 29-room traditional New England inn with a ski-touring center, hot tub, sleigh rides, and on-premises dining. MAP available.

Hillwinds Motor Inn. Box 250, Dow Ave., Franconia 03580; 823–5533. With a restaurant and weekend entertainment, this 30-room motel offers a convenient downtown location.

Horse and Hound Inn. Off Rte. 18, Cannon Mountain, Franconia 03580; 823–5501. A traditional 10-room inn at the base of the mountain with cross-country skiing nearby, on-premises pub and dining, fireplaces. Serves breakfast.

Ledgeland. Rte. 117, Sugar Hill 03585; 823–5341. Country inn and housekeeping cottages with fabulous views; completely equipped; open year-round.

Lovetts Inn by Lafayette Brook. Profile Rd., Franconia 03580; 823–7761. A farmhouse built in 1786 that was restored to a 10-room inn boasting stenciled walls and antiques. There are also 6 country cottages. MAP available.

Sugar Hill Inn. Rte. 117, Sugar Hill 03585; 823–5621. A 10-room, restored 1786 farmhouse offering private baths plus 6 cottages. Stenciled walls add country charm to antiques. Hearty breakfasts include muffins and entree.

Moderate

Cannon View Inn. Rte. 117, Sugar Hill 03585; 823–8039. A small bed-and-breakfast with 3 rooms and private baths. Mountain views from the guest living room with a fireplace. Country breakfasts served.

Gale River Motel. Rte. 18, RFD 1, Box 153, Franconia 03580; 823–5655. A 10-room motel with color TV, free in-room coffee, some cottages with multiple bedrooms.

Hilltop Inn. Rte. 117, Sugar Hill 03585; 823–5695. A 5-room bed-and-breakfast Victorian guest house that features hearty farmers' breakfasts.

Raynor's Motor Lodge. Rtes. 18 and 142, Franconia 03580; 823–9586. A 30-room motel with color TV, free coffee, ski racks; massage and MAP available.

Rivagale Inn. 195 Main St., Franconia 03580; 823–7044. A 14-room New England inn with ski lounge. MAP available.

Stonybrook Motor Lodge. Rte. 18, Franconia 03580; 823–8192. Has 24 rooms with color TV, lodge with game room, ice skating, cross-country skiing. MAP available.

Inexpensive

Blancke's B & B. Rte. 116, Easton 03580; 823–7061. This 19th-century farmhouse offers 5 rooms with shared baths. No smoking.

Franconia Notch Vacation Rentals. Rte. 18, Mittersill Rd., Franconia 03580; 823–5536. Privately owned vacation homes with 2–4 bedrooms; with fireplace, kitchen, linens, furnishings.

Pinestead Farm Lodge. Easton Rd., Franconia 03580; 823–8121. Simple rooms (6 only) in a New England farmhouse; share kitchen privileges.

RESTAURANTS. One can dine quite inexpensively in the region with full meals costing $12–$17 in the *Expensive* category and $7–$12, *Moderate*. Unless otherwise noted, major credit cards are accepted.

Moderate to Expensive

Franconia Inn. Rte. 116, Franconia; 823–5542. Describes its fare as classical cuisine prepared with delicate French sauces. Reservations appreciated.

Horse and Hound Inn. Cannon Mountain, Franconia; 823–5501. Look for old pine and prints and American food with a Continental accent. There's often live music on weekends.

Indian Head Motel Resort. Rte. 3, Lincoln; 745–8000. Prime steaks and ribs done to your liking.

Lovetts Inn. Profile Rd., Rte. 18, Franconia; 823–7761. One of the few places around where jackets are required for dinner, along with reservations.

Sugar Hill Inn. Rte. 117, Sugar Hill; 823–5621. Country gourmet cooking in a country inn atmosphere.

Moderate

Dutch Treat Restaurant/Lounge. Main St., Franconia; 823–8851. Homemade Italian and American food; children's plates.

Hillwinds Sirloin Tavern. Franconia Village; 823–5533. Families enjoy casual atmosphere with fine views; offers fish and steaks.

Rivagale Inn. 195 Main St., Box 97, Franconia; 823–7044. New England–style home cooking.

Village House Restaurant. Main St., Franconia; 823–5912. Something for everyone here, including children's menu.

HOW TO GET AROUND. Access to a **car** is imperative here, since public transportation is limited.

SEASONAL EVENTS. Over Washington's Birthday holiday week in **February,** the Franconia community hosts a *Winter Carnival.*

OTHER SPORTS AND ACTIVITIES. There are 10 miles of **cross-country** terrain right at Cannon and an additional 50 miles in the region. Horse-drawn **sleigh rides** are available at the *Franconia Inn* (823–5542). Also available are **ice fishing, skating, sledding,** and **snowmobiling.** Contact the main lodge, 823–5563.

DAY-CARE FACILITIES. *Cannon's Peabody Base Lodge* (823–5563) will entertain young ones aged 6 months and up, 9 A.M.–noon and 1– 4 P.M. Snacks are provided, but not lunch. The day rate is $16, and reservations are appreciated.

NIGHTLIFE. You can catch live music at *Hillwinds,* 823–5533, and at the *Village House Restaurant,* Main St., both in Franconia, 823–5912.

LOON MOUNTAIN

Rte. 112
Lincoln NH 03251
Tel: 603–745–8111

Snow Report: 603–745–8100
Area Vertical: 2,100 ft.
Number of Trails: 41 on 234 acres
Lifts: 1 four-passenger gondola, 2 triple
*   chairs, 5 double chairs, 1 pony lift*
Snowmaking: 85 percent of terrain
Season: mid-November–April

The dying paper-mill town of Lincoln, NH, got a shot in the arm in 1966, when a former New Hampshire governor, Sherman Adams, began creating Loon Mountain. Ultimately, snow farming grew to be a specialty at Loon, where a reputation for well-groomed slopes brought sufficient people to mandate a limited lift-ticket sale policy on weekends. Today it is the busiest ski area in New Hampshire.

Those who have skied the mountain may be hard pressed to say just why it's their favorite, except perhaps that it brings out the best in people who seem uncommonly civil and happy even while waiting for lifts. Nearly half the terrain here is in the intermediate category, but it's always so well groomed that having a good skiing day here is the norm, although the moguls on Angel Street, a black-diamond trail, are purposely left intact.

Recently Loon developed what it calls North Peak, served by its own triple chair and base lodge and offering spectacular views off the top; it houses the area's most challenging terrain.

The White Mountain Limited is a new four-passenger gondola. Its 7,100-foot service goes to the summit.

A village at the base of the mountain has emerged with the Mountain Club on Loon, a contemporary resort hotel that boasts more than 100 luxury suites and plenty of amenities.

Loon is currently wending its way through the environmental process of preparing for major future expansion.

Practical Information for Loon Mountain

HOW TO GET THERE. Loon Mountain is located on Rte. 112, 2 miles from Lincoln and 80 miles from Manchester. **By car.** Take I-93 to Exit 32 onto Rte. 112 East for 4 miles to Loon Mountain. (To get to the region, see Bretton Woods section above.) Shuttle service can be arranged, generally, from various parts of the region by contacting the lodge where reservations are made.

TELEPHONES. The area code for all New Hampshire is 603.

ACCOMMODATIONS. The *Loon Mountain Lodging Bureau,* Loon Mountain, Rte. 112, Lincoln, NH 03251 (800–227–4191), provides information and reservation service to a number of area accommodations, including its own on-mountain condos. Lodgings in the communities at and around Loon Mountain range from the simple to the sublime. The sublime can largely be found in the condominiums and townhouses at or near slopeside, where all amenities are available at prices ranging from $135 per room per night to $380 for two nights in multiple units. Since most of these offer various packages, they are classified here as *Expensive to Deluxe.* In the other two categories in this listing, rates are based on per person, per night mid-week in hotels, motels, and inns. Expect to pay up to 50 percent more on weekends. For *Moderate,* you'll pay $20–$30; *Inexpensive,* under $20. All lodgings listed are within 5 miles of the ski area.

Expensive to Deluxe

Condominiums at Loon Mountain. Rte. 112, Lincoln 03251; 745–8111 or 800–433–3413. Stay right on Loon: 2-, 3-, and 4-bedroom luxurious condos and townhouses. Fully equipped kitchens, fireplaces; all units tastefully furnished.

Lincoln Station. Box 508, Kancamagus Highway, Lincoln 03251; 745–3401. One hundred seventy-five luxury townhouses, fully equipped. Free shuttle to Loon, plus indoor pool, sauna, whirlpool, ice skating, and paddle tennis.

Mountain Club on Loon. Rte. 112, Lincoln 03251; 745–8111 or 800–433–3413. Exclusive slopeside resort hotel with deluxe rooms, studios, and suites accommodating up to 6 people, with fully equipped kitchen, living/dining area. Fine dining, lounge, and full fitness center on the premises.

Nordic Inn. Rte. 112, Lincoln 03251; 745–2727. Condominiums with fireplaces, plus an on-the-premises spa, health club, indoor pool. Located 1 mile from the slopes.

Rivergreen. Box 696, Lincoln 03251; 745–6261. Condominium resort with superior accommodations with in-room Jacuzzis, full kitchens, living/dining area; accommodates 2–8 people per unit.

Satter Resorts. Box 159, Lincoln 03251; 745–6201. Luxury townhouses and condominiums, studios for 2, and 2-, 3-, and 4-bedroom fully furnished units accommodating up to 10 people.

Moderate

Drummer Boy Motor Inn. Rte. 3, Lincoln 03251; 745–3661. Has 57 motel units, some with kitchenettes, Jacuzzis, and king-size beds. Indoor pool, sauna, Jacuzzi, game room, and exercise room on premises.

Mill House Inn. Box 696, Lincoln 03251; 745–6261. A 100-room full-service luxury inn, with shops and restaurants adjacent; indoor pool, Jacuzzi, and sauna.

Woodstock Inn. Box 118, North Woodstock 03262; 745–3951. Victorian inn decorated with antiques. Warm and comfortable, private and shared bath; all units with cable TV. Restaurants serve breakfast, lunch, and dinner.

Woodward's Motor Inn. Rte. 3, Lincoln 03251; 745–8141. Seventy rooms located in a complete family resort, open-hearth restaurant, indoor pool, sauna, Jacuzzi, exercise room, and racquetball.

Inexpensive

Kancamagus Motor Lodge. Box 505, Lincoln 03251; 745–3365. A 34-room motel, featuring in-room steambaths and cable TV; restaurant on premises serves breakfast.

The Profile. Rte. 3, Lincoln 03251; 745–2759. Has 20 comfortable rooms with cable color TV.

Red Doors Motel. Rte. 3, Lincoln 03251; 745–2267. Thirty rooms with cable TV and in-room coffee; game room, and guest laundry.

Riverbank Motel. Box 314, North Woodstock 03262; 745–3374. Eleven rooms and 3 cottages in a quiet riverside location. All with cable TV and most with kitchenettes and a fireplace unit.

White Mountain Motel. Rte. 3, Lincoln 03251; 745–8924. Has 12 rooms and 3 cottages, all with cable TV and in-room coffee.

RESTAURANTS. At slopeside or in the small communities around Loon Mountain, there is a nice array of dining places serving everything from regional New England dishes to ethnic cuisines. Categories are *Expensive,* $18 and up; *Moderate,* $10–$18; and *Inexpensive,* less than $10. The costs represent the price for an average meal for one person, excluding drinks, tax, and tip. Unless specified, the restaurants accept most major credit cards, but it is wise to check before you go.

Expensive

The Common Man. Lincoln; 745–3463. Rustic farmhouse serves all-American cuisine.

Dickens. Village at Loon; 745–2278. Salad bar, extensive menu, weekend brunch, entertainment.

Woodstock Inn. Woodstock; 745–3951. A glass-enclosed, year-round porch offers candlelight dining. Breakfasts here are sumptuous and range from red flannel hash to eggs Benedict.

Moderate

Half-Baked. North Woodstock; 745–3811. As the name implies, a take-out specialty store with everything from a soup-to-nuts dinner to Italian fare.

Indian Head Motel Resort. Lincoln; 745–8181. Prime ribs, seafood.

The Italian Moose. Lincoln; 745–3339. Casual, family-style dining; Italian specialties.

Mt. Adams Inn. North Woodstock; 745–2711. Polish fare, family dining.

Rachel's. At Loon; 745–8111. Steaks and chops done to your liking.

Woodward's Open Hearth Steak House. Lincoln; 745–8141. Baked stuffed shrimp, among other offerings, besides the steaks.

Inexpensive

Truant's Tavern. North Woodstock; 745–2239. A schoolhouse turned fancy with seafood and sandwiches.

Woodstock Station. North Woodstock; 745–3951. Look for a 10-ounce rib eye steak topped with bearnaise sauce.

HOW TO GET AROUND. A **car** is helpful but not necessary because there is a **shuttle bus** service that operates between the mountain and all condo complexes. There is also a bus that goes to the Mill shopping area. At the mountain, a **steam train** shuttles skiers between the two base areas, about one-third of a mile apart.

SEASONAL EVENTS. January features *Independence Weekend,* a time of special races, games for kids, fireworks, and a torchlight parade. *Spring Fling Weekend* is in mid-**March,** with events such as the Cardboard Box Derby and Loon Egg Hunt.

OTHER SPORTS AND ACTIVITIES. *Loon Mt. Ski Touring* (745–8111) offers 35 km of **cross-country** trails that include sights along an old logging road and treks into the Pemigewasset wilderness. Nature and wilderness tours are offered here throughout the winter. NASTAR races are held daily and surfboard-like devices called **snowboards** are championed here (they aren't at most areas). The snowboard is a single ski about 4 feet long and 1 foot wide that is strapped to the feet for descents of the mountain.

The fitness center at the Mountain Club has an indoor **lap pool, saunas, Jacuzzi, racquetball courts, squash facilities,** and a teen activities center. There's also a health/fitness facility at the Nordic Inn, 745–2727.

Look for **swimming** at Woodward's Motor Inn (745–8141), the Village of Loon Townhouses (745–3401), the Lodge at Lincoln Station (745–3441), Indian Head Resort (745–8181), the Drummer Boy Motor Inn (745–3661), all in Lincoln; and the Alpine Village Townhouses (745–3455) in North Woodstock. Alpine Village and Woodward's Motor Inn (745–8141) also have **racquetball** courts, and there's **tennis** at The Beacon Motel (745–8118) along with swimming in Lincoln. **Ice fishing, skating, sledding,** and **mountaineering** can also be arranged.

HINTS TO THE DISABLED. The *Loon Disabled Skier Program* is an affiliate of National Handicapped Sports. The first lesson is free; thereafter, a nominal fee is charged. Equipment is provided.

DAY-CARE FACILITIES. *Honeybear Nursery* for children 6 weeks to 6 years runs 8:30 A.M.–4:30 P.M. The all-day rate is $30–35. *SKIwee* is available to children 3–8 years and *Mountain Explorers* for children 9–12 years. Full-day rates, including lift tickets, range from $45 to $60, with multi-day discounts available.

NIGHTLIFE. Entertainment in this region includes dancing to rock 'n' roll at the *Loon Saloon* (745–8111), plus comedy night on Sunday and a live band or duo on stage nightly (except Mondays) at the *Granite Bar* in the Mountain Club at the ski area (745–8111), dancing and nightly fun at *Indian Head,* Lincoln (745–8181), and at *Day's Inn* in Campton (536–3520). *Dickens* at the Village of Loon (745–2278) also brings in musicians.

MT. WASHINGTON VALLEY SKI AREAS

ATTITASH

Rte. 302
Bartlett NH 03812
Tel: 603-374-2368

Snow Report: 603-374-0946
Area Vertical: 1,750 ft.
Number of trails: 27 on 220 acres
Lifts: 4 double chairs, 2 triple chairs
Snowmaking: 98 percent
Season: late November–mid-April

Attitash is one of four areas in the Mt. Washington Valley that, because of their proximity to one another, offer interchangeable lift tickets with the purchase of a 3-out-of-4-day midweek pass or any 4-out-of-5-day pass (including weekends). The other areas are Wildcat in Pinkham Notch, Mt. Cranmore in North Conway, and Black Mountain in Jackson, all of which share not only their skiing but their dining and lodging accommodations as well.

Attitash, located on Route 302, 8 miles from North Conway, is an intermediate skier's mountain, with half of its 27 trails, including the 1¼-mile Northwest Passage, marked for the average recreational skier. However, a 42 percent gradient on Idiot's Option has been known to challenge those with a penchant for black-diamond thrills. Kids and beginners like trails with names like Far-Out and Double Delight. A limited lift-ticket sales policy in effect on weekends and holidays helps avoid congestion at the lifts and on the trails.

"New" is the word here, with a 1,000-foot triple chair servicing protected beginner terrain, plus an on-slope place for kids, the Attitots Clubhouse.

The motto of Attitash is "Best skiing in the East, whether it snows or not." With a reputation for quality snowmaking and grooming, added to the "new" feeling of the resort, Attitash is a favorite of many Mt. Washington Valley skiers.

MT. CRANMORE

North Conway NH 03860
Tel: 603-356-5543

Snow Report: 603-356-5543
Area Vertical: 1,167 ft.
Number of Trails: 28 on 185 acres
Lifts: 2 trams, 1 triple chair, 4 double
  chairs
Snowmaking: 100 percent
Season: December–April

One of America's oldest ski areas, started in 1938, Mt. Cranmore may well be the raison d'être for North Conway. It's here that stories abound of skier-laden snow trains puffing up from the cities in the 1930s. The Mt. Cranmore Skimobile, recently exiled to museum status and no longer in operation, was one of the first ski lifts in the United States. For many years, the famed Hannes Schneider Ski School was run by his son Herbert, the area skimeister. The school no longer bears Schneider's name and Herbert no longer runs it (so much for tradition).

The skiing here is primarily in the intermediate range, but don't be surprised if you see old-fashioned leather ski boots and long skis whipping past on its five black-diamond trails.

The mountain is an east-facing slope that catches the sun on cold days, and it is one of the few ski areas in the country that's really located within walking distance of a real village (as opposed to a village created because of skiing). North Conway has over 100 brand-name factory outlets and shops and over 70 restaurants and night spots. Skiers can hit the trails in the morning, wander down to North Conway for lunch and shopping, and spend the afternoon back on the slopes.

WILDCAT MOUNTAIN

Rte. 16
Jackson NH 03846
Tel: 603–466–3326

Snow Report: 800–552–8952 in NH; 617–
965–7991 in MA
Area Vertical: 2,100 ft.
Number of Trails: 30 on 120 acres
Lifts: 1 gondola, 4 triple chairs, 1 double
chair
Snowmaking: 97 percent of terrain
Season: mid-November–late April/early May

With a summit standing at 4,100 feet and a 2,100-foot vertical, Wildcat is well named. It's the next best thing to skiing Mt. Washington in this neck of the woods and is Mt. Washington Valley's biggest ski area. Wildcat is also one of four (including Attitash, Black Mountain, and Mt. Cranmore) that enjoy interchangeable lift-ticket privileges.

Magnificent alpine views are available here even to novice skiers who make descents from the summit. In fact, according to every poll taken, Wildcat always wins the "best scenery in the East" category. From the summit of Wildcat are glimpses of Tuckerman's Ravine across the way. And it was standing on the Mt. Washington side looking over to Wildcat that first inspired some skiers to think of cutting trails on Wildcat.

In 1933, the first race down the Wildcat Trail was held after it was cut by the Civilian Conservation Corps (CCC). Back then, skiers hiked up on fur-lined skis, and if they made three runs a day, they were happy. Today, with the gondola, skiers can make many more runs than they ever imagined in 1933.

Although the trails are narrow, which makes them feel steep, the pitch of the terrain is generally considered enjoyable by upper intermediates. The narrowness of the trails protects skiers and precious snow from the wind. This old-style "trail skiing" is becoming an endangered species in the era of "super trails" and is what makes Wildcat special.

There's a separate area for beginning skiers—the Snowcat Area—that's served by its own triple chair. Children aged 6 and under can ride the chair free, if accompanied by a ticket-bearing parent.

Practical Information for Mt. Washington Valley Ski Areas

HOW TO GET THERE. North Conway is about 130 miles from Boston.

By air. *Continental, Delta, United, USAir,* and *Bar Harbor* airlines fly to the Portland International Jetport, 65 miles away. All major and regional carriers serve Boston's Logan Airport. The regional airport in Fryeburg, ME, 15 miles from North Conway, accepts private aircraft and charters. *Ajax, Avis, Budget, Hertz, National,* and *Thrifty* rental car systems are located at the Portland International Jetport (see Maine chapter for details). All major rental car systems are at Logan. In North Conway, car rentals are available through *Crest Chevrolet* (603) 356–5401; *Freedom Rent a Car* (603) 447–2875; and *Presidential Motors* (603) 356–3136.

By bus. *Concord Trailways* (800–852–3317) offers direct bus service daily from Logan and downtown Boston to North Conway. *Vermont Transit/Greyhound* (800–451–3292) offers daily service to the area via Montreal and Portland.

By car. Take I-95 North to Spaulding Turnpike in Portsmouth NH, to Route 16 north to North Conway. Routes from North Conway to the individual ski areas: Rte. 302 to Attitash in Bartlett, Rte. 16 to Wildcat or Mt. Cranmore in North Conway.

TELEPHONES. The area code for all New Hampshire is 603.

ACCOMMODATIONS. The *Mt. Washington Valley Chamber of Commerce,* North Conway 03860 (356–3171), provides a reservation service for about 100 lodging establishments serving the ski areas. But it should be remembered that the entire valley is a tourist mecca, so you may be staying at a lodging at Attitash, for example, while skiing at Mt. Cranmore. Since most establishments offer packages, lodging rates are based on three nights per person, double occupancy. Categories determined by price for the package (unless otherwise stated) are *Expensive,* $100 and up; *Moderate,* $60–$100; *Inexpensive,* under $60. All lodging is within 5 miles of the slopes unless otherwise noted.

Major credit cards are generally accepted although small restaurants sometimes do not use them. Also, some of the outlet stores accept checks or cash only. Always check first.

Attitash

A special lodging service specifically for the Attitash area can be contacted at 800–223–SNOW.

Moderate

Attitash Mountain Village. Rte. 302, Bartlett 03812; 374–6501. Slopeside 1- to 4-bedroom condos and motel-style rooms, with mountain views, fireplaces, indoor pool, Jacuzzi, sauna, game room, ice skating, color cable TV. Dining on premises; ski packages available.

The Bernerhof Inn. Rte. 302, Glen 03838; 383–4414. Turn-of-century inn has 10 antique-appointed rooms, a Finnish sauna, and some private baths, and serves breakfast in bed. Also look for fine on-premises dining and entertainment. MAP available.

Best Western Storybook Motor Inn. Rtes. 16 and 302, Glen 03838; 383–6800. A 53-room colonial inn with dining room, private baths, sauna, laundry, game room. Especially hearty breakfasts served here.

The Notchland Inn. Hart's Location, Bartlett 03812; 374–6131. A 19th-century inn with 10 antique-filled rooms, private baths, fireplaces, sauna, Jacuzzi, on-premises dining, ice skating. Located about 9 miles from the slopes. MAP available.

The Seasons at Attitash. Rte. 302, Bartlett 03812; 374–2361. Full-service resort with 2- to 4-bedroom condominiums, with fireplaces and full-kitchen facilities. Indoor pool, Jacuzzi, sauna, and restaurant.

Inexpensive

The Country Inn at Bartlett. Rte. 302, Box 327, Bartlett Village 03812; 374–2353. Only 6 rooms in inn, but additional 20 rooms in cottages and 1 efficiency cottage. Cottages have private baths, cable TV. In the lodge are music room, ski racks, and ski tuning bench.

Linderhof Motor Inn. Rte. 16, Box 126, Glen 03838; 383–4334. A Bavarian-style inn offering 33 rooms with 2 double beds, private bath, color TV. Breakfasts available.

The Red Apple Inn. Rte. 302, Glen 03838; 383–9680. Motel accommodations with dining and lounge, cross-country skiing out the back door, fireplace lounge, country breakfasts.

The Villager Motel. Rte. 302, Bartlett 03812; 374–2742. Motel and housekeeping units, two chalets in quiet valley setting.

Will's Inn. Rte. 302, Glen 03838; 383–4239. Knotty pine adds warmth to rooms equipped with cable TV, private baths, and in-room coffee. Meals available.

Mt. Cranmore

Expensive

Darby Field Inn. Bald Hill Rd., Conway 03818; 447–2181. Has 17 rooms (15 with private bath) and what a view of the Mt. Washington Valley! On-premises dining, lounge, cross-country skiing, weekend entertainment. MAP available.

Fox Ridge Resort. Rte. 16, North Conway 03860; 356–3151. A modern resort on a 300-acre hilltop perch. Fine dining, lounge, indoor pool, whirlpool, sauna, color TV. MAP available.

New England Inn. Rte. 16A, Intervale 03845; 356–5541. An 1809 26-room country inn with 14 cottages (9 with fireplaces). Cross-country skiing on premises, sleigh rides, dining. MAP available.

Red Jacket Motor Inn. Rte. 16, North Conway 03860; 356–5411. Modern, if miniature, resort complex set on a hillside. Restaurant, saloon, kitchenettes; indoor pool, whirlpool, sauna, game room, color TV. MAP available.

Snowvillage Inn. Off Rte. 153, Snowville 03877 (near Conway); 447–2818. A pleasant 16-room country inn with cross-country skiing, sauna, library, game room. MAP available.

Moderate

The Buttonwood Inn. Box 3297, Mt. Surprise Rd., North Conway 03860; 356–2625. A secluded 8-room bed-and-breakfast inn with private and semiprivate baths, TV and game rooms, après-ski room with fireplace, hearty breakfasts. MAP available.

The Cranmore Inn. Kearsarge Rd., North Conway 03860; 356–5502. A 25-room inn located near movie theaters, offers 4 suites, 4 private baths, TV room; dining on premises.

Cranmore Mt. Lodge. Box 1194, Kearsarge Rd., North Conway 03860; 356–2044. An 11-room inn with shared baths plus 2-room suite with private bath and TV; also 4 rooms in a barn loft, all with private baths and color TV. On-premises ice skating, tobogganing, snowmobiling, and dining. MAP available.

Eastern Inn. Rte. 16, North Conway 03860; 356–5447. Comfortable, spacious rooms.

Eastern Slope Inn Resort. Rte. 16, North Conway 03860; 356–6321. Downtown location offers 125 rooms, all recently renovated, dining room, pub, sauna, Jacuzzi, year-round pool.

Green Granite Motel. Rte. 16, North Conway 03860; 356–6901. Comfortable rooms, private baths, in-room TV, and Continental breakfasts.

The Merrill Farm Inn. Rte. 16, Box 2070, Conway 03818; 447–3866. Offers 60 rooms with private baths, sauna, Jacuzzi, solar-heated outdoor pool, in-room TV, all in old-fashioned New England setting.

Nereledge Inn & White Horse Pub. River Rd., North Conway 03860; 356–2831. A 1787 inn that serves apple pie for breakfast; 8 guest rooms with shared baths, 2 sitting rooms, dining room and pub.

The 1785 Inn. Box 9, North Conway 03860; 356–9025. A 14-room inn with shared and private baths, 2 guest living rooms, après-ski lounge, breakfasts, and a great place for dinner.

Sunny Side Inn. Seavey St., North Conway 03860; 356–6239. Eleven rooms with private baths available, common living room with fireplace and wood stove in dining room.

Inexpensive

There's a collection of motels in the area with rates under $45 for three nights per person, double occupancy.

Wildcat Mountain

Wildcat's Skier Service Center, Box R, Jackson, NH 03846, offers skiing and lodging packages with nearby motels and inns. Call 603–466–3326 (in NH) or 800–255–6439 for information and reservations.

Expensive

Christmas Farm Inn. Rte. 16B, Jackson 03846; 383–4313. A remodeled 18th-century Cape Cod that's full of antiques. Most of the 33 rooms have private baths; cabins and suites also available. On-premises dining, lounge, game room, sauna. MAP available.

The Inn at Thorn Hill. Box SW, Jackson Village 03846; 383–4242. A 22-room inn on a country road, with dining room, game room, and wax room. With MAP.

Wentworth Resort Hotel. Rte. 16A, Jackson Village 03846; 383–9700 or 800–637–0013. A 50-room hotel in the grand style, located on ski touring route. All rooms with private baths, color cable TV. MAP available.

Whitney's Village Inn. Box W, Jackson 03846; 383–6886 or 800–252–5622. An inn and motor lodge with ice skating, tobogganing, and cross-country skiing nearby. Thirty-one of 37 rooms have private baths, 4 with fireplaces. On-premises dining, lounge, pub, game room.

Moderate

Covered Bridge Motel. Jackson Village 03846; 383–6630 or 800–634–2911. Twenty-six rooms with color TV, social room with fireplace, breakfasts served, sauna, Jacuzzi.

Dana Place Inn. Rte. 16, Jackson 03846; 383–6822 or 800–537–9276. A renovated country inn with some motel units and on-premises dining, lounge, comfortable living room with fireplace; some shared baths.

Town and Country Resort Motel. Rte. 2, Gorham 03851; 466–3315. A full-service resort motel with 153 rooms, indoor pool, restaurant, lounge, and nightly entertainment.

The Village House. Box 359, Jackson 03846; 383–6666. A 10-room inn, with private baths, ski waxing room, greenhouse breakfast porch.

Wildcat Inn & Tavern. Rte. 16 A, Jackson Village 03846; 383–4245. A 15-room traditional country inn offering hot tub and sauna, ice skating, sleigh rides, dining and tavern with weekend entertainment.

Inexpensive

Appalachian Mountain Club. Pinkham Notch Camp; 466–2727. Dorm-style rooms and hearty family-style meals in an environment that recalls skiing "the way it used to be."

RESTAURANTS. Dining out in the Mt. Washington Valley can be a treat to both the palate and the pocketbook. New Hampshire provides tasty food aplenty, not only traditional New England chowders but a wide range of international cuisines as well. Categories based on per-person price range for a full meal exclusive of beverage, tax, and tip are *Expensive,* $20 and up; *Moderate,* $10–$20; *Inexpensive,* $10 and under.

Expensive

The Darby Field Inn. Off Rte. 16, North Conway; 447–2181. Sunset views of the valley are served up with gourmet fare. Candlelight dinner and daily specials.

Inn at Thorn Hill. Jackson Village; 383–4242. A restaurant known for its presentation and sauces; reservations required.

Stonehurst Manor. Rte. 16, North Conway; 356–3113. An international ambience is noticed here, with delicacies like veal Oscar and beef Wellington.

Wentworth Resort Hotel. Rte. 16A, Jackson; 383–9700. Waiters are in formal attire here where a specialty is burgundy rack of lamb. Reservations required.

Moderate to Expensive

Dana Place Inn. Rte. 16, North Conway; 383–6822. European-American choices here and a great place for lunch after taking the Ellis River Trail on cross-country skis from the Jackson Ski Touring Foundation.

New England Inn. Off Rte. 16A, Intervale; 356–5541. Authentic New England preparations are featured, including Vermont turkey; children's menu available.

Moderate

Barnaby's. Rte. 16, North Conway; 356–5781. An extensive menu includes roast beef and salad bar.

Bellini's. Seavey St., North Conway; 356–6331. Pastas, veal, and prime rib featured in elegant or pub setting.

Bernerhof Inn. Rte. 302, Glen; 383–4414. Austrian cuisine served in turn-of-century inn includes fondue by the fire.

Crawdad's at the Eastern Slope Inn. Main St., North Conway; 356–6321. A choice of elegant or pub dining. As the name says, near the slopes.

Horsefeathers. Main St., North Conway; 356–2687. Sustenance, merriment, and cheer is the motto, which it lives up to, offering entertainment as well as vittles.

The Inn at Thorn Hill. Rte. 112, Jackson; 383–9700. Enjoy American food by candlelight.

Nereledge Inn and White Horse Pub. River Rd., North Conway; 356–2831. English beers and an English pub atmosphere.

Red Parka Pub. Rte. 302, Glen; 383–4344. Ribs, seafood, salad bar, and draft beer served in pint jars; this is *the* après-ski place for Wildcat skiers.

Snug Harbor. River Rd., North Conway; 356–3000. A Colonial home with seafood specialties and a children's menu.

Studebaker's. Rte. 16, North Conway; 356–5011. A 1950s decor, complete with waitresses in poodle skirts and lots of neon and Coca-Cola memorabilia. Features pub-style food, steaks, and seafood.

Inexpensive

Checkers. Main St., Conway; 447–5524. Pasta specialties and veal dishes.

Margaritaville. Rte. 16, Glen; 383–6556. Mexican food with some American entrees for the timid. You can eat in the bar or dining room.

Scarecrow Pub & Grill. Rte. 16, Intervale; 356–2287. Generous portions of such delicacies as cioppino and other Italian fare.

Up Country Saloon. Rte. 16, North Conway; 356–9782. Mexican and American fare.

HOW TO GET AROUND. It's preferable to have a **car** in this region, where public transportation facilities are rare or spasmodic. Two trolleys transport visitors to and from Attitash and throughout North Conway for $1. Multiple tickets can be purchased at a saving. (See *How to Get There* section above for car rental information.)

SEASONAL EVENTS. At Attitash, the mountain is race oriented, with the *Lathrop Ski Camp* offering race clinics throughout the season. Just before the ski year ends, an easy giant slalom for skiers 40 years old and up promises a good time during the annual *Old Man of the Mountain Race,* named after that formidable craggy face that's a landmark of the White Mountains.

At Mt. Cranmore, the *Winterfest Winter Carnival* that rolls by annually in **mid-January** brings racers, snow sculpting, fireworks, and a torchlight parade to all the ski areas in the Mt. Washington Valley.

At Wildcat, recreational skiers can ski like the pros the first weekend of **March** during the annual *Wildcat Challenge Dual Format Race.* The *New England NASTAR Championships* are held the last weekend in March. Around **Easter,** there's the *Corn Snow Caper,* a rite of spring that includes silly slaloms, a costume contest, snow volleyball, and more. The *New England Handicapped Sportsmen's Association* also benefits from an annual race held here. *Rites of Spring* with the New England Patriots is co-hosted by Wildcat and Attitash in early **March.** This is a benefit ski race and on-snow volleyball tournament. *Fun for Life* is a benefit for the Dana-Farber Cancer Institute. It is held in late **February.** Three-person teams enjoy races and barbecues.

OTHER SPORTS AND ACTIVITIES. Skiing is just one of many attractions in the Mt. Washington Valley. There are community outdoor **skating** rinks in Jackson, North Conway, and Conway. **Sleigh rides** are available at New England Inn, Intervale, 356–5541.

The following establishments have **health/fitness** centers: North Conway Athletic Club, North Conway (356–5774); 5 racquetball courts, 13 Nautilus machines, full free-weight center, and complete aerobics schedule. Mt. Cranmore Racquet Club, North Conway (356–6301): 2 racquetball, 5 indoor tennis courts, 2 squash courts, 10 Nautilus machines, indoor swimming pool, plus a 48-foot indoor climbing wall, among the highest in the Northeast.

Jackson is also home of the *Jackson Ski Touring Foundation* (383–9355), which coordinates trails and activities of 5 major touring areas offering over 200 km of trails. This is the largest ski touring complex in the East, moving ski touring buffs from inn to inn, around villages, or challenging the mountains on backcountry routes.

The five areas of the center include the center itself, the *Nestlenook Inn and Ski Touring* (383–9443), the *Linderhof Motor Inn* (383–4334), all in Jackson; the *Intervale Nordic Learning Center* on the grounds of the New England Inn (356–5541), and the *Forest Inn* (356–9772), both in Intervale.

For details on night cross-country skiing, backcountry guided tours, and Telemark skiing, contact the *Intervale Nordic Learning Center* (356–5541); *International Mountain Equipment,* North Conway (356–6316); or *Eastern Mountain Sports,* North Conway (356–5433). *International Mountain Equipment* is also the place to contact for details on **ice-climbing expeditions** that are popular in the area.

HINTS TO THE HANDICAPPED. In addition to hosting an annual benefit for the New England Handicapped Sportsmen's Association, the regional chapter of National Handicapped Sports, handicapped skiers receive complimentary lift tickets. At Mt. Cranmore, special lessons are offered to the handicapped, including the hearing-impaired, amputees, and highly motivated retarded children. Call 356–5544 for information.

CHILDREN'S ACTIVITIES. In Attitash, the *Attitots Clubhouse* accepts children from 1 to 6 years, 8:15 A.M.–4:15 P.M. daily. Lunch is available, as are private ski lessons for the older children. The *Attitash Ski School* involves 6- to 9-year-olds in an all-day program that includes lunch and two lessons daily. Young skiers aged 5–14 who want to master the parallel turn can join the *Atticrashers* before moving up to the *Mountaineers,* which introduces racing techniques. The weekend-holiday program operates from mid-December to mid-March. For information on any of these programs, call 374–2368.

The Mt. Cranmore Nursery (356–5543) accepts children aged 1–6 from 8:30 A.M. to 4 P.M. daily for $15 a day. The ski school staff will pick up children from the nursery and take them on the slopes for lessons.

At Wildcat Mountain, the *Kitten Club* (466–3326) accepts children 1 year and up from 8:30 A.M. to 4:30 P.M. Children aged 4 and under can take a private ski lesson for $15 through the club's ski school. *SKIwee,* the nationally recognized learn-to-ski program for children, is available for ages 5–12. Seasonal programs are offered for children who will come with their families frequently to Wildcat.

NIGHTLIFE. The entire area prides itself on bringing in a variety of live enter-tainers. Look for rock 'n' roll, lots of loud music, and the under-30 crowd at *Barnaby's* (356–5781), *Bogie's* (356–2472), *Horsefeathers* (356–2687), *Jackson Square at the Eastern Slope Inn* (356–9466), and *Marcello's* (356–2313) in North Conway; the *Red Parka Pub* (383–4344) in Glen; and *W. W. Doolittle's* (374–6055) in Bartlett, a popular après-ski hangout.

Music on the softer side can be found at *Fox Ridge Resort* (356–3151), the *Darby Field Inn* (447–2181), and *Red Jacket Inn* (356–5411), all in North Conway; and at the *Wildcat Inn and Tavern* (383–4245) and *The Bernerhof* (383–4414) in Glen.

WATERVILLE VALLEY

Waterville Valley NH 03215
Tel: 603–236–8311

Snow Report: 603–236–4144
Area Vertical: 2,020 ft.
Number of Trails: 53 on 226 acres on two
  mountains
Lifts: 1 detachable quad, 3 triple chairs,
  5 double chairs, 1 poma, 1 T-bar, 1
  J-bar, 1 Mitey Mite
Snowmaking: 96 percent of terrain
Season: mid-November–mid-April

Waterville Valley is a self-contained, privately owned, 500-acre resort favored by Bostonians who travel north 2½ hours into New Hampshire's White Mountain National Forest. In fact, this place is inextricably linked to the Kennedy mystique, since the late Senator Robert Kennedy lent some financial backing to the area in the mid-1960s and the Kennedy clan subsequently began skiing here.

As with other New England ski areas, it was the summer wilderness ambience that first drew families to the region. These same families then began to see the possibilities of winter recreation and formed ski clubs to cut a few trails on Snow's Mountain in the mid-1930s. Nearby 4,004-foot Mt. Tecumseh, where the bulk of Waterville Valley's trails are located today, received trail-cutting attention from the Civilian Conservation Corps in the 1930s.

It was the draw of the 1½-mile Mt. Tecumseh Trail that first brought Tom Corcoran, a rising Olympic ski-racing hopeful, to the area in 1948. In 1965, after international competition, he returned to create this destination ski resort.

Over half the area's trails are designed for intermediate-level skiers, with the 3-mile Periphery and nearly mile-long Valley Run two favorites. The steepest trail, with a 38 percent gradient, is Bobby's Run, providing black-diamond challenges along its 3,500-foot length. There are five intermediate trails serviced by a double chairlift and a half-pipe for snowboard skiers on Snow's Mountain.

The village itself is 1½ miles away from the slopes, but there is a free shuttle. At the village are inns, condominiums, restaurants, shops, and rec-reational facilities, along with the Town Square, a five-building re-tail/commercial complex, and the 139-unit Golden Eagle Lodge. All buildings in the village comply with strict zoning codes that call for natu-ral wood exteriors, views from all windows, and nothing higher than four stories.

Mountain guides are available to orient skiers to the area, and much of the social life revolves around the Waterville Valley Ski Week that cou-ples daily on-slope lessons with a moonlight ski touring party, ski races, and entertainment. Families with young children are especially welcome here, with free skiing and lodging midweek (nonholidays) for children aged 12 and under.

Waterville Valley maintains a limited lift-ticket sales policy to keep lift lines to a minimum that it clocks to 15 minutes.

Practical Information for Waterville Valley

HOW TO GET THERE. Waterville Valley is located 70 miles from Manchester and 130 miles from Boston.

By bus. *Concord Trailways* (800–258–3722) provides a daily afternoon trip from downtown Boston and Logan Airport to Plymouth, which is 20 miles from Waterville Valley. Transfers from Plymouth to the village are available by calling the *Waterville Valley Lodging Bureau* at 800–GO–VALLE.

By car. From Boston, take I-93 North to Exit 28, then follow Rte. 49 East 11 miles to Waterville Valley. (See Bretton Woods section above for details on getting to the region.)

TELEPHONES. The area code for all New Hampshire is 603.

ACCOMMODATIONS. The *Waterville Valley Lodging Bureau*, Waterville Valley, NH 03223 (603–236–8371 or 800–GO–VALLE), can make lodging arrangements at inns and numerous condominiums totaling over 6,500 beds within a 5-minute drive of the slopes. All are modern by New England standards, having been built since 1966. Inn rates are per person per night based on double occupancy. Categories determined by price are *Expensive*, $99 and up; *Moderate*, $79–$99. Condominium rates range upward from $115 for a 1-bedroom unit for one night. All lodging is 3 miles from the mountain and serviced by a free shuttle bus that makes continuous rounds.

Golden Eagle Lodge. *Expensive.* Waterville Valley; 236–4551. New 139-suite lodge. Designed in the manner of the grand old hotels of a New Hampshire past with turrets and cupolas. One- and 2-bedroom suites and loft suites offered with hotel amenities. Rooms come with sports-center privileges that include indoor swimming pool, saunas, and whirlpools.

Waterville Valley Condominium Vacations. *Moderate to Expensive.* Waterville Valley; 236–4101. Over 150 1- to 4-bedroom townhouses with well-equipped kitchens, living rooms with fireplaces, and color cable TV. Some have laundry facilities.

Black Bear Lodge. *Moderate.* Waterville Valley; 236–4501. Spacious 106-suite hotel offering 1- and 2-bedroom suites with compact kitchens, bedrooms with double and trundle beds, queen-size wall beds in living rooms. Hotel services include swimming, game room, and sports-center privileges.

Snowy Owl Inn. *Moderate.* Waterville Valley; 236–8383. An 80-room inn with Jacuzzi bathtubs and wet bars in 42 rooms. Complimentary Continental breakfasts include fresh fruit and homemade breads, and there are wine and cheese receptions every afternoon. Guests have free access to a fully equipped sports center.

Valley Inn and Tavern. *Moderate.* Waterville Valley; 236–8336. Look for fresh chocolate-chip cookies and hot-cocoa afternoons and a mint on your pillow at night. Rate includes MAP.

Village Condominiums. *Moderate.* Waterville Valley; 236–8301. Twenty-five easy housekeeping units with dishwasher and disposal, laundry, color cable TV, and choice of 1–5 bedrooms. The units flank a central building housing a game room and saunas.

Windsor Hill Condominiums. *Moderate.* Waterville Valley; 236–8321. Eight 1- to 3-bedroom and 1-bedroom deluxe units.

Silver Squirrel. *Inexpensive.* Waterville Valley; 236–8325. This economical lodging facility maintains down-home hospitality in a serene mountain setting. Cozy lounge with stone fireplace. Within easy walk of shops, restaurants, sports center, and town square.

RESTAURANTS. Since Waterville Valley is a self-contained resort, skiers dine at on-site restaurants in the village itself. Categories for these eating places are *Expensive*, $20 and up; *Moderate*, $10–$20; and *Inexpensive*, less than $10. These price classifications are based on the average cost of a meal for one person, excluding drinks, tax, and tip. All accept major credit cards.

The Valley Tavern. *Expensive.* Waterville Valley; 236–8336. Candlelight dining in a greenhouse ambience. Try the duckling.

Brookside Bistro. *Moderate.* Waterville Valley; 236–4309. Located in Town Square. Serves breakfast, lunch, and dinner. Italian and American cooking. Children's menu. Antique bar.

Schwendi Hutte. *Moderate.* Waterville Valley; 236–8311. A rustic mountain-top log cabin, accessed by chairlift and serving lobster bisque and Bermuda fish chowder, hot drinks, and chocolate dip fruit fondue.

Waterville Valley Yacht Club. *Moderate.* Waterville Valley; 236–8885. The *Rudder Hugger Lounge* with its own 23-foot 1956 wooden Chris Craft has a light menu. The main restaurant features steak, seafood, and duck. Children's menu.

Chili Peppers. *Inexpensive.* Waterville Valley; 236–4646. This Mexican-style eatery located in the Sports Center offers an extensive menu of tangy and spicy fare for lunch and dinner. Children's menu.

Coffee Emporium. *Inexpensive.* Waterville Valley; 236–4021. Serves breakfast, 20 different kinds of coffee; it has a gourmet foods section.

Finish Line Restaurant & Lounge. *Inexpensive.* Waterville Valley; 236–8800. Informal family dining.

Jugtown Deli. *Inexpensive.* Waterville Valley; 236–8662. Sandwiches, salads, fresh baked goods.

Larry's Alpine Pizza & Ice Cream Shoppe. *Inexpensive.* Waterville Valley; 236–4173. Pizza, subs, and ice cream specialties.

Sunnyside Up. *Inexpensive.* Waterville Valley; 236–8311. Mid-mountain cafeteria with chipped beef and blintzes for breakfast; pasta, pizza, and more for lunch.

HOW TO GET AROUND. You can leave your car parked for the length of your stay here, for a free **shuttle** makes the rounds continuously between the village dwellings and the mountain.

SEASONAL EVENTS. An outdoor sunrise **Easter** service begins at 5 A.M. every year. Before that, however, in **February**, WBZ-TV from Boston hosts the *Jack Williams Ski Race* to raise funds to support adoption programs.

OTHER ACTIVITIES. Look for NASTAR recreational **racing**, Wednesday through Sunday, with a coin-op race course open daily. There's an **indoor sports** center at the village with 25-meter indoor and outdoor pools, jogging track, tennis, racquetball and squash courts, and exercise and weight rooms. Village guests can **skate** at a covered ice-skating rink, take **sleigh rides**, and go on moonlight ski tours. The Snow's Mountain chairlift operates on weekends and holidays and the halfpipe is lit for night skiing at these times as well. The *Waterville Valley Ski Touring Center* (236–4666) maintains 105 km (70 km groomed and double-tracked trails) that loop from the center through the White Mountain National Forest, weather permitting.

DAY-CARE FACILITIES. The *Waterville Valley Nursery* accepts children from 6 weeks to 5 years and is open 8:30 A.M.– 4 P.M. daily. Older youngsters can enjoy an on-snow play period or learn to ski in three programs, for ages 3–5, 6–8, and 9–12, through *SKIwee*, a nationally recognized instructional approach to teaching the sport to children.

NIGHTLIFE. The *World Cup Bar and Grill* in the Waterville Valley Base Lodge offers après-ski entertainment daily 4 –6 P.M. *Legends 1291*, Waterville Valley's only year-round dance club, is open daily from 4 P.M. to 1 A.M. (236–8311). Weekend and holiday entertainment are featured at the *Waterville Valley Yacht Club* (236–8885) and the *Brookside Bistro* (236–4309).

New York

If you love New York, as the slogan suggests, you may well fall in love with New York skiing.

While New York lacks many of the destination resorts found in neighboring New England, it makes up for it in the number of areas specializing in day visits. There are—at last count—55 separate alpine ski areas operating.

Of the ski vacation destinations, certainly Lake Placid and Whiteface Mountain head the list. The home of both the 1936 and 1980 Winter Olympic Games, this bustling winter-sports mecca remains electric with sports activity. Hunter Mountain in the Catskills is the Manhattan singles scene moved to the hills, and has been the king of the East's snowmakers for years.

Other major players on the NY ski scene include Gore Mountain, Windham, Whiteface, and Belleayre. Greek Peak and Labrador in the Central Leatherstocking/Finger Lakes area and Holiday Valley and Peak 'n Peak in the Western region are not included here but are noteworthy day areas. New York State also boasts high-quality nordic skiing at a variety of locations.

Too often, skiers put their cars on auto-pilot to head for the Green or White Mountains of New England, bypassing the kinds of places a skier can, well, love.

BELLEAYRE MOUNTAIN SKI CENTER

Box 313
Highmount NY 12441
Tel: 914–254–5600

Snow Report: 800–942–6904 (New York only); 800–431–6012 (outside New York)
Area Vertical: 1,340 ft.
Number of Trails: 23 on 89 skiable acres
Lifts: 3 double chairs, 1 triple chair, 3 T-bars
Snowmaking: 85 percent
Season: late November–late March

Belleayre Mountain Ski Center is owned and operated by the New York State Department of Conservation. The 43-year-old ski area has been pulling skiers up from New York City and New Jersey for enjoyable outdoor recreation and the ambience of the central Catskills.

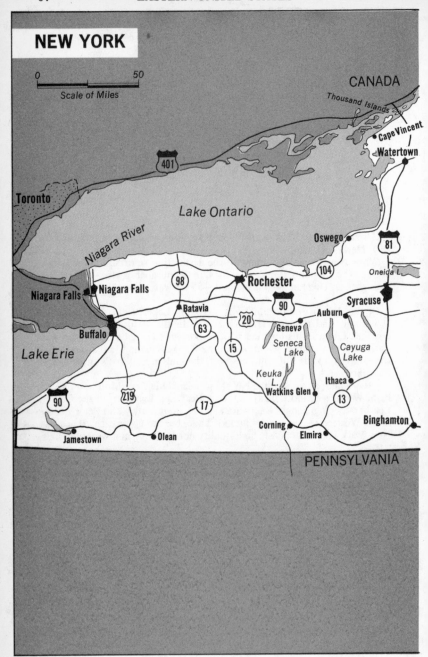

NEW YORK

0   50
Scale of Miles

CANADA

Thousand Islands

Cape Vincent
Watertown

401

Toronto

Lake Ontario

Niagara River

Oswego

104

81

Oneida L.

98

Rochester

90

Syracuse

Niagara Falls
Niagara Falls

Batavia

20

Auburn

63

Geneva

Seneca
Lake

Cayuga
Lake

Buffalo

15

Lake Erie

Keuka
L.

Ithaca

Watkins Glen

13

90

219

17

Corning

Elmira

Binghamton

Jamestown

Olean

PENNSYLVANIA

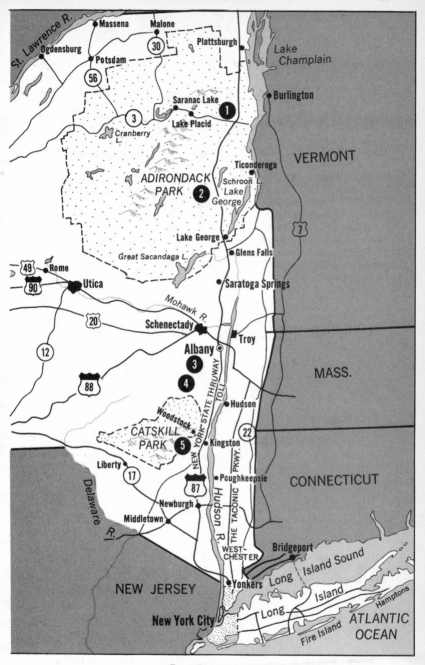

Resorts

Belleayre Mountain, 5
Gore Mountain, 2
Hunter Mountain, 4
Ski Windham, 3
Whiteface Mountain, 1

Skiers who come here are family oriented and find a friendly atmosphere combined with economical lift tickets. Saturday night skiing is also a draw. The mountain tends to be less crowded than some of its Catskill neighbors. The skiing encompasses 23 trails that run first off a ridge line, descending straight down to a central plateau and then descending again to a lower base area. The upper half tends to attract intermediate and advanced skiers while novices prefer the lower mountain and their own learning area. There are base facilities and parking at the top, midsection, and bottom.

Indian lore is strong here, with a favorite novice run called Iroquois and other trails with names like Wanatuska and Utsayantha.

The mountain is a member and founder of "Ski the Catskills," which includes 9 ski areas all within 90 minutes of one another and all accessible from New York State Thruway exits 16–21. These include Big Vanilla at Davos, Bobcat at Andes, Cortina Valley at Haines Falls, Deer Run at Stamford, Holiday Mountain at Monticello, Hunter Mountain at Hunter, Plattekill at Roxbury, and Ski Windham at Windham. (Hunter and Windham are covered in this section.)

And for folks who remember childhood tales and American literature, this is the region that Rip Van Winkle made famous. The mountain is surrounded by small but quaint towns. The area tends to be a popular second home for people from the New York metropolitan area. However, it hasn't yet been discovered as a winter destination resort area.

Practical Information for Belleayre Mountain

HOW TO GET THERE. Belleayre Mountain Ski Center is located in the town of Highmount, some 137 miles from New York City. **By car.** Take the New York Thruway to Exit 19 at Kingston, then onto Rte. 28 west for 38 miles to Highmount. Follow signs to the ski area.

TELEPHONES. The area code for the Belleayre area is 914.

ACCOMMODATIONS. For specific information on establishments in the Belleayre area geared to accommodating individuals and groups of 20 or more, contact the *Belleayre Mountain Lodging Bureau,* Box 313, Highmount, NY 12441; 254–5600 or 800–431–4555. Although most establishments in the area list their rates for a 2-night stay, the following categories are based on a 1-night stay per person, some with MAP: *Expensive,* $75–$100; *Moderate,* $50–$75; and *Inexpensive,* less than $50. All lodging in this listing is within 8 miles of the mountain unless otherwise stated.

Expensive

The Alpine Inn. Alpine Rd., Oliverea 12462; 254–5026. A Swiss-style inn in the Catskills with on-premises nordic skiing, a lighted toboggan run, and snow-tubing. MAP available.

Hanah Country Resort Rte. 30, Margaretville 12455; 586–2100 or 800–752–6494. Gracious dining and delightful accommodations including game room, full spa facilities, cross-country skiing, ice skating, and entertainment on weekends. A MAP plan is offered.

Moderate

Catskill Mountain Lakehouse. Oliverea Rd., Oliverea 12462; 254–5498. Rooms with private baths, snowmobiles for rent, and fireplace room with pool table. MAP available.

Cold Spring Lodge. Oliverea Rd., Big Indian 12410; 254–5711. Cabins with fireplaces, MAP available.

Cooperhood Inn. Rte. 28, Shandaken 12480; 688–9962. A resort with indoor pool, sauna, tennis, and ice skating. MAP available.

Northland Resort Motel. Main St., Fleischmanns 12430; 254–5125. Modern motel rooms with color TV and HBO. MAP available.

Pine Hill Arms Hotel. Main St., Pine Hill 12465; 254–5125. Thirty-five rooms with private baths, located at base of Belleayre Mountain, with dining in greenhouse, sauna, hot-tub spa, and game room. MAP available.

Inexpensive

Butterfields. Main St., Fleischmanns 12430; 254–4966. Clean, modern units and efficiencies. TV, private baths, restaurant, and lounge with life entertainment.

The Colonial Inn. Main St., Pine Hill 12465; 254–5577. A 27-room inn in the Currier & Ives style that offers horse-drawn sleigh rides. MAP available.

Delaware Court Motel. Main Street, Fleischmanns 12430; 254–5090. Affordable motel, cabin, or efficiency units close to Belleayre Mountain; near stores and restaurants. Family discount plans during nonpeak periods.

BED-AND-BREAKFAST TREASURES. Two county organizations maintain lists of these economical establishments in the area. Some are in private homes; others are in lodges or small inns. For detailed information, contact *Bed-and-Breakfast of Delaware County,* Box 36, Stamford, NY 12167 (676–3104); or *Ulster County Bed-and-Breakfast Association,* SR 108, Rte. 42, Shandaken, NY 12480 (688–7101).

RESTAURANTS. Skiers at Belleayre need not spend a fortune to eat well in the area. Most of the fare is standard American, but there are pleasant surprises of Continental cuisine and ethnic dishes as well. In this brief selection, categories are *Expensive,* $30–$50; *Moderate,* $20–$30; *Inexpensive,* less than $20. Prices reflect the cost for a full-course meal for one person, excluding drinks, tax, and tip. Unless specified, the restaurants listed accept most credit cards.

Expensive

The Alpine Inn. Oliverea Rd., Oliverea; 254–5026. A Swiss inn offering Continental fare. Reservations a must.

Roxbury Run Restaurant. Denver; 607–326–7577. Swiss and American specialties including duckling and lobster tails.

Wild Acres Hotel. Highmount Rd., Highmount; 254–9868. A country-club atmosphere with a menu that includes stuffed cabbage. Reservations a must.

Moderate

Big Indian Lodge. Oliverea Rd., Big Indian; 254–5266. Steaks and seafood are served here, as well as hamburgers.

Catskill Mountain Lake House. Oliverea Rd., Oliverea; 254–5498. Sauerbraten and wiener schnitzel are among the specialties here.

Pine Hill Arms Restaurant and Greenhouse. Main St., Pine Hill; 254–9811. A century-old inn has a greenhouse where Cajun dishes are served.

Val d'Isère. Rte. 28, Big Indian; 254–4646. A charming French provincial restaurant that's pricey for the region but not out of line with New York skiers' expectations. Look for escargot, duck à l'orange, chocolate mousse.

Inexpensive

Bob's Ribs. Main St., Phoenicia; 688–2000. Ribs, chicken combination. Kids' specials.

Buzwell's Bakery & Sweet Shoppe. Bridge St., Margaretville; 586–3009. Breakfast and lunch are served in a casual atmosphere. Bakery on the premises.

HOW TO GET AROUND. A **car** is a must here, although a few lodges will provide transportation to the slopes.

OTHER SPORTS AND ACTIVITIES. There is **ski touring** at the area, and **ice skating, snowmobiling,** and **tobogganing** nearby. The lifts operate 6–10 P.M. Saturdays for night skiing. NASTAR races are held weekends and holidays.

HINTS TO THE HANDICAPPED. There is free skiing for the handicapped through Belleayre's Access Pass.

DAY-CARE FACILITIES. The nursery accepts children aged 2–6 for $20 a day, with *SKIwee* program for ages 4–6 involving all day lessons, activities, and lunch.

NIGHTLIFE. Because the ski area isn't yet discovered as a "destination resort," there's nothing nearby resembling a disco or nightclub. However, there is dancing on Saturdays at *Kass' Inn Resort Hotel,* Rte. 30, Margaretville (586–4861), and at *Railz,* Rte. 28, Arkville (586–2992), there's often entertainment.

GORE MOUNTAIN SKI AREA

Peaceful Valley Rd.
North Creek NY 12853
Tel: 518–251–2411

Snow Report: 518–251–2523
Area Vertical: 2,100 ft.
Number of Trails: 41 on 185 skiable acres
Lifts: 1 gondola, 1 triple chair, 5 double chairs, 2 T-Bars, 1 rope tow
Snowmaking: 90 percent of terrain
Season: November–April

Gore Mountain Ski Area is located 25 miles from what is known as the Lake George region of the southern Adirondack Mountains. Although not widely recognized, Gore is one of the oldest ski areas in the East. In 1932, the Winter Olympics in Lake Placid gave impetus to the sport of skiing throughout the region. Attention was regained in 1980 when the Winter Games were, once again, held in Lake Placid.

The merits of this 3,600-foot peak, the second highest (after Whiteface at 4,436 feet) in New York, were duly noted during those first Winter Games. Uphill transport came by way of cars, trucks, and buses to position skiers for descents down trails that were then gentle but narrow. Open slopes were served by rope tows, thought to be the first lifts in the East. Ski trains used to haul as many as 1,500 skiers from Albany to North Creek, where residents opened their homes for accommodations and meals. On one notable day in 1936, the Delaware and Hudson Railroad transported 967 skiers in 14 coaches, and the New York Central carried 850 more in 11 sleepers and 4 coaches.

World War II put a crimp in the evolution of the ski area, but in 1964 attention was again turned to skiing in the region, and the State of New York began developing Gore. In 1984, Gore came under the supervision of the Olympic Regional Development Authority.

North Creek itself, 2 miles away, has a population of 800, and with over 400 beds for tourists, it is moving, albeit slowly, in the direction of accommodating skiers. However, if après-ski and disco-style nightlife is a must for you, you won't find it here. The whole region, town and mountain, lends itself to a family experience, a place where you're more than just a number and people get to know you.

North Creek's claim to fame dates back to the turn of the century and a day when Vice President Teddy Roosevelt was hiking in the area. Roosevelt was contacted by a courier, who advised him that President William McKinley had died. It was from the North Creek train station that Roosevelt was sworn in as President of the United States.

Gore has one of the highest percentages of intermediate terrain—73 percent—of any ski area anywhere, and all the intermediate trails are over a mile long. The favorite is the Cloud Trail, a full 2½ miles long.

From the top of the mountain there are views of Vermont's Green Mountains and the central and high peaks of the Adirondacks.

Practical Information for Gore Mountain.

HOW TO GET THERE. Gore Mountain Ski Area is 40 miles from Glens Falls, 90 miles from Albany, and 40 miles from Fort Edward. It is situated 1 mile from North Creek.

By air. The Albany County Airport is served by *American, United, USAir,* and some commuter airlines. All major rental cars are available at the airport.

By bus. *Greyhound* (793–5052) and *Adirondack Trailways* (793–5525) serve the area.

By car. Take Rte. 87, the Adirondack Northway, to Exit 23; travel north on Rte. 9 to Rte. 28, which leads into North Creek.

By train. There are daily *Amtrak* (800–USA–RAIL) departures from Grand Central Terminal in New York City as well as from the Rensselaer, NY, station to the Gore Mountain/Lake George region via Fort Edward. Special ski packages include rail fare, shuttle transportation, lift tickets, and hotel accommodations.

TELEPHONES. The area code for Gore Mountain is 518.

ACCOMMODATIONS. The *Gore Mountain Region Chamber of Commerce,* Box 84, Main St., North Creek 12853 (251–2612), can give information on some area lodges and on inexpensive bed-and-breakfast establishments in the region. Because this is a popular tourist region, summer and winter, this list does not attempt to include all the accommodations around Lake George, about 25 miles away, but focuses on those closer to Gore Mountain. All those listed in this selection are considered in the *Moderate* category—around $60 per person, based on double occupancy.

Alpine Motel. Main St., North Creek 12853; 251–2451. A motel with restaurant. MAP available.

Black Mountain Ski Lodge. Rte. 8, Peaceful Valley Rd., North Creek 12853; 251–2800. Twenty-five rooms, TV. MAP available.

Conway's Lake Manor. Rte. 8, Chestertown 12817; 494–2211. Motel overlooking Loon Lake, 8 units serving complimentary Continental breakfast. Located 12 miles from the slopes.

Country Road Lodge. Warrensburg 12885; 623–2207. A bed-and-breakfast establishment located 22 miles from the slopes; 5 rooms with wood stove in lounge. All meals available, cross-country skiing nearby.

Garnet Hill Lodge. Off Rte. 28, North River 12856; 251–2821. An old Adirondack lodge in the mountains overlooking Thirteenth Lake. Twenty-six rooms; complete ski touring center; Saturday-night smorgasbord. MAP available.

Gore Mountain Lodge. Rte. 28, North Creek 12853; 251–3444. A 14-room motel 4 miles from the mountain. On-premises dining, lounge with fireplace, live entertainment Friday and Saturday nights.

Highwinds. Rte. 28, North River 12856; 251–3760. An 11-room charming country inn, 2 with private baths. Fireplace in living room. MAP available. Great views of mountains and cross-country skiing network that links with Garnet Hill. Ten miles from the slopes.

Inn on Gore Mountain. Peaceful Valley Rd., North Creek 12853; 251–2111. Sixteen rooms, closest facility to mountain.

The Lakeside Motel. Rte. 8, Chestertown 12817; 494–3965. A 6-unit motel with some efficiencies, overlooking lake. Located 12 miles from the slopes.

Mountain View Hotel. Rte. 28N, Minerva 12851; 251–2529. A 23-room hotel with bar, dining room, and large fireplace. Shared baths. MAP available.

Northwind Motel. Peaceful Valley Rd., North Creek 12853; 251–2522. Groups welcome here; dining room where veal dishes are a specialty. MAP available.

Ridin' Hy Ranch Resort. Sherman Lake, Warrensburg 12885; 494–2742. Lots of activity here with cross-country skiing and horse-drawn sleigh rides. On-premises skiing for beginners, plus spa amenities such as sauna, hot tub, indoor pool. Located 25 miles from Gore. MAP available.

Summit at Gore Mountain. North Creek 12853; 251–3844. The region's only condominiums; with indoor pool, sauna, fireplaces, kitchenettes. Just 1 mile from the mountain.

Valhaus Motel. Peaceful Valley Rd., North Creek 12853; 251–2700. Has 12 large rooms, free coffee, dining room with bar and cocktail lounge.

RESTAURANTS. As in our listing of accommodations, none of the restaurants in our selection approaches being expensive. All are in the *Moderate*, $10–$15, range. The price reflects the cost of a meal for one person; drinks, tax, and tip extra. Most restaurants listed accept major credit cards. (For a wider selection of restaurants in Chestertown, see the Whiteface Mountain section.)

Garnet Hill Lodge. Thirteenth Lake Rd., North River, north of North Creek via Rte. 28; 251–2821. Mountaintop lodge known for cross-country skiing and fine food, especially Saturday evening buffet.

Gore Mountain Lodge. Rte. 28, North Creek; 251–3444. Scandinavian buffet. Lounge with fireplace; weekend entertainment.

Inn at Gore Mountain. Peaceful Valley Rd., North Creek; 251–2111. Look for New Orleans Cajun cooking here, a surprise in the Adirondacks!

Northwind Restaurant. Peaceful Valley Rd., North Creek; 251–2522. A wide-ranging menu featuring veal dishes with a Dutch touch. All food is home-cooked.

Smith's Restaurant. Main St., North Creek; 251–9965. Steaks, chops, and home-baked goods, with German touch.

HOW TO GET AROUND. It is practically mandatory to have a **car** in this region, although some hotels may supply shuttle service. If you do not intend to drive, check when making reservations.

SEASONAL EVENTS. NASTAR races are held Friday to Sunday, and recreational and serious amateur racing are important to the winter calendar. The mountain is designated as an alpine training center operated by the New York Ski Education Foundation, New York's major development program for the U.S. Ski Team. There are also such special events as a *winter carnival* and a *Cocoa Butter Bump Skiing Contest!*

OTHER SPORTS AND ACTIVITIES. An interesting twist on the winter theme—**horseback riding** through the snow. It's popular in this region, with over half a dozen ranch resorts offering such an experience. These include: *Ridin' Hy Ranch Resort,* Sherman Lake, Warrensburg, 494–2742, and *1000 Acres Ranch,* Rte. 418, Stony Creek, 696–2444. All of the above also offer **sleigh rides.**

Cross-country centers are maintained at *Garnet Hill Lodge,* off Rte. 28 on Thirteenth Lake Rd. in North River, 251–2821, 30 km; *Cunningham Ski Barn,* Rte. 28, North Creek, 251–3215, 50 km; *Gore Mountain Ski Area,* 251–2411, 12 km; *Highwinds,* Rte. 28, North River, 251–2706, over 50 km.

Warren County, where Gore is located, maintains a total of over 165 miles of groomed and patrolled **snowmobile** trails that connect to over 300 miles of state and private trails. To check on conditions, call 793–1300.

And for winter **hikers** and **snowshoe** enthusiasts, the *Department of Environmental Conservation,* Box 220, Hudson St., Warrensburg 12885, maintains winter trails. Call 623–3671 for details.

The Sagamore Hotel, 110 Sagamore Rd., Bolton Landing 12814, 644–9400, offers 2 indoor **tennis** courts, **racquetball**, indoor **pool**, and complete **health-spa facilities.**

DAY-CARE FACILITIES. The nursery has been supervised by Helen Cornwall since it opened in 1964. It accepts children aged 2–6 from 8 A.M. to 4:15 P.M. daily, at $3 an hour. The Children's Ski School offers instruction for ages 3–12, with 2-hour lessons for ages 6–12 *(Dino-Mountaineers)* and a Play & Ski Learning Center for ages 2–4 *(The Dinosaur Den)* and ages 3–6 *(Dino-Mites)* to introduce them to skiing. Both facilities can be reached through the main lodge and offer half- or full-day sessions; 251–2411.

NIGHTLIFE. At the Gore Mountain Lodge, Rte. 28, North Creek (251–3444), there's *Mr. B's Après Lounge,* a place to relax off the trails and listen to music before dinner. Or drive 25 miles to the Lake George region where there are a number of places offering live music and dancing.

HUNTER MOUNTAIN

Box 295
Hunter NY 12422
Tel: 518–263–4223

Snow Report: 800–FOR–SNOW
Area Vertical: 1,600 ft.
Number of Trails: 46 on 200 skiable acres
Lifts: 1 quad, 2 triple chairs, 8 double
*   chairs, 1 T-bar, 1 poma, 1 pony,*
*   2 rope tows*
Snowmaking: 100 percent
Season: early November–late April

Two brothers, Orville and Israel Slutzky, were born and brought up in the Hunter Mountain area. They made their fortunes in the construction trade. Then Hunter, a long-time summer mecca for the New York metropolitan area, fell on hard times as major arteries into the Catskills changed and Hunter was no longer on the beaten path.

The Slutzkys, who owned the mountain, offered to give it away for $1 to anyone who would develop it as a ski area. The offer was accepted by Jimmy Hammerstein, of the famous musical family. In fall 1959, the Hunter Mt. Ski Bowl opened. The Slutzkys were brought in to put up the lifts, and it was through their insistence from the onset that snowmaking was factored into the mountain's "must have" mix.

The effort of Jimmy Hammerstein and friends to make skiing work here, however, didn't carry over into fiscal acumen, as the major stockholders, like Paul Newman, Kim Novak, and the members of the Modern Jazz Quartet, albeit avid skiers, were, according to a well-placed Hunter source, "terrible businessmen." The effort, in fact, went down the tubes.

The Slutzkys rode to the rescue once again and for most of the past three decades have owned and operated Hunter, personally making the first runs down the slopes in the morning, day after day, to test the snow conditions. "They love it. They'll be there forever, probably," says the same well-placed source.

Hunter is every person's mountain in more than one way. Over the years, it has tapped into the New Yorkers' penchant for sticking together in groups. Consequently, there are probably more firefighters, police officers, nurses, doctors, and chefs—among other professions and trades—who assemble here to ski together than at any other place in the country. Special events and races have grown up around this stick-together-on-skis phenomenon. The result is that everyone feels he or she belongs at Hunter. And the special-interest groups get larger and larger.

The mountain is divided up by ability level. Hunter One is a learner's area with three double chairs and surface lifts and the large, main base lodge facility. Hunter West is positioned for the advanced skier. And the Hunter Mt. Ski Bowl, the original terrain, is still a free-for-all for everyone, although it tends to attract intermediates.

As ethnic and diverse as the skiers you'll find here is the food service at the Hunter Base Lodge, where staples mean everything, from pizza to sushi.

Hunter is, incidentally, quasi-official headquarters of the ever-growing 70-Plus Ski Club that encourages active participation in alpine skiing by those supposedly "over the hill." An annual race here in honor of these very energetic senior citizens can put younger skiers to shame.

Practical Information for Hunter Mountain

HOW TO GET THERE. Hunter Mountain is located right in the village of Hunter in the Catskills, 120 miles from New York City, making it readily accessible by various modes of transportation.

By car. Take the New York State Thruway to Exit 20 at Saugerties, then follow Rte. 32 north to Rte. 32A and onto Rte. 23A west to the area.

By plane. The Hunter Mt. Airport (518–263–4223) nearby has a 2,550-foot runway that can accommodate single- and twin-engine planes.

By bus. *Adirondack Trailways* (212–947–5300) buses depart from the Port Authority Bus Terminal in New York City twice daily—8:30 A.M. and 6 P.M. The bus trip takes three hours.

TELEPHONES. The area code for Hunter Mountain is 518; for some surrounding towns, it is 914.

ACCOMMODATIONS. The *Hunter Mountain Reservation Center, Inc.,* housed in the base lodge (Box 663, Hunter 12442; 518–263–3827), handles all lodging reservations for hotel, motel, private chalet, slopeside condominium or country inn accommodations. In addition to making reservations, this office can also answer any questions you may have. Since most visitors come to Hunter Mountain on weekend trips, rates at hotels, motels, and lodges are based on a 2-day weekend per person, unless otherwise stated. For those in the *Expensive* category, expect to pay $140–$200; *Moderate,* $75–$140; and *Inexpensive,* $45–$75. (For additional lodging in the area, see *Ski Windham* section. The two ski areas are only 10 miles apart.) All lodging in this listing is within 10 miles of the mountain unless otherwise stated.

Expensive

Antonio's Motel and Resort. County Rte. 16, Platte Cove, Elka Park 12427; 518–589–5197. A country resort from a restored hotel, offering sauna, indoor pool, Jacuzzi, wide-screen TV. MAP available.

Ramada Inn. Rte. 28, Kingston 12401; 914–339–3900. Offers indoor pool, in-room movie channel, and choice of restaurants, 30 miles from the slopes.

Scribner Hollow. Rte. 23A, Hunter 12442; 518–263–4211. Luxurious suites with double-decker living/bedroom combinations, on-premises dining, and indoor pool.

Villa Vosilla Resort and Restaurant. Rte. 23A, Tannersville 12485; 518–589–5060. An older hotel that has added a new motel section, offering indoor pool, complete gym, Jacuzzi, sauna, and game room. MAP available.

Moderate

Auberge des 4 Saisons Hotel-Motel, Rte. 42, Shandaken 12480; 914–688–2223. Thirty-eight rooms (half with private bath), with innlike accommodations in the main house plus a chalet-style motel. Offers French-style cooking. MAP available. Located 20 miles from the slopes.

The Forester Motor Lodge. Rte. 23A, Hunter 12442; 518–263–4555. A motel across the road from Hunter Mountain.

Han's County Line Motel & Restaurant. Rte. 32A, Palenville 12463; 518–678–3101. Standard and deluxe motel rooms; some cooking facilities in cabins.

Howard Johnson's Motor Lodge & Restaurant. Exit 20 off I-87, Saugerties 12477; 914–246–9511. Indoor heated pool and sauna, laundry, and game rooms. Eighteen miles from Hunter Mountain.

Swiss Chalet. Rte. 23A, Tannersville 12485; 589–5445. Cozy, comfortable country hotel with Swiss atmosphere. Dinner nightly featuring Swiss-Continental cuisine.

Villagio Resort. Rte. 23A, Haines Falls 12436; 800–843–4348. A 300-acre traditional Catskill hotel. Lounge, Italian menu, entertainment.

Washington Irving Lodge. Rte. 23A, Tannersville 12485; 518–589–5560. Has 23 rooms, some with private or semiprivate bath, small restaurant, lounge, TV and game rooms.

Inexpensive

Greene Mountain View Inn. Church and South Main Sts., Tannersville 12485; 518–589–9866. Essentially a ski lodge with private baths. Breakfast served, along with buffet-style dinners.

The Hunter House. Rt. 23A, Hunter 12442; 518–263–4611. A hotel that has added modern motel units for a total of 60 rooms, 40 in the hotel.

Redcoat's Return. Dale La., Platte Clove, Elka Park 12427; 518–589–6374. A 14-room inn, 5 rooms with bath; breakfast served.

Sky Top Motel. Rte. 28, Kingston 12401; 914–331–2900. Continental breakfasts and 4 P.M. teatime on weekends. Located 30 miles from Hunter.

Sun-Land Farm Motel. Rte. 23A, Hunter 12442; 518–263–4611. A motel with a main-house public area; piano and small game room.

Vatra. Rte. 214, Hunter 12442; 518–263–4919. A rustic motel-hotel with home cooking. MAP.

Villa Maria. Rte. 23A, Haines Falls 12436; 518–589–6200. An old hotel that has added motel units for a total of 80 rooms; indoor pool, sauna and game room. Breakfast available.

BED-AND-BREAKFAST TREASURES. With an assortment of lodges and country inns situated in the Catskills, visitors are offered a wide choice of bed-and-breakfast establishments. The Hunter Mountain area is no exception. Some places, like the **Albergo Bed & Breakfast** in Windham (518–734–4499), have combined the European touch with colonial amenities. A few others in the area include **The Eggery Inn,** Tannersville (518–589–5363), and **The Hunter House,** Hunter (518–263–4611). Rates at these B&Bs range from $30 to $80 per person. B&Bs are usually not for families and certainly not for all travelers. Be sure to inquire regarding individual credit card policies when making reservations or when checking into the establishment.

DINING OUT. Catskill resorts are well known for their eat-eat-eat type of dining. That's because many of the resorts, particularly those offering package deals, include all-you-can eat provisions with the packages. However, the Hunter area offers visitors the gamut of dining places outside the hotels and resorts. Cuisine ranges from northern Italian to French to American standbys. In this listing, expect to pay $18 to $25 for a full-course dinner for one at a restaurant in the *Expensive* category; *Moderate,* $13–$18; and *Inexpensive,* less than $13. Tips and drinks are extra. Practically all but the inexpensive restaurants accept most major credit cards. However, it is wise to check first.

Expensive

Auberge des 4 Saisons. Rte. 42, Shandaken; 914–688–2223. Obviously French, and one of the better choices in the region, with a 35-year reputation for fine cooking.

Brandywine. Rte. 23, Windham; 518–734–3838. A restaurant with rustic ambience; features northern Italian fare.

Chateau Belleview. Rte. 23A, between Hunter and Tannersville; 518–589–5525. Seafood prepared French style is the specialty, with veal also popular.

Redcoat's Return. Dale La., Elka Park; 518–589–6379. The accent is decidedly British, but very homey with an English touch to the menu.

Moderate

Fireside Restaurant. Rte. 23A, Hunter; 518–263–4216. Sunday omelets a specialty, plus steaks.

Hans County Line. Rte. 23A, Palenville; 518–678–3101. The range is waffles to steaks.

Marianna's Continental Restaurant, Rte. 23A, Haines Falls; 518–589–6011. Italian fare.

The Restaurant. Hunter Mountain; 518–263–4754. Open daily for lunch and for dinner on weekends.

Tannersville Yacht Club. Rte. 23A, Tannersville; 518–589–5455. Sandwiches and snacks, plus the singles scene.

Tequilla's, Rte. 23A, Hunter; 518–263–4863. Mexican fare.

Inexpensive

Pete's Place. Rte. 23, Hunter; 518–263–5469. Chili and burgers are served up here. No credit cards.

P.J. Larkins. Main St., Tannersville; 518–589–5568. Chili and steaks served pub style; also daily specials.

HOW TO GET AROUND. It is wise to have a **car** at Hunter, particularly if you would like to try the slopes at Windham Ski Area, just 10 miles away. However, some of the lodging places supply **shuttle** service to Hunter Mountain. If you don't plan on driving, check with the hotel or condo when making reservations.

SEASONAL EVENTS. The mountain annually hosts a race event called *The Silver Series,* six contests with prizes of up to $250,000. Another popular competition is the *Chef's Race,* held in mid-**January.** It has become so popular that they've had to be firm about having only chefs enter—no kitchen aides allowed!

What may be the largest amateur race in the world is Hunter's annual *Firefighters Race,* held in early **February.** The event draws up to 225 teams with five firefighters on a team going down the course with a 50-foot fire hose.

OTHER SPORTS AND ACTIVITIES. *Villa Vosilla Resort and Restaurant,* Route. 23A, Tannersville (518–589–5060) makes its indoor pool, gym, Jacuzzi, and steam room and sauna available to the public. **Cross-country** skiing is available at *Higher Meadows,* Tannersville (518–589–5361).

CHILDREN'S ACTIVITIES. Hunter offers a child-sitting service at the base lodge, with a specially equipped playroom and a limit of 25 tots. The cost is $18 a day and the service is available from 9 A.M. to 4 P.M. Children ages 5–9 can participate in the *SKIwee/Frosty Ski School* that combines playtime fun and games with on-mountain ski experience. This program is $41 for the all-day (9:30 A.M.–3:30 P.M.) version.

NIGHTLIFE. The "in place" is the *Hunter Village Inn,* Route. 23A, Hunter (518–263–4788), offering live rock bands that please the young crowd. Look for video replays of skiers on Hunter's slopes during happy hour from 3 to 6 P.M. at the *Heart Break Motel,* Main Street in Hunter (518–263–5050); it has live weekend entertainment. There's also action at *Sizzles* on Main Street in Tannersville (518–589–5568).

SKI WINDHAM

C.D. Lane Rd.
Windham NY 12496
Tel: 518–734–4300

Ski Report: 518–734–4300 or 800–729–4766
Area Vertical: 1,600 ft.
Number of Trails: 33 on 210 skiable acres
Lifts: 4 triple chairs, 2 double chairs, 1 pony
Snowmaking: 97 percent of terrain
Season: mid-November–early April

In 1981, Ski Windham made the transition from private club, which it had been since 1965, to a ski resort open to the public. It was purchased by Ski Roundtop, managers of a resort by that name, and Ski Liberty, both in Pennsylvania.

When it was a private club, its clientele tended to be professionals and corporate chiefs, plus a healthy smattering of politicians, all of whom chose Windham to see and be seen. Today the resort is sought after by people who appreciate the quality represented by the original club environment, plus the quality of the snowmaking and grooming of the trails.

The skiing is on 33 primarily fall-line trails. Beginners enjoy a top-of-the-mountain descent on the 2¼-mile Wraparound, the longest trail in the Catskills. Experts prefer the Wheelchair, a steep, moguled run.

The area welcomes skiers of all shapes and sizes, offering free skiing to children 12 or under during non-holiday weekdays. And to make things more comfortable for everyone, a corps of volunteers serves on Ski Windham's Courtesy Patrol Program. Dressed in bright red and blue parkas, wearing "Ask Me" buttons, they can give details on just about anything related to skiing and the resort. In turn, for their time, they earn extra free skiing.

Practical Information for Ski Windham

HOW TO GET THERE. Ski Windham is located in Windham, about a 2½-hour drive from New York City. **By car.** Take the New York State Thruway (I–87) to Exit 21, then west on Rte. 23 for 25 miles to the resort.

By bus. There is *Trailways* service twice a day from Manhattan's Port Authority Terminal (212–947–5300) to the town of Windham.Buses depart daily at 8:30 A.M. and 6 P.M.

TELEPHONES. The area code for this section of the Catskills is 518.

ACCOMMODATIONS. The *Greene County Promotion Department,* Box 527, Catskill 12414 (943–3223), can answer questions about accommodations in the Windham region. The *Ski Windham Lodging Service,* C.D. Lane Rd., Windham 12496 (800–729–7549), can book reservations for properties within 15 miles of Ski Windham. Based on double occupancy, prices range around $120 for *Expensive,* $60–$70 for *Moderate,* and $50–$60 for *Inexpensive* units.

Expensive

Albergo Bed & Breakfast. Rte. 296, Windham; 734–5560. A charming, European-style country inn with 20 antique-furnished rooms and private baths. A full country breakfast is served in the sunroom every morning.

The Evergreen at the Thompson House. Rte. 296, Windham; 734–4510. Luxurious accommodations with telephones and color TV, some suites with Jacuzzis. Cozy lobby fireplace and Continental breakfast.

Hotel Vienna. Rte. 296, Windham; 734–5300. An elegant 30-room hotel within walking distance of 3 gourmet restaurants; offers Continental breakfasts, Jacuzzis, and TV.

Moderate

Colonial Hotel. Rte. 23, Windham; 734–4230. Motel complex with 30 rooms, private baths, color TV, and fireplace in recreation room. Full Continental breakfast.

Country Suite. Rte. 23, Windham; 734–4079. Renovated farmhouse with 10 rooms, fireplace in living room, serving a full home-cooked breakfast.

Windham Arms. Rte. 23, Windham; 734–3000. A 70-room motel with terraces, color TV, telephones, and great views. Also has a recreation room and a coffee shop.

Inexpensive

Cave Mountain Motel. Rte. 23, Windham; 734–3161. Eight-unit modern motel with private entrances, cable TV, Continental breakfast.

Kelly Acres. Rte. 10, Windham; 734–3711. Large country inn with large double rooms. Fireplace and VCR in living room.

RESTAURANTS. Dining in the Windham region is both varied in cuisines and easy on the pocketbook. In this selection, restaurants are listed by price category. Categories are *Expensive,* $13–$20; *Moderate,* $8–$13; and *Inexpensive,* less than $8. These prices are for a meal for one person, excluding drinks, tax, and tip. Most accept major credit cards. (See *Hunter Mountain* section for other choices in the area.)

Expensive

Chalet Fondue. Rte. 296, Windham; 734–4650. Dine on superbly prepared German, Swiss, and Austrian cuisines in an authentic Alpine atmosphere.

La Griglia. Rte. 296, Windham; 734–4499. Northern Italian specialties and fresh game are served here, as well as a Sunday brunch. Rated by some as the best restaurant in the region.

Vesuvio Restaurant. Goshen St., Hensonville; 734–3663. Choose from fresh lobster, veal, fish, and other regional Italian specialties while dining by candlelight.

Moderate

Brandywine. Rte. 23, Windham; 734–3838. Look for northern Italian cuisine such as veal saltimbocca and chicken scarpariello.

Point Lookout. Rte. 23, East Windham; 734–3381. An old stagecoach stop serves European-American food with fresh fish, rack of lamb, veal, steak, prime ribs, and some Mexican dishes.

Thetford's Sir Sirloin Room. Rte. 23, Windham; 734–3322. Prime rib is a specialty here on Saturday nights. Other dishes include fresh seafood, rack of lamb, and veal.

Inexpensive

The Frog's House. Rte. 296, Hensonville; 734–9817. A pub atmosphere with barbecued ribs and chicken.

Garbarino's. Rte. 23, Windham; 734–3914. Located 1 mile from Ski Windham; select from a varied menu featuring pizza, calzones, cutlets, seafood, and pasta.

HOW TO GET AROUND. A **car** is mandatory here, although some inns will provide **shuttle** service to the slopes. Once at the resort, there's a bus to transport skiers from the parking lot to the base lodge. (Limited taxi service is available.)

SEASONAL EVENTS. Fun races, celebrations, and special events are specially tailored for each season, in addition to traditional events like the opportunity to sample local cuisine during the *Taste of Windham* in early **November.** Events include the *Winter Kick-Off Weekend;* the annual *New Year's Eve celebration;* the *Ski Fest,* eight days of races and parties in **February;** and the *Governor's Nephew Cup,* an annual costume fun race in **March.**

OTHER SPORTS AND ACTIVITIES. *Windham Lanes,* South St., Windham (734–3270), offers evening **bowling.** The *White Birches Ski Touring Center,* off Rte. 23 on Navoo Rd., Windham (734–3266), offers 400 acres of private Catskill wilderness for exploration on **cross-country** skis. There are 15 miles of groomed trails at an elevation of more than 2,000-ft. **Snowmobiling** and **horseback riding** are offered at the *Silver Springs Ranch,* Tannersville (589–5559). (See *Hunter Mountain* section for other activities.)

HINTS FOR THE HANDICAPPED. The *Ski Windham Disabled Adaptive Program* encourages people with all kinds of handicaps, including the deaf, blind, and orthopedically impaired, to take part in skiing. Information is available at the Ski School Desk; 734–5070.

DAY-CARE FACILITIES. A Children's Learning Center is open daily from 8:30 A.M. to 4 P.M. for children aged 1 month to 7 years. The day rate is $40. For children

4–13, the *Mini Moguls* and *Mogul Masters* will coordinate a ski lesson through the Children's Learning Center.

NIGHTLIFE. Ski Windham's *Legends Bar* (734–4300), located in the base lodge, is a popular après-ski spot. Look for *Cafe on the Green,* South Street, Windham (734–9917), and *Jimmy O'Connor's,* South Street, Windham (734–4270), to rub elbows with the locals après-ski. *Point Lookout,* Rte. 23 in East Windham (734–3381), and *Seeley's* in Hensonville (734–9892) bring entertainment in on weekends. (See *Hunter Mountain* section for other choices.)

WHITEFACE MOUNTAIN SKI CENTER

Wilmington NY 12997
Tel: 518–946–2223

*Snow Report: 518–946–2223 or 800–462–
6236 (U.S.); 800–858–7782 (Canada)
Area Vertical: 3,216 ft.
Number of Trails: 37 on 142 skiable acres
Lifts: 2 triple chairs, 7 double chairs
Snowmaking: 92 percent of terrain
Season: late November–early April*

Whiteface Mountain is a household word among those who can't get enough of the Olympics. Twice this mountain has hosted the Winter Games, first in 1932 when the town servicing the mountain, Lake Placid, became known as the Winter Sports Capital of the World, and most recently in 1980.

The combination of an exciting mountain (its 3,216-foot vertical is the greatest in the East) and a town whose raison d'être is to woo, wine, and dine tourists makes a ski experience here unforgettable.

The mountain itself is heavy on the "most difficult" side when it comes to trails—44 percent. For intermediates, about 33 percent are marked "more difficult," and beginners can enjoy the rest.

In addition to on-mountain challenges, Lake Placid itself vies for time and attention with its Olympic Center that hosts both sporting events and major entertainers such as Kenny Rogers and Willie Nelson. Mirror Lake, around which the town is clustered, is the setting for ice skating and hockey, and, likely as not, you'll see horse-drawn sleighs on the ice, too.

There isn't another ski town where thrill seekers can arrange for bobsled and luge runs during a break from skiing. And the shopping, as might be expected, can make rainy-day hours pass quickly during a late winter thaw.

Perhaps most noteworthy, however, is the fact that Whiteface Mountain is headquarters for the Olympic Authority and training here goes on year-round. A glass-enclosed elevator to the top of the 90-meter ski jump tower is open to visitors who want to sample views of the Adirondack Mountains and perhaps gain a new-found respect for those who pursue this most daring of alpine events.

Practical Information for
Whiteface Mountain

HOW TO GET THERE. Whiteface Mountain Ski Center is located in the town of Wilmington, 8 miles from Lake Placid.

By bus. *Adirondack Trailways* (518–523–4309) offers daily bus service to the region.

By train. Call the *Amtrak Tour Desk* at 800–USA–RAIL for details on ski train packages that include rail fare, hotel accommodations, lift tickets, and transfers to and from the Westport station. There are also daily departures from Penn Station (New York City) and Rensselaer stations and other locations on the Amtrak system.

By air. *Piedmont Airlines* serves the Adirondack Airport (891–5551) in Saranac Lake, 16 miles from Lake Placid. Airlines serving the Albany County airport include *American, TWA Express* (800–221–2000), *United, USAir,* and some commuter airlines. All major rental cars are available at the airport.

By car. Take the New York State Thruway to I–87 to Rte. 73, Exit 30, to Rte. 86. For auto rental information, contact *Avis* at 253–3506 or 800–331–1212, *Hertz* at 800–654–3131, or Arnie's Service Station (518) 523–3158.

TELEPHONES. The area code for the Adirondacks region is 518.

ACCOMMODATIONS. There are over 50 lodging properties in the immediate area. For general information contact the following: *Lake Placid Convention Bureau,* Olympic Center, Lake Placid 12946; 523–2999. *Lake Placid Chamber of Commerce,* Olympic Center, Lake Placid 12946; 523–2445. *Saranac Lake Chamber of Commerce,* 30 Main St., Saranac Lake 12983; 891–1990. *Whiteface Mt. Chamber of Commerce,* Box 277, Wilmington 12997; 946–2255.

Per-night hotel rates are based on double occupancy. Categories, determined by price, are *Expensive,* $65 and up; *Moderate,* $40–$60; and *Inexpensive,* less than $40. All accommodations in this listing are located within 15 miles of the mountain, unless stated otherwise.

Expensive

Adirondack Inn. 217 Main St., Lake Placid 12946; 523–2424. Beautiful rooms and suites overlooking the lake; free crib or cot for children under 6; restaurant, coffee shop, cocktail lounge; ski plan for individuals or groups.

The Balsam House. Friends Lake Rd., Chestertown 12817 (I–87 Exit 25 to Chestertown); 494–4431 or 800–441–6856. Beautifully restored Victorian inn built in 1865, with 20 uniquely decorated rooms. Gourmet restaurant open to the public, offering French cuisine; MAP available. Worth the 80-mile drive to the mountain.

Best Western Golden Arrow. 150 Main St., Lake Placid 12946; 523–3353. A 74-room resort hotel offering studios, suites; children under 12 free, cribs and cots. Indoor pool, health club, racquetball.

Friends Lake Inn. Friends Lake Rd., Chestertown 12817 (I–87 Exit 25 to Chestertown); 494–4751. A completely restored 1860s inn with 14 rooms, 2 with hot tubs. Restaurant open to the public; on-premises cross-country skiing. MAP. Located about 80 miles from the slopes.

Holiday Inn Grandview Hotel. Olympic Dr., Lake Placid 12946; 523–2556. On hilltop overlooking lake; 182 rooms, children 12 and under free; indoor pool, health spa, and racquetball.

Howard Johnson's Resort Lodge. Saranac Ave., Lake Placid 12946; 523–9555. 92 rooms, children 12 and under free; indoor pool, whirlpool.

Lake Placid Hilton. Mirror Lake Dr., Lake Placid 12946; 523–4411. 178 rooms; children under 18 free, cribs, cots; 2 indoor pools, restaurant, bar, whirlpool.

Lake Placid Manor. Whiteface Inn Rd., Lake Placid 12946; 523–2573. Rustic elegance on the lake, view of Whiteface Mountain, with 38 rooms in 10 lodges and cottages. Restaurant and bar on premises.

Mirror Lake Inn. 35 Mirror Lake Dr., Lake Placid 12946; 523–2544. Colonial decor in 100-room inn; penthouse terrace rooms with cathedral ceilings. Children under 11 free. Offers health club, gourmet restaurant.

Ramada Inn. 12 Saranac Ave., Lake Placid 12946; 523–2587. Ninety rooms; 18 and younger free; indoor pool, whirlpool, restaurant and bar.

Whiteface Resort. Whiteface Inn Rd., Lake Placid; 523–2551. A 360-acre resort on Lake Placid with a 20-km ski touring center, dining, lounge. Has 75 sleeping rooms in motel units, cabins, townhouses, and condominiums.

Moderate

Alpine Motor Lodge. Wilmington Rd., Lake Placid 12946; 523–2180. Neat, clean rooms in 2-story inn; restaurant with German specialties.

The Bark Eater Inn. Keene 12942; 576–2221. A small country inn offering cross-country skiing, breakfast.

Bonnie View Cottages. Bonnie View Rd., Wilmington 12997; 946–2363. Housekeeping cottages 3 miles from Whiteface.

Grand View Motel. Rte. 86, Wilmington 12997; 946–2209. View of slopes and only 4 minutes from skiing.

The Hotel Saranac. 101 Main St., Saranac Lake 12983; 891–2200. Ninety-two rooms in refurbished hotel first opened in 1927, with original lobby preserved—replica of the foyer in the Danvanzati Palace of Florence, Italy. Restaurant is college-operated training facility. Located 20 miles away from Whiteface.

Hungry Trout Motor Inn. Rte. 86, Wilmington 12997; 946–2217. On Ausable River, only a half mile from Whiteface. A combination motel and restaurant.

The Inn at Whiteface. Rte. 86, Wilmington 12997; 946–2232. Right at the ski area, views of slopes. Comfortable accommodations.

Interlaken Lodge. 15 Interlaken Ave., Lake Placid 12446; 523–3180. Victorian setting and relaxing atmosphere with 12 guest rooms. MAP available.

South Meadow Farm Lodge B & B. Cascade Rd., Lake Placid 12946; 523–9369. A small family lodge located on Olympic cross-country trails, serving breakfast.

Stagecoach Inn. Old Military Rd., Lake Placid 12946; 523–9474. A landmark from the stagecoach days, with brass beds, handmade quilts, fireplaces; breakfast served.

Whiteface Mountain Inn. Rte. 86, Wilmington 12997; 946–2155. An old, restored house offering bed-and-breakfast accommodations, shared baths, excellent breakfasts.

Inexpensive

The Constitution Trail Inn. Upper Jay 12987; 946–2276. Only 6 miles from Whiteface, with rooms decorated with Olympic memorabilia.

There are a number of inexpensive motel/motor inn establishments in Lake Placid of which the following are just a sampling: *Carriage House Motor Inn,* Cascade Rd., 523–2260; *Edelweiss Motel,* Wilmington Rd., 523–3821; *Lake Placid Motor Lodge,* Cascade Rd., 523–2817; *Redwood Motel,* Wilmington Rd., 523–2183; and *Village Motel,* Cascade Rd., 523–2150.

RESTAURANTS. There are fine dining spots throughout the Adirondack region, most notably in some of the country inns. Always worth a try for the adventure alone is Hotel Saranac in Saranac Lake, which culinary arts students from Paul Smith's College use as a laboratory-classroom. The emphasis for most restaurants in this region is on straightforward presentation and ample portions. Breakfasts tend to be especially large, perhaps a legacy of the lumbering days when men in the field camps consumed huge breakfasts to start the day. Prices noted are for an average dinner for one person; beverages, tax, and tip extra. *Expensive:* more than $20; *Moderate:* $12–$20; *Inexpensive:* less than $12. Major credit cards are accepted at most places, but it would be wise to check first.

Expensive

The Balsam House. Friends Lake Rd., Chestertown; 494–2828. Elegant dining in a beautifully restored inn built in 1865. Main dining room has candlelight, flowers, and classical music. European chef's specialties include rack of lamb, duckling Chambertin, braised sweetbreads, and Adirondack trout.

Charcoal Pit. Rte. 86 near Cold Brook Plaza, Lake Placid; 523–3050. Fine American fare served in rustic atmosphere with fireplace. Veal Française or veal Normandy may be prepared and flambéed at tableside. Roast duckling also a favorite. Children's menu available.

Friends Lake Inn. Friends Lake Rd., Chestertown; 494–4751. Nicely restored 1860 country inn, reflecting that ambience in the dining room. Daily selections may include snapper en papillote, beef Wellington, or poached salmon with dill hollandaise. Tempting desserts are prepared on the premises.

Interlaken Restaurant. 15 Interlaken Ave., Lake Placid; 523–3180. Dine in a distinctive European atmosphere here, with gourmet menu featuring Swiss and French dishes.

Lake Placid Hilton. Saranac Ave., Lake Placid; 523–4411. Dining room of this hotel offers breathtaking views of the lake and mountains. Menu offers seafood, beef, poultry, and veal dishes.

Lindsay's at the Woodshed. Main St., Lake Placid; 523–9470. Look for French entrees in a setting overlooking the Olympic Arena.

Mirror Lake Inn. 35 Mirror Lake Dr., Lake Placid; 523–2544. Home-baked bread and diverse salad bar accompany fresh seafood and veal dishes here. Meal may end with homemade Adirondack maple nut sundae with pure maple syrup or homemade fudge brownie à la mode. Children's plates available.

Rene's. White Schoolhouse Rd., Chestertown; 494–2904. Casual dining in converted 1917 farmhouse. All items are fresh, homemade European fare, including German and Italian dishes and French desserts. Delicious ice cream is also homemade.

Moderate

Alpine Cellar. Wilmington Rd., Lake Placid; 523–2180. Excellent German cuisine and atmosphere, including sauerbraten, Alpine schnitzel, and roulade, plus homemade breads. Children's plate. Dinners only.

Artist's Cafe. Main St., Lake Placid; 523–9493. Overlook Mirror Lake while enjoying a 16-ounce T-bone steak, surf and turf, or steamed shrimp. Children's menu.

Cascade Inn Restaurant. Cascade Rd. and Rte. 73, Lake Placid; 523–2130. Hearty American dishes; nightly specials. Children's portions available.

Hotel Saranac of Paul Smith's College. 101 Main St., Saranac Lake; 891–2200. Fine dining in the hotel's Regis Room; inexpensive buffet Thursday nights; elaborate Sunday brunch. Bake Shoppe features fresh baked goods daily.

Jimmy's 21. Main St., Lake Placid; 523–2353. Diverse selection of steaks, seafood, chicken, and veal dishes; popular with locals.

Villa Vespa. Saranac Ave., Lake Placid; 523–9959. The town's favorite "nice little Italian restaurant" featuring homemade pastas; fresh seafood daily; unique salad bar. Special pizzas and menu for children.

Inexpensive

Casa del Sol. Rte. 86, east of Saranac Lake; no phone. A Mexican restaurant in the Adirondacks and a favorite of locals. Chili and other traditional Mexican dishes can be tempered to the desired degree of spiciness.

Deer's Head Inn. Rte. 9N, Elizabethtown; 873–9995. The oldest inn in operation in the Adirondacks (since 1818), it reflects German-Swiss influence, with sauerbraten and homemade dumplings a specialty, along with home-baked pies. Children's menu available.

Howard Johnson's. Saranac Ave., Lake Placid; 523–2241. Family-style dining; extensive menu includes inexpensive offerings.

Potluck. Main St., Lake Placid; 523–3106. Specialty foods served in attractive delicatessen setting include hefty sandwiches on hearty breads and pasta salads.

The Wood Parlor at High Peaks Base Camp. Springfield Rd., Upper Jay; 946–2133. Family menu with salad bar. Salmon is a house specialty.

HOW TO GET AROUND. Shuttle service to and from Lake Placid and Whiteface Mountain is available with *Lake Placid Sightseeing* (523–4431). Or contact the following **taxi** services: *Eddie's Taxi,* 523–2024; *Gene's Taxi,* 523–3161; *Jan's Taxi,* 523–1891; and *M&M Limo and Charter Bus Service,* 523–3611.

OTHER SPORTS AND ACTIVITIES. For information on over 100 miles of **ski touring** available in the Lake Placid region, contact the *Adirondack Ski Touring Council,* 523–1365, or *Mt. Van Hoevenberg,* Cascade Rd., Lake Placid, 523–2811. Also available: **snowmobile** rentals and trail rides, *Lake Placid Snowmobiles,* 523–3596; **toboggan** chute rides, 523–2591; **dog-sled** rides, 523–3353; and lessons on the Adirondack **luge,** *Cunningham's Ski Barn, 523–1511.*

NIGHTLIFE. Most of the hotels and dining establishments in the area offer music throughout the evening, in either the lounges or the piano bars. When it comes to places to dance, check out *Mud Puddles* on School Street, Lake Placid (523–4446), which attracts a young crowd. So do *Christies* at the Holiday Inn, Olympic Drive, Lake Placid (523–2556), *Roomers* in the Best Western Golden Arrow, 150 Main Street, Lake Placid (523–3353), and the *Dancing Bears Lounge* in the Hilton, Mirror Lake Drive, Lake Placid (523–4411).

Pennsylvania

THE POCONOS

The Pocono ski areas of Pennsylvania have an advantage that is unique in the East. They're within easy striking distance not only of New York City but also of Washington, D.C., and Philadelphia. In the sense that the ski areas near eastern New Hampshire's North Conway region can all be thought of as one ski resort, so can the 17 resorts of assorted sizes and shapes in the Poconos.

The standards that may apply to "great ski mountains" in other parts of New England don't apply here, since there's not a vertical over 803 feet. But the four areas that, for the purposes of this guide, are legitimate destination ski areas do share in common 100 percent snowmaking coverage. This translates to highly reliable skiing, with efficient lift systems to get the masses of urban skiers up quickly. And it's safe to say from the wealth of condominium development springing up around the mountains that they provide easy-to-get-to weekend alternatives when making the 6- to 12-hour drives into Vermont and New Hampshire may seem a bit much.

The four principal areas are Shawnee Mountain, Camelback, Big Boulder, and Jack Frost Mountain. All are easily accessible from I–80. Two of these, Big Boulder and Jack Frost, are across the road from each other and feature interchangeable lift tickets.

The western Poconos, near Jack Frost and Big Boulder, is a favorite area of cross-country skiers and snowmobilers, with more than 18,000 acres of recreational lands available for exploring. In this Carbon County region, there's the annual "Old Time Christmas Celebration" in a town called Jim Thorpe, a 19th-century community that's sometimes called the "Switzerland of America." This celebration includes townspeople caroling en masse, and a candlelight procession leading to a Christmas tree in the park. Santa is also on board, and old-fashioned steam train rides are available.

The whole region shares in the fun of the annual Pocono Winter Carnival. It's a time for ski reps and retailers to show their wares, for arts councils to pull out their finest exhibits and entertainment, for high school ski teams to compete, and for cross-country and alpine recreational racers to test their skills against the clock. This effort is coordinated by the Pocono Mountains Vacation Bureau, 1004 Main St., Stroudsburg, PA 18360; (717) 421–5791.

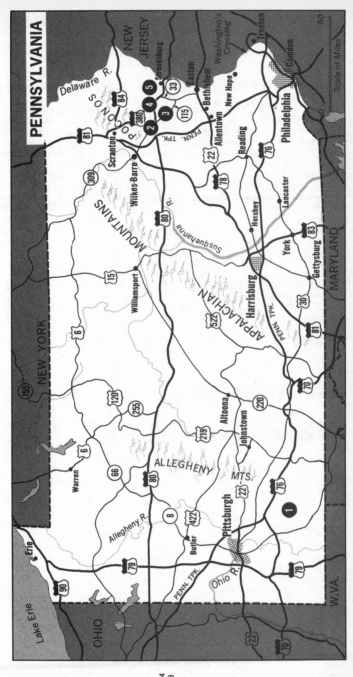

Resorts

Big Boulder, 4
Camelback, 3
Jack Frost, 2
Seven
Springs, 1
Shawnee
Mountain, 5

Practical Information for the Poconos

HOW TO GET THERE. Getting to the Pocono region is accomplished most easily by following the major auto routes through the region.

By car. From New York City, take the George Washington Bridge to I-80 west to the Delaware Water Gap and into the Poconos. An alternate route is to take the best route to I-78 and follow this and US 22 to Rte. 33 north to the Poconos.

By bus. The area is served by *Pocono Mountain Trails,* Blairstown (717-421-1740). *Martz Trailways* (717-421-3040), has stations in Stroudsburg and Mt. Pocono and *Greyhound* has a station in Stroudsburg (717 421-4451).

By plane. The Poconos are served by *Allegheny Commuter, Northwest, United,* and other small commuter lines into ABE Pocono Airport (215-264-2831) in Allentown, and Wilkes-Barre/Scranton Airport (717-655-3077) in Avoca. There are also smaller commuter airports, including the Pocono Mountain Airport in Mt. Pocono (717-839-7161); the Stroudsburg Airport (717-421-8900) and the Birchwood Airpark (717-629-0222), both in East Stroudsburg; and the Cherry Ridge Airport (717-253-5833) in Honesdale.

Pocono Limousine Service (717-839-2111), based in Pocono Summit, services regional and major urban airports (Kennedy, LaGuardia, Philadelphia, Newark, Wilkes-Barre/Scranton, and Allentown/Bethlehem/Easton).

Avis (800-331-2112), *Budget* (800-527-0700), *Dollar* (800-421-6868), *Hertz* (800-654-3131) and *National* (800-227-7368) rental cars are available at Philadelphia, Kennedy, LaGuardia, and Newark airports. Check with the different regional airports to see what rental cars they may have.

TELEPHONES. The area code for the Poconos is 717.

BIG BOULDER SKI AREA

Box 702
Blakeslee PA 18610
Tel: 717-722-0100

Snow Report: 717-722-0100
Area Vertical: 475 ft.
Number of Trails: 11 slopes/trails on 65
  skiable acres
Lifts: 5 double chairs, 2 triple chairs
Snowmaking: 100 percent of terrain
Season: early December–mid-March

JACK FROST MOUNTAIN

Box 703
Blakeslee PA 18610
Tel: 717-443-8425

Snow Resort: 717-443-8425
Area Vertical: 600 ft.
Number of Trails: 20 trails/slopes on 75
  skiable acres
Lifts: 7 double chairs
Snowmaking: 100 percent of terrain
Season: early December–mid-March

They're called The Big Two. Together Big Boulder Ski Area in Lake Harmony (Big Boulder Lake) and Jack Frost Mountain in White Haven boast 31 trails serviced by 14 lifts. Both have 100 percent snowmaking coverage and terrain about equally divided among expert, intermediate, and novice skiers. What the mountains lack in vertical, they make up for in broad slopes and dependable skiing.

Their lift tickets are reciprocal, for both daytime hours and for night skiing at Big Boulder until 10 P.M. Sunday through Friday and until midnight Saturday. And all the slopes are lit! Also unique is a twilight ticket available from noon until 10 P.M. Seniors aged 62 and up ski for only $5; those over age 70 ski free.

Practical Information for Big Boulder/Jack Frost

HOW TO GET THERE. Both are in the western Poconos, Jack Frost 4 miles east of I–80 and the northeast extension of the Pennsylvania Turnpike on Rte. 940; Big Boulder south of the Blakeslee Exit of I–80 on Rte. 903. (See *Practical Information for the Poconos* section, above.)

TELEPHONES. The area code for this region of Pennsylvania is 717.

ACCOMMODATIONS. In this region, the *Expensive* category of accommodations ranges from $50 to $75 per person, based on double occupancy, with some meals included in the higher ranges; *Moderate,* $30–$50; and *Inexpensive,* under $30. All hotels listed are within 6 miles of the slopes unless otherwise stated. Because of their proximity to Camelback Ski Area, Big Boulder/Jack Frost skiers may also choose lodgings from the listings for that resort.

Expensive

The Galleria. Lake Harmony 18626; 722–9111. Offers whirlpool, swimming, and health club in pleasant setting.

Holiday Inn. Rte. 940, Pocono-Lake Harmony, White Haven 18661; 443–8471. Luxurious rooms here in addition to sauna, two restaurants.

Mountain Laurel Resort. Rte. 940, White Haven 18661; 443–8411. Private balconies off rooms, indoor Olympic-size pool, children's activities, and saunas at this noted resort.

Split Rock Resort. Lake Harmony 18624; 722–9111. A lodge and cottages with fireplaces, on-premises indoor swimming, tennis, racquetball, and health club.

Moderate

Blue Heron. On Big Boulder Lake at Big Boulder Ski Area; 800–468–2442. At entrance to the ski slopes, these 2- and 3-bedroom condominiums feature soaking tubs.

Country Place Motel. Rte. 903, Jim Thorpe 18229; 325–2216. Has 14 large rooms with country antiques, on 7 acres.

Harmony Lake Shore Inn. Off Rte. 115, Lake Harmony 18624; 722–0522. Right on lake with color TV, refrigerators, and in-room coffee; snowmobile rentals; minutes from ski area.

Midlake Condominium. Big Boulder 18624; 722–0124. Has 60 2- and 3-bedroom condominiums with fireplaces, offers a shuttle to the slopes.

Pocono Trail Lodge, Rte. 940, White Haven 18661; 443–8461; Has 123 rooms, queen-size and king-size beds available.

Snow Ridge Village. Rte. 940, White Haven 18326; 800–468–2442. Slopeside at Jack Frost; this is condominium living, with cross-country tracks nearby.

Inexpensive

Richie's Motel. Rte. 940, White Haven 18661; 443–9528. Twin double beds, color TV in rooms; 4 separate dining rooms and 3 bars and lounges on premises.

Snowshoe Motel and Lounge. Rte. 940, Blakeslee 18610; 646–2211. Its 17 units are priced for families.

Sullivan's Trail Motel. Rte. 940, Blakeslee 18347; 646–3535. Twenty-five rooms with 2 double beds, color TV in each room.

RESTAURANTS. As in the case of accommodations, skiers at Big Boulder/Jack Frost may want to check out what the Camelback Ski Area may have to offer in the way of restaurants. In this brief listing, only those dining places nearest the Big Two are included. Also, many of the area lodging establishments maintain their own dining rooms that are open to the public. Best to call ahead for reservations. All the restaurants in this listing are in the *moderate* range with a full meal for one person, excluding drinks, tax, and tip costing $10–$15. All but the take-out places accept major credit cards.

Blue Heron Inn. At Big Boulder; 722–9898. Wonderful views and a reputation for good food. Serves lunch, dinner, and Sunday brunch.

Close Quarters. Lake Dr., Lake Harmony; 722–8127. A cozy, comfortable atmosphere with good food.

La Passada Cantina. At Jack Frost Mountain; 443–8494. A Southwestern atmosphere and menu.

Murphy's Loft. Rte. 116, Blakeslee; 646–2813. You will find an authentic log-cabin ambience and good American fare at this cozy restaurant. Popular with families.

Robert Christian's. Rte. 940, Blakeslee; 646–0433. A family restaurant featuring Italian food.

Shenanigans. Lake Dr., Lake Harmony; 722–1100. Offers casual dining and a "baby-boomers" '50's disco.

Village Squire. Rte. 115, Blakeslee; 646–3446. Family-style restaurant with extensive salad bar.

HOW TO GET AROUND. A car is a necessity in this area of the Poconos. However, some lodging places may supply **shuttle** service to the mountains. Check when making reservations.

SEASONAL EVENTS. Jack Frost offers the *52 Association* (for handicapped skiers), a special learn-to-ski program. Big Boulder hosts the *Pennsylvania Freestyle Championships* in early **February.** Everyone in the region enjoys the *Pocono Winter Carnival.* Check with the Pocono Mountains Vacation Bureau, 717–421–5791, for annual dates.

OTHER SPORTS AND ACTIVITIES. Look for **tennis, racquetball,** indoor **swimming,** and **health-spa** facilities at *The Galleria at Split Rock Resort,* off Rte. 534, Lake Harmony, 722–9111.

Mountain Laurel Resort on Rte. 940, White Haven, 443–8411, features an Olympic-size indoor pool and health-spa facilities. And the *Holiday Inn,* Rte. 940, Pocono-Lake Harmony in White Haven, 443–8471, also offers health-spa facilities and pool.

Cross-country skiing is popular in the region, with a 6-mile trail from Big Boulder to Hickory Run State Park and back. At Jack Frost, 15 km of trails are maintained.

In the nearby town of Jim Thorpe, there's cross-country skiing at Mauch Chunk Lake Park with 20 miles of trails, including the Switchback Railroad bed that traces the route of the first gravity railroad in the United States. For trail conditions call the park at 325–3669.

HINTS TO THE HANDICAPPED. Handicapped skiers—blind and amputee—can participate not only in beginner instruction at Jack Frost Mountain but also in intermediate and advanced-level skiing and introductory racing. The programs are endorsed by National Handicap Sports and the Professional Ski Instructors of America. Jack Frost is the only facility in the area to offer this extended learning progression.

For any handicapped skier, the first day on skis, including lift ticket, rental, and lesson, is free. Ensuing days are available at half price. The beginner instructional program is in conjunction with the 52 Association, a nonprofit organization that serves the needs of the severely disabled through its "confidence through sports" concept.

DAY-CARE FACILITIES. There's free babysitting at both areas and free skiing for children under 6 years old (when skiing with an adult). The children's ski school programs at both mountains are dubbed Kids C'N Ski, an animated ski school teaching program that involves children aged 3–5 in a 3-hour winter experience to familiarize them with the concept of skiing. Games and on-snow fun help children get used to ski equipment. The learn-to-ski terrain earmarked for youngsters at both mountains features colorful animated figures visible from restaurant and lounge areas—so mom and dad can relax. Children under 10 can enroll in a full- or half-day of ski and lesson programs.

NIGHTLIFE. The four major resorts in the region all offer music for dancing or entertainment come weekends. These include *The Galleria,* Lake Harmony, 722–9111; *Split Rock Resort,* Lake Harmony, 722–9111; *Holiday Inn,* Rte. 940, Pocono-Lake Harmony, White Haven, 443–8471; and *Mountain Laurel Resort,* Rte. 940, White Haven, 443–8411. Many smaller places around Lake Harmony, such as *Shenanigans,* 722–1100, offer bands and entertainment on weekends also.

CAMELBACK SKI AREA

Box 168
Tannersville PA 18372
Tel: 717–629–1661

Snow Report: 717–629–1661 or 800–233–8100 (in the mid-Atlantic states)
Area Vertical: 800 ft.
Number of Trails: 25 on 125 skiable acres
Lifts: 1 quadruple chair, 2 triple chairs, 8 double chairs
Snowmaking: 100 percent of terrain
Season: mid-December–late March

Camelback is a 2,100-foot mountain in the Poconos offering more skiable terrain on its 25 trails than any of its Pocono neighbors. It recently completed a $3.5 million expansion program with the celebration of its 25th anniversary.

Popular with New Jersey and New York skiers, the mountain has up to 40 percent of its terrain in the "easier" category, 20 percent "most difficult," and the rest flagged for the intermediate skier. The upper third of the mountain is quite steep, with some challenging expert runs like the Rocket.

A virtue of the Poconos ski areas is their commitment to snowmaking, and Camelback is no exception, covering virtually all its 125 acres with machine-made snow from mid-December to late March. It also runs with the philosophy that skiers can't get too much of skiing and opens its slopes for skiing at 7:30 A.M. weekends and holidays, 8:30 A.M. midweek, and from 5 to 10 P.M. nightly.

Practical Information for Camelback

HOW TO GET THERE. Camelback is located 5 minutes from Tannersville via I–80 (exit 45). It is 86 miles from New York City and 90 miles from Philadelphia. (See *Practical Information for the Poconos* section, above.)

TELEPHONES. The area code for Camelback and the Poconos is 717.

ACCOMMODATIONS. Contact the mountain (717–629–1661) for a free lodging directory. There are some 100 rooms right at the slopes and an additional 3,000 in nearby communities. The lodging establishments in this region are very price competitive. Hotel rates are based on double occupancy, per person, mostly MAP.

Categories, determined by price, are *Expensive,* $70 and up; *Moderate,* $40–$70; *Inexpensive,* under $40.

For specific mountainside lodging information, call 629–1661. All those places not mountainside in this listing are located within 10 miles of the mountain unless stated otherwise.

Because of the proximity of the three ski areas in this region of the Poconos, Camelback skiers also may opt for lodgings listed for the Big Boulder and Jack Frost ski areas.

Expensive

Caesars Brookdale Resort. Brookdale Rd., Scotrun; 839–8843. A 250-acre estate with cottages and villas besides the main lodge; 55 suites; dining room and bar; indoor pool, whirlpool, and sauna.

The Chateau at Camelback. Camelback Rd., Tannersville; 629–5900. Located at the base of Camelback Mountain. Spacious rooms and suites; slopeside rooms with balconies overlooking mountain; restaurant, nightclub, lounge, indoor pool, health club.

Crescent Lodge. Rtes. 191 and 940, Cresco; 595–7486. Lodge, motel rooms, and cottages with color TV and phone; 2 dining rooms; cocktail lounge. Located 12 miles from the slopes.

Moderate

Pocono Lodge. Exit 45 off I–80, Tannersville; 629–4100. King-size beds, whirlpool, some deluxe units with fireplaces, color TV (cable).

Towne & Country Motor Inn. Rte. 715, Mt. Pocono; 839–9752. A motel with a nice restaurant and a bar called the *1890 Barn.*

Inexpensive

Alvin's Housekeeping Log Cabins. Rte. 611, Henryville; 629–0667. Four furnished cabins and 4 efficiency units, all with fireplaces, TVs, kitchens and baths. Just 10 minutes to Camelback.

Antlers Lodge & Cottages. Swiftwater Rd., Swiftwater; 839–7243. Twelve minutes from Camelback. Rooms and cottages, cozy bar, home-cooked meals.

Hill Motor Lodge. Rte. 715, Tannersville; 629–1667. Has 72 rooms and a restaurant.

Penn's Wood Motel & Cottages. Rte. 611, Tannersville; 629–0131. Only minutes from Camelback, offering winter ski packages, color TV, and pleasant rooms.

RESTAURANTS. Pocono Mountain trout is the specialty of many restaurants in this area. Price categories for the region are *Expensive,* $15 and higher; *Moderate,* $8–$15; *Inexpensive,* under $8. These prices are for one meal, excluding drinks, tip, and tax. Restaurants in the area accept most major credit cards unless otherwise noted.

Expensive

Brass Door Restaurant. Carriage House at Pocono Manor, Rte. 314; 839–7386. A different environment with a paddlewheel, overhead fans, and overstuffed chairs and a reputation for excellent dining. Reservations suggested.

Chateau at Camelback. Rte. 611, Tannersville; 629–5900. A wide-ranging menu in elegant dining room overlooking mountains.

Crescent Lodge Restaurant. Rtes. 940/191, Cresco; 595–7486. An extensive menu with salad bar, lobster included, and prime rib buffet on Fridays. Entertainment weekends.

Fanucci's Restaurant. Rte. 611, Swiftwater; 839–7097. Northern and southern Italian fare served here, including homemade breads, pastas, and desserts.

Homestead Inn. Sandspring Dr., Cresco; 595–3171. A cozy place with homemade soups, breads, and pies, good choice of entrees.

Johnnie's Pocono Summit Inn. Old Rte. 940, Mt. Pocono; 839–7401. For over 50 years, a reputation for Italian specialties, especially fresh seafood.

Pump House Inn. Rte. 390, Canadensis; 595–7501. Dine in dining room or wine cellar; enjoy French country cuisine, including quiche au fromage and steak au poivre.

Smuggler's Cove Restaurant. Rte. 611, Tannersville; 629–2277. Seafood, steaks, and prime rib are favorites here; separate children's menu; dessert cart and salad bar.

Moderate

Bailey's Cafe and Steak House. Rte. 611, Mt. Pocono; 839–9679. Just like it sounds, a roadhouse atmosphere, but in an Old English Tudor-style building.

Best Western Train Coach Restaurant. Exit 45 off I–80; 629–0113. Authentic railroad dining cars provide the ambience here for steak and seafood specialties.

The Inn at Tannersville. Exit 45 off I–80; 629–3131. A rustic environment offering steaks, chops, and seafood by the fireplace. Locals say it's the best all-around bar scene in the area—365 days a year.

Inexpensive

Cameltop on Big Pocono Mountain. At Camelback, Tannersville; 629–1661. A great place for lunch with panoramic views of the Poconos. Access in winter for skiers only.

HOW TO GET AROUND. Driving your own or a rented **car** is the best way to get around in the Poconos, particularly if your lodgings are far from the mountain. Some of the nearby accommodations, however, do supply **shuttle bus** service. Check when making reservations.

SEASONAL EVENTS. In late **spring** before the snow melts, crazy hats, games, and prizes compete with the corn snow on the trails during annual *Hi-Jinx Day.* And there's a program for recreational skiers designed to hone skiing skills through the *Camelback Challenge Series.*

OTHER SPORTS AND ACTIVITIES. Complete health and exercise facilities, indoor **pool, sauna,** and **whirlpool,** are available at Caesars Brookdale Resort, Scotrun (226–2101), where there's also **ice skating** and **snowmobiling.** Look for hydrospas, indoor roller and ice skating, **racquetball, swimming** and whirlpools at *Strickland's Mountain Inn,* Mt. Pocono, 839–7155. *Pocono Gardens* (595–7431) features a health spa and indoor pool, while *The Chateau at Camelback,* Tannersville (629–5900), has a fully equipped health spa and indoor pool and offers a health staff to help with diet planning and exercise programs.

DAY-CARE FACILITIES. The ski area offers child care in a nursery for $2.50 an hour and the *Cameland Ski School* accepts children aged 4–9 for $65 for a full day of lessons and skiing.

NIGHTLIFE. This is a region where entertainment thrives. For dancing, check out *The Summit,* Rte. 715, Tannersville, 629–0203; *Caesars Brookdale Resort,* Rte. 611, Scotrun, 226–2101; the *Chateau at Camelback,* off Rte. 611, Tannersville, 629–5900; *Memorytown USA,* off Rte. 611, Mt. Pocono, 839–7176 (country-western bands); *Sheraton Pocono Inn,* Main St., Stroudsburg, 424–1930. The *Inn at Tannersville,* Rte. 611, Tannersville, 629–3131, has the reputation of being the best night spot around.

SEVEN SPRINGS MOUNTAIN RESORT

R.D. 1,
Champion PA 15622
Tel: 814–352–7777

Snow Report: 814–352–7777
Area Vertical: 750 ft.
Number of Trails: 30 on 500 skiable acres
Lifts: 2 quad chairs, 7 triple chairs, 2
double chairs, 6 rope tows, 1 pony lift
Snowmaking: 95 percent
Season: December 1–April 1

Seven Springs Mountain Resort is more than a ski area, more than a destination resort, more than a major conference center. It's the American family success story, the stuff of legends having to do with entrepreneurship, dedicated families, and hard work. Its location, 55 miles from Pittsburgh, probably had something to do with it, too.

Seven Springs is Pennsylvania's largest year-round ski resort. Located in Champion, PA, it is spread over 5,000 acres in Laurel Highlands, a region that includes the most substantial mountains in Pennsylvania, dominated by the 2,990-foot peak that draws Seven Springs' skiers. There's another ski area nearby, Hidden Valley Resort in Somerset, that shares its 11 slopes and trails with one of the largest ski touring centers in the state, the Hidden Valley Ski Touring Center (30 miles of groomed trails). Laurel Ridge State Park in Rockwood also has designated a 12-mile cross-country loop. And on state forest and park lands between Routes 31 and 30 on Laurel Ridge there are over 50 miles of groomed snowmobile trails.

The beauty of the region and its year-round potential for recreation were first recognized in 1932 by a German immigrant couple who bought 2½ acres of land for $13. They bought here, perhaps not coincidentally in a natural snow bowl, because the terrain reminded them of their native Bavaria. Perhaps it was the influence of the Schwartzwald that led Adolph Dupre to begin creating his dream. One cabin after another was crafted, creating a getaway in the wilderness for people from Pittsburgh.

By 1935, automobile engine–powered rope tows were helping people up the mountain, and by 1937, the area opened officially for skiing.

Today, the resort offers 30 open slopes and trails that encompass 500 skiable acres. Eleven trails are designated "more difficult" for intermediates, five are earmarked for experts, and 14 are for beginners.

An efficient lift system accommodates skiers, as does snowmaking coverage that can blanket 95 percent of the terrain with machine-made snow.

Because it's such a popular place with urban skiers, the resort offers several lift-ticket options. For example, after 1 P.M., lift tickets sold at the day rate include night skiing until 11 P.M. Or, skiers can purchase a less expensive night lift ticket for skiing from 4:30 P.M. on.

Ski guests are welcomed by Somerset County's largest employer at the 385-room main lodge, where a winter staff of over 1,000 people tend to all details of a ski vacation. There is assorted other lodging with 600 condominiums and townhomes, 26 chalets, and many cabins and suites.

Despite its size and success, the Dupre family still maintains hands-on management, and Helen Dupre, widow of the German entrepreneur, is chairlady of the board. The hospitable clublike environment created over 50 years ago still thrives.

Practical Information for Seven Springs

HOW TO GET THERE. Seven Springs Mountain Resort is 8 miles from Champion and 55 miles from Pittsburgh via the Pennsylvania Turnpike.

By air. The Greater Pittsburgh Airport is served by major airlines. Shuttle service can be arranged from the resort. The Westmoreland County Airport (412–539–8100) in Latrobe, 20 miles away, is served by *Allegheny Commuter Airlines* (800–428–4253). The Seven Springs Airport has a 3,000-ft. paved and lighted runway. Rental car services are available from all major companies at the Pittsburgh Airport. *Thrifty Rental Car* (412–264–1775) is available in the area.

By car. From the east, take Exit 10 (Somerset) off the Pennsylvania Turnpike; turn right off the exit ramp; at the third traffic light, take Rte. 31 west for 7 miles;

turn left at Pioneer Park; after 4 miles and at first stop sign, turn right; drive 5 miles to Seven Springs. From the west, take Exit 9 (Donegal) off the Pennsylvania Turnpike to Rtes. 711 and 31; turn right onto Rte. 711 for 2 miles; follow signs in Champion to Seven Springs.

TELEPHONES. The area code for Seven Springs and surrounding communities is 814.

ACCOMMODATIONS. Although there are inns in nearby Somerset, Donegal, and Ligonier that accommodate Seven Springs skiers, most guests who come to the area stay right at the resort, either in the main lodge or in nearby condominiums, townhouses, and cabins that are under resort management. For reservations and information contact the reservation desk at 352–7777.

Accommodations in the **Seven Springs main lodge** are priced from $130 to $155 per room. Most rooms have private balcony or patio and some offer views of skiing activity.

Mountain Villas and Swiss Mountain condominiums and townhouses range from $610 per week for a 1-bedroom unit to $1,555 per week for a 4-bedroom split-level home. All have complete kitchens with dishwasher, washer and dryer, and TVs.

Cabins with large living rooms, kitchens, bedrooms with bunk beds, and baths can sleep from 14 to 20 people and range from $575 to $800 for two nights.

For off-resort lodgings, there are two inns in Somerset, about 20 miles from the mountain, in the *Moderate* price range, where rates, based on double occupancy, range from $50 to $65 per night, EP.

Holiday Inn. Schaffer St., Somerset; 445–9611 or 800–465–4329. Rooms with phone and color TV with HBO; 23 suites; restaurant and lounge.

Ramada Inn. Exit 10, Pennsylvania Turnpike, Somerset; 443–4646 or 800–2–RAMADA. Renovated motor inn with rooms and 4 suites, restaurant, indoor pool, Jacuzzi, and sauna.

RESTAURANTS. Since Seven Springs is a self-contained ski resort, the dining out here is mostly dining in. Even so, the resort offers a variety of dining accommodations, about 12 establishments, some of which are mentioned here. Price ranges for a full meal for one without tips, tax, or beverages: *Expensive* ranges from $20 to $30; *Moderate,* $8–$20; and *Inexpensive,* less than $8. Two in the *Expensive* category are **Helen's,** where reservations are a must for gourmet fare with a French and Italian touch, and the **Oak Dining Room** in the main lodge, which offers an all-you-can-eat seafood buffet on Fridays and a one-price buffet on Saturdays. The **Slopeside Inn** is a moderately priced restaurant. The **Char 'n Grill Room** *(Moderate)* offers traditional American food, and **Adolph's Cafe** *(Inexpensive)* in the ski lodge features pastries, international coffees, and Belgian waffles. Guests can also snack at the **Coffee Shop** or at the **Pizza and Pastry Place,** both *inexpensive* and both in the main lodge.

And something quite new at ski resorts is a light lunch menu at the resort restaurants, designed to offer only 300 calories to weight-conscious skiers. The menu focuses on high-protein foods and low-calorie desserts. There's also a vegetarian salad bar, and a **Mr. Potato Restaurant** in the base lodge encourages healthy eating with a variety of vegetable toppings for baked spuds.

OTHER SPORTS AND ACTIVITIES. The resort offers **racing** instruction for NASTAR as well as competitions daily. On premises are an indoor **swimming** pool, open weekends until midnight and Mondays–Thursdays until 11 P.M.; **game rooms; bowling** alleys; **minigolf; handball** and **racquetball** courts; **roller skating;** a **health spa** with whirlpool, sauna, and universal gym; **hot tubs** and **massage therapy.**

If **shopping** is high on the list, the on-premises boutiques' stock ranges from clothing to flowers to leather and gifts.

HINTS TO THE HANDICAPPED. To accommodate handicapped guests, Seven Springs sponsors Special Olympics and ski races for the blind.

CHILDREN'S ACTIVITIES. Babysitting can be arranged through the main lodge Customer Service Department. There are also complete organized recreational programs for children starting at age 5. The *Tiny Tots Ski School* for ages 4–7 is a combined program of on-slope instruction, indoor play, and lunch. The full-day program runs from 9 A.M. to 4 P.M. and is $45.

A *Junior Program* for ages 7–12 involves youngsters in 4 hours of instruction from 10 A.M. to 2 P.M. for $40, including lunch.

NIGHTLIFE. There are eight cocktail lounges on the premises, with entertainment usually scheduled in four of them seasonally. Popular here are Top 40 bands and deejays.

SHAWNEE MOUNTAIN

Shawnee-on-Delaware PA 18356
Tel: 717–421–7231

*Snow Report: 717–421–7231 or 800–233–
 4218*
Area Vertical: 700 ft.
Number of Trails: 23 on 80 skiable acres
Lifts: 1 triple chair, 8 double chairs
Snowmaking: 100 percent of terrain
Season: late November–late March

Trail names here have an Indian ring—Pocahontas, Little Brave, and Chief Thunder Cloud. But the activity might be too much for those long-ago natives, especially on an experimental two nights of the year when the mountain forgets (on purpose) to shut off its night skiing lights (usually it's "lights out" at 10 P.M.) and keeps the lifts operating for skiers until 2 A.M.

This area is primarily designed for the beginning–intermediate skier, with many programs and services geared to families and children. Nine trails are marked "easiest," 11 "more difficult," and three "most difficult." A separate beginners' area with its own two lifts keeps the just-learning folks out of the mainstream of the action.

Resort activity focuses on the Shawnee Inn, 2.5 miles from the ski area, and on a collection of resort hotels nearby that, like Tamiment, traditionally bring top-flight entertainment to the Poconos for après-ski diversion.

Practical Information for Shawnee Mountain

HOW TO GET THERE. Shawnee Mountain is located in Shawnee-on-Delaware, 4 miles from Stroudsburg, which is just about the epicenter of the Poconos. Take Exit 52 (the Marshalls Creek Exit) to US 209 north to Shawnee.

TELEPHONES. The area code for the Poconos is 717.

ACCOMMODATIONS. The *Pocono Mountain Vacation Bureau,* 1004 Main St., Stroudsburg 18360 (421–5791), can suggest places to stay close to Shawnee. For information on condominium and vacation-home lodging within walking distance of the lifts, contact *Shawnee Properties,* Shawnee-on-Delaware (717) 421–1500.

Expensive in this region starts at about $75 (with MAP) per person per night; *Moderate,* $40–$75; *Inexpensive,* under $40. All lodgings listed are within 5 miles of the resort unless stated otherwise.

Expensive

Fernwood. Off Rte. 209, Bushkill; 588–6661. This is a year-round resort complete unto itself offering amenities for everybody from families to honeymooners, with indoor tennis and swimming, indoor roller skating, on-premises dining, and nightly entertainment.

Shawnee Villas and Northslope Chateaus. Rte. 209, Shawnee-on-Delaware; 421–1500. Walk to the slopes or take the shuttle from these 2-bedroom townhouses that sleep 6–10 people. Guests have access to all Shawnee amenities and may ski free midweek.

Tamiment Resort and Country Club. Tamiment; 588–6652. Located 10 miles from the slopes, this self-contained resort covers 2,200 acres and has its own lake. On the premises are 4 indoor tennis courts, indoor swimming, snowmobiling, tobogganing, dining, and sometimes big-name entertainment.

Moderate

Glenwood Hotel & Resort Motel. Rte. 611, Delaware Water Gap; 476–0010. A resort offering indoor pool and whirlpool, nightly music for dancing.

Howard Johnson's Motor Lodge. Exit 53 off I–80, Delaware Water Gap; 476–0000. Refurbished rooms, color TV, indoor pool, on-premises dining and lounge; children under 18 free.

Pocmont. Off Rte. 209, Bushkill; 588–6671. Suites in main lodge have whirlpool baths; health club offers steam rooms, whirlpool, and exercise equipment; indoor swimming; on-premises dining and entertainment. Located 8 miles from the slopes.

Shawnee Inn. Rte. 209, Shawnee-on-Delaware; 421–1500. Lodging in 100 rooms close to the mountain, with indoor pool and health spa and on-premises dining with lounge. Free shuttle to slopes and packages including free midweek skiing are available.

Inexpensive

Budget Motel. Exit 52 off I–80, Stroudsburg; 424–5451. A recently built 110-room, motel with color cable TV and ceramic tile baths and showers. Cribs and rollaways available.

RESTAURANTS. A wide variety of dining places to suit every pocketbook is available in the Poconos. Price categories for the region for a meal for one exclusive of drinks, tax, and tip are *Expensive,* $20 and higher; *Moderate* $12–$20; and *Inexpensive,* under $12. Most restaurants accept the major credit cards; call first to be sure.

Expensive

Peppe's Ristorante. Rte. 447, East Stroudsburg; 421–4460. An old-world setting with homemade pastas, other Italian fare. Veal dishes are favorites here.

Top of the World at Saw Creek. Rte. 209, Bushkill; 588–9444. Continental entrees and a seafood menu vie with the views here.

Moderate

Alternative. Rte. 209, East Stroudsburg; 476–0454. Chinese and Polynesian fare, but a reputation for steaks and seafood.

Bailey's Pub & Steakhouse. Main St., Stroudsburg; 424–9120. Classic English pub with treats like "super nachos" and hickory-smoked baby back ribs.

The Country Inn at Stroudsmoor. Off Rte. 191, Stroudsburg; 421–6431. Dinner begins with cocktails by the fire.

Live Lobsters at "The Beaver House." Rte. 611, Stroudsburg; 424–1020. Steak and shore here, with whole Maine lobsters featured.

Saen's Thai Cuisine. Shawnee-on-Delaware; 476–4911. Authentic Thai specialties.

Shawnee Inn Dogwood Room. River Rd., Shawnee-on-Delaware; 421–1500. A beautiful riverside setting with a 100-year-old inn serving American and Continental specialties.

Inexpensive

Hickory Licks Charcoal House. Shawnee Mountain, Rte. 209N; 424–7231. The best in charbroiled entrees and a mountain view. Good for families with children.

Mollie's. Mail St., Stroudsburg; 424–1062. Three meals a day here; basic, hearty food.

HOW TO GET AROUND. If you stay right at the mountain, a car isn't necessary. However, it's preferable to have transportation if lodging in a nearby town. A **shuttle bus** service between the Shawnee Inn and Shawnee Village runs on the hour throughout the resort.

SEASONAL EVENTS. As do the other Pocono ski areas, Shawnee participates in the *Pocono Winter Carnival* every year. The specialty here is a costume carnival day with free season passes going to the winners of various costume categories, and free skiing for everyone who uses imagination in their garb!

OTHER SPORTS AND ACTIVITIES. Several establishments in the area offer **health-spa** facilities, indoor **tennis,** and **swimming.** These include the Shawnee Inn (421–1500), close to the mountain with indoor swimming and affiliated with the mountain Shawnee Racquet Club (424–2333) in Eagle Valley Corners. There are 2 indoor tennis and 2 indoor racquetball courts, a tanning bed, Nautilus fitness center, whirlpool, and saunas. Fernwood (588–6661) and Tamiment (588–6652) in Bushkill have health club facilities for their guests, with gyms, saunas, indoor tennis, whirlpools, and indoor pools. Shawnee Mountain also has **cross-country** skiing.

DAY-CARE FACILITIES. A service called *Little Wigwam Babysitting* charges $3 an hour for children aged 1 year and up. The *SKIwee* instructional program is available for ages 5–12.

NIGHTLIFE. Right at Shawnee Mountain, the *Easy Bumps Saloon* (421–7231) offers entertainment on Friday and Saturday nights. If dancing is in order, then check out *Caesars Pocono Palace Resort* on Rte. 209 in Marshalls Creek (226–2101), *Charlie's Lounge* in the Shawnee Inn, Rte. 209 in Shawnee-on-Delaware (421–1500), *Fernwood* on Rte. 209 in Bushkill (588–6661), *Pocmont* off Rte. 209 in Bushkill (588–6671), and *Tamiment* off Rte. 209 (588–6652). These establishments also offer nightly entertainment and sometimes, on weekends, big-name entertainment.

Vermont

If you like your ski world to look as if it just stepped out of a box of Christmas cards, choose Vermont.

Lovers of big, meaty words call many of the towns and villages of this beautiful state "quintessential." And truly, Vermont is often life in its purest form. Vermont's literal backbone is the Green Mountains, which harbor ski areas and resorts from the Canadian to the Massachusetts borders.

Visit the outlet centers of Manchester in southern Vermont, the mom-and-pop general stores sprinkled across the state, the series of shops specializing in Vermont-made products—a shopper's heaven. Woe be to a visitor who doesn't take an instant "licking" to Ben & Jerry's ice cream or Woody Jackson's cow shirts.

Nowhere east of the Rockies will skiers find as many complete resorts as they will at Killington, a relative "megalopolis" of ski terrain, and its sister to the south, famous Mt. Snow. Killington ranks each year with the huge Colorado resorts in terms of skier visits. Stratton Mountain, Smugglers' Notch, and Jay Peak are self-contained worlds of their own. There are no more traditional ski towns than Stowe and its challenging Mt. Mansfield (give the Goat or Starr your serious attention). Where is there a more charming valley setting than Sugarbush?

Okemo has made its way onto the "national prominence" list with one of the nation's most advanced, successful snowmaking systems and tasteful village development. Bromley still stands for the family traditions of 56 years, as does Bolton Valley to the north. Upstart Magic Mountain continues to appeal to strong skiers and snowboarders, while Mad River Glen revels in its "ski it if you can" image.

Dining and lodging in Vermont is a treat. There's no need to settle for a cookie-cutter condominium, when so many delightful New England inns await your reservation (if you make it early for weekend and holiday trips). Restaurants range from the world-renowned Inn at Sawmill Farm in Dover to the ubiquitous McDonald's at Stowe.

"Moonlight In Vermont" is still the appropriate music on the radio and the glow will remain on skiers long after they leave . . . or move in.

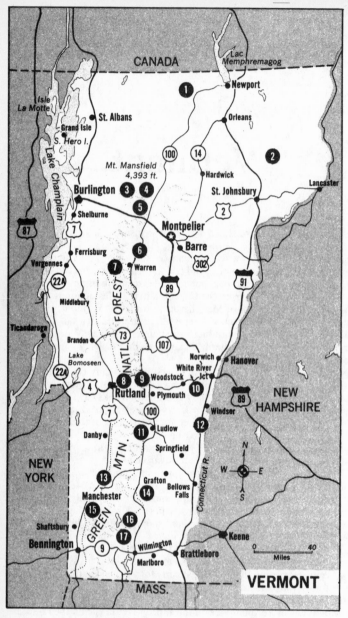

Resorts

Ascutney Mountain, 12
Bolton Valley, 5
Bromley Mountain, 13
Burke Mountain, 2
Haystack, 17
Jay Peak, 1
Killington, 9
Mad River Glen, 6

Magic Mountain, 14
Mount Snow, 16
Okemo Mountain, 11
Pico, 8
Smugglers' Notch, 4
Stowe, 3
Stratton Mountain, 15
Sugarbush, 7
Suicide Six, 10

SOUTHERN VERMONT

ASCUTNEY MOUNTAIN RESORT

Rte. 44
Brownsville VT 05037
Tel: 802–484–7711

Snow Report: 802–484–7711
Area Vertical: 1,530 ft.
Number of Trails: 31 on 100 skiable acres
Lifts: 3 triple chairs, 1 double chair
Snowmaking: 70 percent of terrain
Season: Thanksgiving–April

The people behind Mt. Ascutney, Summit Ventures, Inc., have as much or more interest in producing a resort, per se, as they do a ski area. This mountain, tucked over on Vermont's Connecticut River side in the small village of Brownsville, has been savored by some devoted skiers for years, despite the lack of snowmaking.

Since 1983, however, when Summit took over, that problem has been addressed. Capital construction projects have yielded a first-class condominium hotel, trails have been upgraded, and those who were loyal in the past are Ascutney's cheerleaders today.

The charm of this area is that it's small, very accessible (only 6 miles from I–91), uncrowded, and civilized. There aren't many ski resorts around where guests are greeted at the hotel door and offered assistance with luggage and skis.

Though limited, the black-diamond terrain here on Thunder Road and Fleet Street, among others, can challenge the most expert skier. And for those who like to cruise for a while, there's a meandering 3-mile run.

Practical Information for Ascutney Mountain

HOW TO GET THERE. Ascutney Mountain is one of six ski resorts detailed in this guide that are located in the southern section of Vermont. The others are Bromley Mountain, Haystack, Magic Mountain, Mount Snow, and Stratton Mountain. Ascutney is located on Rte. 44 in Brownsville. Brattleboro and White River Junction are gateways to Ascutney and the other southern Vermont ski resorts.

By air. Direct air service is available on major airlines from Albany, NY, which is 78 miles from Brattleboro. Connecting flights are available from Boston, Hartford, and New York with *Delta Connection* (800–221–1212) and *Northwest Airlink* (800–225–2525) flying into the West Lebanon, NH, airport, 18 miles from the resort. The resort will provide pickup service. Call 484–7711 for details. Precision also flies into the Dillant Hopkins Airport, some 25 miles east of Brattleboro in Keene, NH. Rental car agencies available in Brattleboro are *Hertz* (800–654–3131) and *National* (800–CAR–RENT). In Manchester, rental cars are available from *Hand Chevrolet* (802–362–1754) and *Manchester Motors* (802–362–1808).

By bus. *Vermont Transit* (802–862–9671 or toll free 800–451–3292 in New England), a division of Greyhound, provides service to Brattleboro and to White River Junction, which is 16 miles from Ascutney.

By car. Take I–91 north into Vermont to Exit 8 at Ascutney, some 50 miles north of Brattleboro, and onto Rte. 5 north. A few miles later (watch signs), turn onto Rte. 44A and follow it to Rte. 44. Go west 2 miles to the resort.

By train. *Amtrak* (802–295–7160) service is available to White River Junction.

TELEPHONES. The area code for all Vermont is 802.

ACCOMMODATIONS. Ascutney skiers may choose to stay right at the mountain in slopeside condominiums or they may wander as far as the college town of Hanover, NH, home of Dartmouth, about 24 miles away. *Expensive* per weekend (double occupancy) in the region is $80 and up, with *Moderate* from about $50 to $80. *Inexpensive* is less than $40.

Expensive

Ascutney Mountain Resort Hotel. Rte. 44, Brownsville 05037; 484–7711 or 800–243–0011. A full-service resort hotel encompassing 5 colonial-style buildings and offering hotel rooms plus up to 3-bedroom suites that come with fireplace, living room, kitchen, and deck.

Ascutney Mountain Village Condominiums. Rte. 44, Brownsville 05037; 484–7711 or 800–243–0011. Right on the slopes, these condominiums offer 2-room units that sleep up to 6, with full kitchens.

Ascutney Mountainside Condominiums. Rte. 44, Brownsville 05037; 484–7711 or 800–243–0011. Condominium living offering 2 bedrooms plus sleeping loft, fireplaces or wood stoves, and kitchens with dishwashers and self-cleaning ovens.

The Inn at Weathersfield. Rte. 106, Weathersfield 05151; 263–9217. A 1795 stagecoach stop with private baths, antiques, and working fireplaces; afternoon tea served before 5-course dinner.

Moderate

Holiday Inn. Sykes Ave., White River Junction 05001, 20 miles from the mountain; 295–7537. Après-ski recreation includes indoor swimming, whirlpool, sauna, 2 restaurants and 2 lounges.

Sheraton North Country Inn. Airport Rd., West Lebanon, NH 03784, 18 miles from Ascutney; 603–298–5906. Look for indoor pool and Jacuzzi, plus dining and entertainment.

Inexpensive

Windsor Motel. Rte. 5, Windsor 05089; 674–9964. Color cable TV and in-room coffee plus hospitality to groups.

Yankee Village Motel. Rte. 5, Ascutney 05030; 674–6010. Large family rooms available, in-room coffee, color cable TV, and coffee shop on premises.

RESTAURANTS. Ascutney Mountain offers fine dining at the resort and in the nearby towns of Woodstock and Windsor. Nightly entertainment is available right at the mountain. Price classifications are as follows: *Expensive,* $12–$18; *Moderate,* $8–$12; and *Inexpensive,* less than $8 for a full meal for one, exclusive of tax, tip, and beverage. Most restaurants accept the major credit cards, but check before going.

Ascutney Harvest Inn. *Expensive.* Ascutney Mountain Resort, Brownsville; 484–7711. A 150-seat dining room offering elegant service. Fare ranges from international to traditional American, with a gourmet touch.

The Ascutney House. *Expensive.* Junction of Rtes. 5 and 131, Ascutney; 674–2664. A restored mansion offering fine American cuisine and billing its ambience as circa 1800.

Bentleys of Woodstock. *Expensive.* 3 Elm St., Woodstock; 457–3232. Unusual luncheons and imaginative dinners are served in a casual atmosphere in the heart of this lovely village. There's entertainment most nights.

Skunk Hollow Tavern. *Expensive.* Hartland Four Corners; 436–2139. Assortment of ethnic dishes—menu changes weekly. The pub with fireplace occasionally has entertainment.

The Windsor Station Restaurant. *Moderate.* Depot Ave., Windsor; 674–2052. A restored train station now prepares steaks to your specifications, along with veal dishes.

HOW TO GET AROUND. It is best to have a **car** at this resort. Some of the mountainside lodging places may have **shuttle** service to the surrounding towns, however. Check when making your reservations.

OTHER SPORTS AND ACTIVITIES. The *Sports Center at Ascutney Mountain Resort* (484–7711) has a 35 × 70 ft. indoor, heated swimming pool, sauna, whirlpool, seven tennis courts, two racquetball courts, weight training and aerobics rooms.

Sleigh rides are offered at the *Kedron Valley Inn Stables* in South Woodstock, 457–1480.

And depending on what's happening on a given weekend, Ascutney skiers often cast an eye toward Hanover, NH, where Dartmouth College activities may include college ice hockey or professional entertainers.

DAY-CARE FACILITIES. The *Nursery* (484–7711) accepts children aged 8 weeks to 10 years, 9 A.M. to 4 P.M. daily. Reservations necessary for those under a year old. The *Teddy Bear* program takes ages 3–5 on the slopes for introductory lessons, lunch, and combined nursery program. The *Polar Bear* program takes ages 3–5 who are ready for lift-serviced terrain. *SKIwee* accepts ages 6–12 for ski instruction made fun.

NIGHTLIFE. *Cheddars* at the mountain (484–7711) brings in bands on weekends. The *Winner's Circle Lounge* in the Ascutney Mountain Resort Hotel (484–7711) features jazz musicians on weekends and holidays. *Moguls Nightclub* in Ascutney offers live entertainment. The *Hotel Coolidge* in Ascutney (295–3118) has jazz on Thursday and small bands on weekends.

BROMLEY MOUNTAIN

Box 1130
Manchester Center VT 05255
Tel: 802–824–5522

Snow Report: 802–824–5522
Area Vertical: 1,334 ft.
Number of Trails: 35 on 157 skiable acres
Lifts: 1 quad chairlift, 6 double chairs, 1
*   J-bar, 1 Mitey Mite*
Snowmaking: 84 percent of terrain
Season: November–April

Bromley Mountain has the distinction of being the only south-facing ski area in Vermont. This leads to its claim that it has the earliest and longest-tanned skiers around, and that it's sometimes as much as 10 degrees warmer here than at Stratton, just across the valley. Bromley and Magic Mountain (9 miles away) are owned and managed together.

Bromley is located right on Route 11, which separates its parking area from the ski lifts. While the bulk of Bromley's bed base is in Manchester, Bromley Village has plenty of condominium rentals and one slopeside hotel.

The ski mountain was created in 1937 by Fred Pabst, Jr., of the Milwaukee brewing family. In addition to the mountain itself, Pabst was responsible for some skiing "firsts." He invented the J-bar, pioneered the concept of "snow farming," provided the first base-to-summit snowmaking, and made available the first slopeside nursery facilities.

Bromley is one of those areas that make people of all ages feel welcome, with free skiing for children aged 6 and younger and half-price skiing for seniors aged 65 and older. There's also a Bromley Senior Skiers Club, Box 1130, Manchester Center, VT 05255.

The mountain offers a balanced mix of beginner, intermediate, and expert trails. Bromley's upper east side is serviced by the Blue Ribbon Quad chairlift, and the terrain offered belies the myth that Bromley is merely novice and intermediate. It isn't. On busy days, skiers in the know use the older double chair that still runs in the same direction. Experts find Pabst's Peril and Havoc fun.

Bromley perpetuates the Pabst legacy that everyone is a guest. The warm wooden, old-time base lodge is still a joy—check it out.

MAGIC MOUNTAIN SKI AREA

Londonderry VT 05148
Tel: 802–824–5566

Snow Report: 802–824–5566 or 824–5617
Area Vertical: 1,700 ft.
Number of Trails: 70 on 250 skiable acres
Lifts: 2 triple chairs, 3 double chairs, 1 T-bar
Snowmaking: 80 percent of terrain (on Magic side)
Season: late November–April

Magic Mountain is another in the trio of ski areas that make the Manchester/Stratton region of Vermont such a draw for Northeast city skiers.

Magic Mountain was the dream of Swiss Hans Thorner, who equated it in literary terms to the Magic Mountain of Thomas Mann. His trailcutting was quirky and fun, and he created a mountain full of "magical" tricks (and treats).

In 1985, when Magic Mountain came under new management, there were hints in the wind of dramatic changes to come in the near future. They have. Timber Ridge, a smaller ski area on the back side of Magic Mountain, was purchased by Magic's owners, and trails across the ridge were designed to connect the two. This acquisition, in addition to Magic's own expansion, has more than doubled the trail network. For skiers, this means that the bulk of expert skiing is still on Magic's slopes, while intermediate and novice skiers have their separate Timber-side runs. In addition, the owners have purchased Bromley Mountain, 9 miles away, and now offer a reciprocal lift ticket between Magic/Timberside and Bromley. With this purchase, the Magic skier has a choice of over 100 trails.

Stratton began the snowboarding revolution in the eastern United States, but Magic is wresting away the title. Its permanent half-pipe is open in early December and is the training home to the famed Burton Pro Snowboard Team and several competitions during the season.

STRATTON MOUNTAIN

Stratton VT 05155
Tel: 802–297–2200

Snow Report: 802–297–2211
Area Vertical: 2,003 ft.
Number of Trails: 92 trails on 485 acres
Lifts: One 12-passenger high-speed gondola, 4 quad chairs, 1 triple chair, 6 double chairs
Snowmaking: 62 percent of terrain
Season: mid-November–early May

It's unclear from the archives how Stratton came to be called Stratton, except that many New England place names trace directly back to King George III of England and his pals. The Indian name for the mountain is Manicknung, or "home of the bear." It was a flourishing New England village of 366 people, according to the 1860 census, but as New Englanders discovered other parts of the country, Stratton's population declined. Even in the early part of this century, people struggled to make a living there, primarily through logging.

In 1959, a visionary named Frank Snyder recognized the possibilities of skiing on this mountain and the advantages of the proximity of a southern-based area to the New York metropolitan market. Three years later, Stratton Mountain opened to skiers.

A full 57 percent of Stratton's terrain is designated "more difficult" for the intermediate-level skier who enjoys the mountain's fall-line skiing. The terrain includes a lower mountain, primarily novice-to-lower-intermediate terrain, and an upper mountain, which is intermediate and advanced terrain. This is one of those areas where there's more than meets the eye, and you have to actually get onto the upper mountain to realize how expansive the terrain is. In 1989, Stratton made access to the upper mountain a lot easier with the opening of Starship XII, a 12-passenger high-speed gondola that takes just 7½ minutes from the base to the summit. Stratton also has its own bowl: Popular with intermediates, the Sun Bowl has the added benefit of a southern exposure (read warmth on those chilly Vermont mornings). A 350-seat base lodge has been added to the Sun Bowl, relieving some of the weekend and holiday congestion in the main lodge. There's a quad chairlift, two difficult trails, and expanded snowmaking and parking. A huge Sun Bowl development is in the works, currently undergoing the rigorous Vermont expansion process.

Since the early 1980s, Stratton has been experiencing a renaissance that's included an infusion of more than $75 million for village and mountain modifications (for example, the addition of a 950-car covered parking garage). The result is perhaps a contrast to the traditional ski-country image typified by the Stratton Mountain Boys, ski school instructors of an Austrian bent who entertain here in lederhosen, but the sophistication is working for the area. What makes Stratton a popular destination is its self-contained nature, atop its 4-mile access road.

A 22-acre village core at the base of the mountain houses 60,000 square feet of retail space that includes 30 shops and three restaurants in addition to the covered garage. There's a 91-room condo-hotel, a 108-villa complex called Village Watch, and 34 townhouses.

All three ski areas—Stratton, Bromley, Magic—share the town of Manchester (17 miles from Stratton). Manchester is a collection of factory-direct outlet stores and boutiques, with a number of quality restaurants.

Practical Information for Stratton, Bromley, and Magic Mountains

HOW TO GET THERE. (See *Practical Information for Ascutney Mountain,* above for regional details.) **By car.** Stratton Mountain is located 35 miles from Brattleboro and 4 miles from Bondville. Take I–91 north to Vermont Exit 2 to Brattleboro, then Rte. 30 north to Bondville and turn left at the sign. Bromley Mountain is located 6 miles east of Manchester on Rte. 11. Take I–91 to Exit 6 at Rockingham to Rte. 103 west to Chester, then onto Rte. 11 west for 24 miles to Bromley. For Magic Mountain, continue on Rte. 11 through Chester to Londonderry. Look for signs to the mountain.

TELEPHONES. The area code for all Vermont is 802.

ACCOMMODATIONS. The *Area Lodging Servicer,* Rte. 11, Londonderry 05148 (824–6915 or 800–677–7829), handles reservation requests for lodging in all the mountain towns adjacent to and including Stratton, Bromley, and Magic resorts. In addition, there are slopeside condominiums at Bromley ranging from $420 per unit per person for three nights (including lift tickets). Contact Bromley Mountain, Box 1130, Manchester Center, VT 05255; 824–5522.

Categories for hotel and motel accommodations in the area are *Expensive,* $75 and up; *Moderate,* $45–$75; and *Inexpensive,* $45 and under. All lodgings in this listing are within 25 miles of the three mountains.

Expensive

Barrows House. Rte. 30, Dorset 05251; 867–4455. A comfortable, 200-year-old New England inn with a main house and 8 out-buildings on 11 acres. Sauna, tavern, and restaurant. MAP available.

Bromley Village. Rte. 11, Peru 05152; 824–5458. On-mountain 1- to 4-bedroom condos provide convenient, forget-your-car accommodations.

Dorset Inn. Rte. 30, Dorset 05251; 867–5500. This country inn goes back to 1796, making it the oldest continuously operated establishment of its kind in the state. Located in picturesque village. MAP available.

The Equinox. Manchester Village 05254; 362–4700. A restored 144-room resort hotel in the grand style where the Green Mountain Boys met to plan their siege against the British and where Mrs. Abraham Lincoln once summered. This is a reemerging grande dame with several restaurants and MAP available. Après-ski activities include indoor swimming, Nautilus, and assorted spa amenities.

Liftline Lodge. Stratton Mountain, just off Rte. 30, 05155; 297–2600. Walk to the ski lifts; some apartment units. Hot tub, sauna, spa, gym, lounge, and entertainment on premises, plus a restaurant specializing in wild game. MAP available.

The Reluctant Panther. West Rd., Manchester 05254; 362–2568. Has 13 rooms (some nonsmoking) with king-size beds, 8 with working fireplaces. Couples only. Substantial Continental breakfast, dinners served.

Stratton Mountain Inn. Stratton Mountain 05155; 297–2500. A full-service resort hotel right at the mountain; walk to lifts, other village facilities. Color TV, lounge, dining, entertainment. MAP available.

Stratton Village Lodge. Stratton Mountain 05155; 297–2260. A luxury, 91-room hotel with kitchenettes and walk-to-lifts convenience; also near Stratton recreation and village facilities. MAP available.

Moderate

Alpenrose Inn. Off Rte. 30, Bondville, 05340; 297–2750. A quiet country inn offers 7 rooms, all with private baths. Guests enjoy homemade breakfasts and dinners. MAP.

Birch Hill Inn. West Rd., Manchester 05254; 362–2761. Five rooms with private bath in quiet, relaxing atmosphere; large living room with crackling fire. MAP.

Birkenhaus. Stratton Mountain 05155; 297–2000. An Austrian lodge with 20 double rooms or bunk rooms, all equipped with refrigerators and coffee makers.

Bromley Sun Lodge. Bromley Mountain, Peru 05152; 824–6941. A 51-room hotel on the slopes of Bromley; rooms with 2 double beds; pool, sauna, game room, lounge; ski out your door to slopes.

Bromley View Inn. Rte. 30, Bondville 05340; 297–1459. A 12-room, homey inn near cross-country trails; hot tubs, exercise equipment; hearty breakfasts; MAP available.

Chalet Motel. Rte. 11, Manchester 05255; 362–1622. Has 43 units with 2 queen-size beds and a rollaway couch; refrigerators and coffee makers in rooms. Great for families. Sauna, 2 whirlpool spas.

Dostal's Resort Lodge. Magic Mountain, Londonderry 05148; 824–6700. Walk to Magic Mountain ski slopes from 50-room Austrian hotel/lodge only 9 miles from Bromley and 14 miles from Stratton; heated indoor pool, 2 whirlpool spas. MAP.

Haig's. Rte. 30, Bondville 05340; 297–1300. A lodge at the foot of Stratton Mountain with private baths, ski lockers, fireplaces in rooms; music video, game room, sauna, dancing, and on-premises dining.

Inn at Magic. On mountain, Londonderry 05148; 824–6100. A 25-unit slopeside inn with suites that are popular with families. Amenities include whirlpool, sauna, lounge, restaurant, and fireplaces.

Inn at Manchester. Box 345, Manchester 05254; 362–1793. A Victorian mansion that offers game room and lounge, fireplaces, breakfasts.

Johnny Seesaw's. Rte. 11, Peru 05152; 824–5533. Rustic, casual log ski lodge near Bromley Mountain with accommodations from bunk rooms to cottages with fireplaces; it's a converted roadhouse and speakeasy; game room, lounge with entertainment; favorite of families. MAP available.

Kandahar Resort Lodge. Jct. Rtes. 11 and 30, Manchester Center 05255; 824–5531. A modernized 1841 inn. Offers 2 double beds, TV, and private baths; lounge, sauna, on-premises dining.

Marble West Inn. Box 22, Dorset 05251; 867–4155. In Vermont's marble country, an elegant, 6-guest-room home in the National Register of Historic Places. Near cross-country trails of lovely Merck Forest.

Nordic Inn. Rte. 11, Landgrove 05251; 824–6444. Intimate, 5-room inn with licensed pub, 12 miles of cross-country nearby. MAP available.

Palmer House. Rte. 7A, Manchester 05255; 362–3600. Motel with large rooms, refrigerators, coffee makers, sauna, and Jacuzzi. Ideal for families.

Red Fox Inn. Bondville 05340; 297–2488. A converted barn serves as a dining room for this 10-guest-room Vermont home.

Wiley Inn. Rte. 11, Peru 05152; 824–6600. A 200-year-old inn 1 mile from Bromley; family suites, fireplaces, and homemade raisin bread.

Inns in the *moderate* range offering breakfast include

Bear Creek Resort. Rawsonville 05155 (at base of Stratton Mountain); 297–1700. Look for Jacuzzi, sauna, on-premises dining; free shuttle to the slopes and access to cross-country trails.

Dovetail Inn. Rte. 30, Dorset 05251; 867–5747. A home on the village green turned to bed-and-breakfast, with private baths and fireplaces. Ask for a breakfast basket to be delivered to your room. Near cross-country skiing.

Inn at Sunderland. Rte. 7A, Arlington 05250; 362–4213. A Victorian era farmhouse with old-fashioned high ceilings, ornate woodwork. Breakfast served by fireplace.

Inexpensive

Blue Gentian Lodge. On the Magic access road, Londonderry 05148; 824–5908. All 14 rooms have private baths, fireplace in lounge, playroom, 2 miles cross-country terrain, color TV. Full breakfasts included.

Brook-n-Hearth. Rte. 11, Manchester 05255; 362–3604. A home with individual suites and rooms, private baths, lounge, game room, breakfast available.

Sunny Brook Lodge. State Park Rd., Jamaica 05343; 874–4891. Rooms with double and twin beds, lounge with TV, breakfasts.

White Pine Lodge. Rte. 11, Londonderry 05148; 824–3909. Completely furnished 2- and 3-bedroom apartments with kitchens, some fireplaces; sleep up to 9; cross-country just out the door.

RESTAURANTS. These three ski areas share lodging, dining, and après-ski facilities. *Expensive* restaurants will cost $20–$35 for a meal; *Moderate,* $15–$20; and *Inexpensive,* under $15. Most accept major credit cards, but it would be wise to check before you go.

Expensive

Barrows House. Rte. 30, Dorset; 867–4455. Country inn dining, extensive wine list. Specialties include native pheasant, Vermont lamb. Reservations recommended.

Birkenhaus. Stratton Mountain, Stratton (off Rte. 30); 297–2000. Wiener schnitzel and other Continental preparations in Austrian ambience.

Chantecleer Restaurant and Lounge. Rte. 7, Manchester Center; 362–1616. A varied menu with fondue and frogs' legs Provençale.

Equinox Hotel. Main St., Manchester Village; 362–4700. A grand hotel dining room in refurbished establishment.

Feathers at Bear Creek. Rawsonville; 297–1700. Such items as sweetbreads and pork tenderloin are staples. Reservations suggested.

Four Columns Inn. Rte. 30, Newfane; 365–7713. A country inn offering award-winning dining. Menu includes bouillabaisse and a sauté of rabbit. Reservations recommended.

Mistral's. Rte. 11, near Manchester Center; 362–1779. Jackets suggested here. Rack of lamb for 2 is the house specialty. Dine overlooking the river.

Reluctant Panther Inn. Manchester Village; 362–2568. A select menu includes brace of quail and 5-course, prix fixe dinners. Reservations suggested.

Sage Hill Restaurant. Stratton Mountain Inn, Stratton (just off Rte. 30); 297–2500. Prime ribs prepared with Yorkshire pudding are a specialty.

Three Mountain Inn. Rtes. 30/100, Jamaica; 874–4140. A small New England inn with a French twist to the menu.

Moderate

Cristo's. Main St., Manchester Center; 362–2408. Pizza and pasta.

Dorset Inn. Village Green, Rte. 30, Dorset; 867–5500. New England fare served 3 times daily. Specialties include roast Cornish hen, sautéed fresh calves' liver.

Jamaica House. Rte. 30, Jamaica; 874–4400. Boasts area's largest menu, including fresh seafood and Italian specialties.

Johnny Seesaw's. Rte. 11, Peru; 824–5533. Something for everyone. Home-baked bread served, with all entrees tending toward Yankee.

The Londonderry Inn. Rte. 100, South Londonderry; 824–5226. Dinner menu changes daily, with unusual preparations of old favorites such as curried lamb.

The Mill Tavern. Rte. 11, Londonderry; 824–3247. French fare with a fine hand when it comes to herbs.

Popover's Restaurant & Lounge. Rtes. 30/100, Rawsonville; 297–1146. A limited menu includes frogs' legs with pine nuts and chicken flambéed in Scotch.

Tenderloins Bar & Grill. Stratton Mountain (just off Rte. 30); 297–2200. Located at the Stratton cross-country touring center. Limited menu ranges from beef tenderloin to grilled swordfish.

Inexpensive

Friendly's. Manchester Center; 362–3056. Family dining with good service.

Garlic John's. Rtes. 11/30, Manchester; 362–9843. A long list of Italian specialties, with discounts for children's dinners.

Gurry's. Rtes. 11/30, Manchester Depot; 362–9878. Mostly pizza, burgers, Italian specialties, but steak and seafood also available.

Laney's. Rte. 30, Manchester; 362–4456. Ribs, chicken, pizza, and popovers.

Mulligan's. At Stratton; 297–9293. Charcoal-grilled foods and fast service.

Up For Breakfast. Main St., Manchester Center; 362–4204. Variety of unique breakfasts served upstairs over a store. Bakery.

HOW TO GET AROUND. A **shuttle** bus makes a continuous loop around Stratton, covering the village lodging, sports center, and base lodge. As yet, there is no service between the two other mountain resorts. It would be best to have a car in these parts, particularly if you want to ski at each of the three mountains or enjoy the New England countryside.

HINTS TO THE HANDICAPPED. Through the ski school at Stratton, there's a handicapped-skiers program with one-to-one instruction by a specially trained staff. Bromley can also provide instruction as well as some special equipment for handicapped, blind, and hearing-impaired skiers.

CHILDREN'S ACTIVITIES. Stratton accommodates skiing families through a variety of child-oriented programs. The *Stratton Day Care Center* provides indoor activities and supervision for children aged 6 weeks–5 years at $35 a day. Lunch is included, and the program is open 8:30 A.M.–4:30 P.M. daily. Reservations recommended. Ages 3–6 can join the *Little Cub* program that includes indoor supervision and ski lessons. The *Big Cub* program enrolls youngsters 6–12 in a Junior Ski School for structured lessons, supervised skiing, and lunch.

At Bromley, the state-accredited nursery has been in operation for 42 years, 17 years under the direction of Lorraine Harrington, who minds children ages 1 month to 6 years with tender loving care. The nursery is open from 9 A.M. to 4 P.M.; the full-day fee is $27; the half-day fee, $16.

Bromley's *Junior Ski School* has several programs, including *Nursery Moose Club* for ages 3–5, which meets 9 A.M.–4 P.M. daily, combining nursery activities with ski lessons: the full-day rate is $45; the half-day rate is $25. For ages 6–14, an all-day ski program ranges from $40 to $60.

NIGHTLIFE. The Stratton Mountain Boys perform for après-ski relaxation at the Stratton Mountain Base Lodge (297–2211) right at the mountain. These are ski instructors who are skilled musicians. A Tyrolean Evening spent with "The Boys" is authentic, fun, and as good as anything found in the Alps. A must, after all these years.

Come evening, *Haig's* in Bondville (297–1300) provides a hi-tech environment with video and simultaneous disco.

Alfie's Dancing, Rtes. 11/30, Manchester (362–2637), offers 4 dance floors with music ranging from top-40 to oldies; live bands weekends, and a DJ on board the rest of the week.

Tenderloins Bar & Grill, Stratton Mountain (297–2250) is a nightclub with music for dancing. And a bar called *Cafe Applause* at the Stratton Mountain Inn (297–2200) often has live entertainment.

Mulligan's, located in the Stratton Mountain Village Square, offers après-ski entertainment daily, and a DJ on Friday and Saturday nights. There's also entertainment at *Equinox* (362–4700) and *Dostal's* (824–6700). Dostal's offers contemporary music one night midweek and one night on the weekend.

MOUNT SNOW SKI RESORT

Mount Snow VT 05356
Tel: 802-464-3333

Snow Report: 802–464–2151
Area Vertical: 1,700 ft.
Number of Trails: 84 on 241 acres
Lifts: 2 quads, 6 triple chairs, 8 double
*   chairs, 2 tows*
Snowmaking: 80 percent of terrain
Season: early November–early May

If you're a New Yorker and a skier, chances are you know Mount Snow, a 1,000-acre resort in the Green Mountain National Forest, only 213 miles from Manhattan and within striking distance of millions as an easy-to-reach weekend destination.

Once famous for its outdoor heated swimming pool and Fountain Mountain, a 150-foot geyser that would shoot up from Snow Lake and freeze, the mountain has turned its attention to skiers and provided them with the best possible skiing experience. This is professional ski management at its zenith. Mount Snow is owned and operated by S.K.I. Ltd., the same company that runs gigantic Killington to the north. Skiers have welcomed the changes with open arms.

Today the mountain offers skiing on 84 trails, spread over four interconnected mountain areas. The lift capacity has nearly tripled since the 1960s, with a system of 18 lifts, including two quads and six triple chairs. Snowmaking blankets 80 percent of all skiable terrain, including runs from the summit for all ability levels. Long a favorite of intermediate skiers for its wide, western-style runs, Mount Snow has plenty of skiing for novices and experts, too. Novices can enjoy "easy" runs from the summit, while experts are challenged by the steep North Face that boasts 12 "most difficult" trails.

And as this sunny mountain (the resort where people claim the sun shines 50 percent of the time) grows and thrives, so too do the nearby towns of Wilmington and West Dover, which, as in many other rural New England communities, have been revitalized by winter tourism. They're lined with dozens of shops that sell everything from antiques to handmade Vermont crafts. Other recreational activities such as sleigh rides, snowmobiling, cross-country skiing, and ice fishing are available.

The result today is the ability to move what might seem to be a metropolis of skiers into Vermont, wine and dine them admirably, offer a variety of terrain, shopping, and other activities, and keep them hurrying back for more.

HAYSTACK

RR 1, Box 173
Wilmington VT 05363
Tel: 802–464–5321

Snow Report: 802–464–5321
Area Vertical: 1,400 ft.
Number of Trails: 43 on 180 skiable acres
Lifts: 3 triple chairs, 2 double chairs, 1
*   T-bar*
Snowmaking: 90 percent of terrain
Season: late November–early April

Haystack Ski Area is located only 4 miles from Mount Snow. That's good to remember on Mount Snow's numerous maxed-out days, as the 'Stack limits lift-ticket sales. In fact, a 5-mile nordic-alpine experience is a run along the ridge line that connects the two areas. This is a mountain sporting two peaks and a village of some 100 condominiums, 20 of which are slopeside. A loyal breed of skiers frequents Haystack, with some parents who learned to ski here now introducing their own youngsters to the sport. The children's ski school has a "terrain garden" for easy teaching and offers *SyberVision,* the "monkey see–monkey do" learning method students swear by in Vail.

Haystack's upper mountain is composed primarily of intermediate terrain, with some black-diamond turf. A recent addition of a second base lodge provides more dining, more parking, and easy access to the upper mountain ski terrain. The lower mountain is reserved for novice skiers. In fact, Haystack offers a special lower mountain ticket for first-time and novice skiers. The terrain is rated 35 percent "most difficult," 35 percent "more difficult," and 30 percent "easiest."

Trail names here have a farming theme, such as Hay Fever, Hay Seed, Pitchfork, and Last Straw. Recently a cluster of 10 new trails was added with the theme "The Witches"; these trails have enchanting names such as Merlin, Samantha, and Wizard. And because of the mellow atmosphere, skiers don't feel obliged to dress to the hilt to tackle the slopes. Blue jeans (with long johns underneath) are quite appropriate here.

Haystack received an eleventh hour financial reprieve after letting the word out that the area would not open for the 1990–91 season. Skiers can likely count on continual operation for the future, but no one is sure by whom.

Practical Information for the
Mount Snow/Haystack Region

HOW TO GET THERE. Mount Snow and Haystack are about 30 miles west of Brattleboro, and 5–9 miles north of Wilmington. (See *Practical Information for Ascutney Mountain,* above, for regional details)

By car. Take I–95 north to I–91 to Brattleboro Exit 2 onto Rte. 9. Drive west to Wilmington, where you take Rte. 100 north. At Coldbrook Road, turn left and drive 3 miles to Haystack. For Mount Snow, stay on Rte. 100 for a few more miles into the ski resort.

Buzzy's Taxi Service (802–464–5431) provides 24-hour **taxi** service in the area. **Rental cars** are available through *Mount Snow Vermont Tours Inc.* (802–464–2076).

TELEPHONES. The area code for all Vermont is 802.

ACCOMMODATIONS. *Mount Snow Vacation Services* (802–464–8501 or 800–444–9404), can give specifics on and make reservations for more than 50 inns, lodges, and condominium complexes in the region. There are four separate condominium complexes located at the base of Mount Snow, offering slopeside, walk-to-lift, and mountain view units. Amenities include indoor pool, whirlpool, Jacuzzis, saunas, and exercise-game rooms. A 2-day weekend here starts at $500 per unit.

For Haystack on-mountain lodging, call *Haystack Condominium Rentals* (802–464–5321), or call *Haystack Magazine* and ask for the lodging directory (802–464–5321). In our selection of off-mountain possibilities, rates are per person for a 2-day stay, with meals included. Categories are *Expensive,* $120–$200; *Moderate,* $70–$120; and *Inexpensive,* less than $70. All lodgings listed are within 10 miles of Mount Snow, unless stated otherwise.

Expensive

Andirons Lodge. Rte. 100, West Dover; 464–2114. Dining room, 2 lounges, 3 fireplaces, indoor pool, sauna, whirlpool; game room, in-room movies, cable TV. MAP available.

Deerhill Inn. Valley View Rd., West Dover; 464–3100. Views of Deerfield Valley from 16 guest rooms, some with canopy beds. Afternoon tea is served here. MAP available.

Hermitage Inn. Coldbrook Rd., Wilmington; 464–3511. A 29-room inn that reaches toward the deluxe category, with a dining room that often serves fresh game from its own game farm. There are over 55 miles of cross-country terrain just outside the door. MAP available.

Inn at Sawmill Farm. Rte. 100, West Dover; 464–8131. Lots of elegance; superb meals, wide selection of wines and tasteful furnishings in the luxurious rooms. Restored group of farm buildings.

Inn at South Newfane. Dover Rd., South Newfane; 348–7191. Elegant turn-of-the-century Manor House with 6 rooms.

Longwood Inn. Rte. 9, Marlboro; 257–1545. A 15-room country inn, circa 1700s. Two sitting rooms with fireplaces. Located 19 miles from the slopes.

Snow Lake Lodge. Mountain Rd., Mount Snow; 800–451–4211. The hub of Mount Snow off-slope activities; a full-service resort lodge at the base offering easy access to the slopes. MAP available.

White House of Wilmington. Rte. 9, Wilmington; 464–2135. Turn-of-the-century mansion boasts 8 fireplaces, ski touring center, indoor pool, sauna, steam room; knolltop site with great views.

Moderate

Doveberry Inn. Rte. 100, West Dover; 464–5652. Seven individually decorated guest rooms. Fireplace in living room and home-cooked meals.

Gray Ghost Inn. Rte. 100, West Dover; 464–2474. Has 26 rooms, BYOB lounge, game room, fireplace, TV viewing areas.

Horizon Inn. Rte. 9, Wilmington; 464–2131. Family-run 28-room lodge with game room, lounge, heated indoor pool.

Nordic Hills Lodge. Colebrook Rd., Wilmington; 464–5130. A 27-room inn with game room, 2 lounges with fireplaces.

Nutmeg Inn. Rte. 9, Wilmington; 464–3351. A 1787 country inn by Deerfield River converted to 9-room inn; bar, fireplace, library, delicious home cooking.

Red Cricket Inn. Rte. 100, West Dover; 464–8817. Only things warmer than the home cooking are the 2 fieldstone fireplaces; sauna, cable TV; moonlight horse-drawn sleigh rides and fondue parties. MAP available.

Yankee Doodle Lodge. Rte. 100, West Dover; 464–5591. Twenty-five rooms; children stay free midweek. Whirlpool, in-room TV, BYOB lounge, game rooms, fireplace.

Inexpensive

Misty Mountain Lodge. Stowe Hill Rd., Wilmington; 464–3961. Ten rooms in a farmhouse offering old-fashioned home cooking.

Old Red Mill. Rte. 100, Wilmington; 464–3700. Has 24 rooms, private baths. MAP available.

Whippletree. 1 Tannery Rd., West Dover; 464–5485. Seven rooms; breakfast included in rates.

RESTAURANTS. There are more than 40 restaurants in the region, offering everything from wild game to pizza. In this region a meal for one person costing $30 and more, excluding tips, drinks, and tax, would be categorized as *Expensive;* $20–$30, *Moderate;* and less than $15, *Inexpensive.* In our sampling, major credit cards are accepted unless otherwise noted.

Expensive

Deerhill Inn. Off Rte. 100, West Dover; 464–3100. A small, intimate dining room offering American and European preparations in gourmet fashion.

The Hermitage. Coldbrook Rd., Wilmington; 464–9350. Specials include pheasant, quail, goose, and duckling from on-premises game farm.

Inn at Sawmill Farm. Rte. 100, West Dover; 464–8131. A quiet and formal Vermont country inn with what is generally considered the most prestigious gourmet dining in the valley.

Le Petit Chef. Rte. 100, Wilmington; 464–8437. Country dining with a French touch in renovated farmhouse.

Two Tannery Road. Tannery Rd., West Dover; 464–2707. Look for duckling, veal, seafood, and tasty desserts.

The White House. Rte. 9, Wilmington; 464–2135. An old mansion with 4-season patio lounge offers Continental fare.

Moderate

Andirons/Dover Forge. Rte. 100, West Dover; 464–2114. Three separate dining rooms offering American fare.

Fennessey's Parlor. Rte. 100, West Dover; 464–9361. Steaks, prime rib, and seafood offered here.

Matterhorn of Dover. Rte. 100, West Dover; 464–8011. Prime rib is a specialty, followed by after-dinner sleigh ride.

Poncho's Wreck. South Main St., Wilmington; 464–9320. Mexican food, steaks, fresh fish served in casually rustic environment.

The Roadhouse. Rte. 100, Wilmington; 464–5017. A rustic setting with garden-fresh veggies, homemade bread, and wood stove.

Inexpensive

Deacon's Den Tavern. Rte. 100, West Dover; 464–9361. Super sandwiches, free soup after skiing; live bands weekends.

Elsa's. Rte. 100, West Dover; 464–8425. Deli and restaurant with takeout service. No credit cards.

TC's Tavern. Rte. 100, West Dover; 464–9316. Italian specialties and take-out service. No credit cards.

HOW TO GET AROUND. There is **bus** service between the ski area, Snow Lake Lodge, and base-of-mountain condominiums, although all are within walking distance of the lifts and trails.

SEASONAL EVENTS. Mount Snow hosts three special ski weeks: *Teddy Bear Ski* weeks for families, *Romancing the Snow* for couples, and *Snowbreaks* for college students. There are also *Skiing Discovery Vacations* for new skiers, plus, come **spring**, a *Vermont Products Day,* which includes tastings of local produce. There's also *Daylight Skiing Time* and *Easter* celebrations. Call 802–464–8501 for dates and information.

Haystack hosts a *women's pro ski race* each year and NASTAR racing is available weekends and holidays.

OTHER SPORTS AND ACTIVITIES. Cross-country skiing is available in Wilmington at the *Hermitage Inn,* Coldbrook Rd. (464–3511); *White House,* Rte. 9 (464–2135); *Sitzmark Lodge,* East Dover Rd. (464–8187); and in West Dover at *Timber Creek Condominiums,* Rte. 100 (464–2323). Haystack's 50 km of trails interconnect with Mount Snow's at Hermitage Inn.

Horseback riding and **sleigh rides** are found at the *Matterhorn* on Rte. 100, West Dover (464–8011), in a dinner/sleigh package. *Adams Farm* at the junction of Rte. 100 and Higley Hill Rd. in Wilmington (464–3762) also offers hot chocolate and a trip to a log cabin en route. *Flame's Stables,* Rte. 100, Wilmington (464–8329), and the *Red Cricket Inn,* Rte. 100, West Dover (464–8817), both offer sleigh rides to guests.

Snow Lake Lodge (464–3333) right at Mount Snow, has a **fitness center** open to the public. The *Andirons Lodge* on Rte. 100, West Dover (464–2114), offers indoor **swimming,** sauna, and whirlpool.

Other accommodations with **pools** for guests are the *North Branch Club,* Handle Rd. Ext., West Dover (464–3319); *Encore at the Slopes,* Handle Rd., West Dover (464–3391); *Austrian Haus,* Rte. 100, West Dover (464–3911); the *Horizon Inn,* Rte. 9, Wilmington (464–2131); *White House of Wilmington,* Rte. 9, Wilmington (464–2135); *Mt. Snow Resort Center Condominiums* at the mountain (800–451–4211).

There's a **bowling** alley at *North Star Bowl,* Rte. 100, Wilmington (464–5148); and look for guided **snowmobile** tours at *Wheeler Farm,* Rte. 100, Wilmington (464–5225). *Lake Whittingham* near Mount Snow fills the bill when it comes to **ice fishing**—a do-your-own-thing place.

HINTS TO THE HANDICAPPED. Haystack is equipped with special programs for handicapped skiers including the blind, deaf, amputees, single-limb handicapped, and slightly mentally retarded.

CHILDREN'S ACTIVITIES. Mount Snow takes good care of families, who enjoy the resort's *Teddy Bear Ski Week.* Children 12 years old and under bring a teddy bear or other stuffed friend to obtain a free 5-day ticket. They use a special children's lift, join races, and stage a teddy bear parade. The *Children's Learning Center* is a complete learning facility with a rope tow and terrain garden. *Pumpkin Patch Day Care* provides child-care services for infants to children aged 8. For reservations, call 464–8501. *SKIwee,* the nationally recognized children's learn-to-ski program, is also available here.

At Haystack, the *Little Stack Nursery* accepts children ages 2–6 (toilet-trained only) from 9 A.M. to 4 P.M. For information and reservations, contact the base lodge, 464–5321.

NIGHTLIFE. They don't call Mount Snow the Mountain of Pleasure and the Valley of Fun for nothing. Right on the mountain, *Snow Barn* (464–3333), a nightclub, features live band or DJ entertainment nightly on an oak dance floor. The *Snow Lake Spiral Lounge* in the Snow Lake Lodge, also on the mountain (464–3333), has nightly entertainment and a piano bar. *Deacon's Den,* Rte. 100, West Dover (464–9361), features bands every weekend with a cover charge.

Weekend entertainment comes to *Poncho's Wreck*, South Main St., Wilmington (464–9320), and to the *Andirons*, Rte. 100, West Dover (464–2114). Look for music, too, at *Craft's Inn*, Rte. 9, Wilmington (464–3071), and *Sitzmark Lodge*, Rte. 100, Wilmington (464–3384).

On Saturday afternoons, the place to be is in Wilmington at *North Country Fair* on Rte. 100 (464–5697).

CENTRAL VERMONT

KILLINGTON SKI AREA

Killington VT 05751
Tel: 802-773-1330

Snow Report: 802-422-3261
Area Vertical: 3,175 ft.
Number of Trails: 107 on 721 skiable acres
Lifts: 3.5-mile gondola, 5 quad chairs, 4
*   triple chairs, 6 double chairs, 2 surface*
*   lifts*
Snowmaking: 70 percent of terrain
Season: October–early June

Presently, Killington encompasses six mountains and there are always plans afoot to add more. More trails (107), more lifts (18), and more skiable acres (721) await skiers here than at any other ski area in the East. In fact, this is the place where skiing superlatives have come to roost: more snowmaking, longest season, steepest trail (on Bear Mountain with pitches of up to 62 degrees), longest run (the Juggernaut, 10 miles), and the longest alpine ski trail in the United States . . . the list goes on and on.

And it goes without saying that this area packs the skiers in—but with the finesse that goes along with high-speed lifts, interconnected mountains, and a great variety of terrain. For example, you begin your skiing day where you choose—purchasing your ticket at one of a half-dozen ticket outlets spread out over the six-mountain complex.

A long time ago, early in Vermont's history, a Reverend Samuel Peters stood at the top of Killington Peak, 4,241 feet high, and christened what he saw below *Verd Mont,* meaning "green mountains." Today there's a nifty restaurant at the peak, reached by the 3.5-mile gondola, the longest aerial tram in North America, and the Killington chairlift. From the summit (accessible when snows melt), there are 360-degree views of five states and Canada. But even in winter, the vistas are spectacular and can be enjoyed by novice skiers who can get down from the top of any of the six mountains on trails marked "easiest."

Over the years, the Killington management (S.K.I. Ltd., the same people who own Mount Snow) has gone for what the avid alpine enthusiast most desires—dependable snow conditions on diverse skiing terrain. The result is today's 40 miles of snowmaking trails and enough skiing to keep even the hardiest skier challenged by variety for days.

In addition to trying to provide the best possible skiing experience, the ski area has also paid attention to booking ski-vacation packages. It offers one-stop shopping through a lodging bureau and a travel agency, from which you can obtain lift tickets, ski school vouchers, and rental equipment (773-0755).

There's an emerging village at the base of Snowshed, a teaching-learning hill, where condominiums, hotels and restaurants, shops, and health-spa facilities are mushrooming. But the area for years has depended on the entrepreneurial spirit of innkeepers for miles around to provide the bed base for the ever-growing body of Killington skiers.

There's no ski town, per se, in the sense of a Stowe or North Conway. Skiers gravitate to Rutland or Woodstock for movies and other activities.

But they don't have to leave the mountain to find a wealth of excellent lodging and dining establishments that line the Killington Road, from Route 4 to the mountain.

PICO SKI RESORT

Sherburne Pass
Rutland VT 05701
Tel: 802–775–4346

Snow Report: 802–775–4345
Area Vertical: 2,000 ft.
Number of Trails: 40 on 180 skiable acres
Lifts: 2 quad chairs, 2 triple chairs, 3
    double chairs, 1 poma, 1 T-bar
Snowmaking: 82 percent of terrain
Season: November–early May

Pico Ski Resort sits right on Route 4, a big, bold mountain with long, winding trails spanning its 2,000-foot vertical drop and snatches of glade skiing among the trees. This is primarily an intermediate's choice, with 50 percent of the trails marked "more difficult," 30 percent "most difficult," and 20 percent "easiest."

Although it is a mountain that, over the years, has been run by families and for families, it attracts skiers seeking something a little lower-key in terms of resort ambience than its neighbor Killington.

The mountain was first opened for skiing in 1937 by owners Brad and Janet Mead. Brad Mead brought two novelties to American skiing: the first T-bar to be installed in the United States, and the first Swiss ski instructor, Mr. Karl Acker. Acker coached the Meads' daughter, Andrea, who some years later was to win the first-ever U.S. medal in Olympic ski events, in 1948, and to capture another gold medal in 1952. Acker later bought the resort from the Meads.

Pico celebrated its golden anniversary a few years ago by developing a new base-area village complex on Route 4 and adding two quad chairlifts. The area is being operated by neighboring Killington and a full merger is scheduled to happen by the 1991–92 season.

Practical Information for Killington and Pico

HOW TO GET THERE. Killington and Pico are two of the four ski resorts located in central Vermont that are detailed in this guide. The other two are Okemo Mountain Resort and Suicide Six Ski Area. Rutland is the gateway to these areas. Killington and Pico can be considered a single destination, for they are practically next-door neighbors and are under the same management. A Killington 3–7-day lift pass is valid at Pico during midweek, non-holiday periods. Although they don't offer reciprocal ski-lift tickets, they do share the bounty of lodging and dining in the area.

Pico Ski Resort is on US 4, 9 miles east of Rutland, while Killington is at the junction of US 4 and Rte. 100 in Sherburne, 16 miles east of Rutland.

By air. The Burlington International Airport, 85 miles away, is considered the primary gateway airport for this region, since it is served by all major air carriers and most car rental companies. However, the Rutland Airport has facilities for private aircraft. The Lebanon, NH, airport, 39 miles from Killington, is served by *Northwest Airlink* (800–225–2525) and *Delta Connection* (800–221–1212). *Hertz,* 800–654–3131, provides **rental cars** at both airports.

By bus. *Vermont Transit Lines* (802–862–9671), offers direct daily service through Rutland and to Killington from major eastern cities.

By car. Via Connecticut Turnpike: Take I–95, then I–91 to Bellows Falls, VT. Take Exit 6 to Rte. 103 and follow it to Rte. 100, then north to US 4, and on to Pico, then Killington. Via the New York Thruway: Exit 24 at Albany and take Northway (I–87) to the Fort Ann/Whitehall exit. Pick up Rte. 149 and drive east to US 4, which leads to both ski areas.

TELEPHONES. The area code for all Vermont is 802.

ACCOMMODATIONS. Lodges, inns, and hotels in this area serve both Killington and Pico skiers. The *Killington Lodging Bureau,* Killington Ski Area, Killington 05751 (802–773–1330), can make reservations for lodging and meal packages and can also reserve ski-lift and lesson packages for skiing at Killington. The *Killington Travel Service* (802–773–1330), can book 3-, 5-, and 7-night packages and can arrange airline ticketing. *Pico Lodging Bureau,* Pico Ski Resort, Shelburne Pass, Rutland 05701, (802) 775–1927 or toll-free 800–225–7426 when outside Vermont, can also book reservations.

Condominium lodging is popular in this region, with walk-to-the-slopes accommodations at both Killington and Pico. Based on two people for a 3-night stay, the condominiums start at $105 and range up to $270. A new alpine village, *Sunrise Mountain Village,* off Bear Mountain Rd., Killington 05751 (422–9292), offers a self-contained resort at its nearly 200-unit condominium community near Bear Mountain. In addition to luxury 1- to 4-bedroom condos, the resort offers complete health-spa facilities and on-premises dining at Judd Dugan's. Guests here enjoy ski-on/ski-off access to Bear Mountain, one of Killington's 6 peaks.

Killington Village Condominiums on Killington Rd. (422–3101) provides walk-to-the-slopes convenience with a health spa, pool, and dining for guests staying in suites of 1–4 bedrooms.

There are also many chalets and vacation homes, including the *Hawk Mountain Corporation's* extensive listings of luxury dwellings. Their address is Rte. 100 North, Pittsfield 05762; 746–8911.

Since most lodgings in the area operate on package deals, the rates of establishments listed below are based on 3-night stays per person. Categories are *Expensive,* $120–$200; *Moderate,* $80–$120; and *Inexpensive,* less than $80. All those in the expensive range, as well as many others, include MAP, with one or two meals provided. All lodgings listed are within 10 miles of Killington's slopes unless stated otherwise.

Expensive

Cascades Lodge. Killington Rd., Killington 05751; 422–3731. One of the newer properties, right near the base area. Candlelight dining, lounge with fireplace, and king-size TV. Indoor pool, sauna, whirlpool, exercise and game rooms.

Cortina Inn. Rte. 4, Mendon 05751; 773–3331. A vest-pocket resort located about 8 miles from the slopes with a little of everything. Superb dining; fireplaces in some rooms; indoor pool, sauna, whirlpool, exercise and game rooms. Shuttle to ski area, cross-country skiing.

Grey Bonnet Inn. Rte. 100, Killington 05751; 775–2537. Antiques combine with indoor pool, whirlpools, sauna, tanning room, exercise and game rooms; color TV. Cross-country skiing available.

The Inn at Long Trail. Rte. 4, Mendon 05751; 775–7181. Historic country inn with large hot tub, some fireplace suites, Irish pub.

Inn of the Six Mountains. Killington Rd., Killington 05751; 422–4302. New, full-service inn, with 103 rooms, lounge, indoor lap pool, spa and exercise room, courtesy shuttle to slopes, and on-premises dining.

Killington Village Inn. Killington Rd., Killington 05751; 422–3301. With fireplaces, close to slopes, courtesy shuttle; on-premises lounge and dining.

Little Buckhorn Lodge. Killington Rd., Killington 05751; 422–3314. Family-style meals, home cooking, fireside lounge; 22 rooms, fireplace, lounge sauna.

The Mountain Inn. Killington Rd., Killington 05751; 422–3595. A luxury hotel with whirlpool, steam baths, saunas, game room; on-premises dining, lounge. Walk to slopes.

Mountain Top Inn. Chittenden 05737; 483–2311. A 1,000-acre resort with spectacular views, 50 guest rooms, and 15 cottages; horse-drawn sleigh rides, ice skating, sauna, whirlpool spa, exercise/game rooms, cross-country. About 17 miles from the slopes but worth every minute it takes.

Pico Resort Hotel. At the slopes; 747–3000. Has 150 slopeside condominiums ranging from large studios to 2-bedrooms with lofts and fireplaces. Walk to the lifts, near shops, with many amenities, including *Pico Sports Center* membership.

Red Clover Inn. Off Rte. 4, Mendon 05701; 775–2290. Takes up to 38 guests who enjoy French country cuisine, a favorite dining spot of locals; TV/billiard room.

Red Rob Inn. Killington Rd., Killington 05751; 422–3303. Free shuttle to slopes, outdoor whirlpool, library, game room, sociable lounge with great hors d'oeuvres.

Summit Lodge. Killington Rd., Killington 05751; 422–3535. An antique-decorated inn with racquetball, whirlpool, saunas, massage and game rooms, ice skating; 5 fireplaces, on-premises dining.

Tulip Tree Inn. Off Rte. 4, Chittenden 05737; 483–6213. Located 16 miles from Killington, this is a 24-person-capacity charming country inn.

Moderate

Alpenhof. Killington Rd., Killington 05751; 422–9787. Near slopes, rooms with private baths, dorms and chalets with fireplaces; sauna, whirlpool, game room, video movies; 7-item breakfast buffet and homemade soup in front of fire.

Brandon Inn. Rtes. 7 and 73, Brandon 05733; 247–5766. A 1786 inn that offers horse-drawn sleigh rides and ice skating; on-premises dining. To Killington, it is 28 miles.

Chalet Killington. Killington Rd., Killington 05751; 422–3451. Children under 6 free (except holidays) here; sauna, whirlpool, exercise and game room; Continental breakfasts served.

Comfort Inn of Rutland. 19 Allen St., Rutland 05701; 775–2200. Has 114 rooms, 15 miles from the mountains; indoor pool, sauna, Jacuzzi.

Greenbriar Inn. Rte. 4, Killington 05751; 775–1575. Mountain views, Jacuzzi, sauna, fireplace lounge; each room has private bath, color TV, refrigerator, phone; Continental breakfasts served.

Holiday Inn Centre of Vermont. S. Main St., Rutland 05701; 775–1911. Kids under 20 free in parents' room; indoor pool, health complex; free in-room coffee; on-premises dining. Located 16 miles from the slopes.

Mountain Meadows Lodge. Rte. 4 East, Killington 05751; 775–1010. Large comfortable rooms (for up to 6) with private baths; BYOB lounge, game room, sitting room with color TV; complete ski touring center.

Mountainview Resort. Rte. 4, Sherburne; 773–4311. MAP available in this motor lodge where children under 12 stay free. Suites available.

Rutland TraveLodge. S. Main St., Rutland 05701; 773–3361. Located 15 miles from Killington, there are 75 rooms with luxury apartments and executive suites. Indoor pool, saunas, complimentary coffee in rooms, color TV (cable); on-premises dining.

Inexpensive

Edelweiss Motel and Chalets. Rte. 4 West, Killington 05751; 775–5577. Spacious rooms with color TV, coffee in room, game rooms, exercise area, fireplace lounge, hot tub, sauna; some kitchenettes and some chalets with fireplaces.

Grande Finale. Rte. 4 West, Mendon 05751; 773–2155. An 1853 farmhouse, 11 miles from the slopes, welcomes children under 12 free; rooms with private bath, color TV.

Swiss Farm Lodge. Rte. 100, Pittsfield 05762; 746–8341. A dairy farm that opens its doors to guests, uses own maple syrup and honey. Twelve miles to Killington.

Turn of River Lodge. Rte. 4 East, Killington 05751; 422–3766. A rustic lodge with huge stone fireplace in lounge, set-up bar; rooms with private and shared baths; some dorms; family-style Continental breakfast.

RESTAURANTS. Visitors to this region don't *have* to take all their meals at their lodging places—although most inns and lodges offer fine and substantial fare. If you choose to dine out, there is a wide selection of restaurants, serving not only New England dishes but Continental and ethnic specialties as well. Furthermore, you'll find that the price is right throughout the region. Listings here are based on the following price ranges for a full meal for one person, excluding tips and drinks: *Expensive,* $20–$25; *Moderate,* $12–$20; *Inexpensive,* under $12. Major credit cards are accepted, unless otherwise noted.

Expensive

Annabelles' Restaurant. Jct. Rte. 100 and Rte. 107, Stockbridge; 746–8552. A converted farmhouse offers à la carte and fixed-price menu in greenhouse or just-like-home setting. Reservations suggested.

Cortina Inn. Rte. 4, Mendon; 773–3331. The breakfast buffets here are not to be missed, and dinners range from Continental cuisine to New England specialties. Reservations appreciated.

Hemingway's Restaurant. Rte. 4, Killington; 422–3886. Originally a country home, now an intimate Continental restaurant. Choose from a tasting menu (a great bargain) or order à la carte. Excellent wine menu. Reservations a must, especially on Saturday nights.

The Vermont Inn. Rte. 4, Killington; 775–0708 or 800–541–7795. Enjoy New England and Continental cuisine served fireside in the warm, inviting dining room of this late 1800s farmhouse. Reasonable and varied wine list. The baked stuffed chicken is particularly yummy. Reservations essential. The inn has 14 rooms.

Moderate

Back Behind Saloon Restaurant. Rte. 4, West Bridgewater; 422–9907. A converted railroad car is the setting for casual dining; homemade cole slaw is part of the experience; varied menu.

Casa Bianca Restaurant. Grove St., Rutland; 773–7401. Italian specialties include homemade pastas, veal parmigiana. This is the in place for locals seeking Italian fare.

Countryman's Pleasure Restaurant. Townline Rd., Mendon; 773–7141. It's a country farmhouse offering Austrian specialties such as raspberry—Black Forest tortes and glazed wiener apple strudel. Children's menu.

Ernie's Hearthside Restaurant. 37 N. Main St., Rutland; 775–0856. One of Vermont's best-known restaurateurs, Ernie Royal, presides over the kitchen here, with prime ribs and superb service among the specialties.

Hawks River Tavern. Rte. 100, Plymouth; 672–3811. A tiny restaurant offering creative cuisine.

Red Clover Inn. Off Rte. 4, Mendon; 775–2290. A country inn that's becoming a favorite of the locals. Look for homemade breads, soups, and desserts; veal and seafood specialties.

Sirloin Saloon. Main St., Rutland; 773–7900. Extensive salad bars, children's menu, oyster bar, and seafood/steak specialties.

Inexpensive

Casey's Caboose. Killington Rd., Killington; 422–3795. A large menu served in turn-of-the-century railroad cars. There's literally something for everyone here.

Charity's 1887 Saloon Restaurant. Killington Rd., Killington; 422–3800. Practically everyone turns up here some time for French onion soup, steaks, seafood, quiche, sandwiches.

Pasta Pot. Rte. 4, Killington; 422–3004. Northern- and southern-style pasta dishes, plus vegetarian treatments.

Powderhound Restaurant and Bar. Killington Rd., Killington; 422–4141. Soups, sandwiches, pasta, and the best pizza in Killington (it is also sold in the Killington Base Lodge). Take out or eat in.

Zorba's Tavern. Killington Rd., Killington; 422–3600. Homemade pizza, pasta, subs, spaghetti, and salads; plus pool table, TV, arcade, and jukebox.

HOW TO GET AROUND. Some area lodges provide a **free shuttle** service to and from the slopes. The *Mountain Bus* (422–9713) provides daily (8:30–10:30 A.M. and 3–5 P.M.) service on the mountain road, picking up skiers from lodges and shops and taking them to and from the mountain. This same service operates evenings from 4:30 P.M. to 2:30 A.M.

SEASONAL EVENTS. Killington: The *Bear Mountain Mogul Challenge* attracts upwards of 200 thrill-seekers in early **April** as they set their target on the

62-degree pitches that characterize the steepest terrain in New England. Two other events, a **May Day** Fun Slalom and a **June 1** Fun Slalom, are annual happenings that go a long way to publicize the resort's long-lived ski season.

Pico: The *Harry Chapin Memorial Slalom,* held the last week in **December,** remembers the contribution to Rutland and the Pico Ski Club that the singer made prior to his untimely death. This is an amateur race for young skiers. The *Pico Sunburst Festival* in **March** caps off the winter season.

OTHER SPORTS AND ACTIVITIES. The following establishments have **health-club facilities** open to the public:

Brookside Tennis & Racquetball, 40 Curtis Ave., Rutland; 775–1971. Tennis, racquetball, Nautilus and Jacuzzi, saunas, health bar.

Cortina Health Club, Rte. 4, Mendon; 773–3331. Indoor pool, saunas, game room, masseur, exercise room.

Killington Health Club, Killington Rd., Killington; 422–9370. Lap pool, whirlpools, sauna, steam bath, tanning rooms, racquetball, exercise rooms.

Pico Sports Center, Pico Ski Resort, Sherburne; 773–1786. New facility in Pico Village with 4-lane, 75-foot lap pool; strength and toning center, spa amenities, lounge, nursery, sports shop, and racquet sports to come.

The Spa, 132 Granger St., Rutland; 775–6565. Nautilus, and free weight equipment; sauna, Jacuzzi, and tanning beds.

Summit Lodge, Killington Rd., Killington; 422–3535. 16-person Jacuzzi, whirlpool, 2 saunas, racquetball.

Woodstock Sports Center, Rte. 106S, Woodstock; 457–1160. Indoor pool, whirlpool, Nautilus, racquetball, indoor tennis.

There's **ice skating** at the Summit Lodge and at Hawk Center, Jct. Rtes. 100 and 107; 746–8911.

Ski touring is popular in the region, with the *Killington Gondola* providing access to the 10-mile long Juggernaut Trail. There's also ski touring at *Mountain Meadows Ski Touring Center,* Rte. 4, Killington, 775–7077; *Mountain Top Ski Touring Center,* Mountain Top Rd., Chittenden, 483–2311 (110 km of trails); *Trail Head Ski Touring Center,* Rte. 100, Stockbridge, 746–8038; and *Woodstock Ski Touring Center,* Rte. 106, Woodstock, 457–2114.

Sleigh rides are offered at the Mountain Top Inn and at *Hawk Resort's Salt Ash Colony* on Rte. 100, Plymouth; 672–3811.

HINTS TO THE HANDICAPPED. Both ski resorts offer specialty programs to organizations for the handicapped and can accommodate the handicapped individually through their ski schools. Contact the respective ski resort for detailed information on programs available.

DAY-CARE FACILITIES. Killington. *The Children's Center* (422–3333) provides day-long child and infant care for ages infant–8 years. The charge is $28 for ages 2–8 and $40 for infants. Lunch is included.

Through the center children aged 4–8 can enjoy an *Introduction to Skiing* program that involves a 1-hour lesson, rental equipment, use of beginners' tow, and games. Ages 6–12 are eligible for regular lift and lesson programs that involve a 2-hour class, or they can join the *Superstars All-Day Skiing Program* that includes lessons, lunch, and videotaping, all for $55.

Pico. The *Pico Nursery* accepts 6 months to age 6 from 9 A.M. to 4 P.M. daily. There's optional ski-school instruction. For ages 6–12, the Mountaineering Program offers 4 hours of instruction, lift ticket, and lunch for $39. As participants in Pico's *Mt. Explorer's Club,* ages 3–6 receive special badges.

NIGHTLIFE. Several **on-mountain** (Killington Rd.) hot spots, the *Pickle Barrel,* (442–3035), the *Wobbly Barn Steakhouse* (422–3392), and *The Nightspot* (422–9885), offer nightly live band entertainment and dancing, all with cover charges. *Casey's Caboose* (422–3795) has an après-ski happy hour with the hottest chicken wings in the East!

In Rutland, *The Ritz* at 21 Center St. (775–3365) is the area's first video dance club; cover charge here, too.

Many establishments offer vocal and instrumental soloists as part of the après-ski and dinner ambience. And the *Mountain Inn* on Killington Rd. (422–3595) features honky-tonk piano entertainment. It's probably safe to say that the entertainment overall matches the diversity of ski terrain in the central Vermont region.

OKEMO MOUNTAIN RESORT

RFD #1
Ludlow VT 05149
Tel: 802-228-4041

Snow Report: 802-228-5222
Area Vertical: 2,150 ft.
Number of Trails: 71 on 400 skiable acres
Lifts: 4 quad chairs, 3 triple chairs, 1
*   double chair, 2 pomas*
Snowmaking: 90 percent of terrain
Season: mid-November–mid-April

For years, Okemo Mountain Resort has tantalized the nearby town of Ludlow, at the bottom of its access road, by the possibility that it, too, might someday become the kind of sought-after resort that puts smiles on merchants' faces as it fills their coffers.

Those heady days have arrived and skiers are now convinced that once-sleepy Okemo has gone big-time, mostly due to the efforts of Tim and Diane Mueller, a young couple experienced in developing and managing warm-weather resorts in the Caribbean. An infusion of capital, engineering, and good taste has brought Okemo to life in just a couple of years, allowing Ludlow and the surrounding Black River Valley to serve winter tourists and to weather its transition from a once-thriving textile mill town to tourist center.

Okemo has installed some of the best new lifts in the region as well as a "state-of-the-art" snowmaking system. A road from the summit turns ski trail come winter, offering beginners 4½ miles of gentle terrain. There are two steep gladed areas for more advanced skiers, and some tough terrain such as Double Diamond and Outrage.

Quality is stressed here. Diane Mueller has a personal interest in creating attractive signage and has concentrated on first-rate interior decoration of the condominiums.

A 50-foot clock tower and white stucco archway mark the entrance to the base lodge facilities, around which are clustered a 76-room hotel. A bellman will help with luggage and ski equipment, escort guests to their condominiums, and light the fire in the fireplace.

Practical Information for Okemo Mountain

HOW TO GET THERE. Okemo is located in Ludlow. (See *Practical Information for Killington and Pico, above, for regional details.*)

By car. From points south, take I-91 to Vermont Exit 6 and Rte. 103 west 25 miles to Ludlow. From points east, take I-89 to New Hampshire Exit 9 and NH Rte. 103 through Claremont to Rte. 131 to Rte. 103 west 2 miles to Ludlow. From points west, take Rte. 4 to Rte. 7 to Rte. 103 east, 16 miles to Ludlow.

By bus. *Vermont Transit* (802) 862-9671 provides regular daily bus service to Ludlow.

TELEPHONES. The area code for all Vermont is 802.

ACCOMMODATIONS. *Okemo's Lodging Service,* RFD 1, Ludlow 05149 (228-5571) can arrange accommodations at the 76-room Okemo Mountain Lodge (a complex of 1-bedroom condominiums) in the base area, the slopeside Kettlebrook and Winterplace condominiums (2 and 3 bedrooms), or at any of the more than 48 establishments offering over 5,000 beds within a 15-mile radius of the mountain. Rates are based on double occupancy per person, per night. Categories, determined by price, are *Expensive,* $100 and up; *Moderate,* $60–$100; *Inexpensive,* under $60. All lodgings listed are within 5 miles of the mountain unless stated otherwise.

Expensive

Black River Inn. 100 Main St., Ludlow 05149; 228–5585. A stately brick home catering primarily to couples is enjoying the new life generated in town by the ski resort. MAP available.

Castle Inn. Box 157, Proctorsville 05153; 226–7222. Quarrystone construction marks this turn-of-the-century inn complete with oak paneling, hand-carved plaster ceilings, and old-time elegance. MAP available.

Combes Family Inn. R.F.D. 1, Ludlow 05149; 228–8799. Ten rooms in total, divided between motel units (with 2 double beds, no phones or TVs), and rooms in inn with hall baths. Package plans available.

Echo Lake Inn. Box 154, Ludlow 05149; 228–8602 or 800–356–6844. A rambling turn-of-the-century structure offers country elegance. Tavern, game room, steam bath. MAP available.

The Governor's Inn. 86 Main St., Ludlow 05149; 228–8830. This 100-year-old house was once home to a former Vermont governor. Today it offers creative gourmet fare and a notable afternoon teatime. With MAP.

Kettlebrook Condominiums. R.F.D. 1, Ludlow 05149 (on Okemo Mountain); 228–5571. Sixty-six slopeside homes in New England contemporary design, 1–3 bedrooms, with fireplaces; convenient to skiing. Children 12 and under stay free.

The Mill Hotel. 145 N. Main St., Ludlow 05149; 228–5566. A restored 19th-century mill now houses 1–3 bedroom condo-hotel units with kitchens and fireplaces.

Okemo Inn. R.F.D. 1, Box 133, Ludlow, 05149; 228–8834. An 1810 structure at the base of the mountain, filled with American antiques, the inn has 11 guest rooms and a sauna.

Okemo Mountain Lodge Condominiums. R.F.D. 1, Ludlow 05149 (Okemo Mountain); 228–5571. Seventy-six one-bedroom efficiency units clustered courtyard style around main ski lodge. No charge for children 12 and under. Walk to lifts.

Okemo Lantern Lodge. Box 247, Proctorsville 05153; 226–7770. Victorian gingerbread is still alive and well in this antique-filled dwelling that offers MAP.

Moderate

Golden Stage Inn. Box 218, Proctorsville 05143; 226–7744. Built in 1795. Country quilts and plants decorate this 10-room inn (6 with private baths). MAP available.

Jewell Brooke Inn. Rte. 100 South, Ludlow 05149; 228–8926. A 10-room inn near a pond, private and shared baths. Breakfast served.

Old Town Farm Inn. R.F.D. 4, Chester 05143; 875–2346. Breakfast served in a colonial farmhouse offering 10 guest rooms (3 with private baths). About 15 miles from the slopes.

The Timber Inn Motel. Rte. R.R.1, Box 1003, Ludlow 05149; 228–8666. Modern and cozy. You'll find a sauna, Jacuzzi, color TV, and a restaurant.

The Winchester Inn. 53 Main St., Ludlow 05149; 228–3841. An 1813 colonial inn with dining room and lounge.

Inexpensive

There's a host of motels in the inexpensive range. These are the *Abby-Lyn Motel,* Junction Rtes. 106/10, North Springfield 05150, 886–2223; *Inn Towne Motel,* 112 Main St., Ludlow 05149, 228–8884, and *Best Western Ludlow Colonial Motel,* 43 Main St., Ludlow 05149, 228–8188.

RESTAURANTS. Dining out in the Okemo Mountain area presents the visitor with choices similar to other ski areas in central Vermont. Restaurants nearest the resort may be a bit pricier, but all in all, the average remains about the same. So does the fare. Categories, determined by price, are based on a full meal for one person, exclusive of tax, tips, and beverages: *Expensive,* $15 and up; *Moderate,* $9–$15; *Inexpensive,* less than $9. Most places accept American Express, MasterCard, and Visa unless otherwise noted.

Expensive

The Castle Inn. Rte. 103, Proctorsville; 226–7222. The mahogany Oval Dining Room is the setting for such entrees as roast duckling grand marnier in this architectural landmark.

The Governor's Inn. 86 Main St., Ludlow; 228–8830. Chef Deedy Marble was named 1 of 4 "outstanding innovative chefs in Vermont." Dinners begin at 6 with hors d'oeuvres in the parlor, followed by a single 7 P.M. seating in a Victorian dining room with waitresses in period dress. Braised quail and sherried apricot soup may be on the menu. Reservations are requested.

Michael's Seafood and Steak Restaurant. Rte. 103, Ludlow; 228–5622. Beef and seafood preparations are served here along with a well-stocked salad bar.

Nikki's Restaurant. Foot of Okemo Mountain access road, Ludlow; 228–7797. Offers regional fare ranging from New England pork fillet to grilled Atlantic swordfish; eclectic interior.

Moderate

Black River Inn. 100 Main St., Ludlow; 228–5585. A 5-course menu-du-jour begins at 7 P.M. in this 1835 country inn. Seating by reservation only.

Echo Lake Inn. Box 154, Ludlow; 228–8602. Fresh herbs and spices from a summer garden garnish home-cooked winter meals.

Okemo Lantern Lodge. Box 247, Proctorsville; 226–7770. Call by 4 P.M. for a reservation and look forward to New England and Continental cuisine.

Priority's Restaurant. Inn at Clock Tower, base area; 228–2800. Serves salads, steaks, chicken, seafood, and pasta. Children's menu. Live entertainment plus Sports Bar.

Winchester Inn. 53 Main St., Ludlow; 228–3841. A 14-item menu includes seafood, steaks, lamb, and veal.

Inexpensive

Chuckles. Rte. 103, Ludlow (near Okemo access road); 228–5530. Lobsters and prime ribs served in relaxed setting.

Harry's Cafe. Rte. 103, Mt. Holly; 259–2826. Look for clambakes on Wednesdays, with stir fry and Mexican fare also on menu.

Okemo Inn. R.F.D. 1, Ludlow; 228–8834. Family-style meals with traditional baked breads and homemade soups. Make reservations a day in advance.

HOW TO GET AROUND. You'll need a **car** to get to the resort; however, once at Okemo, everything is within walking distance of the slopes and trails. The resort provides **shuttle** service from the lower parking lots to the base lodge.

SEASONAL EVENTS. *Okemo Ski and Swing Spring Spree,* a celebration of the arrival of the first day of spring, is composed of races and mogul contests. There's a '50s beach party at night. NASTAR races are held at noon daily (except Monday).

OTHER SPORTS AND ACTIVITIES. There's **ice fishing** on nearby Echo Lake. The Plymouth Village Ski Touring Center in Plymouth and Fox Run Ski Touring Center in Ludlow both offer **cross-country** terrain.

CHILDREN'S ACTIVITIES. Okemo's state-approved *Day-Care Center* (228–4041) is open for children aged 12 months–8 years. Ages 3 and 4 can get an *Introduction to Skiing* through a special program that costs $10 a day. The center is open from 8:30 A.M. to 4:30 P.M., free (including lunch!) Monday through Friday and non-holiday periods. On weekends and holidays, the cost is $30 (with lunch) for a full day, $15 (with snack) for a half day. *SKIwee,* the nationally recognized program to help children learn to ski, is offered here. And Okemo has created a children's race course called Hot Dog Hill that involves following an instructor over moguls, around turns, and through tunnels, with colorful cartoon characters greeting young skiers along the way.

NIGHTLIFE. Through the influence of the ski resort, the town of Ludlow is just beginning to come alive at night, with at least three establishments offering entertainment, usually live bands, on weekends. These are *Priority's Restaurant,* Inn at Clock Tower at the base area, 228–2800; *Michael's Seafood and Steak Restaurant,* Rte. 103, Ludlow, 228–5622; *Pot Belly Pub,* Main St., Ludlow, 228–8989; and *Dadd's,* on the mountain road (228–9820).

SUICIDE SIX SKI AREA

Woodstock VT 05091
Tel: 802–457–1666

Snow Report: 802–457–1622
Area Vertical: 650 ft.
Number of Trails: 19 on 100 skiable acres
Lifts: 2 double chairs, 1 J-bar
Snowmaking: 50 percent of terrain
Season: mid-December–March

A jump away from the Village of Woodstock, with its Paul Revere church bells and covered-bridge New England atmosphere, is Suicide Six, known in an earlier day (and on current topographical maps) simply as "Hill 6." It was here in 1937 that Bunny Bertram opened what is America's oldest continually operating ski tow. The area, which was then little more than a heart-stopping, steep, open slope, was sold in 1961 to Rockresorts. Today it provides family-oriented skiing on 19 trails.

Trails range from the scenic beginners' run, "Easy Mile," to the sheer drop of "The Face," training ground for generations of Olympic and national trainees from nearby Dartmouth College.

Perhaps the main reason to come to this area, however, is that it's a wonderful excuse to spend time in Woodstock, either at the elegant Woodstock Inn, enjoying tea, perhaps, or wandering down the colonial-homelined streets. For connoisseurs of pretty towns, this one rates high on most lists. It's charming without being quaint, sophisticated (and pricey) without being trendy.

Practical Information for Suicide Six

HOW TO GET THERE. Suicide Six Ski Area is 3 miles north of Woodstock. (See *Practical Information for Killington and Pico,* above, for regional details.)

By car. Take I–91 into Vermont to Exit 9, then US 5 north to Rte. 12, which leads into Woodstock.

By bus. Woodstock is served daily by *Vermont Transit,* 802–862–9671.

By train. *Amtrak* (802–295–7160) runs to White River Junction, 15 minutes away.

By air. *Delta Connection* (800–221–1212) and *Northwest Airlink* (800–225–2525) service the West Lebanon, NH, airport, 20 minutes from Woodstock.

TELEPHONES. The area code for all Vermont is 802.

ACCOMMODATIONS. The region offers a wide assortment of lodging establishments, ranging from motels to bed-and-breakfasts, guest houses, and cabins. The best source of local lodging information (and to book accommodations) is the *Woodstock Chamber of Commerce,* 18 Central St., Woodstock, VT 05091 (457–3555). There are also a number of bed-and-breakfast treasures scattered throughout the region. Reservation services for these places are handled through *Vermont Bed and Breakfasts,* Box 1, East Fairfield VT 05448 (827–3827).

Rates for hotels and inns listed here are based on double occupancy, with many places including breakfast and some having MAP. Categories determined by price are *Expensive,* $80 and up; *Moderate,* $60–$80, and *Inexpensive,* less than $60. All lodgings in this listing are roughly within 10 miles of the slopes unless stated otherwise. Guests staying in Woodstock can also conveniently ski Killington and Okemo.

Expensive

Carriage House of Woodstock. Rte. 4 West, Woodstock 05091; 457–4322. An informal, friendly, country inn with comfortable rooms. Welcomes children and serves Continental breakfasts.

Charleston House. 21 Pleasant St., Woodstock 05091; 457–3843. A brick Greek revival townhouse listed with the National Registry of Historic Places. Has 7 rooms with private baths and old-fashioned, comfortable beds. Large sumptuous breakfasts (look for family Christmas china during the holidays) or Continental breakfast served in bed.

Clay Gates Farm. North Bridgewater Rd., Bridgewater 04034; 672–5294. An 1830 estate on 200 acres with views of the Ottauquechee Valley. Four rooms with private baths are available on this working farm with Morgan horses. No children permitted; serves large country breakfasts.

The Jackson House. Rte. 4, Woodstock 05091; 457–2065. An 1890 Victorian landmark with 11 antique-furnished rooms, 9 private baths; fireside parlor, library. Breakfasts served.

Kedron Valley Inn. Rte. 106, South Woodstock 05071; 457–1473. Rooms (6 with working fireplaces) dispersed among 1828 inn, 1822 tavern, or log cabin lodge. Skating on pond; on-premises dining with classical French cuisine that emphasizes local Vermont products.

Quechee Bed and Breakfast. Rte. 4, Quechee 05059; 295–1776. A 1795 former coach stop overlooking the Ottauquechee River. Has 6 antique-filled rooms with private baths. Easy walk to Quechee Village and the scenic gorge.

The Quechee Inn at Marshland Farm. Club House Rd., Quechee 05059; 295–3133. A 1793 Vermont farmstead with 24 guest rooms, private baths; breakfasts served, dinners by reservation.

Woodstock Inn and Resort. US 4, on the Village Green, Woodstock 05091; 457–1100. Luxurious colonial-style inn, handsome quilts on beds. Fine dining by candlelight; night-time sleigh rides; coffee shop and lounge. Indoor sports center.

Moderate

The Corners Inn. Rte. 4, Bridgewater Corners 05035; 672–9968. Early American decor in this 6-room inn.

Echo Lake Inn. Rte. 100, Tyson 05149; 228–8602. An authentic colonial inn has welcomed travelers for 175 years; 25 modern rooms.

1830 Shiretown Inn. 31 South St., Woodstock 05091; 457–1830. Has 3 comfortable rooms with private baths; hearty country breakfasts.

The Inn at Weathersfield. Rte. 106S, Weathersfield 05151; 263–9217. A 1795 stagecoach stop with 10 rooms; serves afternoon tea. Located 21 miles from Woodstock.

Lincoln Covered Bridge Inn. Rte. 4, West Woodstock 05091; 457–3312. A country inn with 6 guest rooms, private baths, choice of queen, king, or twin beds; breakfasts served.

October Country Inn. Eight miles west of Woodstock, Bridgewater Corners 05035; 672–3412. A 10-room rambling farmhouse with home cooking.

Thomas Hill Farm B&B. Thomas Hill, Woodstock 05091; 457–1067. Three rooms with private and shared baths.

Three Church Street. 3 Church St., Woodstock 05091; 457–1925. Ten rooms with private and shared baths in an 1800 house in the heart of the village. On the National Historic Register.

The Village Inn at Woodstock. US 4, Woodstock 05091; 457–1255. A Victorian mansion with 9 guest rooms, oak wainscoting, tin ceilings; dining room.

Woodstock B&B. River St., Woodstock 05091; 457–3896. Nine rooms, private baths and suites, large whirlpool, laundry, walk to village.

Inexpensive

Abbott House. 43 Pleasant St., Woodstock; 05091; 457–3077. Five rooms in 100-year-old village home full of antiques.

Liberty Hill Farm. Rte. 100, Rochester 05767; 767–3926. A working dairy farm with cross-country trails at the door, 5 guest rooms, shared bath; farmstyle breakfasts and dinners.

Shire Motel. Pleasant St., Woodstock 05091; 457–2211. Has 18 comfortably appointed rooms.

RESTAURANTS. Since the region is hardly a self-contained resort, visitors here have a choice of places to dine out, either in country elegance, family-style, or old world settings. Offerings are just as varied—Vermont turkey and other regional fare to Continental cuisine and ethnic specialties. The price classifications of the following restaurants are based on the cost of an average three-course dinner for one person for food alone; beverages, tax, and tip would be extra. *Expensive:* $20 and up; *Moderate,* $10–$20. Most places accept major credit cards, but it would be wise to call ahead first.

Expensive

Barnard Inn. Rte. 12, Barnard; 234–9961. An inn offering Continental cuisine under the direction of a Swiss chef; jackets required for men.

The Prince & the Pauper. Woodstock Village; 457–1818. The evening starts in the lounge and moves to a candlelight dinner that has a Continental touch. Reservations essential. Award winner in state culinary competition.

The Quechee Inn at Marshland Farm. Club House Rd., Quechee; 295–3133. Country elegance overlooking Ottauquechee River; entrees varied but always come with freshly baked rolls and desserts. Jackets and reservations requested.

Woodstock Inn. Rte. 4, Woodstock; 457–1100. A formal but not stuffy atmosphere where chefs regularly win "Taste of Vermont" awards for culinary excellence. Three specials nightly in addition to extensive menu.

Moderate

Bentleys Restaurant. Elm St., Woodstock; 457–3232. Plants, antique wood, and an interesting menu mark this establishment.

Corners Inn. Bridgewater; 672–9968. Pastas, seafood, steak, and veal. Casual, fireside atmosphere. Gold-medal winner in state culinary competition.

Enes' Table at Valley View Motel. Rte. 12, Woodstock; 457–2512. Family restaurant specializing in Italian food; reservations appreciated.

Lincoln Covered Bridge Inn. Rte. 4, Woodstock; 457–3312. Northern Italian specialties are favored here, and after-dinner coffees are a must. Reservations requested.

Rumble Seat Rathskeller. Woodstock East; 457–3609. Located in the cellar of the 1834 Stone House; offers European-style dining.

The Village Inn of Woodstock. 41 Pleasant St., Woodstock; 457–1255. Roast fresh Vermont turkey and homemade desserts are only the beginning here; also enjoy natural oak woodwork, tin ceilings, and stained-glass windows. Reservations requested.

HOW TO GET AROUND. Because Suicide Six is not a self-contained ski resort, it is best to have a **car**—particularly if you would like to explore some of the Vermont countryside. Some accommodations, however, have **shuttle** service to the ski area. Check when making reservations, for driving mountain roads during ski season can be hazardous.

SEASONAL EVENTS. The *Woodstock Inn & Resort* offers a wassail celebration in early **December** that includes a lavish medieval feast, King Arthur style, and a torchlight parade plus lighting of a yule log and Christmas tree.

OTHER SPORTS AND ACTIVITIES. *The Woodstock Ski Touring Center,* Rte. 106, Woodstock, 457–2114, is headquartered at the Woodstock Country Club and its **cross-country** trails cover 75 km of terrain in the Green Mountains. **Sleigh rides**

are available through the *Woodstock Inn and Resort,* on the Green, Woodstock, 457–1100. Sleigh rides are also at *White Birch Farm,* off Stage Rd., Barnard, 457–2768; *Quechee Inn,* Club House Rd., Quechee, 295–3133; *Kedron Valley Stables,* Rte. 106, South Woodstock, 457–1480; and *Salt Ash Stables,* Rte. 100, Plymouth, 672–3811.

The Woodstock Inn and Resort's new Sports Center is located 1 mile south of Rte. 4 on Rte. 106 in Woodstock, 457–1160. Facilities include indoor tennis, squash, racquetball, whirlpool, lap pool, steam, sauna, massage, exercise and aerobics room, complete restaurant and bar.

DAY-CARE FACILITIES. There are no facilities for child care at the area. For information on baby-sitters in the region, call *Otts Tots,* 114 Main St., Quechee, 295–1610; or the *Unitarian-Universalist Church Nursery School,* Rte. 4, Woodstock, 457–2557. The Woodstock Inn provides names of baby-sitters for guests only.

NIGHTLIFE. About four times a year, there's dancing at the Woodstock Inn on the Green in Woodstock, but the rest of the time look for disco action at *Bentleys Restaurant,* Elm St., Woodstock, 457–3232.

NORTHERN VERMONT

Six of the northern Vermont ski resorts of Bolton Valley, Jay Peak, Mad River Glen, Smugglers' Notch, Sugarbush, and Stowe joined together with hotels and motels of Burlington to form "Ski the Classics—Jet to Burlington." Their goal is to further promote northern Vermont as a destination vacation region easily reached through the Burlington International Airport. They have worked with airlines to provide inexpensive air fares and plan to have an interchangeable lift ticket available for the 1988–89 season. Contact any one of the participating resorts or the *Lake Champlain Regional Chamber of Commerce*, Box 453, Burlington, VT 05402, (802) 863–3489, for more information.

BOLTON VALLEY RESORT

Bolton Valley VT 05477
Tel: 802–434–2131 or 800–451–3220 in eastern U.S.

Snow Report: 802–434–2131
Area Vertical: 1,600 ft.
Number of Trails: 43 on 120 skiable acres
Lifts: 1 quad chair, 4 double chairs, 1 Mitey Mite
Snowmaking: 40 percent of terrain
Season: November–mid-April

The newest of Vermont's major ski resorts may also be the state's oldest ski area. A world traveler and colorful character named Edward Bryant came through Vermont after World War I. He began carving ski trails 2,600 feet up on Bolton Mountain. Strapped into 7-foot skis with a Sou'wester on his head, he christened his work the Heavenly Highway and Bolton Mountain trails and invited his friends to come skiing. He also built a rustic cabin called Bryant Lodge. This was in the late 1920s. Along came the Great Depression and then World War II. He tried but failed to get financial backing to put in a rope tow and base lodge, and he died in 1951.

For years after, the only activity on Bolton Mountain was lumbering. In 1964 a University of Vermont graduate, Ralph Des Lauriers, started re-creating Bryant's dream.

Today, 43 trails are concentrated on Ricker Mountain and Timberline, adjacent to Bolton, and the trails that Bryant cut are part of the resort's extensive cross-country network.

Bryant would be amazed to see the self-contained resort village that has developed in 20 years, only minutes from downtown Burlington, the largest city in Vermont.

The resort takes its name from the nearby town of Bolton, chartered by King George III in 1763. Settlers then paid an annual tax of one ear of Indian corn and looked after the towering white and other pine trees suited to mast making. A century later, in 1847, Irish immigrants by the hundreds staged a demonstration called the Bolton Revolt. They wanted their pay for work they had done on the Central Vermont Railroad, called the Iron Ligament, that snaked through the nearby Winooski Valley.

The first hostelry in town was the James Moore Tavern, an establishment commemorated by one of the same name at the resort. And local lore has been kept alive by the likes of the Bolton Outlaw, a trail named in honor of early poachers in the area, and the Beech Seal Trail, derived from punishment inflicted on trespassers by a beechwood wand wielded by Vermont's early lawmakers, the Green Mountain Boys. Another trail, Peggy Dow's Hymn Book, has a long story all its own, and Bear Run recalls Bolton's first inhabitants.

If you've guessed the mood is folksy here, you're right. Likely as not, Des Lauriers is found mingling in the dining room with guests, ready to tell stories of the day's skiing. Couples and families appreciate this mid-sized resort as much for what there isn't as for what there is—crowds non-existent, staff friendly but not stodgy.

Practical Information for Bolton Valley

HOW TO GET THERE. Bolton Valley is one of 7 ski resorts located in northern Vermont that are detailed in this guide. The others are Burke Mountain, Jay Peak, Mad River Glen, Stowe, Sugarbush, and Smugglers' Notch. Burlington is the gateway to these resorts and Bolton is closest.

By air. The Burlington International Airport, (802) 863–2874, is served by *CommutAir, Continental, Delta Connection, Northwest Airlink, TWA Express, United,* and *USAir.* The airport's Ground Transportation desk, (802) 863–1889, can give details on shuttle service to the various ski areas. Bolton Valley provides its own shuttle service to its guests, (802) 434–2131. Car rental agencies located at the airport are *Avis* (864–0411 or 800–331–1213), *Budget* (658–1211 or 800–527–0700), *Hertz* (864–7409 or 800–654–3131), and *National* (864–7441 or 800–328–4567).

By bus. *Vermont Transit* (802) 862–9671 serves Burlington and most adjacent towns.

By car. From Albany, NY, take I–87 north to Exit 19 onto Rte. 109; travel east to Fort Anne, NY, onto Rte. 4 to Whitehall; then take Rte. 22 north to Vergennes and onto Rte. 7 into Burlington. To drive to Bolton from the north, take Exit 11 off I–89. From the south, take Exit 10 off I–89; follow Rte. 2 to the Bolton Valley access road, then drive 4 miles to the resort.

TELEPHONES. The area code for all Vermont is 802.

ACCOMMODATIONS. There are more than 1,250 beds in two lodges, an inn, and condominiums within walking distance of the lifts and trails. Rates at these establishments are based on double occupancy. Categories, determined by price, are *Moderate,* ranging from $75 to $125 per night.

Black Bear Inn. Bolton Valley; 434–2126 or 800–395–6335. A 24-room slopeside country inn appointed with handmade quilts and wall hangings. Children under 6, free.

The Lodge at Bolton Valley. At the slopes; 434–2131. This 146-room hotel is located steps from the tennis courts and alpine ski trails in the middle of the beautifully landscaped resort village center. Kitchenettes, fireplaces, balconies, and mountain views in many units. Children under 6 stay free.

Trailside Condominiums. Bolton Valley Resort; 434–2769. More than 120 completely furnished 1- to 4-bedroom units with fireplaces (wood is free), private decks, and color TV. Cribs are provided at no charge and daily maid service is available for a small fee.

RESTAURANTS. There's a tendency for guests to stay put at this self-contained resort because there is little besides the resorts attractions nearby. Although there are numerous restaurants in both Burlington and Montpelier, most guests consider the 20-mile drive to either city too much to take after a hard day's skiing. Besides, the lodge dining rooms offer a wide selection from light meals to full-course dinners. Expect to pay $20 and up at an *Expensive* place; $10–$20 at a *Moderate;* and less than $10, *Inexpensive.* This is for a full meal for one excluding drinks, tax, and tips.

Lindsays. *Expensive.* Lodge at Bolton Valley; 434–2131. Candlelight dinners especially suited to couples and other adult groups. Nouvelle cuisine. Dinner by reservation only. A magna cum laude graduate of the American Culinary Institute presides. It shows.

The Black Bear Lodge. *Moderate.* Bolton Valley; 434–2161. Country-inn style dining features regional cooking. Dinner by reservation only.

Fireside Restaurant. *Moderate.* Bolton Valley Lodge; 434–2131. Candlelight dining and menu offering classic American fare with fresh fish daily. MAP available. Chefs won culinary honors in annual "Taste of Vermont" competition.

Bumps. *Inexpensive.* Bolton Valley Lodge; 434–2131. Deli with Mom-style desserts, daily specials.

Cafe Cortina. *Inexpensive.* Bolton Valley Lodge; 434–2131. Light meals include soups, sandwiches, pasta, salads, pizza. Take-out also available.

James Moore Tavern. *Inexpensive.* Bolton Valley Lodge; 434–2131. Hearty hot sandwiches and full-course lunches overlooking slopes. The French onion soup gets kudos.

Sports Club Lounge. *Inexpensive.* Bolton Valley Sports Center; 434–2131. Light meals and gourmet munchies.

Also available at two cafeterias are light meals, breakfast, lunch, and dinner. Weather permitting, there's also *al fresco* dining on ribs and chicken at the slopeside **Barbecue.**

HOW TO GET AROUND. Since this is a legitimate, self-contained destination resort with the slopes within walking distance, having a car here is unnecessary.

SEASONAL EVENTS. Ski season officially begins with the Bolton Valley *"Thanksgiving Extravaganza,"* when the resort offers free skiing to its lodging guests. Several weeks during the year are tabbed as *"Fun On the Snow Weeks,"* for beginning skiers. On Wednesdays, Saturdays, and Sundays, NASTAR is available, and *Carnival Weekend* occurs the last weekend in **January,** with family fun including ski races, a torchlight parade, and more. *Springthing Weekend* falls in late **March,** as it has for years, with music on the slopes, outdoor barbecues, and other rites-of-spring activities.

OTHER SPORTS AND ACTIVITIES. Partly because of its base elevation, at 2,150 feet the highest in the state, the resort's 6,000 private acres are blessed with early and late season snows. This means that its 100-km **cross-country** center gets snows earlier and later than other ski touring centers in Vermont and, increasingly, people come here because of the combination of extensive alpine and cross-country terrain. A 14-km wilderness trail is open at times, connecting to Stowe Valley and the Trapp Lodge complex there. Those interested in Norpine and Telemarking can purchase a one-ride lift ticket that brings skiers to a 3,400-ft. elevation for a 5-mile descent. Guided backcountry tours can be arranged by calling 802–434–2131.

The Sports Center that's within walking distance of restaurants and lodging houses two **tennis** courts, an indoor pool, Jacuzzi, sauna, tanning room, and lounge.

HINTS TO THE HANDICAPPED. The *Sports Center* and activities at the Bolton Valley Lodge are accessible to the handicapped, and the lodge is one of the few at a ski area that is served by an elevator. The sports center can be contacted at the main lodge, 434–2131.

CHILDREN'S ACTIVITIES. Because the resort lends itself so well to the family ski experience, Bolton Valley emphasizes programs for children. The *Honey Bear Nursery,* open from 8:45 A.M. until 4:30 P.M., accepts infants and children up to age 6. Advance reservations are urged (434–2131). Children aged 3 to 5 in the program enjoy outside preski play. The cost is $38 ($20 for a half day) per child. *Bolton Bears & Cubs (SKIwee program)* for ages 6–12 takes youngsters on the mountain from 9:30 A.M. until 2 or 3 P.M. (depending on age) with supervised instruction and skiing, lunch, and camaraderie. The program is $34 a day for ages 5–7; $40 for ages 7–12.

Kids Night Out and evening nursery hours offer twice-weekly respite to parents who may yearn for quiet getaway time. Children ages 6 to 11 get together Wednesdays and Saturdays for dinner, movies, crafts, and organized fun.

NIGHTLIFE. Bolton offers night skiing every night except Sunday. The *James Moore Tavern* in the Bolton Valley Lodge is different from night to night. One evening may be subdued folk music; the next evening, the rafters will be ringing to rock 'n' roll. This is the resort's social center, with video games downstairs for youngsters and the slopes lit for night skiing from 6 to 11 P.M. nightly (except Sunday). The *Sports Center* also hosts social activities, with bridge and backgammon tournaments and volleyball matches vying for attention with Trivial Pursuit wars.

BURKE MOUNTAIN

Box 247
East Burke VT 05832
Tel: 802–626–3305

Snow Report: 802–626–3305
Area Vertical: 2,000 ft.
Number of Trails: 30 on 130 skiable acres
Lifts: 1 quad chair, 1 double chair, 2
* pomas, 1 J-bar*
Snowmaking: 35 percent of terrain
Season: December–April

Burke Mountain, with a 2,000-foot vertical, is a monadnock. This means that it's a free-standing mountain unrelated to nearby mountains. From the peak there are views of Mount Mansfield (Stowe), Jay Peak, and even Mount Washington over in New Hampshire, plus vistas of surrounding farmlands in valleys formed by glaciers millennia ago.

The mountain first attracted attention as a recreation area back in the 1930s, when the Civilian Conservation Corps (CCC) built a fire lookout tower at the top and an access road that subsequently became the key to a few ski trails that were developed. After this quiet start, a group of local people bought the mountain and put in a lift in an effort to create activity for the community. Three ownership changes later, the mountain has evolved into today's 30 trails, mostly in the upper intermediate range and with a popular hill for novice skiers, though there is a good supply of expert ski terrain. The Burke Mountain Academy has turned out a number of top-level racers, including current U.S. Ski Team star Diann Roffe.

The area attracts primarily family skiers who drive up from Massachusetts and Connecticut. There's a loyal following of people who favor the low-key ambience that this increasingly popular resort still offers.

Practical Information for Burke Mountain

HOW TO GET THERE. Burke Mountain is located 1 mile east of the town of East Burke. (For regional details, see *Practical Information for Bolton Valley,* above.)

By car. Take I–91 to Exit 23 to Rte. 114 north to East Burke.

By bus. *Vermont Transit,* (802) 862–9671, serves Lyndonville, 5 miles away.

By air. *Caledonia State Airport,* (802) 626–3353, in Lyndonville offers a 3,300-ft. runway for private aircraft.

TELEPHONES. The area code for all Vermont is 802.

ACCOMMODATIONS. Part of Burke's charm is that it is still relatively undiscovered, with some condominiums at the mountain and a sprinkling of small motels and inns in nearby East Burke and Lyndonville. For lodging reservations and information call 800–541–5480. *Expensive* here is $50 and up per room per night, double occupancy; *Moderate,* $35–$50; and *Inexpensive,* less than $35. All lodgings are within 5 miles of the mountain.

Expensive

Burke Mountain. Slopeside condominiums; 800–541–5480. Choice ranges from private room with bath to studios, efficiencies, and 1- to 4-bedroom units, some with lofts. Units available for 2-night stays for 4–11 people.

Moderate

Changing Seasons Motel. Rte. 5, Lyndonville; 626–5832. A motel offering Jacuzzi and sauna plus cable TV.

Colonnade Motor Inn. Rte. 5, Lyndonville; 626–9316. Forty rooms with phones, cable TV; only 6 miles from the mountain.

The Old Cutter Inn. On Burke Mountain, East Burke; 626–5152. A small country inn with fireplace in après-ski lounge; 9 rooms, one apartment; MAP available.

Inexpensive

Burke Green Guest House. RR 1, East Burke; 467–3472. An 1840 farmhouse with a bed/sitting room that holds up to 6. Bed and breakfast hospitality.

The Garrison Inn. Burke Hollow Rd., East Burke; 626–8329. Just 5 minutes from mountain, inn with private baths, living room with fireplace, and hearty breakfasts.

House in the Wood. One mile from ski area, East Burke; 626–9243. On-premises recreation room with fireplace and shuffleboard; children welcome and meals available.

RESTAURANTS. Continental and ethnic cuisines complement Vermont staples such as roast turkey, griddlecakes with pure maple syrup, and country-style sausage. Price ranges in this listing are based on a full dinner for one person, excluding drinks, tax, and tip: *Expensive,* $12–$15; *Moderate,* $9–$12; *Inexpensive,* less than $9. Unless otherwise specified, most major credit cards are accepted.

The Old Cutter Inn. *Expensive.* On Burke Mountain, East Burke; 626–5152. A Continental touch to the menu; dinners only.

The Pub Outback. *Moderate.* East Burke Village; 626–5187. Casual dining "outback" of Bailey's Store. Daily specials for lunch and dinner.

Trinket's Restaurant. *Inexpensive.* At Changing Seasons Motor Lodge, Rte. 5, Lyndonville; 626–5832. An all-American menu with hamburgers a staple. Credit cards for motel guests.

HOW TO GET AROUND. Public transportation is scarce in the region, so it's best to have a car.

SEASONAL EVENTS. Burke is home to the *Burke Mountain Academy,* which accepts 60 students in grades 9–12 who are interested in developing ski-racing skills while pursuing their studies. Because of the intensive race-training that goes on here season-long, skiers can often view these students whizzing by or involved in any number of a series of amateur racing events.

OTHER SPORTS AND ACTIVITIES. *Total Fitness Inc.,* 58 Broad St., Lyndonville, 626–5430, offers an indoor pool, sauna, spas, tanning booth, isokinetic machines, Olympic weights, treadmills, bicycles, and a trek machine.

The *Burke Mountain Ski Touring Center* at the mountain maintains 60 km of **cross-country** trails. There's **skating rink** at the Burke base lodge facility.

DAY-CARE FACILITIES. The *Burke Mountain Nursery* (626–3305) accepts children aged 4 months–7 years for $6 an hour or $20 all day.

NIGHTLIFE. Live entertainment is offered weekend nights at *Gumby's* on Depot Street (626–3064) and at the *Packing House Lounge* on Hill Street (Rte. 5) in Lyndonville (626–8777).

JAY PEAK SKI RESORT

Jay VT 05859
Tel: 802–988–2611

Snow Report: 802–988–2611 or 800–451–
*   4449 in the U.S. and Canada*
Area Vertical: 2,153 ft.
Number of Trails: 39 trails on 275 skiable
*   acres*
Lifts: 1 aerial tram, 1 quad, 1 triple chair,
*   1 double chair, 2 T-bars*
Snowmaking: 80 percent of terrain
Season: mid-November–early May

Skiers looking for an international flavor at an American ski resort might well head to northern Vermont's Jay Peak, only a few miles from the Canadian border. They speak French as well as English up here, and, in fact, a sister ski resort, Mont St-Sauveur, northwest of Montreal, is under the same management. In the past few years, the Canadian owners have brought a European flair to what's called Vermont's Northeast Kingdom, a region distinguished by its wild beauty that's occasionally interrupted by pockets of civilization. Jay itself is a four-corners town with a country store and an inn, and the nearest town of any size is Newport, 20 miles away.

In this rural, farm-oriented country, 32-year-old Jay Peak Ski Resort is carving out a name for itself, offering a large mountain experience without the resort rush experience that sometimes comes with more populated areas. The Canadian Maritime winds do their share to make sure there's lots of snow at Jay. The two distinct mountains that form the ski resort also help in that moist air tends to move over the mostly flat terrain before it bumps into the mountains and drops its load of water and, in winter, snow. When it is raining just about everywhere else in the region, Jay gets snow.

The resort itself is service-oriented; for example, the Hotel Jay offers valet unloading, a courtesy patrol, and attentive guest services. There's a high repeat business here, good marks for an area that takes a little longer to get to.

Practical Information for Jay Peak

HOW TO GET THERE. Jay Peak Ski Resort is located 4 miles from Jay, 45 miles from St. Albans, and 75 miles from Burlington. (For regional details, see *Practical Information for Bolton Valley,* above.)

By train. *Amtrak* (800–872–7245) serves St. Albans from most eastern cities in the United States.

By bus. *Vermont Transit* stops at the Troy General Store (802–862–9671), 8 miles from Jay. If you're staying at the Hotel Jay, call 800–451–4449 to arrange for shuttle service to the hotel.

By car. From eastern New England, take I–93 north to I–91, get off at Exit 26, and follow signs to Jay. From New York take I–87 to Rouses Point and follow Rte. 105 east from St. Albans.

TELEPHONES. The area code for all Vermont is 802.

ACCOMMODATIONS. One of Jay's claims to fame is that it offers a ski vacation experience the way it was 20 years ago: uncrowded, hassle-free skiing and comfortable country accommodations. However, growth and expansion have also moved north, and, in the past few years, 64 slopeside condominiums have joined 20 older units and the Hotel Jay to provide 700 skiers with slopeside beds. There's also a collection of inns and motels nearby; all are listed in a central lodging guide. Contact the *Jay Peak Area Association,* Jay, VT 05859 (802–988–2611).

There are some lodging bargains to be found here. *Expensive* lodgings are limited, with the Hotel Jay offering a slopeside room at $70 per person per night, double occupancy, with MAP. *Moderate* is from $40 to $60; *Inexpensive,* less than $40. All lodgings are within 10 miles of Jay Peak, unless stated otherwise.

Expensive

Hotel Jay. Jay Peak; 988–2611. Located at the base of Jay Peak, with 48 rooms, all with private baths, color TV, and balconies. Lounge, dining room, living room with fireplace, game room, sauna/Jacuzzi. A definite Continental touch in evidence here.

Moderate

Alpine Haven. Rte. 242, Montgomery Center; 326–4567. Offers 2- to 6-bedroom chalets, located 6 miles from Jay.

Black Lantern Inn. Rte. 118, Montgomery; 326–4507. Built as a stagecoach stop in 1803 and located 12 miles from the slopes. Soups to desserts are all homemade; taproom, TV room, fireplace room available for relaxation.

Inglenook Lodge. Rte. 242, Jay; 988–2880. Large rooms with private baths, dining on the premises, just 1 mile from skiing; sunken fireplace lounge, indoor pool, sauna, and racquetball courts.

Inn at Trout River. Rte. 118, Montgomery Center; 326–4391. An 11-room country inn, with private baths; on-premises dining, pub.

Jay Peak Condominium. Rte. 242, Jay 05859; 988–2611. Two-bedroom condominiums with modern kitchens, fireplaces, fold-out sleeper couches, and on-the-slopes convenience.

Jay Village Inn. Rte. 242, Jay; 988–2643. A country inn near the mountain, combination rooms with suites offering private baths. On-premises dining and player piano in Barney's Pub & Fireplace Lounge.

Inexpensive

Eagle Lodge. Rte. 242, Montgomery Center; 326–4518. A Vermont-style lodge run by Vermonters, with home-cooked meals served buffet style.

Gramp Grunts Motel. Rte. 118, Montgomery Center; 326–4572. Look for heated waterbeds with down comforters, color TV, queen-size beds, modern baths, and large towels.

Greymour Dorm. Rte. 118, Montgomery Center; 326–4794. Reputation as the top ski dorm in the East; maintains 2 vans for shuttle from Amtrak and Burlington airport. 18 rooms with fireplace, pool table, sauna.

In addition to a sprinkling of motels, there are also guest houses (including chalets and apartments) with costs ranging per unit or room from $13 to $100. One of these is the *Gingerbread Chalet,* off Rte. 242, Jay (988–4363).

RESTAURANTS. Eating, and eating well, is fairly easy to do in this region if you are on a moderate budget. A full dinner for one, exclusive of drinks, tax, and tip, is the model for the following price categories: *Expensive,* over $20; *Moderate,* $10–$18; and *Inexpensive,* under $10. Following is a selection of what the area has to offer. Unless otherwise specified, restaurants accept major credit cards.

Expensive

On the Rocks. Rte. 58, Hazen's Notch, Montgomery Center; 326–4500. One of Vermont's most talked-about places; fine food and ambience. Reservations for dinner a must.

Moderate

The Belfry. Rte. 242, Montgomery Center; 326–4400. Formerly an old school-house, now a combination pub/restaurant, offering casual fare such as steaks, potato skins, fresh fish.

Black Lantern Inn. Rte. 118, Montgomery; 326–4507. Candlelight dining here with varied menu. Reservations requested.

Heermansmith Farm Inn. Coventry Village, Coventry; 754–8866. A country setting for fine dining enhanced by slate stone fireplace. Reservations suggested.

Hotel Jay. Jay Peak; 988–2611. Right at the mountain is one of the finest restaurants in the area, offering a complete menu, including seafood, beef, and veal; excellent wine selection.

Inglenook. Rte. 242 (Upper Mountain Rd.), Jay; 988–2880. An American setting with unusual appetizers, good wine selection.

Inn on Trout River. Rte. 118, Montgomery; 326–4391. Candlelight dining, with veal specialties. Dress is "smart" casual.

Jay Village Inn. Rte. 242, Jay; 988–2643. A country inn with candlelight ambience. Menu offers rack of lamb rosemary and steak au poivre; reservations suggested.

Inexpensive

The Border Dining Room & Lounge. N. Main St., Derby; 766–2213. Menu in both French and English, with choices of seafood, steaks, and New England dinners; entertainment Friday and Saturday nights; fresh seafood and roast beef buffet Fridays.

Mill Hollow Pub. Rte. 100, Westfield; 744–6512. Fare ranges from steak to pizza. No credit cards.

HOW TO GET AROUND. It is best to have a **car** in this region. However, some accommodations may have **shuttle** service to the ski area. If you don't plan to drive your car (or a rented one), check with the hotel when making reservations.

SEASONAL EVENTS. As far as the mountain management knows, Jay has the only downhill event for amateur racers in the East—the *George Syrovatka International Downhill,* held in mid-**March.** It attracts speedy skiers in numbers of up to 150 and ages ranging from 9 to 62.

OTHER SPORTS AND ACTIVITIES. There are numerous opportunities for **cross-country** skiing, at the *Jay Peak Ski Touring Center* at the mountain (988–2611), with over 20 km of trails; *Hazens Notch Ski Touring,* Rte. 58, Montgomery Center (326–4708), with 30 km of groomed trails and 12 km of maintained trails; *Heermansmith Farm Ski Touring Center,* Coventry Village, Coventry (754–8866), a 14-km trail system; and *Cross Country* at Cedarwood, Rte. 242, Jay, 15 km of trails. **Snowmobiling, sledding, ice fishing,** and **skating** are also available in the region.

HINTS TO THE HANDICAPPED. The aerial tram is accessible to the handicapped by an elevator. The Jay Peak Ski School (988–2611) will also give instruction and assistance to handicapped skiers upon request.

CHILDREN'S ACTIVITIES. The *Child Care Center* (988–2611) at Jay Peak accommodates children aged 2–7, providing indoor fun and games. It's open from 9 A.M. to 4 P.M. daily. Rates are $16 a day per child. Add $16 for two 45-minute lessons in conjunction with Learn to Ski programs through *Kinderschool* and *SKIwee.* There is free child care for guests of the Hotel Jay and Jay Peak Condominium.

NIGHTLIFE. Saturday nights, there's action right at Jay Peak, with live bands playing music for dancing at the inn. In nearby Montgomery, a place called the *Slovatkia Inn* at the end of Rte. 242 (326–4690) has disco entertainment with an occasional sprinkling of live bands. At *On the Rocks,* Rte. 58 in Hazen's Notch, Montgomery Center (326–4500), there's piano music on Saturdays.

STOWE

Stowe VT 05672
Tel: 802–253–7311

Snow Report: 800–63–STOWE
Area Vertical: 3,360 ft.
Number of Trails: 45 on 378 acres
Lifts: 1 gondola, 1 quad chair, 1 triple
    chair, 6 double chairs, 1 Mitey Mite
Snowmaking: 63 percent of terrain
Season: mid-November–late April

It's Stowe's Diamond Anniversary in the 1991–92 season, a celebration of 75 years as the legendary "Ski Capital of the East." Stowe Ski Resort is a two-mountain complex, Mt. Mansfield and Spruce Peak, situated 6 miles north of the village of Stowe. This is where eastern skiing was born and, along with Sun Valley, Idaho, where Americans became aware of the sport for the very first time.

In addition to the highest peak, Mt. Mansfield, the main mountain and its companion, Spruce Peak, offer a healthy mix of expert, intermediate, and novice terrain. The variety is enhanced by the fact that 32 of the resort's 45 trails are more than 1 mile in length.

Mt. Mansfield is known for "the front four," a quad of super expert trails recognized as one of skiing's true tests. Spruce Peak is a wide-open intermediate and novice paradise. The Stowe Ski School operates classes for all levels on Spruce.

Stowe is a marriage of New England skiing tradition and modern skiing technology. The resort has been acclaimed as one of the nation's top 10 resorts by both skiers and writers. The great variety of skiing, combined with the après-ski ambience of the Stowe area, makes the package work. Restaurants and lodging establishments line the mountain road and can satisfy every palate or wallet.

Stowe is a favorite spot of senior citizens. The resort offers discounted tickets to persons between 65 and 69 and free skiing for those 70 and older.

Practical Information for Stowe

HOW TO GET THERE. Stowe is in north-central Vermont, 40 miles from Burlington and 10 miles from Waterbury. (For regional details, see *Practical Information for Bolton Valley,* above.)

By car. Take I–89 to Exit 10, then follow Rte. 100 north to Stowe.

TELEPHONES. The area code throughout Vermont is 802.

ACCOMMODATIONS. The *Stowe Area Association Lodging Bureau,* Box 1320, Stowe, VT 05672 (253–7321 or 800–245–TOWE), can make arrangements for lodging at some 60 accommodations, ranging from bunk rooms to luxurious inns. For some reason known only, perhaps, to real estate sales people, condominium development hasn't quite caught on in this area yet. The few condos that are here range from $120 to $350 a night.

There are two ski dorms: the *Round Hearth,* R.R. 1, Box 2240, Stowe (253–7223), and *Winterhaus,* R.D. 1, Stowe (253–7731), that offer lodging, breakfast, and dinner for only $25–$30 per person per night.

Country inns, hotels, and a sprinkling of resorts take up the lion's share of visitors' attention. In the selection below, *Expensive* includes those with rates from $85 upward per person, based on double occupancy (with MAP); *Moderate,* $60–$85; and *Inexpensive,* under $60. All lodgings in this listing are within 10 miles of the slopes.

Expensive

Edson Hill Manor. Off Rte. 108, Stowe; 253–7371. There are 40 km of ski touring trails here; rooms with fireplaces, on-premises dining. Parts of Alan Alda's movie *Four Seasons* were shot here. MAP available.

Green Mountain Inn. Main St., Stowe; 253–7301. An authentic country inn, some rooms with canopy beds; offering game room, sauna, Jacuzzi, and formal and casual dining. MAP available.

Inn at Thatcher Brook Falls. Rte. 100, Waterbury; 244–5911. There's a romantic get-away atmosphere in this 1899 Victorian country inn; private baths and gourmet dining room.

Stoweflake Resort. Rte. 108, Stowe; 253–7305. A 75-room resort hotel with some condominiums; indoor pool, Jacuzzi, health spa.

Ten Acres Lodge. Luce Hill Rd., Stowe; 253–7638. Individually decorated rooms and dining by candlelight; comfortable, elegant decor; spacious rooms, 2 queen-size beds, some 2-room suites. MAP available.

Toll House Inn. Rte. 108; 253–7311. A slopeside inn plus condominium complex with chairlift to Mt. Mansfield. Rooms (all spacious, some 2-room suites) include steam bath and refrigerator. MAP available.

Topnotch at Stowe. Rte. 108, Stowe; 253–8585. They don't make many places nicer than Topnotch, first because of its dramatically high perch, second because of the generous size of both room and bath, with guest rooms resembling mini-suites, equipped with a library and sitting area. Afternoon tea is served here, with four indoor tennis courts, indoor pool, and a health spa. MAP available.

Trapp Family Lodge. Luce Hill Rd., Stowe; 253–8522. Home of the *Sound of Music* Von Trapp family. An elegant lodge has replaced one destroyed by fire a few years ago; on-premises dining and only a short walk from the Austrian tearoom and spectacular alpine views. MAP available. Cross-country skiing is the favorite activity here.

Moderate

Anderson Lodge. Rte. 108, Stowe; 253–7336. A small Tyrolean-style inn with an Austrian chef. MAP available.

Butternut Inn. Rte. 108, Stowe; 253–2477. Antiques, afternoon tea, and quail for dinner come with cozy rooms and pine-paneled ambience. Some chalets available. MAP available.

Golden Eagle Resort Motor Inn. Rte. 108, Stowe; 253–4811. Oversized beds and fireplaces, balconies, some kitchenettes; sauna, whirlpool, and exercise room. MAP available.

Mountaineer. Rte. 108, Stowe; 253–7525. Enjoy a heated indoor pool and candle-light dinners, plus a fireside lounge and game room. MAP available.

The Salzburg Motor Inn. Rte. 108, Stowe; 253–8542. Comfortable accommodations near cross-country skiing and indoor tennis and pool, with a game room, lounge, and on-premises dining. MAP available.

Scandinavia Inn & Chalets. Rte. 108, Stowe; 253–8555. Kids love the video games, on-premises dining with family-style meals, sauna, and Jacuzzi. MAP available.

Siebeness Lodge. Rte. 108, Stowe; 253–8942. A hot tub, fireplace lounge, and cross-country skiing right out your door are specialties here.

Ski Inn. Rte. 108, Stowe; 253–4050. A country inn offering good food.

Town & Country Motor Lodge. Rte. 108, Stowe; 253–7595. In town near the shops and movies, offering an indoor pool, game room, sauna, and Jacuzzi.

Inexpensive

Fiddler's Green Inn. Rte. 108, Stowe; 253–8124. Private or connecting baths in old-fashioned inn; complimentary hors d'oeuvres.

The Gables Inn. Rte. 108, Stowe; 253–7730. Antiques, country bedrooms, wide plank floors, hot tub, and game room.

Grey Fox Inn. Rte. 108, Stowe; 253–8921. Casual and comfortable 18-room inn with game room and sauna, serving homebaked bread and desserts.

Logwood Inn. Off Rte. 108, Stowe; 253–7354. Lodge—genuine log construction—and chalets.

Quality Inn. Rte. 100, Stowe; 253–7355. A 48-room resort hotel with exercise room, lighted skating pond, sauna, Jacuzzi, and free shuttle to the slopes.

Spruce Pond Inn. Rte. 100, Stowe; 253–7087. A country inn where reservations are requested for dinner; offers cross-country skiing.

Stowe Bound. Rte. 100, Stowe; 253–4515. Colonial guest house and sheep farm offers German cooking with natural foods.

The Yodler Motor Inn. Rte. 108, Stowe; 253–4836. Some kitchenettes available in motel accommodations offering home cooking.

BED-AND-BREAKFAST TREASURES. The Stowe area hosts several of these accommodations for the budget minded. Not all bed-and-breakfasts have rooms with baths; most lack TVs and telephones. But all offer warm hospitality. A selection of them, all in Stowe, is listed here.

The following B&Bs range from $55 to $100 per room per night: *Inn at Brass Lantern,* Rte. 100, 253–2229; *Raspberry Patch,* Randolph Rd., 253–4145; *1860 House* in Stowe Village, 253–7352; *Stowe-Away,* Rte. 108, 253–7574; *Golden Kitz Lodge and Hotel,* Rte. 108, 253–4217; *Bittersweet Inn,* Rte. 100, 253–7787; *Nichols Lodge,* Rte. 100, 253–7683; the *Pub at Stowe,* Rte. 108, 253–8669; and *Timberholm Inn,* off Rte. 108, 253–7603.

RESTAURANTS. In addition to restaurants referred to briefly in the Accommodations listings above, the community offers some 40 eateries with French, Italian, German, Greek, Hungarian, English, and New England fare. For entrees only, *Expensive* would be $17 and up; *Moderate,* $10–$16; and *Inexpensive,* less than $10.

Expensive

Isle de France. Rte. 108, Stowe; 253–7751. Classic fine dining with French decor in the main dining room. Also offers bar menu.

Stowehof Inn. Edson Hill Rd.; 253–8500. The Alpine architecture is complemented by European cuisine in this secluded mountain inn, although the dining room has an Early American motif, with a large stone fireplace and high beamed ceilings.

Tanglewoods. Waterbury; 244–7855. Distinguished and original American and European dishes (including venison) in old Vermont barn.

Ten Acres. Luce Hill, Stowe; 253–7638. An old New England inn that delivers Continental preparations with local ingredients such as Vermont-grown lamb.

Topnotch at Stowe. Rte. 108, Stowe; 253–8585. A dramatic setting with award-winning fare, extensive wine selection, formal and informal dining.

The Trapp Family Lodge. Luce Hill, Stowe; 253–8511. The famous singing Trapp Family presence is alive here, with a main dining room in the handsome rebuilt main lodge and the nearby Austrian tea room in which the pastries rival their Alps counterparts.

Villa Tragara. Rte. 100, Waterbury Center; 244–5288. Superbly prepared Italian cuisine in elegant and bright rooms.

Moderate

Alpine Lodge. Rte. 108, Stowe; 253–7700. German and other international dishes receive the gourmet touch here.

Cafe Mozart. Pond Rd., Stowe; 253–9900. European pastries and freshly ground coffee follow American and Continental meals.

Charda Inn. Rte. 100, N. Stowe; 253–4598. This is a late-18th-century brick dwelling turned restaurant with gracious hospitality.

Foxfire Inn. R.D. 2, Stowe; 253–8459. A long, long menu featuring southern Italian cooking with a lecture, if you wish, on what constitutes each dish!

H.H. Bingham's Restaurant & Broken Ski Tavern. Rte. 108, Stowe; 253–7311. A slopeside location plus New England fare add up to a comfortable family-style dining atmosphere.

Hob Knob. Rte. 108, Stowe; 253–8549. Fresh salmon and roast duckling prepared to order.

The Partridge Inn. Rte. 108, Stowe; 253–8000. Look for Cape Cod seafood specialties.

Restaurant Swisspot. Main St., Stowe; 253–4622. Authentic beef and cheese, plus chocolate, fondues—all served in Swiss ambience.

Stoweflake Inn. Rte. 108, Stowe; 253–7355. Prime rib, fresh fish, and Yankee cooking in main dining room; light menu in lounge.

Stubb's. Rte. 108, Stowe; 253–7110. Innovative menu in fireside surroundings.

Town & Country Lodge. Rte. 108, Stowe; 253–7595. New England, family-style, casual dining; salad bar.

Trattoria La Fest. Rte. 108, Stowe; 253–8480. Colorful and festive, run by Italian family of restaurateurs. Country-style Italian food.

The Whip at Green Mountain Inn. Main St., Stowe; 253–7301. Serves breakfast, lunch, and dinner, with an emphasis on fresh seafood and light meals. Great desserts.

Whiskers. Rte. 108; 253–8996. A Victorian mansion that's kept the old-fashioned touches of Tiffany-style lamps and antiques, with a menu ranging from prime ribs to seafood (including lobster), plus salad bar.

The Yodler. Rte. 108, Stowe; 253–4836. New England hot buffet dinner is featured on Saturdays.

Inexpensive

The Bistro at Topnotch. Rte. 108, Stowe; 253–8585. Still the same great views, but this time with more casual dining, offering fondues and salad bar.

Estia Pizza Restaurant. Rte. 108, Stowe; 253–7880. There's Greek food here in addition to pizzas, with an emphasis on fresh ingredients.

The Shed. Rte. 108, Stowe; 253–4364. An extensive menu in a casual greenhouse environment; wonderful waffle-and-omelet bar during Sunday brunch.

Stowe Away. Rte. 108, Stowe; 253–7574. Vegetarian, seafood, and Mexican dishes on the menu here, served fireside.

Stowe-wich Shop. Rte. 108, Stowe; 253–7770. Sandwiches, crisp salads, homemade soups. Take out or sit in.

HOW TO GET AROUND. Stowe provides free **shuttle bus** transportation between the ski area and Stowe Village every half hour and continuously between the Mansfield and Spruce base lodges. The mode? Molly's Trolly—refurbished, antique trolleys! In addition, many of the hotels in the area provide free shuttles to the ski area. Check when making reservations.

Sullivan's Taxi, 253–9440, and *Lamoille Taxi,* 253–9433, provide service in the Stowe area.

SEASONAL EVENTS. *Stowe Winter Carnival Week,* usually held in mid-**January,** has been popular since 1921. Known as "king of the winter carnivals," the events range from black-tie affairs to dog-sled races, church suppers, and snow sculpting. The Wintermeister is part of the fun. This is a winter triathlon involving cross-country, giant slalom, and speed skating. Serious ski racers of all ages flock here for various events throughout the season, and **Easter Sunday** sees a gondola ride to the top of the mountain for a service and an optional ski down, with costume parade.

OTHER SPORTS AND ACTIVITIES. The *Mt. Mansfield Touring Center* (253–7311), along with the *Trapp Family Ski Touring Center* on Luce Hill (253–8511), *Edson Hill Manor,* off Rte. 108 (253–7371), and *Topnotch at Stowe,* Rte. 108 (253–8585), offer 150 miles of interconnecting **cross-country** trails. A 4-mile recreation path in and around Stowe Village, popular in snowless weather for **jogging** and **cycling,** also attracts cross-country enthusiasts.

Sleigh rides are available from *Stowehof* on Edson Hill (253–9722) and the Trapp Family Lodge (253–8511). There's **skating** in town at the *Jackson Arena,* and public indoor **swimming pools** at the *Town & Country Motor Lodge,* Rte. 108 (253–7595), the *Salzburg Inn,* Rte. 108 (253–8541), the *Peacock Motel,* Rte. 100 (253–7244), and *Stoweflake,* Rte. 100 (253–7355). Other accommodations offering swimming, to guests only, are *Notchbrook Resorts,* Rte. 108 (253–4882), *Mountainside Resort,* Rte. 108 (253–8610), and *Sullivan Real Estate,* Rte. 108 (253–8132).

The Topnotch (253–8585) has four **indoor tennis** courts open to the public; the *Green Mountain Inn Health Club,* Main St. (253–7301), offers **racquetball,** Jacuzzi, whirlpool, steam and dry sauna, Nautilus and exercise equipment; the *Golden Eagle,* Rte. 100 (253–4811), has the same facilities as the Green Mountain Inn except for racquetball.

CHILDREN'S ACTIVITIES. A day-care center called *Pooh's Corner* is located at Spruce Peak and operates in conjunction with the *Winnie the Pooh Ski School* to involve children aged 3–12 in ski lessons. The rate is $36 a day. *Kanga's Pocket,* a nursery, accepts children aged 1 month to 3 years at a daily rate of $36. The center is open from 8:30 A.M. to 4:30 P.M. The *Stowe Ski School* hosts a Mountain Adventure Program for ages 7–12 that includes instruction, supervised skiing, and lunch, from 9:30 A.M. to 3:30 P.M.

NIGHTLIFE. There's an endless list of restaurants and inns that offer piano bars, duos, and folk guitar-style entertainment nightly. *Stowehof* on Edson Hill Rd. (253–9722) and the *Trapp Family Lodge* on Luce Hill (253–8511) both offer romantic evening sleigh rides. Live band music of all varieties is available in town at *B. K. Clarks,* Rte. 108 (253–9300), jazz, rhythm and blues; the *Matterhorn Night Club,* Rte. 108 (253–8198), has music from the '40s and '50s; and the *Rusty Nail Saloon,* Rte. 108 (253–9444), offers top-40 and hard rock. The *Stoweflake* (253–7305), *Town & Country* (253–7595), and *Topnotch* (253–8585) all offer entertainment in their lounges.

MAD RIVER VALLEY

SUGARBUSH SKI RESORT

R.R. Box 350
Warren VT 05674–9993
Tel: 802–583–2381

Snow Report: 802–583–SNOW
Area Vertical: 2,600 ft. (North), 2,400 ft.
(South)
Number of Trails: 80 on 386 skiable acres
Lifts: 3 quad chairs, 3 triple chairs, 6
double chairs, 4 surface lifts
Snowmaking: 46 percent of area
Season: early November–late April

In Vermont's Mad River Valley, or "The Valley," as it's known locally, three distinct mountains compete for attention with fine restaurants and shops, all comfortably at home in a bucolic working-farm community.

The mountains are Sugarbush South and Sugarbush North— comprising Sugarbush Ski Resort in Warren—and Mad River Glen in Waitsfield. The valley itself is narrow, marked by a river of the same name, white-steepled churches, country schoolhouses turned boutiques, and carefully preserved covered bridges.

Sugarbush emerged in 1957–58, quickly becoming the "in" place for the East's sophisticated skiers, and was dubbed at one time "mascara mountain" for its collection of chic. With this sophistication came folks like Armando Orsini, the New York restaurateur who converted a hay-barn with crystal chandeliers and strains of Vivaldi into today's Common Man Restaurant, a very uncommon place; and Henri Borel, proprietor of Chez Henri, one of the most elegant French restaurants in Vermont.

Twenty years later, Solon Automated Services purchased Sugarbush and its neighbor (then Glen Ellen, now Sugarbush North) and began planning trails and lifts that would connect the two mountains. This connection is still a few seasons away, but a courtesy shuttle scoots skiers back and forth.

When the resort first opened, there were perhaps 50 beds nearby for skiers; today the collection of condominiums alone at the base of Sugarbush totals 2,400 beds. And as with other healthy resort communities, country inns and lodges in the locale are thriving.

Management claims that Sugarbush/South Basin is a ski area built for skiers and by skiers. All the trails on Sugarbush, itself a giant bowl, come to a central hub at the base. Experts stick to the upper levels, intermediates to the middle, and novices enjoy the lower terrain.

An advantage to upper-level skiers offered by both mountains is upper-elevation lift service that allows them to stay put near the top, avoiding long runs back to the base in order to get back to the exciting terrain.

At Sugarbush North, novice skiers can ride to the summit to enjoy spectacular 360-degree views. Here the Rim Run, a 2½-mile trail down the spine of the Green Mountains, exposes Camel's Hump and Mt. Mansfield (Stowe) on the right, and the Adirondacks of New York and Lake Champlain on the left. On a clear day, New Hampshire's White Mountains are also visible. Overall, 19 percent of the trails are in the "easiest" category, 47 percent are in the "more difficult" category, and 34 percent are in the "expert" category.

Skiers of all ages are very much at home here with free ski programs for youngsters aged 6 and under and for senior citizens aged 70 and older.

Like previous owners, the newest proprietors of Sugarbush are attentive to many of the smallest details that can make the difference between a nice and an excellent ski vacation experience. For example, there's the convenience of a cable TV system that provides 24-hour information on ski conditions, nightlife, and events in the area. This is available in many of the nearby accommodations.

MAD RIVER GLEN

Rte. 17
Waitsfield VT 05673
Tel: 802–496–3551

Snow Report: 802–496–2001 or 800–696–2001 in VT
Area Vertical: 2,000 ft.
Number of Trails: 33 on 85 skiable acres
Lifts: 3 double chairs, 1 single chair
Snowmaking: 15 percent of terrain
Season: mid-December–mid-April

Mad River Glen is one of the three ski mountains (Sugarbush South and Sugarbush North are the other two) that make the Mad River Valley one of Vermont's most popular winter destinations. Mad River doesn't have the glitter and glamor of its next-door neighbors, but its low-key, just-give-'em-good-skiing approach to running a mountain produces loyal fans who come back generation after generation.

One of the reasons it exacts great loyalty from its skiers, perhaps, is due to bumper stickers that say: "Mad River Glen—Ski It If You Can." Management, however, says not to be intimidated: "You can!"

The mountain was developed—about as much as it still is today—back in 1949. Its specialty is steep, twisting, fall-line trails, a favorite of New

York investment banker Roland Palmedo who first saw potential in this Vermont mountain.

Today's owner, Betsy Pratt, says she doesn't see much need to change what people keep coming back for—the challenging terrain as well as a dedicated crew of chairlift operators and cafeteria staff who have been serving Mad River skiers for years. JoAnn Eurich, for example, is celebrating her 31st year as a Mad River staff member, beginning as a dishwasher and now helping manage the base lodge restaurant.

Although there is some lodging at the base of the mountain, Mad River is happy to share the largesse of the valley with its skiers.

The terrain includes 40 percent "most difficult" trails, 40 percent "more difficult" trails, and 20 percent "easiest" trails. The trails are named after animals, with birds and periwinkles going to the beginning skiers, and Panther, Lynx, and Catamount the purview of the experts.

Practical Information for
Sugarbush and Mad River Glen

HOW TO GET THERE. Sugarbush is located in the town of Warren, 45 miles from Burlington and 20 miles from Waterbury. Mad River Glen is located 5 miles from Waitsfield, on Rte. 17. (For regional details, see *Practical Information for Bolton Valley,* above.)

By car. To get to both resorts, take I–89 north to Exit 9 at Middlesex, then onto Rte. 100B south, which merges into Rte. 100. At Rte. 17 follow the signs to each resort.

TELEPHONES. The area code for all Vermont is 802.

ACCOMMODATIONS. Sugarbush Village is a mature resort village at the base of Sugarbush that's characterized by a greater variety of condominium architecture than you'll find at any other resort in the state. Although most of the 2,400 condo beds are in the village, condominium complexes also dot surrounding hills and sprout along the Sugarbush Access Rd. to the mountain. In addition, there are numerous country inns and lodges in the three valley towns of Warren, Waitsfield, and Fayston. The Sugarbush Valley boasts some 6,000 guest beds in all.

Sugarbush Reservations, Sugarbush Ski Resort, Warren, VT 05674–9993, (802) 583–3333 or 800–53–SUGAR, can assist in providing information and making reservations at both resorts and can give details on airfares and car rentals. In the region the per-person, per-night rate, double occupancy, in the *Expensive* range is $55–$100; *Moderate,* $35–$75, and *Inexpensive,* $30 and under. All lodgings in this listing are within 8 miles of the slopes unless stated otherwise.

Expensive

The Bridges Resort & Racquet Club. Sugarbush 05674; 496–4441. Accommodates up to 600 guests in 1- to 3-bedroom condominiums with fireplaces, fully appointed kitchens, indoor pool, saunas, game room, indoor tennis and squash courts, party lounge. Free shuttle to the slopes.

Sugarbush Inn. Sugarbush Access Rd., Warren 05674; 583–2301. Elegant 45-room country inn with beautifully decorated private and public rooms. Offers a complete Sports Pavilion with indoor pool, sauna, Jacuzzi, ice skating, and free shuttle to slopes, plus cross-country skiing and ice-skating rink nearby. MAP available.

Sugarbush Village Condominiums: Snow Creek, Glades, Paradise, Southface, Summit. Box 234, Sugarbush Village, Warren 05674; 583–3000. These 1- to 3-bedroom dwellings, including some hotel suites, have private baths, and most are within walking distance to the slopes, are convenient to activities, and offer shuttle bus service.

Tucker Hill Lodge. R.F.D. 1, Box 147, Waitsfield 05673; 496–3983. Country sophistication, excellent dining, extensive cross-country center. Accommodates 60. MAP.

Waitsfield Inn. Rte. 100, Waitsfield 05673; 496–3979. Romantic country inn decorated with antiques. MAP available.

Moderate

Beaver Pond Farm. Box 306, Golf Course Rd., Warren 05674; 583–2861. Serves country breakfast and après-ski complimentary hot cider and munchies. A restored farmhouse for 10.

Honeysuckle's Inn. Rte. 100, Moretown 05660; 496–6200. Victorian-style bed-and-breakfast inn, with après-ski tea and baked goods served in front of a crackling fire.

Lareau Farm Country Inn. Rte. 100, Waitsfield 05673; 496–4949. A 150-year-old farmhouse with antiques, country breakfasts.

Madbush Resort. Rte. 100, Waitsfield 05673; 496–3966. A traditional inn with the modern touches of a hot tub, sauna, cable TV. Some 4-person lofts.

Mad River Barn. Rte. 17, Waitsfield 05673; 496–3310. Offers cross-country skiing and sauna. Spacious guest rooms, children under 10 sleep free in same room with parents. MAP available.

Millbrook Lodge. Rte. 17, Waitsfield 05673; 496–2405. An 1865 farmhouse turned country inn with antiques, hand stenciling, and quilts. MAP.

Newton's 1824 House Inn. Rte. 100, Waitsfield 05673; 496–7555. Casually elegant country inn with 6 guest rooms, private baths, gourmet breakfasts, and cross-country trails.

Old Tymes Inn. Rte. 100, Waitsfield 05673; 496–6200. Small bed-and-breakfast inn, with fireside bar and fine dining.

Powderhound Resort. Rte. 100, Warren 05674; 496–5100. A combination of condominium convenience with country inn ambience; 2-room suites with kitchenettes, color TV; dining, lounge game room, hot tub, and shuttle.

Round Barn Farm. Box 247, East Warren Rd., Waitsfield 05673; 496–2276. Elegant country inn in rural setting, offers full breakfasts.

Snow Goose Inn and Restaurant. Rte. 100B, Moretown 05660; 496–3532. A contemporary inn offering waterbeds, private baths, candlelight dining, and desserts before bed.

Sugartree Country Inn. Sugarbush Access Rd., Warren 05674; 583–3211. A bed-and-breakfast, decorated with handmade quilts, ruffles, and other country touches.

Inexpensive

Carpenter Farm. Box 2710, Meadow Rd., Moretown 05660; 496–3433. Inn at a working dairy farm with private and shared baths. MAP available.

Christmas Tree Inn. Sugarbush Access Rd., Warren 05674; 583–2211. Handmade quilts and the Vermont country ambience; Continental breakfast included.

Golden Lion Riverside Inn. Rte. 100, Warren 05674; 496–3084. Private baths, queen and double beds in spacious rooms. Continental breakfast.

The Hydeaway. Rte. 17, Waitsfield 05673; 496–2322. One of the original valley lodges offering tavern and ice skating. MAP.

Mooselips Motel. Rtes. 17/100, Waitsfield 05673; 496–3937. Two-room suites sleep up to 6, with cable TV and phones in room. On-premises dining, large-screen TV, video jukebox, pool table in lounge.

Pitcher Inn. Box 408, Warren 05674; 496–3831. A 26-bed inn downtown in village, great breakfasts.

Schultze's Ski Lodge. Rte. 100, Moretown 05660; 496–2366. A lodge with semi-private baths, breakfast that includes homemade breads. Kitchen privileges at dinner time.

South Hollow Farm. R.R. 1, Box 287, Warren 05674; 496–5627. Restored farmhouse; sledding and cross-country. Breakfasts served.

Wait Farm Motor Inn. Rte. 100, Waitsfield 05673; 496–2033. Ten motel rooms with cable TV and private baths; village location.

Weathertop Lodge. R.D. 1, Box 151, Waitsfield 05673; 496–4909. Family-run lodge with sauna, hot tub, and fitness room; serves breakfast.

Wilder Farm Inn. Rte. 100, Waitsfield 05673; 496–6541. Restored New England farmhouse with cozy living room and library with fireplace. Continental breakfast.

RESTAURANTS. The Mad River Valley is establishing a reputation not only for outstanding skiing but for exemplary dining experiences. *Expensive* here means meals costing $17–$22; *Moderate,* $11–$17; and *Inexpensive,* less than $11. An unusual twist in a ski resort community is the *Green Mountain Coffee Roasters Cafe and Espresso Bar,* in the Mad River Green Shopping Center on Rte. 100 in Waitsfield (496–5470), where you can enjoy fine coffees, along with croissants, pastries, and chocolate truffles. Major credit cards are accepted, unless otherwise noted.

Expensive

Chez Henri. Sugarbush Village, Warren; 583–2600. An authentic French bistro offers veal sweetbreads in a rich wine sauce and a noontime French onion soup that's as close to the real thing as you'll find in New England.

The Common Man. German Flats Rd., Warren; 583–2800. A barn turned posh serves European fare to strains of Vivaldi under crystal chandeliers.

The Onion Patch at Sugarbush Inn. Sugarbush Access Rd., Warren; 583–2301. Two restaurants here. The Terrace Room is a greenhouse setting; the Onion Patch serves steaks and seafood.

The Phoenix. Sugarbush Village, Warren; 583–2777. Stained glass and wonderful, myth-making desserts. Reservations requested.

Sam Rupert's Restaurant. Sugarbush Access Rd., Warren; 583–2421. A greenhouse atmosphere with interesting menu.

Tucker Hill Lodge. Rte. 17, Waitsfield; 496–3983. Fresh seafood is a specialty, as are interesting and unusual preparations of old New England favorites.

Waitsfield Inn. Rte. 100, Waitsfield; 496–3979. Classic and American culinary traditions here.

Moderate

Beggar's Banquet. Rte. 100, Fiddlers Green, Waitsfield; 496–4485. Noted for hearty soups, salads, entrees, plus Mexican night on Sundays.

The Den. Rte. 100, Waitsfield; 496–8880. Look for house steaks and seafood.

D. W. Pearl's. Rte. 100, Waitsfield; 496–8858. Soup and salad bar, great breakfasts.

Huckleberry's. Rte. 100, Warren; 496–5100. A family restaurant with an Italian and northern European flair. Reservations requested.

JJ's Pub. Mad River Green, Waitsfield; 496–8887. Casual pub with local flavor; soups, burgers, light entrees.

Mad River Barn. Rte. 17, Waitsfield; 496–3310. Informal dining with homemade breads and desserts.

Millbrook Inn. Rte. 17, Waitsfield; 496–2405. Eclectic menu includes authentic Indian cuisine and gourmet vegetarian dishes.

Mother Machree's at Gallagher's. Jct. Rtes. 17/100, Waitsfield; 496–8800. Dine here and skip the cover charge at Gallagher's bar later on.

The Odyssey. Sugarbush Village, Warren; 583–2001. Pizza and homemade Italian specialties.

Olde Tymes. Sugarbush Village, Warren; 496–3875. Green Mountain memorabilia transform a long-time farmhouse and classic menu.

Reveille at the Pitcher Inn. Warren; 496–3831. Unique and delicious breakfasts (only).

RSVP. Bridge St., Waitsfield; 496–7787. Homemade pizza and other specialties.

HOW TO GET AROUND. There is a **shuttle** between Sugarbush and Sugarbush North that runs every 15 minutes. Many area lodges also provide free shuttle service to the slopes. Free fun shuttle runs every night from 5:30 P.M. to 12:15 A.M.

SEASONAL EVENTS. At Mad River Glen, a prespring ritual is the *Mogul Contest and Groundhog Watch* on **February** 2, Groundhog Day. Family races are popular throughout the season, and in mid-**March** there's an annual *Telemark Festival.*
At Sugarbush there's a full calendar of events. *March Madness* in late **March** brings a full week of events, including races, mogul contests, and more. Toward

the end of the season, a *triathlon,* combining canoeing, cycling, and cross-country skiing, is held. For details, call the local Chamber of Commerce (496–3409).

OTHER SPORTS AND ACTIVITIES. Ski touring is popular in the Mad River Valley at *Tucker Hill Lodge,* Waitsfield, 496–3983; the *Rossignol/Sugarbush Inn Ski Touring Center,* Warren, 583–2301; *Blueberry Lake Cross Country Center,* Warren, 496–6687; and *Ole's Cross Country Center,* Warren, 496–3430. In all, there are nearly 150 km of marked and groomed trails.

The *Sugarbush Sports Center* (583–2391), one of the finest facilities of its kind at a ski resort in New England, offers three tennis, two squash, and two racquetball courts; an indoor pool, exercise room with universal gym and Nautilus, saunas, steam room, Jacuzzi, and whirlpool. There's also an outdoor ice skating rink with rentals.

The *Bridge's Resort and Racquet Club* in Warren (583–2922) provides a heated pool, saunas, one racquetball and two tennis courts to the public.

Competitive amateur skiers can pit themselves daily against the clock on a Dual Automatic (coin-op) Race Course that is a modified giant slalom challenge. This program is available on both mountains.

HINTS TO THE HANDICAPPED. Although neither Sugarbush nor Mad River Glen has any formal handicapped programs, the ski school at each resort can accommodate skiers with disabilities or impairments on a one-to-one basis. Contact the main lodge at each resort for specific information and reservations. Sugarbush, 583–2381; Mad River Glen, 496–3551.

DAY-CARE FACILITIES. At Sugarbush, the *Valley Day School Nursery* (583–2495) accepts infants on up from 8:30 A.M. to 4:15 P.M. daily at $4.50 per child per hour, with reduced rates for additional children from the same family. State-certified facilities at the resort include a special crib room for infants. For older children, there's a ski playground dubbed the *Mogul Mouse Land,* where youngsters under age 6 can ski free. The *Sugar Bear* is a program for children up to 10 years old that includes supervised skiing and lunch.

At Mad River Glen, a nursery called the *Cricket Club* (496–2123) offers an all-day—8 A.M.–4 P.M.—child-care program with ski instruction available.

NIGHTLIFE. Find lively après-ski entertainment nightly at *Gallaghers,* Jct. Rte. 17/100 in Waitsfield (496–8800), part of a complex that includes dining at Mother Machree's, and in the *North* and *South Base Lodges* at Sugarbush (583–2381) on weekends. The *Bass Tavern* (583–3100) on the Sugarbush Access Rd. in Warren houses a disco, and the elegant *Chez Henri Restaurant* in Sugarbush Village (583–2600) also provides disco entertainment.

One of the most popular night spots in the valley is *The Blue Tooth* on the Sugarbush Access Rd. in Warren (583–2656), billing itself as a cozy mountain saloon. *Edison's Studio* on Rte. 100 in Waitsfield (496–2336) shows movies nightly, with deli food and cocktails available.

The *Wunderbar* in the Valley House at Sugarbush Ski Resort (583–2381) is home to a folk singer, and a number of inns feature nightly entertainment, usually of the mellow folk rock or piano bar style.

SMUGGLERS' NOTCH RESORT

Smugglers' Notch VT 05464
Tel: 802–644–8851 or 800–451–8752

Snow Report: 802–644–8851
Area Vertical: 2,610 ft.
Number of Trails: 56 on 325 skiable acres
Lifts: 4 double chairs, 1 handle tow
Snowmaking: 38 percent of terrain
Season: late November–mid-April

According to the people at Smugglers', the name refers to a colorful character who enjoys a rich lifestyle but who does so without paying the duty customarily charged. Actually, "the Notch" is the closest thing to a hairpin curve in Vermont and is, except in winter, the route linking Stowe to Smugglers'. A historical archives story has it that in the 1800s goods were smuggled through the Notch—hence the name.

Three interconnected mountains, Madonna (2,100-foot vertical), Sterling, (1,500-foot vertical), and Morse (1,150-foot vertical), are the skiing peaks here. The concentration of expert-level skiing is on Madonna, with a 54 percent pitch on a black-diamond stretch called Freefall. Nearly half the overall terrain is rated for intermediates, and the easiest trails for novice-beginners are concentrated on Morse Mountain. Sterling offers both open and gladed trails; the 2.5-mile Rum Runner is a favorite of lower intermediate skiers.

Because all the vacation activity is focused on a self-sufficient condominium village at the base of the mountains, Smugglers' Notch has recognized its value to families as an easy-to-get-around resort. Cars can be parked and forgotten because everything is within walking distance of the condominiums.

Village amenities include, in addition to sports facilities, a post office, country store and deli, child-care center, sports shop, lounges, and a variety of restaurants. Smugglers' is designed as a walk-about village with centralized activities, though nightclubs and restaurants in town remain a lure.

Activities for guests seem endless, much like a "Club Med for Families." Late afternoons mean sipping hot chocolate, snowgolf, and broomball with celebrity Mogul Mice guests. A different family night program is offered each evening ranging from a New Games Festival to Wacky Hat Bingo to a sledding party. Entertainment is offered to parents later in the evening. The capper for a ski week or weekend is the Thursday and Saturday torchlight parade and fireworks show.

Smugglers' is indeed a resort that means what it says about a family playing together.

Practical Information for Smugglers' Notch

HOW TO GET THERE. Smugglers' Notch is 28 miles northeast of the Burlington International Airport and 5 miles southwest of Jeffersonville on Rte. 108.

By air. (For regional details, see *Practical Information for Bolton Valley*, above.) Call the resort at 644–8851 to arrange for limo service at the airport.

By car. From Burlington, take Rte. 15 east to Essex Junction and Jeffersonville and Rte. 108 south to Smugglers'.

TELEPHONES. The area code for all Vermont is 802.

ACCOMMODATIONS. Lodging choices are made simple at this self-contained village. You either want a private motel-type room with bath, a 5-bedroom condominium with fireplace, or something in between. Some condominiums are efficiencies with a kitchenette, and there are deluxe studios. Daily maid service is optional. Two-night per-person weekend rates, including lift tickets for two days of skiing and lessons, start at $165, depending on the size, luxury of the unit, and number of people in the party. "Mini-vacation" (3-day, 3-night) packages are available.

RESTAURANTS. Guests take their meals at on-premises and local restaurants. Given the limited number of restaurants, there are really only two price ranges: *Moderate,* $10–$15 per person, and *Inexpensive,* less than $10. The expensively

priced exceptions are the **Golden Horse at the Windridge Inn** (644
Cheval D'Or (644–5556), which serve classic French cuisine.

Bandito's Cantina and Restaurant. *Moderate;* 644–8884. Friendly,
sphere with flair for Tex-Mex. Take-out available.

The Club Cafe. *Moderate;* 644–8851. Slopeside location. Breakfast wi
noon buffet, après-ski, light fare at night.

The Crown & Anchor Pub Restaurant. *Moderate;* 644–2900. An Eng
ambience features à la carte dining.

Smugglers' Notch Inn. *Moderate;* 644–2412. Old New England inn serving Continental cuisine. Daily dinner, Sunday brunch.

Three Mountain Lodge. *Moderate;* 644–5736. A log lodge with quilt decor serves family meals—seafood and traditional fare.

The Village Restaurant. *Moderate.* 644–8851. Features American cuisine in a warm country atmosphere.

Base Lodge Cafeteria. *Inexpensive;* 644–8851. The place for everybody's favorite hamburgers and hot dogs.

The Brewski. *Inexpensive;* 644–5432. Casual lodge and restaurant. Serves pizza, salads, and sandwiches. Take-out available.

Jana's Cupboard. *Inexpensive;* 644–5454. Family diner featuring country-style breakfasts, lunch, and dinner specials.

McPherson's Pub. *Inexpensive;* 644–8851. Hot sandwiches, chili, and Mexican food are specialties.

The Village Cafeteria. *Inexpensive;* 644–8851. Daily breakfast and lunch specials, cafeteria style.

HOW TO GET AROUND. On busy days, a **shuttle** will take guest skiers from the lower mountain to the upper-mountain lifts. The village itself provides walk-to-everything convenience.

OTHER SPORTS AND ACTIVITIES. There are two indoor **tennis** courts; a heated indoor **aqua center** with a pool, saunas, and hot tub; **sleigh rides** and outdoor games such as broomball, snow soccer, and **ice skating** to complement the skiing. Snowboarders and telemarkers are welcome on the slopes. The resort also maintains over 23 miles of **cross-country** trails. *Nordland Villa,* one of the condominium clusters, also has a Scandinavian spa that includes a hot whirlpool, steam room, and massage by appointment; bathing suits are mandatory.

HINTS TO THE HANDICAPPED. The ski school staff here is equipped to work with blind skiers through the BOLD program. Call the resort for information: 644–8851.

CHILDREN'S ACTIVITIES. *Alice's Wonderland Child Care Center* is open to children aged 6 weeks–6 years from 8:30 A.M. to 4:30 P.M. The *Discovery Ski Camp* provides a full day of ski lessons, mountain games, sleigh rides, and storytelling for ages 3–6 years. The all-day *Adventure Ski Camp,* for ages 7–12, offers supervised ski instruction, ski treks, fun races, mountain adventure games, and a hot lunch. The *Explorer Ski Program* for ages 13–17 offers teenagers skiing adventures and games.

Part of the fun of the Smugglers' children's programs is a *Cookie Monster Race* held Thursdays and Sundays. Wee racers run an obstacle course, and at check points they have to eat chocolate chip cookies! Everyone's a winner with buttons and prizes.

NIGHTLIFE. Because this is a self-contained village, guests tend to stay put day and night, and after-dinner action takes place throughout the village. Nightly entertainment at the *Smugglers' Lounge* can be a piano player or a comedy routine; there's relaxed piano-bar music from 4 to 6 P.M. at the *Club Lounge,* followed by nightly live entertainment from 9 P.M. to 1 A.M.; and a DJ is on board with music for dancing and sing-alongs at *The Snow Snake.* On weekends and some other occasions, a live rock band appears at *The Meeting House.*

MIDWESTERN UNITED STATES

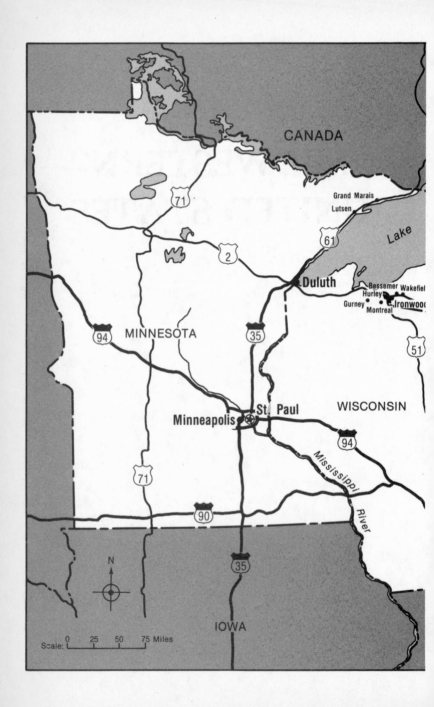

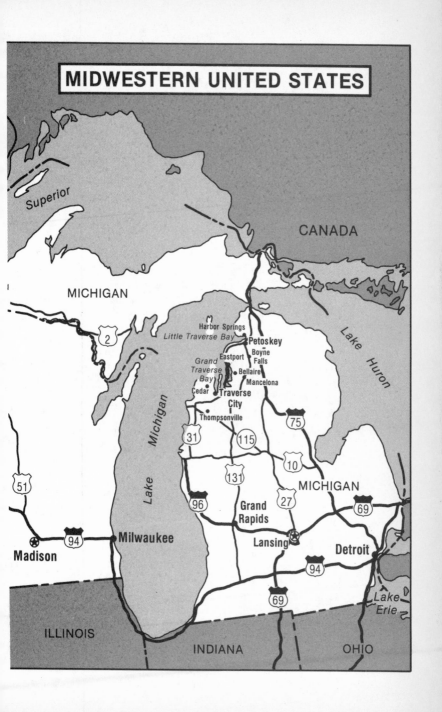

MIDWESTERN UNITED STATES

MIDWESTERN UNITED STATES

As in the Eastern United States, modern snowmaking technology at most Midwest ski areas provides winter recreational fun for millions. The long-established Midwest summer resort communities that combine the beauty of lakes and mountains are rapidly becoming sensitive to the advantages of selling snow.

There is absolutely no rule of thumb to go by in choosing what will be the "right" resort for your ski vacation. Families will lean toward the availability of children's programs and amenities; young people will especially want a choice of après-ski activity; ski fanatics will look for a variety of challenging terrain; new-to-the-slopes skiers will look for sound ski instructional programs. And there are, of course, many other variables to consider.

The right mind set, however, is perhaps the most important variable.

Just like theater, not every ski area is a heart-of-Broadway experience. But you can enjoy some fine performances in the few Midwest ski resort areas. And it's putting forth their best that motivates the folks behind the skiing you're bound to enjoy.

With most Midwest ski destinations located in Michigan, we've divided that state into Lower and Upper Peninsula, with the latter spilling over to a select area in Wisconsin.

Michigan

LOWER PENINSULA

In the northwestern corner of Michigan's Lower Peninsula are four ski resorts, all of which use the Traverse City/Grand Traverse area as their hub. They are Shanty Creek/Schuss Mountain Resort, Crystal Mountain Resort, and Sugar Loaf Resort. Also part of the ski roster (but not reviewed in this guide) is The Homestead in Glen Arbor, which offers 15 trails serviced by 3 chairs and a rope tow and cross-country skiing. (For details call 616–334–5000.)

Traverse City itself is the tourist center of this part of Michigan, with a cosmopolitan environment and lots of professionals enjoying the recreation the region offers. Primarily, the tourist facilities, both lodging and dining, are geared to warm-weather water pursuits; however, an increasing number recognize the popular winter tourist attraction called snow that falls in great abundance in the region, and many offer off-season rates during the winter months for cross-country and alpine skiers and snowmobile enthusiasts.

Traverse City also enjoys the title of Cherry Capital of the World. A one-time lumbering center, it also made history when wood from this region rebuilt Chicago after the famous Chicago fire.

Guests come here year-round to enjoy the accomplishments of students at the Interlochen Arts Academy, and a winter event, the North American VASA Race, attracts the top U.S. cross-country skiers and those from 11 foreign countries.

CRYSTAL MOUNTAIN

Thompsonville MI 49683
Tel: 616–378–2911 or 800–321–4637

Snow Report: 616–378–2911
Area Vertical: 375 feet
Number of Trails: 23 or 70 skiable acres
Lifts: 1 quadruple chair, 2 triple chairs, 2
*   double chairs, 2 rope tows*
Snowmaking: 95 percent of terrain
Season: late November–early April

Crystal Mountain is a self-contained resort on Michigan's Lower Peninsula that combines its 23 alpine trails with a 30-km cross-country facility

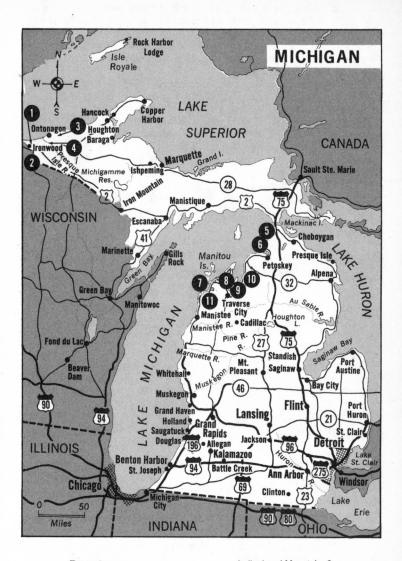

Resorts

Big Powderhorn, 1
Blackjack, 4
Boyne Highlands, 6
Boyne Mountain, 10
Crystal Mountain, 11

Indianhead Mountain, 3
Nub's Nob, 5
Schuss Mountain, 9
Shanty Creek, 8
Sugar Loaf, 7
Whitecap Mountain, 2

that also provides access to an additional 15 km of state-maintained trails. There's not only night skiing on 13 mountain trails, but 4 kilometers of cross-country trails are lit, along with widened, groomed tracks for cross-country skating.

The area vertical is big by Midwest standards, with trails primarily in the intermediate category (45 percent), 25 percent marked for novices, and 30 percent for advanced skiers.

Beginning skiers are still catered to here, with a free rope tow and beginner's area open all the time. Four children's programs take care of newborns through age 16. Children sleep and ski free midweek.

There's an innovative way to sell lift tickets here, called "Ski by the Hour," with tickets sold in 4-hour time increments, to attract day skiers who can't or don't want to ski the full day.

Crystal Mountain has been in the business of attracting skiers for 30 years, but skiing in the area actually came about in the early 1950s when a local high school principal rigged up a rope tow in his own backyard, then caught ski fever and went looking for bigger mountains. Today there is on-premises lodging for over 500 skiing folk, plus an indoor pool and fitness center.

SCHUSS MOUNTAIN RESORT

Schuss Mountain Rd.
Mancelona MI 49659
Tel: 616–533–8621 or 800–748–0249

*Snow Report: 616–533–8621 or 800–748–
0249*
Area Vertical: 450 ft.
Number of Trails: 17 on 50 skiable acres
*Lifts: 1 triple chair, 3 double chairs, 2 rope
tows*
Snowmaking: 100 percent of terrain
Season: late November–March

SHANTY CREEK

Shanty Creek Rd.
Bellaire MI 49615
Tel: 616–533–8621 or 800–748–0249

*Snow Report: 616–533–8621 or 800–748–
0249*
Area Vertical: 250 ft.
Number of Trails: 13 on 50 skiable acres
Lifts: 2 double chairs, 1 rope tow
Snowmaking: 100 percent of terrain
Season: December–March

Schuss Mountain and Shanty Creek are under the same management, which makes sense because the two are only 3½ miles down the road from each other. They offer the skier two resorts literally for the price of one, since guests have access to all the amenities at both resorts. Transportation is provided between the two. Both, therefore, are fortunate to be positioned in the snowbelt that graces this part of the northern Lower Peninsula of Michigan, but both still rely heavily on snowmaking to augment Mother Nature's largesse.

Schuss has been around since 1968, when it got a lot of publicity for marketing itself as the Kingdom of Schuss, complete with a village square entered over a moat and through a covered gatehouse. Vestiges of this romance still remain, but, over the years, the resort has become a full-service, year-round facility. The architecture at Shanty Creek is newer, but on winter weekends the rates stay the same for reciprocal lift and lodging packages.

Although there are two expert slopes at Shanty Creek, the bulk of the terrain here is geared to the beginner–intermediate skier, while that at Schuss Mountain is for the intermediate–advanced skier.

Between the two resorts, the complex offers 650 accommodations, including on-mountain hotels, condominiums, and chalets/private homes.

SUGAR LOAF RESORT

Cedar MI 49621
Tel: 616–228–5461 or 800–748–0117

Snow Report: 616–228–5461 or 800–748–0117
Area Vertical: 500 ft.
Number of Trails: 20
Lifts: 1 triple chair, 5 double chairs, 1 J-Bar
Snowmaking: 80 percent of terrain
Season: late November–mid-March

Sugar Loaf is a year-round resort 18 miles northwest of Traverse City. The skiing terrain on the back face of the mountain overlooks Lake Michigan and the Manitou Islands, with a series of gladed runs up to a mile in length for both intermediates and beginners. The front face has shorter and steeper trails including "Awful-Awful," touted as the Midwest's steepest slope. In all, the 20 downhill slopes offer 20 percent "easiest" terrain with "more difficult" and "most difficult" at 40 percent each, comprising the rest of the slopes. The 500-foot vertical is hefty for the Midwest. Snowboarders have their own half-pipe, and snowboarding lessons are available.

Twenty-six kilometers of cross-country terrain weave through the mountain's base area, offering skiers a choice of either alpine or cross-country skiing. Another option: Eighty percent of the mountain is lit for night skiing.

Practical Information for
Lower Peninsula Ski Resorts

HOW TO GET THERE. By air. Cherry Capital Airport (616–947–2250), 3 miles southeast of Traverse City, is served by 3 commuter carrier lines: *Northwest Airlink* (800–225–2525), from Detroit; *American Eagle* (800–433–7300), from Chicago's O'Hare Airport; and *Midway Airlines* (616–947–2401), serving Chicago's Midway Airport. Air service to the region is weather dependent, so be sure to check daily flight plans. Car rentals are available from *Cherry Capital Cab* (616–941–8294), *Hertz* (616–946–7051), and *Ugly Duckling* (616–941–8445). *Grand Traverse Limousine* (616–929–1559) in Traverse City provides a **shuttle** limousine service. The Antrim County Airport in Bellaire can service a variety of planes, including a DC-9, for skiers going to Shanty Creek or Schuss Mountain. Frankfort City Airport in Benzie City can service up to a small private jet on its 3,250-foot-long runway. This airport is 16 miles from Crystal Mountain. At the base of Sugar Loaf there is also a 4,300-ft. all-weather airstrip.

By car. From Detroit, follow I-75 north to Grayling; then Rte. 72 west to Kalkaska, and north on US 131. Two of the ski areas—Shanty Creek and Schuss

Mountain Resort—are within a few miles of each other off US 131. To get to Crystal Mountain, stay on Rte. 72 to Traverse City, then take Rtes. 31 and 115 to the ski area. For Sugar Loaf, follow Rtes. 72 and 22 out of Traverse City.

TELEPHONES. The area code for this region of the Lower Peninsula is 616.

ACCOMMODATIONS. An organization has been established to give information and book reservations at many establishments in the region. It's called *Michigan RSVP* (Reservation Service & Vacation Planning) and it can be contacted at 8727 Palaestrum, Williamsburg, MI 49684; 800–748–0576. An informative brochure listing resort information is available from the Michigan Travel Bureau. Call 800–5432–YES for a free copy.

At Sugar Loaf **mountainside,** there are 150 rooms in the base lodge and another 150 rooms in townhouse accommodations. Rates, including lift tickets, start at $59 per person per night, double occupancy. Up to three children 18 and under sleep and ski free when sharing accommodations with two paying adults in the hotel. Contact *Central Reservations,* Sugar Loaf Resort, Cedar 49621; 800–748–0117. Mountainside lodging at Shanty Creek and Schuss Mountain is coordinated through *Schuss Mountain Resort,* Schuss Mountain Rd., Mancelona 49659; 587–9162. Condominium prices range from $110 to $180 per night, depending on the size of the unit, and private homes range from $165 to $220.

In this selection of accommodations, those listed under Traverse City Area could serve skiers at all four areas. However, Crystal Mountain, located 28 miles away from Traverse City, has a cluster of accommodations near the mountain. They are listed separately. *The Traverse City Chamber of Commerce,* 202 Grandview Parkway, Traverse City 49684; 947–5075, can be contacted for additional assistance.

Hotel rates are based on double occupancy. Categories, determined by price, are *Expensive,* $70 and up; *Moderate,* $40–$70; and *Inexpensive,* less than $40.

Traverse City Area

Expensive

Grand Traverse Resort Village. US 31, Acme 48610; 938–2100. Geared for holidays, with indoor pool, sauna, Jacuzzi, exercise equipment, whirlpool, indoor racquetball and tennis courts; ice skating and cross-country skiing; condominium and motel accommodations.

Waterfront Inn/Best Western. 2061 US 31, Traverse City 49684; 938–1100. A modern motel facility with an indoor pool, prides itself in offering fine dining.

Moderate

Chateau Reef. Box 295, Suttons Bay 49682; 271–3634. Near a quaint, artsy village, 14 units on the beach, some housekeeping units.

Colonial Inn. 460 Munson Ave., Traverse City 49685; 947–5436. A 44-unit motel with in-room heart-shaped whirlpools, on-premises sauna, Jacuzzi and exercise room.

Fox Haus Motor Lodge. 704 Munson Ave., Traverse City 49685; 947–4450. An 80-unit motel with some housekeeping units, sauna, game and exercise rooms.

Heritage Inn. 417 Munson Ave., Traverse City 49685; 947–9520. A 21-unit motel that offers special senior rates and is known for friendly hospitality and free coffee.

Park Place Hotel. Corner of Park and States Sts., Traverse City 49685; 946–5000. A local landmark that rises 10 stories and offers top-of-the-building dining.

Pine Crest Motel. 360 Munson Ave., Traverse City 49685; 947–8900. A 32-unit motel located near Northwestern Michigan College.

Shanty Creek-Schuss Mountain Resort. Mancelona 49659; 533–8621 or 800–748–0249. Two separate lodging facilities, 3½ miles apart. Continuous free shuttle service between properties; 650 rooms, condos, suites, and chalets; fully equipped health club, indoor-outdoor pools with Jacuzzis.

Shoreside Inn. 5841 US 31, Acme 49610; 938–1888. A 16-unit motel on the water on East Bay Beach; near marina.

Sugar Loaf Resort. Cedar 49621; 800–748–0117. Over 200 units in hotel, condominium, and townhouse accommodations, some with fireplaces; sauna, Jacuzzi.

Inexpensive

The following establishments fall into the inexpensive category during the winter months, which is considered off season in the Traverse City region. In Traverse City (49685): *Bayshore Motel,* 833 E. Front St., 946–4798; *Best Value Motel,* 828 East Front St., 947–4330; *Cedar Lake Motel,* 11998 West Bayshore Dr., 946–7442; *Days Inn,* 429 Munson Ave., 941–0208; *D'Orr Haus Motor Lodge,* 894 Munson Ave., 947–9330; *Driftwood Motel,* 1861 US 31, 938–1600; *Ranch Rudolf,* 6841 Brownbridge Rd., 947–9529; *Sleepy Hollow Motel,* 939 S. Memorial, 943–4740.

Outside town are *Granada Inn,* 720 N. Cedar, Kalkaska 49646, 258–9131; *Knollwood,* 5777 US 31, Acme 49610, 938–2040; *Maple Lane Resort,* 8720 Dorsey Rd., Empire 49630, 334–3413.

BED-AND-BREAKFAST TREASURES. In Traverse City, these establishments include *The Broadbrick Inn,* 6369 Secor, 946–0650; *The Cider House,* 5515 Barney Rd., 947–2833; *Painted Pony Inn,* 8392 West M–82, 947–9117; *Warwickshire Inn,* 5037 Barney Rd., 946–7176.

Crystal Mountain Area

The Brookside Inn. *Expensive.* US 31, Beulah 49617; 882–7271. Look for canopy-covered waterbeds, a Polynesian spa, and rooms with log stoves, some with saunas and steam baths.

Hotel Frankfort. *Expensive.* Main St., Frankfort 49635; 882–7271. Under the same management as Brookside Inn, with similar amenities.

The Beach House. *Moderate.* Beulah 49617; 882–5075. A one-time boarding house with antiques and rooms overlooking Crystal Lake.

Crystal Mountain. *Moderate.* Rte. M-115, Thompsonville 49683; 378–2911. Has 147 hotel rooms and luxury condo units plus 21 chalets in a resort setting.

Harbor Lights Complex. *Moderate.* Main St., Frankfort 49635; 352–9614. A 38-room motel and 6-unit condominium complex.

Sunny Woods Resort Motel. *Moderate.* US 31, Honor 49640; 325–3952. Offers motel accommodations.

Hammer's Riverside Resort. *Inexpensive.* US 31, Benzonia 49616; 882–7783. Individual housekeeping cabins.

Mountain Valley Motel. *Inexpensive.* Cadillac Hwy., Thompsonville 49683; 378–2990. A 20-unit motel with indoor swimming pool.

Pine Knot. *Inexpensive.* US 31, Beulah 49619; 882–7751. A motel with some kitchenette units.

The Plaza Motel. *Inexpensive.* US 31, Benzonia 49616; 882–4314. Housekeeping units.

Rosier's Motel. *Inexpensive.* US 31, Benzonia 49616; 882–4891. A modern, 13-unit motel.

RESTAURANTS. Throughout this region of the Lower Peninsula, the visitor will find many places to dine out. What he or she won't find, however, are high prices. In this selection, restaurants are listed by price category: *Expensive,* $12 and up; *Moderate,* $7–$12; *Inexpensive,* less than $7. Unless otherwise specified, those listed in the moderate and expensive ranges accept the major credit cards.

Expensive

Hannah Lay Room. Grand Traverse Resort Village, US 31, Acme; 938–2100. Gourmet French cuisine served in a quiet, romantic atmosphere. Some items prepared tableside.

Hilton Shanty Creek. Bellaire; 533–8621. American and European cuisine with breathtaking hilltop view.

The Jordan Inn. 228 Main St., East Jordan; 536–2631. European country cuisine.

Reflections Restaurant & Lounge. 2061 US 31, Traverse City; 938–2321. Waterfront views and fresh seafood specialties.

The Rowe Inn. On East Jordan Rd., Ellsworth; 588–7351. One of the area's best, offering European-flair dining.

Tapawingo. Lake St., Ellsworth; 588–7971. Michigan-grown foods of the season are specialties.

Trillium Restaurant and Nightclub. Grand Traverse Resort, US 31, Acme; 938–5455. Views of Grand Traverse Bay served up with regional American cuisine.

Moderate

Bowers Harbor Inn. 13512 Peninsula Dr., Traverse City; 223–4222. Elegant dining in century-old mansion, extensive wine list. Reservations suggested.

Campbell's of Torch. East Torch Lake at Clam River, Torch River; 377–4171. Family dining, with emphasis on Italian foods, chicken, and seafood.

Crystal Mountain. Rte. M–115, Thompsonville; 378–2911. Look for 20 percent discount for seniors between 5 and 6 P.M.

Dills Olde Towne Saloon. 4235 Union, Traverse City; 947–7534. A century-old lumbering saloon offers seafood and fresh meats.

Embers on the Bay. 5555 US 31, Acme; 938–1300. Famous for 1-pound pork chops.

Hearthstone Restaurant. M–88, 2 miles south of Bellaire; 533–6531. Steaks and chops.

La Senorita. 1245 S. Garfield Ave., Traverse City; 947–8820. Mexican foods to warm the inner skier.

Park Place Hotel. 300 East State, Traverse City; 946–5000. Choice of old-fashioned dining or an 1890s pub menu.

The Pinestead Reef. 1265 US 31, Traverse City; 947–5493. Views of East Bay over dinner.

Scheldes. 2030 S. Airport Rd. and 714 Munson, Traverse City; 946–0981. Steaks and seafood.

Sugar Loaf Resort. Cedar; 228–5461. Choice of Tonelli's Pizzeria & Finer Delicatessen or the Four Seasons Dining Room with extensive menu.

Inexpensive

Bonanza Family Restaurant. 1112 S. Garfield Ave., Traverse City; 941–7472. Salad bar and family-style dining.

Cheepeng. 3650 US 31 South, Traverse City; 947–2803. Cantonese and Mandarin choices.

China Fair. 1357 S. Airport, Traverse City; 941–5844. Cantonese, Mandarin, and Szechuan choices.

Sleders Family Tavern & Victorian Porch. 717 Randolph, Traverse City; 947–9213. Open since 1882, so they must be doing something right.

Union Street Station. 117 S. Union, Traverse City; 941–1930. Vegetarian, some ethnic specialties.

U & I Lounge. 214 E. Front St., Traverse City; 946–8932. The place for Greek food.

Crystal Mountain Area

Moderate

The Brookside Inn. US 31, Beulah; 882–7271. Look for country-cured ham and antique-filled walls.

The Cabbage Shed. Elberta; 352–9843. Homemade soups are specialties in this rustic, homey setting.

The Sail Inn. US 31, Benzonia; 882–4971. Seafood specialties and a salad bar displayed in a sailboat lure patrons here.

The Wildflower. Crystal Mountain Resort, Rte. M–115, Thompsonville; 378–2911. Popular cuisine served up with salad bar.

INFORMATION SERVICES. For information on the region, contact the *Traverse City Chamber of Commerce,* 202 E. Granview Parkway, Traverse City, MI 49684; 947–5075. For details on facilities near Crystal Mountain, contact the *Benzie County Chamber of Commerce,* Box 204, Benzonia, MI 49616; 882–5802.

HOW TO GET AROUND. A **car** would be extremely helpful, especially if you intend to ski all four areas. However, there is some **shuttle** service available. A free shuttle, for instance, makes regular runs between Schuss Mountain and Shanty Creek, a 3½-mile trip. Some lodging establishments in the region may also supply shuttle service. If you do not intend to drive, be sure to check when making reservations.

SEASONAL EVENTS. Sugarloaf has hosted 11 consecutive *Michigan Special Winter Olympic Games* for participants 8 years and older in early February. For information call 774–3911. Two major *biathlons* are held here in January and February.

Shanty Creek-Schuss Mountain activities begin in December with *Spense Bock Youth Race Camp.* In February, the *50k White Pine Stampede,* a cross-country race, is held during the first week; a *10k event* to benefit Easter Seals is held in the fourth week. The first weekend in March is *Tropicana Kids Day* at **Shanty Creek,** with fun events for the entire family. The *Slush Cup Weekend* is held in March at **Schuss Mountain;** it involves an obstacle race plus a slalom over a pond of ice cold water. Something called a *Tutti-Frutti Contest* goes on at about the same time, involving stuffing fruit into snowsuits.

OTHER SPORTS AND ACTIVITIES. At **Crystal Mountain** there's an **indoor pool** and **fitness center, sleigh rides, movies,** and moonlight **cross-country** safaris, all offered as complimentary activities.

At **Schuss,** there is **cross-country** skiing available with 50 km of trails connecting to Shanty Creek's ski-touring network, for a total of 59 km of terrain. Schuss also has horse-drawn **sleigh rides** during the week, as well as **saunas** and indoor **pools.**

At **Shanty Creek** there are two **racquetball** courts, indoor pools, and a fully equipped **health spa** with sauna, steam room, and Nautilus.

Sugar Loaf has an **indoor pool,** whirlpool, and **Nautilus room. Jazzercise** classes are available, as are fireside **sing-alongs** and **hayrides.**

NASTAR races are a staple at all four resorts.

HINTS TO THE HANDICAPPED. All the "Big Four" ski resorts participate in programs for the handicapped. At Crystal Mountain, for instance, racing events are conducted for the *Blind Outdoor Leisure Development* (BOLD) program. Special attention is also given at the resorts for people with other physical disabilities or impairments. Contact the base lodge at each ski area for details.

CHILDREN'S ACTIVITIES. Crystal Mountain claims its day-care programs aren't just depositories for kids. *Hot Shots* is an intensive instructional program for kids aged 11–16. The *Mountain Midget* program for ages 3–4 combines nursery care, lunch, snacks, and equipment with supervised skiing activities in a special terrain garden. Gentle inclines and walk-up mats facilitate learning and development of coordination. Children, ages 5 and up, can enroll in a 10 A.M.–4 P.M. program that includes instruction, lots of skiing fun, lunch, and hot chocolate. *The Nursery* offers day care for newborns to age 5 from 9 A.M. to 5 P.M. daily. At **Schuss Mountain** day care is available at $8 for a half day, $15 for a full day. The *Ski Academy* takes children aged 5–10 and involves them in half-day and full-day instructional fun on snow.

At **Shanty Creek,** kids ages 5–10 can join the *Kids' Academy* for a lesson/ski experience from 10:30 A.M. to 4 P.M. The nursery accepts infants to age 10 from 9:30 A.M. to 12:30 P.M. and from 1:30 to 6:30 P.M.

At **Sugar Loaf,** the *Kids Club* offers all-day supervision on skis for ages 4–12. A nursery accepts non-skiing youngsters under 4 from 9 A.M. to 5 P.M. daily. Cost is $15 per child.

For detailed information and reservations, contact the base lodge at each ski resort.

NIGHTLIFE. Bands light up the Traverse City night at the *Holiday Inn,* 615 East Front St. (947–3700), offering top-40 and easy listening entertainment. Look for jazz at the *Union Street Station,* 117 S. Union St. (941–1930).

There's entertainment also at *JRR's Warehouse Saloon,* 205 Lake, Traverse City (941–4422). There's showband entertainment in the *Trillium Nightclub* at Grand Traverse Resort in Acme (938–5455), Tuesday through Saturday, with the music switching to jazz under the stars in a glass-enclosed nightclub on Sunday and Monday evenings.

Nightlife is focused right at the mountains, too, with entertainment Monday–Saturday nights at Shanty Creek and Schuss. Trios are the standard fare at Shanty Creek, and live contemporary music at Schuss. You will also find après-ski activities at Sugar Loaf Resort and Grand Traverse Resort Village.

For skiers at Crystal Mountain, the *Hotel Frankfort* in Frankfort (352–4303) offers a dinner theater. Folk singers appear at the *Cabbage Shed* in Elberta (352–9843). There's live entertainment on the third floor of the base lodge.

The lodge at Sugar Loaf features Friday- and Saturday-night rock 'n' roll, an après-ski guitar player daily, and some entertainment midweek.

LITTLE TRAVERSE BAY REGION

Three ski resorts in northwestern Michigan share the attractions of the Little Traverse Bay Region, whose claim to fame is year-round recreation. These are Boyne Highlands and Nub's Nob, both in Harbor Springs, and Boyne Mountain, about 25 miles south in Boyne Falls.

Like most of their midwestern counterparts, these ski areas augment nature's bounty with snowmaking systems that cover over 90 percent of the skiable terrain, ensuring seasons that last from late November to mid-April.

Since the 1800s, this region of Michigan has been primarily in the summer resort business, thanks to the beauty of Lake Michigan. However, in the past 25 years, it has also grown to be the winter capital of the Midwest.

BOYNE HIGHLANDS

Harbor Springs MI 49740
Tel: 800–462–6963

Snow Report: 800–462–6963
Area Vertical: 520 ft.
Number of Trails: 27 on 225 skiable acres
Lifts: 1 high-speed detachable quad, 3
*   quadruple chairs, 4 triple chairs, 2 rope*
*   tows*
Snowmaking: 100 percent of terrain
Season: late November–mid-April

BOYNE MOUNTAIN

Boyne Falls MI 49713
Tel: 800–462–6963

Snow Report: 800–462–6963
Area Vertical: 460 ft.
Number of Trails: 18 on 325 skiable acres
Lifts: 4 quadruple chairs, 6 double chairs, 1
*   triple chair, 1 rope tow*
Snowmaking: 100 percent of terrain
Season: late November–mid-April

These two resorts are under the same ownership and, although about 25 miles apart, they offer interchangeable lift tickets and similar programs and amenities.

Boyne Mountain, home of the first chairlift in northern Michigan, was founded in 1947 by Everett Kircher and, in 1963, he purchased and greatly expanded and developed Boyne Highlands, which now features the first high-speed detachable quad chairlift in Michigan. Together both hills comprise 10,000 acres in Charlevoix and Emmet counties.

Much of the skiing at Boyne Mountain is geared to the advanced skier, with 45 percent "most difficult," 30 percent "more difficult," and 25 percent "easiest terrain." At Boyne Highlands the split among all three skiing levels is about equal.

There's night skiing on Wednesdays and Saturdays at Boyne Mountain and Tuesdays and Fridays at Boyne Highlands. On Saturday mornings, first-time skiers are eligible for free ski lessons at both areas.

At Boyne Highlands there's access to two cross-country trails via a ride on a chairlift with a total of 26 km of ski touring terrain overall. And at Boyne Mountain, look for 13 km of tracked and groomed ski-touring terrain.

NUB'S NOB

Harbor Springs MI 49740
Tel: 800–878–NUBS

Snow Report: 616–526–2131
Area Vertical: 427 ft.
Number of Trails: 18 on 150 skiable acres
Lifts: 3 double chairs, 2 triple chairs, 1
    quadruple chair, 1 rope tow
Snowmaking: 100 percent of terrain
Season: late November–early April

If there was ever any question about where good snow's to be found, the answer lies at Nub's Nob. Nub's Nob made skiing history when its snowmaking crew took their guns to the 1984 Winter Olympic Games at Sarajevo. Today, James Bartlett, general manager, sticks close to home, protecting his 150 skiable acres with machine-made snow.

The mountain has been serving skiers for over 30 years, offering 30 percent "easiest" terrain, 40 percent "more difficult" terrain, and 30 percent "most difficult" terrain. An intermediate run called Sno-Pro is the longest of its type in the area, offering skiing the whole family can enjoy together, along with vistas of Lake Michigan and Little Traverse Bay. The slopes of Nub's Nob South are relatively protected from the northwest winter winds that can really blow here.

The resort offers night skiing from 6 to 10 P.M. Thursdays, Fridays, and Saturdays (after the holidays) and NASTAR is popular here.

In addition to turning out great snow, Nub's Nob pays attention to the details like offering palatable cafeteria food. Specialties include a chicken sandwich (without the skin) and others geared to low-cholesterol diets.

Practical Information for
Little Traverse Bay Resorts

HOW TO GET THERE. Boyne Highlands and Nub's Nob are both located approximately 5 miles from Harbor Springs, 10 miles from Petoskey, and 275 miles from Detroit. **By car.** From Detroit, take I–75, Michigan's principal north–south highway, and follow it most of the way northward. At Indian River, go east on Rte. 68, which leads into Rte. 31. Follow signs to the two resorts. For Boyne Mountain, leave I–75 at Gaylord, then go west on Rte. 32 and a short distance north on Rte. 131 to the ski resort.

By air. The Emmet County Airport (539–8441) is serviced by *American Eagle* and *Missauba* airlines. At the airport, car rentals are available from *Hertz* (800–654–3131) and various limousine services. Also, within walking distance of the Boyne Mountain ski area is a paved and lighted 4,200-ft. airstrip for private aircraft.

TELEPHONES. The area code for the Little Traverse Bay region of Michigan is 616.

ACCOMMODATIONS. Lodging at **mountainside** has all sorts of possibilities in condominium and hotel settings. Each of the main lodges at the two ski resorts can serve as central reservations for mountainside and other lodgings. At Boyne Highlands, *Bartley House* on Hedrick Rd. (526–2183) offers 65 rooms in a hotel setting with all the amenities of a resort. The *Boyne Highlands Inn* (526–2171) at that mountain has 165 rooms in a Swiss alpine motif, and the *Heather Highlands Inn* (526–2171) offers deluxe condo-hotel living.

At Boyne Mountain, there's a choice of 235 rooms between the *Boyne Mountain Lodge* and *Mountain Villa Condominiums,* all offering walk-to-the-slopes convenience. There are also some mini-suites available. Contact the lodge for details, 549–2441.

The *Boyne Country Convention and Visitors Bureau,* Box 694, Petoskey, MI 49770 (800–456–0197 or 348–1810), also provides information on lodgings most accessible to the three ski areas.

There are a number of condominium/private home complexes open to skiers. In this region, categories by price are *Expensive,* $70–$100, which is the category of mountainside accommodations listed above; *Moderate,* $50–$70; and *Inexpensive,* less than $50. The rates are per person per night, based on double occupancy in a hotel room, 1-bedroom, or studio condo.

Expensive

Birchwood Farm Estate. Box 497, Harbor Springs 49740; 526–2156. These private homes are fully equipped and have 3 to 5 bedrooms.

Graham Real Estate. Main St., Harbor Springs 49740; 526–6251. 2–3 bedroom homes, most with fireplaces.

The Harborage. 500 Front St., Boyne City 49712; 800–456–4313. A condominium marina on Lake Charlevoix with 2–4 bedroom units. Whirlpools.

Harborside Inn. Main St., Harbor Springs 49740; 526–6238. 24 luxury suites with fireplaces, whirlpool baths, kitchens, color TV.

Stafford's Bay View Inn. US 31, Petoskey 49770; 347–2771. A 104-year-old Victorian country inn with 30 rooms, private baths, on-premises restaurant.

Wildwood on Walloon. 2775 Wildwood Harbor Rd., Boyne City 49712; 582–9616. Three- to 6-bedroom condos with fireplaces on Walloon Lake.

Moderate

Alpine Resort. 1116 W. Gruler, Petoskey 49770; 347–8501. Cabins or chalets that sleep up to 12 in well-appointed units with fireplaces.

Best Western Inn. US 131, Petoskey 49770; 800–528–1234. An 85-unit motel with indoor pool, whirlpool, exercise room, cable TV.

Birchwood Inn. M–119, Lake Shore Dr., Harbor Springs 49740; 800–530–9955. forty-four rooms overlooking Little Traverse Bay; cable TV; one of the area's better restaurants, too.

Days Inn. Rtes. 31/131, Petoskey 49770; 347–8717. Enjoy indoor pool, Jacuzzi, and TV with HBO at this 92-unit motor lodge.

Hamlet Village Resort Homes and Condos. Pleasantview Rd., Harbor Springs 49740; 526–2641. Both resort homes and condos, accessible to chairlifts; cross-country skiing on properties.

Harbor Cove. Box 544, Harbor Springs 49740; 800–678–1036. Cross-country ski out the door of these 2–4-bedroom townhouses.

Hideaway Valley Condominiums. Box 544, Harbor Springs 49740; 347–7347. A secluded wooded setting for these 3–4-bedroom townhouses; cross-country skiing and snow-mobiling on premises.

Holiday Inn. US 131, Petoskey 49770; 800–HOLIDAY. A 144-room motel with indoor swimming, sauna, whirlpool, and color TV.

Stafford's Perry Hotel. Bay and Lewis Sts., Petoskey 49770; 800–456–1917 or 347–4000. An 1899, completely restored hotel in historic gaslight shopping district. Restaurant, cocktail lounge, indoor whirlpool.

Trout Creek Condominiums. Pleasantview Rd., Harbor Springs 49740; 800–678–3923. Fine views of Boyne Highlands from these 1–3-bedroom condo units, adjacent to cross-country trails.

Inexpensive

Clarion Terrace Carriage Inn. 216 Fairview, Petoskey 49770; 800–530–9898 or 347–2410. Fully restored 1911 Victorian inn. Private baths, restaurant, Continental breakfasts.

Coach House North. US 31, Petoskey 49770; 347–8281. A 20-room motel only 6 miles from Nub's Nob.

Econo Lodge. US 131, So. Petoskey 49770; 800–748–0417 or 348–3324. Sixty-two rooms adjacent to entertainment center and restaurant, indoor pool.

Green Roof Motor Inn. West US 131, So. Petoskey 49770; 348–3900. Has 134 rooms in basic inn. Restaurant at Holiday Inn next door. ·

Sundown Motel. 525 W. Mitchell St., US 31, Petoskey 49770; 348–4380. Sound-proof rooms, near restaurants and lounges, holds groups of up to 100.

RESTAURANTS. Because this is a four-season resort area, there's a collection of fine restaurants, with *Expensive* meals costing $14–$21; *Moderate,* $10–$14; and *Inexpensive,* less than $10. Again and again, you will find white fish on the menu in both fancy and plain eateries. This is a regional favorite. Most major credit cards are accepted, but check first, particularly at the inexpensive places.

Expensive

Arboretum. M–119, Lake Shore, Harbor Springs; 526–6291. As the name suggests, a tropical environment with varied menu ranging from fish to lamb.

One Water Street. 1 Water St., Boyne City; 582–3434. Gourmet dining on the docks of the scenic lake. Considered one of the area's finest restaurants.

Stafford's Pier Restaurant. 102 Bay, Harbor Springs; 526–6201. Lunch and dinner are served in a modern setting on Lake Charlevoix.

Walloon Lake Inn. 4178 West St., Walloon Lake; 535–2999. A country inn overlooking the lake, offering gourmet dining with emphasis on fresh local fish.

Moderate

Andante. 321 Bay St., Petoskey; 348–3321. Upscale dining, Midwest cuisine, dinner only.

The New York. 101 State, Harbor Springs; 526–6285. Since 1904, a Victorian setting with hardwood floors and Tiffany-style lamps. Eclectic menu.

Northwood Restaurant. US 31, Oden; 347–3894. This is the place to come for fish 'n' chips. No liquor service.

Shelde's. 1315 US 31, No. Petoskey; 347–7747. For breakfast, lunch, or dinner. Steak restaurant with liquor service.

Teddy Griffin's Road House. 5025 Hedrick, Harbor Springs; 526–7805. Casual dining from pizza to steak.

Inexpensive

Bar Harbor. 100 State, Harbor Springs; 526–2671. A bar that serves up hamburgers to its hungry customers.

La Senorita. 1285 US 31, No. Petoskey; 347–7750. Mexican specialties for breakfast, lunch, and dinner. Best chicken wings in town. Cocktails.

Mitchell St. Pub. 426 E. Mitchell, Petoskey; 347–1801. Popular hang-out with good sandwiches and an extensive beer selection.

HOW TO GET AROUND. If you book at one of the mountainside accommodations, a vehicle is hardly necessary. Some of the hotels and other lodgings in the surrounding area may supply **shuttle** service to the slopes. Check when making your reservations. However, a **car** allows you to try your skiing skills at any of the three slopes.

SEASONAL EVENTS. At Nub's Nob a torchlight parade on **New Year's Eve** adds a thrilling and romantic glow to the slopes. Boyne Highlands hosts the *National Pro Ski Racing Team* in **January.** Also at that ski area, mid-**March** brings on *Crazy Spring Day Celebration.* At Boyne Mountain there's a *Spring Carnival* right after **St. Patrick's Day,** with live entertainment in the afternoons, special bands in the evenings, a costume party, and on-slope events. Similarly, Nub's Nob is festive in **March,** with a *Mardi Gras* that brings out the costumes, contests, and goofy fun.

OTHER SPORTS AND ACTIVITIES. There are outside heated pools, two outdoor Jacuzzis, and ice skating available at Boyne Highlands. Also sleigh rides can be arranged through *Sogonosh Stables* in Harbor Springs, 526–5766. The *Little Traverse Racquet Club,* 611 Woodview Dr., Petoskey (347–5450), offers indoor tennis, racquetball, and a health spa.

At Boyne Mountain and Boyne Highlands, look for outdoor heated pools, outdoor Jacuzzis, ice skating, and saunas. Call Boyne Mountain 526–2171 or Boyne Highlands 549–2441, or 800–GO–BOYNE for either resort.

Throughout this region you will find extensive facilities for ice skating, sledding, cross-country skiing, and snowmobiling.

CHILDREN'S ACTIVITIES. Youngsters aged 8 and under ski free when accompanied by a parent. Both this resort and Boyne Mountain also take pride in their *Austrian Children's Program* that involves children in lessons, lunch, dinner, and evening activities. The full-day program begins after breakfast and continues until 9 P.M. For ages 3–6 there's a nursery at each resort that operates 9 A.M. to noon and 1–5 P.M. Babysitters for toddlers can also be arranged.

At Nub's Nob, children 12 years old and under ski free—except holidays, evenings, and weekends. Nursery available daily except Wednesdays and every day during holidays. Open 8:30 A.M. to 5 P.M. for children age 3 months to 5 years. Call Nub's Nob (526–2131) for details.

For any of the on-premises programs, contact the base lodge at each of the three resorts.

NIGHTLIFE. There are live bands weekends at Boyne Mountain's *Day Bar* and nightly in its *Snowflake Lounge.* At Boyne Highlands, look for a trio performing six nights a week in the *Slopeside Lounge* and Warren Miller ski movies, two nights a week. Also at Boyne Highlands, from 4–7 P.M. Saturdays the troops are called out to rock 'n' roll at the *ZOO Bar.*

The *Holiday Inn,* US 131, Petoskey (347–6041), offers entertainment. There's a live band that plays at *Hoppy's of Harbor Springs,* Pleasantview Road (562–2189). A favorite place is *Victory's* in Petoskey, US 131 (347–4927), which has a live band Wednesday through Saturday nights.

UPPER PENINSULA

BIG POWDERHORN MOUNTAIN

Bessemer MI 49911
Tel: 906–932–4838

Snow Report: 906–932–4838
Area Vertical: 622 ft.
Number of Trails: 23 on 180 skiable acres
Lifts: 8 double chairs
Snowmaking: 90 percent of terrain
Season: late November–early April

BLACKJACK

Bessemer MI 49911
Tel: 906–229–5115
Reservations: 800–848–1125

Snow Report: 906–229–5115
Area Vertical: 465 ft.
Number of Trails: 16 on 90 acres
Lifts: 4 double chairs, 2 rope tows
Snowmaking: 60 percent of terrain
Season: late November–April

INDIANHEAD MOUNTAIN AND BEAR CREEK

Wakefield MI 49968
Tel: 906–229–5181

Snow Report: 906–229–5181
Area Vertical: 638 ft.
Number of Trails: 19 on 160 skiable acres
Lifts: 1 triple chair, 1 quadruple chair, 3
*   double chairs, 2 T-bars, 2 beginner lifts*
Snowmaking: 90 percent of terrain
Season: late November–early April

WHITECAP MOUNTAIN

Box D
Montreal WI 54550
Tel: 715–561–2227

Snow Report: 715–561–2227
Area Vertical: 400 ft.
Number of Trails: 33 on 450 skiable acres
Lifts: 1 quadruple chair, 4 double chairs, 2
*   rope tows*
Snowmaking: 80 percent of terrain
Season: Thanksgiving–early April

Blackjack is a mile as the crow flies from Indianhead, and Big Powderhorn is only 5 miles away. These three ski areas and a fourth, Whitecap, in nearby Montreal, Wisconsin, constitute a group called Big Snow Country, located on the western tip of the Upper Peninsula of Michigan. The region is characterized by rugged hills with a wilderness forest near Lake Superior's south shore.

Because of its northern location, the area's residents resemble their Canadian neighbors in speech characteristics, although the region is strongly ethnic, with a blend of Finns, Italians, and Slavs who came decades earlier to work the iron and copper mines.

The romance of the territory was captured in Edna Thurber's novel about the lumber industry, *Come and Get It,* and some old-timers still recall the roaring '20s when Al Capone and his brother ran a hotel in the area and there were almost as many bars as residents on Silver Street in Hurley, still the place for après-ski action with 28 bars for the population of 2,200.

The region's ski areas attract skiers from Chicago, Milwaukee, and Minneapolis-St. Paul. "Thank God Wisconsin is flat," says an Indianhead spokesperson who cherishes the Milwaukee market.

Because of the snowbelt that hugs the lake's south shore, the region gets reliably heavy snowfalls averaging 211 inches a year. However, snowmaking is also used at all the areas. Once on the mountains, skiers discover they're actually on a ridgeline facing west and looking out toward Lake Superior beyond the Ottawa National Forest.

The four resorts offer interchangeable lift tickets and naturally share their lodging and dining facilities. Blackjack encourages snowboarding with its own half-pipe.

Practical Information for the Upper Peninsula Areas

HOW TO GET THERE. By car. The four resorts are all accessible from major markets: from Milwaukee, Wisconsin, take Hwy 5, or 45; Minneapolis, US 2; Chicago, 51. Big Powderhorn Mountain is located off US 2, 2 miles from Bessemer; Indianhead is 1½ miles from Wakefield; Blackjack is 6 miles east of Ironwood; and Whitecap is 10 miles west of Ironwood. Look for signs for each turn-off.

By air. There is regularly scheduled service by *Great Lakes Airlines* into the Ironwood Airport (906–932–5808) from Chicago. Each ski area provides **shuttle** service for its guests.

By bus. *Greyhound* provides service to the Ironwood bus depot (906–932–4221) from Wisconsin and Illinois; *Four Star Bus Lines,* from Minneapolis-St. Paul; and *Wisconsin-Michigan Trailways,* from Wisconsin, Michigan, and Minnesota.

TELEPHONES. The area code for the three Michigan mountains is 906, and for Whitecap Mountain, Wisconsin, it is 715.

ACCOMMODATIONS. The Big Snow Country organization assists skiers with both snow reports (800–BSC–7000) and lodging (906–932–4850). The address is US 2 East, Ironwood, MI 49938.

There are lodging operations connected with all four mountains. They are *Big Powderhorn Lodging Association,* Powderhorn Rd., Bessemer, MI 49911 (800–222–3131), servicing 3,000 beds within 1½ miles of the mountain, mainly in chalets and condominiums; *Blackjack Lodging Reservation Inc.,* Blackjack Rd., Bessemer 49911 (800–848–1125), servicing 450 beds, mostly condominiums; *Whitecap Mountain Management Co.,* Box E, Montreal, WI 54550 (715–561–2776), servicing an estimated 650 slopeside beds, mostly condominiums with some motel units; and *Indianhead Reservations,* Indianhead Mountain, Wakefield, MI 49968 (800–3–INDIAN), servicing a combination of chalets, lodge rooms, and condos for up to 1,200.

Because of the mix of lodging available, mountainside accommodations can be considered inexpensive to upper moderate, predicated mostly on the number of people per unit.

Expensive in this region is $70 and up per room per night, with *Moderate* $40–$70, and *Inexpensive,* less than $40. All lodgings listed are within 15 miles of at least one of the four areas' slopes.

Expensive

Indianhead Valley Condos & Chalets. At Indianhead Mountain; 906–229–5113. Right at slopes. Deluxe lodgings featuring fireplaces, hot tubs, and saunas.

Powdermill Inn. Off US 2, Bessemer 49911; 906–932–0800. This is an A-frame, chalet-type building of logs and glass; the rooms offer access to indoor swimming, a whirlpool, sauna, restaurant, and game room.

Moderate

Circle Hills Resort. Rte. 513, Ironwood 49938; 906–932–3857. Luxury condominium living includes access to indoor pool, restaurant, and lounge.

Haven North Condos. Off Hwy. 51, Hurley, WI 54534; 715–561–5626. Completely furnished 1–3-bedroom condos with fully equipped kitchens, cable TV, maid service, fireplaces; access to indoor swimming and saunas at Holiday Inn across the street.

Hiawatha Lodging. US 2, Ironwood 49938; 906–932–5416. This is a lodging referral service offering a variety of establishments with some including health-spa and swimming amenities.

Holiday Inn. Off Hwy. 51, Hurley, WI 54534; 715–561–3030. Offers indoor recreation center with pool, whirlpool, saunas, exercise equipment, restaurant, and lounge; snowmobile trails out front door.

Towne House Motor Inn. Half-block off business Rte. 2, Ironwood 49938; 906–932–2101. A downtown location with weekend entertainment, restaurant, lounge; some king-size beds; newest facility in town.

Inexpensive

Armata Motel. US 2, Ironwood 49938; 906–932–4421. Features 12 ground floor units with color TV, tubs and showers; car plug-ins.

Comfort Inn. US 2, Ironwood 49938; 906–932–2224. New facility with indoor pool and Jacuzzis in some rooms.

Crestview Motel. US 2, Ironwood 49938; 906–932–4845. In-room coffee, cable TV, and free use of sauna come with rooms.

Davey's Motel. US 2, Ironwood 49938; 906–932–2020. Twenty-four motel and housekeeping units, color TV, daily family rates, and special welcome to snowmobilers.

Hedgerow Lodging. US 2, Bessemer 49911; 906–663–6950. Individual A-frame chalets with kitchens.

Super 8 Motel. US 2, Ironwood 49938; 906–932–3395. Typical chain motel. Whirlpool on premises.

RESTAURANTS. Whether you dine in Michigan or in Wisconsin, you can expect fine German and Scandinavian dining rooms serving fresh fish from the abundance of waterways in this region. Restaurant price categories are *Expensive,* $12 and up; *Moderate,* $8–$12; and *Inexpensive,* under $8. The price is an average cost for one meal for one person, excluding drinks, tax, and tip.

Expensive

Powdermill Inn. Powderhorn Rd., Bessemer; 906–932–0800. A copper-and-stone fireplace, cathedral ceilings, and lots of glass add character to the inn that offers a full menu specializing in steaks.

Moderate

Alpen Inn. Big Powderhorn Mountain; 906–667–0211. A country setting on the side of a ski trail; diners can choose from a full menu and watch the night skiers schussing down the trails under the lights.

Blackjack Inn. Blackjack Mountain; 906–229–5115. Warm paneling adds coziness to this inn that faces the slopes; family fare is the menu's theme.

Branding Iron. Silver St., Hurley, WI; 715–561–4562. Grill your own steaks here, or they'll do it for you.

Caribou Lodge. Big Powderhorn Mountain; 906–932–4714. A salad bar and buffet are the draw here, in addition to action on the slopes.

China Sea Palace. US 2, Ironwood; 906–932–1322. This is a hexagon-shaped log building that serves up Chinese specialties.

Circle Hills Resort. Rte. 513, Ironwood; 906–932–3857. This is a small restaurant with lounge that offers a full menu.

Connie's Supper Club. Silver St., Hurley, WI; 715–561–9807. Italian specialties are the draw here, as well as steaks.

Liberty Bell Chalet. Half-block off Main St., Hurley, WI; 715–561–3753. Caesar salad, Italian offerings, and the ubiquitous pizza are musts here.

The Lodge Restaurant. Off US 2, Indianhead; 906–229–5181. There are great buffets, fish fries, and ethnic fare here.

Snowflake. Big Powderhorn Mountain; 906–932–4838. The Wednesday smorgasbord is popular; a full menu offered other nights.

Towne House Motor Inn. Suffolk St., Ironwood; 906–932–2101. Red and black is the motif here, with a lounge, salad bar, and special nights focusing on Mexican cuisine and surf and turf.

Inexpensive

Angelo's Pizza. Rte. 2, Ironwood; 906–932–2424. Deep-pan pizza gives this place a name.

Don & GG's. US 2, Ironwood; 906–932–2312. A lounge that serves pub fare, including hearty sandwiches.

Windjammer. Silver St., Hurley, WI; 715–561–9800. The lounge here is shaped like a ship; the food is American and Italian.

HOW TO GET AROUND. A **car** is a necessity in the region. However, some lodging establishments, particularly those at the mountains, may furnish **shuttle** service. Check when making your reservations.

SEASONAL EVENTS. A regional calendar features *New Year's torchlight parades* on **December 31** at Big Powderhorn, Blackjack, and Whitecap; *winter carnivals* in mid-**January** at Blackjack and Whitecap; followed by *spring carnivals* in early **March** at these two areas. **St. Patrick's Day** is big at both as well.

OTHER SPORTS AND ACTIVITIES. The *Indianhead Health & Racquet Club* (906–229–5151) offers an indoor **pool, racquetball,** Nautilus, aerobics, tanning bed, and sauna.

At Big Powderhorn Mountain, look for an indoor pool and saunas, an **ice-skating** rink, and **sleigh rides.** Whitecap has a heated and lighted indoor **tennis** court.

Cross-country skiing abounds in this region, with 30 km of groomed trails at Big Powderhorn, reached by a free shuttle from the mountain. Whitecap has 20 km of trails, and Blackjack has 32 km. For additional information on cross-country skiing, call *Big Snow Country* (906–932–4850). NASTAR is offered at all four ski areas.

Snowmobiling is also popular in the region, and *Big Snow Country* (906–932–4850) can provide specifics on where trails are maintained and marked.

Ice skating is offered at the community college in Ironwood, 906–932–0602.

HINTS TO THE HANDICAPPED. Free use of outriggers, lessons, and lift tickets are available at Indianhead (906–229–5181) to amputees and the blind. In fact, there's an amputee on the resort's ski patrol who works with the handicapped in between patrol duties. Big Powderhorn (906–932–4838) also offers free skiing to the handicapped.

CHILDREN'S ACTIVITIES. At Indianhead, there's *Kinder Country* which includes all-day baby-sitting and lunch for ages 2½ and up, with ski lessons available for ages 4–12. The hours are 9 A.M. to 4 P.M.

They call it *Kinderschool Program* at Big Powderhorn Mountain, with baby-sitting for ages 2 and up and lessons for ages 4 and up.

At Blackjack, a *Kinderkamp Nursery* offers child care to ages 2 and up when parents purchase lift tickets. Evening baby-sitting is also available to Blackjack lodging guests. A *Kinderschool Program* is also available at Whitecap.

Contact the base lodge at each of the ski areas for information and reservations.

NIGHTLIFE. There's plenty of après-ski activity in the region, with a number of establishments offering dancing and entertainment. In 1990, the governor called Hurley the town with "the best nightlife" in the state. Check it out for yourself. There are D.J.'s and live bands. Some of the livelier establishments include *Alpen Inn* at Big Powderhorn Mountain, 906–667–0211; *Booby Hatch,* 2 blocks off US 2, Bessemer, 906–663–4694; *Branding Iron,* Silver St., Hurley, WI, 715–561–4562; and *Caribou Lodge,* Big Powderhorn Mountain, 906–932–4714.

A favorite place of the young crowd is *Horse's Corral,* Silver St., Hurley, WI; 715–561–9945. Live bands play at *Towne House* on Suffolk St., Ironwood; 906–932–2101.

There's also music aplenty at *Dudley's Saloon* at Indianhead Mountain, 906–229–5181; *Logger's Lounge* at Blackjack Mountain, 906–229–5115; *Powdermill Inn,* Bessemer, 906–932–0800; *Ski High* at Indianhead Mountain, 906–229–5181; *Snowflake* at Big Powderhorn Mountain, 906–932–4838; and *The Vertical Drop,* Indianhead Mountain, 906–229–5181.

Minnesota

LUTSEN MOUNTAIN

Box 128
Lutsen MN 55612
Tel: 218–663–7281

Snow Report: 218–663–7281
Area Vertical: 1,008 ft.
Number of Trails: 27 on 200 skiable acres
Lifts: 1 gondola, 4 double chairs, 1 poma lift, 1 T-bar
Snowmaking: 80 percent of skiable terrain
Season: Thanksgiving–April

Lutsen, located on the north shore of Lake Superior, is the largest ski area in mid-America, spread over 1,500 acres and incorporating four large mountains.

These are Ullr, with runs for beginning and intermediate skiers; Eagle Mountain, with extra-long runs and spectacular views of Lake Superior and the surrounding wilderness; Mystery Mountain, with a summit deck and mile-plus runs; and Moose Mountain, offering the most challenging terrain and the area's greatest vertical drop.

The mountains themselves rise over 1,000 vertical feet above the shore of the world's largest freshwater body, Lake Superior. The views from the summit span hundreds of miles of blue water contrasted with the rocky coast of Minnesota's North Shore. The Superior National Forest, a wilderness area with moose, bear, and timber wolves, borders the ski area.

The base mountain village includes a total of 88 condominiums, a 30-unit hotel, and a recreation area; all along the Lake Superior shore are a variety of lodges and condominiums offering accommodations, food, and entertainment.

Because of its proximity to Lake Superior and its peculiar climatic conditions, the area receives twice the natural snowfall of the inland areas of northeastern Minnesota, and by early December, most of the mountain's trails are assisted by an efficient snowmaking system drawing water from the scenic Poplar River that roars by through gorges and over falls and rapids.

Practical Information for Lutsen Mountain

HOW TO GET THERE. Lutsen Mountain is located 1 mile from the town of Lutsen on Minnesota's North Shore of Lake Superior. It is 90 miles northeast of Duluth and about 75 miles south of the Canadian border. It is some 240 miles north of Minneapolis-St. Paul.

By car. From Minneapolis-St. Paul, take I–35 north through downtown Duluth to London Rd. (US 61). Follow 61 to Lutsen, then take County Rd. 36, left, to Lutsen Mountain.

TELEPHONES. The area code for northern Minnesota is 218.

ACCOMMODATIONS. Both on-mountain and all along Hwy. 61 bordering Lake Superior's North Shore, there is a variety of accommodations. Categories of condominiums are based on per-night prices for a studio or 1-bedroom unit: *Expensive,* $150 weekend or $125 midweek; *Moderate,* $100 weekend or $75 midweek; *Inexpensive,* $60 and under. All lodgings listed are within 10 miles of the slopes unless stated otherwise.

Expensive

Blue Fin Bay on Lake Superior. US 61, Tofte 55615; 663–7296 or 800–Bluefin (in-state). Located on a point jutting out into Lake Superior, offering lakeside motel units and townhouses; restaurant and lounge.

Gull Harbor Condominiums. US 61, Tofte 55615; 663–7205 or 800–223–2048 (in-state). Luxury condominiums on a cliff overlooking Lake Superior; sauna and whirlpool.

Sea Villas. US 61, Lutsen 55612; 663–7212 or 800–232–0071. Luxury condominiums right on Lake Superior and part of Lutsen Resort. Private lakeside decks offer spectacular views of the lake.

Village Inn and Resort (at Lutsen Mountain). County Rd. 36, Lutsen 55612; 663–7241 or 800–642–6036 (in-state). Nestled in the valley of Lutsen Mountains ski area, efficiency–3-bedroom housekeeping condominiums offer ski in, ski out convenience to both cross-country and alpine facilities; pool, whirlpool, fireplaces.

Moderate

Aspenwood Resort-Motel. US 61, Tofte 55615; 663–7978 or 800–322–6169. European and housekeeping plans available in complex that includes whirlpool, sauna, game room, homemade pizza shop, and lounge.

Best Western Cliff Dweller. US 61, Lutsen 55612; 633–7273. One-bedroom units overlooking Lake Superior. Restaurant on premises.

Cascade Lodge. US 61, Grand Marais 55604; 387–1112 or 800–322–9543 (in-state). Main lodge and log cabins with fireplaces overlooking Lake Superior and surrounded by Cascade River State Park; cross-country trails nearby; housekeeping and MAP available.

Chateau LeVeaux Condominium Resort & Motor Inn. US 61, Tofte 55615; 663–7223 or 800–445–5773. Motel units and housekeeping condos with fireplaces; pool, whirlpool, sauna, game room.

Lutsen Resort. US 61, Lutsen 55612; 663–7212. A rustic, old-lodge atmosphere right on Lake Superior, with pool, whirlpool, saunas, recreation room, dining room, lounge, cross-country trails; housekeeping and MAP plans available.

Shoreline Motel. Broadway, Grand Marais 55604; 387–2633 or 800–247–6020 (in-state). A multistory motel located on the bay downtown; great views.

Solbakken Resort. US 61, Lutsen 55612; 663–7566. Secluded housekeeping cabins nestled on Lake Superior's shore, offering spacious lake homes with fireplace and economical kitchenette motel units; access to cross-country trails.

Thomsonite Beach. US 61, Lutsen 55612; 387–1532. Small and large luxury housekeeping apartments and guest house with fireplaces, decks, and kitchens; plus motel units, all nestled on the shore of Lake Superior, with access to cross-country trails.

Inexpensive

East Bay Hotel. US 61, Grand Marais 55604; 387–2800. Located right on the bay in downtown Grand Marais, 20 miles from Lutsen; on-premises restaurant and bar.

Fenstad's Resort. US 61, Little Marais 55604; 226–4724. Housekeeping lakeshore cabins on the beach and rocky shoreline; fireplaces and kitchens; groomed cross-country trails outside the door. Located about 23 miles from the slopes.

Sandgren Motel. US 61, Grand Marais 55604; 387–2975. Motel units right in town.

RESTAURANTS. Dining out in this region is still reasonably easy on the pocketbook. Most restaurants offer American fare, with a regional favorite being fresh fish hauled in from Lake Superior. Restaurants are listed here by category, according to the price of a full meal for one without tax, tip, or beverage. *Expensive,* $15–$20; *Moderate,* $9–15; *Inexpensive,* less than $9. Major credit cards are accepted at restaurants in the expensive and moderate categories.

Expensive

Birch Terrace & Terrace Lounge. 6th Ave W./Hwy 61, Grand Marais; 387–2215. One of area's most beautiful and historic restaurants. Music on Saturday evenings. Local specialties for lunch and dinner.

Blue Fin Bay Restaurant. US 61, Tofte; 663–7296. Fine dining on a point jutting out into Lake Superior; varied menu with sandwiches available in the Bridge Bar.

Lutsen Resort Dining Room. US 61, Lutsen; 663–7212. Right on Lake Superior; fine dining in a beautiful lodge atmosphere, varied menu. Serves breakfast, lunch, dinner.

Moderate

Cascade Lodge Restaurant. US 61, Grand Marais; 387–1112. A superb view of Lake Superior from the popular full-service dining establishment offering extensive American menu.

Harbor Light Supper Club. US 61, Grand Marais; 387–1142. A supper club offering dancing with live music on weekends, imported wines and liquor, varied menu.

Upper Deck Restaurant. US 61, Grand Marais; 387–1597. A full-service restaurant offering an American menu; located on the harbor with great view of Lake Superior.

Village Inn Restaurant & Saloon. At Lutsen Mountain in Village Inn; 663–7241. Ski in for lunch or dinner. Family dining and cocktails, Open 8 A.M. till midnight.

Inexpensive

Best Western Cliff Dweller Restaurant. US 61, Lutsen; 663–7273. Good food in a warm but casual atmosphere, family dining overlooking Lake Superior.

Cross River Cafe. US 61, Schroeder; 663–7208. Good home-cooked meals.

Lutsen Mountains Chalet Cafeteria. County Rd. 36, Lutsen; 663–7281. Breakfast and lunch for skiers, including sandwiches, chili, soups, hamburgers, and beverages.

Sven & Ole's Pizza. 9 W. Wisconsin, Grand Marais; 387–1713. Pizza in a Norwegian atmosphere; sandwiches, salads, and soups are also available for both sitdown or takeout.

HOW TO GET AROUND. Access to a **car** is a necessity in this region. Some of the lodging establishments, however, may supply **shuttle** service to the mountain. Check when making reservations.

SEASONAL EVENTS. In the annual *Koo Koo Can-Am Speed Skiing Race,* held in **December,** downhill skiing speeds of more than 70 mph are reached as competitors ski in an all-out tuck from top to bottom of Koo Koo run on Eagle Mountain.

The *Moose Mountain Downhill,* held in early **January,** is the only professional downhill race in the Midwest.

OTHER SPORTS AND ACTIVITIES. In the region is a 200-km **cross-country** network called the *North Shore Trail System.* For information call the Lutsen-Tofte Tourist Association, 663–7804. The *Grand Marais Municipal Pool,* Tourist Park (US 61), is an Olympic-size indoor **pool. Ice fishing** is an option in this region, as is photographing the ice formations, sunrises, and fierce Nor'easter storms that frequent the lake.

HINTS TO THE HANDICAPPED. The Moose Mountain Downhill Race, an annual event, accommodates handicapped skiers with a special division for them. For information, contact the main lodge, 663–7281.

DAY-CARE FACILITIES. *Kinder School* (663–7281) is open to ages 3–5 and is offered daily. The program includes five hours of indoor and outdoor play, with a minimum of two hours instruction by a ski school instructor specially trained to teach children. Cost for full day is $32; half-day is $20.

NIGHTLIFE. The *Harbor Light Supper Club* in Grand Marais (387–1142) offers music for dancing that includes country rock and swing. Lutsen Mountain's *Chalet Bar* (663–7281) brings in variety entertainment and specializes in rock 'n' roll.

For those seeking a quiet background-music atmosphere, the *Bridge Bar* at the Blue Fin Bay Restaurant in Tofte (663–7296) features duos and soloists and lots of folk music.

WESTERN
UNITED STATES

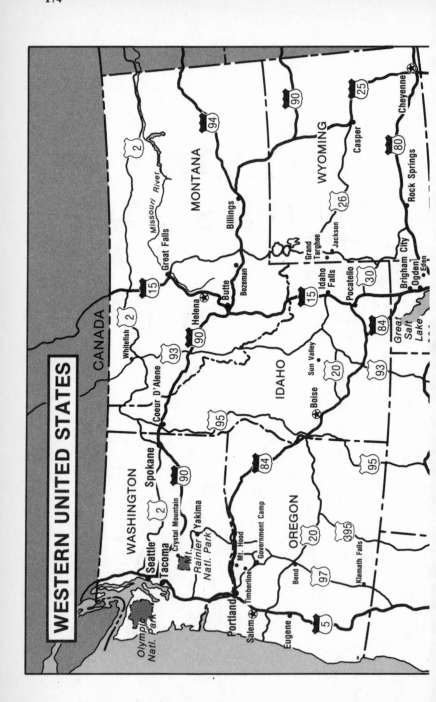

WESTERN UNITED STATES

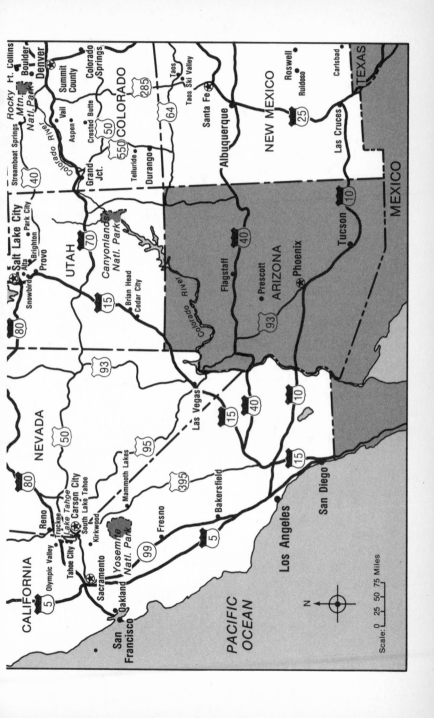

WESTERN UNITED STATES

by
ROSEMARY FRESKOS and DIANA HUNT

Rosemary Freskos has been writing for national ski publications for over 10 years. She is a member and past president of the U.S. Ski Writers Association. She was also publisher and owner of Ski Sun, *a tabloid for skiers in the Midwest.*

Diana Hunt writes for national and Rocky Mountain publications and is a member of the U.S. Ski Writers Association, Aviation/Space Writers Association, and Colorado Press Women.

The mountain ranges of the Western United States offer some of the best skiing in the world. A grandiose claim, perhaps, but with good reason. Certainly, Europe has its unique ambience, and Quebec and New England, their provincial flavor. But the Rockies consistently have the best snow conditions.

When planning a ski vacation, it is comforting to know that even in low snowfall years, skiing in the Western United States is still superior to all others. When nature doesn't cooperate, most western ski resorts, with heavy investments in snowmaking and grooming equipment, are able to augment the natural snowfall. Machines, each costing upwards of $100,000, manicure the slopes to maintain smooth, packed powder conditions. And when the famed "champagne powder" falls, the powderhounds are lined up waiting for the lifts to open so they can be the first to cut their tracks into the soft, fluffy snow. The phenomenon of powder (Utah has the driest and usually the most) occurs when Pacific storms pass over the deserts of Nevada and Utah's Great Basin, where they lose much of their moisture before hitting the Rocky Mountain barrier. The resulting snow is so light and dry that it floats away from your skis. Those who have mastered the technique of powder skiing (lessons *do* help) gladly forsake sleep to get at this snow.

In addition to the skiing, the guest facilities at Western resorts are among the best to be found anywhere, offering many options from secluded rustic cabins to condominiums and hotels. The luxury of world-class resorts such as Vail, Aspen, and Deer Valley is impressive, not only for the exquisite decor of lodgings and restaurants, but for the attention to niceties for skiers: tissue boxes at the lift areas, free corrals to guard skis, computer boards to illustrate the status of lifts and runs, and boot warmers in rest rooms.

Activities other than skiing are plentiful. Vacationers can find both active and sedentary diversions. With the advent of high-speed lifts, skiers are finding that they get so much more skiing done early in the day that by early afternoon they're ready to try other activities. This is the time to go for a Sno-Cat ride, try some hot-air ballooning, play a set or two of tennis, or visit the spa. Virtually all the larger resorts now provide non-skiing activities for all ages.

There is no better place for round-the-clock amusements than the Lake Tahoe–Reno area. From the pristine Sierra grandeur of 22 ski areas to the neon glitter and gaming tables, this area has it all. Heavenly Valley, the biggest area, even allows you to ski in two states: California and Nevada.

Do you like the vast ski circuses of Europe? Try Utah's Interconnect. Do you want to stay in a city with an array of other activities in addition to skiing? Go to Salt Lake City or Reno. Do you want a lot of sunshine with your skiing? Head south to New Mexico or west to California and Colorado; they have the winter sun. Would you prefer old-fashioned, less glamorous skiing? You can find it in Oregon, Wyoming, and Alta, Utah. A quiet retreat for low budgets? Try Big Sky, Montana, and Winter Park, Colorado. An old Western mining town with cowboys? Ride into Steamboat Springs, Telluride, and Purgatory in Colorado.

Clearly, the Rockies resorts cater to all lifestyles; the only problem is picking the one that's right for you. When planning your trip, ask a lot of questions and consider an all-inclusive package vacation. Choosing an off-peak time may make one of those high-priced resorts very affordable. January is a good time to go for savings. April, when it's usually warm and sunny, is another bargain time. If you can, you should try to experience a Rockies resort at Christmastime. Although the prices are about 15 percent higher than usual, the torch light parades, Santas on skis, and brilliant firework displays turn resorts into fantasylands.

One final note: If you go skiing in Colorado inquire about buying discount lift tickets in some Denver supermarkets and retail outlets such as 7-Eleven. Resorts such as Keystone, Copper Mountain, Breckenridge, and Vail/Beaver Creek can be skied with considerable savings through these promotions. Colorado Ski Country USA®, an association of 28 Colorado areas, has detailed, current information on opening and closing dates, rates, and snow conditions. Write to them at 1560 Broadway, Suite 1440, Denver, CO 80202, or phone (303) 837–0793; snow report, (303) 831–SNOW. They also have an information booth and receptionists to greet visitors at Denver's Stapleton and Grand Junction's Walker Field airports; call (303) 398–5398.

California

MAMMOTH MOUNTAIN SKI AREA

JUNE MOUNTAIN SKI RESORT

MAMMOTH MOUNTAIN

Box 24
Mammoth Lakes CA 93546
Tel: 619–934–2571

*Snow Report: 714–955–0692 (Orange
County) or 619–231–7785 (San Diego)*
Area Vertical: 3,100 ft.
*Number of Trails: over 150 open slopes,
bowls, and trails; longest run 2.5 miles*
*Lifts: 2 gondolas, 5 quad chairs, 7 triple
chairs, 14 double chairs, 1 T-bar, 1
poma*
Snowmaking: none
Season: November–June

JUNE MOUNTAIN

June Lake CA 93529
Tel: 619–648–7733

*Snow Report: 714–955–0692 (Orange
County); 619–231–7785 (San Diego)*
Area Vertical: 2,950 ft.
*Number of Trails: 30 runs on 25 trails;
longest run 2.5 miles*
*Lifts: 1 tram, 2 high-speed quads, 5 double
chairs*
Snowmaking: 10 percent of terrain
Season: Thanksgiving–Easter

Mammoth Mountain is Southern California's busiest ski area because its vastness and variety can accommodate the 15,000 skiers that show up on an average weekend. This resort is one of the largest in the country, with over 150 open slopes, bowls, and lifts that keep all levels of skiers satisfied. Forty percent of the terrain is intermediate, and beginner and advanced terrain each comprise 30 percent of the 3,500 skiable acres. Even the main lodge is mammoth: the three-level structure houses skiing services and lockers. The "hill" is so big that beginning skiers should consider going up with an instructor or guide for the first day to learn their way around.

June Mountain, a half-hour drive from the town of Mammoth Lakes, is less challenging for experts but has plenty of intermediate and beginner runs. More sheltered than Mammoth Mountain, June's mid-winter daytime temperatures rarely drop below 25 degrees F. And the lift ticket is interchangeable with Mammoth's. Mammoth's top elevation of 11,053 feet keeps the snow cold and the average snow depth at 10 to 15 feet each season. For fair-weather skiers, Mammoth has a "summer" season that lasts until June or July. Clothing becomes minimal for maximum exposure to tanning rays.

California's surfers looking for a winter high naturally gravitate to snowboards. The Storm Riders snowboard shop, run by Mammoth, has board rentals, sales and instructors. June has a world-class half-pipe and an Alpine Adventure Course just for snowboarders. Snowboarding is allowed on all runs at both areas, and lift tickets cost the same as for skiers.

Lodging closest to the mountain is quiet and convenient, but the action gets better 4 miles down the road, in town. With over 126 hotels, condos, and lodges, the area has something for everyone. Mammoth's *Travel Planner* magazine lists all lodging, along with photographs, prices, and other useful information on the region. Write or call the area for a copy.

Practical Information for
Mammoth Mountain/June Mountain

HOW TO GET THERE. By air. *Alpha Air* offers daily service between Mammoth and Los Angeles, Burbank, and Orange County airports; call 800–824–2610 or, in California, 800–421–9353. Round-trip airfares from Los Angeles to Mammoth are about $188–$270. Rental cars are available from the Mammoth Lakes airport.

By car. From Los Angeles, it is a 300-mile, 6-hour drive via US 395 to Rte. 203 to Minaret Rd. From the San Francisco area, take Hwy. 80 to US 395, or Hwy. 50 to South Lake Tahoe, then Hwy. 19 or Hwy. 89 to US 395. In the spring, when Tioga Pass is open, the drive goes through Yosemite.

By bus. *Greyhound Bus* serves the town of Mammoth Lakes twice daily from the north and south. *Hot Dogger Tours* has scheduled service between Mammoth and Los Angeles, Orange County, and Mojave; call 714–523–5982 or 213–698–6211.

TELEPHONES. The area code for the Mammoth Lakes area is 619.

ACCOMMODATIONS. There are 30,000 rooms in Mammoth Lakes, 4 miles from the ski area, as well as several condo complexes on the route up to it. The following handle bookings for most of the properties in the area: *The 1–800 Mammoth Resort and Reservations & Realty Co.,* 800–MAMMOTH or (619) 934–4541; *Mammoth Reservations Bureau,* 800–462–5571; *Mammoth Sierra Reservations,* 800–325–8415. The best locations are close to the Warming Hut II, near chair 15, or on the shuttle route.

The categories are based on per-night rates: *Expensive,* up to $230 for a 1-bedroom condo; *Moderate,* $84–$140; *Inexpensive,* $32–$84 for motel rooms. A few dorm rooms are available at lower rates. Many lodges offer group rates and mid-week or week-long-stay discounts.

Mammoth Mountain Inn. *Expensive–Moderate.* Nearest to slopes and day lodge. The hotel has room service, cable TV, a spa, and 2 restaurants. Also has 1- and 2-bedroom condos. Three-night hotel packages start at $199. Call 800–228–4947 for information.

Other *expensive* properties include the new **Snowcreek Resort** (800–544–6007 or 934–3333), located on the edge of town, and the walk-to-the-lifts **1894 Condos** (800–421–1849 or 934–7525), which have 1- to 4-bedroom units and feature 3-night packages starting at $190.

In the *moderate* category, the **Sierra Nevada Inn** (800–824–5132 or 934–2515) has hotel and condo units with 3-night packages from $183.

For *inexpensive* lodging: The **Rivendell Inn B&B** (934–2873) is a short walk from restaurants and shops. The **Travelodge** (800–255–3050 or 934–8576), the last lodge on the route to the ski areas, has studios and 2-bedroom units, some with kitchens, and also offers an indoor pool and spa. **Ullr Lodge** (934–2454) is a motel with kitchen facilities.

June Mountain also has lower-price lodging—two reservation services to contact are **June Lake Properties** (800–648–JUNE) and **June Mountain Reservations** (800–648–2217). From the **Reverse Creek Lodge** (800–762–6640) you can walk to the lifts.

RESTAURANTS. At the ski area there are six cafeteria-style restaurants. In town there are over 50 restaurants, from haute cuisine to deli. Most take major credit cards. Price categories are based on an average dinner for one. *Expensive,* $15–18; *Moderate,* $10–15; *Inexpensive,* less than $10.

Convict Lake Restaurant. *Expensive.* Located 2 miles up the road at the Convict Lake turnoff of Rte. 395; 934–3803. Mammoth's romantic escape—elegant decor, classic cuisine with fine wine.

Mountainside Grill. *Expensive.* In the Mammoth Inn, across the parking lot from the ski area's main lodge; 934–2581. American and Continental dishes are served in an airy, open dining room with exposed beams. The wine list is extensive and the pepper steak recommended. Reservations suggested.

Roget's. *Expensive.* Hwy. 203 and Minaret Rd.; 934–4466. Considered by many to be the finest restaurant in the area; only dinners are served here. The cuisine is Continental with unusual flourishes. Reservations necessary.

Good Stuff. *Moderate.* In the Old Mammoth Mall; 934–1734. Health food prepared fresh for breakfast and lunch.

Mogul Steak House. *Moderate.* Old Mammoth Rd. across from the Mammoth Mall; 934–3039. Homemade soups, salad bar, steaks, seafood, poultry; dinners only.

Ocean Harvest. *Moderate.* Old Mammoth Rd.; 934–8539. Prime seafood, steak, and chicken, mesquite-broiled. You can dance the night away downstairs in the Ocean Club.

Shogun. *Moderate.* In the Sierra Center Mall; 934–3970. Mammoth's only sushi bar serves traditional Japanese cuisine. Reservations recommended.

Angels. *Inexpensive.* Old Mammoth Rd.; 934–7427. A local's favorite for hefty portions of delicious barbecue and great desserts. Take-out and children's menus.

Berger's. *Inexpensive.* Minaret Rd.; 934–6622. Giant hamburgers, homemade chili, chicken and ribs. Take-out menu.

Swiss Cafe. *Inexpensive.* Old Mammoth Rd.; 934–6196. Family restaurant with good homemade soups. Start here with an early breakfast before hitting the slopes; fresh croissants, muffins, the usual eggs and pancakes.

HOW TO GET AROUND. Mammoth has expanded its **free shuttle bus** service with four routes looping between town and various points at the ski area and parking lots. It operates every 15 minutes between 7 A.M. and 6 P.M. There is also hourly service between Mammoth Lodge and the town center until 1 in the morning. Call 934–0687 or 934–2571 for schedule. The *Mammoth Cab Company,* 934–3346, offers charter and **taxi** service in the village. A tip: If you park close to chairs 2, 4, 10 and 15, you can ski back to your car.

SEASONAL EVENTS. Christmas is celebrated with *Spectacular Night of Lights,* a *Parade of Carols and Lights,* a *Messiah* performance, and an *Arts and Crafts Festival.* In **January** the Village Ski Championships—spiced with local rivalries—begin. The **OP Pro Snowboard Race** takes place at June Mountain during the season.

OTHER SPORTS AND ACTIVITIES. *Mammoth Adventure Connection* (934–0606, office at Mammoth Inn) can arrange **ballooning, dog sledding, cross-country**

skiing, snowmobiling, and more. There are many miles of **cross-country trails;** try *Sierra Meadow,* 934–6161, or *Tamarack,* 934–2442. Rentals are available at the slopes and in town.

There is **bobsledding** near Mammoth Mountain. **Snow sleds** are available at *Kittredge Sports,* 934–7566, or *Filson's,* 934–2517; **sleigh rides** from *Sierra Meadows,* 934–6161. There are 200 miles of **snowmobile** trails; for information call *DJ's Snowmobile Rentals,* 935–4480. **Tobogganing** and **tubing** are also available.

Racing is a big deal here. There are mid-week race camps and 3- and 5-day camps. The *Alpine Athletic Club* is a racing program for adults. Each Wednesday sees an FIS-style World Cup amateur slalom and giant slalom. NASTAR races and classes are offered along with a Marlboro Pay Race Course. Call Mammoth Race Department for a brochure of events, 934–0642.

DAY-CARE FACILITIES. The Mammoth Mountain Inn operates the *Small World Day Center,* a state-licensed facility with learning-and-play programs for youngsters from infant to 12 years old. Cost for a full day is $37 for infants up to 2½ years and $34 up to 12 years. A half-day of ski school for 3- to 12-year-olds is $50; price includes day care from 8 A.M. to 5 P.M. and lunch. Call 934–0646 for reservations.

NIGHTLIFE. Up at the ski area, the *Yodler,* across from main lodge, has a large-screen TV and a lively bar. *Mammoth Inn*'s bar is less rustic but just as lively. The rest of the après-ski watering holes are in town (where there's also a movie theater). *Whiskey Creek,* Main St. and Minaret (934–2555), has dancing, as does *Rafters* on Old Mammoth Rd. (934–2537). *The Western Saloon* (934–8587) is a sports bar with 5 giant TVs, pool, shuffleboard, foosball, plus chili and burgers at low prices.

OTHER CALIFORNIA SKI AREAS

Besides Mammoth/June Mountain and the ski areas to be detailed in the Tahoe Basin chapter, there are 15 other ski areas in Central and Southern California. Droves of Southern Californians descend on these areas because they are nearby—less than 2 hours from the ocean. The four areas named below attract about 1.3 million skiers annually. Reservations for weekend skiing should be made through the areas or with Ticketron or Teletron, as there is a limit to the number of skiers allowed at some areas. All have 150 to 200 acres of skiable terrain that is mostly beginner–intermediate. All allow snowboarding, and all except Bear Mountain have night skiing. Mountain High is most accessible but Bear and Snow Summit, located in the resort town of Big Bear Lake, offer more activities and lodging. Snow Valley, a smaller area, is just off the highway on the way to Big Bear. For more information or accommodations at these areas contact *Ski Southern California,* 9550 Warner Ave. #250, Fountain Valley, CA 92708, (714) 964–6073.

Bear Mountain. Box 6812, Big Bear Lake, CA 92315, (714) 585–2519. Snow report: (714) 585–2517.

Mountain High. Box 428, Wrightwood, CA 92397, (619) 248–5801. Snow report: (213) 460–6911 from LA.

Snow Summit. Box 77, Big Bear Lake, CA 92315, (714) 866–5766. Snow report: (213) 613–0602, from LA.

Snow Valley. Box 2337, Running Springs, CA 92382, (714) 867–2751. Snow report: (714) 867–5151.

The Tahoe Basin

CALIFORNIA/NEVADA STATE LINE

The Lake Tahoe region was a year-round playground for the Indians long before the white man came with casinos and ski lifts. Today, however, this pristine lake is surrounded by 19 ski resorts (the largest concentration of ski facilities in the country) and is one of the world's most beautiful vacation spots.

The California-Nevada state line bisects Lake Tahoe. The towns of South Lake Tahoe, CA, and Stateline, NV, are at the south end of the lake and closest to Heavenly Valley, the largest of Tahoe's ski areas. The two towns are separated only by one main street, so the big-name gambling, entertainment, and bargain dining of Nevada's casinos are just minutes from the strip of motels and lodges that line the route to the ski area on the California side. There are 10,000 rooms in every price category, from spartan motels to the luxury of Harrah's, with its five-star awards from Mobil and AAA. *The Lake Tahoe Visitor's Authority,* Box 16299, South Lake Tahoe, CA 95706 (916–544–5050 or 800–822–5922), will give lodging information on this area but cannot make reservations.

Along the north and west shores of Tahoe, there are 11 alpine and seven cross-country areas. Skiers looking for cross-country trails will find a virtual paradise in this region's wilderness and state-park trails, first-class resorts, and cozy ski centers. Three of the better-known areas include: **Royal George** (916–426–3871), North America's largest groomed track system with 317 km on 77 trails. The resort has two rustic mountain inns (the Wilderness Lodge offers 30 private rooms), eight warming huts, a surface lift, and an Interconnect Trail leading from the lodges to the track system. The resort is an hour's drive west of Reno, off I–80. **Tahoe Donner Cross Country** (916–587–9484) features lighted nighttime nordic skiing with 65 km of double-tracked trails. There is a day lodge and the Coyote Cafe, which serves homemade cuisine. Tahoe Donner is located 4 miles northeast of Truckee. Just 2 miles from Tahoe City, the **Tahoe Nordic Center** (916–583–9858) is known for its scenic Lakeview trail. There are four warming huts, plus a day lodge and a deli that bakes bread and cookies daily.

Moving south from Reno, the first of Tahoe's alpine areas is Mt. Rose, a day mountain with the area's highest elevation, just 22 miles from downtown. The larger areas are 45 minutes to 1½ hours' drive from Reno and

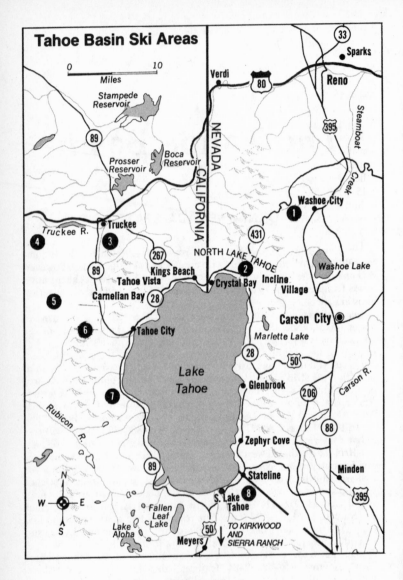

Tahoe Basin Ski Areas

0　　　　Miles　　　10

Resorts

Alpine Meadows, 6
Diamond Peak, 2
Heavenly Valley, 8
Homewood, 7
Mount Rose, 1
Northstar-at-Tahoe, 3
Squaw Valley USA, 5
Sugar Bowl, 4

include Diamond Peak in Nevada and Northstar-at-Tahoe, Squaw Valley, and Alpine Meadows, all in California on the lake's north shore.

The towns along the north shore of the lake, such as Incline Village, Tahoe City, and Tahoe Vista/Kings Beach, have a number of lodges and motels that offer packages. Interchangeable lift tickets are offered by Squaw Valley, Alpine Meadows, Northstar, Diamond Peak, Sugar Bowl, Mt. Rose, and Homewood. In 1991, a 3-day pass cost $108. Information and a booklet describing the properties can be obtained from the *Tahoe North Visitors and Convention Bureau*, Box 5578, Tahoe City, CA 95730 (800–824–8557 or 800–822–5959 in California). For information on activities and ski facilities, call *Ski Tahoe North* at 800–824–6348.

As an alternative to staying on the north and south shores of Tahoe, consider Reno. Winter is the low season there and many hotels offer discounts and ski packages. Food, especially at the casino "buffets," can be ridiculously inexpensive ($5.95 dinners!). Skiers staying in Reno will have a 45–60-minute drive to the ski areas; a car is necessary, or you can take a shuttle bus. *Sierra Nevada Gray Line* (800–822–6009) runs a ski shuttle between downtown Reno and Tahoe's North Shore. Cost is $15 adults, $10 children under 12.

There are more than 40 full-service hotels in this region. Listed here is a sampling of Reno's accommodations: **Bally's,** 800–648–5080, 2-night package—$86. **Flamingo Hilton,** 800–648–4882, 2-night package—$89. **Sands Regency,** 800–648–3553, 2-night package—$76. Hotels without casinos are: **Quality Inn,** 800–762–5190, 2-night package—$89. **McCarran House,** 800–548–5798, 2-night package—$37.50. These prices are per person, double occupancy mid-week, and include lift passes, some meals, and car-rental discounts. **Circus Circus,** 800–648–5010, has rooms $18 and up, Sunday through Thursday. It is a fun place for families. The best way to get additional information on the Reno area is to contact the *Reno/Sparks Convention and Visitors Authority's Information and Reservation Referral Service* at 800–FOR–RENO or the *Tourism Department*, Box 11430, Reno, NV 89510. They will send you an informative Travel Planner.

There's plenty of sightseeing, too, including the *William Harrah Foundation Automobile Museum*, (702) 788–3242, the *Wilbur D. May Museum and Arboretum, Liberty Belle Saloon's* slot machine collection, and the new 5-acre *Great Basin Adventure. Tahoe Tours*, (702) 832–0713, and *Silver State Stage Lines*, (702) 348–7121, have group tours; call for rates and schedules.

Twelve air carriers serve Reno, with 61 daily scheduled departures. Charter service and air taxis are also available.

Many car-rental agencies are represented at the airport: *Action*, (800) 633–4117; *Alamo*, (800) 327–9633; *Avis*, (800) 331–1212; *Budget*, (702) 758–2543; *General*, (800) 327–7607; *Hertz*, (800) 654–3131; *Lloyds*, (800) 654–7037; *National*, (800) CAR–RENT.

Amtrak stops in the heart of Reno on East Commercial Row at Lake Street. The *California Zephyr* is the most scenic train ride in America, crossing three mountain ranges on its 2,427-mile transcontinental journey. Call 800–USA–RAIL or the Reno Ticket Office, (702) 329–8638, for reservations and information. Amtrak also stops in nearby Truckee.

ALPINE MEADOWS SKI AREA

Box 5279
Tahoe City CA 95730
Tel: 916–583–4232

Snow Report: 916–583–6914
Area Vertical: 1,800 ft.
Number of Trails: 100 trails over 2,000
    acres on two mountains; longest trail is
    2.5 miles
Lifts: 1 high-speed quad, 2 triple chairs, 8
    double chairs, 2 pomas
Snowmaking: on 145 acres of beginner and
    intermediate trails (1,400 vertical feet)
Season: mid-November–Memorial Day

Alpine Meadows is a ski cruiser's paradise. Most of the intermediate runs are on the front side, with varying degrees of pitch and slant, and are groomed to perfection every night. There are powder areas and steep challenges for experts, particularly Wolverine Bowl. Experts should also look for Art's Knob, Our Father, and Scott Chute.

Skiers can follow the sun around the mountain for the best exposure; good spring corn snow is found in the Sherwood area and on Scott Peak. The quickest way onto the slopes is to buy lift tickets at the base of Subway Chair. The base lodge includes a cafeteria, full-service restaurant, bar, repair and ski shop, and a large sundeck. Alpine Meadows has the longest spring skiing season in the Tahoe area and sunshine an average of 80 percent of the entire ski season. It also has the distinction of having Tahoe's most reliable skiing conditions. Alpine also runs regular shuttle service to and from lodging properties in both the North and South shores of Lake Tahoe.

Practical Information for Alpine Meadows

HOW TO GET THERE. By car. Tahoe City is 6 miles and Reno is 45 miles from the ski area via I–80. San Francisco is 200 miles west; Sacramento is 120 miles. Take I–80 east to Hwy. 89, South Exit, Tahoe City/Squaw Valley. Follow Hwy. 89 to Alpine Meadows Rd.; it is 13 miles from Truckee to the ski area. For more details and maps, contact the *California State Automobile Association*, Box 19, Tahoe Vista, CA 95702, 916–540–4245.

By air. The gateway airport is Reno, which is served by most major carriers. The Lake Tahoe Airport, on Hwy. 50, is often closed to flights in winter and is therefore not reliable for skiers. Small planes can land at the Truckee-Tahoe Airport, 2 miles east of Truckee, 10 miles north of Lake Tahoe; aircraft tie-down area, 24-hour flight operations.

For Reno **car rental** companies, see the *California/Nevada State Line* section at the beginning of this chapter. In Lake Tahoe, rental companies are *Dollar* and *National* through the *Tahoe North Visitors and Convention Bureau; Thrifty,* 916–587–2588; and *Budget,* 916–583–8941.

By train. *Amtrak* stops in Truckee; for schedule call 800–USA–RAIL, or in California only, 800–872–7245.

By bus. *Trailways,* 916–323–4511, and *Greyhound,* 916–323–4511, provide eastbound and westbound service to the Truckee depot on Commercial Row.

TELEPHONES. The area code for this region of California is 916, and for all Nevada it is 702.

ACCOMMODATIONS. Call the *Tahoe North Visitors and Convention Bureau,* 800–TAHOE–4–U or 800–824–6348, or write to them for information and reservations at Box 5578, Tahoe City, CA 95730. They handle 115 properties along the North Shore from Truckee to Incline, including facilities near Alpine Meadows.

Condo and room-rate categories are based on per person, double occupancy rates. *Expensive,* $90–$250; *Moderate,* $70–$90; *Inexpensive,* $50–$70.

Alpine Place One and Two. *Expensive.* A short distance from the slopes; 583–8213. Condos of 2, 3, and 4 bedrooms, with fireplaces, TVs, kitchens, baby-sitting, and day care. Shuttle bus available to the slopes, a quarter of a mile away.

Best Western Truckee Tahoe Inn. *Moderate.* In Truckee; 587–4525 or 800–824–6385 (CA only). 100 rooms and suites. Hot tub, sauna, exercise room, free movies, complimentary breakfast, free shuttle. Midweek discount packages.

Alpine Motor Inn. *Inexpensive.* At the base of Alpine Meadows Rd. along the Truckee River; 583–4266. Continental breakfast, hot tub, racquetball courts at an additional charge; 2-night minimum.

For lodgings other than along the North Shore, see the *California/Nevada State Line* section, at the beginning of this chapter.

RESTAURANTS. In the ski area itself, *Kealy's Pub* (583–5177) in the base lodge serves hearty fare and the mid-mountain lodge has an *Alpine Deli.* The restaurants listed below are the best in the area in their price ranges; see *Squaw Valley* section for more dining options. For an *Expensive* meal here for one person, expect to pay $20 and more; *Moderate,* $10–$20; and *Inexpensive,* less than $10. All accept most major credit cards.

River Ranch. *Expensive.* Hwy. 89 at Alpine Meadows Rd., Tahoe City; 583–4264. Fresh seafood, roast duck, and rack of lamb are among the Continental dishes served in this picture-filled and candlelit dining room. The après-ski bar is one of the best in the Alpine Meadows area. Reservations recommended.

Swiss Lakewood. *Expensive.* Hwy. 89 South in Homewood, 6 miles south of Tahoe City; 525–5211. Cowbells, pitchforks, and flickering table candles set the tone at this 18-year-old rustic establishment. Try the beef Wellington (order when you make your reservations, which are necessary) or the popular duck à l'orange. An extensive menu features unusual hors d'oeuvres. Closed on Mondays, except for holidays.

Gar Woods Grill & Pier on the Lake. *Moderate.* 5000 N. Lake Blvd., Carnelian Bay; 546–3366. Located right on the water (there's even valet boat parking in summer), the name comes from the nostalgic garwood boat photos scattered throughout the restaurant. The cuisine is Continental, with fresh seafood, prime rib, steaks. A popular dish is the "hot rock"—your meat is cooked tableside on a hot granite rock. Reservations recommended.

Pfeiffer House. *Moderate.* One-half mile south of Tahoe City, along I–80; 587–1377. An old-time favorite of frequent Tahoe skiers; menu features schnitzel and sauerbraten; dinner only.

Bacchi's Inn. *Inexpensive.* 2905 Lake Forest Rd., 1 mile north of Tahoe City; 583–3324. Your choice of 42 Italian entrees are served up family-style. All-you-can-eat minestrone soup, bread, antipasto, etc.—for one price—and a congenial environment make it a great place to take hungry kids (and adults). Bacchi's has been in business for 70 years so it must be doing something right to keep those families coming. No credit cards accepted.

HOW TO GET AROUND. *Alpine Meadows* operates a free daily **shuttle** pickup service with over 40 stops on the North Shore, 916–581–8341. *Tahoe Area Regional Transit* (TART) operates a public **bus** on a daily schedule, except Sundays, in the North Lake Tahoe area, 916–581–6355.

SEASONAL EVENTS. *Snowfest* is the big **winter** celebration all along the North Shore, with hundreds of events taking place in early **March.** *The Great Ski Race* is held the first Sunday in **March** and follows a scenic and historic ski route from Lake Tahoe to Truckee, 30 km away. It is the largest cross-country ski event in California, with nearly 1,000 entrants. For information, write Tahoe Cross-Country Ski Center, Box 1632, Tahoe City CA 95730; 583–0484.

OTHER SPORTS AND ACTIVITIES. See the *California/Nevada State Line* section at the beginning of this chapter for **cross-country skiing** options. The *Cobblestone Cinema* in Tahoe City features current movies. Also in Tahoe City are numerous art galleries, and the *North Tahoe Fine Arts Council* puts on productions throughout the year; call 546–5562 or 583–9048.

DAY-CARE FACILITIES. Check with the Chamber of Commerce, 583–2371. The *Children's Snow School* takes youngsters aged 3½–6; full-day lessons are $52.

NIGHTLIFE. *River Ranch* has a cozy lounge. There is no dearth of night spots around Lake Tahoe, Tahoe City, Truckee, Tahoe Vista, South Lake Tahoe, Incline Village, Sparks, or Reno; it's a matter of how much a person can take. Pick up the local newspapers for the latest happenings.

DIAMOND PEAK SKI RESORT

Box AL
Incline Village NV 89450
Tel: 702–832–1177

Snow Report: 702–831–3211
Area Vertical: 1,840 ft.
Number of trails: 35 runs on 655 skiable
*   acres; longest run 2.5 miles*
Lifts: 1 quad, 6 double chairs
Snowmaking: 80 percent of terrain
Season: mid-November–April

Incline Village is easily the richest town in Nevada. It's a quiet, sophisticated little place, where the residents own the ski area. Situated at the end of Crystal Bay, 2 miles from Stateline, Nevada, this 9 square miles of rustic splendor owes 65 percent of its tourism to Northern California and 15 percent to Southern California. Its appeal boasts one thing the California ski areas lack: casino gambling.

A multimillion-dollar expansion doubled the size of the resort in 1987. The five-phase plan is expected to be completed by 1996. The opening of "Diamond Peak," one of Tahoe's largest ski expansions in over a decade, has put this resort in Tahoe's big leagues. The mile-long quad chair to the top of Diamond Peak opens up over 300 new acres of skiable terrain, eight new runs, and some of the basin's best tree skiing. The advanced terrain is a refreshing change for this once timid resort.

The Child Ski Development Center is the showcase of base area improvements. It is an innovative teaching center structured to improve knowledge of skiing and winter safety. Diamond Peak specializes in affordably priced family programs for both alpine and nordic skiers.

A 3-story, 12,000 square-foot base lodge provides skier services, banquet and meeting facilities, an elegant but casual après-ski bar, and a ski shop. Development plans call for a restaurant at the top of Diamond Peak overlooking the lake and valley, 3,500 feet below.

Practical Information for Diamond Peak

HOW TO GET THERE. By air. Reno is the gateway to the area. An airport shuttle bus is available to Incline Village/ *Hyatt Regency Lake Tahoe.* The drive takes about 45 minutes; inquire about reservations when you book your hotel rooms.

By bus. *Sierra Nevada Stagelines,* (702) 359–1750, operates a daily shuttle from the major properties in Reno to the ski area.

By car. From Reno take Hwy. 431 for about 35 miles over Mt. Rose. From Sacramento and San Francisco take I–80 over the Donner Summit to Truckee and then to Tahoe.

TELEPHONES. The area code for Incline Village and Reno is 702.

ACCOMMODATIONS. The center of attention at the area is the new **Hyatt Regency Resort and Casino,** Lakeshore and Country Club Dr.; 831–1111 or 800–228–9000. The Hyatt is a full-service hotel with a casino and several restaurants and bars. Prices range from $99 for a standard double to $250 and up for 2-bedroom suites. There are midweek packages; two nights and three days start at $85 per person. Kids stay for free.

There are numerous condos of varying sizes at Incline Village. For rates and reservations, call 800–GO–TAHOE.

RESTAURANTS. There are a few restaurants at Incline Village. Categories, based on the price of a full dinner for one, excluding tax, tips, and beverages, are *Expensive,* $30 and up, and *Moderate,* $25 and under. Most restaurants accept the major credit cards.

Hugo's Rotisserie. *Expensive.* In the Hyatt; 831–1111. Elegant atmosphere and Continental cuisine.

Spatz at Incline Village. *Expensive.* 341 Ski Way in the lift building; 831–8999. Sophisticated dining with great views.

Alpine Jacks. *Moderate.* In the Hyatt; 831–1111. Coffee shop with good food.

Italian Village Restaurant. *Moderate.* 570 Lakeshore Blvd.; 831–1480. Family dining with a pleasant atmosphere.

Las Panchitas. *Moderate.* 930 Tahoe Blvd.; 831–4048. Traditional Mexican food and a lively bar.

Watercress. *Moderate.* 800 Tahoe Blvd.; 831–6769. Mandarin and Szechuan specialties.

OTHER SPORTS AND ACTIVITIES. *Incline Cross Country Ski Center,* 832–1150. Located off Hwy. 431 on the Executive Golf Course with gently rolling terrain on 15 km of groomed double-track trails. A day lodge has a rental/accessory shop and food service from 9 A.M. to 5 P.M. daily.

CHILDREN'S ACTIVITIES. The Child Ski Development Center has a program for children aged 3–7. PSA's "Great Escape" ski packages have a kids-ski-free promotion for children aged 12 and under. Call 800–223–2929 for information.

NIGHTLIFE. Most partying is low key and "at home." The *Hyatt* offers the closest bars and casino, with additional casinos in North Lake Tahoe, 1 mile away. *Testa Rosa* is a disco and bar in town with live entertainment.

HEAVENLY VALLEY SKI RESORT

Box 2180
Stateline NV 89449
Tel: 916–541–1330 or 800–2–HEAVEN

Snow Report: 916–541–SKII
Area Vertical: California—3,600 ft.,
Nevada—2,900 ft.
Number of Trails: over 20 square miles
Lifts: 1 aerial tramway, 1 high-speed quad,
7 triple chairs, 9 double chairs, 6
surface lifts
Snowmaking: 62 percent of runs
Season: mid-November–mid-May

Unique among ski areas, Heavenly lies in two states—California and Nevada. In terms of skiable acreage, it is the largest ski area in the United States, with nine peaks, 5½ runs, and an amazing 3,600-foot vertical drop. It is a balanced mix of half intermediate, one-quarter beginner, and one-quarter expert terrain. It is often called the "upside-down" mountain because most of the beginner and intermediate terrain is located at upper elevations—a treat for those who don't usually get a chance to ski or see the view from the summit. There are well-groomed runs, wide-open bowls, and timbered glades. Mott Canyon, on the Nevada side, is an ungroomed run with lots of trees and cliffs to test out the experts' abilities. The ski area stretches along the south shore of what has been called the most beautiful alpine lake in the world.

In 1988, Heavenly added four chairlifts, one a high-speed quad, to its Nevada side. These improved access to the less-crowded Nevada slopes. The snowmaking system was also expanded to cover all the new lifts, as well as most of the major runs on the California side of the mountain.

Heavenly claims to have the "world's largest snowmaking system"—just in case the annual snowfall doesn't reach its average 300 to 500 inches. Yet there are other practical reasons for Heavenly's investment in snowmaking. Because Heavenly Valley receives sunshine 80 percent of the season and daytime temperatures are often above 30 degrees, the snowmaking ensures better skiing conditions throughout the season.

If all this beauty is too much and you feel the need of concrete beneath your boots, Reno, South Lake Tahoe, and Stateline are not far away for 24-hour après-ski diversion. On top of that, summer is high season in the gaming casinos. Wintertime prices to lure skiers to the tables and entertainment are ridiculously low by Colorado or Utah standards. You can get a dinner special for the price of one drink in the glitzy resorts of Vail, Aspen, and Deer Valley.

However, even paradise has its flaws—San Franciscans relentlessly pursuing their pleasures blanket the entire area on weekends. The base lodges on the California side are usually crowded, but the Nevada day lodges are rarely so jammed. It is worth the steep 3-mile drive on Route 207, Kingsbury Grade Road, to get to the Nevada side for shorter lines and more ski runs.

Practical Information for Heavenly Valley

HOW TO GET THERE. By air. *American Airlines* serves South Lake Tahoe airport from major California cities. It is a short drive to the ski area via taxi, rental car, or bus. Reno's Cannon International Airport is 55 miles from Heavenly, and is served by major national and international airlines. *LTR Stagelines* has daily scheduled **bus** service between the Reno airport and South Lake Tahoe hotels, motels, and casinos. Call 702–588–6633 for schedules and fare information. Rental cars are also available.

By bus. *Greyhound Bus Lines* has 12 daily buses between South Lake Tahoe and San Francisco; 14 daily buses between Reno and San Francisco. The Lake Tahoe terminal can be reached at 916–544–2241.

Heavenly's free ski shuttle buses run throughout the South Shore daily to both base facilities. A *Skier's Shuttle* bus also operates in South Lake Tahoe. One-way fare is $1. For more information call *City Bus Information*, 916–544–2266. Some casino hotels have complimentary 24-hour shuttles to the ski areas.

By car. Heavenly is 180 miles east of San Francisco via I–80 to Sacramento, then US 50 to South Lake Tahoe. Reno is approximately 75 minutes away via US 395 and 50.

TELEPHONES. The area code for the Heavenly area is 916; for all Nevada it is 702.

ACCOMMODATIONS. *Heavenly Central Reservations* can book airline, lodging, and lift packages with various airlines and major hotels and condos. Call 800–2–HEAVEN or 702–588–4584. Buses pick up skiers from Heavenly, Kirkwood, and Sierra Ski Ranch. For motel or hotel reservations only for any of the 10,000 rooms in the South Lake Tahoe area, call the Visitors Bureau, 800–822–5922 in California and 800–824–5150 outside California. For a free travel planner, write *South Lake Tahoe Visitors Bureau,* Box 17727, South Lake Tahoe CA 95706.

Hotel rates are per night, double occupancy: *Expensive,* $70–$90; *Moderate,* $60–$80; *Inexpensive,* under $60. Prices are usually lower Sunday through Thursday; weekend rates are higher.

Most properties offer multiday lift-ticket packages that are a great saving over the per-night rates. There are three rate scales for the three seasons: *regular* season runs from mid-January through the end of March; *value* season starts at the beginning of the season through the second week in December, the first two weeks in January, and April on; and *holiday* season, when prices soar, is Christmas/New Year's and President's weekend in February. The following is a small sampling of lodges and hotels that offer packages. The prices given are for 7-night/6-day lift-and-lodging packages per person, double occupancy. They should be used as an approximate guide; prices *will* fluctuate.

Best Western Station House Inn. 916–542–1101. Has standard rooms, spa, restaurant, breakfasts, less than 2 miles to skiing. Packages from $444.

Eagle's Nest Inn. 800–233–6378. Ski-in, ski-out European-style hotel on Nevada side. Packages from $931.

Lakeland Village. 800–825–8246. Lakeside resort condos with heated pools, saunas, hot tub. Located 1½ miles from Heavenly. Packages from $547.

Ridge Tahoe. 800–243–2836. At the slopes. With deluxe rooms, health club, pool, indoor tennis, racquetball, restaurant. Packages start at $683.

The following "big three" casino hotels are all *expensive.* They are opulent, with huge, richly appointed guest rooms (Harrah's have two bathrooms). All offer a variety of restaurants, lounges, and bars, as well as swimming pools, health clubs, and tennis courts. Leaving is the hard part.

Caesars Tahoe. Box 5800, Stateline, NV; 708–588–3515 or 800–648–3353. A 7-night ski package starts at $588.

Harrah's Tahoe. Box 8, Stateline, NV 89449; 702–588–6611 or 800–648–3773. Luxury suites with butler service. A 7-night ski package is $607.

Harvey's Resort. Box 128, Stateline, NV 89449; 702–588–2411 or 800–648–3361. First casino at Lake Tahoe and the largest. Seven-night ski package is $527.

The California side of town has a large selection of lodging (without gambling) in all categories.

Tahoe Beach and Ski Club. *Moderate.* Box 1267, So. Lake Tahoe, CA 95731; 800–822–5962. Studio and 1-bedroom units with microwave kitchens. Restaurant, lounge, spa, sauna.

Lazy S Lodge. *Inexpensive.* Box 7676, So. Lake Tahoe, CA 95731; 916–541–0230. Cottages with kitchenettes and fireplaces, or standard rooms.

The Montgomery Inn. *Inexpensive.* Box 18245, So. Lake Tahoe, CA 95731; 800–624–8224. Nicely furnished units with private baths, cable TV, kitchen suites, hot tub. Five minutes to casinos and Heavenly.

RESTAURANTS. Heavenly has plenty of places to eat in between skiing. On the California side, the base lodge, *Top of the Tram* (2,000 ft. above ft. above Lake Tahoe), and Sky Meadows (at the base of Sky Chair) both have cafeterias, barbecues, and dining rooms and cocktail service. On the Nevada side, *Boulder Base Lodge, Stagecoach Lodge* (at the base of Stagecoach Lift), and *East Peak Midmountain Lodge* (the base of East Peak and Dipper chairs) have eats and drinks and outdoor sundecks.

Restaurants are listed in order of price category. *Expensive,* $20 and up; *Moderate,* $12–$20; *Inexpensive,* less than $12. These prices are for a meal for one person, excluding drinks and tip. The above listed on-mountain cafeterias are inexpensive and generally do not take credit cards. Other sit-down restaurants honor most major credit cards. The buffets at the casinos in South Lake Tahoe are considered great bargains; check them out, but don't bet your skis. For other restaurants in the South Lake Tahoe area, see section on *Kirkwood.*

Christiana Inn. *Expensive.* Across the road from the Tram at Heavenly Valley at 3819 Saddle Rd.; 916–544–7337. A country-style inn serving gourmet meals by the fireside; popularized by *Bon Appétit* and *Cosmopolitan* magazines; major credit cards; reservations.

Eagle's Nest. *Moderate.* At the Nevada base area, 472 Needle Peak Rd.; 702–588–6492 or 702–883–6478. Features American and Italian dishes amid Victorian ambience.

Scoozi. *Moderate.* Ski Run Blvd.; 542–0100. One of the better Italian restaurants in the area. Nice ambience, close to the slopes.

Carlos Murphy's. *Inexpensive.* 3678 Hwy. 50; 542–174. Serves 3 meals daily and Sunday brunch. Mexican-American food.

Garden 'n Grill. *Inexpensive.* 1080 Emerald Bay Rd.; 541–6409. Serves lunch and dinner. Homemade soups, salad bar, Italian combos, burgers, and fish.

HOW TO GET AROUND. A complimentary **shuttle bus** runs between the California base lodge and accommodations in the area and from the casinos to the Boulder base lodge in Nevada, 7 A.M. to 5:15 P.M. For schedule information, call the ski area, 541–1330.

SEASONAL EVENTS. The major event in **January** is the *U.S. Pro Challenge.* In early **February** the *Plymouth/Harrah's Celebrity Ski Classic* is held. In **March** there is a *Top Gun Mogul competition,* open to international professional mogul skiers. The annual *Silver Dollar Super G* race is open to USSA-licensed racers in **April.**

OTHER ACTIVITIES. Snowboarders are allowed only on the Nevada side of Heavenly Ski Resort.

In town there are bowling alleys and movie theaters, and many factory-outlet stores for some interesting shopping are located at the intersection of Hwy. 50 at Hwy. 89. The shops are open seven days a week.

For an unusual, close-up look at Lake Tahoe, book onto the rather grand old sternwheelers, the *Tahoe Queen* or the M.S. *Dixie* (leaving from Zephyr Cove). Cruises offer a bit of adventure, dining, drinking, and live music. Call for reservations aboard the *Dixie* at (916) 588–3508 or 882–0786. The *Tahoe Queen* cruise heads across the lake to the North Shore ski resorts, even in winter; call (916) 541–3364.

CHILDREN'S ACTIVITIES. The California Main Lodge operates a day-care center from 8:30 A.M. to 5 P.M. daily, on a first-come, first-served basis for children aged 2–4 years. The program includes lunch and costs $49 for the day.

Heavenly's L'il Angels Children's program is offered at the California and Boulder base lodges for ages 4–12. Call the program at (916) 541–1330 for details.

NIGHTLIFE. The California base lodge has live music and dancing. In town, the *89th St. Bar & Grill* and *Rojo's* have live entertainment and dancing. The casinos all feature lounge acts and revues for various tastes. *Crystal Cabaret* at Caesars is all glitter; *Harrah's* revue is a sizzler. The mainstay of nightlife in town, of course, is the gambling, from the luxurious Harrah's to the more homey *Bill's Casino.* Big-name entertainment usually is headlined at *Caesars* and *Harrah's.*

KIRKWOOD

Box 1
Kirkwood CA 95646
Tel: 209–258–6000

Snow Report: 209–258–3000
Area Vertical: 2,000 ft.
Number of Trails: 65 trails on 2,000 acres;
    longest run is 2.5 miles
Lifts: 4 triple chairs, 6 double chairs, 1
    surface lift
Snowmaking: none
Season: mid-November–May

Kirkwood is south of Lake Tahoe by a mountain peak or two and only 30 minutes from the town of South Lake Tahoe. The Sierra Crest rises 2,000 feet above Kirkwood's mountain meadow, providing some of the most diverse skiing terrain in the country. There is everything—chutes, good steep pitches, tree skiing, open bowls, and gentle novice terrain on the Hay Flats. The panoramic view from the top of Wagon Wheel chairlift, at 9,800 feet, is from the High Sierras to the central valley of California. In terms of skier visits, Kirkwood has now developed into the third largest in the Tahoe area.

The resort is well suited to families and those who prefer a quiet atmosphere. The village consists of six condominiums at the base of the lifts. Two base lodges have rental and ski shops, cafeterias, and sit-down restaurants.

Practical Information for Kirkwood

HOW TO GET THERE. For transportation to South Lake Tahoe and Reno, see *Heavenly* section. Kirkwood is 30 miles southwest of South Lake Tahoe on Hwy. 88 at Carson Pass. **By car.** From Reno, take US 395 south to Minden, then Hwy. 88 west to Kirkwood. It is about 1½ hours from Reno's Cannon International Airport. The skier's **shuttle** provides scheduled service from South Lake Tahoe locations to Kirkwood Ski Resort; call 258–6000 for schedules. **Taxis, rental cars,** and complimentary casino/hotel **vans** are also available.

TELEPHONES. The area code for the Kirkwood area is 209.

ACCOMMODATIONS. *Kirkwood Central Reservations,* Box 1, Kirkwood, CA 95646, 258–7000, can arrange moderately priced lodging at one of the six local complexes—a total of 104 condominiums—owned and operated by Kirkwood. For accommodations in nearby South Lake Tahoe, see *Heavenly Valley.* For lodging information and rates for the South Lake Tahoe area, call 800–822–5922.

Ski packages are available for downhill skiers as well as cross-country skiers with a 3-night, 3-day lift pass midweek starting at $218 (weekend $256), per person, double occupancy. Five-day packages start at $336. Lodgings range from studios to 3-bedroom condos with kitchens, fireplaces, and the usual resort amenities.

Base Camp, across the street from Solitude and Cornice Lifts in the main base area, has 1- and 2-bedroom condos.

Edelweiss, at Kirkwood's Timber Creek base area, offers access to Hole in Wall and Bunny Chair lifts; 1-, 2-, and 3-bedroom condos, some with lofts.

The Meadows, various condo units located midway between Timber Creek and the Red Cliffs Lodge, has a comfortable common area including a spa.

Thimblewood, close to the Timber Creek base area, features 1-bedroom, 1-bath condos; views of Kirkwood Meadow; health club, conference facilities, restaurant.

Whiskey Run, adjacent to Red Cliffs day lodge at the base area, has 2-bedroom, 3-bath condos with ski-in/ski-out accessibility.

RESTAURANTS. There are four restaurants and five bars in the village of Kirkwood. There is also a new chef who is a graduate of the California Culinary Academy and has received accolades for the progressive American cuisine he now prepares at the Cornice Cafe. In addition to those near the lodges, there is a big selection of restaurants in South Lake Tahoe, a short drive away.

Price categories are based on a meal for one, excluding beverages and tip. Restaurants are listed in order of price category. *Moderate,* $10–$15, and *Inexpensive,* less than $10. All restaurants listed accept major credit cards unless otherwise noted.

Moderate–Inexpensive

Cornice. At the base of chairs 5 and 6; 258–7373. Features gourmet California cuisine with moderate prices. Favorites are baked brie with garlic and red peppers and a frozen white-chocolate mousse. Cornice serves lunch and dinner and has a bar for après-ski evening entertainment.

Kirkwood Inn. On Hwy. 88 at the resort entrance; 258–7304. This rustic building dates back to 1864. Lunch and dinner are served daily; barbecue and sandwich specials.

Red Cliffs Day Lodge. At the base; no phone. Large cafeteria serving full breakfasts and lunches.

HOW TO GET AROUND. If you stay in the village of Kirkwood, no transportation is needed. Everything is within walking distance, including the grocery store and restaurants. A **shuttle bus** runs along Kirkwood Meadows Drive throughout the day. The town of South Lake Tahoe operates a 24-hour free transportation system on the US 50 corridor and in the area's residential neighborhoods; call 916–544–2266 for fares and schedules.

SEASONAL EVENTS. The area hosts a series of three cross-country races in **December** and **January,** a **New Year's Eve** Torchlight parade, the *Coca-Cola Cup* recreational race in **February,** and an assortment of recreational ski races on a daily basis.

Check the *South Lake Tahoe Chamber of Commerce,* 3066 US 50 (541–5225), for up-to-date information; closed Sundays. The *Visitors Coupon Information Center,* 4093 US 50 (544–0374; 800–237–3536), hands out complimentary packages with discounts for dining and entertainment.

OTHER SPORTS AND ACTIVITIES. Kirkwood has one of the largest **cross-country** centers in the country. Eighty km of groomed track cover some 4,000 acres. The interconnecting trail system provides a challenge for all ability levels and includes pine forests, open meadows, and ridges with spectacular views of the Sierra Nevada crest. Lessons, clinics, guided tours, and video reviews are available; for information call 258–7248.

DAY-CARE FACILITIES. For children 3–6 years and out of diapers, there is child care available at *Red Cliffs* lodge; 9 A.M.–4:30 P.M. with lunch, $30; half-days with lunch, $20. Cost is $5 per hour with a 2-hour minimum. The *Mighty Mountain* takes children, 4–12, who are ready to ski out to the slopes from Red Cliffs lodge; all day (10:30 A.M.–4 P.M.) $45 with lunch. *Mogul Mountain* has its own grooming and its own platter lift. For reservations and information, contact the ski school at 258–6000.

NIGHTLIFE. *Zak's Bar* in the Red Cliffs day lodge has great nachos and is open till midnight. On Friday and Saturday, Zak's features music and dancing. The *Cornice* bar stays open until the customers leave and occasionally has live entertainment. Kirkwood doesn't offer much bar hopping, but the determined can drive the 30 miles to South Lake Tahoe for plenty more.

NORTHSTAR-AT-TAHOE

Box 129
Truckee CA 95734
Tel: 916–562–1010

Snow Report: 916–562–1330
Area Vertical: 2,200 ft.
Number of Trails: 49; longest is 2.9 miles
Lifts: 2 high-speed quad chairs, 3 triple
      chairs, 3 double chairs, 2 surface lifts
Snowmaking: top to bottom on 110 acres
Season: Thanksgiving–April

Northstar is called the Sierra's most complete destination resort. It gears itself for the family vacation with a classic distribution of ski terrain—25 percent beginner, 25 percent expert, and 50 percent intermediate. The north-facing, wind-protected bowls offer some of the best powder skiing around. Steep chutes; long, lazy meandering runs; and fantastic scenery keep everyone happy. Lift-ticket sales are limited so that on sell-out days, lift-line waits should be no more than 20 minutes.

There are plenty of amenities off the slopes as well. The Village Mall houses shops and meeting facilities. The Mid-Mountain Day Lodge has a sundeck with a barbecue pit and restaurants. The Recreation Center is great for après-ski relaxation with spas, saunas, exercise rooms, and game rooms.

Lake Tahoe's North Shore is 6 miles by road, and the naughty California/Nevada border is only 15 miles away.

Practical Information for Northstar-at-Tahoe

HOW TO GET THERE. The Truckee/Tahoe airport is only 3 miles from Northstar and the *Amtrak* stop in Truckee is about 6 miles away on California Hwy. 267. *Sierra Tahoe Aviation,* (916) 587–4433, comes into Truckee. Reno is 40 miles southeast and San Francisco is 196 miles west. Major national airlines serve Reno's Cannon International Airport, (702) 785–2575.

TELEPHONES. The area code for Northstar-at-Tahoe is 916; for all Nevada it is 702.

ACCOMMODATIONS. Lodging on the North Shore stretches from Incline Village to Tahoe City. Many of the establishments include interchangeable lift tickets valid at 7 areas. For specific information on the 80 or so lodges in the region, contact the *Tahoe North Visitors and Convention Bureau,* Box 5578, Tahoe City, CA 95730; (916) 583–3494 or 800–TAHOE–4 U.

For reservations at Northstar call (916) 587–0200 or 800–533–6787. Lodging categories are for double occupancy. *Expensive,* $100 and up; *Moderate,* $50–$100; and *Inexpensive,* under $50. Packages of 3–6 nights are available and include lift tickets. Studio to 4-bedroom condos with full kitchens, fireplaces, hot tubs, saunas, and shuttle service throughout the complex range from $108 per night for a studio to $264 for a 4-bedroom; 3- and 4-bedroom houses range from $270 to $360 per night.

River Run Condominiums. *Expensive.* On the access road to Alpine Meadows overlooking the Truckee River; 583–0137. Nightly rates for accommodations ranging from 1-bedroom to 3-bedrooms with a loft.

Pepper Tree Inn. *Moderate.* Box 29, downtown Tahoe City; 800–624–8590 or 800–824–5342 in CA). Just a short walk to shops and restaurants. Recently remodeled rooms—king-size beds, hair dryers, irons, and other amenities. Heated pool, hot tub, laundry.

River Ranch. *Moderate.* Box 197, Tahoe City; 583–4264. Set on the Truckee River, all rooms have a view; antique furnishings; complimentary breakfast.

Tamarack Lodge. *Inexpensive.* Box 859, Tahoe City; 583–3350. Features rustic-style rooms and housekeeping cabins. Restaurant.

RESTAURANTS. The closest towns with a variety of restaurants for the North Shore are Tahoe Vista, Carnelian Bay, Tahoe City, Kings Beach, and Truckee. On the mountain, *Big Springs* day lodge has a cafeteria, snack bar, and hot dog bar. Nearby is a wine and cheese house. In the base area's Village Mall are *Schaffers' Mill* restaurant, *Pedro's Pizza Parlor,* and *Sam's Deli.* Nearby *The Basque Club Restaurant* offers price-fixed, family-style Basque cuisine for dinner. It is in the Northstar Clubhouse; 587–0260. Following is a selection, listed by price category, determined by the cost of a full dinner for one, excluding tax, tips, and beverages. *Expensive,* $20–$30; *Moderate,* $10–$20; and *Inexpensive,* less than $10.

Le Petit Pier. *Expensive.* 7250 N. Lake Blvd., Tahoe Vista; 546–4464. A classic French restaurant with set menus, attentive service, and a romantic setting with lake views.

Wolfdales. *Expensive.* 640 N. Lake Blvd., Tahoe City; 583–5700. One of the best in the area. Three-star California cuisine with a Japanese flair. Reservations suggested.

Jakes-on-the-Lake. *Moderate.* Boatworks Marina at 780 N. Lake Blvd., Tahoe City; 583–0188. It is "in" and reservations are recommended; diners can watch the colors over the lake change with the sunset; mostly seafood, dinners only.

Squeeze Inn. *Inexpensive.* Main St., Truckee; 587–4814. Serves a great variety of omelets for breakfast and lunch.

HOW TO GET AROUND. A free skiers' **shuttle** is available between Incline Village, Tahoe Vista/Kings Beach, and Northstar; call (916) 562–1010.

SEASONAL EVENTS. Santa plays a big part in Northstar's four-day **Christmas** celebration, especially when he passes out candy to the children in ski school, child-care centers, and any and all skiers on the slopes. The *Truckee Sled Dog Races* are held each **February** at the airport. The races feature over 70 teams from the western U.S. with the huskies covering distances of 3–14 miles. Weight pulling is exciting, too; the record for one dog is 1,600 pounds. *Snowfest* lasts for 10 days in early **March,** with more than 100 events taking place at various North Shore locations.

OTHER SPORTS AND ACTIVITIES. The *Northstar Cross Country and Telemark Center* maintains 45 km of double-track **cross-country** trails and skating lanes. Guided tours, gourmet ski tours, off-track tours, telemark lessons, races, and clinics are scheduled throughout the season. The tracks wind through forests overlooking the Martis Valley and the Sierra Nevada. Skiers will see *Schaffers' Camp,* once the hub of frenzied activity during the West's logging era. Northstar Center, Box 129, Truckee, CA 95734: 587–0273.

Snowmobiles can be rented from *Mountain Lake Adventures* in Incline Village, 831–4202. *North Tahoe Regional Park,* 546–7248, in Tahoe Vista, rents snowmobiles and **sleds.**

CHILDREN'S ACTIVITIES. The children's program offers all-day lessons for children 5–12. The price of $45 includes 5 hours of lessons and lunch. Call *Ski School* at 562–0270. For younger kids who are toilet trained, a licensed child-care center at the base mall has all-day activities and a learn-to-ski program. Reservations recommended. Call 587–0278.

NIGHTLIFE. The *Alpine Bar* in the village has live entertainment. There is the usual gambling, big-name entertainers, and hot spots in Incline Village and Truckee. There are also bars overlooking the lake for quiet drinks. See other Lake Tahoe areas for more information.

SQUAW VALLEY USA

Box 2007
Olympic Valley CA 95730
Tel. 916–583–6985

Snow Reports: 916–583–6955
Area Vertical: 2,850 ft.
Number of Trails: all open bowls
   encompassing 8,300 acres
Lifts: 16 double and 7 triple chairlifts, 1
   gondola, 2 detachable quads, 150-
   passenger tram, 4 pony tows
Snowmaking: 80 acres (off 3 lifts)
Season: mid-November–early May

Squaw Valley is immense. Nestled among six Sierra mountain peaks overlooking Lake Tahoe, Squaw has thousands of acres of open skiing on an average annual snowpack of 450 inches and receives plenty of warm California sunshine. This world-class resort was the site of the 1960 Olympics and is in the process of regaining its reputation for high standards of skiing and lodging. The 1990–91 season saw the opening of the 405-room, all-season Resort at Squaw Creek, with its own quad chairlift and run to its base across the valley from Squaw's Village. This new resort offers all the amenities you could imagine. At the top of the tram the new Bath and Tennis Club adds another dimension to on-mountain dining and year-round amenities, with an Olympic-size ice-skating rink and six tennis courts.

Although Squaw is well known for steep and challenging skiing, 70 percent of its terrain is perfect for novice and intermediate skiers. They can ride the tram to the top and ski vast, open slopes without having to ride another chairlift. Last season 300 acres of new ski terrain were opened, and new snowmaking now covers Big Red, Searchlight, Squaw Creek, and the pony-tow lifts from top to bottom.

Practical Information for Squaw Valley

HOW TO GET THERE. The closest gateway by **air** is Reno's Cannon International Airport, served by 12 carriers. Daily **shuttle service** from the airport to Truckee and the North Shore is available from *Aero Trans Vans,* 702–786–2376; and *See Tahoe Tours,* 702–329–2205 or 916–546–3293. **Taxis** can be hired from *North Shore Taxi,* 546–3181; *T.C. Cab,* 583–TAXI; and *Truckee Taxi,* 587–6336. See the *California/Nevada State Line* section at the beginning of this chapter for **rental car** companies in Reno. By automobile, Squaw lies 200 miles east of San Francisco via I–80 and Highway 89, 5 miles north of Tahoe City.

Amtrak's *California Zephyr,* called the most scenic **train** ride in America, stops daily in Reno and Truckee (6 miles from Squaw Valley), mornings westbound, evenings eastbound. Call 800–USA–RAIL for reservations and information. For Reno ticket office, call 702–329–8638. *The Transcisco* is a tour train operating between the Bay area, Truckee, and Reno. A lounge car features a live band and dancing. Service is offered every weekend and on Wednesdays. Reservations: *Transcisco Tours,* 555 California St., San Francisco, CA 94104; 415–477–9700.

TELEPHONES. The area code for Squaw Valley is 916; for Reno, it is 702.

ACCOMMODATIONS. For information on lodgings, contact *Squaw Valley Central Reservations,* Squaw Valley USA, Box 2007, Olympic Valley, CA 95730; call 800–545–4350, or locally, 916–583–5585. A shuttle to the ski area is available from all lodge locations in North and South Shore and Truckee. Rate categories are based on the per-night cost of a hotel room: *Expensive,* $85–$195; *Moderate,* $45–$85; *Inexpensive,* $32–$45. All properties offer 3-, 5-, and 7-day packages.

Olympic Village Inn. *Expensive.* Box 2648, Olympic Valley; 916–581–6000 or 800–VILLAGE. Outdoor heated swimming pool and 5 outdoor spas, restaurant, and bar. Nightly rates also available.

Resort at Squaw Creek. *Expensive.* Box 3333, Olympic Valley; 800–545–4350. Deluxe, ski-in, ski-out accommodations. Fitness complex, heated outdoor pools and spas, ice-skating rink, restaurants.

Squaw Valley Inn. *Expensive.* Box 2407, Olympic Valley; 916–583–1576. Ski-in, ski-out, next to the cable car. Restaurant, swimming pool, hot tub, adjacent to village.

Squaw Valley Lodge. *Expensive.* 916–583–5500 or 800–922–9970. This development at the base of Super Squaw lift has a full-facility health club. Six-day lift tickets available.

Granlibakken Resort. *Moderate.* Box 6329, Tahoe City, CA 95730; 916–583–6203. Eight miles from the area; saunas, hot tubs, full breakfast daily. One-bedroom condos and bedrooms available.

Mayfield House. *Moderate.* An old Tahoe residence beautifully restored and refurbished in Tahoe City, 8 miles from Squaw; 916–583–1001.

Sunnyside Lodge/Restaurant. *Moderate.* 1850 W. Lake Blvd.; 583–7200. On West Shore, 10 mi. from the slopes. Circa 1930 lodge, completely redone to a bed-and-breakfast, with 23 rooms and suites.

The Hostel at Squaw Valley. *Inexpensive.* 800–544–4723. At the base, walk to lifts. Accommodates up to 100 persons: bunks and shared baths. Remember to bring your own sleeping bag.

Tahoe City Inn. *Inexpensive.* 790 N. Lake Blvd, Tahoe City; 583–3494. Most rooms have private Jacuzzis and lake views. Popular with honeymooners.

RESTAURANTS. Variety is the spice of food fare at Squaw Valley, where cuisine ranges from Continental to ethnic to basic American. *High Camp Bath and Tennis Club* at the top of Squaw's Cable Car has three restaurants serving breakfast, lunch, and dinner: *The Terrace (Inexpensive)* is a cafeteria with sweeping views of Lake Tahoe; *Alexanders (Moderate)* has table service for lunch and cocktails; the *Poolside Cafe (Moderate)* offers elegant atmosphere for lunch and dinner with incredible views and sunsets. Call 583–2555 for all three restaurants.

Restaurant categories listed here are based on a meal for one, with beverages and tips extra. *Expensive,* $20 and up; *Moderate,* $10–$20; *Inexpensive,* less than $10. All restaurants listed take major credit cards unless otherwise noted.

Glissandi. *Expensive.* Resort at Squaw Creek; 800–545–4350. Neo-French haute cuisine in an intimate, semi-formal setting. Run by former owners of La Cheminee, one of California's top restaurants.

Wolfdales. *Expensive.* 640 N. Lake Blvd., Tahoe City, a 20-minute drive from Squaw; 583–5700. One of the best, if not the best, in the area. Their specialty is fish dishes with Japanese touches. Reservations suggested. Open Fridays, Saturdays, and Sundays only.

Cascades Restaurant. *Moderate.* Resort at Squaw Creek; 800–545–4350. Regional American cuisine in a casual setting. Scenic views of Squaw Peak.

Hardscramble Creek Bar & Grill. *Moderate.* Resort at Squaw Creek; 800–545–4350. Bistro-style cafe with oak-burning pizza oven. Good for snacks and for hearty soups in afternoons. In the evening the live music keeps things jumping.

Jimmys. *Moderate.* Squaw Valley base lodge; 583–2614. Imaginative omelets, sandwiches, soups. Sit-down service for lunch and dinner.

Clocktower Cafe. *Inexpensive.* Squaw Valley base lodge; 583–2614. Inexpensive for casual dining. Usually good fare.

La Chamois. *Inexpensive.* Squaw Valley; 583–5404. Not French, as you may assume, but a pizza, soup, and sandwich shop. No credit cards.

HOW TO GET AROUND. The village core of Squaw is all ski, so everything is within walking distance. **Shuttle buses** provide transportation among the hotels and into Tahoe City and Truckee as well.

SEASONAL EVENTS. *Snowfest* is the second largest winter carnival in the United States (the first is in St. Paul). It takes place throughout the North Lake Tahoe area at the beginning of **March.** Activities include ski races, dances, wine tastings, tournaments, and parades. For details of which activities are scheduled at various resorts, contact Snowfest, Box 7590, Tahoe City, CA 95730; 916–583–7625.

OTHER SPORTS AND ACTIVITIES. Every ski area has its **amateur races.** But at Squaw there is a tremendous variety of events for skiers of all ages and abilities. Contact race services at 583–6985.

For **night skiing,** the Searchlight slopes are illuminated on Fridays and Saturdays all season.

For **cross-country skiing** contact *the Resort at Squaw Creek Nordic Ski Center,* 583–5585.

Ice skating is a popular activity here. At the Olympic ice pavilion, at the top of Squaw's cable car route, the views are spectacular. The rink is open to the public daily with skate rentals. Down in the valley, the Resort at Squaw Creek also has a new rink and rental shop.

Sightseeing and **gambling** in nearby Reno are big draws for the ski resorts in the area.

CHILDREN'S ACTIVITIES. Squaw's philosophy is that skiing is a family affair. To that end, the *Papoose Snow School* provides a way for parents to enjoy skiing while children aged 3–5 spend the day in an entertaining and educational environment. The schedule includes supervised activities that introduce children to skiing; also arts and crafts, exercises, storytelling, and rest periods. Skiing takes place in a specially designated area. Children must be toilet trained. *Ten Little Indians Infant Care* offers state-licensed, supervised activities for the 6-month to 3-year-old child. The fee for both age groups is $47 per day and includes lunch and snacks. Reservations are necessary; call 583–0119.

Snow School sessions begin at 8:30 A.M. or 1 P.M. Call the school's office at 583–4743 for information.

NIGHTLIFE. The active pace of the day does not diminish after dark. In addition to the activities in the new facilities at the top of the tram (open until 10 P.M.), *Bar One* at the base of Squaw Valley, 583–6985, features live music. The *Olympic Village Inn* has comedy nights. The *Opera House Cinema* has first-run feature films. *Bullwhackers Pub* at Squaw Creek Resort has pool tables, sports videos, and a wide selection of regional beers. *Hardscramble,* Squaw Creek Resort's après-ski café, has dancing to live music till 1 A.M.

OTHER LAKE TAHOE SKI AREAS

The Lake Tahoe area has a number of smaller ski hills.

Homewood Ski Area. Box 165, Homewood, CA 95718; 916–525–7256. Six miles south of Tahoe City on Hwy 89. Vertical drop: 1,650 feet. Longest run: 2 miles. Lifts: 2 double chairs, 2 triple chairs, 1 quad chair, 5 surface lifts. Two day lodges, day-care center. Friendly, family-oriented area with 1,260 acres of skiing. Fifteen percent beginner, 50 percent intermediate, 35 percent advanced.

Mount Rose Ski Area. Box 2406, Reno, NV 89505; 702–849–0704. Twenty-two miles southwest of downtown Reno on Rt. 431. Vertical drop: 1,450 feet. Forty-one runs on 900 acres. Summit: 9,700 feet. Longest run: 2.5 miles. Lifts: 1 quad chair, 3 triple chairs, 1 double chair. Two day lodges, cafeterias, bar, rental shop.

Sierra Ski Ranch. Box 3501, Twin Bridges, CA 95735; 916–659–7535. Vertical drop: 1,500 feet. Longest run: 3.5 miles. Lifts: 1 detachable quad, 2 triple chairs, 8 double chairs. Two Thousand acres on 3 mountainsides. Variety of instructional and lodging packages offered. Two day lodges, cafeteria, complimentary shuttle to South Lake Tahoe. No alcoholic beverages allowed on premises.

Sugar Bowl Ski Resort. Box 5, Norden, CA 95724; 916–426–3651. Vertical drop: 1,500 feet. Longest run: 2 miles. Lifts: 7 double chairs, 1 quad chair, 1 gondola. More than 50 years old, the historic lodge just steps from the lifts has recently been renovated, with hotel rooms, restaurants, and a bar. New licensed child care. Five-day ski-week packages and Skiers Bed & Breakfast package.

Colorado

ASPEN AREA

ASPEN MOUNTAIN

Box 1248
Aspen CO 81612
Tel: 303–925–1220

Area Vertical: 3,267 ft.
Number of Trails: 625 acres of groomed
trails at Aspen Mountain, longest run 3
miles; 402 acres of groomed trails at
nearby Buttermilk/Tiehack, part of the
Aspen complex
Lifts: On Aspen Mountain: 1 gondola, 7
chairlifts. On Buttermilk/Tiehack: 6
chairlifts
Snowmaking: 35 percent of terrain
Season: mid- to late-November–mid-April

Aspen. To skiers, the name conjures the same fantasies as New York does to theater buffs. For over 40 years, this little town has been the "ultimate" in ski destinations. The celebrities provide as much of the dazzle and glitter as do all the other attractions of Aspen. Like New York, when the sun goes down, the restaurants and night spots, over 100 of them, fill up with the potpourri of well-heeled visitors who can indulge themselves in some of the finest eating establishments in any ski town and, indeed, in most cities.

A walking tour of the town—the center is a traffic-free mall—can be filled with discoveries and amazement for even the most jaded shoppers. Average mortals can see items in shops with price tags that stagger the imagination. But there are plenty of the usual souvenir shops also, most of the ubiquitous T-shirt variety. Nonskiers will not feel out of place here; there is so much else to do.

Aspen Mountain has seen $17 million in improvements since 1985. The big attraction is the Silver Queen gondola, with its 3,267 vertical-foot rise to the top. Besides speeding the flow of experts who challenge the steep face of Ajax, as the mountain is known, the gondola gives beginners a chance to go up, ski the gentle runs at the top, then ride back down and be able to brag about "skiing Aspen Mountain."

The other two mountains, Buttermilk and Snowmass, are part of the same corporation, yet they have their own separate personalities. (See

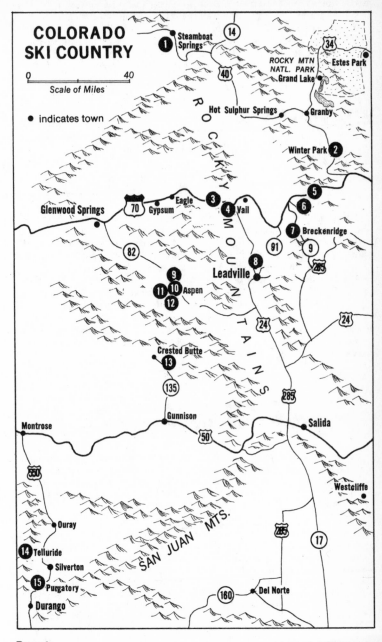

COLORADO SKI COUNTRY

0 _____ 40
Scale of Miles

● indicates town

Steamboat Springs ❶

ROCKY MTN NATL. PARK
Estes Park
Grand Lake
Granby
Hot Sulphur Springs

Winter Park ❷

Glenwood Springs
Gypsum
Eagle
❸
❹ Vail
❺
❻
❼ Breckenridge
91
9
❽
Leadville
❾
⓫ ❿ Aspen
⓬
Crested Butte
⓭
135
Gunnison
Montrose
Salida
Westcliffe
Ouray
⓮ Telluride
Silverton
⓯ Purgatory
Durango
Del Norte

Resorts

Arapahoe Basin, 5
Aspen Highlands, 9
Aspen Mountain, 10
Beaver Creek, 3
Breckenridge, 7

Buttermilk, 12
Copper Mountain, 8
Crested Butte, 13
Keystone, 6
Purgatory/Durango, 15

Snowmass, 11
Steamboat Springs, 1
Telluride, 14
Vail, 4
Winter Park/Mary Jane, 2

Snowmass section.) Lift tickets are interchangeable and include The Highlands (not owned by Aspen). Buttermilk, long a favorite of the locals, now has a racing arena and is home to the Vic Braden Ski College.

Strict zoning and sky-high costs have, in the past, limited the development of new lodging facilities in Aspen. But in 1989, the new 92-room Little Nell Hotel opened at the base of Aspen Mountain, and a 292-room Ritz Carlton is scheduled to open for the 1991 season.

ASPEN HIGHLANDS

Box T
Aspen, CO 81612
Tel: 303–925–5300

Area Vertical: 3,800 ft.
Number of Trails: 500 acres, longest run 3 miles
Lifts: 9 double chairs, 2 pomas
Snowmaking: on 40 acres
Season: Thanksgiving–mid-April

The Highlands, while part of the Aspen complex, is a privately owned and operated ski area on a separate mountain that sits between Aspen and Buttermilk mountains. It has some spectacular skiing, especially for advanced and intermediate skiers. A new area called Olympic Bowl has 65 acres of open trail and glade skiing with an 800-foot vertical.

Multiple-day area lift tickets are interchangeable with Aspen, but Highlands also offers its own daily and multiday tickets. Kids 12 and under ski free when accompanied by skiing parents.

There is no significant lodging near the base; skiers stay in Aspen-area lodges. Skiing packages for Highlands can be booked through *The Aspen Resort Association,* 800–262–7736 or 800–421–7145 in Colorado, and *Aspen Ski Tours,* 303–925–9500.

Practical Information for Aspen and Aspen Highlands

HOW TO GET THERE. Aspen is in the White River National Forest, 205 miles from Denver. **By air.** *Continental Express* and *United Express* fly from Denver to the Aspen/Snowmass Airport 4 miles from town. During the winter season, *United Express* operates nonstop flights into Aspen from Los Angeles, Chicago, and Dallas/Ft. Worth. Taxis are available between the airport and town lodging. Taxis and limos are also available for the ride from Denver's Stapleton Airport to Aspen.

By bus. *Greyhound-Trailways* runs between Denver and Aspen and Grand Junction and Aspen; call 800–237–8211 for information. *Aspen Limousine and Bus Service* provides the same service; call (303) 925–2400. Reservations are suggested.

By train. Daily transcontinental service on *Amtrak* stops at Glenwood Springs. Without prior arrangements, the taxi to Aspen is $55; however, divide that among five people and it's $11 per person. Eastbound trains arrive at 3 P.M. and westbound trains at 1 P.M. Make advance reservations through Amtrak or your travel agent to book a *Mellow Yellow Taxi* at a special rate between Glenwood Springs and the Aspen area, (303) 925–2282. *High Mountain Taxi* also serves this route, (303) 925–8294.

By car. It is 145 miles from Denver via I–70 to Glenwood Springs, then Hwy. 82 into Aspen. From Colorado Springs, take Hwy. 24 to Hwy. 82, 160 miles. From Grand Junction, take I–70 east to Glenwood and Hwy. 82 to Aspen, 140 miles.

TELEPHONES. The area code for Aspen is 303.

ACCOMMODATIONS. Contact the *Aspen Resort Association,* 700 S. Aspen St., Aspen, CO 81611; 800–262–7736, or in Colorado, 800–421–7145 (international telex, 705580 ASPENRESORT UD), for lodging reservations. The *Aspen Skiing Company* also has a reservations center that books lodging year-round. Call 800–525–6200. *Coates, Reid and Waldron,* 720 E. Hyman Ave., 800–22–ASPEN or 924–1400, the largest management company in Aspen, lists many condos and home rentals in the moderate range.

Lodging in town is within a maximum of an eight-block walk to the base of Aspen Mountain; also the free shuttle runs regularly through town to the mountain and to Buttermilk, Snowmass, and Aspen Highlands. Many hotels have shuttle service to and from ski areas and the airport. The listings here will give an idea of the range of lodgings available. Price categories are for regular season rates for a room based on double occupancy. *Expensive,* $185–$600; *Moderate,* $75–$185, and *Inexpensive,* under $75. During "Value" season, November through mid-December and early April and January, rates are discounted. During the Christmas holidays, rates are more expensive.

Expensive

Aspen Club. 1450 Crystal Lake Rd.; 925–8900. A condominium complex specializing in physical fitness, a half-mile from town, with 2-bedroom units with fireplaces. Restaurant, cocktail lounge, fitness center, pool, sauna, hot tubs, steam rooms, running track, and indoor tennis.

The Gant. 610 West End Ave.; 925–5000. One- to 4-bedroom units in this condominium resort. Two heated pools, whirlpools, saunas, and 5 all-weather tennis courts.

Hotel Jerome. 330 E. Main St.; 920–1000 or 800–331–7213. This historic hotel has been completely restored to its 1800s Victorian splendor. Twice-daily maid service, concierge, and elegant restaurants. Centrally located in town.

Lift One. 131 E. Durant Ave.; 925–1670. Full-service condominiums at the base of Aspen Mountain; 1- to 3-bedroom units. Pool, sauna, Jacuzzi. Convenient to restaurants and night spots.

Little Nell Hotel. At the base of Aspen Mountain; 800–525–6200. Totally new, just steps from the gondola. Understated elegance throughout: fireplaces in rooms as well as out-of-the-ordinary service that satisfies the most discerning appetites. Not ostentatious; for those who don't flinch at nightly rates up to $1,600.

Molly Gibson Lodge (formerly Aspen Ski Lodge). 101 W. Main St.; 925–3434. One- and 2-bedroom units with outdoor decks. Some have kitchenettes, fireplaces, Jacuzzis. Heated outdoor pool and hot tubs, breakfast.

Moderate

Aspen Manor Lodge. 411 S. Monarch St.; 925–3001. Small, modern lodge, close to mall and lifts. Heated pool, sauna, whirlpool, complimentary Continental breakfast.

Innsbruck Inn. 233 W. Main St.; 925–2980. Charming old-world inn at the bus stop. Heated pool, whirlpool, sauna, breakfast buffet, friendly owner-operation.

Skiers Chalet. 233 Gilbert St.; 920–2037. Just 100 yards from the finish line of all Aspen World Cup races. The 1A chairlift is at the back door. Heated pool, refrigerators, and restaurant on the premises.

St. Moritz Lodge. 334 W. Hyman Ave.; 925–3220. A 1930s lodge with European flavor. Apartments, rooms with private baths, inexpensive dorm rooms with shared baths. Fireplace in lobby, TV lounge, library, and game rooms; après-ski refreshments, but no restaurant. Heated pool, sauna, Jacuzzi. Condos are also available.

Inexpensive

Little Red Ski Haus. 118 E. Cooper Ave.; 925–3333. Friendly Victorian house, recently renovated; complimentary breakfast; 3 lounges, quad and single rooms.

Snow Queen Lodge. 124 E. Cooper St.; 925–8455. Small, cozy Victorian bed-and-breakfast, centrally located within walking distance of town. Outdoor hot tub and lodge parlor with TV.

T Lazy 7. Write: Box 240, Aspen CO 81612; 925–7254. Spartan apartments with kitchens located just outside town. This working ranch is wonderful for children to explore. Twice weekly barbeques feature country-and-western entertainment for the whole family: $40 adults, $30 children. A shuttle bus connects the ranch to town and the ski areas. Heated outdoor pool, Jacuzzi, sauna; no TV or telephone in rooms.

Tyrolean Lodge. 200 W. Main St.; 925–4595. Central location, free ski buses at the door. Large studio rooms and kitchenettes.

RESTAURANTS. On Aspen Mountain, the mountaintop *Sundeck* offers the usual ski fare with indoor and outdoor seating. *Bonnie's Restaurant,* mid-mountain in Tourtelotte Park, serves good ol' American food and delicious European specialties. The outdoor deck is *the* place to meet and to be seen. *Ruthie's* is near Ruthie's Run, with cafeteria-style service plus gourmet dining in *Darcy's.*

On Buttermilk, *Cafe Suzanne,* located at the bottom of lift 3, features French country food, outdoor tables, wine, and beer. *The Cliffhouse,* at the top of lifts 5 and 2, offers cafeteria-style dining and a sundeck with a spectacular view. *Base Restaurant* at the bottom of lift 1 features cafeteria-style dining and a sundeck. *Anneliese's,* located at the bottom of lift 4 at Tiehack, has cafeteria-style dining, a sundeck, wine, and beer.

In town, there are over 80 restaurants, most of them excellent and most with prices comparable to New York or San Francisco. *Expensive* restaurants run around $18–$30 for entrees; *Moderate,* $12–$18; *Inexpensive,* under $12. All restaurants listed take major credit cards unless otherwise noted.

Expensive

Syzygy's (pronounced siz-i-je). 520 E. Hyman Ave.; 925–3700. The name of this restaurant is an astronomical term that describes 3 or more heavenly bodies within a solar system—here, it applies to the 3 elements that make up a stellar restaurant: food, decor, and service. With a very attentive staff, an elegant art deco motif (the dining room is divided by sheets of glass with water running over them), and creative cuisine (grilled ahi with red chili pesto and lettuce-wrapped spring rolls in mango sauce is just one of many unusual dishes), Syzygy's fits its billing. The restaurant's "star" quality is further justified by its clientele: celebrity watchers will be awed by the Aspen glitterati who frequent the place—making reservations a must.

Pinons. 105 S. Mill St. (upstairs); 920–2021. Located in a landmark building and decorated in the popular Santa Fe/western style (with rawhide-wrap handrails, stucco walls, and pink lighting), Pinons continues to please diners with it's fresh American cuisine. Entree specialties include macadamia nut–breaded ahi in a fresh burre butter sauce and elk tenderloin with a pink peppercorn sauce; as an appetizer try the lobster stroodle. But if you want to sample these delicacies you'll have to plan carefully: The restaurant is closed the last two weeks in April; all of May, June, and October; and for three weeks in November.

Moderate

Asia. 132 W. Main St.; 925–5433. Szechuan, Mandarin, and Hunan dishes make up the menu but the setting is what's really special about Asia. Located in a historic house (100-plus years old), the bar is from Liverpool and the 150-year-old ceiling is a sheet of stained glass. Free delivery 7 days a week (except in May, when it's closed).

Cache Cache. 205 S. Mill St.; 925–3835. "Flavors from Provence" (how the management describes the cuisine) are served in this comfortable peach-hued restaurant. Grilled salmon with tomato basil niçoise olive purée served over spinach and grilled eggplants is a typical special. Dinner only; reservations recommended.

Pepi's Hideout. 130 W. Cooper St. in the Fireside Lodge; 925–8845. The specials change nightly but the cuisine is mainly Continental, prepared by a team of Swiss chefs. Check out the beveled glass in the bar, formerly of the Bank of Aspen. The atmosphere is cozy with a fireplace in the bar. Reservations recommended.

Primavera. 600 S. Spring St. in the Aspen Club Lodge; 925–6602. At Primavera, you'll get a good view of the mountain while you eat light and healthfully—pastas, seafood, and salads dominate the menu. And all the light entrees should leave you with enough room for the delicious cheesecake.

Wienerstube Restaurant. 633 E. Hyman Ave.; 925–3357. For 27 years, Wienerstube has been turning out some of the yummiest breakfasts and lunches in Aspen— blueberry crêpes with vanilla cream sauce, eggs Benedict, Viennese pastries, and raisin bread pudding are just a few of the Austrian specialties you'll find here. Dinner is served from July through the end of March. Closed Mondays.

Inexpensive

La Cocina. 308 E. Hopkins Ave.; 925–9714. *The* place for Mexican food: the blue corn tortilla and posole is a favorite. Popular with Aspenites—so you know it's good. No reservations accepted.

Home Plate. 333 E. Durant Ave.; 925–1986. Prime rib, pastas, fried chicken breast, and daily vegetarian specials attract a lot of families—as do the availability of children's portions. Be sure to taste one of the homemade desserts.

Little Annie's. 517 E. Hyman Ave.; 925–1098. The generous portions of American food served here—pastas and grilled meats and chicken—are in sync with the Old West flavor of the wood and glass interior. Popular with the local crowd; no reservations are accepted; children's menu.

Skiers Chalet Steak House. 710 S. Aspen St.; 925–3381. In business since 1951, the Skiers Filet Mignon Specials—which make up almost 40 percent of the restaurant's sales—keep the people coming back for more (the convenient location close to Lift 1-A doesn't hurt either). Other entrees include lobster and chicken specials.

HOW TO GET AROUND. There is free **bus** service around town and to the ski areas of Aspen Mountain (in town), Buttermilk, Aspen Highlands, and Snowmass. **Taxis** (*Mellow Yellow,* 303–925–2282, or *High Mountain,* 303–925–5245) and **horse-drawn sleighs** from the mall are other means. Aspen is compact enough to **walk** nearly everywhere, and the center of town is a mall with no vehicular traffic permitted. Unless you're staying at a remote lodge or a friend's house, you won't need a car.

SEASONAL EVENTS. *Winterskol* is the annual **January** carnival. The *Subaru Aspen Winternational* is in **March**; it features the top amateur racers in world competitions on Aspen Mountain. *Snowmass/Aspen Banana Season* is in **April,** with parties, contests, special events, and discounted lodging.

OTHER SPORTS AND ACTIVITIES. There are guided and unguided **cross-country** tours on the *Tenth Mountain Trail,* a hut-to-hut European-type experience covering 100 miles of terrain in the White River National Forest between Aspen and Vail. Contact *Paragon Guides,* Box 130, Vail, CO 81658 (949–4272), *Elk Mountain Guides* Box 10327, Aspen, CO 81612 (923–6131), or the *Tenth Mountain Trail Association,* 1280 Ute Ave., Aspen, CO 81611 (925–5775). Moonlight dinner tours, cookhouse lunches, and cross-country lessons are available at Ashcroft, a ghost town 12 miles up Castle Creek Rd. There are 30 km of cross-country trails. Check *Aspen Cross Country Center,* c/o Ute Mountaineer, 308 S. Mill St., Aspen, CO 81611 (925–2145). A system of well-equipped shelters in the *Alfred A. Braun Hut System* connects Aspen with Crested Butte. Cost is $15 per person per night; call 925–7162. Ski rentals are available from *Ute Mountaineer,* 925–2849.

Snowshoe rentals are available from *Ute Mountaineer;* in fact, all kinds of touring equipment can be rented there.

In season, there are **Sno-Cat tours** on Aspen Mountain. Call the *Aspen Skiing Company* reservations center at 925–4444 or 800–525–6200.

CHILDREN'S ACTIVITIES. Aspen Mountain has no child-care or children's ski school facilities, but several in-town nursery services are available; call 925–1940 for information. *Aspen Sprouts* day care takes 2–5-year-olds, and is located at the Aspen Airport Business Center. The program includes art, games, and music; call 920–1055. Buttermilk Mountain operates the *Powder Pandas Ski School* for ages 3–6. Beginner to advanced instruction, rental equipment, private ski hill, lunch and snacks. Reservations suggested; call 925–1220. The daily rate is $50; 5-day programs cost $235. Aspen Highlands has a *Snowpuppies* program for 3–6-year-olds. Lessons, lunch, and lift tickets cost $46 a day or $195 for 5 days. For reservations call 925–5300. Also, see *Snowmass* section for children's programs there.

At *Pitkin County Library,* 120 E. Main St., preschool story hour is Tuesday mornings, toddlers on Wednesday mornings. A Tuesday afternoon read-aloud program for 6–10-year-olds is also available. A children's film program is held here

Friday afternoons from the end of December to early March; call 925–7124. Teens will enjoy hockey or figure skating at the *Aspen Ice Garden,* open 7 days a week; 925–7485.

The *Aspen Center for Environmental Studies* at the Hallam Lake Wildlife Sanctuary (925–5756) offers guided walks and snowshoe hikes Monday–Friday and an open house on Sunday afternoons; animals and educational displays.

NIGHTLIFE. It's impossible to describe the variety and selection Aspen offers—you'll not be bored here—but a few of the most popular places are covered below. The early après-ski crowd heads for *Shlomos* (in the Little Nell Hotel) and the *Tippler* (right off the lifts at 535 E. Dean), where, as the night progresses, the scene gets younger and wilder. The *Paragon* (419 E. Hyman) blares disco or live music until the wee hours. *Andre's* (312 S. Galena) is also a rocking disco although its former status as a celebrity hangout is on the wane. The current in-places for rubbing elbows with Aspen's rich and famous are the bars at *Mezzaluna* and *Pinon's* (see *Restaurants*). *Little Annie's* and *O'Leary's Pub* (517 and 521 E. Hyman respectively) are favorite low-key gathering spots.

For those of a more cultural bent, an old favorite for dinner theater is the *Crystal Palace,* 300 E. Hyman Ave., 925–1455. There are also four movie theaters in town.

SNOWMASS

Box 1248
Aspen CO 81612
Tel: 303–923–2085
    Central Reservations: 800–332–3245;
    Aspen Skiing Co. reservations: 800–525–6200

Snow Report: 303–925–1221
Area Vertical: 3,615 ft.
Number of Trails: 1,500 acres of tree-lined
    trails; longest run 3.7 miles
Lifts: 3 high-speed quad chairs, 9 double
    chairs, 2 triple chairs, 2 platter pulls
Snowmaking: 55 most heavily trafficked
    areas
Season: late November–mid-April

The wide-open valley that is Snowmass is no longer Aspen's stepsister, "Snowmass-at-Aspen," but has its own distinctive personality. Snowmass is a premier year-round resort.

What sets Snowmass apart is that literally everything is near the base lifts. Except for a few far-flung condos, you can walk everywhere. Lodging is situated so you can put your skis on at the door and ski down to the chairlift.

On the mountain, skiers will find the "Big Burn" area to be a paradise for cruising. The smooth runs are geared to intermediate or advanced-beginner skiing and seem to go on forever. The new (1986) Big Burn SuperChair goes from the base to the top in just 8 minutes, and two other high-speed quads on Fanny Hill and the Coney Glade area have alleviated lift lines considerably. Although not considered as challenging as Aspen Mountain, the bumps of Campground and High Alpine and the faces of the Hanging Valley Wall provide thrills for expert skiers. Actually, 9 percent of the area is rated easiest, 51 percent more difficult, 18 percent most difficult, and 22 percent expert.

The village has enough diversions, shopping, dining, and nightlife that one need never venture down the road to Aspen, and many families find it easier just to stay at Snowmass for their visit. There are a number of special programs for children at the area, but be aware that costs here are at the upper end of the scale. The experience is luxurious in all aspects, though, and merits the expense. The key is to check on "value season" dates during early December, January, and April.

Practical Information for Snowmass

HOW TO GET THERE. Snowmass is in the White River National Forest, 200 miles southwest of Denver. **By air.** All major airlines fly into Denver's Stapleton Airport; connect via *United Express* or *Continental Express* to the Snowmass/Aspen Airport. In winter, there are flights into Grand Junction and connecting ground transportation to the airport. Courtesy cars, taxis, and limousines are available at the airport; so are **rental cars:** *Avis,* 800–331–1212; *Budget,* 800–527–0700; and *Hertz,* 800–654–3131.

By bus. *Greyhound-Trailways* has daily schedules to the Snowmass/Aspen Airport and into Aspen from Denver and from Grand Junction; call 800–237–8211 for information.

By train. *Amtrak's* California Zephyr stops eastbound at 3:15 P.M. and westbound at 1:30 P.M. in an extravagantly scenic route from Denver across the Rockies. Advance arrangements should be made for connecting ground transportation from Glenwood Springs to Snowmass through Amtrak or your travel agent. Call Amtrak at 800–USA–RAIL or in Denver at (303) 893–3911.

By car. Go west on I–70 from Denver to Glenwood Springs, then Hwy. 82 to Snowmass, 200 miles. From Grand Junction it is 128 miles east on I–70 to Glenwood, Hwy. 82; 10 miles west of Aspen on Hwy. 82, 6 miles west of the Snowmass/Aspen Airport.

TELEPHONES. The area code for Snowmass is 303.

ACCOMMODATIONS. Contact *Central Reservations* at Box 5566, Snowmass Village, CO 81615; 800–332–3245, or, in Colorado, 800–237–3146 and 303–923–2010, for accommodations in the village. In addition, there are nearly 8,000 pillows in Aspen, 12 miles down-valley. Contact the Aspen Skiing Co. reservations center at 800–525–6200, for information. (Also, see section on *Aspen*).

A sampling of what's available follows. All properties are ski-in, ski-out with the exception of the Snowmass Club, which is 3 miles away on the golf course; a free shuttle service runs between the mountains and the club. Rates are based on double occupancy for a 1-bedroom condo. *Expensive,* $175–$225; *Moderate,* $110–$175; *Inexpensive,* $90 and up. (You won't find suitable lodging here for under $90 per night.)

Expensive

Crestwood. Box 5460, Snowmass Village; 923–2450. Attractive condominium complex with 1–3-bedroom units featuring fireplaces and private balconies with barbecues; some with saunas. Heated pool.

Snowmass Club. Drawer G-2, 0239 Snowmass Circle, Snowmass Village; 923–5600. Ski lodge and villas at base of Snowmass Mountain ski area. Spacious rooms and condominium units with private balconies. Restaurant, bar, lounge. Indoor and outdoor tennis courts; squash and racquetball courts; indoor and outdoor pools; health club; dog sledding.

Woodrun Place. 0425 Wood Rd., Snowmass Village; 923–5392. Luxurious condominium accommodations, with all the amenities.

Moderate

Stonebridge Inn. Box 5008; Snowmass Village; 923–2420. Rooms with restaurant and lounge.

Timberline. Box I–2, Snowmass Village; 923–4000. Condominium units with rustic Western atmosphere. Restaurant on the property.

Inexpensive

Pokolodi Lodge. Box B–2, Snowmass Village; 923–4310. Family-oriented lodge on hillside, 50 yards from ski lift. Pool and Jacuzzi. Restaurants nearby.

Snowmass Inn. 923–4202. Comfortable accommodations.

RESTAURANTS. Six restaurants are on the mountain. *Sam's Knob* is a typical cafeteria; upstairs is a fairly good sit-down restaurant, *CeCe's Point of View.* The expanded *Ullrhof,* at the base of the Big Burn, serves the usual ski fare, as does *Elk Camp* cafeteria. *High Alpine* also offers a buffet line, and an elegant restaurant, *Gwyn's,* gives reasonable value for high-quality food, large portions, and a fine wine list.

Expensive restaurants have entrees for $15–$25; *Moderate,* around $10; *Inexpensive,* $5–$9. Nearly all accept credit cards, but call to be sure.

Expensive

Chez Grandmere. 0016 Kearns Rd.; 923–2570. Exclusive establishment that has room for only 34 at its once-nightly seating. Price-fixed, 5-course meal.

Krabloonik. At the dog kennels (see "Other Sports and Activities" below); 923–3953. In spectacular setting and with homespun atmosphere, serving gourmet game cuisine. Ski in for lunch; dinner reservations required.

Il Poggio. In Village Mall; 923–4292. Northern Italian fare; overlooking the mall. Open for lunch.

La Boheme. In Village Mall; 923–6804. Former chef to the Royal Jordanian family and at Aspen's Hotel Jerome, Maurice Coutourier offers the finest in French cuisine. Reservations suggested.

Moderate

Hite's. In Village Mall; 923–4989. Country-fresh cooking for breakfast and dinner. Reservations suggested.

La Pinata. 65 Daly La.; 923–2153. Good Mexican food and margaritas.

Pippin's. In the Hotel Wildwood, 40 Elbert La.; 923–3550. Steak and lobster. Elegant dining with wonderful views and a harpist.

Shavanos. 20 Village Sq.; 923–4292. New American and Continental food; overlooks Snowmass Mall.

Timberline Restaurant. Snowmass Village; 923–4004. Affordable family dining with a cozy atmosphere. European and American cuisine.

The Tower Restaurant. On the Mall; 923–4650. Serves pasta, seafood, steaks—a lot of food for the money.

Inexpensive

Mama Maria's Pizza & Subs. Snowmass Center; 923–5250. Serves pizza, subs, and antipasto salads.

Mountain Dragon. On the Mall above Sports Kaelin; 923–3576. Specializing in Mandarin and Szechuan cuisines.

Pour La France. 0016 Kearns Rd; 923–5990. For soups, salads, pastries, specialty coffee drinks. Take-out service available.

Sno Beach Cafe. 45 Village Mall; 923–2597. Features cheese omelets, soups, salads, quiches, and sandwiches.

Stew Pot. 15 Village Mall; 923–2263. Featuring homemade soups, stews, homemade bread, and sandwiches.

The Timber Mill. 105 Village Sq. 923–4774. Cafeteria-style breakfasts and lunches.

HOW TO GET AROUND. Intravillage **bus** service is available at no charge between the day-skier lot and Lift One; check the *Transportation Department* at 923–6363 for specific times. The *Roaring Fork Transit Agency* offers daily bus service between Snowmass and Aspen, with many stops in between. *Aspen Skiing Company* runs free shuttle buses between Snowmass, Buttermilk, and Aspen from 8 A.M. to 4:45 P.M. for skiers; schedules are posted at the Snowmass Bus Stop and the Information Booth, or call 925–8484, 923–2085, or 923–5400.

Aspen Limousine (925–2400) or *High Mountain Taxi* (925–TAXI).

SEASONAL EVENTS. January is time for the winter celebrations—in Aspen and Snowmass it's *Winterskol,* featuring Telemark cross-country, torch-light parade, and the Mad Hatter's Ball. Banana Season coincides with *Spring Carnival* in early April, when everyone goes bananas in the warm sunshine.

OTHER SPORTS AND ACTIVITIES. Over 50 km of maintained **cross-country** trails linking the Snowmass Club Touring Center and Owl Creek Trail to Aspen's Buttermilk Mountain are free. The *Aspen/Snowmass Nordic Council* grooms the trails; for more information call 925–4790. Rentals, tours, and lessons at the Snowmass Club Touring Center, 925–3148.

The largest full-time **dog-sled** kennel in the world is in Snowmass. Visitors can take a half-day dog-sled ride pulled by 13 huskies from *Krabloonik Kennels* and then top it off with a gourmet game meal in Krabloonik Restaurant's hand-hewn log cabin. Advance reservations required, 923–4342.

Snowmobiles are available to rent in the Maroon Creek Valley at *T-Lazy-7 Ranch,* 925–4614. **Horse-drawn sleighs** whisk guests to a secluded mountain cabin for a barbecue and western entertainment; departures 5:30 and 8 P.M. Reserve in advance at the Information Booth in the Mall, or call 923–2000, ext. 249.

If you want to get above it all, take a **hot-air balloon ride** in the morning; it includes complimentary champagne upon landing. Call *Unicorn Balloon Company,* 925–5752, for information and reservations.

For other activities, there's **swimming** in one of 47 heated outdoor pools and Jacuzzis for guest use in the village. Those staying in the Snowmass Club have use of the full-service athletic club and indoor tennis courts, and they can have a Personal Fitness Profile done to improve their athletic performance and eating habits.

CHILDREN'S ACTIVITIES. Snowmass is geared to families, and there are excellent facilities for kids. Winter programs include the *Snowmass Cubs* (18 months–3½ years), with snow play indoors and out with hot lunch and snacks, and *Big Burn Bears* (3½ years–kindergarten age), with ski instruction, hot lunch, snacks, and lift ticket. Rates are $50 a day, $225 for five days. Evening rates are $5 per hour, per child; dinner included. Hours: 8:30 A.M.–4:30 P.M. daily. Evenings: 5:30–11:00 P.M. For reservations call 800–525–6200.

Ski classes for children from post-kindergarten age through pre-teens meet at the Ski School Youth Center at 9:30 A.M. for lessons, special races, and picnic; call 923–4873.

A teen program for 13–19-year-olds is exclusive at the Ski School. Grouped by ability, students are led by an instructor through lessons, videotaping, racing, picnics, and after-ski activities, including sleigh ride barbecues; call 923–4873.

NIGHTLIFE. Snowmass is more sedate than its neighbor Aspen, so for heavy nightlife and the singles scene, head for Aspen. But "downtown" Snowmass Village isn't entirely quiet. The après-ski crowd heads for *Timber Mill,* 105 Village Sq., for live music until 5:30 P.M. or so. The *Tower Magic Bar* puts on a spontaneous magic show 7 nights a week. The *Piano Bar* in the *Snowmass Club,* 0239 Snowmass Club Circle, is quietly elegant, but for members only. The new *Cowboys,* in the Silvertree Hotel, features nightly country-western dancing and an unusual gourmet menu.

The *Repertory Theater* performs for six weeks in winter; for tickets, call the ticket hotline, 923–2618.

CRESTED BUTTE MOUNTAIN RESORT

Box A
Mt. Crested Butte CO 81225
Tel: 303-349-2333 or 349-2211

Snow Report: 303–349–2323
Area Vertical: 2,300 ft.
Number of Trails: 82 on 827 acres plus 60
    acres of nonlift-served expert terrain
Lifts: 3 triple chairs, 1 enclosed double
    cabin, 5 double chairs, 3 surface lifts
Snowmaking: 40 percent (off 11 lifts)
Season: November–April

Unlike the other Colorado mining towns, Crested Butte never became a ghost town. The old town is seductive, with its carefully maintained Victorian buildings glowing softly in the evenings under gas street lights. *SKI* magazine named it the "best for lovebirds," one of North America's most romantic resorts. This rather remote town, in the Gunnison Valley, is listed as a National Historic District.

Crested Butte's weatherbeaten Victorian buildings reflect the price of survival in the harsh high-country winters. But behind the sometimes rough-hewn 1880s facades are gourmet restaurants, boutiques, and art galleries. Here you'll fit right in wearing jeans and sweatshirts: the flashiest outfits seem to be in the ski-shop windows. You'll hear classic Grateful Dead tunes every time you ride the minibus to town, and you can still buy a beer for less than $2.

The ski area, Mt. Crested Butte, is 3 miles up the road from the town. Here the condos are modern, with views of the Elk Mountain Range and Ragged Wilderness Areas that will take your breath away. The ski area is actually the other side of Aspen Mountain, and hardy cross-country skiers make their way across the summit in winter; hikers and horseback riders do it in summer. A dirt road between Aspen and Crested Butte is open only in summer and is a 2½-hour scenic drive via Kebler pass.

The area's self-proclaimed fame stems from its 475 acres of expert, ungroomed, backcountry terrain, the Extreme Limits. The expert terrain complements the maintained trails that emphasize intermediate (53 percent) and beginner (27 percent) skiing. The ski school is one of the best in the country (ask about the Learn to Ski Free program).

Crested Butte is also known in nordic circles as the telemarking capital of the United States; it was here that the telemark turn was reborn, and telemarkers will often swish by you on the slopes. The resort area is building up its nordic reputation by creating a varied system of cross-country trails and a downtown nordic center.

Practical Information for Crested Butte

HOW TO GET THERE. Crested Butte is in the Gunnison National Forest, 230 miles southwest of Denver. **By air.** Gunnison is the closest gateway, 30 miles downvalley in west central Colorado. *American Airlines* offers nonstop jet service daily to and from the Dallas/Ft. Worth and Chicago hubs. *Delta Airlines* has direct service into Gunnison from Atlanta on Saturdays and Sundays. *Continental Express* and *United Express* also offer daily flights to Gunnison from Denver; both airlines offer through fares to Gunnison on connecting flights from other cities. Information and reservations are available through *Crested Butte Vacations,* 800–544–8448, or through the airlines or agents.

From Gunnison Airport, *Alpine Express* offers **taxi** service (303–641–5588) to Crested Butte. Several major **car-rental** agencies have offices at Gunnison Airport, including *Hertz, National,* and *Budget.*

By bus. *Greyhound-Trailways,* 800–237–8211, runs from Denver, Colorado Springs, and Grand Junction to Gunnison.

By car. It is a 5-hour drive over Monarch Pass from Denver via US 285, US 50, and Rte. 135. From Colorado Springs, the trip is 196 miles.

TELEPHONES. The area code for Crested Butte is 303.

ACCOMMODATIONS. There are 6,000 pillows in a large variety of condominium complexes and lodges in the towns of Crested Butte and Mt. Crested Butte. Contact *Crested Butte Vacations,* 349–2222 or 800–544–8448, to arrange lodging, lift tickets, ski rental, and lessons. Accommodations categories are determined by price. *Expensive,* $150 for a 1-bedroom condo, up to $320 for a 3-bedroom condo; *Moderate,* $130–$145 for a 2-bedroom condo; and *Inexpensive,* about $40 per person per night in a lodge room.

Crested Mountain Village. *Expensive.* 21 Emmons Rd.; 349–7555. Located on Warming House hill, each unit has a whirlpool, fireplace, and use of heated pool and health spa.

Grande Butte Hotel. *Expensive.* Box 5006; 349–7561, 800–341–5437, or 800–441–2781 in Colorado. This 263-room luxury hotel is ski-in/ski-out at the base of Keystone and Silver Queen lifts. Two restaurants, lounges, and bars, plus an indoor pool, spa, and sundeck. The rooms are spacious with closet kitchens stocked for light cooking, plus it has whirlpool baths and terraces that overlook the slopes. Convenient to all mountain activities. The recreation department for guests features supervised activities for children from 4 to 11 P.M.

Irwin Lodge. *Expensive.* Box 457; 349–5308 or 800–2–IRWIN–2. An exclusive resort favored by powder hounds, Irwin Lodge's piece of paradise is accessible only by Sno-Cat or snowmobile. Guests stay in a rustic 24-room, 1-suite lodge where the view alone is worth the price. Sno-Cats take downhill skiers to untracked runs, and guides lead cross-country skiers into Colorado's back country. Snowmobiling, ice fishing, and snowshoeing are also possible, and the lodge has 2 outdoor hot tubs for day's end. Packages include activities, all meals and transportation from Crested Butte (there's nowhere else to go).

Penthouse. *Expensive.* 21 Emmons Rd., atop the Conference Center; 349–7555 or 800–433–5684. Primarily 1-bedroom units with slanted, wood ceilings, a pool and hot tubs. Tops at this resort is the 3-bedroom, 3-bath condo with a 2½-story living room with a rock-wall fireplace, private hot tub, private deck, and sauna.

Mountain Sunrise Condominiums. *Moderate.* 15 Marcellina La.; 349–2828. Attractive townhouses located several blocks from the slopes. Skiers can take the shuttle bus, walk, or drive to the main lot; Jacuzzi and sauna.

Plaza Condominiums. *Moderate.* 11 Snowmass Rd.; 349–6611 or 800–433–5684. Spacious complex has sauna, outdoor hot tubs, restaurant; a 4-minute walk to the lifts.

Elk Mountain Lodge. *Inexpensive.* 129 Gothic Ave.; 349–5114. In the town of Crested Butte; features Victorian-style lodge rooms with private baths.

Manor Lodge. *Inexpensive.* Gothic Ave.; 800–826–3210 or 800–548–2454 in Colorado. Central base area location with a short walk to lifts. Offers 57 rooms with TVs, phones, kitchenettes; hot tub, sauna, restaurant, bar, and laundry facilities.

RESTAURANTS. Most of the good restaurants are in town, but several lively après-ski spots are at the mountain. Restaurants are listed in order of price category, determined by the price of a full meal for one, excluding drinks, tax, and tip. *Expensive,* $13–$20; *Moderate,* $8–$12; and *Inexpensive,* less than $8. Major credit cards accepted unless otherwise noted.

Penelopes. *Expensive.* 120 Elk Ave; 349–5178. A long-time favorite of locals and visitors in the know, it is a cheery, sunny place with lots of ferns and antiques; Sunday brunch is especially good.

Soupçon. *Expensive.* 127 Elk Ave.; 349–5448. Small, elegant log cabin in an alley behind the Forest Queen; basically a French menu; try the roast duck.

Artichoke. *Moderate.* In Treasury Center; 349–6688. Mediocre Mexican fare.

Bacchanale. *Moderate.* 208 Elk Ave.; 349–5257. Delightful Italian dishes.

Forest Queen. *Moderate.* 129 Elk Ave.; 349–5336. In the morning, you can get a big traditional breakfast; at night, the restaurant serves seafood specialties.

Jeremiah's. *Moderate.* Mt. Crested Butte; 349–7555. Serves both breakfast and dinner. Beef is the house specialty. The poolside bar is open 3–10 P.M. and serves appetizers.

Max Moretti's. *Moderate.* In Treasury Center; 349–7195. Deli and croissant bakery.

Powderhouse Bar & Grill. *Moderate.* 130 Elk Ave.; 349–5494. Delicious traditional Mexican dishes such as mesquite-roasted kid are served up here.

Slogar. *Moderate.* Second Ave. and Whiterock St.; 349–3765. A very popular place despite the limited menu. Serves family-style meals: fried chicken with fresh biscuits.

Angelo's. *Inexpensive.* 501 Elk Ave.; 349–5708. Pizza; no credit cards.

Tincup. *Inexpensive.* Mt. Crested Butte; 349–7555. Slopeside breakfasts and lunches.

Wooden Nickel. *Inexpensive.* 222 Elk Ave.; 349–6350. A must—serves hearty portions of steak, ribs, lobster; a local favorite with a noisy, rah-rah atmosphere.

HOW TO GET AROUND. The *Mountain Express* resort **shuttle** operates free of charge from 7 A.M. to midnight between town and the mountain. Call 349–5616 or 6298 for schedule. Having a car gives visitors more flexibility.

SEASONAL EVENTS. *College Ski Week* is always in early **January.** The infamous *Al Johnson Memorial Uphill-Downhill* race is held in early **April,** while winter is "flushed out" by celebrating *Flauschink* also in early **April.**

OTHER SPORTS AND ACTIVITIES. The **cross-country's** Telemark turn is said to have been rediscovered and is taught here. Cross-country skiing is important here, with groomed tracks, instructors, tour guides, and extensive trails into the back country. Contact the *Nordic Center,* in downtown Crested Butte, 349–6201.

For **sleigh rides** throughout town or on outlying roads, call 349–2211. Indoor **tennis** is available at *Skyland Resort and Country Club;* **racquetball** is available at Skyland or the *Crested Butte Athletic Club.* Several companies in town offer **snowmobile** rides. If you wish to go **horseback riding,** call 349–5765. For **dog-sled tours,** call 349–6598.

CHILDREN'S ACTIVITIES. The *Children's Ski Center* is located in the Whetsone Building, 349–2209, and is open from 8:30 A.M. to 4 P.M. Nursery care is available for ages 6 months to 3 years for $35 full day. The *ABC ON SKIS* program, ages 3–6, costs $42 for a full day and includes lesson, lunch, rentals, and indoor and outdoor activities. The *Butte Busters* program is for ages 7–12 with group lessons costing $37 with lunch or $27 for a half day, no lunch.

A "Kids Ski Free" package is available, but there are date restrictions; contact the area for details.

NIGHTLIFE. *Black Bear Bar,* 11 Snowmass Rd., has delicious pizza during après-ski. *Rafter's,* in the Gothic Building at the base area, offers dancing till wee hours, often to live music. *The Roaring Elk* in the Grand Butte Hotel has live music, dancing, and big-screen TV. Local favorites in town are *Donita's Cantina, Kochevar's, Oscar's,* and *Talk of the Town. Eldorado Cafe* has entertainment nightly. Crested Butte's new *Center for the Arts,* 349–7487, brings a steady stream of entertainment during the tourist seasons.

The *Crested Butte Mountain Theatre,* 132 Elk Ave., 349–5685, has performances year-round. The *Crested Butte Society,* 349–6355, sponsors activities for artists, dancers, and musicians. Contact the *Crested Butte Chamber of Commerce* for information, 349–6438.

PURGATORY-DURANGO

Box 666
Durango CO 81302
Tel: 303–247–9000 or
   800–525–0892

Snow Report: 303–247–9000
Area Vertical: 2,029 ft.
Number of Trails: 640 skiable acres, longest
   run 2 miles
Lifts: 4 triple chairs, 5 double chairs
Snowmaking: 100 acres served by 3 lifts
Season: late November (Thanksgiving)–
   mid-April

Durango, in southwest Colorado, has long been a summer tourist destination. Purgatory Ski Resort came to life in 1965 and the winter season has increased in importance since then. The ski resort cemented its ties to the town in 1990 by changing its official name to "Purgatory-Durango, the warmth of the Southwest."

Purgatory is popular with skiers from Arizona, New Mexico, Texas, and Southern California because of its proximity to those states. Beginners have their own special 7-acre area at Columbine Station, while intermediates enjoy 50 percent of the mountain's runs. New techniques for grooming the steep, 35-degree slopes mean that intermediates can try them while they're nice and flat before the big bumps that are formed every few days rise up. Many Durango locals seek out the steep chutes, moguls, and powder glades that constitute 30 percent of the area. The Legends has excellent tree and glade skiing.

The Village at Purgatory-Durango is constantly adding to its still-new base-area improvements. There are nine condo and hotel-type lodges at the base, with rooms for 2,000 skiers slopeside and an additional 1,000 in nearby condos, which are served by shuttle buses.

Most of the action, however, is 25 miles away in Durango. Durango's 12,000 residents and scores of tourists have access to almost unlimited recreational opportunities. Here, in the "Banana Belt" of Colorado ski areas, five out of seven days are sunny and the average precipitation of 18.6 inches annually usually comes in the form of winter snow and summer showers. Set in the Animas Valley, Durango is surrounded by the San Juan Mountains.

Practical Information for Purgatory-Durango

HOW TO GET THERE. Purgatory-Durango is located in the San Juan National Forest, 340 miles southwest of Denver, 25 miles north of Durango.

By air. La Plata Airport, 20 miles south of Durango and 45 miles south of Purgatory, is the gateway to Purgatory-Durango. Direct flights are scheduled from Denver, Dallas/Ft. Worth, Albuquerque, and Phoenix on *America West, Mesa Airlines, Continental Express,* and *United Express.* Common fare rates are available from Denver to Durango in conjunction with package tours; charter flights also go into La Plata. There are also fly-free programs and incentives from Denver and Albuquerque. Call 800–525–0892 for details. Call 259–LIFT for schedules; prices subject to change without notice. Rental cars are available. Some hotels offer free shuttle service.

By bus. The *Lift* regularly runs between Durango and Purgatory, $5 round-trip. Call 259–LIFT. Charters are available by contacting *Purgatory/Durango Central Reservations,* 800–525–0892.

By car. From Denver to Purgatory-Durango is a 340-mile drive via US 285, US 150, and US 550 in the southwest corner of the state. From Grand Junction it is 150 miles south on US 50 and US 550. Flagstaff, Arizona, is 319 miles to the south, Albuquerque is 212 miles via Hwy. 44 to US 550; Phoenix, 456 miles. Durango is 25 miles south on US 550. **Rental cars** available at La Plata Airport are *Avis,* 800–331–1212; *Budget,* 800–527–0700; *Dollar,* 800–421–6878; *Hertz,* 800–654–3131; *National,* 800–328–4567.

TELEPHONES. The area code for Purgatory is 303.

ACCOMMODATIONS. At Purgatory-Durango, there are accommodations for 2,000 people, with more planned for the future. In Durango, there are over 10,000 pillows, with prices for all pocketbooks. Midway between the ski area and town is a world-class resort, **Tamarron** (Box 3131, Durango, CO 81301). Accommodations are deluxe, there are 13,000 sq. ft. of conference facilities and two gourmet restaurants. Call 800–525–5420; in Colorado 247–8801. Tamarron offers a free shuttle to Purgatory and into Durango; call (303) 259–2000.

Purgatory/Durango Central Reservations, Box 3496, Durango, CO 81302, 800–525–0892, represents a majority of lodging both in town and at Purgatory. The following is a sample of what's available. *Expensive,* $69 (for a lodge room) to $350 a night (depending on the size of the unit); *Moderate,* $45–$165; and *Inexpensive,* under $45.

Expensive

Cascade Village. 50827 Hwy. 50 North; 259–3500. A mile north of Purgatory; 2-bedroom units available.

Edelweiss Condos. At the base; 247–9000. Spacious luxury 3- and 4-bedroom units. A lodge room is $69 per night.

Purgatory Village Hotel. At the base; 247–9000 or 800–879–7874. King-size lodge rooms, studios, and 1-, 2-, and 3-bedroom units. Very luxurious.

Red Lion. 501 Camino del Rio; 259–6580. New inn and conference center located on the river.

Sitzmark Condos. At the base; 247–9000. Units include 3 and 4 bedrooms; studios run $80–$120 per night. No amenities.

Moderate

Angelhaus. Box 666, Durango, at base of Purgatory Mountain; 247–8090. Reasonably priced 1- and 2-bedroom condominiums.

Best Western Lodge at Purgatory. 49617 US 550, Durango; 247–9669. Western-style lodge; restaurant and lounge.

Purgatory Townhouse Condominiums. Box 37, Durango; 247–0026 or 800–223–ISKI. Studio, 1-, and 2-bedroom units at the base area.

Strater Hotel. 699 Main Ave., Durango; 247–4431. Built in 1882 and authentically restored, this is an outstanding facility with 93 antique-filled rooms. Amenities include an on-site restaurant, bar, and Jacuzzi.

Inexpensive

Alpine North Motel. 3515 Main Ave., Durango; 247–4042. Basic motel facility.

Budget Inn Motels. 3077 Main Ave., Durango; 247–5222. Basic rooms at low prices.

Spanish Trail Motel. 3141 Main Ave., Durango; 247–4173. Some 2-bedroom units with kitchens.

Western Star. 3310 Main Ave., Durango; 247–4895. Great budget option for families: a room with 2 queen-size beds and a full kitchen starts at $37 per night, double occupancy.

RESTAURANTS. With over 60 restaurants in Durango and a half-dozen at the mountain plus the restaurants at Tamarron, one need not go hungry. **At the mountain,** *Farquahrts North* in the village serves lunch, dinner, and drinks at moderate prices. *Powderhouse* is mid-mountain next to Pitchfork, with outdoor barbecues and home-style favorites; *Dante's* is mid-mountain by Chair 5, with cafeteria, sit-down dining in a greenhouse atmosphere, and *Dante's Den and Lounge. Sterling's,* in the Village Center, is a cafeteria, with outdoor sundeck and lounge. *Heaven-Eleven Deli* and *Mesquite's Bar & Grill* are also in the center.

Expensive restaurants have entrees running $15–$25; *Moderate,* $9–$15; *Inexpensive,* below $9. All restaurants listed take major credit cards unless otherwise noted.

Expensive

Ariano's. 150 E. Sixth St.; 247–8146. Traditional Italian dining features homemade pastas.

Cafe Cascade. At the Cascade Village condos, 2 miles north of resort; 259–3500. Features great seafood and daily dinner specials in an elegant dining room.

The Ore House. 147 Sixth St.; 247–5707. One of the oldest restaurants in town; rustic and casual with an extensive wine selection.

The Palace. 1 Depot Pl.; 247–2018. Victorian decor with a wide variety of entrees.

The Red Snapper. 144 E. Ninth St.; 259–3417. Fresh seafood, prime ribs, oyster bar. Have a drink in the bar below the atrium.

Sweeney's Grubstake. 1644 County Rd. 203; 247–5236. At the north end of town, serves steaks, seafood, and huge salads.

Moderate

The Atrium. 21382 Highway 160; 385–4834. Basic American fare.
The Continental. 658 Main Ave.; 259–2888. Classic Continental cuisine for lunch and dinner. Jazz bar upstairs.
Francisco's. 619 Main Ave.; 247–4098. For Mexican food, steaks, and seafood. Children's menu available.
Golden Dragon. 970 Main Ave.; 259–0956. Oriental food to eat in or take out.
Randy's. 152 E. Sixth St.; 247–9083. Prime rib, seafood, steaks, and bar.

Inexpensive

Father Murphy's. 636 Main Ave.; 259–0334. Pub atmosphere, serving sandwiches, burgers, and soups. No credit cards.
Griego's Taco House. 1400 E. Second Ave.; 247–3127. The name says it. No credit cards.
Mr. Rosewater's Delicatessen. 552 Main Ave.; 247–8788. Typical deli fare.
Olde Tymer's. 1000 Main Ave.; 259–2990. Casual surroundings, with menu of burgers, soups, pasta.
Pronto's. 160 E. Sixth; 247–1510. For Italian food and pasta buffet.

HOW TO GET AROUND. Major **car** rental agencies are at the Durango airport (see *How to Get There*) and many visitors opt for the convenience of their own vehicles. A **shuttle** service operates regularly to and from Purgatory and within Durango on all major arteries. Tamarron runs a regular free shuttle between the resort, Purgatory, and town.

SEASONAL EVENTS. *Snowdown Winter Carnival* is celebrated late **January** through early **February.** The last weekend in February brings the *NFL Player's Association Ski Invitational for the Disabled.* Mid-**March** brings the *Pro-Am Bump Off* mogul-skiing championship as well as the *Wolverton Days Nordic Championships.*

OTHER SPORTS AND ACTIVITIES. *Purgatory Cross-Country Touring Center* maintains 16 km of **trails** across US 550 from the entrance to Purgatory Village. Lessons, rentals, Telemark clinics are available; a lesson-rental package costs $25; trail fee $5. An alpine daily lift ticket is exchangeable for this cross-country package. Call director Ineka Boyce, 247–9000.

DAY-CARE FACILITIES. Call 247–9000 at Purgatory-Durango Ski Resort for information and reservations. The *Teddy Bear Camp* operates during ski season for children 2 months–6 years of age. Day care is $38 a day, $28 a half-day, lunch included. The ski school is $38 a day, $28 a half-day with lunch and ski lessons; skis and boots are available with the program. Children should be provided with adequate warm clothes, goggles, and sunscreen. Reservations are required.

Older children can go into the ski school, $43 a day with lunch and lift ticket; lift tickets (12 and under) are $27 a day, and a season's pass for children 12 and under is only $75.

NIGHTLIFE. Yes, there is life after skiing, at least if you go into Durango. The *Diamond Belle Saloon,* 699 Main Ave., a historic Durango landmark, is right out of the Old West—those swinging doors have been swinging for over a century; elegant Victorian atmosphere, ragtime piano. The *Old Muldoon,* 561 Main Ave., is for popcorn and for meeting singles. *Sundance,* 602 Second Ave., features country-western dancing, live music, and a Western flavor—you'll feel comfortable in your cowboy hat and boots. *Carver's Brewpub,* 1022 Main Ave., brews beer on-site in a micro-brewery. Pilsner, stout, ale, and seasonal specials. *Farquahrt's Downtown,* 725 Main Ave., has good pizza and live rock, reggae, and world-beat bands.

There are even night-time activities that do not have to do with drinking. Bowl at *Durango Bowl,* 800 South Camino del Rio; 259–1012. See a movie or attend the live theater—*Abbey,* year-round (128 E. Sixth St., 247–2626). Touring musicians often stop in town on the way to Albuquerque or West-Coast concert dates.

STEAMBOAT SPRINGS

2305 Mt. Werner Circle
Steamboat Springs CO 80487
Tel: 303–879–6111

Snow Report: 303–879–7300
Area Vertical: 3,600 ft.
Number of Trails: 101 trails on 2,500 acres,
　　longest run 3 miles
Lifts: 1 eight-passenger gondola, 1 quad
　　chair, 7 triple chairs, 9 double chairs, 1
　　ski school chair, 1 Mighty Mite
Snowmaking: on 365 acres served by 11 lifts
Season: late November (Thanksgiving
　　weekend)–early April

Visitors to Steamboat Springs find many different experiences awaiting them. They can stay right at the base of Mt. Werner in one of the modern lodges and ski on the four peaks of the mountain that has enough variety to keep skiers of every skill level happy. They can shop the mall stores and eat and drink in the establishments that are all within walking distance of one another in the vacation village. They can even ski a run with Billy Kidd, former Olympian and director of skiing at Steamboat, who welcomes guests for a 1 P.M. run down the mountain, in season. The trip up the mountain was made faster and warmer with the installation of the "Silver Bullet" gondola in 1986. From base to mid-mountain takes only 9 minutes—just enough time to get acquainted.

Without the glitz and snobbery of some other major ski areas, Steamboat has always welcomed visitors with a low-key friendliness. In recent years, the area has promoted a kids-stay-and-ski-free program, which has attracted a lot of families.

But a visit is not complete without a trip into "town," a couple of miles west of the ski village. Here, 5,000 residents cling to a small-town way of life. You won't find a McDonald's—the town refused to let the franchise in. (But there is a Wendy's.) In the 60-odd bars and restaurants, you'll find a lot of "American" food, and you may even be able to sit down and chat with one of the many cowboys who work in the neighboring ranches of the Yampa Valley. If you're on a budget, lodging in town is less expensive than at the ski area.

The Howelsen Hill Ski Area looms over the town, lit up at night for skiing. It is the oldest ski area in continuous use in Colorado and has produced more Olympians than any other North American ski area. In addition to alpine, it offers cross-country and jumping facilities.

Over 100 hot springs bubble up in the area. In town two pools are heated to 103 degrees by the mineral waters—a perfect place for weary skiers to soak their tired bodies!

Practical Information for Steamboat Springs

HOW TO GET THERE. Steamboat Springs is in the Routt National Forest, 157 miles northwest of Denver.

By air. Several airlines service the airport at Steamboat Springs. Daily, non-stop jet service from Dallas/Ft. Worth, Chicago, and Los Angeles and Saturday service from San Jose and Newark is offered by *American Airlines. Northwest Airlines* flies daily from Minneapolis/St. Paul. *America West* flies three days a week from Phoenix. Daily flights from Denver, from Houston (Saturdays only) and from Newark via Cleveland are available on *Continental Airlines.* All offer connecting service from over 200 cities into Steamboat's *Yampa Valley Regional Airport,* at Hayden, 22 miles from the resort. *Continental Express* has 50-passenger DASH-7s with several daily flights to Bob Adams STOLport (5 miles from the resort) from Denver. Ground transportation from the STOLport and the regional airport includes *Alpine Taxi, Panorama Coaches, Trailhead Transit,* and *Ultimate Limousine.* Rental cars are available at both airport locations. All can be reserved through *Steamboat Reservation Services,* 800–922–2722.

By bus. *Greyhound Trailways* has year-round daily service. Departures are from Denver terminal, at 8:30 A.M. and 9:30 P.M. (arrive at 1:25 P.M. and 1:55 A.M.). The one-way cost is $30; round-trip, $57. Call 303–293–6555 for reservations. To get to Greyhound's 19th St. terminal from Stapleton Airport take RTD city bus at lower-level gate 11; the bus runs every half-hour daily and costs $1.50. Call 800–366–7433 for schedules. *Steamboat Express* buses have daily service from Stapleton. Cost is $44 on Saturday and $39 other days, one way. Call 800–922–2722 for reservations.

By car. From Denver, Steamboat is about a 3-hour drive over all-weather highways. Take I–70 West to the Silverthorne exit, then north on Colorado Hwy. 9 to Kremmling, then west on US 40 to Steamboat. For road conditions call 639–1234.

From Grand Junction, drive east on I–70 to Hwy. 131 at Wolcott, then onto US 40 in the valley, a total of 200 miles. From Laramie, Wyoming, it is 122 miles via Hwy. 230, Hwy. 127, Rte. 14, and US 40.

TELEPHONES. The area code for Steamboat Springs is 303.

ACCOMMODATIONS. *Steamboat Reservation Services,* Box 774408, Steamboat Springs, CO 80477, 800–922–2722, has one-call capability for a variety of ski-package plans and lodging and transportation reservations. Twenty lodges are within walking distance of the slopes and an additional 55 hotels, condominiums, and townhouses make up a total of 15,500 pillows in town and at the base area.

Several property-management companies lease condos and townhouses in the area. A 1-bedroom condo in regular season (February–April) runs $95–$200 per night; in the "value" season, these prices drop to $75–$180. A 2-bedroom unit, regular season, costs $185–$300; value season, $140–$250. Here are a few to try; price categories will vary.

Pine Reservations. Box 881565, Steamboat Springs, CO 80477; 800–325–5571 or 800–879–4175 in Colorado. Over 10 different locations on the mountain are managed by Pine. Pets are welcome in some units.

Steamboat Lodging Management Co. Box 4406, Steamboat Springs, CO 80477; 800–822–7669 or 800–922–7669 in Colorado. Manages *Snow Flower's* studios, 2- and 4-bedroom units next to the gondola and *Golden Triangle's* loft condos.

Steamboat Resorts. Box 2995, Steamboat Springs, CO 80477; 800–525–5502 or 800–332–5533 in Colorado. Manages 9 properties in all price ranges.

Rates for hotel rooms are based on double occupancy; *Expensive,* $120–$300; *Moderate,* $80–$120; and *Inexpensive,* under $80. Usually, the more expensive the unit, the closer it is to the lifts.

Expensive

Bear Claw Condominiums. 2420 Ski Trail La.; 879–6100. Top-of-the-line accommodations, right against the lifts and partway up the mountain.

Sheraton at Steamboat. 2200 Village Inn Ct.; 879–2220. Right in the center of the village mall, next to the gondola. A restaurant and cafeteria are on the premises.

Thunderhead Lodge. 35215 Mt. Werner Way; 879–2220. At the ski area, with heated pool.

Moderate

Best Western Ptarmigan Inn. 2304 Après-Ski Way; 879–1730. Adjacent to gondola station at base of Mount Werner. Family-style restaurant and lounge; heated pool and sauna; games room and ski shop.

Glen Eden Ranch. 54737 Routt County Rd. 129, Clark; 879–3906. Located 18 miles north of town; rustic cabins with kitchens and fireplaces; free shuttle to ski area.

Harbor Hotel. 703 Lincoln; 879–1522. Renovated Victorian-style rooms; comfortable place.

Holiday Inn. 3190 S. Lincoln; 879–2250. A mile from the base area gondola; free shuttle service, outdoor pool, restaurant, and cocktail lounge.

Scandinavian Lodge. Box 5040; 879–0517. Above the ski area, ski to the lifts and ski tour out the back door. Prices include 3 outstanding meals.

Inexpensive

Clermont B&B. Box 774927; 879–3083. Full breakfast, 2 rooms share a tub. Convenient in-town location.

Rabbit Ears Motel. 201 Lincoln Ave.; 879–1150. Close to downtown restaurants and shopping; take shuttle to ski hill.

Quality Inn Overlook Hotel. 1000 Highpoint Dr.; 303–879–2900 or 800–228–5151. Located midway between the town and the slopes. Hotel rooms and 2-story suites.

RESTAURANTS. The *Thunderhead* facility, at the upper terminal of the gondola, has a third-floor cafeteria, *BK's Corral,* with a barbecue sundeck. The second floor has *Hazie's,* a gourmet restaurant serving lunch daily; and *Cafe Thunderhead,* the children's ski-school cafeteria. *The Stoker Bar,* on the first level, is also a good lunch spot. First-on-the-mountain skiers take the gondola up at 8:15 A.M. and have breakfast at BK's, to be ready for the slope's opening, at 9 A.M. Tuesday through Saturday you can ride the gondola up for a starlit dinner at *Hazie's* or a family-style barbeque at *BK's.*

Rendezvous Saddle Restaurant in the Priest Creek area has seating for 600 inside and outdoors; included inside is the dining room *Ragnar's,* noted for its fine food and Norwegian specialties; make reservations during February and March; 879–6111.

At or near the base area are 14 restaurants.

Entrees at *Expensive* restaurants are $13–$16; *Moderate,* $9–$12; *Inexpensive,* under $9. All restaurants listed take MasterCard and Visa unless otherwise noted.

At or Near The Slopes

Cipriani's. *Expensive.* In the Thunderhead Lodge, 35215 Mt. Werner Way; 879–2220, ext. 1220. Features northern Italian cuisine, good wine list. Reservations recommended.

Mattie Silk's. *Expensive.* In Ski Times Sq., 1890 Mount Werner Rd.; 879–2441. A delightful, split-level restaurant featuring veal, pork, duck, and lamb in a candlelit atmosphere. Fifty imported beers. Children's menu. Reservations suggested.

Remington's. *Expensive.* In the Sheraton, 2200 Village Inn Ct.; 879–2220. Overlooking the Headwall of the ski area. Children's menu available. Open winters only, reservations recommended.

Dos Amigos. *Moderate.* 1910 Mount Werner Rd.; 879–4270. An old-time hangout in Steamboat. Good Mexican food and lots of activity. Dinner only. Children's menu.

Soda Creek Cafe. *Moderate.* In Thunderbird Lodge, 35215 Mt. Werner Way; 879–2220. Specializes in German food; also burgers and sandwiches. Cheerful atmosphere and German beers and wines. Children's menu.

The Tugboat. *Inexpensive.* 1860 Mount Werner Rd.; 879–9990. Another local favorite. Noisy, western atmosphere serving burgers and beer. Open for three meals.

In and Around Town

The Coral Grill. *Expensive.* In the Sundance Plaza on Angeler Dr. off Hwy. 40; 879–6858. A popular après-ski spot where you can sample appetizers such as gourmet pizza and shrimp dumplings while you watch TV in the sports bar. Dinner selections include a variety of fresh, grilled seafood; chicken teriyaki; Maryland crab cakes. Reservations needed.

Gorky Park. *Expensive.* 57½ Eighth St.; 879–9939. Go back to the time of the czars in this opulently furnished, burgundy-and-pink "salon" where pirogi, blini, and other Russian dishes are served with attentive care. The crowning jewel here, though, is the vodka menu: you'll find 27 different flavors, from strawberry to horse-radish. Try as many as you dare—to some the delights are worth the potential hang-over—but be sure to designate a driver. Reservations suggested.

L'Apogee. *Expensive.* 911 Lincoln St.; 879–1919. The exquisite French cuisine, extensive wine list, and deep-burgundy and green Victorian decor set the tone for one of Steamboat's most respected—and expensive—establishments. Serves an ex-cellent rack of lamb and fresh smoked rainbow trout. Another bonus is that you can buy vintage wines by the glass—a rare treat in most fine restaurants.

Harwig's Grill. *Moderate.* 911 Lincoln St. (in the same building as L'Apogee, above); 879–1980. A true bargain: you get gourmet-class food (such as lamb burgers or peapod and feta cheese salad with oil-and-vinegar nut dressing) prepared by L'Apogee's kitchen staff at moderate prices in a casual, social setting.

Pine Grove. *Moderate.* 1465 Pine Grove Rd.; 879–1190. This 75-year-old barn has been turned into a homey western restaurant. Exotic game is the draw: Alaskan caribou, Australian wild boar, Norwegian moose, and South Dakota black bear are among the selections. For the less adventurous, chopped steak, broiled chicken, and lobster tails are also on the menu. Moderately priced wine list, plus children's por-tions available.

Cantina. *Inexpensive.* 818 Lincoln Ave.; 879–0826. Mexican food and pizza. Crowded with locals for breakfast; good margaritas in the evening.

Canton Chinese Restaurant. *Inexpensive.* 720 Lincoln Ave.; 879–4480. Great Chinese food at great prices.

The Shack. *Inexpensive.* 740 Lincoln Ave.; 879–9975. Good for a quick breakfast or lunch.

HOW TO GET AROUND. *Steamboat Springs Transit* (SST) connects points west of the city limits to town and to the ski area; check schedules at lodge, but extra **buses** are put on during ski season; 50¢ a ride, but for savings, buy tokens in quantity at any lodge or store. For schedule information, call 879–3717. For **taxis,** call *Steamboat Taxi Service,* 879–2800.

SEASONAL EVENTS. There is usually something special going on in cowboy country. Three- and six-day *Billy Kidd Race Camps* are scheduled throughout the winter. In mid-**January,** the most unusual ski area event happens—the *Cowboy Downhill;* top rodeo riders from the Pro Rodeo Tour come up from Denver's annual National Western Stock Show and try their skill. The oldest continuous *Winter Car-nival* in the West takes place for a week in early **February,** with a fun mixture of cowboys, skiers, and hot-air balloons. Spring officially arrives in early **April** with the *Steamboat Springs Stampede.*

OTHER SPORTS AND ACTIVITIES. Cross-country skiing is avidly pursued in Steamboat. Besides ski touring from the Scandinavian Lodge, the *Ski Touring Center* maintains 12 miles of trails; guided tours on Rabbit Ears Pass, moonlight tours by appointment; lessons, call 879–8180. Other lodges that offer cross-country skiing are *Bear Pole Ranch, Dutch Creek Guest Ranch, Glen Eden, Home Ranch, Post Ranch, Red Barn Ranch,* and *Vista Verde Guest Ranch.* Anyone can ski here—it's open forest land.

Ski powder by **Sno-Cat;** call the *Steamboat Powder Cats,* 879–5188.

Dog sledding is nearby at *Dog Sled Adventures,* 879–5280. **Ice fishing** is at Steam-boat and Dumont Lakes; license required, call 879–1870 for information. **Ice skat-ing** is at Howelson Hill in town. **Sledding** is also popular at Howelson Hill for young children; call 879–4300.

Sleigh rides go from *All Seasons Ranch,* 879–2606; *Double Runner Ranch,* 879–6459; *El Rancho,* 879–9988; *Red Barn Ranch,* 879–4580; *Vista Verde Guest Ranch,* 879–3858. **Snowshoeing** expeditions head out from Elk River, Red Barn, Vista Verde, and Post ranches. **Snowmobiles** can be rented at Dutch Creek, Elk River, Post, and Red Barn ranches.

Enjoy **hot mineral pools** any time of year in town at the public pool and at the *Steamboat Springs Health & Recreation Association,* 879–1828. *Strawberry Park Hot*

Springs, 4 miles north of town, features mineral springs in a natural setting. Year-round early morning **balloon rides** are available through four hot-air balloon companies—*Balloon Colorado,* 879–4932; *Balloons Over Steamboat,* 879–3298; *Balloon the Rockies,* 879–7313; and *Pegasus Balloon Tours,* 879–7529.

HINTS TO THE HANDICAPPED. For ski instruction by appointment for the visually impaired and some physically disabled, contact the *Steamboat Ski School,* 2305 Mount Werner Circle, Steamboat Springs, CO 80487; 879–6111.

CHILDREN'S ACTIVITIES. The *Kids Ski Free Program* stipulates that one child under 12 can ski free with a parent who purchases 5 or more day lift tickets and who is staying a minimum of five nights at a participating Steamboat Chamber/Resort Association lodging property. Children also stay free in the same room with their parents and will have free ski rentals when their parents rent skis for the same period of time. The offer is not valid during the Christmas/New Year's holiday. Call Steamboat Ski Corporation for more details, 879–6111.

In addition, the *Kiddie Corral Child Care* provides day care for children 6 months to 6 years of age; $32 a day or $28 a half day, plus $4 for lunch. The *Kiddie Corral Ski School* is for young skiers 3–5 years of age who are toilet trained. Lunch, lift privileges, and lessons, $43 a day, $32 a half day, $120 for three days, or $165 for five days. Ground floor, Gondola Building; 879–6111, ext. 216.

The Ski School has lessons for kids 6–15. Group lessons are $26 for two hours, $43 for all day (includes lunch). For details, call 879–6111, ext. 222.

Kids seem to be the only ones who have energy for night skiing; take them to Howelsen Hill in town; Tuesdays–Fridays, 6–9 P.M. Otherwise, the *Kiddie Corral* will take care of them at its night nursery; see above.

Off the slopes, children will enjoy the Hydro Tube and swimming at the *Steamboat Springs Health & Recreation Association,* Lincoln St., in town; 879–1828.

If you want to leave junior at home while you party, many lodges provide a list of qualified baby-sitters; inquire at the front desk or call the Chamber/Resort Association for a list; 879–0880.

NIGHTLIFE. Much of the late-night action is close to the slopes. At the base, *The Inferno* is the rowdiest spot where the emphasis is on heavy duty après-ski imbibing. The *Tugboat Saloon* in Ski Time Square attracts a slightly more subdued crowd and has a pool table in the back. Here things stay lively into the wee hours and there is often live entertainment and dancing. A few doors down is *Dos Amigos* where the margueritas and tequila shots flow—the nachos and salsa are good, too. For a more conservative time, try the *Observatory* in the Thunderhead Lodge, which has a comfortable lounge with a fireplace.

In town, the *Coral Grill* has a sports bar. On Saturday and Sunday, the *Old Town Pub* becomes a get-down-and-dirty rock 'n' roll bar. If vodka's your vice check out *Gorky Park* on Eighth Street. Also on Eighth Street is the *Loop* for rock 'n' roll. Farther afield, the *Glen Eden Ranch* (see *Accommodations*) has a cozy lounge with country-and-western music.

Bowlers can head to *Sno Bowl II* just west of town; call 879–9840 for a lane. The movie theater has first-run films. The *Steamboat Arts Council* holds dance concerts and melodramas, and there are other local talent displays throughout the year; call 879–4434.

SUMMIT COUNTY

Four of Colorado's best ski areas are located in Summit County, about 80 miles west of Denver: Breckenridge, Copper Mountain, Keystone Resort, and Arapahoe Basin. Although each area has its own distinct personality, the bonus here is that all are located within a short drive of one another and Summit County provides free transportation to skiers among the areas. You can cruise the slopes at Copper one day, ski the challenging

A-Basin the next, enjoy Breckenridge's three peaks the next, and spend an evening night skiing at Keystone. In all, there are eight mountain peaks, 54 lifts, over 250 trails, and nearly 4,000 acres of skiable terrain. Summit County offers a "Ski the Summit" pass, good for all four areas. For details, contact any of the ski areas, or *Ski the Summit,* Box 267, Dillon CO 80435 (303) 468–6607.

BRECKENRIDGE

Box 1058
Breckenridge CO 80424
Tel: 303–453–2368

Snow Report: 303–453–6118
Area Vertical: 2,583 ft.
Number of Trails: 1,519 acres, 110 runs;
*   longest run 3 miles*
Lifts: 4 high-speed quads, 1 triple chair, 9
*   double chairs, 1 platter pull*
Snowmaking: on 430 acres
Season: mid-November–mid-April

In the 1860s, the town of Breckenridge was the center of a group of villages and mining camps that sprung up during the gold rush. The town thrived as a mining center; in fact, the largest single gold nugget ever found in Colorado—weighing 13 pounds 7 ounces—was found here in 1887.

After World War II, the majority of the mining operations stopped, and the town was soon considered a ghost town. Local legend has it that until 1936, the town was not legally considered a part of the United States, having been overlooked by governmental surveyors. Residents are fond of recalling the days of the "Kingdom of Breckenridge" and musing about what might have been had the town remained "sovereign."

In 1961, the Breckenridge Ski Area opened and began the rebirth of this charming town. The skiing spans three peaks, each accessible by its own high-speed quad lift (two quads on Peak 9) and all interconnecting. The easier trails (21 percent) and the "more difficult" trails (32 percent) are spread over Peaks 8 and 9, so intermediates and beginners get a lot of different terrain to cover. The "most difficult" runs are connected on Peak 10 and the Back Bowls of Peak 8 and make up nearly 47 percent of the total runs. Here you can find a lot of easy cruising runs and the steep-n-deeps; efforts have recently been made to upgrade the difficulty of the harder runs while maintaining plenty of intermediate slopes. Two of the three base areas extend right into the town (you can walk to the lifts from Main Street), where the Victorian buildings and mining town atmosphere happily persist.

Practical Information for Breckenridge

HOW TO GET THERE. The resort is located in the Arapaho National Forest, 85 miles west of Denver.

By air. Stapleton Airport in Denver is the gateway. Limousines, taxis, and charter coaches are available from Stapleton upon request. For transportation to Breckenridge, see below.

By chauffeured vans. *Resort Express,* 800–334–7433, and *Skiers Connection,* 668–0200, cost approximately $25 one way.

By car. A 90-minute drive west via I–70 from Denver, through the Eisenhower Tunnel, which cuts through the Continental Divide, to exit 201, Colorado Rte. 9, about 9 miles from Frisco. From Colorado Springs, it is 105 miles via US Hwy. 285 and Colorado Hwy. 9. Two **rental car agencies** have drop-off services in Breckenridge: *Dollar Rent-a-Car,* 303–453–2000, and *Budget,* 800–247–9510.

TELEPHONES. The area code for Breckenridge is 303.

ACCOMMODATIONS. The *Breckenridge Resort Chamber* represents 95 percent of the available lodging and is the central reservations facility. Call 800–221–1091; 453–2918, in Colorado; 0–800–89–74011, from the United Kingdom toll free; or fax 303–453–7238. Write Box 1909, Breckenridge, CO 80424. *Executive Resort Rentals, Inc.,* manages units in many of the area condominiums, including several economy accommodations. Call 800–662–5368, or write 203 N. Main St., Box 1700, Breckenridge, CO 80424. There are more than 100 condominium complexes, motels, and family-style lodges in the town and base area of Breckenridge, and 23,000 people can be housed.

"Ski Free/Stay Free" packages are offered by some of the lodges and the area. Purchase three or five days of skiing and lodging and get the fourth or sixth day free. Not available during holidays. Prices for double-occupancy hotel accommodations start at $165 per person for the 4-day package and $260 for 6 days. Four people in a 2-bedroom condo can pay as little as $210 each on the 4-day package and $355 for 6 days. Call the ski area for details.

The following list should give you an idea of what's available. Price categories are based on per-night, double-occupancy costs, but always remember to check for packages. *Expensive,* ranging from $90 to $350 per night, depending on the size of the unit; *Moderate,* $75–$115; *Inexpensive,* $50–$75.

Expensive

Beaver Run. 620 Village Rd., Breckenridge; 453–6000 or 800–525–2253. Luxurious, ski-in, ski-out property at the base of Peak 9. It includes a complete commercial center, pool, hot tubs, saunas, steam and exercise rooms, and day care. Try to get one of the studios with your own whirlpool spa.

Hilton Hotel. 550 Village Rd.; 800–321–8444. Top of the line slopeside property with 6,000 square feet of meeting space, indoor pool, Jacuzzi, health club, and restaurant.

Park Place. 325 Four O'Clock Rd.; 800–221–1091. Spacious 2-bedroom units, hot tubs. Easy access to shuttle, town, and slopes; access to pool, whirlpool, hot tub, sauna.

Village at Breckenridge. 535 South Park St.; 800–321–8552 or 800–643–2997 in Colorado. Condominium resort complex between the banks of the Blue River and the base of the ski lifts, cross-country, ice skating.

Moderate

Four O'Clock Lodge. 550 Four O'Clock Rd. in Upper Four Seasons Village; 453–6228. Within walking distance of the slopes and town, studios to 3-bedroom lofts. Access to an amenities area with pool, whirlpool, sauna, hot tub.

Wedgewood Lodge. 535 Four O'Clock Rd.; 800–521–2458. Victorian townhomes located as a ski-home property, features fireplaces, hot tubs, sauna.

Inexpensive–Moderate

Fireside Inn. 114 French St.; 453–6456. Restored Victorian home in town with dorms, private rooms, and family-style group dining.

RESTAURANTS. There are 4 on-mountain restaurants and 17 picnic tables, plus a brown-bag room and a bar; 3 restaurants at the base area; and over 50 restaurants in town. Entrees in *Expensive* restaurants listed below run $15–$19; *Moderate,* $8–$15; and *Inexpensive,* under $8. All restaurants listed take major credit cards unless otherwise noted.

Expensive

Breckenridge Cattle Co. At Village at Breckenridge, Main St. and South Park Rd.; 453–2000. Serves ribs and steaks and has a good wine selection and view of Maggie Pond.

Briar Rose. 109 E. Lincoln St. 453–9948. Serves wild game, prime ribs, seafood, and steaks.

Brown Restaurant. 208 N. Ridge St.; 453–0084. In the Brown Hotel, an old restored Victorian building said to have housed a ghost or two. Outstanding food and service in homey dining room. Try the stuffed shrimp for an excellent, unusual taste.

St. Bernard Inn. 103 S. Main St.; 453–2572. Northern Italian specialties—pastas, bread, and soups made daily on the premises. Over 175 varieties of wine in its cellars. Victorian setting with classical music. Pub opens at 3 P.M. Dinner only.

Spencer's. Beaver Run Resort; 453–6000. Continental cuisine with unusual veal, seafood, and game dishes; à la carte prices; dinner only.

Whale's Tail. Main St. in town; 453–2221. Good seafood and a popular happy hour.

Moderate

Adams Street Grill. 10 Adams St.; 453–6805. Serves steaks and seafood and has an oyster bar. With two decks: one faces the slopes, the other the street.

Fatty's. 106 N. Ridge St.; 453–9802. The oldest pizzeria in town. Also features other Italian dishes. Take-outs available.

Gold Strike Saloon. 450 S. Columbine Rd.; 453–2000. Overlooks Maggie Pond. Family-priced roast beef, fondues, sandwiches, nachos.

Poirrier's Cajun Cafe. 224 S. Main St., 453–1877. Authentic Cajun specialties. Open for lunch, dinner, and cocktails.

Tillie's Restaurant. 215 S. Ridge St.; 453–0669. Victorian atmosphere with stained glass and marble. Steaks, burgers, daily specialties. No credit cards.

Weber's. 200 N. Main St.; 453–9464. German specialties served in authentic Bavarian atmosphere with excellent service.

Inexpensive

Breckenridge Brewery. 600 S. Main St., 453–9148. Micro-brewery serving burgers and sandwiches. Pool table.

Downstairs at Eric's. 111 S. Main St., 453–1401. Serves pizza and Italian dishes. Over 50 varieties of beer.

Gold Pan Restaurant & Bar. 150 N. Main St.; 453–9761. Mexican dishes. Breakfast and dinner.

Jeremiah's. 325 S. Main St.; 453–6969. Serving breakfast, lunch, and homemade ice cream.

HOW TO GET AROUND. Everything in the town of Breckenridge is within walking distance. There is free **shuttle** service to the three bases at the ski area, to town, and between lodges. The *Summit Stage* is a free **shuttle bus** serving all the Summit County ski areas (including Keystone, Copper, and A-Basin), as well as the towns of Dillon, Frisco, and Silverthorne. Call 453–2368 at Breckenridge for details.

SEASONAL EVENTS. Every ski season is punctuated by the *World Cup Freestyle Competition* in **January.** The *ULLR Festival,* a Norwegian winter carnival honoring the Norse god of snow, and the *Snowboarding Championships* will be held in **January,** as well as the *International Snow-Sculpting Competition.* Telemark returns and the *Summit Telemark Series* features cross-country competitions in early **March.** The annual *Snowshoe Races* are held during the season, and in **April** there is a *Figure 8 Powder Competition.*

Breckenridge also offers four all-inclusive *Women's Ski Seminars* taught by and for women. Contact the Ski School for specifics and costs, 453–2368.

OTHER SPORTS AND ACTIVITIES. The Breckenridge Nordic Center, 453–6855, has 23 km of groomed trails for all ability levels.

For groups of 25 or more, the Obstacle Course Race is great fun. There is also **helicopter skiing** (453–2368) on nearby peaks. **Ice skating** (453–2000; rentals at Recreation Sports (453–2194); **ice fishing** (453–2194 for information); **sleigh riding** with Alpine Adventures (453–0111), Tiger Run Tours (453–2231), and Breckenridge Nordic Center; **Sno-Cat riding** (453–2368 or 453–2231); **snowmobiling** from Tiger Run TV (453–9690).

DAY-CARE FACILITIES. Nursery and child care is available for children aged 2 months and older; call 453–2368 for rates and reservations (necessary).

NIGHTLIFE. For those who can stay up and party after a day of skiing, Breckenridge does have bars, discos, and live entertainment. *Shamus O'Toole's Roadhouse Saloon,* 115 S. Ridge, is famous in these parts for its rowdy, get-down-and-dirty atmosphere. It offers live entertainment nightly. *Josha's,* 500 S. Park, 453–4146, is a popular night spot, with dancing to D.J. music. *Village Pub* in the Bell Tower Mall has live entertainment, good après-ski and late night; *The Mogul Georgian Square,* Main St., Breckenridge, features live rock and a great dance floor. *Tiffany's,* in the Beaver Run Resort, has a disc jockey spinning tunes and gets a very respectable dance crowd most weekends.

COPPER MOUNTAIN

Box 3001
Copper Mountain CO 80443
Tel: 303–968–2882 or 800–458–8386

Snow Report: 303–893–1400 (in Denver), or
    303–968–2100, ext. 6900
Area Vertical: 2,760 ft.
Number of Trails: 76 trails on 1,200 skiable
    acres; longest run 2.8 miles
Lifts: 2 high-speed quads, 6 triple chairs, 8
    double chairs, 4 surface lifts
Snowmaking: on 270 acres served by 4 lifts
Season: mid-November–late April

Like so many other modern ski resorts in Colorado, Copper Mountain was originally a small mining town. John Wheeler moved his family to the Snake River Valley in 1879, where he seemed to own or run all the necessities in the little settlement. The mining camp, set amid the 13,000-foot peaks of the Ten Mile Range, soon became known as Wheeler. The mines yielded only low-grade copper ore, but one mine at the summit of the sloping mountain that dominates the valley gave the area the name Copper Mountain.

There were even a few skiers back then—hardy men like Father Dyer (an itinerant preacher) and contract mail carriers. But the ore ran out, and only a few weathered cabins remained in Wheeler. In 1972, the valley was rediscovered by ski-area developers, and Copper Mountain opened its first lift.

The village is a self-contained community at the base of the mountain that has won AAA's 4-diamond rating. Everything is within walking distance, and the number of accommodations and dining options grows every year. The mountain itself seems to have been created to be a ski resort. The terrain is naturally divided among advanced (35 percent), intermediate (40 percent), and beginner (25 percent) areas, with Spaulding Bowl and Union Bowl for the experts. Both Spaulding and Union plus two other advanced bowls, Hallelujah and Resolution, are above timberline and offer the better skier some of the most challenging terrain in Summit County.

Practical Information for Copper Mountain

HOW TO GET THERE. Copper Mountain is in the Arapaho National Forest, 75 miles west of Denver.

COLORADO

By air. Denver's Stapleton Airport is the gateway with connections b
below) or rental car. The two major airlines in Denver are *Continental E*
United. All major car agencies are represented at the airport.

By bus. *Trailways, American Limousine,* and *Resort Express* all shuttle
Stapleton Airport and the ski area. Call Apex Travel at 968–2310.

By car. Take I–70 west from Denver 75 miles through Eisenhower Tunnel to
Exit 195. The resort claims that there are no mountain passes to cross from Denver,
but this is misleading; Eisenhower Tunnel cuts through the Continental Divide at
11,600 ft. and climbing from 5,280 ft. at Denver is no small task. Alternatively,
you can go via Loveland Pass. From Colorado Springs, it is 90 miles via US 24
and Colorado Rte. 9; from Grand Junction, 180 miles east on I–70 to Exit 195.

TELEPHONES. The area code for Copper Mountain is 303.

ACCOMMODATIONS. There are approximately 2,800 beds in 22 hotel and condominium units plus a 225-room Club Mediterranée in the village. A new day
lodge/conference center is scheduled to open in January 1991. Reservations are
made through *Copper Mountain Lodging Services,* Box 3001, Copper Mountain,
CO 80443; 800–458–8386. If they're booked, additional lodging is available at the
mountain and in the surrounding Summit County area through the *Copper Mountain Resort Association,* 800–525–3891 outside Colorado, or 968–6477.

Nearly all the lodges have a choice of *expensive* to *moderate* hotel rooms and
condos. The average price runs $43 per person, maximum occupancy. For example,
Mountain Plaza and **Village Square** are both at the base of the mountain, and have
saunas, shops, and Jacuzzis. A 1-bedroom apartment at either is $150 per night;
a studio with kitchen, fireplace, and pull-out sofa, or a hotel room, is $100 a night.

Inexpensive motels can be booked in nearby Frisco at **A & B Court Apartments,**
310 Main St. (668–3587), or **Sky Vue Motel,** 305 S. Second Ave. (668–3311). In
Dillon, the **Tenderfoot Motor Lodge** (22784 U.S. Hwy. 6, 468–2254) is moderately
inexpensive.

Club Med runs from mid-December to mid-April. For current rates contact a
travel agent or Club Mediterranée, 50 Beeler Pl., Copper Mountain, CO 80443;
800–528–3100 outside Colorado, 968–2161 in state.

RESTAURANTS. *Solitude Station,* mid-mountain, offers the skier hearty cafeteria-style fare, as does the *Center Cafeteria* at the base area; upstairs from the latter
is *Jacques' Loft,* which offers a limited menu and après-ski lounge. *B-Lift Pub* is
open for three meals a day, mostly burgers. *Union Creek* also has a cafeteria for
skiers.

Ten other restaurants in town offer a variety of cuisines at reasonable prices. Entrees at *Expensive* establishments are $9–$17; *Moderate,* $7–$10; *Inexpensive,* under
$6. All restaurants listed take major credit cards unless otherwise noted.

Expensive

Barkleys. 620 Main St., Frisco; 668–3694. Good steaks, prime ribs, chicken, and
Mexican specialties. Reservations recommended.

Blue Spruce Inn. 120 W. Main St., Frisco; 668–5243. A fine Continental restaurant with a cozy, fireside atmosphere.

Farley's. 104 Wheeler Pl., Copper Mountain; 968–2577. Specializes in prime
ribs, steaks, nightly specials. Reservations recommended.

Pesce Fresco. Mountain Plaza, at center of village; 968–2882, ext. 6505. An elegant restaurant offering a variety of pastas and fresh seafood entrees.

Moderate

O'Sheas. In the village center; 968–2882, ext. 6504. Western atmosphere with
hearty breakfast, lunch, and dinner buffets. Nightly country/rock entertainment.

Rackets. In The Copper Mountain Racquet and Athletic Club; 968–2882, ext.
6386. This southwestern grill features an extensive salad bar, seafood, prime ribs,
and pastas. Dinner only.

Inexpensive

The Clubhouse. Base of B Lift; 968–2882, ext. 6514. Swiss fondue dinners with
complimentary wine. Also chocolate or cheese dessert fondues. Friday and Satur-

day dinners, 1 seating only. Also has daily breakfast and lunch buffets for $4.25 and $4.95, respectively.

The Copper Saloon. Snowbridge Square; 968–2020. Features pan-fried T-bone steaks and a variety of western specialties. Lunch and dinner. Après-ski entertainment offered several days a week.

The Deli. Mountain Plaza Bldg., 968–6168. Croissant sandwiches, soups, ice cream, chocolates. Lunch only. Call for credit card information.

Vlasta's Pizza. Snowbridge Sq., 968–2323. Deli foods, breakfast, lunch, and dinner.

The Gate. 104 Wheeler Pl.; 968–BAND. Mexican entrees and appetizers. Daily lunch, dinner, and après ski. Live rock 'n' roll Wednesday–Sunday.

HOW TO GET AROUND. Within the Copper Mountain Resort complex, a free **shuttle bus** runs from 7 A.M. until 11 P.M. and makes stops at various points on the village route. *Summit Stage,* a free **shuttle bus** service, goes to all the major towns and ski areas in Summit County; at Copper, call 968–2882. Also available is *Summit Taxi Service,* 668–3565.

SEASONAL EVENTS. Early season ski clinics in **December** and **January** have become a standard. Numerous cross-country clinics and events are held during the season. The annual *Ski and Surf Snowboard Race Series* runs every two weeks from **mid-December to mid-March.** Call 968–2882 for further details on diversified ski programs and the unique ski school.

OTHER SPORTS AND ACTIVITIES. Cross-country skiing is available on 25 km of maintained double tracks at Union Creek. A track pass is $8 for adults and $6 for children and senior citizens. A combination K-lift/Track pass is $14. **Moonlight tours** followed by a Swiss-style dinner, **backcountry tours** and an "Eat, Ski and Be Merry program" are just a few of the nordic special events. Rentals are available, call 968–2882, ext. 6342 for details.

Ice skating on West Lake is held noon to 9 P.M., no charge; skate rentals at *Turning Point Sports/Gorsuch Ltd.* in Village Square, 968–2048. **Sleigh rides** follow the base of the mountain daily except Sunday; call 968–2232 for reservations.

The $3 million *Copper Mountain Racquet and Athletic Club* offers **racquetball, Nautilus equipment, weight room, aerobics,** and **pool** with four 25-yard lap lanes, **saunas, hot tubs,** a **massage therapist,** two **indoor tennis courts,** nursery, restaurant and bar. Daily fees for resort guests; call 968–2882.

CHILDREN'S ACTIVITIES. Call for day-care information, 968–2882, ext. 6345. *Belly Button Babies* is for tots 2 months to 2 years. *Belly Button Bakery* operates daily for kids 2 years and up, teaching them cooking, baking, arts and crafts, and outdoor snow play.

Junior Ranch is a learn-to-ski program for 4-, 5-, and 6-year-olds. A full day of supervised indoor and outdoor activity with lunch costs $38; $27 for a half day. First-time skiers only. Ski equipment needed; reservations recommended (968–2882). *Senior Ranch* is a ski school program for 7–12 year olds, beginners to hotshots. All-day instruction with lunch is $38; $27 for half day. *Newcomer* packages for children are for those who have never skied. They include lift tickets, lessons, and ski rentals; one day costs $37. For children who have skied before, the lift/lesson/rental package price is $48 per day. Copper's Ski School, by the way, is top-notch.

NIGHTLIFE. The nightlife won't overwhelm you at Copper Mountain, but some good sounds come from the background guitar music at *Pesce Fresco. Clubhouse,* at B-Lift, features live entertainment Tuesdays–Sundays, 3:30–7:30 P.M. Rock and Top 40 are featured in *Jacques' Loft* in the Center, Tuesdays–Saturdays, 9 P.M.–1 A.M. *O'Shea's,* in the Copper Junction Building at the base area, has live country-western music during the winter only. Movies are put on twice-weekly by the Resort Association; call for schedules and location, 968–6477. The Center features après-ski entertainment six nights a week. VCR rentals and two game rooms (Snowbridge Building and Copper Junction) round out après-ski life.

KEYSTONE RESORT/ARAPAHOE BASIN SKI AREA

Box 38
Keystone CO 80435
Tel: 303–468–2316

*Snow Report: 303–572–SNOW (Denver
   direct); 303–468–4111 (outside Denver)*
*Area Vertical: Keystone: 2,340 ft. Arapahoe
   Basin: 1,670 ft.*
*Number of Trails: Keystone: 71 on 1,075
   skiable acres, including open bowl and
   glade skiing. Arapahoe Basin: 29 on
   350 acres plus open bowl skiing*
*Lifts: Keystone Mountain: 2 six-passenger
   gondolas, 4 quad chairs, 3 triple chairs,
   6 double chairs, 3 surface lifts.
   Arapahoe Basin: 1 triple chair, 4
   double chairs*
*Snowmaking: Keystone: 100 percent of area.
   Arapahoe Basin: none*
*Season: Keystone: late October–late April.
   Arapahoe Basin: late November–
   mid-June*

Keystone is the ultimate planned village. This four-season resort consists of the Keystone Lodge and 800 condominium units mostly clustered around a central lake and immaculate village. Every building has been constructed of materials and colors that blend with the environment, maintaining a feeling of the natural landscape.

Skiing at Keystone is available on three mountains and three faces. Keystone Mountain is located less than a mile from the main section of the resort village. The front face offers many terrific cruising runs; the intermediate (65 percent) and beginner (20 percent) trails are evenly spread out over the face, giving even beginners a wide variety of trails and areas to cover. North Peak, adjacent to Keystone Mountain, offers the advanced skier some challenging terrain; 71 percent of its runs are rated "most difficult." The Outback, behind Keystone Mountain and North Peak, opened in 1990 with 300 ungroomed acres of above-timberline bowls and trails for high-intermediate and advanced skiers. Two quad chairs serving North Peak and the Outback, a mountain-top restaurant, and a gondola from the summit of Keystone to summit of North Peak are scheduled to open in the 1991–92 season.

And then there's Arapahoe Basin, located a few miles from Keystone Village. A-Basin, as it is commonly known, was a day area before it was acquired by Keystone's corporation. Now, though still frequented by many Denver skiers, it provides an area for Keystone's guests who seek steeper and more difficult runs than can be found at Keystone Mountain. Because of its proximity to the Continental Divide, A-Basin gets an average of 360 inches of snow annually and is usually open until June.

Beginners and intermediates can find only a few suitable runs at the top (10 percent) of this 12,450-foot mountain and should go up if only for the spectacular view. Experts can revel in the steep runs and an ungroomed area called Pallavicini, an open bowl that narrows into a steep gully that can fill with powder snow. A-Basin is also known for its encouragement and support of snowboarding, an up-and-coming form of skiing.

Base facilities at A-Basin consist only of a cafeteria, lounge, ski shop, child-care center, and ski school office. The facilities at Keystone are quite extensive. The ski school is renowned, and Keystone is home to the Phil and Steve Mahre Training Centers.

One special facet of Keystone is that it is the only area in Summit County that offers night skiing until 10 P.M. The enclosed six-passenger gondola is the lift that makes this possible even on cold winter evenings.

Practical Information for Keystone

HOW TO GET THERE. Keystone is in the Arapaho National Forest, 75 miles west of Denver.

By air. Denver's Stapleton Airport is the closest gateway, with scores of airlines from all major American cities, and rental cars available. Scheduled **chauffeured van** service via *Resort Express* is available from the airport for $26 per person one way; call 800–451–5930. Keystone offers free round-trip transportation with their 5-night or longer packages.

By car. Drive 75 miles west from Denver via I–70, through Eisenhower Tunnel, to Exit 205, then 6 miles east on US 6. In good weather, go through the spectacularly scenic Loveland Pass by exiting I–70 just before the tunnel, and taking US 6, past Loveland and Arapahoe ski areas to Keystone. From Colorado Springs, it is 125 miles via I–25 and I–70; from Grand Junction it is 180 miles east on I–70 over Vail Pass to Exit 205, then 6 miles east on US 6.

By bus. *Trailways* has daily bus service from Denver's airport to Frisco, with some schedules direct to Keystone. It's a short taxi ride from Frisco to Keystone.

TELEPHONES. The area code for Keystone is 303.

ACCOMMODATIONS. For reservations nationwide, call 800–222–0188, or write *Keystone Central Reservations,* Box 38, Keystone, CO 80435. In Denver, call direct: 534–7712. Information for all accommodations: 468–2316.

Categories are determined by price. *Expensive,* $130–$165 per night for hotel rooms; $130–$550 per night for studio units to 4-bedroom condos. *Moderate,* $125–$470 per night for studios to 4-bedroom condos. *Inexpensive,* $110–$370 for studios to 4-bedroom condos. Ask for "Premium" when making reservations at an expensive establishment, "Deluxe" at moderate establishments. Keystone also has many packages that offer tremendous savings. Call central reservations for details.

Expensive

Keystone Lodge. Box 38; 468–2316. Keystone's full-service hotel, the lodge holds awards for the superiority of its guest facilities. Each of the 152 rooms has a mountain view; the heated indoor–outdoor pool has complete cocktail service. There is a sauna and whirlpool. No pets.

Most of the following accommodations range from studio units to 4-bedroom condos. Private homes are also for rent. **Argentine, Plaza, Mall, Edgewater,** and **Lakeside** are all on the Keystone Lake at the center of the village; a 2-minute shuttle ride to the mountain.

Willows, Decatur, Montezuma, and **Lenawee** are on the east side of Keystone Lake; a 2-minute walk to village center and a 2-minute shuttle ride to the mountain.

Chateaux d'Mont (Lancaster Lodge) is at the base of Keystone Mountain.

Ski Tip Lodge. This restored 1860s stagecoach stop offers one of the most unusual lodging opportunities in the county. Located deep in the woods near the resort, the Ski Tip has several rooms for overnight guests in addition to gourmet dining. Spend some time in the living room with its huge fireplace; this is the real meaning of après-ski. Call (303) 468–4202 for information and reservations.

Moderate

Pines, Soda Spring, Homestead/Lodgepole, Quicksilver, Tennis Townhouses, St. John; a 5-minute walk from the village center; no pets.

Inexpensive

Flying Dutchman, Wild Irishman, Key Condo, Keystone Gulch. These are standard accommodations, but hardly cheap. Farther from the village, they don't have the wonderful views. The *Key Condo,* however, is at slopeside.

RESTAURANTS. At the base of the mountain is *Gassy's,* open for lunch and dinner. Good crepes can be had from the *Greatest Crepe Wagon,* parked at the base area. *Last Lift Bar* is good for snacks and drinks. The *Summit House* at the top of Keystone Mountain is a multileveled cafeteria and soup bar, with outdoor barbecues in good weather. *Mountain House* and *River Run Plaza* offer cafeteria food.

Entrees in *Expensive* restaurants will run $17–$20; $10–$15 in *Moderate;* under $10 in *Inexpensive.* All restaurants listed take most major credit cards unless otherwise noted.

Garden Room. *Expensive.* In the Keystone Lodge; 468–2316. For Continental meals prepared tableside. Reservations recommended.

Bighorn Steakhouse. *Moderate.* In the Keystone Lodge; 468–2316. Serves steaks, fresh fish, soup, and breads and offers a 28-item salad bar.

Commodore. *Moderate.* At Keystone Lake; 468–4295. For seafood; reserve in advance. Beautiful views of the ice rink.

Der Fondue Chessel. *Moderate.* In the Summit House at the top of Keystone Mountain; 468–4130. For a fun evening of food and entertainment, order the fondue and some German beer or wine and listen to the oompah band. Open only 5–9 P.M. You can ski down the mountain when you're done eating; the less adventurous can always take the enclosed gondola down.

Ida Belle's. *Moderate.* Overlooking Keystone Lake; 468–4289. Burgers as well as Italian-American dishes. Reservations accepted.

Edgewater Cafe. *Inexpensive.* In Keystone Lodge; 468–4127. Open in winter for three meals. Reservations accepted.

Last Chance Saloon. *Inexpensive.* Argentine Plaza, Keystone Village; 468–9501. Good pizzas and a young crowd. Full bar, dancing, live entertainment.

Outside Keystone Resort

Blue Spruce Inn. *Expensive.* 12 West Main, Frisco; 668–5243. Known for its Continental menu, steaks and ribs.

Keystone Ranch. *Expensive.* At the Keystone Resort golf course in the resort, a few miles from Keystone Village; 468–4161. Outstanding 6-course dinners, fixed price of $32, all in an elegant ranch setting. Reservations recommended.

Ski Tip Lodge. *Expensive.* On Montezuma Rd., 2 miles east of Keystone Village; 468–4202. Dining in a cozy guest ranch—the oldest in Colorado. A warm atmosphere with hearty down-home cookin'.

Old Dillon Inn. *Moderate.* 305 Dillon La., Silverthorne; 468–2791. Mexican food, loud music, and weekend entertainment make this the most popular hangout for locals.

Claim Jumper. *Inexpensive.* 805 North Summit Rd., Frisco; 668–3617. For pizza and chicken.

Whiskey Creek. *Inexpensive.* 912 North Summit Rd., Frisco; 668–5595. For Mexican food and fine margaritas.

HOW TO GET AROUND. A free **shuttle** operates continually from the Keystone Lodge and all condos to the village, Mountain House, River Run Plaza, Arapahoe Basin, Keystone Ranch and Ski Tip Lodge for dinner. For information, call the *Transportation Center,* 468–4200. Within Summit County, the free **bus** service, *The Summit County Stage,* runs from Keystone to the neighboring "Ski the Summit" areas of Breckenridge and Copper Mountain and the neighboring towns of Dillon, Frisco, Silverthorne, and Breckenridge from mid-November until late April.

SEASONAL EVENTS. *Spring skiing* is celebrated at Arapahoe Basin in **April** and **May** with beach parties.

OTHER SPORTS AND ACTIVITIES. Cross-country skiing is on 26 miles of prepared trails. Lessons and tours by day or evening offered. Contact Jana Hlavaty, Keystone Resort, Box 38, Keystone, CO 80435; 468–4275.

Helicopter skiing is available through *Colorado Heli-ski* of Frisco; call 668–5600.

Ice skating is popular on Keystone Lake; the *Keystone Ice Rink* is the largest maintained outdoor facility in the country. Call 468–2316, ext. 3980.

DAY-CARE FACILITIES. Kids 12 and under stay free in the same lodge room or condominium with their parent, provided minimum occupancy is not exceeded. The *Children's Center* in the Mountain House at the base of Keystone Mountain will take care of children from 2 months. It is open 8 A.M.–5 P.M. daily; advance reservations required, 468–4182. Care for infants 2 to 11 months and 12 months and up can be arranged. Call for rates. Evening baby-sitting may be reserved through the Children's Center.

At Arapahoe Basin, the center accepts children 18 months and older from 8:30 A.M.–4:30 P.M. daily; call 468–4182 for reservations.

Snow Play Program, 468–4182, is for children 3 years and older. It offers sledding and skating. Children should be toilet-trained and dressed for outdoors. Keystone Mountain only.

Junior Ski School is for ages 3–12 and includes lift ticket, equipment rental, and 2½ hours of lessons. Call the ski school for prices and reservations, 468–4170.

NIGHTLIFE. You won't disco the night away in Keystone, but there are several lounges for après-ski and après-dinner drinks. The *Tenderfoot Lounge,* in the Lodge, is elegant, with a spectacular view of the Gore Range. *Ida Belle's* occasionally has live entertainment and *Last Chance Saloon* usually has nightly entertainment and dancing. See *Restaurants* section for addresses.

TELLURIDE

Box 307
Telluride CO 81435
Tel: 303–728–3856 and 800–525–3455

Snow Report: 303–728–3614
Area Vertical: 3,155 ft.
Number of Trails: 45 on 735 acres, longest run 2.85 miles
Lifts: 1 quad, 7 double chairs, 2 triple chairs, 1 poma
Snowmaking: 120 acres served by 4 lifts
Season: late November (Thanksgiving)–mid-April

The town of Telluride has a rich mining history, which remained economically important to the area until 1978. Butch Cassidy robbed his first bank here in 1889. But since 1973, most of the excitement has come in the form of 18 special events hosted in Telluride, a town whose slogan is "Make it a festival." The summertime Telluride Bluegrass and Jazz festivals are legendary. But it's winter that brings the tourists to this challenging mountain.

Telluride has four distinct areas tailored for various skill levels. The broad, gentle runs of Meadows are great for beginners. Sunshine Peak's rolling slopes and wide trails attract both beginners and intermediates. Served by three lifts, Gorrono Basin offers good cruising runs for intermediates. The Face is Telluride's ultimate. Its expert runs like "The Plunge" and "Spiral Stairs" have been named, in many ski publications, as some of the toughest in the country, able to challenge any expert. However, with the advent of new grooming techniques, it may be possible for some intermediates to sample the excitement of these runs.

In the past Telluride was coveted for its remoteness. A new airport, perched at 9,068 feet and touted as the highest commercial strip in the

United States, has ended Telluride's isolation. As a result of the anticipated increase in the number of tourists, a billion-dollar community is growing, 8 miles from the mountain. The centerpiece is the Doral Resort & Spa, a $90 million complex slated to open in winter 1992. With residential lots starting at $150,000 and homes going for $3 million, it's easy to envision Telluride becoming the new Aspen. Celebrities already choose it for the excellent skiing, the availability of real estate, and the low-key friendliness that pervades the town. Residents really do not want another Aspen here, and they are fighting to preserve their community—a battle that in the wake of increasing development may prove to be as challenging as skiing Telluride's slopes.

Practical Information for Telluride

HOW TO GET THERE. Telluride is located in the Uncompahgre National Forest, 325 miles southwest of Denver.

By air. Telluride's new airport, located 5 miles from town, has daily round-trip flights from Denver, Albuquerque, and Phoenix on *Mesa Airlines.* Montrose (67 miles south), Durango (125 miles south), and Grand Junction (127 miles north) airports are gateways to Telluride also. *America West* flies to Phoenix and Austin/Durango daily. Other daily service is offered from Denver by *United Express,* 800–821–7126, and *Continental Express,* 800–525–0180. *Delta's Sky West,* 800–453–9417, has non-stop flights on Saturdays and Wednesdays from Los Angeles to Telluride. *Telluride Transit* meets all flights with 24-hour advance reservations in Montrose, Grand Junction, and Durango. For information on schedules, contact the Telluride Ski Resort, Box 307, Telluride, CO 81435 (303) 728–3856.

By bus. *Trailways* serves Montrose. *Telluride Transit* provides ground transportation to Telluride with 24-hour advance reservations, (303) 738–4105, or Telluride Central Reservations Transportation Desk, 800–525–3455. The Montrose/Telluride trip is $15 per person one-way; Durango/Telluride, $35 per person one-way; Grand Junction/Telluride, $30 per person one way.

By car. Denver is a long drive on US 285, US 50, US 550, and Rtes. 62 and 145. Durango is 125 miles south via Rte. 145, Rte. 62, and US 550; Montrose is 67 miles north via US 550, Rte. 62, and Rte. 145. Grand Junction is 125 miles north via US 789, US 550, Rte. 62, and Rte. 145. **Car rentals** from Montrose include *Budget,* 800–527–0700; and *Hertz,* 800–654–3131; in Grand Junction, *Avis,* 800–331–1212, *Budget, Hertz,* and *National,* 800–328–4567; in Durango, *Budget, Avis,* and *Hertz.*

TELEPHONES. The area code for Telluride is 303.

ACCOMMODATIONS. *Telluride Central Reservations* handles lodging, information, and reservations for all properties in town: Box 1009, Telluride, CO 81435; 800–525–3455; 728–4431 in Colorado. For details on rentals at the new Telluride Mountain Village Resort contact *Telluride Mountain Village,* Box 11163, Telluride 81435; 800–544–0507. The base of the ski area is four blocks from town, six blocks from Main Street condos.

The following price categories are based on per-night rates; you can expect better value for longer stays. *Expensive,* $150–$575; *Moderate,* $80–$150; and *Inexpensive,* $50–$80.

Bachman Village. *Expensive.* 105 S. Davis, near entrance to town; 728–4226. The new, deluxe, Victorian-style homes here are ideal for 6 to 8 people.

Ice House Hotel. *Expensive.* 310 S. Fir St.; 800–544–3436. A new, 42-room lodge with luxurious furnishings. You can walk to the Oak Street Lift.

LuLu City Condos. *Expensive.* 728–4387. Most condos are liftside. All units have phones, TV, hot tubs, steam showers, and saunas.

Pennington's Mountain Village Inn. *Expensive.* 100 Pennington Court, Mountain Village; 800–543–1437. Elegant bed-and-breakfast with private baths.

San Sophia Bed & Breakfast. *Expensive.* 330 W. Pacific St.; 800–537–4781. Contemporary decor is featured in this lovely inn. Known for sumptuous breakfasts and après-ski offerings.

Telluride Mountain Village. *Expensive.* 800–544–0507. There are several new condominiums at the new Mountain Village that offer a variety of amenities and services. Call for details.

Graysill Condos. *Moderate.* Liftside; 728–4431. Fine accommodations with Jacuzzis, washers/dryers; 2-bedroom units available.

Ore Station Lodge. *Moderate.* 260 S. Aspen; 728–4311. Studio to 3-bedroom condos, furnished in antiques and oak furniture.

Telluride Lodge. *Moderate.* 666 W. Colorado Ave., at the base of the area; 728–4446. Condominium units 4 blocks from historic downtown; common hot tub.

Tom Boy Inn. *Moderate.* 728–3871. Located in town. Glass-enclosed spa and steam room. Former Best Western Inn.

The Dahl House. *Inexpensive.* Box 695, Telluride; 728–4158. A restored 1890s miners' boarding house. Furnished with antiques in the bed-and-breakfast area. Some rooms share baths. Also has studios and 1- and 2-bedroom condos.

Johnstone Inn. *Inexpensive.* 403 W. Colorado Ave.; 800–752–1901 or 728–3316. Three blocks from Coonskin Lift. A Victorian-style bed-and-breakfast establishment.

New Sheridan Hotel. *Inexpensive.* Box 980, 231 W. Colorado Ave.; 728–4351. Smack in the middle of town, this is a Victorian beauty built in 1895 and completely remodeled in 1991. Free ski shuttle to mountain, 6 blocks away.

RESTAURANTS. At the mountain, cafeteria food is available at the *Prospector Base* and the *Sausage Shack* at mid-mountain. The *Gorrono Ranch Restaurant* is also popular. Several restaurants in town will prepare box lunches for skiers. *The Galloping Goose Gourmet,* 728–3063 or 728–6500, will stock your condo with groceries for your arrival.

For a small town, Telluride has a relatively large number of restaurants and bars—at last count, 20 in town plus three at the base or middle of the mountain. *Expensive* restaurants have entrees ranging from $15–$25; *Moderate,* $10–$15; *Inexpensive,* under $10. Call restaurants for credit card information.

Expensive

La Campagna. Pacific St.; 728–6190. In Victorian house, this elegant restaurant specializes in fine Italian cuisine. Reservations suggested.

La Marmotte. 150 San Juan Ave.; 728–6232. Quaint and rustic, this restaurant serves alpine favorites.

Powderhouse. 226 W. Colorado Ave.; 728–3622. Traditional Telluride restaurant in Victorian setting. Dinner only; reservations necessary.

Silverglade. 115 W. Colorado Ave.; 728–4943. The specialty is California style mesquite-broiled fresh fish.

Moderate

Athenian Senate. 123 S. Spruce St.; 728–3018. Good selection of Greek dishes, including a vegetable moussaka with tofu, eggplant, mushrooms, and a creamy kasseri-cheese topping. The fun begins with traditional Greek dancing and breaking of plates.

Excelsior Cafe. 200 W. Colorado Ave.; 728–4250. Marvelous Continental breakfasts; soups, fondues, espresso, pastries until 10:30 P.M.

Floradora Saloon. 103 W. Colorado Ave.; 728–9937. Extensive lunch and dinner menus. Char-broiled burgers, salad bar. Open late.

Hongu's Lotus Petal. S. Spruce St.; 728–5134. Asian cooking with the accent on healthy dishes. Breakfast, lunch, and dinner.

Leimgruber's Bierstube & Restaurant. 573 W. Pacific Ave.; 728–4663. European atmosphere, open from 7 A.M. to 11 P.M.

Sofio's. 110 E. Colorado Ave.; 728–4882. Telluride's Mexican restaurant.

Inexpensive

Baked-in Telluride. 127 S. Fire; 728–9902. Light fare. *The* place for fresh bagels in the morning.

Eddies, 300 W. Colorado Ave.; 728–5335. Traditional New York–style pizza, gourmet pizza, and desserts.

Telluride Country Club. 333 W. Colorado Ave.; 728–6344. Steak, seafood, and cook-your-own on a charcoal grill.

HOW TO GET AROUND. A free **shuttle bus** makes the loop from town to the mountain—Coonskin lift and Mountain Village base—every 40 minutes in ski season; a free bus circulates in town every 10 minutes during ski season and summer festivals. **Taxis** are available by calling 728–6667. Nearly everything is within walking distance, and the base area is only 4 blocks from most lodges.

SEASONAL EVENTS. The *Sonoma County Wineries* and Telluride host a week-long wine/ski festival the last week in **January.** *Coonskin Carnival* is Telluride's answer to the winter blahs in early **February.** *Spring Fling* heralds spring's arrival at the end of **March.**

OTHER SPORTS AND ACTIVITIES. *The Nordic Center Guides* introduces **cross-country** skiers to the backcountry with picnics and lessons; 10-km and 17-km ski tracks. Trail fee is $5, equipment rental available, $10 a day. Telemark lessons are available on the mountain for $22. Inquire about guided tours through *Central Reservations,* 728–3455, or 800–525–3455 outside Colorado. For those who like to ski tour the backcountry on their own, call 728–3041 for information on trails from the town park to Lizard Head Pass and Sunshine and Wilson mesas.

Heli-skiing is available, even for the not-so-fantastic skier; contact *Heli-Trax,* 728–4909, and find the hidden basins in the San Juan Mountains. **Ice skating** is available on the town park; skating parties every Wednesday evening with a bonfire and music; rentals from Olympic Sports at $4 a pair, 226 W. Colorado Ave.; 728–3501. **Roller skating** all year at the *Quonset Hut,* Columbia and Townsend, 728–4477, rentals $2.50 a pair.

HINTS TO THE HANDICAPPED. Skiing is free for those with sight or hearing impairment or with a variety of other physical handicaps. For details and reservations, contact the Ski School, 728–4424.

DAY-CARE FACILITIES. Children 2 months and up are cared for at the *Village Nursery,* at Meadows base facility. Open from 8:30 A.M. to 4:30 P.M. Care for infants under 1 year costs $6 an hour or $35 for a full day. For children 1 year and up the cost is $30, all day, with lunch; $20, half-day. Multi-day rates are lower. The *Snowstar* program offers day care for 3- and 4-year-olds, including snow play, ski lessons, rentals; full day, $40. Two *Telstar* programs are for 5- to 7-year-olds and 8- to 12-year-olds. All-day lesson including lunch, lifts, and snacks costs $50; with rentals, $60. Call 728–4424 for the Village Nursery and Children's Center.

NIGHTLIFE. Although visitors may not be overwhelmed by the choice, there are enough evening activities to keep most busy during their stay. *Fly Me to the Moon Saloon,* 132 E. Colorado Ave., features live music, a dance floor, pool, and pizzas from 3 P.M. to 3 A.M. *O'Bannon's Irish Pub* is open till 2 A.M. and serves soups and sandwiches till closing. *Roma Bar and Cafe* rocks with live music, and happy hour lasts all day and night, Monday through Thursday.

VAIL/BEAVER CREEK

VAIL

Box 7
Vail CO 81658
Tel: 303–476–5601, 800–525–3875 outside
Colorado

Snow Report: 303–476–4888/4889
Area Vertical: 3,250 ft.
Number of Trails: 120 trails on 3,834
*   developed acres, longest run 4.5 miles*
Lifts: 1 gondola, 1 enclosed high-speed
*   quad, 5 detachable high-speed quads, 2*
*   fixed grip quads, 2 triple chairlifts, 8*
*   double chairlifts, 2 surface lifts*
Snowmaking: on 332 acres
Season: late November–late April

In just 25 years, through a combination of size, quality, and service, Vail has grown into one of the greatest ski resorts in the world. This fact was underscored by Vail's hosting of the 1989 World Alpine Ski Championships, the "olympics of alpine skiing." Vail is only the second area in the United States to be awarded its bid to host the championships (the first was Aspen in 1950) and it rose to the occasion grandly and with ease.

In the beginning, Gore Valley was home to ranchers and miners who remained after the gold and silver rushes of the late 1800s subsided. The white man's intrusion drove out the Ute Indians, the original residents, who left angrily, setting "spite fires" to thousands of acres of timberland.

The result gave Vail the famous "back bowls," over 4,000 acres of open glades beyond the front side of the mountain, which were expanded, *doubling* the size of Vail's terrain. In late 1988 Vail opened China, Siberia, Teacup, and Mongolia bowls, adding 1,881 acres to the existing 800 acres of Sun Up and Sun Down bowls. This is mostly ungroomed terrain for intermediate (36 percent) and advanced (64 percent) skiers. Add that to 120 groomed runs on over 1,000 acres, and you have a variety of skiing that boggles the mind. Skiing at Vail for a full week will allow most people only to scratch the surface of what's available.

Because Vail has seven express quad chair lifts that make up the largest high-speed network in the world, skiers can log more mileage here in less time than at other areas with slower lifts. Many skiers dislike high-speed lifts because they increase skier traffic on the runs; at Vail, the expanse of terrain belittles this concern. The management's "keep the skier in mind" level of planning is another factor. Thus snowboarders have their own "park," featuring a half-pipe and berm, each over 300 feet long.

Take, as another example, families. A recent high-level-of-service-for-our-skier development at Vail was the opening of a children's ski center at the Golden Peak base (one of four base areas). The new, airy building was designed for maximum ease and utility in providing one-stop day care and children's ski instruction. In addition, the Children's Mountain Adventures, an on-mountain maze of ski-through attractions designed to teach skiing skills (the "adventures" are scattered on different parts of the mountain and are linked by two western frontier story themes), have been upgraded and expanded. The ski school is rated one of the world's best with over 900 instructors and state-of-the-art teaching methods.

The plethora of available off-mountain activities rivals the skiing here. Shopping is an art form in Vail Village: The pedestrian-only "mall" at the base is sprinkled with numerous shops and restaurants; its Bavarian architecture, while not original for a ski village, can be charming, particularly for first-time visitors.

Vail Associates, the owner of Vail and of neighboring Beaver Creek, has additional plans in the works to expand services for skiers. For example, look for things like mobile cafeterias in the bowl areas that serve ethnic food: imagine lunching on chicken lo mein and wonton soup while sitting atop China Bowl. Gimmicky yes, but it'll be a unique skiing experience—and that's what you'll find at Vail.

Practical Information for Vail

HOW TO GET THERE. Vail is in the White River National Forest, 100 miles west of Denver.

By air. The Vail/Eagle County Airport is 35 miles west of Vail on I–70. From December through March *American Airlines* offers daily, non-stop service from Dallas/Ft. Worth and Chicago O'Hare with connections from 61 cities. *America West* has daily service from Phoenix and Saturday service from Los Angeles International. For reservations call *Vail/Beaver Creek Reservations,* 800–237–0643; *American Airlines,* 800–433–7300; or *America West,* 800–247–5692. For private-pilot information at Vail/Eagle County Airport, call 303–524–7700 or 949–5480.

Denver's Stapleton airport is served by most major airlines and is a hub for *Continental Airlines,* 800–525–0280.

Ground-service-transportation companies serving both airports with regular and charter **shuttle buses** are: *Colorado Mountain Express,* 800–525–6363; *Louie's Casual Cabs/Vail Transportation Inc.,* 800–992–8294; *Resort Express,* 800–334–7433; *Skiers Connection,* 800–824–1104; and *Vans to Vail,* 800–222–2112. The trip takes about 2½ hours from Denver's Stapleton and costs $25–$30. The Vail/Eagle County airport is located about 45 minutes from Vail; cost is $18.

By bus. *Greyhound/Trailways,* 800–322–2754 or (303) 476–5137, serves the Vail Transportation Center from downtown Denver and Stapleton Airport and from Grand Junction.

By car. From Denver, Vail lies 100 miles west on I–70. From Grand Junction, it is 150 miles east on I–70; Colorado Springs is 145 miles away via I–25 and I–70. *American International,* 800–527–0202; *Budget,* 800–527–0700; and *Thrifty,* 800–367–2277, are the **rental car companies** in Vail; all the major rental car companies are at the Denver airport.

TELEPHONES. The area code for Vail is 303.

ACCOMMODATIONS. Twenty thousand guests can be accommodated within a 5-mile radius of Vail Village. Contact *Vail/Beaver Creek Reservations,* Box 7, Vail, CO 81658, 800–237–0643. During busy periods there are long waits to get information from Vail's reservation number. Calling directly to the properties is recommended for faster service.

All establishments are in the village, within walking distance of the slopes, shopping, and dining.

In this listing, price categories are determined by the size of the unit as well as the amenities offered. *Expensive:* $200–$1,000 per night; *Moderate:* $125–$500 per night for double rooms and 1–3-bedroom condos; *Inexpensive,* $85–$200 per night, depending on the size of the unit. Package rates based on per person, double occupancy, and include seven nights' lodging, lifts, and transfers to airport. Prices range from $674 to $2,221 during the regular season.

Expensive

The Lodge at Vail. 174 East Gore Creek Dr.; 476–5011 or 800–223–6800. Close to the lifts and village center. European ambience and service; 162 units—rooms and condos—2 restaurants, lounge, swimming pool, saunas, 16-person Jacuzzi. The complimentary breakfast buffet for guests is one of Vail's best.

Marriot's Mark Resort. 715 W. Lionshead Circle; 476–4444 or 800–228–9290. Rooms and condo units, 200 yards from the gondola. Restaurants, lounges, athletic club, racquetball courts, swimming pool, and meeting rooms.

Sonnenalp Hotel. 20 Vail Rd.; 476–5081 or 800–654–8312. Two hundred yards from Vista Bahn in Vail. Recently expanded, 172 hotel rooms, 2-bedroom condos; conference facilities, 3 restaurants, 2 lounges.

Vail Hotel & Athletic Club. 352 E. Meadow Dr.; 476–0700 or 800–822–4754. Just 100 yards from the lifts and the center of town, with a full range of amenities, including newly remodeled rooms and condos. Conference facilities, dining room, and one of Vail's best health clubs with an indoor pool.

The Westin Hotel. 1300 Westhaven Dr.; 476–7111 or 800–228–3000. In the Cascade Village adjacent to a new quad lift. Formal gourmet restaurant, *Alfredo's*. Two outdoor pools, use of Cascade Club facilities; indoor tennis, racquetball, weights, and the like. Convention facilities.

Moderate

Lion Square Lodge. 660 W. Lionshead Pl.; 476–2281 or 800–525–5788. Twenty-five yards from gondola and Chair 8. Includes 90 condos, 28 rooms and suites. Conference facilities, restaurant, lounge, heated pool, and Jacuzzi.

L'Ostello. 705 Lionshead Circle; 476–2050 or 800–283–8245. Formerly the Enzian Lodge, in 1991 this inn was totally renovated. Only 100 yards from the Lionshead lifts, with 50 rooms, conference facilities, a private gym, an outdoor pool. On-premises dining and a jazz lounge.

Manor Vail Lodge. 595 E. Vail Valley Dr.; 476–5651 or 800–525–9165. Located 50 yards from the Golden Peak lifts, offering individually decorated studio and 2-bedroom condo units with kitchens and ski storage. Perfect location for families with kids—Golden Peak Children's Center is steps away. Amenities include outdoor heated pool, small private gym, messages, fine on-premises dining (the buffet breakfast is included in the room rate). The lodge is undergoing a major lobby renovation and expansion of its conference and dining facilities, which should be completed for the 1991–92 season.

Montaneros. 641 Lionshead Circle; 476–2491 or 800–444–VAIL. A 42-unit, deluxe condo complex 50 yards from the gondola lift. Multi-bedroom units have fireplaces. Outdoor pool, whirlpool, sauna, covered parking.

Mountain Haus. 292 E. Meadow Dr.; 476–2434 or 800–237–0922. A luxurious hotel/condominium in Vail Village, 2 blocks from the Vista Bahn lift. One- to 4-bedroom units with fireplaces. The outdoor pool is heated; there is a steam room with masseur, plus a sauna and Jacuzzi.

Vail Racquet Club Condominiums. 4690 Racquet Club Dr.; 476–4840. At base of Vail Pass in East Vail. Units with fireplaces and balconies with barbecues. Restaurant, 3 indoor tennis courts, squash and racquetball courts, health spa, exercise room.

Inexpensive

Best Western Vailglo Lodge. 701 W. Lionshead Circle; 476–5506. Near shopping mall, 300 feet from the gondola; 34 hotel rooms. Received the AAA 3-diamond award and the Mobil 3-star rating.

Days Inn. 2211 N. Frontage Rd.; 800–325–2525. Two miles west of Lionshead ski area. Health club with pool and sauna. Free shuttle service.

Holiday Inn/Holiday House. 13 Vail Rd.; 476–5631. Located 300 yards from the Vista Bahn in Vail. Has 120 hotel rooms and 21 condos; 2 restaurants, a lounge, and conference facilities; free parking.

Roost Lodge. 1783 N. Frontage Rd.; 476–5451. A long-time favorite of those on a budget. Bus or drive or village.

RESTAURANTS. Dining in Vail presents another array of choices—more than 115 restaurants and bars. On-mountain food service includes cafeterias at *Mid-Vail* (outdoor barbecues in good weather), *Eagle's Nest, Golden Peak,* and *Lionshead Gondola Building.* Snack facilities are at *Far East Shelter* at Lift 14 (also outdoor barbecues) and *Wildwood Shelter* at Lift 3. Full-service, sit-down restaurants are *The Cook Shack* at Mid-Vail (nouvelle cuisine, expensive, reservations necessary), *The Wine Stube* at Eagle's Nest (international dishes), and *Trail's End* in the gondola building (breakfast, lunch, and children's dinners).

Because many restaurants have à la carte menus (appetizer, entree, salad), price categories are based on a full meal for one, exclusive of beverage and tip. *Expensive,* $30–$40; *Moderate,* $18–$30; and *Inexpensive,* under $18. All restaurants accept most major credit cards unless otherwise noted.

Expensive

Alfredo's. In the Westin Hotel, 1300 Westhaven Dr.; 476–7111. Northern Italian cuisine in an elegant setting. Serving dinner and Sunday brunch. Reservations suggested.

Ambrosia. 17 E. Meadow Dr.; 476–1964. Extensive Continental menu and good dessert selection served in a French provincial setting. Dinner only. Reservations recommended.

Chanticler. In Vail Spa Building, 710 W. Lionshead Circle; 476–1441. French atmosphere and food, extensive wine list; covered parking available.

Gourmet Room. In the Sonnenalp Hotel; 476–5656. Daily 5-course gourmet menu featuring Continental specialties.

The Left Bank. 183 Gore Creek Dr.; 476–3696. Très French and très expensive, with only 2 seatings each night. Reservations needed several weeks in advance; dinner only in winter.

L'Ostellos. 705 Lionshead Circle; 476–2959. Awarded a 5-star rating by the *Denver Post.* Sophisticated, modern ambience is the setting for northern Italian Specialties. Adjacent jazz lounge features entertainment.

Tea Room Alpenrose. 100 E. Meadow Dr.; 476–3194. German specialties and mouth-watering pastries. Lunch and dinner.

The Wildflower. In the Lodge at Vail, 174 E. Gore Creek Dr.; 476–5011. Sunny spot with silk flowers all around, serving American cuisine, à la carte dinner only. Reservations recommended.

Moderate

The Chart House. 610 W. Lionshead Circle; 476–1525. Known for its steaks and salad bar, this is one of the largest restaurants in Vail. No reservations.

KB Ranch Co. 660 Lionshead Pl.; 476–1937. Casual dining: pasta, steaks, and seafood; biggest salad bar in Vail. Great view of Lionshead.

Lord Gore Restaurant. 595 E. Vail Valley Dr.; 476–4959. Located in the Manor Vail Lodge, this elegant yet casual restaurant serves Continental classics and game dishes—including the best rack of lamb Provençale in town. The floor-to-ceiling windows offer fantastic views of the Golden Peak base area. Children's menu available; reservations suggested.

Siamese Orchard. 12 S. Frontage Rd.; 476–9417. Fine Thai and Southeast Asian cuisine. Dinner only.

Uptown Grill. 472 Lionshead Circle; 476–2727. Santa Fe–style decor, with California cuisine for lunch and dinner.

Vendetta's. 291 Bridge St.; 476–5070. Located in the Plaza Lodge, Vendetta's is a long-time favorite for fine Italian food.

Inexpensive

Blu's Ltd. 193 E. Gore Creek Dr.; 476–3113. Innovative egg dishes, pasta, fresh fish, and sandwiches. Serves breakfast, lunch, and dinner.

May Palace. 223 E. Gore Creek Dr.; 476–1657. Mandarin and Szechuan cuisine and a bar that features Polynesian drinks. Serves lunch and dinner.

Montauk. 549 W. Lionshead Mall; 476–2601. Featuring Vail's largest selection of fresh seafood and an oyster bar.

Vail Village Inn Pancake House. 68 S. Frontage Rd.; 476–2207. Part of a national chain with true '50s-diner decor. One of the most popular items is Santa Fe Skillet, an egg dish with cheese and chilis. Eggs Benedict and omelets are also favorites. Open 6 A.M. to 9 P.M.

HOW TO GET AROUND. Within Vail Village is a free **shuttle bus** service, the third-largest municipal bus system in the state. Between Vail and Beaver Creek, the shuttle costs $1. For information, call 476–7000. The village is planned as a pedestrian mall, and shops, dining, lodging, and the base area are all within walking distance; however, if you're carrying skis and boots, it can sometimes be a long walk.

SEASONAL EVENTS. A number of events are held throughout the **winter** and **spring,** such as the *International Dog Sled Races,* the *Pro Men's Tour Races,* the *Grand Marnier Chefs Race,* and the *Women's Ski and* Spa Weeks. Call the area for a list of exact dates.

Early March brings a week of events that fills the town with celebrities: *Jerry Ford Invitational Ski Classic, Legends of Skiing,* and a *World Cup* race.

OTHER SPORTS AND ACTIVITIES. The **cross-country** skiing center, 476–5601, teaches basic-to-advanced track skiing and use of touring skis; Telemark clinics are held; full or half-day tours are available. Gourmet lunches (Thursdays only) and a Vail-to-Red Cliffs tour for six or more people can be planned by advance registration; call 476–3239, ext. 4380. A recreational **bobsled course** over 3,500 feet long is located near Golden Peak. Call Vail Associates, 476–5601, for details. **Snowboarding** is allowed on all runs at Vail/Beaver Creek.

Piney River Ranch, 8 miles from Vail, offers **snowmobile** excursions, **Sno-Cat** tours, and backcountry ski tours: 884 Spruce Ct., Vail, CO 81658; 476–3941. **Sleigh rides** are available on *Vail Golf Course* from 4–8 P.M.; the cost is $12 plus an optional dinner at Satch's restaurant in the clubhouse. Call 476–1330 for details and reservations. Contact *Eagle River White Water* for winter **river rafting** and **jet boating** on the Colorado River, 60 miles west of Vail; 476–3296. *Paragon Guides* offers 4–6-day ski-touring trips along the scenic 10th Mountain Division trail hut-to-hut route. Call 476–0553 for details. *Dobson Ice Arena* in Lionshead, 476–1560, has public **skating,** $3 per half hour, and skate rentals, $1, in addition to instruction in figure skating and hockey. It is also the home of the John Curry Skating Co.

Several lodges offer private **health-club** facilities. The *Vail Athletic Club* and the Westin Hotel's neighboring *Cascade Club* are two of the largest, with complete weight rooms, racquetball courts, and so on. Cascade has indoor tennis courts.

Vail Village has over 80 shops and boutiques, including Gucci, Ralph Lauren, several art galleries, and shops specializing in handcrafted items. **Shopping** can be a full-time activity here.

For a nice diversion, visit the *Colorado Ski Museum,* located between Vail Village and Lionshead; exhibits portray the history of Colorado skiing and the individuals who made it happen. Call 476–1876 for hours. The *Vail Public Library,* 292 W. Meadow Dr., 479–2183, is a quiet haven; here you'll find plush seating, a fireplace, and an excellent selection of periodicals and books.

HINTS FOR THE HANDICAPPED. For ski instruction by appointment for people who are blind or have other physical disabilities, contact *Vail Ski School,* Box 7, Vail, CO 81658; 476–5601, ext. 4324.

DAY-CARE FACILITIES. There are a number of baby-sitting services; lodges maintain lists of qualified sitters, and the *Vail Youth Services* (479–2291) in the Lionshead Parking Structure Building provides sitters.

The Vail/Beaver Creek Children's Ski Center has created a unique program. On both mountains, there are snow parks that are "off-limits" to adults. The parks have historical themes; children can wander through Indian Villages, Dragon's Breath Mine, race courses, and mogul fields. There is even a Children's Mountain Map for youngsters to chart their own paths. Sport Goofy, the Disney character, is part of the ski school team and makes frequent appearances on and off the slopes. Evening activities include a family dinner and entertainment night, and there are "Just for Kids" events. Call the Family Activities Hotline, 479–2048.

The *Children's Ski Center* is available for 3- to 12-year-olds at three locations: Golden Peak, Lionshead, and Beaver Creek. Prices run from $58 for a full day of instruction plus lunch, to $155 for a 3-day package.

The *Small World Playschool* is available for children ages 2 months to 6 years for $45 per day. Call 479–2044 for details.

NIGHTLIFE. There are many night spots in Vail. Some of the biggies include *Nicks,* 228 Bridge St., where the disc jockey spins rock and pop tunes—a hot spot with the locals for dancing. The *Altitude Club,* in the Doubletree Hotel, is popular with the younger disco crowd; it has a weekend cover charge. *Bogie's Nightclub,* at the Marriott Mark Resort in Lionshead, features two bars, Vail's largest dance floor, and music by a disc jockey. *Cyrano's,* on Bridge St., has dancing to live bands ranging from rock to reggae to New Wave; there's a $3 cover charge at the door. *Sheikas,* located beneath the Gasthof Gramshammer, has a European club flavor and features dancing to live pop bands; cover charge. *Mickey's,* in the Lodge at Vail, is an institution. Piano man Mickey Poage plays pop and classical tunes most nights in this cozy bar. The *Sundance Saloon* in Lionshead, at the Sunbird Lodge, is a genuine "neighborhood" bar that features country rock bands every Friday and Saturday night. Pool tables are available for nondancers. The newest spot for top-name jazz entertainment is *Babau's Cafe,* in L'Ostello building, 476–2050. Open for dinner and snacks 5–11 P.M. and nightly jazz from 8 P.M. to closing. Since it has the same kitchen as L'Ostello's restaurant, you can sample the 5-star light-dining cuisine at inexpensive prices.

BEAVER CREEK RESORT

Box 915
Beaver Creek, CO 81620
Tel: 800–525–2257; from Denver, 949–5750

Snow Report: 303–476–4888
Area Vertical: 3,340 feet
Number of Trails: 51 trails on 830
        developed acres, longest run 2¾ miles
Lifts: 1 high-speed quad, 5 triple chairs, 4
        double chairs
Snowmaking: on 243 acres
Season: late November–mid-April

Beaver Creek celebrated its 10th anniversary in 1991. It has become one of America's most elegant ski resorts. Guests at Beaver Creek can enjoy some of the most luxuriously appointed lodgings to be found anywhere. They are chauffeured around the village in Cadillac limos and served cookies and hot beverages at the lift base each morning at 10.

On the mountain, the lift lines are usually short and there is a good mix of trails: 23 percent beginner, 43 percent intermediate, and 34 percent advanced. The mountain is great for cruising and is a favorite of the locals, who prefer the unhurried, serene atmosphere to the more crowded one over at Vail, 10 miles to the east.

Ten years later Beaver Creek is still expanding. The Grouse Mountain development will open the 1991–92 season with an additional 100 skiable acres of intermediate and advanced terrain and a high-speed quad lift. Located on a ridge between Larkspur Bowl and the Birds of Prey runs on Beaver Creek Mountain, it also will offer excellent glade skiing. "Ripsaw," an advanced run with 1,400 feet of vertical drop, located east of chair 4 in Rose Bowl, opened in 1990. These improvements are part of a long-range plan that includes more skiable terrain, a performing-arts center, and an ice rink.

The Village Plaza at the base of the mountain is 4 miles from the town of Avon. There are a number of interesting shops, an art gallery, the Village Hall and Conference Center, and the elegant Park Plaza condos that are designed to resemble a tiny European village. In the past three years about a half-dozen new, deluxe properties have sprung up around the Village Plaza, all with easy access to the lifts, bringing the number of hotels and condominiums to 17. Gerald Ford, Jimmy Connors, and Mats Wilander are some of the celebrities who own homes in Beaver Creek.

The continuing development of real estate in this area has been west of Vail into the Beaver Creek/Avon area and its neighbor, Arrowhead, with a golf course and estate-type homes. In 1988, Arrowhead opened its own ski area, which shares the western side of Beaver Creek's mountain. Primarily intended for the residents but also open to the public, the terrain is mostly intermediate. There are 80 acres with six trails served by a super chair. Base-lodge dining and ski instruction are available. For more information, call Arrowhead at 303–476–1972.

Practical Information for Beaver Creek

HOW TO GET THERE. By air. See information for Vail.

By bus. *Trailways Transportation Center,* 303–476–5137, provides frequent service from Denver and Grand Junction to Vail, where you can take a shuttle bus to Beaver Creek during the winter season for $1.

By car. Beaver Creek is 10 miles west of Vail, at the Avon exit off I–70 in the White River National Forest. By car, it is 110 miles or about a 2-hour drive west from Denver on I–70. From Grand Junction it is 100 miles east on I–70. **Rental cars** are available from agencies at Denver's airport. In Avon there is *Budget,* 800–527–0700; *Dollar Rent-A-Car,* 800–421–6868; *Hertz,* 800–654–3131; *National,* 800–328–4567; and *Thrifty,* 800–367–2277.

TELEPHONES. The area code for Beaver Creek is 303.

ACCOMMODATIONS. Guests can choose lodging in the Beaver Creek resorts or in the town of Avon, which has both economical and luxury units. All bookings can be made through *Vail/Beaver Creek Reservations,* Box 925, Avon, CO 81620; 800–525–2257.

The Beaver Creek resorts offer 7-night/6-day packages (with lift tickets) from $850 to $1,375 per person. Lodges in Avon and Eagle, several miles from the lifts, are less expensive, from $600 to $1,000 for a 7-night package. Nightly rates are $300 to $500 at the mountain and start at $110 in town. During the "value season" (late November through mid-December, January, and mid-April), rates are discounted. Check with individual lodges for dates and prices.

Three new condominiums, all located slopeside on Beaver Creek Mountain, offer deluxe 3- to 6-bedroom units: *The Meadows, Highlands Lodge,* and *Highland Slopeside.* They are all expensive, but exquisitely appointed with ski-in, ski-out convenience. Contact *East-West Hospitality Corp.,* 1000 S. Frontage Rd. West, Vail, CO 81657; 303–949–5071, for information. Or, call Beaver Creek reservations, 800–525–2257. Some of the deluxe Beaver Creek lodges near the lifts are:

The Charter at Beaver Creek. At the base of Beaver Creek Mountain, 120 Offerson Rd., Box 5310, Avon; 949–6660. One-, 2-, and 3-bedroom condominiums with fireplace and balcony. Spa and health club with indoor lap pool. Conference rooms, fine dining room, lounge, outdoor pool, golf course.

Creekside at Beaver Creek. Box 2017, Avon; 949–7071. Two-bedroom condos, indoor and outdoor pools.

Hyatt Regency Hotel. In the Village Plaza; 949–1234. With 298 rooms and suites. Conference facilities for 1,200 people. Complete health facilities, a full-service restaurant, and entertainment lounge.

The Inn at Beaver Creek. At the base; 800–525–2257. Intimate hotel with 45 units. There is an outdoor pool and hot tub, and indoor sauna and steam room. Located steps from the chairlift.

Park Plaza. Box 36, Avon; 800–525–2275. In the heart of Village Plaza, with 2- and 3-bedroom condominiums and full hotel services. Complimentary breakfast plus an on-premises bar and grill.

Avon lodges in the deluxe category include **Avon Center, Beaver Creek West,** and **Falcon Point.** Other, more economical lodging can be found at the **Christie Lodge, Sun River, Sunridge,** and the **Comfort Inn.** The town of Minturn, midway between Vail and Avon, now has bus service, so you may wish to stay at the **Eagle River Inn,** one of the best bed-and-breakfasts in Colorado. Located right on the river banks, with only 12 rooms. Rooms cost from $79 to $175 per night. Information and reservations for all these lodgings can be obtained from the Vail/Beaver Creek Central Reservations number, 800–525–2257.

RESTAURANTS. *McCoy's* in the base lodge serves breakfast and lunch, cafeteria-style. The bar has a big selection of exotic coffees and hot chocolate drinks, as well as hors d'oeuvres. Live entertainment begins here in the late afternoon for the après-ski crowd.

The *Spruce Saddle Lodge,* mid-mountain, serves breakfast and lunch, cafeteria-style. Upstairs, the *Rafters* offers elegant sit-down service and a Continental menu with an extensive wine list. Reservations are suggested, 949–5750.

At *Expensive* restaurants listed below, entrees cost $18–$24; *Moderate* restaurants' entrees cost $6–$18. All restaurants listed accept Visa and MasterCard unless otherwise noted.

Beano's Cabin. *Expensive.* On the mountain; 949–5750. Reached by Sno-Cat or sleigh ride, Beano's offers 2 seatings a night for chicken, trout, or steak dinners. One price includes everything, even transportation, to this rustic, but sumptuous, hewn-log building set in the mountain wilderness. Reserve far in advance, for it's very popular—and worth it.

First Season. *Expensive.* In the Charter in the village; 949–6660. Continental cuisine, dinner only; reservations recommended.

Legends. *Expensive.* In the Poste Montane Lodge in the village; 949–5540. Noted for a variety of fresh seafood flown in daily. Reservations necessary.

Mirabelle. *Expensive.* At the entrance to Beaver Creek, 55 Village Rd., Avon; 949–7728. By far, the most outstanding restaurant at the resort. French cuisine served in a restored wooden Victorian farmhouse, once the largest residence in the town of Avon and a place of some social importance at the turn of the century. Some claim it is the finest restaurant in the mountains—no small compliment. No credit cards accepted; reservations are a must.

Golden Eagle Inn. *Moderate.* Downstairs in the Village Hall; 949–1940. The same ownership as the Tyrolean Inn in Vail, it features a Tyrolean menu and take-out entrees. Serves both lunch and dinner.

LeRoy's. *Moderate.* In the Park Plaza in the village; 949–5750. Family dining, barbecues, burgers, fajitas; casual setting for lunch and dinner.

Terrace. *Moderate.* In the Charter in the village; 949–6660. Charming family restaurant serving breakfast and dinner.

Avon has a few restaurants in the *moderate* category that serve the basic chicken, steak, pizza, and sandwiches. *Paddy's, Hole-in-the-Wall, Ironside Pizza, Rug's Pub,* and the *Stone Creek Inn* are the best. Nearby in Minturn, two popular restaurants are *The Saloon,* Mexican food, and the *Minturn Country Club* with cook-your-own steaks. Both offer economical dining. See also the restaurants in Vail.

HOW TO GET AROUND. Skiers can park in lots in Avon and take the **free shuttle buses** that make frequent runs up to the area from various pickup points in town and at the lodges. **Bus service** to Vail and Minturn costs $1. Guests at Beaver Creek have free **limos** on call for intravillage travel after 5 P.M.

OTHER SPORTS AND ACTIVITIES. Cross-country skiing at *McCoy Park* offers spectacular mountain views and 30 km of set tracks with marked runs for various abilities. Rentals available at the base lodge; group and private lessons and gourmet tours are available. Call 800–525–2257 for additional information.

Resolution SnoTours offer rides in an enclosed SnoCat so that you can enjoy the mountain scenery before sitting down to a gourmet meal in a secluded mountain setting. They also offer great **backcountry skiing** experiences by SnoCat and helicopter.

The *Beaver Creek Activities Desk,* 949–5750, ext. 4636, can also arrange **snowmobiling, dog sledding, hot-air ballooning,** and **sleigh rides.**

An overnight stay at *Trapper's Cabin* near McCoy Park is "camping" in luxury. A new log cabin with accommodations for up to 10 is reached on cross-country skis. A caretaker acts as guide and gourmet chef for dinner and breakfast. Guests can ski to Beano's Cabin and have lunch in a private dining room. Call 949–5750 for reservations.

DAY-CARE FACILITIES. The *Small World Play School,* 949–5750, runs a program for infants, 2 months and up. Advance registration is recommended. *Junior Village,* 949–4929, operates half-day enrichment programs for ages 3–5. Located in Avon.

For toilet-trained children, the *Children's Skiing Center* meets at the Village Hall; lunch and ski lessons provided, ages 3–12. Call *The Children's Center,* 949–2304, for rates. The Walt Disney character, *Sport Goofy,* invites families to join in special activities during the week. Special areas on Vail and Beaver Creek mountains are reserved for children's skiing. See the Vail section for further details.

NIGHTLIFE. Evenings in Beaver Creek tend to be on the quiet side, with people lounging in front of a fire or soaking in hot tubs. *Drinkwater Park* in the Village Hall has live entertainment and 100 different kinds of beer at the bar. The *Forum Bar* at The Charter is good for quiet, elegant evenings. The new Hyatt's entertainment lounge, *The Crooked Hearth,* specializes in gourmet pizzas, fondue, and snacks until 11 P.M.; the *Lobby Bar* is open until 11:30 P.M.

WINTER PARK/MARY JANE

Box 36
Winter Park CO 80482
Tel: 303–726–5514, 800–453–2525 for
    reservations outside Colorado, 303–
    726–5587 for reservations inside
    Colorado

Snow Report: 800–621–SNOW or 303–726–5514
Area Vertical: 2,200 ft.
Number of Trails: 106 trails on 1,115 acres, chartered Sno-Cat skiing on 220 acres, longest run 3.9 miles
Lifts: 4 quad chairs, 3 triple chairs, 12 double chairs
Snowmaking: 16 trails on 250 acres
Season: mid-November–mid-April

In the beginning, the opening of the Moffatt Tunnel in 1928 brought the first skiers to Winter Park. Enthusiastic Denverites rode the train as far as West Portal Station (so named because it is the tunnel entrance on the west side of the Continental Divide). They would hike up the mountain and ski down, making perhaps two runs a day and staying overnight in the railroad construction shacks. Winter Park ski area was born in 1940. It became part of the Denver Mountain Parks system in 1940. Today the resort is still owned by the City of Denver, administered by a volunteer board of directors, and run as a not-for-profit entity—unique in resort operations in this country.

Winter Park has changed its image considerably in the past few years. From a day area for Denver skiers, it is in the process of growing into a full-fledged destination resort with all the amenities of a "ski town." There is still a distance problem in that the two ski areas of Winter Park and Mary Jane are a few miles away from the town of Winter Park. Many day skiers never realize the town is on the road *past* the areas. But the shops, restaurants, and lodges keep growing from the town toward the mountain, offering more and more choices to entice skiers to spend a few days.

The skiing is really superb because the *three* interconnecting areas of Winter Park, Vasquez, and Mary Jane offer something for every level of skier within their own spaces and do not interfere with one another. Winter Park is composed of 44 percent beginner terrain, 45 percent intermediate, and 11 percent expert; and Vasquez Ridge offers 26 percent beginner,

58 percent intermediate, and 16 percent expert terrain. Apollo Flats is reserved for beginners only; the runs are long and gentle. The top of the mountain has fun, cruising runs for intermediates. The weekends tend to be crowded, since day skiers and groups flock here. Midweek is much quieter. Mary Jane does not get as crowded, mostly because its runs are rated 40 percent expert, 55 percent intermediate, and 5 percent beginner. From the top, Mary Jane's vertical is 2,200 feet down to the Winter Park base. The tough bump run, "Outhouse," is patrolled to keep skiers with less than 185 cm skis off it, so as not to spoil the symmetry of the moguls.

Practical Information for Winter Park/Mary Jane

HOW TO GET THERE. Winter Park is 67 miles northwest of Denver in the Arapaho National Forest.

By air. Denver's Stapleton Airport is the closest gateway for all major airlines. From the airport, *Trailways* and the *Express (Gray Line)* serve Winter Park; call *Winter Park Central Reservations* for schedules, 800–453–2525. *Home James,* (303) 726–5060, and *Vanex Van Service,* (303) 726–8015, provide on-call and scheduled service.

By bus. *Greyhound-Trailways* serves Winter Park and nearby Fraser from downtown Denver and the airport; call (303) 292–6111 or 800–237–8211.

By train. *Amtrak's* transcontinental California Zephyr serves Winter Park daily; train depot is in Fraser, 2 miles from the town of Winter Park, 4 miles from the ski slopes. Most lodges provide free shuttle service. The area shuttle bus, *The Lift,* (303) 390–LIFT, meets all trains, no charge; *Home James* taxi service is also available, (303) 726–5060.

On Saturdays and Sundays from Christmas until early April, the *Winter Park Ski Train* arrives from Denver at the base area at 9:30 A.M. It waits on a siding for the return trip at 4:15 P.M. In 1988, the eight existing 1915 vintage cars were replaced with 14 new ones, seating up to 775 passengers in first- and coach-class. First-class round-trip fare is $40, and coach is $25; a one-way ticket costs $23. The trip takes 2¼ hours and travels through spectacular mountain scenery. Cafe cars offer snacks and beverages. The train is so reliable that it has missed running only five times in 50 years of service. Call (303) 296–ISKI for reservations; groups should call (303) 296–4754.

By car. Winter Park is 67 miles northwest of Denver via I–70 to Exit 232, then onto US 40 over Berthoud Pass to the ski areas; the town is 2 miles farther. All major **rental car** agencies are represented at the Denver airport. In Winter Park there is *Hertz,* (303) 726–8993 or 800–451–4844, and *National,* 800–328–4567.

TELEPHONES. The area code for Winter Park is 303.

ACCOMMODATIONS. *Winter Park Central Reservations* handles the majority of lodging in the Fraser Valley; write Box 36, Winter Park, CO 80482; call 726–5587 or 800–453–2525 outside Colorado. Categories, determined by price, are: *Expensive,* $90–$140 a night, for studios to 2-bedrooms; *Moderate,* $80–$100 for 1-bedroom condos, double occupancy, to $37 per person for a 2-bedroom, 4-person occupancy; *Inexpensive,* $10–$30 per room, double occupancy. All properties listed below are in the town of Winter Park unless noted otherwise.

Expensive

Beau West Bed & Breakfast. Box 3156, 148 Fir Dr.; 726–5145. Situated less than 500 yards from the base, this eclectically decorated but intimate 3-room B&B offers magnificent views of the Continental Divide, and superlative homemade breakfasts prepared fresh daily by owner/baker Greg Baca.

Crestview Place. Box 3095; 726–9421. Two- and 3-bedroom units.

Iron Horse Resort Retreat. 257 Grand County Rd. 70; 726–8851. Winter Park's only ski-in, ski-out property offers full hotel service, a health club, restaurant and lounge. Studios to 2-bedrooms.

Moderate

Hi Country Haus Condominiums. Box 3095, 78727 US 40; 726–9421. Located 2 miles from ski hill. All units with fireplaces. Games room, indoor pool, sauna, Jacuzzi.

Meadowridge. Box 3123, Winter Park Ranch; 726–8822. Condominium resort community, 4½ miles west of ski area. One- to 3-bedroom units, each with fireplace and sun deck. Restaurant, bar, pool, sauna, and whirlpool, tennis and racquetball courts, ice rink.

Snowblaze Athletic Club. Box 404, 79104 US 40; 726–5701. Full athletic-club facilities, sauna in every condo. Two-bedroom, 4-person units available.

Timber Run Condominiums. Box 1356, Forest Trail; 726–9421. Two-bedroom, 4-person units.

Winter Park Tennis Club. Next to Meadowridge complex, Box 377, 628 Cranmer, Fraser; 726–9703. Huge condominiums with wonderful views.

Inexpensive

Alpenglo Motor Lodge. 78641 US 40; 726–5294. Basic accommodations, on a per-person basis.

Morning Star Ranch. 933 Grand County Rd. 8; 726–8118. In the woods, only 10 minutes from the ski area. Small, country-style facility; double occupancy.

Olympia Motor Lodge. 78572 US 40; 726–8843.

Sundowner Motel. 78869 US 40; 726–9451.

Viking Lodge. 78966 US 40; 726–8885.

YMCA of the Rockies (Snow Mountain Ranch). Box 558, 1344 Grand City Rd., Granby; 887–2152. A real bargain, 20 minutes from Winter Park with miles of cross-country trails and an indoor Olympic-size pool. Rustic cabins are $10 a night per person.

A number of mountain inns serve breakfast and dinner family-style; most cost in the range of $33–$60 a night per person with two meals. Contact: *Arapahoe Lodge,* 78594 US 40, 726–8222; *Beaver Village,* 79303 US 40, 726–5741; *Brenner's Ski Chalet,* Box 15, 219 Vasquez Rd., 726–5416; *Timber House,* 196 Grand County Rd. 716, 726–5477.

RESTAURANTS. There is a broad selection of eateries for such a small town. At the ski area, the Mary Jane Center has *Pepperoni's Pizza and Sports Bar* and *The Club Car,* a full-service restaurant. In the lower level of Mary Jane Center is a cafeteria for quick snacks and barbecues, open weekends and holidays only. On the Winter Park side, the midmountain *Snoasis* is a cafeteria, and downstairs is *Mama Mia's* pizzeria; at the base, *West Portal Station* is a cafeteria and has an après-ski lounge, the *Derailer Bar.* The *Coffee & Tea Market* serves croissant sandwiches, homemade soups, salads, and divine pastries for sit-down or take-out; a small bar carries the beverage of your choice.

Entrees at the *Expensive* restaurants listed below run $17–$30; *Moderate,* $7–$17; *Inexpensive,* under $6. All restaurants listed take the major credit cards unless otherwise noted.

Expensive

Expectations at the Slope. 1161 Winter Park Dr., Old Winter Park; 726–5727. Fine Continental food served in a small dining area. Dinner only. Reservations suggested.

The Peck House. Empire; 569–9870. Thirty miles south of the ski area on US 40 (but worth the trip), this original stagecoach house, established in 1862, is the oldest hotel still operating in Colorado. Fine dinners served in the Victorian dining room. Reservations recommended. Rooms are available—some are said to be haunted.

Moderate

The Continental Divide. Cooper Creek Sq.; 726–4900. Italian cuisine and a stocked salad bar in an elegant dining room.

Deno's Coachman Tavern and Restaurant. 78911 US 40; 726–5332. A favorite local hangout featuring American dishes, late-night snacks, burgers.

Gasthaus Eichler. Park Place; 726–5133. Classic German food in a European atmosphere. Good fattening desserts. Breakfast and dinner.

Lani's Place. Cooper Creek Sq.; 726–9674. Light, cheery oaken surroundings. Mexican specialties, also take-outs. Lunch and dinner.

Restaurant on the Ridge. At Meadowridge Resort; 726–9411. Continental menu for dinner, including oysters, other seafood, and chicken Wellington. An elegant place. For breakfast and lunch, the menu is Mexican (with other specialties). Sunday brunch, children's menu. Reservations recommended for dinner.

The Shed. 78672 US 40; 726–9912. Good steaks; also chicken and burgers. Dinner and breakfast. No reservations.

Inexpensive

Carver Brothers Bakery. 93 Grand County Rd.; 726–8202. Egg breakfasts, fresh pastries; lunch and dinner selections include soups, stews, sandwiches. No credit cards.

Fontenot's Cajun Deli. 78711 US Hwy 40; 726–4021. Po' boys and deli sandwiches.

Hernando's Pizza Pub. 78260 US 40; 726–5409. Features pizza and other Italian dishes served in a casual atmosphere around a huge fireplace. Carry-outs available. Lunch and dinner.

The Kitchen. 78542 US 40; 726–9940. Hearty breakfasts, some Mexican specialties served at this local favorite. Casual spot for breakfasts only. No credit cards.

HOW TO GET AROUND. During ski season *The Lift,* a free **shuttle bus,** connects all the lodges to the town and to the ski areas of Winter Park and Mary Jane; runs every 20 minutes; 726–5514 or 8253.

SEASONAL EVENTS. There always seems to be something happening at Winter Park. Because of its nonprofit status, the area hosts more than its share of civic and amateur, as well as pro, events. In **December,** Christmas festivities include a visit by Santa, Christmas Eve church services at the base area, and a torchlight parade. The *First Interstate Bank Cup* is the pro race held in early **February,** while a variety of pro and amateur qualifier races are held throughout February. *The Golden Bunny Race* for kids highlights **Easter,** the *Mascot Race* (college mascots racing in full costume) is in early **April,** with *Spring Splash* (attempting to ski over a pond of water) closing the season in mid-April.

OTHER SPORTS AND ACTIVITIES. Available in **Sno-Cat skiing** (conditions permitting) in Parsenn Bowl above the Mary Jane area. Racing clinics, mountain guides, freestyle, and jumping programs are available; for some seldom-skied, hard-to-find challenging terrain, sign up with the "Jane Gang," the ski instructors on the Mary Jane Mountain. Never-Ever ski packages, NASTAR Clinics, Over-30 Bump Clinic, Women's Workshops (Tuesdays and Saturdays), and the Ski Blast Weekend workshops are offered through the ski school.

Cross-country enthusiasts can head for nearby Idlewild, 726–5564, with a nordic center in the town; *Snow Mountain Ranch/YMCA of the Rockies* with 26 miles of groomed trails and a 3-km lighted loop, 887–2152; *C Lazy U Ranch* near Granby with an outstanding trail system, 726–3344; or the *Soda Springs Ranch* near Grand Lake, about 30 miles from Winter Park, 627–8011; and Devil's Thumb Ranch, north of Fraser, 726–8231, offer cross-country facilities.

Snow tubing at *Frasier Valley Sports Center,* 726–5954, is uncontrolled fun; $5 ($7 after 6 P.M.) an hour for an inner tube and rope tow. **Snowmobiling** is available from *Beaver Village,* 726–9247; including guided trip up to the summit of the Continental Divide; also available from Snow Mountain Ranch/YMCA. **Ice skating** is available at Beaver Village (skate rental for a small fee), and Snow Mountain Ranch, 887–2434, with $3–$4 per hour skate rental. **Sleigh rides:** *Jim's Sleigh Rides* with campfire and hot chocolate stop, 726–5527; stops at a rustic barn for dinner. **Rac-quetball, swimming,** and **weightlifting** can be enjoyed by guests of Snowblaze, Meadowridge, and Iron Horse. **Roller skating** and **basketball** are available year-round at Snow Mountain Ranch, along with indoor miniature golf.

DAY-CARE FACILITIES. For reservations for programs listed below, call 726–5514. An infant nursery for children 8 weeks to 18 months is available at the ski area on a limited, space-available basis; parents must provide lunch. The nursery for children 1–8 years includes all-day supervision and lunch for $35 a day.

Some lodges can arrange for qualified baby-sitters. *Fraser Creative Learning Center,* 726–5681, has planned activities, Monday through Friday. Call for reservations.

CHILDREN'S ACTIVITIES. Children 3–4 years old, mature enough to ski, and toilet trained can be part of *Penguin Peak:* $45 a day includes all-day supervision, games, ski lessons, play, and lunch; $52 a day includes rental equipment. *Ski Scouts* is for kids 5–7: 3 hours of instruction, lunch, lift ticket, and progress card; $45 a day ($52 with rental equipment), $120 for three days, $165 for five days. The *Rangers* are 8- to 13-year-olds: lessons, lift ticket, lunch, and progress card are included at the same prices as the Ski Scout program. Children 5 and under receive a free lift ticket, and 6- to 13-year-olds are entitled to a $15 lift ticket.

NIGHTLIFE. Nighttime activities are as casual as the lifestyle in Winter Park. After skiing, late evening usually finds music and dancing at *The Slope,* 1161 Winter Park Dr., in Old Town Winter Park. The *Stampede,* 145 Forest Trail Rd., has recorded disco music, dancing, and an oyster bar, and is a good meeting place. If you want to run into your ski instructor or other locals, head for *Deno's* on US 40, no entertainment but lots of lively conversation. *Gasthaus Eichler,* on US 40, celebrates "Stammtisch Hour" from 5 to 6 P.M. by the fireplace with special German après-ski treats.

Idaho

SUN VALLEY

Sun Valley Company
Sun Valley ID 83353
Tel: 800–SUN–VALY

Snow Report: 800–635–4150
Area Vertical: 3,400 ft.
Number of Trails: 70 on 1,275 acres
Lifts: 3 high-speed quads, 5 double chairs, 8
*   triple chairs*
Snowmaking: 20 percent of terrain
Season: late November–early May

Sun Valley celebrated its golden anniversary in 1986. For 55 years, it has been synonymous with style and glamour.

Before 1936, there was no destination ski resort in the United States. Averell Harriman, chairman of the board of the Union Pacific Railroad, set out to find a place to build a self-sustaining resort in the European tradition served by his railroad. In a rather remote Idaho valley of sheep ranches, he found his ideal combination of mountain terrain and valley floor near the ramshackle mining town of Ketchum. He wanted people to ride his train beyond the Mississippi River, and this resort idea might even get the more adventurous off the train and onto the slopes.

The Sun Valley Lodge opened for business a few days before Christmas 1936. The original concept was to offer exquisite food, impeccable service, and nightly entertainment in a mountain region that was neither too high, too windy, too remote, nor too near a town. The elegance established at the beginning has always attracted celebrities, from East Coast notables to Hollywood stars. Hemingway, Cooper, Gable, Colbert, Crosby, Garland, Monroe, Eastwood, and Duchin have all added glitter to this already glamorous resort.

All this and skiing, too. Baldy and Dollar mountains are groomed to perfection. There is a 3-mile run, and there are five on-mountain restaurants (complete with etched glass and brass, even in the cafeterias). Skiers can follow the sun through a day of skiing on the different faces of the mountains. The world's first chairlift went into service in Sun Valley, with a design based on a device used to load bananas onto fruit boats. Now skiers can hop on the high-speed quads that replaced the Warm Springs and Christmas double chairs and get to the top much faster than was previously possible. There is also a quad on the Greyhawk run, where races are held.

247

In the 1940s, the Union Pacific sold some of the 4,300 acres around Sun Valley for development. In 1964 the railroad sold the resort. This was the start of major changes, and Sun Valley has since been developed as a vacation village for families while still attracting the rich and famous. Condos, lodges, and hotels are in several locations—around the original Sun Valley Lodge, near Baldy, and in the town of Ketchum. With a year-round population of 3,000, Ketchum is unpretentious but has quaint restaurants, western bars, and art galleries. Because the local population is so small, there are no weekend lift lines. Nearly all the skiers are destination visitors.

Sun Valley today is established as a cultural center as well as a summer and winter destination. One thing that won't change—the omnipresence of Baldy Mountain.

Practical Information for Sun Valley

HOW TO GET THERE. By air. Gateways to Sun Valley are Salt Lake City, Boise, Idaho Falls, and Twin Falls. *Horizon Airlines* flies to Hailey (12 miles from Sun Valley) from Salt Lake and Boise. Call 800–453–2737. Charter flights are available from Salt Lake City, Boise, and Idaho Falls into Hailey. *Sky West* (Delta's connection) flies from Salt Lake City to Sun Valley four times daily, year-round.

Bus service is available to Sun Valley from Salt Lake City, 5 hours via *Lewis Bros. Stages*, 801–359–8677; and *Greyhound-Trailways*, 801–328–8121. From Twin Falls, a 2-hour ride, call *D Bus Company*, 208–733–8003, or *Sun Valley Stages*, 208–733–3921. Boise, 3 hours away, has bus service on *Apollo Transit*, 208–336–7240; *Greyhound-Trailways*, 208–343–7531; and *Sun Valley Stages*, 208–733–3921. Idaho Falls, 3 hours' drive, serves Sun Valley via *Greyhound*, 800–528–0447; *Sun Valley Stages*, 208–733–3921; and *Teton Stage Lines*, 208–529–8036.

Rental cars from *Avis, Hertz,* and *National* may be dropped off in Sun Valley. All other agencies book round trips only. *Avis,* 800–331–1212; *Hertz,* 800–654–3131; *National,* 800–328–4567.

You can also rent a car from most major agencies in Twin Falls and Boise; call the 800 numbers, above, for details.

For additional assistance, call the Sun Valley reservations office, 800–SUN–VALY.

TELEPHONES. The area code for Sun Valley and most of Idaho is 208; for Salt Lake City and all Utah, it is 801.

ACCOMMODATIONS. Lodging is grouped into four areas around the mountain complex. For reservations and information on all accommodations, write the *Sun Valley Company,* Sun Valley, ID 83353; 800–635–8261 in the U.S., 800–632–4104 in Idaho.

The most *expensive* and luxurious accommodations are in the tiny village of Sun Valley. Each lodge in the core village is adjacent to the shopping and restaurant mall. Nightly rates (without lift ticket) at the Sun Valley Lodge are $125–$275; at the Sun Valley Inn, $100–$190; at Lodge Apartments and Wildflower, $115–$390; at Elkhorn Village condos, $100–$280. These rates start with a standard hotel room and go up to suites and 4-bedroom condos.

Sun Valley Lodge and Inn received the AAA Four-Diamond Award for 1985. The *Lodge* is a full-service hotel with glass-enclosed, heated swimming pool, massage, sauna, newly appointed interior, the Duchin Lounge, and *Gretchen's Restaurant.* It is considered the hub of activity in the village. Seven nights starts at $616 for a standard room per person, double occupancy. Includes 5-day lift ticket.

The *Inn* is a Tyrolean-like hotel with family-style cafeteria, 2 restaurants, meeting room, bell service, telephones, and glass-enclosed heated pool. Seven-night packages start at $525.

The luxury *Lodge Apartments* are adjacent to the Lodge, available in 1-, 2-, and 3-bedroom units. Cozy living rooms, fireplaces, kitchens, telephone, daily maid service. Rates from $980 per person double occupancy for a parlor suite to $581 per person for 6 people in a 3-bedroom condo (a 7-night package with a 5-day lift ticket).

Wildflower Condominiums are similar in appearance and have the same rate structure. The shuttle bus takes approximately 15 minutes to Baldy, 5 minutes to Dollar Mountain—an ideal beginner's hill.

A bus ride over the hill from the Sun Valley village takes you to **Elkhorn Village** (more condominiums) and the **Elkhorn Hotel.** Contact the *Elkhorn Resort at Sun Valley,* Box 1067, Sun Valley, ID 83353; 622–4511 or 800–635–9356, 800–632–4101 in Idaho. **Village I** and **II, Atelier, Snowcreek, Dollar Meadows,** and **Cottonwood** all have studio to 4-bedroom units. Studio rates are $525; a 2-bedroom unit with 4 people, $511; and a 4-bedroom with 8 people, $420, all per person for a 7-night package with 5 days' worth of lift tickets. In all units, children under 11 stay free when in the same room with parents. Special packages are available during Singles Week, Snowball Week and Winter Carnival in January and Ski Club Week in March. Skiers who are better than beginners will want to take the 10-minute shuttle ride to the Mt. Baldy, Warm Springs, stop.

Moderate lodging is found in Warm Springs at the base of Mt. Baldy—it's a short walk to the lifts. Prices range from $63 for a studio up to $315 for a 4-bedroom suite. Contact *Warm Springs Resort,* Box 228, Sun Valley, ID 83353; 726–8274 or 800–635–4404.

The fourth area is the town of Ketchum itself. Contact *Sun Valley Ketchum Central Reservations,* Box 979, Sun Valley, ID 83353; 726–0147 or 800–634–3347. Lodging is moderately priced. The **Tamarack Lodge** (Box 2000, Sun Valley, ID; 726–3344) is just a few blocks from the center of town and has a small indoor pool.

Christiana Lodge (Best Western). *Moderate.* 209 Walnut, Ketchum ID 83353; 800–534–3241. A few minutes' walk from a variety of shops and restaurants. About a 7-minute shuttle ride to Mt. Baldy.

Most of the hotels and lodges in each area have some *inexpensive* rooms for under $40 a night. Group rates often bring prices down to the inexpensive level.

RESTAURANTS. For information and reservations for all Sun Valley restaurants, stop by the concierge in the Lodge lobby between noon and 8 P.M. daily or call 622–4111, ext. 2435. Restaurants are listed in order of price category: *Expensive,* $15–$25; *Moderate,* $8–$15. These prices are for a meal for one person, exclusive of drinks and tip. All but the inexpensive restaurants, snack bars, and cafeterias accept major credit cards.

Expensive

Lodge Dining Room presents elegant dining in a grand manner. White-glove service, French cuisine, extensive wine list. *Do* dress for the part. Live entertainment nightly. For reservations call 622–4111, ext. 2150. Sunday brunch—a must—is served from 8:30 A.M. until 2 P.M.; no reservations for brunch.

Christiana Lodge. 209 Walnut St., Ketchum; 726–3388. Huge upholstered couches against a 2-story rock wall. Expect a leisurely dinner, Continental menu; reservations recommended.

Moderate

Gretchen's. In the Lodge; 622–4111, ext. 2144. Open for lunch and dinner, Saturdays until midnight. A family place, American menu, no reservations required.

The Ore House. Sun Valley Mall; 622–4111, ext. 2471. Features steak, seafood, salad bar, happy hour-and-a-half.

Ram Dining Room. Sun Valley Mall; 622–4111, ext. 2225. Serves wild game specialties. Reservations not required.

River Street Retreat. 12 River St., Ketchum; 726–9502.

HOW TO GET AROUND. The village itself is quite compact and an automobile is unnecessary. Condos are within easy walking distance of Sun Valley Village, but the lodges do provide complimentary **bus** service. Continuous round trips by bus go from the village and the lodges to Dollar and Baldy mountains. The Sun Valley–Ketchum area provides free public buses within the Sun Valley, Elkhorn, Ketchum, and Warm Springs areas. Taxis are also available. The two ski mountains are several miles from the Sun Valley area. Warm Springs is near Mt. Baldy.

SEASONAL EVENTS. In **January,** there is a *New Year's Eve* celebration with a big-band sound, *Singles Week* is mid-month, and *Winter Carnival* and the *Duchin Celebrity Cup Invitational* take place at the end of January. In **March** the *North American Airlines Ski Federation* visits the area.

OTHER SPORTS AND ACTIVITIES. For those who want to improve or just brush up, the ski school will accommodate. Classes with private or group instruction are available. NASTAR races run every Tuesday through Friday.

If skiers can pry themselves off Baldy, they will find some of the finest **cross-country** skiing in the country. There are groomed trails as well as guided backcountry **tours** and **helicopter skiing** to find your own wilderness. Cross-country skiers can enjoy 25 miles of groomed trails around the golf course and up Trail Creek Canyon at the *Sun Valley Nordic Center.* Trail fee is $10 ($7.50 half-day). Children and senior citizens ski at reduced prices. Equipment rental is $13; for children, $8. The ski school gives instruction in all facets of cross-country skiing and has a complete rental shop. If it's forests you want, head for Wood River Valley, Galena, and Busterback Ranch tour centers. If you are a strong nordic skier, go with the *Sun Valley Trekking Company,* which offers hut-to-hut skiing in the Sawtooth Wilderness area. Actually, accommodations are in domed tents called yurts and the dinners are scrumptious. For information on any of the above, call *Sun Valley Nordic Ski Touring Center* at 622–4111, ext. 2250 or 2251, or write Box 272, Sun Valley, ID 83353. The *Sun Valley Cross-Country Ski Association* publishes a free map and guide to the entire backcountry area. Write the association at Box 3636, Sun Valley, ID 83353 for a copy.

Close behind skiing comes **ice skating.** Sonja Henie starred here in the movie *Sun Valley Serenade* in 1941, and skating has been alive and well ever since. The huge rink behind the lodge rents skates. Skating goes on year-round with an indoor rink; competition hockey on weekends. Information at The Lodge.

The town of Ketchum has become a thriving **arts** community, with a ballet foundation, two theater groups, and first-class preparatory schools. It is the kind of unpretentious resort town where Mariel Hemingway can walk down the street without a second glance from anyone.

There's **bowling** in the lodge basement, first-run **movies,** and special **theater** and **dance** performances at the Opera House and, of course, the perfect après-ski relaxation in the glass-enclosed heated **pools** at the inn and lodge; cocktail service at the lodge pool. The *Ketchum Community Library* on Spring Street has a good collection of Hemingway's works and historical books on ski instruction.

DAY-CARE FACILITIES. *Playschool* is a program of planned activities for children, including swimming, ice skating, and 2 hours of ski school. Call 622–4111 for details or go to the blue building north of the Sun Valley Mall. Children 5 years and older are enrolled in the *Sun Valley Ski School.* Ski/play activities are designed to teach sound skiing fundamentals while having fun. The *SKIwee* national program is also part of the children's ski program.

NIGHTLIFE. The *Ram Bar* features après-ski Mondays through Fridays, with live entertainment nightly. There is entertainment nightly at the lodge dining room and the *Duchin Lounge* also has après-ski and live, late-night entertainment. Check out some of the western bars in Ketchum, such as *Whiskey Jacques.*

Montana

THE BIG MOUNTAIN

Box 1400
Whitefish MT 59937
Tel: 406–862–3511 or 800–858–5439, in
    Canada call 800–637–7547

Snow Report: 406–862–3511
Area Vertical: 2,170 ft.
Number of Trails: 50 runs on 4,040 skiable
    acres; longest run is 2.5 miles
Lifts: 1 high-speed quad, 4 triple chairs, 1
    double chair, 1 T-bar, 1 platter lift
Snowmaking: none
Season: late November–April

In the glacier country of northern Montana, Big Mountain is just that.
Although only 6,770 feet at the summit (lower than the base elevations
of the Colorado ski areas), Big Mountain is the predominant geographic
feature hereabouts. From the nearest town of Whitefish, 8 miles away, the
ski trails on the mountain are clearly visible. Families from the northern
Rockies and Canada are attracted to the area because of the reasonable
costs, and the area promotes that image.

On weekends, Calgarians (the city is only 320 miles away) descend by
the busload on Big Mountain. But since they installed Montana's only
high-speed quad lift there are virtually no lift lines. Children 12 and under
stay free at most lodges when accompanied by an adult.

The back side of the mountain has 11 trails, primarily intermediate. The
mountain is rated 55 percent intermediate, 25 percent beginner, and 20
percent advanced. There is "endless" out-of-bounds skiing for advanced
skiers—at their own risk of course—that is accessible from the lifts, a feature not found at most ski areas. For details, check with the ski patrol.
The average snowfall is 200 inches a year, so there is always good natural
cover here. There is night skiing Wednesday through Sunday on 25 percent of the mountain.

The base area has condominium lodging, grocery and specialty stores,
nine restaurants and bars, and a ski shop. The Summit House, a large,
two-story on-mountain lodge with cafeteria and ski shop, is open Wednesday and Saturday for dinner. Guests ride in gondolas to the top and dine
overlooking Glacier National Park.

Practical Information for Big Mountain

HOW TO GET THERE. By air. Glacier Park International Airport in Kalispell is 19 miles from Big Mountain, and is served by *Delta* and *Horizon* airlines. Rental cars are available at the airport.

By car. Big Mountain is 8 miles north of Whitefish, off US 93. Kalispell, at US 93 and US 2, is 23 miles; Glacier National Park is 28 miles; Missoula is 137 miles via Hwy. 93N; Great Falls, 230 miles; Spokane, WA, 270 miles; and Calgary 320 miles. The fly-and-drive option is best done from Missoula, which is well served by most major airlines. Cars can be rented there for the scenic, 2½-hour drive to Big Mountain.

By bus. Charter buses ply between Calgary and Big Mountain for weekend and week-long trips. A daily bus runs from Whitefish to the area; call (406) 862–9494 for schedules.

By train. *Amtrak's Empire Builder* stops daily both eastbound and westbound in Whitefish, just 8 miles from the slopes. Call the ski area for transportation to and from the station. Car rentals are available, too.

TELEPHONES. The area code for all Montana is 406.

ACCOMMODATIONS. Fifteen hundred guests can stay within walking distance of the slopes. Skiers should pick up major provisions for their condos in Whitefish, but the grocery store at the slopes will stock condos with necessities if you call in advance and place an order. Call *Big Mountain Central Reservations,* 862–3511 or 800–858–5439, and in Canada 800–637–7547, for all base lodging; it will also assist on lodging in Whitefish. Hotel rates are per room, based on double occupancy. Categories, determined by price, are *Expensive,* $75 and up; *Moderate,* $50–$75; and *Inexpensive,* $32–$50. Condominium lodging is about the same range for a studio or 1-bedroom.

Anapurna Alpine Homes. *Expensive.* Box 55; call central reservations. These are a variety of units at the base of the area, all within walking distance of the lifts. Some are ski-in, ski-out. All units are rented on a nightly basis, with a discount for 5 nights or more.

Edelweiss. *Expensive.* At slopeside; contact central reservations. This is the newest, poshest accommodations at the area.

Grouse Mountain Lodge. *Expensive.* 1205 Hwy. 93W, Whitefish 59937; 862–3000; or in Montana, 800–621–1802; outside Montana, 800–321–8822. Highly recommended by AAA, this resort overlooks the golf course; large rooms, bar, and grill.

Kandahar Lodge. *Expensive.* Box 1659; phone central reservations. Amenities include sauna, Jacuzzi, cedar-wood decor, single hotel rooms or 3-bedroom condos; located above the ski area road near the entrance to the parking lot, a short walk to the base area and can be skied to from Triple Three Chairlift; also served by a shuttle bus.

Alpinglow Inn. *Moderate.* Base area overlooking Flathead Valley; 862–6966 or central reservations. Amenities include saunas, heated pool, whirlpools; nightly and package rates with meals available.

Chalet Motel. *Moderate.* 6430 Hwy. 93S, Whitefish; 862–5581. In town; has pool.

Duck Inn. *Moderate.* 1305 Columbia Ave., Whitefish; 800–344–2377. Ten rooms on a riverfront setting at one price, $57 a night. Continental breakfast included. Rooms have fireplaces, brass beds, and deep tubs. Jacuzzi and car rental on premises.

Allen's Motel. *Inexpensive.* 6540 Hwy. 93S, Whitefish; 862–3995.

Downtowner Motel & Health Club. *Inexpensive.* 224 Spokane Ave., Whitefish; 862–2535. Guests have free use of the club with Jacuzzi, weight room, sauna, and daily aerobics classes.

The Hibernation House. *Inexpensive.* A bed-and-breakfast lodge in the base village, within walking distance of the lifts. Call central reservations for details.

Mountain Holiday Motel. *Inexpensive.* Box 302, Whitefish; 862–2548. 34 rooms with indoor pool, sauna, and Jacuzzi.

RESTAURANTS. There is a cafeteria, the *Alpinsnack,* and four restaurants at the base with a good selection in the town of Whitefish. Since dining at the base is rather limited, we list only two categories here: *Moderate,* $10–$18; and *Inexpensive,* less than $10. Those prices are based on the cost of an average dinner for one person for food alone; beverages, tax, and tip extra. Major credit cards accepted.

Alpinglow Inn. *Moderate.* At the base area; 862–6966. Overlooks the picturesque Flathead Valley through high glass windows; open to the public for breakfast.

Kandahar Cafe. *Moderate.* At the base area; 862–6098. European atmosphere with daily specialties.

Mountain House Grille. *Moderate.* At the base area; 862–3511, ext. 244. Serves 3 meals a day, steaks, seafood, and chicken specialties, in the dining room; the atrium offers a great mountain view.

Moose's. *Inexpensive to moderate.* On the mountain; 862–7771. Serves soup, pizza, and sandwiches 10 A.M.–10 P.M. daily. Live music.

Bierstube. *Inexpensive.* At the base area; 862–3028. A bit rowdy, but serves the best burgers in these parts. Open daily until 10 P.M. with live music.

Hellroaring Saloon and Eatery. *Inexpensive.* At the base; 862–3511. Open for lunch, aprés-ski and dinner. The bar is lively.

HOW TO GET AROUND. Everything is accessible from the small base village by foot. A bus makes the regular run between Whitefish and Big Mountain for $2; call 862–9494 for details. Check with central reservations as to which lodges on the mountain road have free **shuttle** service. Otherwise, a **car** is convenient.

SEASONAL EVENTS. Each **January** the *Glacier Sprints and Glides* highlight Whitefish. Whitefish *Winter Carnival* takes place in early **February** each year, with parades, street games, contests, races, and dog-sled and balloon rides. In **March** the *Doug Betters Winter Classic* features pro football players and the media racing each other for charity. *Spring Rendezvous* is at the end of **March**. *Media Appreciation* week, also in **March,** is when local personalities battle it out on Big Mountain's race course. Call the area for details.

OTHER SPORTS AND ACTIVITIES. A full-service Nordic Center is at the base with 15 km of groomed and tracked **cross-country** trails. Additional **ski touring** is in nearby Flathead National Forest and Glacier National Park. Ski rentals are available at *The Big Mountain Ski Shop;* call 862–3511. **Sleigh rides** are available during the week; call 862–2538 for information. Nearby is **snowmobiling, ice skating, Sno-Cat rides;** check with the ski area at 862–3511 for details.

DAY-CARE FACILITIES. *Kiddy Korner* has child-care facilities at the ski area. It takes kids of all ages, even in diapers, for $2.50 an hour, $2 out of diapers, second child $1.25 an hour; call 862–3511 for further information. Advance notice is required for children under 1 year. There is an excellent ski instruction program for children also. Call *Big Mountain Ski School* at 862–3511 for information. Prices range from $12 for a half-day lesson to $60 for a 10-lesson package.

NIGHTLIFE. At the base village, there is music at *Moose's, Hellroaring Saloon and Eatery,* and the *Bierstube.* Whitefish has a number of lively night spots.

BIG SKY RESORT

Box 1
Big Sky MT 59716
Tel: 406–995–4211, 800–548–4486, 800–
   548–8096 (group information)

Snow Report: 406–995–4211, ext. 2400
Area Vertical: 3,030 ft.
Number of Trails: 65 miles of groomed
   trails, longest run 3 miles
Lifts: 2 four-passenger gondolas, 2 triple
   chairs, 4 double chairs, 2 rope tows
Snowmaking: 20 percent of terrain
Season: mid-November–mid-April

Montana's skiing atmosphere is unlike that of its faster-paced neighboring states to the west. Friendly and relaxed, with a variety of night spots, it meets the needs of serious skiers and provides low-key socializing. A lot of Midwesterners and Canadians find Big Sky more convenient, less expensive, and less crowded than the other large Rockies resorts.

Big Sky (just look up to see where it got its name) was a dream of Chet Huntley—half the Huntley-Brinkley news team. When he retired from television, Huntley moved to this pristine mountain land and forged his ski area. He *is* the history of the ski business in this part of the world.

Big Sky is a good intermediate mountain and people move around well so that crowds are rarely in evidence. There are open bowls and tree-lined and meadow runs with confidence-building slopes for beginners, skilled intermediate runs, and "steep-and-deep" terrain off the new Challenger Lift. The ability mix is 20 percent beginner, 50 percent intermediate, and 30 percent advanced.

Skiers can follow the sun by starting at Mad Wolf chair, heading to the bowl or gondola 2; and toward afternoon, skiing the front side and Ram's Head Chair. The new Southern Comfort triple chair, on the southeast face of Andesite, has sunny exposure all day. Experts can ride the Challenger Lift to reach the Little Rock Tongue for open bowl skiing or tight tree turns. You should check with the ski patrol for extreme chutes that are open.

Practical Information for Big Sky

GETTING THERE. By air. The closest commercial airport is Bozeman. Scheduled flights are via *Northwest, Delta,* and *Continental* airlines. Rental cars are available from *Avis, Hertz, Budget, National,* and *American International.* Shuttle buses, run by *Karst Stages,* meet most major flights and provide transportation to Big Sky accommodations. Its office is at the airport.

By car. Big Sky is 45 miles south of Bozeman, 18 miles north of Yellowstone National Park. From Bozeman, drive west on Rte. 307 about 10 miles, then south on US 191. Highways are kept in good driving condition in winter; motorists can get weather information and road reports on all radio stations or call in-state 800–332–6171 or out of state (406) 444–6339. Within a 100-mile radius of Bozeman call (406) 586–1313.

TELEPHONES. The area code for all Montana is 406.

ACCOMMODATIONS. There are over 1,000 hotel rooms and condos at Big Sky, with many more beds a short distance away in Meadow Village. Call or contact *Big Sky Management,* Box 1, Big Sky, MT 59716; 800–548–4486 or (406) 995–4211.

Hotel rates are per person, based on double occupancy. Categories, determined by price, are *Expensive,* $65–$150; *Moderate,* $40–$65; and *Inexpensive,* less than $40.

The Huntley Lodge at Big Sky. *Expensive.* Call the ski area for details. A resort hotel at the base of the lifts with a spectacular view of the Spanish Peaks and Lone Mountain. Condominium hotel suites offer the best of both types of accommodations. Heated outdoor pool and Jacuzzi, saunas, weight room, nightly poker games, live entertainment, convention facilities. The lodge is the center of most activity at Big Sky.

Lone Mountain Ranch. *Expensive.* Box 145, Big Sky 59716; 995–4644. A few minutes down the road from the ski area, this rustic but deluxe property consists of log-and-stone cabins with all conveniences; meals in the ranch dining room. It draws primarily cross-country skiers, but downhillers are permitted as well; weekly rates with meals only.

Buck's T-4 Lodge. *Moderate.* Box 895, Big Sky 59716; 995–4111 or 800–528–1234. Best Western establishment; has lounge, restaurant, Jacuzzi, free shuttle service to the ski area.

Golden Eagle Lodge. *Inexpensive.* Box 8, Big Sky 59716; 995–4800. Rooms have 4 beds. Located 6 miles from slopes. New grill area, game room.

Mountain Lodge. *Inexpensive.* Box 46, Big Sky 59716; 800–831–3509 or 995–4560. Rooms have 4 beds; price includes lift tickets; basic and clean. A short walk to the slopes.

In Bozeman there is a choice of moderate and inexpensive motels, including a **Grantree Inn, Holiday Inn, Super 8,** and **Best Western.**

RESTAURANTS. There are over 15 restaurants and places to drink at Big Sky, and several more are within a short driving distance. Prices are moderate in comparison with other ski resorts. The price classifications of the following restaurants are based on the cost of an average three-course dinner for one person for food alone; beverages, tax, and tip extra. *Expensive,* $18–$28; *Moderate,* $12–$18; *Inexpensive,* less than $12. Major credit cards are accepted.

First Place. *Expensive.* Meadow Village Center; 995–4794. Considered the best spot by locals; fireside dinners with Continental dishes only, including seafood, veal, game, steaks; reservations requested.

Lone Mountain Ranch. *Expensive.* Rte. 64, 6 miles from the ski area; 995–4644. Has the best sleigh-ride dinners ever; gourmet meals prepared on a wood-burning stove, light by kerosene lantern; fixed price. Guests at the ranch get first chance, but it is possible to make a reservation.

Andiamo. *Moderate.* In the Arrowhead Mall; 995–2220. Exquisite Italian cuisine presented in a lovely setting at the foot of the slopes. Enjoy classical guitar music while dining.

Bucks T-4. *Moderate.* A few miles from the base, there is a dinner shuttle; 995–4111. A fun and popular place where many locals go. Continental dinners and pizza available.

The Lodge Dining Room. *Moderate.* 995–4211. Serves buffet breakfast and Continental dinners. Reservations suggested, especially for the Austrian folklore dinners when Austrian ski-school instructors entertain.

Whiskey Jack. *Moderate.* At the ski area base, with a great view of the mountain; 995–4211. Considered the best on-mountain place for lunch and inner. Fun atmosphere with music.

Corral. *Inexpensive.* US 191; 995–4795. Features family-style dining, open 7 A.M. to 9 P.M. with breakfast all day; children's menu.

M.R. Hummers. *Inexpensive.* Mountain Mall at the base of the slopes; 995–4543. Popular, packed with skiers; good sandwiches, snacks, steaks, ribs, lunch and dinner.

Mountain Lodge. *Inexpensive.* Base area; 995–4560. Famous for its pizza; also good hamburgers and sandwiches. Open for breakfast, lunch, and dinner.

HOW TO GET AROUND. Shuttle buses run between the base area, the condominium complexes, and Meadow Village. The Huntley Lodge and some condos are at the base area within walking distance. There are daily **buses** to *Yellowstone* and the *airport.* However, if skiers want to do any exploring outside the area, a **car** is recommended.

SEASONAL EVENTS. In early **December,** the *Five Dollar Day Promotion* combines with Lone Mountain Ranch's *St. Nick's Nordic Days.* **January** is *Western Winter Carnival* time and *Viking's Revenge X-C citizens race.* Qualifier races for USSA classified racers for the Junior Olympics also take place in **January.** **February** is the time for the *Dirt Bag Ball,* the season's biggest bash to benefit the Ski Patrol. We're told that you should wear "your finest polyester." On **April** 1, the *Lone Peak Lookout Super Triathlon* is held. In **mid-April,** the *Spring Carnival celebration* brings two days and nights of music and on-snow merriment.

OTHER SPORTS AND ACTIVITIES. **Sleigh rides** available from Lone Mountain Guest Ranch (995–4644). **Cross-country skiing** at the area offers 13 nordic trails with 45 miles of terrain; also from Lone Mountain Ranch and into Yellowstone National Park; **Sno-Cat tours** and **snowmobiling** are available at Yellowstone as well (contact the Huntley Lodge). Bring your own skates to enjoy the **skating rink** behind Buck's T-4 lodge.

DAY-CARE FACILITIES. Children 1 year and older can go to the *First Run Child Care Center* on the lower level of the Mountain Village Mall for programmed activities and lunches. Children 3–5 years can join the *Ski Club,* which offers a full day of skiing and other recreational activities. Call Big Sky Resort at 995–4211.

NIGHTLIFE. In Mountain Village Mall, check into *Whiskey Jack* for loud music and a young crowd. *Scissor Bill's* and *M.R. Hummers,* both at the base area, offer happy hours and live entertainment. *Chet's Bar* in The Lodge usually has live entertainment. *Buck's T-4* also offers music on some evenings.

New Mexico

TAOS SKI VALLEY

Box 90
Taos Ski Valley NM 87525
Tel: 505–776–2291

Snow Report: 505–776–2916
KKIT radio weatherline: 505–758–4267
Area Vertical: 2,612 ft.
Number of Trails: 71
Lifts: 1 quad, 1 triple chair, 6 double
chairs, 2 surface lifts
Snowmaking: 23 percent of acreage
Season: Thanksgiving–late April

The ambience of Taos Ski Valley is as close to a European one as can be found in an American ski resort. The resort's founder, Ernie Blake, planned for a limited number of lodges nestled in the small valley containing the ski area. Most of the owners of these establishments come from Swiss, French, and German ancestry and steadfastly adhere to old-world traditions. Many guests become regulars, returning year after year. Lodges often require reservations long in advance.

The town of Taos offers yet another ambience, all in traditional adobe architecture. This is an old, Indian pueblo, rich in historical sites and galleries of the many artists who call it home.

The 12,000-foot tree line of the southern Rockies is twice that of the Alps. Part of the magic of Taos's skiing is the variety of hidden powder bowls, glades, and chutes, beginning at 11,819 feet and plunging to the village below at 9,207 feet. All this snow, 321 inches annually, under normally blue skies and warm sun!

There is beginner and intermediate skiing at Taos, but it is not as easy as the blue and green runs of most other areas. Fifty-one percent of the runs are rated expert, 25 percent are intermediate, and 24 percent are beginner.

Most skiers sign up for ski lessons, the best way to learn this tough mountain. The ski school is one of the most respected in the world: Ski instructors from other areas come here for refresher courses. The first run visible from the base is the famed "Al's Run," a gravity-defying vertical plummet flanked by several others of equal difficulty. But, a large sign assures first-timers, "Don't panic—we have easy runs, too!"

Practical Information for Taos

HOW TO GET THERE. By Air. Albuquerque is the closest commercial airport, served by most major airlines. *Mesa Airlines* has scheduled flights from Albuquerque to Taos; call 800–637–2247.

By car. Skierized **rental cars** are available from *Avis, Budget, Dollar, Hertz, Rich Ford,* and *National* at the Albuquerque airport. From Albuquerque, Taos is a 3-hour drive, 147 miles away. Denver's Stapleton Airport is 281 miles away, or nearly a 6-hour drive; Colorado Springs airport is a 5-hour drive or 216 miles away.

By shuttle. *Faust's Transportation,* (505) 758–3410, and *Pride of Taos Tours,* (505) 758–8340, run shuttles between the airport and the ski area twice a day.

TELEPHONES. The area code for all New Mexico is 505.

ACCOMMODATIONS. Packages are offered for three to seven days. Most popular in this rather remote resort is the 7-day Learn-to-Ski-Better package, which includes lodging, three meals a day, 6-day lift ticket, and six days of lessons. You can stay slopeside or in the old Indian town of Taos and visit the pueblo which has been continuously inhabited since 1200. For reservations contact the *Taos Valley Resort Association,* Box 85, Taos Ski Valley, NM 87525; 800–992–SNOW (7669) or 776–2233 within New Mexico; or *Taos Central Reservations,* Box 1713, Taos, NM 87571, 800–821–2437, or 758–9767 within New Mexico. Categories, based on price range for the package, are *Expensive,* $930–$1,070; *Moderate,* $451–$800; *Inexpensive,* less than $250.

Hotel Edelweiss. *Expensive.* On the slopes; 776–2301. Features a 7-day ski package with breakfast and dinner, 6 days of lifts, and lessons; double occupancy.

St. Bernard Condos, 776–8506, or **Hotel,** 776–2251. *Expensive.* Both on the slopes; 7-day ski package with 3 meals a day, 6 days of lifts and lessons, double occupancy.

Thunderbird Lodge and Chalets. *Expensive.* On the slopes; 776–2280. Offers full 7-day ski packages.

Austing Haus. *Moderate.* Box 8, Taos Ski Valley, NM 87525; 776–2649. Two miles from the slopes; 7-day packages with 2 meals daily, lifts, and lessons; hot tub, restaurant, and game room.

Quail Ridge Inn. *Moderate.* Box 707, Taos, NM 87571; 800–624–4448 or 776–2211. A family resort and conference center, 14 miles from Ski Valley in Taos; has a lounge and restaurant, racquetball, tennis, phones, pool, hot tub, sauna, fireplaces. Offers a 4-day package with lift tickets for a 1-bedroom.

Villacito Condos. *Moderate.* Box 49, Arroyo Seco, NM 87514; 776–8778. Located 13 miles from the slopes; large units with hot tubs, washer/dryer, and phones. Offers 7-day package with 6 days of lift tickets and lessons.

Abominable SnowMansion. *Inexpensive.* Box 3271, Taos, NM 87571; 776–8298. A dormitory facility 10 miles from the slopes. Rate includes 7 nights' lodging, 6 days of lift tickets, and lessons. There are hearty home-cooked meals; bed-and-breakfast packages also available.

El Pueblo Lodge and Condos. *Inexpensive.* Five blocks from the historic plaza, 758–8700 or 800–433–9612. Newly redecorated with heated pool, hot tub, refrigerators, and kitchenettes. Complimentary Continental breakfast.

RESTAURANTS. Since many ski packages include meals, most visitors opt to stay at Ski Valley to eat. The hotel's restaurants take some "outside" reservations; most are in the expensive range, listed below. There are also many good restaurants in Taos—reached via the daily shuttle service—to lure skiers from the mountain. In this selection, restaurants are listed by price category. *Expensive,* $15–$25; *Moderate,* $8–$15; *Inexpensive,* less than $8. These prices are for an average meal for one, excluding beverages, tax, and tip. All restaurants in the moderate and expensive categories accept major credit cards.

Expensive

The Brett House. In the historic Dorothy Brett house, Ski Valley Rd. at the blinking light in Taos; 776–8545. International dishes of seafood, lamb, steak, beef Wellington, chef's choices; intimate atmosphere. Reservations required.

Carl's French Quarter. At the Quail Ridge Inn on Ski Valley Rd.; 776–8319. Serves original Cajun and Continental specialties. Dinner theater on weekends. Reservations recommended.

Doc Martin's. Taos Inn, Paseo del Pueblo Norte, Taos; 758–2233. The Spanish influence is felt here like nowhere else; the historic inn oozes with authenticity. The menu offers superb northern New Mexican dishes and seafood, extensive wine list; reservations are recommended.

Sagebrush Inn. Paseo del Pueblo Sur, Taos; 758–2254. Award-winning menu includes steaks, prime rib, seafood, vegetarian dinners, salad bar, Chinese dishes. Live entertainment nightly; reservations a must.

Moderate

Apple Tree Restaurant. 123 Bent St., Taos; 758–1900. Intimate and charming with 4 dining rooms; the best *chile rellenos* in Taos, Hunan-style shrimp, good seafood, steaks, desserts, wine list; serves Sunday brunch 10 A.M.–3 P.M.; reservations recommended.

The Garden Restaurant. On the Plaza in Taos; 758–9483. Extensive selection of Mexican, Italian, and vegetarian items; beer and wine.

La Cigale. In the Pueblo Allegre Mall, Taos; 751–0500. French-style bistro serving breakfast, lunch, and dinner. Specialties include fondues, ratatouille pepper steak, fresh-baked bread, and pastries.

Phoenix Restaurant. Taos Ski Valley at the base of Kachina Lift; 776–2291. Serves hamburgers, chili, soups, sandwiches, beer and wine. View of the highest peaks in New Mexico.

Rhoda's Restaurant. Ski Valley Resort Center; 776–2005. Casual dining with great view of Al' Run. Daily specials include New Mexican dishes, game, pastas, and fresh fish. Full liquor service. Lunch and dinner daily.

St. Bernard Rathskeller. At the ski area; no phone. Serves sandwiches, home-made soups, stews; eat inside or on the sundeck.

Inexpensive

Comidas del Mante. S. Santa Fe Rd., between Randall Lumber and Ranchero Boots in Taos; 758–9317. Mexican cooking.

Mainstreet Bakery. Guadalupe Plaza, Taos; 758–9610. Delicious "health food."

Resort Center Cafeteria/Tenderfoot Katie's. At the base. Homemade soups, salads, sandwiches, and grilled food. Open for breakfast, lunch, and dinner.

Rickey's. Paseo del Pueblo Sur, Taos; 758–3589. A Taos-style menu that is a laundry list of home-cooked food, from Mexican dishes to pork chops and mashed potatoes to every type of sandwich.

Whitefeather Whistlestop. At the base of the Number 6 chairlift; no phone. Serves pizza, sandwiches, snacks.

HOW TO GET AROUND. *Faust's Transportation* (758–3410) and *Pride of Taos* (758–8340) offer local *bus, taxi,* and *charter* service. A daily skiers' **shuttle** serves the Taos motels, the Town Ticket Office, and the ski slopes (reservations required). On Tuesday and Thursday, a shopping shuttle takes guests from the Ski Valley to Taos. Many of the local merchants stay open on ski-shuttle nights.

SEASONAL EVENTS. The *Marlboro Coin-Op Race Course* operates daily throughout the ski season. NASTAR races are held on Wednesday, Thursday (adults), and Friday (children). *Ernie Blake's birthday* is celebrated annually in late **March** with a mountain treasure hunt, fireworks, and music.

OTHER SPORTS AND ACTIVITIES. The big thing at Taos Ski Valley is the ski school. Owner Ernie Blake's philosophy is that skiers must learn more here than they could anywhere else. So whether you are a beginner or an expert, to be part of the scene you take part in the ski school program. For those who have never skied, there is the Yellow Bird Program.

In Taos, the many **art galleries** are worth visiting. The *Millicent Rogers Museum,* 4 miles north of Taos off Rte. 522, near blinking light, 758–2462, displays Hispanic and Native American arts and gifts. First-run **movies** are featured at the Plaza Theatre and High Society Cinema; 758–9715. Guided **snowmobile** tours are conducted at *Moreno Valley Recreation* in Angel Fire; 758–3088 or 377–2321. *Native Sons* in Taos, 758–9342, also offers snowmobile and **cross-country** ski tours. An hour from Taos via US 64 and US 285 south, treat yourself to the *Ojo Caliente Mineral Springs* and therapeutic **massage.** It is open 8 A.M. to 7 P.M. daily; call 583–2233 for an appointment.

DAY-CARE FACILITIES. Usually, baby-sitting arrangements can be made for infants younger than 3 years at the lodging facilities. At the ski area, several programs are available. *Kinderkare* provides daily care for infants 6 weeks to 3 years. The 3- and 4-year-olds are in a program that includes an hour of skiing in the morning and in the afternoon plus various outdoor and indoor activities and lunch rest time; 5- and 6-year-olds meet for 2 hours of ski lessons in the morning and afternoon plus lunch.

The *Junior Elite Program* is for 7–12-year-olds with 2 hours of ski instruction in the morning and afternoon plus a weekly ski school race and videotape critique. All lift tickets and ski school classes can be purchased at the ski school office or next door at the ticket office. Call Taos Ski Valley, 776–2291, for free information and schedules.

NIGHTLIFE. Most of the nightlife centers on the ski lodge activities. Many have nightly entertainment, everything from country-western to jazz. After a hard day of keeping up with instructors, most skiers call it an early night.

The Taos Resort Center's top floor houses the *Martini Tree Bar,* featuring après-ski appetizers and music and entertainment daily.

The *Thunderbird Lodge,* Taos Ski Valley (776–2291), holds a jazz festival each January with the country's top performers, something jazz buffs should keep on their calendar. It equals any gig seen in New York.

For those who do drive or take the shuttle into Taos, there are several places with lively activity. *Kachina Lodge,* 758–2275, features music from punk to country during the week.

Ogelvie's Bar and Grille, on the Plaza, 758–8866, is a good gathering spot, especially on weekends when live entertainment is featured; unusual drinks.

Adobe Bar, in Taos Inn, 758–2233, has a Sunday-night music series and a Wednesday-night jazz program. Good for artist watching—R.C. Gorman spends some time here and also often dines at the Brett House.

OTHER NEW MEXICO SKI AREAS

ANGEL FIRE RESORT

Drawer B
Angel Fire NM 87710
Tel: 505–377–2301 or 800–633–7463

Area Vertical: 2,180 ft.
Number of trails: 51
Lifts: 4 double chairs, 2 triple chairs
Snowmaking: 60 percent of area
Season: Thanksgiving–Easter

Angel Fire appeals to Texas and Oklahoma skiers because it is only a 5-hour drive from Amarillo. In fact, many Texans own condos near the resort. For skiers who want a change of scene from Taos, Angel Fire offers solid intermediate and beginner runs, all smoothly groomed. The 3½-mile

"Headin' Home" is a fun slope for beginners to practice on. Experts have some good runs too, about 19 percent of the terrain. It's worth the drive here from Taos if you're into sampling various areas.

There are over 600 condo units in the area. The Legends Hotel, a deluxe 158-room facility at the lifts, offers spacious rooms—each can accommodate a family of four. There is an indoor pool and Jacuzzi, two restaurants, and some shops on the premises. Two adults and two children can stay for two nights and three days plus skiing for about $315. (Kids 12 and under stay free.) Call 800–663–7463 for information.

SKI APACHE

Box 220
Ruidoso NM 88345
Tel: 505–336–4356

Snow Report: 505–257–9001
Area Vertical: 1,800 ft.
Number of Trails: 38
Lifts: 5 triple chairs, 2 double chairs, 1
*   four-passenger gondola*
Snowmaking: 30 percent of area
Season: Thanksgiving–Easter

This resort is owned by the Mescalero Apache Tribe and is located on the 12,003-foot Sierra Blanca Peak, the sacred mountain of the tribe. It is second to Taos in the number of visits by skiers to New Mexico. Most of the skiers are from Texas, Arizona, Arkansas, Oklahoma, and Mexico.

There is good beginner and intermediate skiing, and 45 percent of the area is rated "most difficult," ensuring something for everyone. Several new trails on Elk Ridge are now serviced by a new chairlift. The southwestern location means lots of dry powder and sunshine. Great sightseeing nearby includes Carlsbad Caverns, White Sands National Monument, and the Space Hall of Fame in Alamogordo.

The closest major airport is in El Paso, Texas, about 100 miles away. The Sierra Blanca Regional Airport, outside Ruidoso, is serviced by Mesa Airlines. With a paved and lighted runway, it is capable of handling 727-type aircraft. The towns of Ruidoso and Alto offer lodging in condos, cabins, hotels, and motels; but the main attraction is the luxurious four-star **Inn of the Mountain Gods,** 800–545–9011, owned by the Mescalero Apache Tribe. Ski packages including lift tickets begin at $127 per night, double occupancy.

Oregon

MT. BACHELOR

Box 1031
Bend OR 97709
Tel: 503-382-2442
Reservations Information: 800-547-6858
   or 382-8334 in Oregon

Snow Report: 503-382-7888
Area Vertical: 3,100 ft.
Number of Trails: 54 on 6,000 acres
Lifts: 3 high-speed quads, 1 high-speed triple
   chair, 4 triple chairs, 1 double chair, 2
   poma lifts
Snowmaking: none
Season: mid-November–July

Like the entire Pacific Northwest, the weather and snow conditions at
Mt. Bachelor can be changeable; rain slickers sold in many sport shops
are an indication of its fickleness. But spring and summer skiing are among
the best anywhere.

The Pacific Northwest destination resorts aren't anything like the slick
resorts of California and Colorado. These areas draw mainly families from
Canada and the northwestern United States, with fewer choices of lodges
and restaurants in the immediate vicinity of the ski areas. Yet they are
not without their charm. The views from these ancient volcanoes are totally different from the Rockies or the Alps in that each mountain stands
alone, with the other volcanic cones off in the distance. The summit of
Mt. Bachelor provides a 360-degree panoramic view, with the Three Sisters, Hood, St. Helens, and Rainier standing like faraway sentinels.

The skiing at Bachelor's summit is 360 degrees, too. If one side isn't
good, just traverse to another. So skiers won't get lost in a sudden white-
out, there's a cat track—Catchline—that brings skiers to the front side
of the mountain. Closer to the base of Bachelor, there are fine tree skiing,
glades, powder runs in Outback, and groomed trails.

The summit chair opens the area to summer skiing and to passengers
with nothing more than shoes on their feet. The lift actually operates
through Labor Day, shutting down for just a few months until the beginning of the season in November. This is high desert country, and the "in"
thing during spring and summer is to ski the summit in the morning, then
head down to Bend, 20 minutes and many thousands of feet in elevation
away, to golf, tennis, raft, or hike.

Surrounding the base of the mountain are six day lodges (five with their
own restaurant, parking, rental shop, and ticket office) plus a guest services
building with ticket office, rest rooms, and lockers. Some tips on which

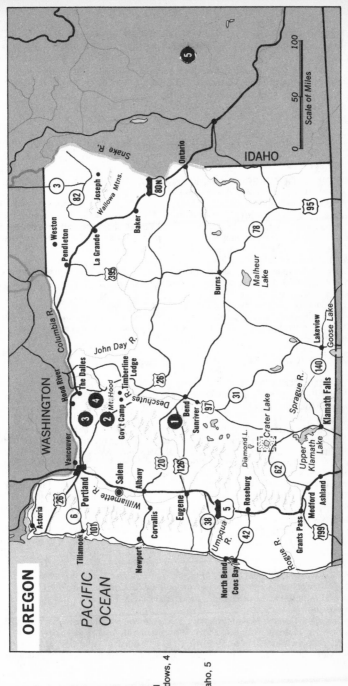

OREGON

PACIFIC OCEAN

IDAHO

WASHINGTON

Scale of Miles
0   50   100

Resorts

Mt. Bachelor, 1
Mt. Hood Meadows, 4
Ski Bowl, 2
Timberline, 3

Sun Valley, Idaho, 5

lodges to use: day-care facilities are in Sunrise Lodge and West Village; Blue Lodge has easy access to beginner and intermediate trails; the West Village Lodge is closest to the expert runs; and powder freaks can usually be found on the Cinder Cone and Outback. At mid-mountain (at 7,800 feet between the Pine Marten and Outback chairlifts), the Pine Marten Lodge has a restaurant and a ski shop.

Practical Information for Mt. Bachelor

HOW TO GET THERE. Mt. Bachelor is 22 miles west of Bend, on scenic Century Drive. Bend is in the center of Oregon.

By air. *United Express,* 800–241–6522, services Redmond/Bend from Portland with connections to other Northwest cities; it also has three daily non-stops into Redmond/Bend from San Francisco. Airport **limousine** service goes into Bend, 15 miles from the airport. **Rental cars** at the airport are *National,* 800–328–4517, and *Hertz,* 800–654–3131. Private aircraft can land at Sunriver Airport, 17 miles from Bend. Hertz cars are available.

By car. Bend is at the junction of US 97 and US 20. It's 3 hours from Portland via US 26 and US 97. From Seattle, it is 334 miles, 7 hours, via I–5 to Portland, then US 26 to US 97.

By bus. *Greyhound* operates from Portland to Bend daily.

By train. *Amtrak's* Coast Starlite serves West Coast cities from Seattle to San Diego. The train stops in Chemult, south of Bend, with limousine or rental cars from there.

TELEPHONES. The area code for all Oregon is 503.

ACCOMMODATIONS. For all lodgings near the ski area, contact the *Central Oregon Reservations Center* at 800–547–6858 or 382–8334 in Oregon. There are no accommodations at the base of the mountain, but there are some lodges and motels along Century Drive leading to the base and a wide variety of lodgings in the town of Bend, 22 miles away. Sunriver, a smaller community 18 miles away, also has a selection of accommodations for a total of 3,500 beds in the general area. All offer 7-night packages, which include one day of free skiing. Rates are based on double occupancy. Categories, determined by price for the package, are: *Expensive,* $300 and up; *Moderate,* $200–$300; and *Inexpensive,* less than $200.

Inn of the Seventh Mountain Condos. *Expensive.* On Century Dr., 14 miles from Mt. Bachelor; Box 975, Bend; 382–8711, 800–452–6810 in Oregon, 800–547–5668 in western states. Suites with kitchen, fireplace, TV; whirlpools, saunas, ice skating rink; bus service to the mountain.

Sunriver Resort. *Expensive.* On Century Dr., 18 miles from Mt. Bachelor; 800–547–3922 in Oregon, 800–452–6874 elsewhere in the United States. The resort also has bus service to the area, heated indoor swimming pool, Jacuzzis, store, golf course.

Best Western Entrada Lodge. *Moderate.* Century Dr., Bend; 382–4080. Borders Deschutes National Forest, 2 miles west of Bend. Charming rooms with color TV; Jacuzzi, sauna, heated pool. Full breakfast available. Free après-ski refreshments in season.

Inn of the Seventh Mountain Lodge. *Moderate.* Same address and phone number as Seventh Mountain Condos, above. TV; restaurant, lounge, snack bar.

Riverhouse Motor Inn. *Inexpensive.* On US 97, north of Bend; 389–3111. Seventeen suites; restaurants and lounge, sauna, Jacuzzi. Cross-country skiing and snowmobiling available.

RESTAURANTS. Seven on-mountain restaurants are in the day lodges and the Nordic Lodge. Sunday champagne brunch is a tradition at the main lodge. However, après-ski activities take place in the individual lodges as well as in Bend and in Sunriver. Restaurants are listed here in order of category, determined by the price of a full dinner for one, excluding drinks, tax, and tip. *Expensive,* $15–$25; *Moderate,* $7–$15; *Inexpensive,* less than $7. All sit-down restaurants accept major credit cards.

Expensive

Le Bistro. 1203 N.E. Third St., Bend; 388–7274. In a redecorated church; gourmet menu features saddle of lamb and scampi; closed Sundays and Mondays.

Skiers Palate—South Sister Restaurant. In the mid-mountain Pine Marten Lodge; 382–2442. Provides an elegant dining experience with a breathtaking view of the Cascade Mountain range.

Moderate

The Ore House. 1033 N.W. Bond St., Bend; 388–3891. Features that plush San Francisco style of all restaurants in the Ore House chain; good steaks, salad bar; open daily.

Pine Tavern. 967 N.W. Brooks, on Mirror Pond, Bend; 382–5581. The town's oldest tavern, serving American menu, Sunday brunch; reservations required.

The Riverhouse. 3075 N. US 97, Bend; 389–8810. French and Continental cuisine; open 7 days a week, 3 meals a day.

Inexpensive

Bentley's American Grill. 119 N.W. Minnesota, Bend; 389–9878. Serves brunch and lunch; hamburgers, soups, salads.

Bonanza. 1245 S. US 97, Bend; 389–2852. Features the largest salad bar in central Oregon, all-you-can-eat soup and salad; children's menu.

Mexicali Rose. 301 N.E. Franklin, Bend; 389–0149. As the name implies, south of the border dishes, as hot as you want 'em.

Poppy Seed Cafe. At the Inn of the Seventh Mountain; 387–8711. Good for fish and chips, sandwiches, family-style dinners; airy atmosphere, with plenty of greenery.

HOW TO GET AROUND. A free, super **express shuttle** runs nonstop from the Mt. Bachelor's downtown office on Century Drive in Bend to West Village Lodge at Mt. Bachelor. For schedules, call 800–547–6858 or 503–382–8334, in the state. The more expensive lodges have complimentary bus service; otherwise a car is necessary. TLC, The Limousine Company, has a chauffeured presidential **limousine** for hire; 389–5202. Call-A-Cab **taxi** service is 382–1687.

SEASONAL EVENTS. A Thanksgiving cross-country ski clinic is an annual **November** activity. In **January** are the *Cascade Winter Festival* and the *North American Pro Tour Race.* In **March,** the *Oregon State Special Olympics are held here.* **May** starts the "Summit Season" (usually the best skiing at the summit) with reduced ticket prices; the *Pole Pedal Paddle Pentathlon, Mt. Bachelor AdultCamps,* and *Bob Woodward's Summer X-Country Camp* also are in May. *Cross-Country US Ski Team* spring training camp is in late May–early **June** and *Mt. Bachelor Summer Ski Camps* for adults and juniors are May–**July** in the summit's permanent snow fields. For details on any event, call the ski area at 382–2442 or 382–2607.

OTHER SPORTS AND ACTIVITIES. Besides skiing for 10 months of the year, there is an extensive **nordic trail system.** Fifty km of machine-groomed, marked, and patrolled trails begin near the main parking lot at Bachelor and lead into the Deschutes National Forest. The Nordic Lodge at the base, adjacent to the main lodge, has snacks, ski school, rentals, and repairs. Daily trail pass is $8.50 for adults, $4.50 for children 12 years old and under, $4.25 for seniors. Lessons in telemarking and racing are available.

Snowmobile trails are marked to Elk Lake and Cascade Lakes. Also, tours are available through Sunriver Resort; call 382–2124, ext. 418. **Sleigh rides** are from the Inn of the Seventh Mountain, 382–8711; also *Wildcat Packers and Outfitters* run sleigh and dinner rides, 389–9458. Pick up a copy of *Our Town* guide to Bend and vicinity for the latest in activities and events as well as maps of the area.

DAY-CARE FACILITIES. There are two day-care centers at Mt. Bachelor, at West Village and Sunrise lodges. Rates are $22 to $25 per day for ages 6 weeks–

7 years; reservations recommended; 382–2607, ext. 2138. Planned activities; lunch must be provided by parents. For advance booking, write Mt. Bachelor Day-Care Center, Box 1031, Bend, OR 97709. Children's ski school is for youngsters 7–12; *Tiny Tracks* is a ski school for ages 4–6, 3-hour lesson, $49 with rentals. Contact the ski school at 382–2607, ext. 2116.

NIGHTLIFE. The town of Bend is usually hopping, and depending on the crowd at the Inn of the Seventh Mountain and Sunriver Resort, those places can be lively as well. *El Crab Catcher* at the Seventh Mountain has après-ski hour with ski movies, entertainment, and dancing; 389–2722. *The Riverhouse* features bands from the Northwest, happy hour; 389–3111. The *Pine Tavern,* 382–5581, and *DeJola's,* 338–1288, are often packed with après-skiers.

OTHER OREGON SKI AREAS

Mt. Hood is another of those extinct volcanoes that dominate the Oregon landscape. The 11,245-foot mountain has three day-ski areas on its slopes—Mt. Hood Meadows, Timberline, and Ski Bowl. Mt. Hood is about 70 miles east of Portland via Hwy. 84N and Hwy. 26. Ski Bowl is the smallest and closest to Portland; Timberline has nice beginner and intermediate terrain for both summer and winter skiing, while Mt. Hood Meadows is the most diverse, with runs for all ability levels.

MT. HOOD MEADOWS

Box 470
Mt. Hood OR 97041
Tel.: 503-337-2222

Snow Report: 503-227-SNOW
Area Vertical: 2,777 ft.
Number of Trails: 48 on 2,000 acres,
  longest run 3 miles
Lifts: 1 quad chair, 1 triple chair, 7 double
  chairs, 1 rope tow
Snowmaking: none
Season: mid-November–mid-May

There are some 2,000 skiable acres on the eastern flank of Mt. Hood. Included is a good mix of groomed slopes, gentle beginners, fun intermediate cruisers, and short—but—steep advanced terrain. Most of the skiing is in the trees, protected from the wind. The Texas Chair serves areas above timberline, but runs only when weather conditions permit. The most famous run is Heather Canyon, a 3-mile-long outback trail for experts, reached from the Texas and Shooting Star chairs. There is night skiing from five of the lifts on the front of the mountain.

The main base lodge and a smaller lodge below the Meadows Chair include bars, a deli, snack bar, and bakery; there is usually live entertainment during the late afternoon hours. Rental skis are available.

TIMBERLINE SKI AREA

Timberline Lodge OR 97028
Tel: 503-272-3707

Snow Report: 503-222-2211
Area Vertical: 2,000 ft. winter, 2,500 ft.
  summer
Number of Trails: 31 on 1,000 acres
Lifts: 5 double chairs, 1 triple chair
Snowmaking: none
Season: mid-November–mid-April,
  mid-May–Labor Day

Obviously, what separates Timberline from other ski areas is the full summer ski season. Skiing in summer starts 1,000 feet higher than in winter, from 6,000 to 8,500 feet on the treeless section of Mt. Hood for glacier skiing. Temperatures can range from blizzards to swimsuit sun. Lifts open early in the morning and close early in the afternoon to avoid the mushy midday conditions. Nearly 50 race camps hold clinics here each summer, and Olympic team members and hopefuls attend. With limited summer uphill capacity, the lift lines can get incredibly long in summer. Each race camp stakes out a portion of the hill to run gates. Unfortunately, this does not leave much room for the casual skier.

Winter skiing is in the protected wooded area. The longest run, Magic Mile to the bottom of Victoria Station, is 1¼ miles. Ablility mix is 30 percent novice, 50 percent intermediate, and 20 percent advanced. A permanent halfpipe for snowboarders is adjacent to the Betsy chairlift. Three chairlifts are lighted for night skiing, Wednesdays through Saturdays during the winter.

The Wy'East day lodge sells tickets, food, and drinks and has rental equipment. But the main attraction of Timberline is the grand old Timberline Lodge. No visit is complete without a tour or an overnight stay at this architectural marvel, a National Historic Landmark. Accommodations range from chalet dorm-type quarters starting at $55 to deluxe rooms at $140, per night, double occupancy. The lodge has a swimming pool, hydro-spa, sauna, and game room. The Cascade dining room and two bars provide food and beverage service. They also offer conference facilities for up to 300 people. Several ski packages are offered. For reservation information call (503) 272–3311; in Oregon, call 800–452–1335; in Washington, Nevada, Idaho, Utah, and northern California, call 800–547–1406.

Timberline is 55 miles east of Portland, and 180 miles south of Seattle. *Mt. Hood Express* provides transportation to and from the airport in Portland; call (503) 622–5554.

SKI BOWL

Box 400
Government Camp OR 97028
Tel: 503-272-3522

Snow Report: 503–224–9221
Area Vertical: 1,400 ft.
Number of Trails: 31 on 400 skiable acres
Lifts: 4 double chairs, 7 tow ropes
Snowmaking: none
Season: late November–mid-April

The terrain consists of mostly open slopes, north facing. This is the oldest ski area on Mt. Hood. Two day lodges have cafeterias, and the West Lodge has a bierstube.

Ski Bowl is the area closest to Portland, about 53 miles east on US 26.

Utah

Seven Wasatch Front ski areas are within an hour of the international airport of Salt Lake City. The canyons stretch like fingers from the Great Salt Lake, each catching the Pacific storms, which have been dried after moving across the Sierra. Little Cottonwood Canyon, home of Alta and Snowbird, catches the majority of the storms, and in an average year can get over 40 feet of snow. Four ski resorts are described in detail here, followed by a listing of seven other ski areas as well as the Ski Utah Interconnect, an evolving network of backcountry routes connecting several of the Utah ski areas.

ALTA

Alta UT 84092
Tel: 801–742–3333

Snow Report: 801–572–3939
Area Vertical: 2,050 ft.
Number of Trails: open and bowl skiing on
*   2,200 acres, longest run 3½ miles*
Lifts: 8 double chairs, 3 rope tows
Snowmaking: none
Season: mid-November–April

Alta, Utah's oldest ski area, celebrated its 50th anniversary during the 1988–89 season. Since 1938, when North America's third chairlift was installed at Alta, this area has remained true to a policy of emphasizing quality rather than quantity. It has not put in a lot of high-speed lifts to reduce waiting time in lines because this would increase the traffic on the runs. Not having to look over one's shoulders all the way down a crowded slope is worth a few extra minutes' wait to Alta's skiers. Alta also has one of the lowest priced lift tickets of any major resort—$21 for all lifts for both adults and children (based on the idea that they occupy the same amount of space on the mountain). The sole "modernization" at Alta has come in the form of the ski area's acknowledgement of the widespread use of "plastic" for payment: You can now buy your lift ticket with MasterCard or Visa. Most of the area lodges, however, do not accept credit cards, so be sure to check first.

The slopes are comparable to some in Europe, where the trails are not formally marked. Skiers negotiate downhill according to their own whims and stamina. Despite its fame for steep and deep powder fields, there are

269

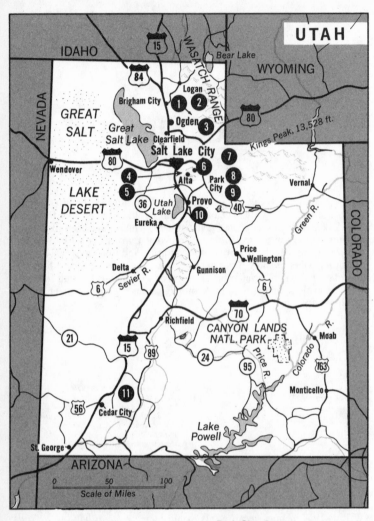

Resorts

Alta, 4
Brian Head, 11
Brighton, 6
Deer Valley, 9
Nordic Valley, 1

Park City, 8
Powder Mountain, 2
SnowBasin, 3
Snowbird, 5
Solitude, 7
Sundance, 10

plenty of less-advanced slopes. "Crooked Mile" is a groomed, mile-long, undulating run that is great for beginners. Actually, except for Albion, the beginners' lift, skiers of varied abilities can ride up all the lifts and ski down on a run suited to their level.

The skiing terrain is rated 25 percent beginner, 40 percent intermediate, and 35 percent advanced—far more advanced terrain than any other destination area except perhaps Taos in New Mexico (the two are soulmates). When you first see the mountain, the advanced runs face you. However, many intermediate runs are not apparent from the base area. There is also plenty of expert-only, off-trail terrain, but check with the ski patrol to see if the routes are open. The Utah Interconnect is caught here, as well as a ski route to Snowbird, a mile and a half west.

Practical Information for Alta

HOW TO GET THERE. Alta is 26 miles southeast of Salt Lake City, just past Snowbird, at the end of Little Cottonwood Canyon.

By air. Major airlines serve Salt Lake's International Airport (for a list of the airlines and rental car companies, see *Practical Information for Park City*). *Hosking Helicopter* lifts skiers to Alta in just 15 minutes for approximately $300.

By bus. *Utah Transit Authority* provides scheduled bus service from the airport to Alta for $6; from downtown it's $3 one way. Call 801–263–3737 for information and schedules. Hotels in the downtown area have buses that leave for the ski areas every 10 minutes in the morning; return buses depart from the ski areas just as frequently in the late afternoon. *Canyon Transportation* (801–942–1108) has service from the airport to Alta. *Lewis Brothers* (801–359–8677) has **limousine** service; *City Cab* (801–363–5014), *Ute Cab* (801–359–7788), and *Yellow Cab* (801–521–2100) will take skiers for their usual mileage fee.

By car. From downtown Salt Lake, take Route 500 South to I–15 southbound to I–215 eastbound (Exit 302). Follow I–215 to Exit 6, then follow the signs to the Little Cottonwood Canyon ski areas. It can be a quick 45-minute drive from the airport, but if it's snowing and there is avalanche danger, it could take longer. The narrow mountain road is sometimes temporarily closed during storms.

TELEPHONES. The area code for all Utah is 801.

ACCOMMODATIONS. All lodges (excluding condominiums) operate on modified American and full American plans, with packages of three, five, or seven nights. Contact *Alta Travel & Reservation Service,* Alta, UT 84092; 801–742–0404. All lodges can be contacted individually by writing to them at Alta, UT 84092, or calling their numbers in this listing.

A popular alternative is to stay in Salt Lake City and drive up each day to ski. There are 10,000 beds in Salt Lake City—everything from deluxe to motel-cheap. Contact the *Utah Travel Council,* Council Hall/Capitol Hill, Salt Lake City, UT 84114 (801–533–5681), for a list of accommodations.

Since Alta's lodging is limited, rates charged by all lodges and condos are similar. Actual prices depend on the size of the room and amenities. Quite a few rooms in these lodges still have shared baths. If you want your own, be sure to request it. Most of the lodges pride themselves on serving outstanding cuisine. Meals are considered a high point in the day. For those accommodations that require you to go on a meal plan, a 25 percent tax-and-gratuity charge is added to the bill.

A studio condo runs from $160 to $175 per night for two. A 7-day package costs about $700 per person and includes meals. There are also $800 7-day packages for more deluxe rooms. Inquire at each lodging for exact package plans.

Alta Lodge. 742–3500. Ski-in, ski-out accommodations from dorm rooms to deluxe rooms with fireplaces and balconies, saunas, whirlpools, bar; often called the classic ski lodge; MAP plan only.

Alta Peruvian Lodge. 742–3000 or 800–453–8488. With huge outdoor pool and Jacuzzi, sauna; rooms range from dormitory style to 2-bedroom suites; full American plan only. Some of the best dining in Alta.

Blackjack Condominium Lodge. Situated between Alta and Snowbird; 742–3200. Free shuttle to both ski areas, fireplaces, game room; accommodations range from studios to 3-bedroom units.

Goldminer's Daughter Lodge. At the base of the lifts, next to the parking lot; 742–2300 or 800–453–4573. Has ski and repair shop, hot tubs, sauna, game room, new exercise room, bar, cafeteria; MAP.

Hellgate Condominiums. Halfway between Alta and Snowbird; 742–2020. Free shuttle to slopes, free garage space and firewood; 1- and 2-bedroom condos.

Rustler Lodge. 742–2200. With heated pool, hot tubs, sauna; another classic lodge with accommodations ranging from dorm rooms to large suites; MAP plan.

Sugarplum Condos. Located between Snowbird and Alta; 943–1842. Newest and very luxurious. Accommodations vary from townhouses to cottage units. Many have individual hot tubs, laundry facilities, and garages. At the high end of the price scale.

RESTAURANTS. Since the lodges all serve breakfast and dinner (some include lunch), meals are usually taken where you stay. If you are staying elsewhere and want to eat at one of the lodges, you can make reservations, provided the lodges are not booked with their own customers. The *Alta Lodge, Alta Peruvian,* and *Rustler* are all known for their good food. Prices are moderately expensive, in the $10–$20 range for a full meal, exclusive of beverage, tax, and tip. The two on-mountain cafeterias are the *Alpenglow* and the *Albion Grill;* both are open for lunch.

Chic's Place, near the base of the Germania lift in Watson's Shelter, is an excellent sit-down restaurant—nothing fancy, just good, home cooking at affordable prices. Call 742–3037 for reservations. The *Shallow Shaft,* in the center of Alta, 742–2177, offers a Continental menu.

HOW TO GET AROUND. Once at the ski area, one can walk or take the free **shuttle bus** to lifts, lodges, and restaurants. Those staying in condos would want a **car** if they intend to eat out.

SEASONAL EVENTS. Spring skiing in "corn snow" is one of the few promoted events, since the snow outlasts the visitors.

OTHER SPORTS AND ACTIVITIES. There is unlimited terrain for **cross-country** skiers; instruction is available through the *Alf Engen Ski School;* 742–2600. For the Interconnect, see the section on Ski Utah Interconnect.

CHILDREN'S ACTIVITIES. The *Children's Ski School* meets at the Albion Ticket Office at 10 A.M. and 2 P.M. daily; call ski school, 742–2600. The *Children's Center,* located upstairs in the Albion ticket and ski school building and operated by *Vesle Barne Day Care Inc.,* is for youngsters 2–12 years. Open from 9:30 A.M. to 4:30 P.M.: lessons, lunch, and day-care are available; call 742–3042.

NIGHTLIFE. Contrary to popular opinion, one can drink alcoholic beverages in Utah—you just have to know how. State liquor stores sell packaged liquors, beer, and wines; locations can be found in the local telephone directory under "Utah State Government." The stores accept cash only and are closed on Sundays and holidays.

In designated restaurants, minibottles of liquor with setups and wine by the glass can be sold to patrons. You can also bring your own bottle of corked wine; there may be a corkage charge.

Private clubs are establishments that sell drinks over the bar to members and guests; consider the membership fee a cover charge. The Chamber of Commerce has a list of private clubs.

Evening hours at Alta, however, revolve around lodge life. There may be movies planned, folk dancing, special talks, costume parties, bridge or chess games, or just conversation and marshmallow-toasting by the fire.

DEER VALLEY RESORT

Box 1525
Park City UT 84060
Tel: 801–649–1000 or 800–424–3337

Snow Report: 801–649–2000
Area Vertical: 2,200 ft.
Number of Trails: 56 trails on 900 acres
Lifts: 1 high-speed quad, 9 triple chairs, 1
*   double chair*
Snowmaking: on 24 percent of skiable
*   terrain*
Season: December–March

Deer Valley doesn't mind being called the most expensive of Utah's resorts. The area celebrated its 10th anniversary in 1990, and it continues
to develop an image of exclusivity by setting high standards for all its services. The base lodge, for example, is so luxurious that even the faucets
in the public rest rooms are of a fancy, gold-plated type. Architecture and
appointments throughout the area are outstanding.

All creature comforts are attended to. Lift ticket sales are limited, so
no one has to wait in line. Attendants are close at hand to assist with unloading skis, getting into bindings, and helping load up at the end of the
day. Ski storage overnight is complimentary.

Deer Valley is actually three mountains—Bald Mountain, Flagstaff, and
Bald Eagle Mountain, with 15 percent of the area designated as beginner
terrain, 50 percent intermediate, and 35 percent advanced. That plentiful
Utah powder is groomed to perfection, with no catwalks, no flat run-outs,
few moguls. The 1990 investment in new lifts, trails, and snowmaking,
as well as expanded base facilities totaled in excess of $6 million. When
it has developed fully, Deer Valley will have 80 ski runs and 15 lifts on
1,200 acres of terrain with a capacity of 8,000 skiers on all three mountains.

Olympic gold medal winner Stein Eriksen holds forth as the director
of skiing. His input is seen in all aspects of what is as close to ski perfection
as possible. Two day lodges, Snow Park at the base and Silver Lake at
mid-mountain, have all the amenities, including elaborate buffets (go easy
on the excellent lunches or you'll have a hard time getting back out on
the slopes!), dining, rentals, ticket office, child care, a photo shop, and ski
school, all set in brass and wood and etched glass. Information desks are
located in Snow Park and Silver Lake day lodges. Marquees at the top
of Bald Mountain and outside the two day lodges give current information
on trail conditions and restaurant usage.

Deer Valley is adjacent to the old mining town and current ski town
of Park City. Many of the original Victorian-era buildings have been renovated, giving the town a charming frontier ambience. There is a wide
choice of shops, restaurants, lodging, and nightlife.

Practical Information for Deer Valley

HOW TO GET THERE. The nearest airport is Salt Lake City International,
served by major national carriers. (See *Practical Information for Park City.)*
By bus. From the airport, *Lewis Brothers Stage* serves Park City with buses, vans,
limos; call (801) 359–8677 for schedules. Their *Red Horse Express* has scheduled

service hourly to Park City. *Park City Transportation* serves Park City with regularly scheduled service; call 800–637–3803.

By car. Located next to Park City, Deer Valley is a 45-minute drive via I–80 from Salt Lake City International Airport. **Rental cars** from the airport include *Alamo,* (801) 539–8780 or 800–327–9633; *American International,* (801) 322–2488 or 800–527–0202; *Hertz,* (801) 539–2683 or 800–654–3131; *National* (801) 539–0200 or 800–CAR–RENT.

TELEPHONES. The area code for all Utah is 801.

ACCOMMODATIONS. Rentals at Deer Valley are available by the day or week. For accommodations, contact *Deer Valley Central Reservations,* Box 3149, Park City, UT 84060, 800–424–DEER or 801–649–1000. Condominiums form clusters at the base area of Snow Park Village and at mid-mountain at Silver Lake Village. Concierge, valet, and daily maid service are available at all lodgings. *Expensive* is the word for this resort: Expect to pay $100–$300 for 1-room lodgings and $400–$840 a night for 2-bedroom suites.

Listed below are the accommodations available at the resort. For less expensive lodgings, one can stay in Park City. For all listings below you can book through Deer Valley Central Reservations.

Cache. In the Silver Lake area, condos with glassed-in Jacuzzis; walking distance to lifts.

Goldener Hirsch Inn. In Silver Lake Village, adjacent to lifts; 649–3373 or 800–252–3373. A 20-suite hotel with luxuries comparable to the famed Stein Ericksen Lodge: heated, indoor parking; hot tubs and sauna; private decks off huge suites featuring handcrafted European furnishings with down comforters and fireplaces. The inn was modeled after its namesake in Salzburg, and an Austrian influence predominates here. The restaurant serves complimentary breakfast to guests and is open to the public for breakfast, lunch, and dinner.

La Maconnerie. Has 3- and 4-bedroom suites, swimming pool, Jacuzzis; ski-in, ski-out.

Pinnacle. Haw 4- and 5-level apartments with saunas, pool tables, outdoor Jacuzzis.

Stein Eriksen Lodge. Mid-mountain at the Silver Lake Village; 649–3700 or 800–453–1302. Top of the line in this top-of-the-line resort. It could be considered downright ostentatious with so much custom work and spaciousness. It's a ski-in, ski-out lodge at mid-mountain Silver Lake Village. Old-World elegance, massive beams, huge fireplaces, health club, pool, afternoon tea.

RESTAURANTS. Dining seems to be as important as skiing at Deer Valley. In fact, it is definitely the highlight of a skiing vacation here, with fine Continental or American cuisine offered at the posh lodges. There are two on the mountain—the Snow Park Lodge at the base and the mid-mountain Silver Lake Lodge. (See reviews, below.) Price categories, based on an average three-course dinner for one, excluding tip or drinks, are: *Expensive,* $20–40; *Moderate,* $10–$20; *Inexpensive,* less than $10. All restaurants accept major credit cards.

Expensive

Café Mariposa. In Silver Lake Lodge; 649–1005. A blend of classic and current cuisine elegantly served by a crackling fire. Fixed-price menu from 6 P.M. to 10 P.M. nightly.

Glitretind Restaurant. In the Stein Eriksen Lodge; 649–3700. Oozes with Norwegian atmosphere. Old World specialties and smorgasbord; serves breakfast, lunch, and dinner; reservations suggested.

Goldener Hirsch. In the Goldener Hirsch Inn; 649–7770. Continental cuisine with an Austrian accent. Appetizers include such delicacies as smoked Baltic sea tray, raclette, and beef tartare. Venison and game birds are served with herb-and-wine sauces. Open for breakfast, lunch, and dinner. Recommended for sit-down skier's lunch (*moderate* price category)—the homemade soups and salads are especially good.

Stag Lodge Restaurant, In the Stag Lodge, Silver Lake; 649–2421. French Provençal restaurant, open for 3 meals a day; creative dishes change weekly; winner of the Silver Spoon Award from Gourmet Diners Club of America; reservations required for dinner.

Moderate

Birkebeiner Cafe. In the Stein Eriksen Lodge; 649–3700. An à la carte menu featuring homemade pastries, soups, stews, and daily specials.

Inexpensive

The Huggery. In Snow Park Lodge; 649–1000. Complete natural breakfast buffet with grilled items. Lunch and afternoon snacks served. Site of nightly seafood buffet, prix fixe $30 adults, $18 children.

McHenry's. In Silver Lake Lodge; 649–1000. Same delicious food as the Snuggery (see below) but has sit-down service for lunch and dinner. Take out available.

The Snuggery. In Silver Lake Lodge; 649–1000. This self-service buffet offers Continental breakfast and lunch daily, but don't be fooled by the fact that it's essentially a cafeteria—it has perhaps the best on-mountain food available in the country and keeps pace with the finest restaurants in the area. Look for a plentiful salad bar, sandwiches, pizza, and a variety of hot items (one of the most interesting is the Southwestern turkey chili) plus a memorable carrot cake.

The Stew Pot. In Deer Valley Plaza; 645–STEW. Features stews, soups, sandwiches, salads for lunch and dinner; open until 9 P.M.

HOW TO GET AROUND. If skiers want to visit Park City in the evenings, a **car** is necessary. The *Park City Transit* **shuttle bus** operates between the ski lodges and condos and into Park City daily. In Deer Valley itself, everything is within walking distance or a lift ride.

SEASONAL EVENTS. The *Steve Garvey Celebrity Classic* and the *Coca-Cola Cup Race* are the two annual events. In **January,** *Masters Race* is held. Call for dates and details.

OTHER SPORTS AND ACTIVITIES. Guests at Stein Eriksen Lodge can use the health club and tackle an exercise program under an instructor's direction. Most of the lodges have **swimming pools. Ski racing** is set up on a race course run at the base of Bald Mountain; practice on the self-timed course, then race in the *Medalist Challenge;* race clinics available. Race tickets purchased at the course. (For additional activities, see *Practical Information for Park City.*)

CHILDREN'S ACTIVITIES. Snow Park Lodge at the base area has a child-care center with separate areas for different age groups. For children 3–12, there is a daily schedule of indoor and outdoor activities; half- and full-day programs, with or without lunch. The nursery accepts infants 6–24 months; call for reservations, 649–1000.

The ski school accepts children for group lessons all day with lunch; for youngsters under 4, private lessons only. Contact the *Ski School* at 649–1000; ext. 1638.

NIGHTLIFE. There are several lounges for quiet, elegant evenings with friends. The *Après-Ski Lounge* in Snow Park Lodge is open from 1 P.M. to 6 P.M. daily. It serves beer and cocktails. *Troll Hallen Lounge* in Stein Eriksen Lodge features hors d'oeuvres until midnight. *The Stag Lodge Lounge* in the Stag Lodge is open daily from 10 A.M. to 11 P.M.

A good selection of wines, champagnes, and liquor can be purchased at Silver Lake's *Wine & Spirit Shop.* Open Monday–Saturday, 10 A.M.–11 P.M.

PARK CITY SKI AREA

Box 39
Park City UT 84060
Tel: 801–649–8111
Reservation Information: 800–222–PARK

Snow Report: 801–649–9571
Area Vertical: 3,100 ft.
Number of Trails: 83 on 2,200 acres
Lifts: 1 gondola, 5 triple chairs, 8 double
     chairs
Snowmaking: on 350 acres
Season: mid-November–end of April

Unlike many resorts that have been developed specifically for the skiing crowd, Park City has a colorful and flamboyant past. The town sprung up as a mining camp when a rich silver strike was discovered in 1872. For half a century the mountains surrendered $400 million in silver, establishing many fortunes, including that of George Hearst, father of publishing magnate William Randolph Hearst.

Visitors can walk down a preserved Main Street district that is listed on the National Register of Historic Places. With 85 shops and boutiques, a dozen art galleries, 45 restaurants, and 20 clubs and bars, this is the best place in the state for après-ski nightlife.

Park City is one of six official U.S. Ski Team alpine training centers and is headquarters for the U.S. Ski Team and the U.S. Ski Association. The Park City Ski Area sponsors more U.S. Ski Team members than any other company in the world. Thus, it comes as no surprise that Park City is Utah's largest ski area, with 2,200 acres of skiable terrain, including 650 acres of open bowls and 83 trails (17 percent easier, 49 percent more difficult, and 34 percent most difficult. Skiers from beginners to experts will have fun at Park City because the terrain is so diverse. There's a new access to the summit: you can take the Pay Day lift from the base to the new Crescent quad then up to the Pioneer triple chair to the Summit House restaurant. From here, there are plenty of blue runs down. Or advanced skiers can take the Jupiter Access to the Jupiter bowl—a must for all experts—with steep terrain consisting of wide open faces, chutes through trees, gullies, cornices, and cliffs. The new high-speed quad Prospector lift (reached from the King Consolidated lift) takes you to some tough black runs surrounded by blues that wind through trees and glades—perfect for skiers of varying abilities.

The Town Lift goes to mid-mountain from the old Coalition Mine Building near Main Street; this is the best way up from downtown and the best way down if you're pooped at day's end but still want to sample the après-ski activities in town.

Practical Information for Park City

HOW TO GET THERE. Park City is 27 miles east of Salt Lake City.

By air. *Delta Airlines* has its hub in Salt Lake; in addition, the airport is served by *American, America West, Continental, Northwest, Pan Am, TWA,* and *United,* plus several commuter airlines—*Alpine, Horizon/Alaska,* and *Sky West.*

By bus. *Greyhound,* (801) 355–4684, serves Salt Lake City from all over the U.S. The area is well served by scheduled bus from the airport and some downtown pickups. *Lewis Brothers,* (801) 359–8677 or 800–826–5844, serves the area from both locales; their "Red Horse" departs from the airport and returns from Park City every half-hour; $24 round trip, $13 one way. *Park City Transportation* (800–637–3803) and *Key Transportation* (800–678–2360 or 801–328–2360) offer **van service** to and from Park City and the surrounding ski areas. Bus service leaves for Alta and Snowbird weekends on demand at 8 A.M., returns 5 P.M.; $14 round trip.

By train. *Amtrak's* California Zephyr pulls into downtown Salt Lake City from the West Coast and from Denver; call 800–USA–RAIL.

By car. Take I–80 from Salt Lake to Rte. 224, a 40-minute drive on good highways. Major **rental car** firms are located at the airport: *Avis,* 800–331–1212 or (801) 539–1117; *Budget,* 800–527–0700 or (801) 363–1500; *Dollar,* 800–421–6868 or (801) 596–2580; *Hertz,* 800–654–3131 or (801) 539–2683; *Pay Less,* 800–327–3631 or (801) 596–0851; *National,* 800–328–4567 or (801) 539–0200; *Ute,* 800–328–4567 or (801) 328–5709; *Thrifty,* 800–367–2277 or (801) 595–6677; and *Agency,* 800–321–1972 or (801) 534–1622.

Park City isn't out of range of a **cab.** Call *City Cab,* (801) 363–5014; *Ute Cab,* (801) 359–7788; or *Yellow Cab* (801) 521–2100.

TELEPHONES. The area code for all Utah is 801.

ACCOMMODATIONS. There is a total of 12,000 pillows in a 5-mile radius of Park City. *Park City Ski Holidays,* Box 4409, Park City, UT 84060 (649–0493 or 800–222–PARK), is an affiliate of the ski area and represents 2,500 lodging units. *Advance Reservations, Inc.,* Box 1179, Park City, UT 84060 (649–7700 or 800–453–4565), represents most of the other properties, including bed-and-breakfast establishments and deluxe homes.

In our list, *Expensive* ranges from $90 to $250 for 1-bedroom suites, double occupancy; *Moderate,* $50–$90; and *Inexpensive,* less than $50.

Expensive

Blue Church Lodge & Townhouses. In Park City's historic district, near Main Street and within walking distance of the Town Lift 649–8009; Condos and hotel rooms with antique country charm; fireplaces, lounge, indoor and outdoor spas, game room. Listed on the National Register of Historic Places.

The Resort Center Lodge and Inn. At the base; 800–824–5331 or 649–0800. Ninety luxurious ski-in/ski-out condos from 1 to 4 bedrooms. Fitness center, ice skating, shops, and restaurants.

Silver King Hotel. 1485 Empire Ave.; 800–331–8652 or 649–5500. Deluxe condos at the base. Indoor/outdoor pool, underground parking, sauna, whirlpool, Continental breakfast.

Moderate

Old Miners' Lodge Bed & Breakfast. 615 Woodside Ave. ⅛ mile to the lifts; 800–648–8068 or 645–8068. This 1893 building is in the historic district, restored to the original trappings; includes full breakfast, wine or cider after skiing, use of community living room and library, outside hot tub; each room is named after a historic Park City person.

Park Station Condominium Hotel. 950 Park Ave.; 800–367–1056 or 649–7717. Located next to the Town Lift and within walking distance of Old Town. A full-service hotel plus condo units. Jacuzzi, ice-skating rink.

Prospector Square Hotel. Conference Center and Athletic Club; 800–453–3812 or 649–7100. This is a complete facility just a few minutes by bus from downtown Park City and the lifts, includes 100 hotel rooms, 180 studio units, seven 3-bedroom condos and 5 private homes. Guests have use of the athletic club with pool, Jacuzzi, masseuse, steam room, gym, racquetball courts, sauna, weight training room, and lounge.

The Yarrow Hotel and Conference Center. 1800 Park Ave.; 800–327–2332 or 649–7000. A short bus ride to town and the lifts. A full-service hotel with swimming pool, sauna, Jacuzzi, ski rental and repair, and a National Car Rental office.

Inexpensive

Alpine Prospector's Lodge. 151 Main St.; 649–9975 or 649–3483. Close to restaurants and shops; 16 rooms, 4 baths, sauna, lounge.

Star Hotel. Main St.; 649–8333. In business for over 60 years. Family-style living with breakfast cooked to order and dinner included in room rate.

RESTAURANTS. Park City has restaurants to suit all tastes and budgets. *Expensive* restaurants have entrees in the $18–$40 price range; *Moderate,* $10–$18, and *Inexpensive,* less than $10. Most take major credit cards. See the Deer Valley section for additional listings; Deer Valley is about a 10-minute drive from Main Street, Park City.

On **on-mountain** eateries, all in the inexpensive-moderate range, include *Summit House,* at the top of the gondola and the Prospector, Pioneer, Motherlode, and Thaynes chairlifts; *Snow Hut,* at the bottom of Prospector; *Midmountain Restaurant,* recently renovated and moved 4,000 feet up the mountain to the Pioneer lift area; and *Base Cafeteria,* in the gondola building.

Alex's. *Expensive.* 442 Main St.; 649–6644. Fine Continental dining. A la carte menu or fixed-price dinners for $22. Cozy, below-sidewalk-level location.

Cafe Terigo. *Moderate.* 424 Main St.; 645–9555. Extensive appetizer menu. Entrees emphasize chicken and seafood-and-pasta combos. Killer desserts.

Cisero's Ristorante Bar. *Moderate.* 306 Main St.; 649–5044. Classic Italian cuisine. Shellfish, veal dishes, and pasta are recommended.

The Depot. *Moderate.* 660 Main St.; 649–2102. The Cafe menu features Austrian specialties. The Pub is open until midnight with piano music and an inexpensive menu of appetizers and light entrees costing $1–$7.

Sirloin & Seafood. *Moderate.* 151 Main St.; 649–7482. In addition to beef-n-reef, entrees include creative chicken dishes, rack of lamb, and barbecued ribs. Bonanza salad bar. An early-bird dinner is offered 5:30–6:30 P.M. for $10.

Baja Cantina. *Inexpensive.* Park City Resort Center; 649–BAJA. Park City's requisite Mexican restaurant serves large portions for lunch and dinner; no reservations.

La Flamme. *Inexpensive.* 255 Main St.; 645–9333. Classic fondues—2-serving minimum—offered nightly.

A Matter of Taste. *Inexpensive.* 530 Main St.; 645–7246. European deli with gourmet items for eat-in or take-out. Continental breakfasts served. Open 8 A.M. to 10 P.M. daily.

Ziggy's. *Inexpensive.* In the Resort Center; 649–2776. A $7 all-you-can-eat breakfast begins at 7:30 A.M. Soups, salads, sandwiches, pizza, and pasta for lunch and dinner. Great for snacks, too.

HOW TO GET AROUND. A car is neither necessary nor desirable. A free **shuttle bus** serves the lodges, historic Main Street, and the base area between 7:45 A.M. and 12:30 A.M. Call *Park City Transit* (649–6660) for details. *Park City Taxi* (649–8567) is available from 7 A.M. to midnight; call for service.

SEASONAL EVENTS. The **Christmas Eve** torchlight parade is the highlight of the holiday festivities. Each **February** is the local winter carnival. *World Cup races* are held in **March** or **November.** There is usually a *U.S. Ski Team Celebrity Classic* in February or **April.** An **Easter** egg hunt and sunrise service round out the year.

OTHER SPORTS AND ACTIVITIES. Recreational **racing** is usually big at most areas—NASTAR is run daily on an electronically timed race course. Group races and obstacle races can be arranged by prior notice; contact the ski area marketing department, 649–8111. The ski areas of Deer Valley and Park West are a snowball's throw away and worth a day or two away from Park City's slopes.

Cross-country ski with the *Norwegian School of Nature Life,* in Main Street Memorial Building, New Park Cyclery, Emporium Plaza and Rte. 248 at Kearns Blvd.; 649–2320 or 649–9461. Ski lessons, long and short day tours, cabin treks into the Uinta Mountains, and overnights are all available.

Piute Creek Cross Country, at the Upper Loop Rd., offers tranquil and secluded guided day **tours,** overnight bunk and breakfast tours, and rentals from a rustic base camp.

White Pine Ski Touring Center, at the Park City Golf Course (645–7555), has complete services, 9 km of prepared **track,** group and private **instruction,** overnight **excursions,** and a rental and repair shop.

Park City Sleigh Company, in the Park Meadows Racquet Club (649–3359), runs a half-hour **sleigh ride** to an old barn where you'll enjoy a Western barbecue dinner complete with guitar music; $37 adults, $22 children. The *Snowed Inn,* on Hwy. 224 (649–5713), offers a sleigh ride/dinner adventure for $35 adults, $20 children. Reservations required.

Ice skaters can enjoy *The Skaters Center* at Park City Resort Center, an outdoor rink at the base of the mountain; open seven days a week, rental, lessons, broomball; 645–7555.

CHILDREN'S ACTIVITIES. *Kinder-Ski-Kare* at the ski area, for children enrolled in ski school lessons, provides supervised play for ages 3–6; call 649–8111, ext. 314. *Merry Pop-ins* offers baby-sitting service in hotels and condos for infants and children at any time of day or night; contact them at Box 39, Park Meadows Plaza D-100; 649–5900. *Miss Billie's Kids Campus,* Star Route, across from Park West Ski Resort, takes care of children up to age 9; licensed by the state; call 649–9502.

NIGHTLIFE. Park City visitors not only ski here, they party. But to join in you will need to keep Utah's new liquor laws in mind. Liquor can *no longer* be brought into restaurants (except for corked wines purchased in the state). Instead, in most restaurants and bars, liquor is sold in sealed minibottles (airline size) with setups for mixed drinks. Many bars and lounges are private clubs where liquor is sold by the drink. You will need to buy a membership to partake; two-week visitor cards are available at most bars for a nominal fee. You can buy alcohol for personal consumption in state stores (Park City's are in Prospector Sq., and at 524 Main St. and are open Monday through Saturday 10 A.M. to 10 P.M.) or in package agencies located in many lodges and hotels.

Main Street sees plenty of action, and most lodges have lounges or bars with entertainment. Favorites include *Steeps at the Base,* in the Resort Center, and *The Club,* in the Park City Racquet Club. *"Z" Place,* on Main Street, 645–9200, books some big names to entertain in the 2nd-level concert hall that seats about 1,200. It's also available for private parties. The lower level has a sports bar, video arcade, and bowling alley.

For live entertainment, plays and musicals, head for the Egyptian Theater, 328 Main St. Movie buffs can see the latest films at *Holiday Village Cinemas III,* 1776 Park Ave.

SNOWBIRD SKI AND SUMMER RESORT

Snowbird UT 84092
Tel: 801–741–2222 or 801–521–6040 in Salt Lake City

Snow Report: 801–742–2222 or 801–521–6040
Area Vertical: 3,100 ft.
Number of Trails: 38 designated trails, longest run 2.5 miles
Lifts: One 125-passenger tram, 7 double chairs
Snowmaking: none
Season: end of November–mid-June

Snowbird popularized skiing in Utah. Starting in the 1970s, the cognoscenti of the skiing world descended on the newly opened planned resort. Snowbird, the giant killer, catered to the upscale crowd, a group far different from that at neighboring Alta. Today, the skiing crowd is more a mix of in-fashion types and utilitarian-clad Midwesterners.

From narrow Little Cottonwood Canyon, four stark concrete buildings dominate the base area while the huge tram makes a dramatic climb to the top of Hidden Peak. The terrain is vast, consisting of two north-facing bowls with 1,900 acres. With 50 percent advanced or expert runs, it is as challenging as Alta. But there are delightful civilized intermediate and beginner runs through stands of spruce and pine, and one can buy a less-expensive lift ticket valid for chairlifts only. The tram serves the mostly strong intermediate-to-expert terrain of Peruvian Gulch and Gad Valley. Beginner skiers cluster around Chickadee chair. Ask the tram operator or locals about off-trail skiing and the chute to Alta.

Because the area can be intimidating, the establishment has provided free guided tours to help newcomers find the runs best suited to their ability. Tours depart daily from the Plaza Deck. The extended spring and summer skiing is usually off the Gad 1 chairlifts or alternatively from the aerial tram.

Practical Information for Snowbird

HOW TO GET THERE. Snowbird is located in Little Cottonwood Canyon 45 minutes from the airport and 35 minutes from downtown Salt Lake City. See *Practical Information for Park City* for airlines, bus and train services, and rental cars; see *Practical Information for Alta* for driving directions and bus information.

TELEPHONES. The area code for all Utah is 801.

ACCOMMODATIONS. The village consists of four lodges, the tram building, and shops, boutiques, and groceries in Snowbird Center. Reservations for any of Snowbird's lodges is made through *Snowbird Corporation,* Little Cottonwood Canyon, Snowbird, UT 84092; 800–453–3000 or 801–532–1700; 800–742–2222 outside the continental United States. Snowbird lift vouchers with packages are exchangeable at Alta, Park City, and Deer Valley (the last two have an additional charge). Nightly rates and packages of three, four, five, and seven nights are available.

Salt Lake City has 10,000 beds plus restaurants and culture. The 35-minute drive from downtown is not difficult except when it's snowing; there is extreme avalanche danger in the narrow canyon, and Rte. 210 is often closed or clogged with cars. The *Utah Travel Council,* Council Hall/Capitol Hill, Salt Lake City, UT 84114, 801–533–5681, has information on a stay in Salt Lake.

The following lodges fall under the *Expensive* (nightly per-room rates of $240–$350 for a suite; per-person costs of $700–$1,400 for a 7-night package) and *Moderate* (nightly per-room rates of $150–$300 for a 1-bedroom or studio; per-person rates of $640–$710 for a 7-night package) categories. The Cliff Lodge has dormitory accommodations for $24–$40 per night. Call the Snowbird Corporation for details.

The Cliff Lodge is a full-service hotel with meeting and convention space and a total of 532 rooms from 2-bedrooms to a corner deluxe suite. The top floor houses the Cliff Spa. This health club is open to the public. It is a complete spa facility, with herbal wraps, massage therapy, lap pool, weight room, whirlpool, and beauty shop. There are several restaurants (see listings) in the hotel, as well as an underground garage.

Iron Blosam Lodge has time-shares, with limited rental rooms; 2 pools, steam room, Jacuzzi, weight room, saunas, physical therapist, game room, valet parking. Each room has its own balcony, from studio units with 1 bed to a 2-story loft suite.

The Lodge at Snowbird has a pool, saunas, valet parking; 160 condos with a choice of dormitories, bedrooms, and loft suites.

Turramurra Lodge has the usual heated swimming pool, saunas, valet parking, within easy walking distance of the center. Each of the 73 units, ranging from standard bedroom units to 2-level loft suites, has a private balcony.

RESTAURANTS. There are only eight private clubs and eight public restaurants at the base and one on the mountain, but there is a good variety. Unless otherwise noted, the phone number for all restaurants is 742–2222. A state liquor store is in Snowbird Center. Uncorked wine can be brought into restaurants, where a corkage fee is charged. A Snowbird Club membership costs $5 and will allow you to drink liquor. *Expensive* is in the $15–$35 range; *Moderate,* $10–$15; and *Inexpensive,* less than $10. Major credit cards accepted.

The Aerie. *Expensive.* Atop the Cliff Lodge. High-tech, Oriental decor, a spacious bar with live entertainment in the evening, and a cozy fireplace. Menu features Continental dishes of veal Oscar, salmon; also Italian and barbecue nights; huge breakfast buffets.

Forklift. *Moderate.* Level 3 of the Snowbird Center. Open for 3 meals a day; beef, fish, pasta entrees for dinner; burgers, soups, and salads for lunch.

Lodge Club. *Moderate.* Level 1 of the Lodge at Snowbird. An intimate club serving veal, chicken, beef, good appetizers.

Mexican Keyhole. *Moderate.* In the Cliff Lodge. Features superb Mexican dishes; cozy decor.

The Steak Pit. *Moderate.* Level 1 of the Snowbird Center. Specializes in great steaks; also seafood and unlimited salad fixings. Often crowded, so dinner reservations are necessary (521–6040).

Wildflower Restaurant. *Moderate.* Level C of Iron Blosam Lodge. The newest restaurant at the resort; family-oriented, with entrees from sandwiches to fish; breakfast and dinner only.

Birdfeeder. *Inexpensive.* Level 3 of the Snowbird Center. A quick snack bar on the outdoor plaza.

Mid-Gad. *Inexpensive.* Located at the top of the Mid-Gad chair. Good for lunch without having to come down the mountain.

HOW TO GET AROUND. Everything is within easy walking distance. *BART* (Bird Area Rapid Transit) provides free **shuttle service** to and from the main and Gad Valley parking areas and the Snowbird Center for day skiers and lodge guests. A shuttle operates to Alta every 30 minutes for $1 one way during skiing hours. Transportation to Park City may be arranged through the lodge front desk.

SEASONAL EVENTS. Festivities always take place during **Christmas;** *Winterfest* is celebrated from mid- to late **January;** and the *Telemark Series* is in mid-**April.** *NASTAR* races are every Tuesday, Thursday, and Friday.

Spring skiing season is the first two weeks in **May,** with terrain open in the Gad Valley. **Summer skiing** goes to **mid-June,** with Little Cloud Chairlift and the aerial tram open from 7:30 A.M. to 1 P.M. daily. Summer race camps are open to intermediate and advanced skiers of any age from the month of May; the fee is approximately $600 and includes instruction, ski conditioning such as hiking, swimming, tennis, ski films, and lectures, meals, and lodging; contact *Snowbird Ski School Office* at 742–2222 or 521–6040, ext. 4170.

OTHER SPORTS AND ACTIVITIES. Nordic and alpine **touring** is available along the ridges on the upper half of Little Cottonwood Canyon. Most of the **cross-country** skiing leaves from Alta and White Pine.

Helicopter skiing into virgin powder snow is available through *Wasatch Powder Guides* (742–2800).

CHILDREN'S ACTIVITIES. At Snowbird lodges, children under 13 stay free in your room, and one child skis free with each adult lift ticket purchased. Complimentary child care is available for guests of the Cliff Lodge. Children enrolled in the Children's Ski School are also cared for when not in lessons; they must be 3 years old and toilet trained. *Kinderbirds* takes 4–5 year olds for ski lessons and supervised activities. There is a Cookie Dual Race for all kids in ski school every Thursday afternoon on Chickadee, followed by an ice-cream party.

In-room baby-sitting services for infants to 3 years of age are available with two weeks' prior notice to the individual lodge or by calling 801–742–2222.

NIGHTLIFE. Evening entertainment centers on the lodge lounges. Particularly popular is *The Aerie Lounge,* with a great raw seafood bar and live entertainment, on Level 10 of the Cliff Lodge. The *Lodge Club,* Pool Level of the Lodge at Snowbird, is lively after skiing. The *Tram Room Bar,* Level 1 of the Snowbird Center, has live entertainment, pool tables, large screen TV; the loudest place in the village, good for burning up any extra energy.

OTHER UTAH AREAS

Brian Head Ski and Summer Resort
Box 190008
Brian Head UT 84719
800–27–BRIAN or (801) 677–2035
In the south of the state, this area is only
150 miles north of Las Vegas and an
easy trip for Californians; a low-key
family resort.

Brighton Ski Resort
Brighton UT 84121
(801) 943–8309
25 miles up Big Cottonwood Canyon
from Salt Lake City just past Solitude. A skier's delight, with plenty of
variety, fun chutes, and bargain lift
rates. Well worth the trip for a day's
skiing.

Nordic Valley
Box 178
Eden UT 84310
The third area near Ogden.

Powder Mountain
Box 68
Eden UT 84310
Near SnowBasin, in the Golden Spike
Empire.

SnowBasin
Box 200, Dept. UP
Huntsville UT 84317
In the "Golden Spike" area near Ogden.

Solitude Ski Resort Company
Box 17557
Salt Lake City UT 84117
23 miles up Big Cottonwood Canyon
from Salt Lake City; similar atmosphere to Alta but on a smaller scale;
a bonus here is that you'll find mogels
aside groomed runs—when you get
tired just ski to the middle of the trail
for some relief.

Sundance
R.R. 3, Box A–1
Sundance UT 84604
South of Salt Lake, near Provo, is Robert Redford's ski area. Always active
in the performing arts, the area is a
family-oriented resort. It's been a
sleeper, but is on the verge of expansion and promotion.

SKI UTAH INTERCONNECT

The Interconnect could well be North America's largest skiable area.
Actually, locals have skied this route for years, but few tourists dared venture into the backcountry.

Because the resorts of the Wasatch Front—those closest to Salt Lake
City—are only a few miles apart as the crow flies but miles away via circu-
itous canyon roads, the idea of tying the areas together by a network of
trails is an exciting one. Ski Utah currently combines five resorts interconnected by back–country routes that offer the magnificent scenery of the
Wasatch Range. Skiers must be accompanied by a Forest Service–
approved guide and must be of advanced skiing ability, able to navigate
in various snow conditions. The tour routes feature skiing in each of the
areas visited as well as on the terrain between them, which is ungroomed
and not patrolled (hence the need for guides trained in avalanche control
and safety). Two tours are offered: the **five-area tour** begins at Park City
and includes Solitude, Brighton, Alta, and Snowbird. Approximately 8
hours in length, it operates Monday, Wednesday, Friday, and Sunday.
Cost is $95 per person. The **four-area tour** begins at Snowbird and includes
Alta, Brighton, and Solitude. Approximately 6 hours long, it operates on
Tuesday, Thursday, and Saturday and costs $85 per person.

Group size varies from six to 14 skiers. Prices include lunch and return transportation to point of origin. Skiers will receive Ski Utah Interconnect Adventure pins upon completion of the tour. Reservations must be made in advance and guaranteed with a credit card number. Call (801) 534–1907, 8 A.M.–6 P.M. Monday–Friday, or write Ski Utah Interconnect, 307 West 200 South 1003, Salt Lake City, UT 84101.

Washington

CRYSTAL MOUNTAIN RESORT

Box 1
Crystal Mountain WA 98022
Tel: 206–663–2265 or 800–852–1444 (in
    Washington)

Snow Report: 206–634–3771 or 206–634–
    0200
Area Vertical: 3,100 ft.
Number of Trails: 32 trails on 1,400 acres
    (plus 1,000 acres backcountry)
Lifts: 1 high-speed quad, 1 quad chair, 3
    triple chairs, 5 double chairs
Snowmaking: none
Season: mid-November–mid-April

Ski conditions in Washington State are like those in Oregon—unpredictable. Surely, there is far less danger from sunburn than at Colorado and California areas: Northwestern U.S. winters are normally cloudy and damp. Crystal Mountain's amenities are bare boned, compared with other major resorts. Yet the lodges and restaurants thankfully are clustered around the base of Crystal Mountain, the only such setup in the Pacific Northwest. But if you ski hard enough, a hot Jacuzzi and clean sheets are all that is important.

And you can ski hard at Crystal; at 7,000 feet, it is the state's highest resort. There is a lot of expert terrain, plus 1,000 acres of ungroomed, unmarked territory. Much of the steep and deep resembles more famous areas—such as Snowbird or Jackson—but the snow is laden with that Northwest wetness. There are extensive open areas as well as glade skiing. In addition to the advanced skiing, beginners and intermediates have 17 runs, 57 percent of the mountain.

The day lodge has two restaurants. There are also two other restaurants, two pools, a hot tub, sauna, grocery, and ski shop at the base area. If you are looking for a low-key area or one that caters to Seattle day trippers, Crystal Mountain is the place.

Practical Information for Crystal Mountain

HOW TO GET THERE. Crystal Mountain is in the Mt. Baker-Snoqualmie National Forest, on the northeast boundary of Mt. Rainier National Park. It is 76 miles from Seattle, 64 miles from Tacoma, and 67 miles from Sea-Tac International Airport. Sea-Tac is served by major national and international air carriers.

By car. Take I–5 south from Seattle to Exit 142A to Auburn, follow Rte. 164 to Rte. 410, east for 33 miles to the Crystal Mountain turnoff; go 6 miles up the road to the resort. Rte. 410 is closed to the east during winter months.

A **bus** runs twice daily from Enumclaw on Rte. 410; call (206) 663–2265 for schedules and rates.

TELEPHONES. The area code for Crystal Mountain is 206.

ACCOMMODATIONS. Lodging at Crystal Mountain is moderate by ski area standards. Prices range from $36 per night midweek to $140 for a 2-bedroom condo. Five-night packages, with lodging and lifts, start at $213 per person, double. Reservations can be made by calling 800–852–1444 or (206) 663–2558 for all accommodations except the Alpine Inn. All lodgings are at the ski area, and all guests register at the Silver Skis Chalet office (listed below).

Alpine Inn; 663–2262. Basic accommodations with shared or private bath (5-day package with breakfast and dinner from $268).

Crystal Chalets; 663–2558. Comfortable chalets nestled in the trees, with fireplace; sleep 1–4 people; some meal packages available.

Crystal House Hotel; 663–2558. Offers standard rooms by the night from $70 (1–4 persons). Located in the heart of the valley.

Silver Skis Chalet; 663–2558. Modest lodge geared for families or groups. A standard unit contains kitchen-living area and fireplace and sleeps 2–6 people; heated outdoor pool.

Village Inn; 663–2558. Next door to Crystal House, features country-style compact rooms; some meal packages.

RESTAURANTS. Since Crystal Mountain is a self-contained ski resort, visitors generally take their meals at the resort restaurants, where dining costs are *moderate* by ski resort standards, ranging from $7 to $15 for a dinner for one person, excluding tip, beverages, and tax. All restaurants can be reached through the resort's main telephone number, 663–2265.

Alpine Inn Restaurant has a varied menu and a fine wine selection; open 7 days a week serving 3 meals a day until 9 P.M.

Crystal Inn Dinner House features fine dining; open until 9 P.M. weekdays and 10 P.M. weekends.

Rafters is a full-service restaurant in the new lodge serving breakfast, lunch, and après-ski hors d'oeuvres.

Sporting Elk Deli in the Alpine Inn serves snacks in the European rathskeller tradition.

The Summit House, perched at the top of Crystal Mountain at 6,872 ft., is the highest restaurant in Washington State. Who cares if you ski or not? Just relax and enjoy the spectacular view of 14,410-ft. Mt. Rainier in the distance. Fast foods during ski season; full-service "sunset dinners" during the summer.

HOW TO GET AROUND. Everything at the ski area itself is within walking distance, so no transportation is needed. Shuttle **buses** are provided for transportation to and from the parking lots.

SEASONAL EVENTS. The **New Year's Eve** Torchlight Parade is an annual party. The *City League Team Race Series* program pits business rivals against each other on Wednesday and Sunday races during **January** and **February,** with finals held in early **March.** *Snow Golf* is in early **April**—test your clubs on snow while skiing (tournament with prizes).

OTHER SPORTS AND ACTIVITIES. The *Crystal Mountain Athletic Club* provides instruction for serious racers for national and international competition. Contact the club at 11425 136th Ave. East, Puyallup, WA 98373; 848–6389. **Cross-country** lessons are available at the ski school, as are downhill lessons.

DAY-CARE FACILITIES. *Crystal Mountain Childcare Center* (663–2300) is open from 8 A.M. to 4:30 P.M. for ages 2–7 years. Call for rates; reservations recommended. It is located in the Poolside Building next to the Crystal Inn Restaurant. Infants under 2 years are accepted midweek only for $16 a day or $2.50 an hour; reservations required.

NIGHTLIFE. Besides the restaurants there is *Rafters Lounge,* with entertainment Saturdays and Sundays. The *Pub* serves beer and wine on the D level of the day lodge. The *Crystal Inn Saloon* features live bands Friday and Saturday nights till 2 A.M. *The Sporting Elk Cellar,* in the Alpine Inn, is great for après-ski or deli snacks.

Wyoming

GRAND TARGHEE SKI RESORT

Alta WY via Driggs ID 83422
Tel: 307–353–2304

Snow Report: 800–443–8164
Area Vertical: 2,800 ft.
Number of Trails: 26 groomed trails, 3,000
*   skiable acres*
Lifts: 3 double chairlifts, 1 rope tow
Snowmaking: none
Season: mid-November–mid-April

Grand Targhee is on the "sunny side of the Tetons." Situated on the Idaho–Wyoming state line, Grand Targhee nestles up to the Teton Peaks, which soar high as a dramatic backdrop. The Teton Valley once was a battleground for Indians, fur trappers, and mountain men. Today, the valley is a thriving tourist and farming community.

Targhee's west slope of the Tetons has the reputation for being warmer than Jackson Hole, yet it receives more snow, an average of 500 inches yearly. The powder skiing is about the best you can find, with lots of open terrain and without the terrifying pitches of Jackson Hole—perfect for cruising through virgin powder after a fresh snowfall. Intermediate terrain makes up 70 percent of the mountain, 10 percent is beginner, and 20 percent is advanced. Besides the groomed trails, there are glades, bowls, and acres and acres of open skiing. Targhee runs daily Sno-Cat skiing excursions to its second mountain. This powder adventure gives skiers, guides, and patrolmen 1,500 acres and 2,800 feet of vertical to themselves. Snowboarders have a permanent half-pipe, along with lessons and rentals. There is also a full-service Nordic Skiing Center on site. New base facilities opened in 1990. Forty percent larger than those destroyed by a 1989 fire, they feature the latest safety codes and guest services. The new base is still only 50 yards from the lifts and the area has shops, restaurants, and an outdoor heated pool.

Expanded jet service to Jackson, WY, and Idaho Falls, ID, makes Targhee more accessible than ever before. The view from the summit includes three states, two national parks, the Jedediah Smith Wilderness, and the three Tetons as they were first seen by the French fur trappers in the 1820s. Locals who know their powder flock to Targhee, but the slopes stay uncrowded, the ambience is uncommercial, and the prices are relatively low.

287

Practical Information for Grand Targhee

HOW TO GET THERE. By air. Fly into Idaho Falls, ID, 87 miles to the west, on *Delta* or *Sky West* airlines via Salt Lake City. Or fly into Jackson, 42 miles to the east, direct from Chicago or Dallas/Ft. Worth on *American Airlines. Delta, Continental,* and *United Express* also fly into Jackson. (See *Practical Information for Jackson Hole*). With 48 hours' notice, the resort shuttle will meet incoming and outgoing flights; $20 one way, minimum of two people; children 12 and under are free with parents. For large groups, *TW Services,* 307–344–7311, runs charter buses as does *Teton Stage Line,* 208–529–8036. Traveling time is about an hour and a half from Jackson and 2 hours from Idaho Falls. Cars can be rented at the airport or in Targhee. General aviation (including private and charter flights) can use Driggs Airport, 13 miles from Grand Targhee. The runway is asphalt, 5,200 ft. long, and at 6,200 ft. elevation. Call *Grand Valley Aviation,* 208–354–8131. With 48 hours' notice, a resort van will meet incoming flights; $20 one way.

By car. From Idaho Falls it is 87 miles via Rtes. 26, 31, and 33 to Driggs, then 12 miles up the narrow, winding road to Grand Targhee. From Jackson Hole it is 42 miles over Teton Pass and up Targhee Road, the only one to the area. From Salt Lake City it is a 5-hour drive.

The *Targhee Express* **bus** goes between Targhee and Jackson every day. Call 800–443–8146 or 307–733–3101.

TELEPHONES. The area code for all of Wyoming is 307; for this section of Idaho it is 208.

ACCOMMODATIONS. The base area is a small western village with three lodges, four restaurants, a bar, a Kid's Club, five shops, outdoor heated pool, and hot tub. On packages of three days or longer, one child per paid adult skis free when staying in the same lodging unit.

Rates at Grand Targhee are in the *moderate* category compared to other resorts. On a 5-night, 4-day package with lift tickets included, for example, the **Targhee Lodge** is $295 per person, double occupancy. The **Teewinot Lodge** is around $325. The **Sioux Lodge Apartments** have studios for about $500 per person on the same package.

Combination packages to ski both sides of the Tetons are available. Start at Targhee to sharpen your technique, then tackle Jackson Hole. Call Grand Targhee Resort, 800–443–8146 or 307–353–2304, for information and reservations.

Lodging is also found in Driggs. Moderately priced ski packages are available at the **Best Western,** 426 N. Main St., Driggs, ID 83422; 800–528–1234; in western states, 800–252–2363, or 208–354–2363. The **Teton Teepee Lodge** in Alta, WY, via Driggs, 307–353–8176, offers complete packages, including meals, lift tickets, lessons, and transportation to the area.

Inexpensive ($18–$35 per night) Driggs lodging is found at the **Pines Motel,** 105 S. Main St.; 208–354–2774. In Victor, 7 miles south of Driggs, in the **Timberline Motel** at 38 W. Center St.; 208–787–2769.

RESTAURANTS. At the base of Grand Targhee and in the Teton Valley, restaurants lean toward the *Inexpensive* and *Moderate* categories, ranging from $7 to $16 for a dinner for one. In the moderate category, **Skadi's Fine Dining at Targhee** serves Continental food in an informal atmosphere. **Martin's Sleigh Ride Yurt Dinner** is a must for visitors—a sleigh ride followed by a dinner in a tent. Reservations necessary; call the resort at 307–353–2304. The **Beer and Brat Stand** on the lodge deck is open for lunch on sunny days. In the *Inexpensive* category are **Salsa de Border Mexican Restaurant, Cicero's Bistro,** and **Wild Bill's Grill.** All the above restaurants are conveniently located at the base of the mountain.

In Teton Valley, there is an Oriental restaurant that could be considered *expensive.* **Lost Horizons,** 353–8226, on the Wyoming side of the state line, is at the bottom of the road leading to Grand Targhee. Dining is an evening's experience; shoes are taken off at the door, drinks are served downstairs while diners go upstairs for a 10-course meal and a fabulous view of the Tetons through enormous windows. Fixed menu costs $30 per person.

Moderate (a full dinner for one costing $10–$25) restaurants include the **Knotty Pine,** 208–787–2276, for American food; and **Victor Steak Bank,** 208–787–2277, for American-style meats and some seafood.

Inexpensive (a full dinner for one costing under $10) places include **Joe's Place,** 208–354–2293, for homemade pizza and simple dinners; **Macho's,** 208–354–9981, for Mexican food; **O'Rouke's,** 208–354–8115, for burgers and pizza; and **Pierre's Rendezvous,** 208–354–2347, which also serves as the valley's only liquor store.

HOW TO GET AROUND. In Grand Targhee all facilities are within 50 yards of the lifts, so you can sleep late and still be the first on the lift. By staying in Driggs, the curvy, narrow 12-mile road must be negotiated twice a day—good enough reason for staying at the resort.

SEASONAL EVENTS. Each **December** the *Junior Olympics* hold qualifications; in **January** the *Idaho Area VII Special Olympics* and *Powder 8 Snowboard Contest* are scheduled; **March** sees the *Pro-Am* race.

OTHER SPORTS AND ACTIVITIES. Special complimentary **evening programs** include movies, a wine-and-cheese party, a casino night, and sleigh rides so guests can be entertained every night of the week. On Saturday night, the *Kid's Club* is open so parents have the evening to themselves.

Day trips are available to Yellowstone National Park, 90 miles north; Teton National Park, 50 miles east; National Elk Refuge, 50 miles east in Jackson; and **cross-country** trips surrounding Grand Targhee. Cross-country lessons are available for both track and telemark skiing for $40 per hour (private) and $18 (group). Back-country avalanche course and Telemark ski camps are offered. Rentals available.

Scenic **glider rides** are available year-round from *Grand Valley Aviation,* 208–354–8131. A flight over Grand Targhee goes for $65. A 206 Turbo carrying one to five passengers costs $145 per hour.

DAY-CARE FACILITIES. Children's programs are available during ski hours at the *Kid's Club* for $20 per day, including snacks and lunch. Ski-school classes are available for toddlers to 12-year-olds.

NIGHTLIFE. The resort's complimentary activities each evening are about all there is to do. The *Trap Bar,* in the Lodge, has nightly live music. For movie buffs the General Store has VCRs and videos for rent.

JACKSON HOLE SKI RESORT

Box 290
Teton Village WY 83025
Tel: 307–733–2292

Snow Report: 307–733–2291
Area Vertical: 4,139 ft.
Number of Trails: 58 on 2,500 acres
Lifts: 1 tram (63 passengers), 1 high-speed
quad, 2 pomas, 1 triple chairlift, and 5
double chairs
Snowmaking: on 2 percent of terrain
Season: early December–early April

Jackson Hole is actually a valley 10–40 miles wide and 50 miles long. The name refers to the resort on Rendezvous Mountain. The small village at the ski area is called "Teton Village," while the bigger town of Jackson is 12 miles away. They are at the foot of the Grand Teton Mountains, part of the Gros Ventre (pronounced gro-vont) Range. These are big, jagged, and impressive peaks; no rounded foothills loom as an approach to the ski runs. Jackson Hole has recently been trying to dispel the image that it originally gained of being only for experts.

An $8 million improvement plan begun in 1987 added two new lifts that provide skiers with an alternative to the long tram ride to the top of Rendezvous Mountain. This saves the extra $2 cost for the tram. One is a high-speed poma lift that takes skiers from the base of Rendezvous Bowl to the top of the mountain, at 2,500 feet and 900 feet vertical, in 3½ minutes. The other is a quad chair from the base of Laramie Bowl to high on the East Ridge, where skiers can ski into Tensleep Bowl to the north and the bottom of Rendezvous Bowl to the south.

This is the biggest lift-served vertical drop in North America, 4,139 feet. The resort covers 2,500 acres, with more than a hundred miles of runs. Only 22 miles are groomed, intermediate runs on Après Vous Mountain, and less than that for beginners. The rest is an expert's paradise. Rendezvous Bowl, served by the 63-passenger tram, is filled with couloirs and chutes, bowls, cliffs, the Hogbacks, all covered with ungroomed powder. And, if that's not enough, guides will take strong skiers to "secret" powder spots in the backcountry when conditions permit. Of course, you'd expect to find a top-notch ski school at an area like this, and you do. Skiers quickly develop their skills here so they can tackle the more challenging runs.

The abundant wildlife and natural beauty make cross-country skiing especially delightful. Trailheads from Teton Village go through Grand Teton National Park. Yellowstone Park is also nearby, accessible by snowcoach, snowmobile, or cross-country skis.

Practical Information for Jackson Hole

HOW TO GET THERE. By air. *American Airlines* has one flight daily between Dallas/Ft. Worth and Jackson, via Salt Lake City. From Chicago, American has nine round trips a week operating during ski season only. *Delta Airlines,* has nonstops from Salt Lake City. *Continental/Continental Express* has nonstops from Denver. *Sky West* and *Mesa Airlines* also fly from Denver. Jackson Hole shuttles meet every incoming commercial flight and drop off for departures. They service several points in the Teton Village and Jackson Hole area. The airport is 22 miles from Teton Village, the base area of Jackson Hole Ski Area, and 11 miles from the town of Jackson.

By car. Jackson Hole is 550 miles from Denver. Take I–25N to I–80W, to US 191, to US 89. From Salt Lake City, follow I–80 to Rte. 189, then to Rte. 89. From Idaho Falls, 100 miles to the west, take US 26 to Rtes. 31 and then 22.

TELEPHONES. The area code for all Wyoming is 307.

ACCOMMODATIONS. *Jackson Hole Central Reservations,* Box 20304, Jackson, WY 83001, 800–433–6931, can book your entire vacation, including airline tickets, accommodations, lift tickets, car rentals, and après-ski activities. Teton Village, at the base of Jackson Hole Ski Area, has several inns, a condo-style hotel, and a youth hostel. For the diehard skiers, the hostel is the place to be—a bed to fall into at the end of a hard ski day without a lot of late-night activity.

Condos, guest ranches, and resorts are found between Teton Village and the town of Jackson. In Jackson itself, there are numerous motels, coupled with down-home cowboy nightlife.

Although nightly rates may be available, Jackson Hole is just too far to travel to stay for just a day or two. The properties in Teton Village are all within a 5-minute walk of the lifts. Prices vary with amenities and season; rates quoted below are per person based on double occupancy.

Expensive

Alpenhof. Box 288, Teton Village, WY 83025; 733–3242. The closest to the lifts; heated outdoor pool, hot tubs, saunas, massage by appointment, game room, laundry facilities. A 7-day package, double occupancy, costs $440–$1,358 per person.

The Inn at Jackson Hole. Box 328, in Teton Village; 733–2311 or 733–3657. A full-service hotel with heated outdoor pool and Jacuzzi. A 7-day package runs $360–$920. Spacious houses are also available in the complex.

The Jackson Hole Racquet Club. Star Route, Box 362A, Jackson; 733–3990. A complete, year-round condominium resort complex. Guests have use of the athletic club with sauna, Jacuzzi, steam room, jogging track, lap pool, Nautilus, cross-country on the new Arnold Palmer championship golf course. A 1-bedroom condo or a 1-bedroom with loft goes for $150 and up. The club is located between the ski area and town.

The Spring Creek Ranch. Box 3154, Jackson, WY 83001; 2 miles from Jackson, 10 miles from Jackson Hole; 733–8833 or 800–443–6139. This resort on top of East Gros Ventre Butte is highly rated by AAA; there are condominiums, inn rooms, conference center.

Moderate

Americana Snow King Resort. Box SKI, Jackson; 733–5200. Has its own small Snow King ski area in the town of Jackson, a good practice hill with $20 lift tickets ($14 for children).

Crystal Springs Inn. Box 250, Teton Village; 733–4423. Motel-type lodging, 100 feet from aerial tram. A 7-day package costs $381–$444.

Sojourner Inn. Box 348, Teton Village; 733–3657. A European-style lodge with pool, sauna, Jacuzzi, game room. The newly decorated Mountain Lodge offers nicer rooms. Seven-day packages are $430–$616.

Wort Hotel. Box 89, Jackson; 733–2190. A half-block from the elk antler arches, this is a highly rated hotel.

RESTAURANTS. There are six restaurants in Teton Village, including two on the mountain. The atmosphere in the village is a combination of Austria and the Wild West. In Jackson, where there are numerous eateries, it is pure Wild West. Restaurant categories are *Expensive,* $15–$20; *Moderate,* $8–$15; *Inexpensive,* less than $8. These prices are for one meal for one person, exclusive of drinks or tip. Those in the expensive and moderate categories accept major credit cards.

Expensive

The Alpenhof Restaurant. In the Alpenhof; 733–3242. Wyoming's highest-rated restaurant; features veal, seafood, wild game, and delicious pastries. Serves 3 meals.

Steigler's Restaurant. At the Jackson Hole Racquet Club; 733–3990. Features Austrian specialties, topped off with apple strudel and Williams pear brandy.

Moderate

La Fondue. In the Sojourner Inn; 733–3657. An intimate restaurant featuring cheese, beef, and chocolate fondues; reservations suggested.

The Mangy Moose (733–4913) in Teton Village is a must. Everyone eats or drinks here at least once during a visit. Menu includes crab legs, barbecued ribs, salad bar. Dinner only.

The Steak House. In the Sojourner Inn; 733–3657. Supposedly has the best prime ribs in the area.

Dinner sleigh rides begin at the Tram building and go up Après Vous Mountain to a heated log cabin for a steak dinner. For reservations for the 2-hour dinner, call 733–6657.

In Jackson, the **Blue Lion,** 733–3912, is informal, featuring Continental cuisine and a full-service bar. The **Cadillac Grille,** 733–3279, on the west side of the town square, serves Mexican, Italian, and Chinese dishes in a 1940s art deco atmosphere. **Lame Duck,** 733–4311, 8 blocks east of the town square, has a wide variety of Szechuan, sushi, and sashimi—even American dishes and take-out service.

Inexpensive

At the slopes, **Valley Station Cafeteria** in the Tram building, no phone, features daily specials, good spaghetti dinners, all you can eat for $7.95. **The Village Store,** 733–4733, has breakfast and lunch as well as après-ski deli service. **Bear Claw Cafe,** 733–8715, serves breakfast, lunch, and après-ski buffalo burgers, soup, chili, and snack items. **Rocky Mountain Oyster,** downstairs from the Mangy Moose, 733–5525, has burgers, sandwiches, and skiers' specials for under $5.

On the way to Jackson on Village Road, the **Calico Pizza Parlor,** 733–2460, features delivery service to Teton Village and the Aspens.

In Jackson, **La Chispa Mexican Cafe,** downstairs from the Cowboy Bar, features standard and new Mexican dishes. **New York City Sub Shop,** 733–4414, serves Big Apple–style sandwiches and Philly cheese steaks.

HOW TO GET AROUND. Amenities and facilities are spread out in the 12 miles between the ski area and the town of Jackson. The local **bus** system is called *START* and runs daily between Teton Village, the Racquet Club, and town from 7 A.M. to 12 midnight. There is a $1 charge to ride the bus; books of 10 tickets may be purchased for $5 at the customer service center in Teton Village, Jackson Hole Racquet Club, or the Wort Hotel in Jackson. **Rental car** agencies in Jackson are *Avis,* 733–3422; *Budget,* 733–2206; *Dollar,* 733–9226; *Hertz,* 733–2272; *Jackson Hole Car Rental,* 733–6868; and *National,* 733–4132.

SEASONAL EVENTS. In **January,** the *NCAA Championships* are held. The now-famous *Powder 8 Championships* are the highlight each **February.** Held in Cody Bowl on Rendezvous Mountain, expert powder skiers swirl down the mountain to form the most perfect set of figure-eights for the judges. In **March,** the *National Para-ski Championships* are held. Parachutists try to steer to a landing point on the mountain and hit a disc only a few inches in diameter; points for this are combined with points in a ski race to determine the winner.

Then there is the annual *Pole-Paddle-Paddle* competition in **April.** Only for the hardiest, it starts off with a timed race down Rendezvous Mountain, followed by a 10-km nordic leg, a 20-mile bicycle run, and finally a 9-mile kayak paddle in the icy spring waters.

OTHER SPORTS AND ACTIVITIES. Skiing is the primary draw, of course. The *Ski the Big One* program awards pins for those who ski 100,000 or 150,000 vertical feet in any one week, or 300,000, 500,000 or 1 million vertical feet in a lifetime at Jackson Hole. Contact the *Marketing Department,* 733–2292, for details. The *Ski Week* instructional programs provide people with the same instructor for a week of maximum learning. Five half-day and full-day packages are available, with video tape evaluation. Also *Mountain Experience* classes, alpine guides, and ski-racing camps. Contact *Ski School* director Pepi Stiegler, 733–2292.

There are four **nordic touring** centers, each with lodging: *Jackson Hole Karhu Center* at Teton Village; *Spring Creek Ranch; Togwotee Mountain Touring Center,* 45 miles north of Jackson; and *Teton Mountain Touring* at Grand Targhee, an hour's ride on the other side of Teton Pass. **Cross-country** skiing goes through Grand Teton National Park, Yellowstone National Park, and Bridger-Teton and Targhee National forests. Rental equipment is available, as are lessons, videos, clinics, and ski tours. Call 800–443–6931 for information on all the touring centers.

There is **snowmobiling** in Yellowstone, Granite Hot Springs (the water is 100° F), Grand Teton, and Togwotee Pass (snowmobile maps available at the Jackson Chamber of Commerce); **sleigh rides** of 45 minutes into the largest remaining elk herd in the United States at the National Elk Refuge; **helicopter skiing** or a snowcoach ride into Yellowstone National Park—have lunch, see the geysers and the elk and bison foraging in the steam. Pick up a free copy of *The Village Focus* for the latest in activities, events, and schedules.

CHILDREN'S ACTIVITIES. The *Ski School* features the SKIwee program for children 4–12 years old. This is a special child-centered teaching approach with games and ski instruction. *Kinderschule* has day care for all kids over age 2, lunch included. Children from 3 to 5 years old can be enrolled in group ski lessons held from 10–11:30 A.M. and 2–3:30 P.M. For advanced beginners only.

NIGHTLIFE. It all starts at the *Mangy Moose* in Teton Village—good view, good entertainment, and noisy crowd. A little more sedate is *Dietrich's Bar and Lounge* in the Alpenhof; cozy, ski movies, drink specials. *Wingback Lounge* at the Inn is comfy, too. *Stockman's Lounge* in the Sojourner Inn features ski movies, free hors d'oeuvres, drink specials.

For later-night activity, Jackson is the place and cowboy is the theme. The *Million Dollar Cowboy Bar* is rowdy and rough, where you can shoot a game of pool; live entertainment to 2 A.M. The *Silver Dollar Bar* and the newly remodeled *Rancher* complete the "Bermuda Triangle" of popular Western bars. The *Shady Lake Saloon* in Americana Snow King Resort features live entertainment; ladies night Monday with free champagne. Or just walk down Jackson's wooden sidewalks, push open a swinging door, and find your own saloon. In Wilson, rub elbows with the cowboys at the *Stagecoach.*

EASTERN CANADA

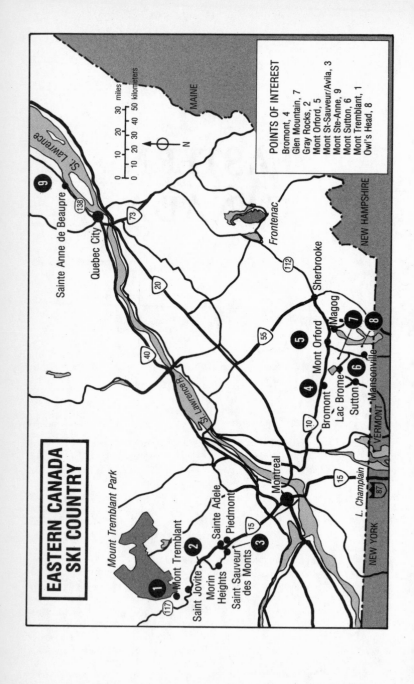

EASTERN CANADA SKI COUNTRY

POINTS OF INTEREST
Bromont, 4
Glen Mountain, 7
Gray Rocks, 2
Mont Orford, 5
Mont St-Sauveur/Avila, 3
Mont Ste-Anne, 9
Mont Sutton, 6
Mont Tremblant, 1
Owl's Head, 8

MAINE

St. Lawrence

Frontenac

N

0 10 20 30 miles
0 10 20 30 40 50 kilometers

Sainte Anne de Beaupre

Quebec City

138

73

20

40

55

112

Sherbrooke

Magog

Mont Orford

5

7

8

4

Bromont

Lac Brome

6

Sutton

Mansonville

10

NEW HAMPSHIRE

VERMONT

Mount Tremblant Park

Mont Tremblant

1

Saint Jovite

Morin Heights

Sainte Adele

Piedmont

2

Saint Sauveur des Monts

3

15

117

St. Lawrence R.

Montreal

15

L. Champlain

87

NEW YORK

EASTERN CANADA

Quebec

by
GUY THIBAUDEAU

The words of French-Canadian poet Gilles Vigneault are most befitting to winter in Quebec. Says Vigneault: "Mon pays ce n'est pas un pays, c'est l'hiver!" (My country is not a country, it's winter!)

Quebec is a land of winter, and while the summers are warm and pleasant, the winters are long and snowy. It is the capital of skiing in Canada. It does not have the vertical elevation and the scope of Western Canadian resorts, but it has more ski areas per capita and more ski facilities than most other provinces or states in North America.

There are more than 100 alpine areas and about twice as many cross-country centers catering to everyone's needs. From the lofty, unexplored peaks in the Gaspésie to the impeccably groomed ski highways of Gray Rocks, from small historical villages where the locals don't ski but are experts at hospitality to modern 20th-century cities, skiing in Quebec runs as deep as the snow that covers its mountains. It's a celebration of winter done with a zest and *joie de vivre* that makes a skiing vacation in Quebec something very special. It's called "Skiing à la Française" and its unique flavor has kept winter visitors coming back year after year.

Of the 6.5 million inhabitants of Quebec there are more than 800,000 alpine skiers and 1.6 million cross-country skiers. Skiing here, more than in any other province of Canada, is a way of life.

Quebec boasts seven distinct ski regions:

The Laurentians, north of Montreal, have 26 alpine and as many cross-country areas.

The Eastern Townships, southeast of Montreal and north of the U.S. border, contain 10 alpine areas and half a dozen good cross-country centers.

The Quebec City region has four alpine centers.

The Outaouais, north of the national capital Ottawa, has five areas.

Charlevoix, a developing region northeast of Quebec City, contains two alpine areas and plenty of off-trail skiing.

Lanaudière, northeast of Montreal, has seven areas running parallel to the Laurentians.

The Gaspésie, in the Gaspé Peninsula at the mouth of the mighty St. Lawrence River, has nine alpine areas.

For North Americans, a ski vacation in Quebec is the closest thing to a European holiday. And while Quebec areas are no match for the Alps, life in Quebec combines the comforts and standards of North America with the charm and cosmopolitan atmosphere of the Old World. French is the official language of Quebec, but you'll have no trouble being understood in English except in a few remote villages east of Quebec City on the North Shore.

Quebec has a preponderance of great eateries. Deluxe restaurants abound in Quebec City, Montreal, and surrounding regions. In North America, the only other cities to rival Montreal for food are New York and San Francisco; in Canada, it has no match. The best onion soup this side of Paris and local specialties, such as French-Canadian *tourtière* and *ragout* all the way to the more common chicken barbecue, are sure to tempt and please all tastes.

Montreal is the economic hub of the province. With a population of more than 2.5 million, it is the most cosmopolitan of Canadian cities. Being one of Canada's first cities, its architecture was strongly influenced by the French and the British.

Some of Montreal's landmarks are Mont Royal, the mountain in the heart of the city. Several lookouts will give you a scenic, bird's-eye view of the city from various angles. Mont Royal also has a 7.5-kilometer cross-country trail beautifully maintained by the city. From it are scenic views of downtown Montreal; you can almost touch the highrises.

Quebec City is the second largest city in Quebec. Its population of 650,000 is mostly French. The Upper Town overlooks the St. Lawrence River and is mostly residential. The Lower Town harbors industrial and commercial facilities.

Of particular interest is Old Quebec, with its cobblestone streets and protected garrison, a well-preserved testimony of colonial days. Fine restaurants, bars, and bistros provide visitors to Quebec with an even more genuine taste of French Quebec.

Lately, the exchange rate for Americans traveling to Quebec has been extremely favorable, and with skiing rates in the province already lower than in the U.S., a treasure of bargains awaits the budget-conscious traveler.

Since 1983, the tourism branch of the Quebec Government has been strongly supportive of skiing, encouraging and subsidizing the necessary infrastructure to make skiing in Quebec competitive with the rest of eastern North America.

Modern facilities are second to none. Quads and high-speed quad chairs are sprouting up every year at the more popular resorts to whisk a maximum number of skiers to various mountain tops, ensuring more time on the slopes. High-speed detachable quads are revolutionizing uphill technology. The difference between a fixed triple and a detachable quad is more than one more skier on the chair. It is almost as revolutionary as was the change from the rope-tow to the T-bar. The detachable quad allows you to board the chair when it is moving very slowly. You board as easily as you sit on a park bench. When the chair clamps onto the main cable, the chair accelerates to a speed more than double that of a fixed chair. Hence more comfort, more capacity, more safety, and less time waiting in the lift line.

Despite dependable winters, all of Quebec's major resorts have snowmaking covering from 50 to 100 percent of their skiing terrain. The popularity of skiing in Quebec and the relatively high level of proficiency of Quebec skiers has made snowmaking as necessary as lifts to prevent sharp-edged carved turns from breaking through to the ground.

Quebec's leading destination resorts are principally Mont Ste-Anne near Quebec City, Mont Tremblant, and Gray Rocks in the Laurentians north of Montreal; the Eastern Townships centers are Mont Sutton, Mont Orford, and Bromont.

If skiing continues to develop successfully, more areas now on the drawing board are likely to become reality. Le Massif at Petite Rivière St. François could become a giant in the same league as Killington, Vermont. Vertical in excess of 2,600 ft., there are plans for up to 14 lifts. And Mont Ste-Anne continues its aggressive development that could, in the next decade, increase the mountain's capacity by 40–50 percent. It is Quebec's flagship resort.

Skiing in Quebec has long been discovered by its residents. Skiing à la Française is fast becoming a contender in the North American ski market and a destination unlike anywhere else on this continent.

Travel information can be obtained by calling *Tourism Quebec* at 800–443-7000 from the U.S., and 800–361–6490 from Ontario and the Maritimes.

Note: Remember, all prices quoted in the Eastern Canada section of this guide are in **Canadian dollars.**

The Laurentians

Skiing as a sport originated in Norway in the late 1800s, but it was via the Laurentian Mountains north of Montreal that skiing made its foray into the North American continent.

Early in 1879, a Norwegian who had recently immigrated to Montreal appeared on skis. For Montrealers, who were most familiar with snowshoes in those days, skis were seen as a variation of the snowshoes and were in fact named "Norwegian snowshoes." At 9 feet long, 6 inches wide, with a toe-strap and a foot board, they made curious-looking snowshoes.

Although skiing had made an early appearance in Montreal, it was only in the early 1900s that it began to develop as a sport. In 1904, the Montreal Ski Club was formed with 50 members. In 1909, skiing was part of the Montreal Winter Carnival. But it was after World War I that skiing finally took off. By 1920, the Montreal Ski Club Annual described skiing as "the king of winter sports in Montreal."

From the 1920s to the 1940s, ski trains took skiers north. Trails were opened for cross-country skiing by another Norwegian immigrant, Herman Smith-Johannsen, nicknamed "Jackrabbit" for his quickness and agility on skis. Johannsen is known as the "father of Laurentian skiing." He, more than anyone else, promoted skiing by blazing trails, organizing competitions, and coaching. At age 102 Johannsen was still skiing; at 110, he was still promoting skiing. He died in his 112th year on January 6th, 1987.

Another greatly influential figure in the development of Laurentian and North American skiing was Louis Cochand, who came to the Laurentide Inn in Ste. Agathe in 1911 from Switzerland to give the "first ski lessons in Canada and North America."

In 1932, Alex Foster installed the first mechanical ski tow in North America. The first T-bar in the Laurentians was installed at Gray Rocks in 1934. In 1938, Mont Tremblant inaugurated the first chairlift in Canada.

Skiing has since become the region's leading industry. There are now more than 26 alpine skiing areas with over 100 lifts, including the most modern in lift technology, high-speed (detachable) quad chairs. Every year, the snowmaking capacity is increased at the major resorts. All major areas now have at least 50 percent of their skiing terrain covered with machine-made snow.

More enchantment came to the high country with night skiing. Late afternoon and night skiing is as popular as day skiing in the Laurentians, particularly in the St-Sauveur–Ste. Adèle region where seven of the ten areas that offer night skiing are found. What a pleasure for the avid skier for whom ski days are always too short! And what a sight for those who just enjoy sitting in a comfortable lounge with a view of the brightly lit hills.

Cross-country skiing is also very popular in the Laurentians, with hundreds of kilometers of trails linking villages such as Ste. Agathe, Val David, Val Morin, Ste. Adèle, Ste. Marguerite, Morin Heights, and St-Sauveur. Within meters of every lodge and hotel, there is a trail that permits you to link up with the main network. The Laurentians are a wonderland for the cross-country skier.

The Laurentian Mountains are blessed with abundant snow and good snow retention. Boosted by snowmaking, the season extends from mid-November to mid-April.

You will find professional ski schools at all major resorts. All full-time instructors are members of the Canadian Ski Instructors' Alliance.

There is lodging for every taste and budget in the Laurentians—from resort hotels, inns, and motels to condominiums, chalets, and youth hostels. From all-inclusive ski week packages to weekday and weekend specials, Laurentian hospitality is available everywhere at affordable prices. Eating in the Laurentians is legendary as it is throughout most of Quebec. And nighttime activities are as diversified as the skiing itself.

Getting around in the Laurentians is simple enough. The toll-free Laurentian Autoroute 15, paralleled by Highway 117, is the backbone of the region, with towns and villages strewn along the way from St. Jerome, the gateway to the Laurentians, to Ste. Jovite, the end of the run for alpine skiers. Nowadays the Laurentians are the playground of Montrealers. Numerous lakes, coupled with skiing in winter, have made the region the most popular four-season cottage country for thousands of residents of southwestern Quebec. And because of the region's proximity to Montreal—less than one hour's drive—more and more are making the Laurentians their permanent residence.

Colonized in great proportion by the Catholic Church and Curé Labelle who promoted the extension of the railway north of St. Jérome in the late 1800s, the region has long since lost its frontier character. With the advent of the railway came growth to the region and the development of tourism. From the 1930s to the early 1950s, the famous Laurentian Ski Trains shuttled thousands of skiers every weekend to ski the hills of St-Sauveur, Morin Heights, Ste. Marguerite and Ste. Adèle.

The construction of the autoroute in the mid-1950s opened the region to automobile traffic and marked the end of the ski train era. Efforts to revive the ski trains in the 1970s during the gas shortage failed. Skiers were too spoiled by the luxury of driving directly to the hills.

The Laurentians are home to more than 26 alpine areas between St. Jérome and Mont Tremblant. There are hundreds of miles of cross-country ski trails linking every village and hotel. The greatest concentration of skiing is between St-Sauveur and Ste. Agathe. Off that 25-mile stretch of Hwy. 117 or Autoroute 15, there is a choice of some 20 alpine areas and probably 500 miles of cross-country skiing. A map-filled booklet describing all the best Laurentians cross-country centers is published by *Ski de Fond Laurentides Inc,* 514–436–4051, and is available at many sports shops, convenience stores, and other commercial outlets throughout the region.

GRAY ROCKS

Box 1000
St. Jovite PQ JOT 2H0
Tel: 514–861–0187 or 819–425–2771

Snow Report: 819–425–2771
Area Vertical: 190 meters (620 ft.)
Number of Trails: 18
Lifts: 1 quad, 3 double chairs
Snowmaking: 85 percent of trails
Season: mid-November–early May

In terms of statistics, this mountain is a shrimp compared with the giants with which it competes for skiers every year. But in terms of its success, it rates with the best. This is where the season begins for most skiers around Montreal, and it has consistently been among the first areas in Quebec to open with good conditions year after year.

Snowmaking and grooming are an art here, and excellence in snow conditions is the number-one priority. And for good reason: with a relatively small vertical the area must offer distinctively and consistently better skiing conditions to succeed.

Snowmaking begins at Gray Rocks in early November and runs unabated until early March. Neither storm, wind, nor extreme cold will stop the snow factory at this area. The snow guns shut down only when temperatures rise above freezing. Snow is built up 10–15 feet thick in spots most vulnerable to the spring sun. Snow reserves are built up near lift terminals to be transported, as needed, when the season stretches into late April and May. One year there were leaves on the trees and flies on your neck, but skiers were still schussing.

The mountain's 18 runs on three different exposures offer a very pleasant skiing experience. And although the trail length is limited, there is something for everyone, from beginner to advanced. The west side pitches, "Devil's Dip" and "Bon Voyage," will make you realize that skiing at Gray Rocks is not only for beginners. A quad and three double chairs service the area, which was challenging enough in the 1950s to produce Canada's first international ski star, Lucille Wheeler, who in 1958 won gold medals in giant slalom and downhill at the FIS Games in Bad Gastein, Austria.

But Gray Rock's reputation is built on more than just great skiing. In 1951, Gray Rocks packaged a week of skiing, including lessons and accommodations, for the Ski Club of Washington, DC. The Ski Week was invented. From that point on, the area has been filled to capacity from mid-November to mid-April with skiers and would-be skiers whose main purpose is to learn to ski or improve their technique while having fun doing it.

The Snow Eagle Ski School built by Real Charette has no equal in the East. At full capacity, there are 50 certified Canadian ski instructors dishing out the "bend zee knees" to over 500 guests. The ski school and its instructors are fully integrated into the ski week activities in much the same way as the G.O. (activities director) at a Club Med. In fact, the ski vacation concept at Gray Rocks is an all-inclusive one where the package covers most expenses, save for bar bills. Today, Gray Rocks' renowned ski week includes accommodations for seven days/six nights, 19 meals from Sunday lunch, unlimited use of ski lifts, and 22 hours of ski instruction.

It was also on the modest slopes of Gray Rocks that the modern North American skiing technique evolved. In the mid-1940s, an Austrian immigrant named Luggi Foeger escaped Nazi-occupied Austria, settled at Gray Rocks, and began to teach the Arlberg skiing technique that he had learned in St. Anton from its creator, Hannes Schneider.

This family-operated area was developed somewhat accidentally at the turn of the century, when an American named George Wheeler built a sawmill that led to a profitable construction business. Enchanted by the beauty of the area, many of Wheeler's friends came up to visit while enjoying the good hunting and fishing in the region. In 1906 the Wheelers built the inn that is still an integral part of the much-extended complex.

Guests of Gray Rocks are treated to nothing but the best. Meals feature extensive table d'hôte menus of French and French-Canadian cuisine for gourmets and gourmands alike. Skiing is usually enough for most to work off the extra meal calories, but for those who need more exercise, there is a complete fitness center, including a lap-pool, sauna, whirlpool, and numerous exercise machines such as Lifecycle bikes, rowing machines, and the Nordic-Track cross-country skiing simulator.

Located within sight of famous Mont Tremblant, Gray Rocks lures skiers who wish to test their newly acquired skiing skills before taking on longer, more demanding slopes.

Although skiing is what has made Gray Rocks world famous, the inn is busy year-round. Situated on the shores of Lac Ouimet, the beautifully flowered property covers more than 2,000 acres, including a scenic 18-hole golf course, 22 Har Tru tennis courts, and a tennis school that is associated with the Van der Meer Tennis University and is building a reputation to match the ski school.

Practical Information for Gray Rocks

HOW TO GET THERE. Montreal is the gateway to the Laurentians and to Gray Rocks.

By car. Montreal's two major airports are Dorval, for North American traffic, and Mirabel, for international destinations. The latter is conveniently located 20 minutes north of Montreal at the gateway to the Laurentians. However, few flights from the United States terminate at Mirabel. All North American traffic runs through Dorval, but a few international airlines, such as *Aerolinas Argentinas* from Buenos Aires and Rio de Janeiro via New York; *Sabena* from Chicago; *Lan Chile* from Santiago, Miami, and New York; and *Royal Air Maroc* from Morocco via New York's John F. Kennedy Airport terminate at Mirabel and have pick-up rights from U.S. gateway cities. Flying into Mirabel is preferable if you are not planning to visit Montreal.

Dorval offers a full slate of **car rental** companies including the big four: *Avis,* 800–331–1212; *Budget,* 800–527–0700; *Hertz,* 800–654–3131; and *Tilden,* the Canadian affiliate of *National,* 800–328–4567.

By air. Located 120 km (about 80 miles) north of Montreal, Gray Rocks is easily accessible via Laurentian Autoroute 15, a toll-free expressway that is linked to all of Montreal's major highways. Follow the autoroute to the end, where it merges with Hwy. 117. Follow signs to Mont Tremblant and you will arrive at Gray Rocks.

TELEPHONES. The area code for Gray Rocks is 819; for Montreal, it is 514.

ACCOMMODATIONS. Gray Rocks is the complete resort and vacationers stay at the *Gray Rocks Inn* or at adjacent *Le Chateau,* a smaller but equally attractive lodge on the lake less than a mile from the inn. Both are on the American Plan, which includes lodging, meals, and much of the recreation. The inn is the center of all activity for ski and tennis weeks and is the larger of the two. The chateau's dining room and lounge are smaller and more intimate, offering a nice change of pace. Daily rates run from $98–$165 based on double occupancy and type of accommodation. Weekly rates run from $715–$1,042 on the American Plan. Weekend rates are also available.

RESTAURANTS. Because of the all-inclusive nature of a Gray Rocks vacation, all meals are taken at the hotel. The menu is different every day and about the only complaint ever voiced is that there is too much to eat! Nonetheless, if you wish to sample local restaurants in the region, there are a number of excellent ones at adjacent Mont Tremblant. (See *Mont Tremblant* section for suggestions.)

HOW TO GET AROUND. Everything is quite centrally located around the inn and you are always within walking distance of all facilities. However there are free **shuttle vans** to take you and your equipment to any point on the property should you need assistance or be unable to walk. This van is in regular service between the chateau and the inn, a distance of less than a mile.

SEASONAL EVENTS. *Canadian Ski-Laser Yachting Championships* are usually held on the first or second weekend in **May.** This unique event combines alpine skiing on the slopes of Gray Rocks one day with a Laser class sailing regatta on adjacent Lac Oumet the next. The combination of snow on the slopes and sailboats on the lake makes for a spectacular sight. On that weekend, the golf course and tennis courts are often open with skiers purchasing a day lift ticket entitled to use all facilities that are open.

Every **summer,** the *Gray Rocks Tennis School* teams up with the world-famous tennis school, *Van der Meer Tennis University,* for special, intensive week-long sessions. Information on dates and programs are available by writing or phoning Gray Rocks.

OTHER SPORTS AND ACTIVITIES. Cross-country skiing is quite plentiful around Gray Rocks. The area maintains 18 km of track-set trails on its golf course and from there you can tie in with the 90-km St. Jovite–Mont Tremblant Ski Club network. Nearby Domaine St. Bernard, which is run by monks, also offers a fine network in a most scenic environment.

Gray Rocks has a fully equipped fitness center that includes a lap **pool, whirlpools, sauna,** a dance **aerobics** room with regular classes, and a fully equipped **gym** with Nautilus, Global Gym, Nordic Track equipment, rowing machines, ergometers, and Monarch stationary bicycles. In addition, Gray Rocks offers fitness tests and computerized nutrition analyses.

Sleigh rides, movies, and a complete and diversified fare of indoor activities and entertainment are organized in conjunction with **ski weeks.**

Ski weeks at Gray Rocks usually have an optional ski day at Mont Tremblant. Another area worth visiting in the region is Mont Blanc in St. Faustin on Hwy. 117. St. Faustin is the first village south of Ste. Jovite and you will pass Mont Blanc on the left side of the highway as you drive up. With a vertical rise of 300 meters, it is the second highest peak in the Laurentians. Two triple chairs, one double chair, and four surface lifts service 25 runs, 12 of which have snowmaking. After Mont Tremblant this area offers the most challenging slopes in the Laurentians.

NIGHTLIFE. You need not look very far for nightlife at Gray Rocks. Live music and nightly entertainment make it the place where outsiders come for a good time. The *Thirsty Eagle Bar* is the focal point of the region's après-ski life. Here, you're as likely to meet someone from Florida up for the annual ski trip as you are to meet a ski instructor from one of the neighboring lodges. The bar has two main live periods: after skiing between 4 and 6 P.M. and in the evening from 8 P.M. on. There are also discos at the *Villa Bellevue Hotel,* just a mile up the road from Gray Rocks and at the base of Mont Tremblant. (See *Mont Tremblant* section.)

MONT ST-SAUVEUR/AVILA

Box 910
St-Sauveur-des-Monts PQ JOR 1RO
Tel: 514–227–4671

Snow Report: 514–277–4671
Area Vertical: 700 ft.
Number of Trails: 33 on 100 acres
Lifts: 3 high-speed quads, 1 triple chair, 3
  double chairs, 1 T-bar, 1 Pony lift
Snowmaking: 70 percent of the trails
Season: mid-November–mid-April

Back in 1934, an American named Fred Pabst, son of the Milwaukee brewer, installed the first permanent ski lift on the slopes of St-Sauveur, and for a time Hill 70 was one of the most famous ski hills in eastern Canada.

As the area grew in popularity, a group of businessmen joined Victor Nymark in 1945 to create Uphill Ltd. Four years later, in 1949, they imported from Austria the first T-bar to be installed in North America and St-Sauveur-des-Monts became the cradle of skiing in eastern Canada. That first T-bar on Hill 70 was soon followed by tows on Hills 67–72, which are to this day the main ones at the area.

Nowadays, the 700-foot vertical of Mont St-Sauveur, with its 450 acres, has been totally retrofitted. Slopes have been widened and recut, old lifts repositioned, and brand-new ones installed to handle the many skiers who make this the most popular area in the Laurentians. Among the area's seven lifts, two high-speed quads ensure both a rapid ascent and a good capacity. A modern snowmaking system covers 70 percent of the skiing terrain and a fleet of the most sophisticated grooming machines guarantees the best possible conditions.

Although Mont St-Sauveur was not the first to offer night skiing, it was the first to make it the big deal that it now is. From "candlelight" skiing on one or two runs in 1973, the area now offers night skiing on 19 of its 24 runs, backed up by over 1.1 million watts of lighting power.

In elevation, several neighboring areas approach Mont St-Sauveur's vertical, but the length of the runs is not what draws crowds to the area. Mont St-Sauveur is the place to be as well as the place to be seen. The first area in Quebec to pay attention to details and to market its skiing through activities and promotions, it has attracted skiing's leaders. The crowds have followed. If a star is going to be seen skiing anywhere, it's likely to be at St-Sauveur. If a picture of a bikini-clad skiing beauty is to make the front page of the Montreal papers announcing the arrival of spring skiing, it is likely to have been shot at Mont St-Sauveur.

The base lodge, built in 1978, is a combination stage and jewel box. It is the focal point of all activities at the area, which occasionally can make for some congestion even though it was almost doubled in size in 1985. But services are built with crowds in mind and even on the busiest day you can eat, rent your skis, and purchase your ticket without waiting too long.

In summer 1987, Mont St-Sauveur acquired the adjacent Avila Ski Center, adding nine new runs, for a total of 33. Although both areas are run separately, skiers purchasing a Mont St-Sauveur ticket gain free access to Avila. Transfer from one area to the other is made easy through interconnecting trails. With its 33-trail network, the Mont St-Sauveur/Avila complex is the largest in the lower Laurentians.

Practical Information for Mont St-Sauveur/Avila

HOW TO GET THERE. By air. Montreal's two major airports are Dorval for North American traffic and Mirabel for international destinations. The latter is most conveniently located 20 minutes south of St-Sauveur at the gateway to the Laurentians. Most North American flights terminate at Dorval. However, a few international carriers such as *Aerolinas Argentina, Sabena, Lan Chile,* and *Royal Air Maroc* have pick-up rights at some major U.S. gateway cities, such as New York, Chicago, and Miami. Flying into Mirabel is preferable if you are not planning to visit Montreal.

Dorval offers a full slate of **car rental** companies including the big four: *Avis,* 800–331–1212; *Budget,* 800–527–0700; *Hertz,* 800–654–3131; and *Tilden,* the Canadian affiliate of *National,* 800–328–4567.

By car. Montreal is the gateway to the Laurentians and to Mont St-Sauveur. Located 60 km (about 40 miles) north of Montreal, it is easily accessible via Laurentian Autoroute 15. Take Exit 58 off the Laurentian autoroute and follow signs to Mont St-Sauveur.

TELEPHONES. The area code for the Mont St-Sauveur region of Quebec is 514.

ACCOMMODATIONS. *Village Mont St-Sauveur,* slopeside condominiums, are available through Mont St-Sauveur, Box 910, St Sauveur-des-Monts PQ, JOR 1R0; 514–227–4671. These beautifully appointed ski-in, ski-out condos are furnished with sleeping accommodations for up to six people. Attractive 2–5 day packages are available, including lift tickets, accommodations, and the option of lessons and rentals.

Most of the above condos are in the *expensive* category (above $75 per person per night), depending on the time of year, number of persons per unit, and number of consecutive days' stay. Prices, however, begin as low as $32 per person per day based on four people in a 2-bedroom unit. Other categories in this listing are *Moderate,* $50–$75, and *Inexpensive,* less than $50 per night.

Auberge St. Denis. *Expensive.* 61 St. Denis; 227–4602 or toll free 800–361–5724. Located midway between the slopes and the village's main street, this charming French-Canadian lodge offers 42 luxurious rooms, including 24 executive suites, plus exceptional French cuisine.

Manoir St. Sauveur. *Expensive.* 246 Chemin du Lac Millette; 227–1811 or toll free from the United States and Canada 800–361–0505. This 200-room hotel opened in the winter of 1988–89. The largest hotel in the valley, it features oversize rooms, in-room movies, underground parking, indoor pool, exercise room, squash courts, and more. Located within view of Mont St-Sauveur, it's about a 2-minute car or shuttle bus ride from the slopes.

Auberges des Ameriques. *Moderate.* 101 Principale; 227–1831. Located within a 5-minute drive from the slopes, this inn has 32 comfortable rooms (no kitchenettes or fireplaces in rooms). Special packages are available. The auberge is well known for its restaurant *Le Boulevard des Océans,* which specializes in seafood and steak.

L'Auberge de la Vallée. *Moderate.* 520 Principale; 227–5998. Dining room, bar, ski week packages.

Hotel Chateaumont. *Moderate.* 50 Principale; 227–1821. This recently opened (1987–88) inn has 32 luxurious rooms with fireplaces. Also has sauna and exercise room and offers packages. It is located approximately 5 minutes by car from St-Sauveur's slopes.

Motel Jolibourg. *Moderate.* 60 Principale; 227–4651. Motel with panoramic view; rooms with fireplaces. Rates include Continental breakfast.

Motel des Pentes. *Moderate.* Box 789, 12 Laning St.; 227–5351. In the village, this motel is located within 5 minutes of the area on Hwy. 364 which runs through the village. Most units have kitchenettes. Chalets with 2 or 5 bedrooms plus fireplace and kitchenette are also available on a weekly basis.

Motel le 60. *Moderate.* 600 Chemin des Frênes; 227–4880. You can't miss it. Located at exit 60 of the Laurentian autoroute, the exit for St-Sauveur-des-Monts. Rooms with fireplaces and kitchenettes; packages available.

Pension du Cap. *Inexpensive.* 270 Chemin Constantineau; 227–3424. Low-cost, clean bed and breakfast with good atmosphere and pleasantly located on the Simon River. Less than 10 minutes from ski areas.

RESTAURANTS. If there is something St-Sauveur is famous for, other than skiing, it is the quality and diversity of its dining establishments. Whatever your taste or budget you'll find numerous places to suit you. Price categories are as follows: *Expensive,* $20–$30; *Moderate* $15–$20; *Inexpensive,* less than $15. These prices are for one meal, excluding drinks, tips, and taxes. Restaurants accept most major credit cards unless indicated otherwise.

Expensive

La Gascogne. 358 Principale; 227–5171. Fine French cuisine and excellent rack of lamb.

Gibby's. 414 Principale; 227–2623. Excellent steaks and seafood served in style. Dining room has 3 fireplaces. Meal portions are large and most orders come with appetizers. Reservations recommended, particularly weekends and holidays. Dinners only.

Da Tulio's. 389 Principale; 227–4313. Italian haute cuisine, considered the best in the region. Always a busy place; reservations recommended. Dinners only.

Marie Philip. 352 Principale; 227–2171. A very highly rated French nouvelle cuisine restaurant for diners of discriminating taste and broad means. Reservations necessary.

Moderate

Le Biftheque. Rue de la Gare, corner Chemin de la Vallée, 227–2442. The largest steakhouse in the Laurentians, Le Biftheque is affiliated with one of Montreal's best-known beef eateries. From steaks to side dishes to prices, you can count on it. Open for both lunch and dinner.

Le Charbon De Bois. 314 Principale; 227–6465. Specializes in steaks.

Le Jardin des Oliviers. 239 Principale; 227–2110. Exceptionally fine French-Provençale cuisine served with a personal touch. Lunch and dinner; 7 days a week.

Le Kindli. 22 Lafleur North; 227–2229. Swiss with some French cuisine featuring raclette, fondues, steaks, veal, and brochettes. Closed Tuesdays.

La Vieille Ferme. 967 Principale; 227–3083. Typical old-time French-Canadian farmhouse serving steaks and seafood and featuring roast beef dinner Sunday evenings.

Moderate–Inexpensive

Le Chalet Grec. 138 Principale; 227–6612. Greek specialties; bring your own wine.

Le Jardin Lee. 163 Principale; 227–2828. Not French, but fine Chinese food.

Restaurant la Boheme. 251 Principale; 227–6644. One of the village's most popular eateries. Small and intimate, it serves an unusual selection of fine food and wine. In addition to steaks, veal, and brochettes, it serves fine couscous and paella. No reservations. Eat early if you don't like waiting in line.

Inexpensive

Bentley's. 235 rue Principale, corner de la Gare; 227–1851. Under the same ownership as Moe's (below). Offers lighter fare: finger foods, chicken wings, salads, etc. A fun, relaxed spot everyone will enjoy.

Giorgio's. Highway 364 and Laurentian Autoroute; 227–3151. Italian and rock-bottom ("How can you do it, Giorgio?") prices—and good too.

Moe's. 21 de la Gare in the heart of St-Sauveur; 227–8803. Since this New York–style deli and bar opened in March 1989 it has been the busiest and most popular of all St-Sauveur restaurants, serving hearty fare, including the best smoked meat sandwich for miles, excellent pizzas, steaks, and other deli-cacies. Wait 'til you see the size of your plate!

Pizzaiolo. 64 de la Gare; 227–4422. Pizza parlor featuring over 20 different varieties. Bring your own wine; a convenience store around the corner sells it.

St. Hubert Barbecue. Located at the southbound entrance to the Laurentian Autoroute; 227–4663. It serves a most delicious barbecued chicken, accompanied by a special sauce. Great for families; special children's menu.

HOW TO GET AROUND. It is best to have a **car** at your disposal, since there is no public transportation within St-Sauveur. However, **taxi** service is available through *Taxi des Pays d'en Haut*, 229–3535 or 227–3000.

SEASONAL EVENTS. *Mid-Summer Madness* takes place every **August.** It's a ski race on crushed ice terminating in the area pool. Points are given for speed and style. Although there are few regularly scheduled major events at Mont St-Sauveur, some activity of interest takes place almost daily.

OTHER SPORTS AND ACTIVITIES. Cross-country skiing is a popular activity in the St-Sauveur Valley with trails starting on the outskirts of the village. Some enjoyable trails begin from the *Chalet Pauline Vanier* (Community Center) off de l'Eglise and behind the Parish of St-Sauveur Town Hall. A more organized trail network is located in adjacent Morin Heights, 6 km north of St-Sauveur via either Hwy. 364 or Chemin de l'Eglise. The *Centre de Ski de Fond Morin Heights* (Morin Heights Cross-country Center) offers a wide variety of track-set trails for all abilities. Call 226–2417 for information.

Skating is also available on rinks adjacent to village schools.

Shopping. The St-Sauveur Valley has developed so much in recent years that there is almost as much shopping as there is skiing in the region. The town caters to shoppers with 6 major shopping areas—all in a town with only 4,000 permanent residents. The areas include the area along rue Principale; Galeries des Monts, located off Hwy. 364, the most popular shopping center with the town's only liquor store; the newly opened Carrefour des Trois Villages, across from the Delta Hotel; Le Faubourg, a converted bar and hotel, home to a number of indoor boutiques; Promenades St-Sauveur, located off rue Principale near the church; and Promenades de la Vallée, recently transformed into factory-outlet stores.

NIGHTLIFE. Après-ski activity around St-Sauveur revolves around a few key bars. *Les Vieilles Portes,* 185 Principale; 227–2662. "Operated for skiers by skiers" is their slogan, a good cozy bar where the locals meet regularly after skiing in a friendly atmosphere. Specials offered on different nights, such as free spaghetti Monday nights.

Common's Bar, on Lac Echo Rd. in Morin Heights; 226–2211. Features live, rock 'n' roll bands every weekend.

Nuits Blanches Bar, 762 Principale; 227–5419. Just what its name implies, a late-night, late-action bar frequented more by the "beautiful people" than the hard-core skiers who are normally tucked in when this place starts to shake.

La Louisianne-Bourbon Street, Located on Hwy. 117 between Piedmont and Ste. Adèle, 229–2905, this is the most active bar in the region, drawing from all neighboring villages. Loud rock 'n' roll music, and plenty of dancing.

Bar Resto-Polo, 307 Principale; 227–2430. A good late-night spot often featuring live entertainment.

OTHER SKI AREAS IN THE ST-SAUVEUR VALLEY

Although Mont St-Sauveur is the leading area of the lower Laurentians, the St-Sauveur Valley, with neighboring Ste. Adèle and Morin Heights, is home to another nine major areas that can offer the vacationing skier plenty of variety. All are within a 10–15-minute drive.

Avila (227–4671) was purchased by Mont St-Sauveur in 1987. It is run as a separate area, but purchasing an all-day lift ticket at Mont St-Sauveur gives you free access to Avila. It is located at the easternmost end of Mont St-Sauveur with interconnecting, cross-over trails. It has a vertical of 185 meters (600 feet), nine snowmaking runs, one high-speed quad, one double chair, one T-bar, and night skiing every night. Its base lodge, although unsightly, is big and functional and has a good bar and restaurant for those who want more than burgers and fries for lunch.

Mont Habitant (227–2637) is a good family area located on the same range as Mont St-Sauveur but at the western end. Its 170-meter vertical drop includes eight well-groomed snowmaking runs serviced by a quad, one double chair, and one T-bar. There is night skiing every night on all the trails. In 1986, the area rebuilt a new base lodge that is one of the loveliest in the Laurentians. It has an excellent bar and restaurant for full meals.

Ski Morin Heights (226–1333) is in Morin Heights, a small municipality due north of St-Sauveur on Hwy. 364. This area opened in 1981 and has been growing steadily in popularity. At 214 meters of vertical with 22 trails serviced by four triple chairs, one double chair, and one T-bar, and 100 percent snowmaking, it is, with Mont St-Sauveur, one of the best areas in the region. Situated in a bowl, all trails converge around an attractive, comfortable recently expanded base lodge and a spacious multilevel sun deck. The lodge offers a full health club including squash courts, sauna, and whirlpool. There is night skiing every night of the week. Daycare facilities are also available on the premises.

Mont Olympia (227–3523) is in Piedmont, just east of Mont St-Sauveur. It has a fine array of beginners' slopes, wide and gentle. Opened in 1988, a new mountain offers the more advanced skiers some of the steepest pitches in the lower Laurentians. It has 21 runs served by one quad, one triple chair, and four T-bars, with a vertical of 174 meters and night skiing on 16 runs.

Mont Gabriel (229–3547), located off Hwy. 117 between Piedmont and Ste. Adèle, is one of the first ski areas built in the Laurentians. With a 192-meter vertical drop and 20 runs on four different mountain sides (although 90 percent of the time, only two sides and 15 trails are available), it offers a variety of slopes for all categories of skiers. Two of the best bump runs in the region are Tamarack and O'Connell. The area has snowmaking and night skiing seven nights a week on both north and south faces. Lifts include two quadruple chairs, one triple chair, and five T-bars.

The Chantecler (229–3555) in Ste. Adèle has been renovated, refitted, recut, and redone. Built around a 200-room resort hotel—a very attractive mini-chateau—it should appeal to the ski week vacationer looking for a full-service hotel right on the mountain. The area has skiing on four mountains although skiers gather around the hotel's Mountain No. 1, where five gentle beginners' slopes allow for both day and night skiing, and on Mountain No. 4, where nine more trails offer a wider variety of slope difficulty for all abilities. Mountain No. 2 is basically a teaching mountain with very gentle slopes. The 195-meter vertical is serviced by two quadruple chairs, one triple, two doubles, and two poma lifts. The base facility at the bottom of Mountain No. 4 was recently renovated.

On a busy weekend to get away from it all, you might retreat to the following smaller areas where children outnumber adults. **Mont Christie** (514–226–2412) in St-Sauveur north of the main village on Hwy. 364; **Bellevue Ski Hill** (514–226–2003) in the center of Morin Heights on Hwy. 364 north of St-Sauveur; and **Hills 40 and 80** (514–229–2921) in Ste. Adèle, just off Highway 117.

Parallel to the Laurentian Autoroute, Hwy. 117 is the backbone of the Laurentian region. Off it there are many quaint and interesting villages, such as Mont Rolland, Val Morin, Val-David, and the municipalities of

Ste. Adèle and Ste. Agathe. Each offers its own selection of activities and a variety of fine eating spots.

MONT TREMBLANT

Mont Trembland PQ JOT 1Z0
Tel: 819–425–8711

Snow Report: 800–461–8711
Area Vertical: 2,131 ft.
Number of Trails: 33 on 300 acres
Lifts: 1 high-speed quad, 1 quadruple chair,
*   2 triple chairs, 4 double chairs, 1*
*   T-bar, 2 poma lifts*
Snowmaking: 45 percent
Season: end of November–early April

The legend of Mont Tremblant is as mighty as the mountain itself. Among the earliest settlers in the region were Algonquin Indians who sought refuge from the warring Iroquois tribe on the shores of Lac Tremblant. It was one of these old Indian legends that gave the mountain its name, Mont Tremblant, "the trembling mountain." The Indians called it Manitou-Ewitchi-Saga, the Mountain of the Dread Manitou. Manitou was the Indian god of the wilderness who, in his wrath, caused the great mountain to tremble "with tempest and falling rock" when he was aroused by the infringement of man on the sanctity of the wilds and the animals inhabiting it.

The historical legend of Mont Tremblant in no way surpasses the skiing legend of Tremblant. Mont Tremblant was developed by Philadelphia millionaire Joseph Ryan, who first explored the mountain in 1932 with American newsman and travelogue producer, Lowell Thomas, and another American, Harry Wheeler, owner of neighboring Lac Ouimet Club (now Gray Rocks). Together they planned the resort that would become, during World War II, a favorite of North American skiers as much for its skiing as for its gourmet food and French ambience. In 1939, the resort opened with a single chair, the second in North America; the first was erected at Sun Valley, Idaho, a year earlier.

Over the years, the area has evolved into a major destination resort. Sitting majestically at the end of the Laurentian Autoroute yet only 90 minutes from Montreal, Mont Tremblant is the highest peak in the Laurentians. From its summit, it commands a spectacular panorama of lakes, mountains, valleys, and forests. It also provides the highest skiable vertical in the province of Quebec, over 2,100 feet.

In the early days, Tremblant was known for its narrow, difficult, twisting trails that started at the top in a forest of dwarfed frozen spruce trees. The frozen trees are still there, but few of the original trails can be found. In the 1970s and early 1980s, a major retrofit saw both the lift and trail networks upgraded and modernized. Many of the narrow, twisting chutes have been recut to favor faster, longer turns. As a result, intermediate and advanced skiers can often enjoy the same trails while skiing them somewhat differently.

Mont Tremblant is like two mountains atop each other. And before skiing it, you must be prepared to deal with what locals consider almost four mountains: the upper north and south sides and the lower north and south sides, each providing skiing for all abilities.

Long known for its difficult skiing, Mont Tremblant has gone a long way to overcome its reputation in order to please the beginning skier. The north side slopes, Sissy Schuss and Fuddle Duddle are among the best teaching slopes for the novice skier. On the south side the Nansen runs top-to-bottom—over 3 miles—and is both an excellent beginners' run and a fun cruiser to get you to the south side base at day's end.

Intermediate and cruising trails are wide at Tremblant and tend to draw both the intermediate and advanced skier. Given a touch of fresh powder, there are no better runs than Beauchemin and Lower Duncan on the north side, and Beauvallon and McCullough on the south side.

Expert skiing is found mostly on the upper mountain sections although the area's two toughest mogul trails, Expo and the Flying Mile, are on the lower sections of the north and south sides, respectively.

The area's lift system is basically made up of chairs: doubles, triples, and two quads, each one servicing the upper or lower section of the area. The high-speed quad installed in 1989 has reduced the bottom-to-top ride on the south side to less than 9 minutes (it used to be 45 minutes). A similar lift is being planned for the north side.

With an advanced snowmaking system covering 45 percent of the area, Mont Tremblant now guarantees vacationing skiers good skiing on the key trails.

Mont Tremblant, the highest summit in the Laurentians, is often exposed to some tough weather and you should come prepared with your warmest gear. A common fact of life in the high mountains: you never know till you get there what awaits you at the top!

Despite the charming and distinctive French-Canadian atmosphere that heightens the experience of a skiing vacation here, Mont Tremblant in recent years has not kept up with the North American standards for hospitality, service, and for what Quebec has built a reputation on—good food. It has survived on the fact that it is the highest peak in the Laurentians and in the province of Quebec.

Practical Information for Mont Tremblant

HOW TO GET THERE. Montreal is the gateway city to the Laurentians and Mont Tremblant.

By air. See *Practical Information for Gray Rocks,* above.

By car. From Montreal by **car,** take Laurentian Autoroute 15 to Ste Jovite. From there, you'll see the mountain in the distance on your right, and the road is clearly marked.

By bus. The *Voyageur Bus Line* also serves the Mont Tremblant region daily. For rates and schedule, call 514–842–2281. The main Montreal bus terminal is downtown at 505 de Maisonneuve East. Voyageur also operates special day trips to the area.

TELEPHONES. The area code for Mont Tremblant is 819; for Montreal, it is 514.

ACCOMMODATIONS. *Mont Tremblant Reservations* is a central reservations center for hotels, chalets, and condominiums in the area. It represents 10 major hotels and 40 different private chalets and condominiums. For information, contact Mont Tremblant Reservations, Box 240, Mont Tremblant, PQ, J0T 1Z0; 819–425–8681.

Rates are per person, based on double occupancy, modified American Plan in Canadian dollars: Categories, determined by price, are: *Expensive,* $75 and up; *Moderate,* $50–$75; *Inexpensive,* less than $50. The mailing address for all is the same—Mont Tremblant PQ, J0T 1Z0.

Mont Tremblant Lodge. *Expensive.* 425–8711; 800–461–8711 from Quebec, Ontario, and the United States. Part of the Mont Tremblant complex, this is the only slopeside accommodation. Four hundred rooms are available in your choice of French-Canadian chalets or condos. The lodge offers various package options.

Cuttle's Tremblant Club. *Moderate to Expensive.* 425–2731 or 800–567–8341 from Quebec and Ontario and 800–363–2413 from the United States. A relaxed smaller lodge in the complex with accommodations in either rooms in the main lodge or adjacent condominium units. Two- and 5-day ski week packages including lessons with the hotel's own ski school. Overlooking Lake Tremblant, Cuttle's is renowned for its gourmet dining and cozy atmosphere; less than 3 miles from the mountain.

Pinoteau Village. *Moderate to Expensive.* 800–567–8341 from Quebec and Ontario or 800–363–2413 from the United States. Features 88 luxurious and fully equipped condominium units less than 1 kilometer from Mont Tremblant. Complimentary shuttle ensures transport to and from the ski slopes.

Hotel-Motel Villa Bellevue. *Moderate.* 426–2734 or 800–567–6763 from Quebec, Ontario, and the Maritimes. Located 3 miles from Mont Tremblant's south side, Villa Bellevue is one of the oldest inns of the region operating since the early 1920s. It offers 88 rooms in either hotel or motel units, or chalets. It is owned and has been operated by the Dubois family, a prominent and very sports active family in the region for 3 generations. Development director Luc Dubois coached the Canadian alpine ski team from 1971 to 1976, and during the year as many as 10 family members take part in making guests feel at home. Winter packages are 2 and 5 nights, MAP. Villa Bellevue operates its own ski school and free transportation to and from the mountain. Cross-country ski weeks are also offered. The hotel has a sports complex that includes a lap pool, a sauna, a Jacuzzi, and an exercise room.

Chateau Beauvalon. *Inexpensive.* 425–7275. Owned and operated by Judy and Alex Riddell, long-time skiers of Mont Tremblant, this is a ski lodge as it was meant to be. Originally an annex of Mont Tremblant Lodge, the 15-room chateau has maintained its original French-Canadian charm. Bar, dining room, and a cozy fireplace make it a place for those who prefer a more intimate atmosphere. Cash or personal checks. No credit cards.

Other accommodations in the region, all in the *Moderate–Inexpensive* range, include the following.

L'Abbée du Nord. 425–8394. Country inn with four rooms. The inn, a historic site, was the house of one of the past parish priests of Mont Tremblant. Dining room features ribs and French specialties, rack of lamb, and fresh fish daily.

Chalet des Chutes. 425–2738. Motels and chalets less than a mile from the slopes.

Motel Mountain View. 425–3429. A few minutes' drive from Mont Tremblant; 44 units, 10 with fireplace.

RESTAURANTS. Good food—French and French-Canadian cuisine—has been a drawing card for the area since its beginnings. Ski-week lodges generally offer table d'hote fares with four or five choices daily and usually a once-a-week special buffet dinner. The area also offers a good selection of restaurants for all tastes. Restaurant categories are *Expensive,* $20 and up; *Moderate,* $10–$20; *Inexpensive,* less than $10. These prices are for one meal, exclusive of drinks, tips, and tax. The following restaurants accept most major credit cards unless indicated otherwise.

La Pinede. *Expensive–Moderate.* At the Mountain View Motel on Rte. 327 between St. Jovite and Gray Rocks; 425–8015. French and Continental cuisine; table d'hôte ranges from $15 to $20.

La Table Enchantée. *Expensive–Moderate.* On Rte. 117 at Lac Duhamel; 425–7113. Authentic French cuisine served in a quiet atmosphere.

Cafe de la Gare. *Moderate.* Located in Mont Tremblant Village; 425–3343. Serves hearty French-Canadian fare and excellent breakfast. V only.

Restaurant O Wok. *Moderate.* 878 Ouimet, St. Jovite; 425–8442. Does not serve Irish-Chinese cuisine as its name implies. If you are in the mood for excellent Chinese food, O Wok is the only choice in the area.

Antipastos. *Inexpensive.* 444 St-Georges, St. Jovite; 425–7580. An old train station off the main street features the region's best version of Italian cuisine. Pizza fresh from a brick oven is the specialty although the pasta dishes deserve special mention.

St. Hubert Bar-B-Q. *Inexpensive.* 330 Ouimet, St. Jovite; 425–2721. A must stop for out-of-province visitors not accustomed to the typically Quebecois barbecued chicken in special sauce. The restaurant is part of a chain with branches in other Canadian provinces as well as some states, including Florida. Good for the family.

HOW TO GET AROUND. Most lodges operate their own learn-to-ski weeks and their own ski school. As a result, all have **shuttle** transportation to and from the mountain. Most accommodations serving Mont Tremblant are within 5 miles of the area and so are restaurants. **Car rental** is also available from *Location Jean Gagné,* 425–2767. Reserve well in advance because it has few cars. Getting around to other lodges or restaurants or to shops in St. Jovite is best done by **taxi.** Contact *Taxi Mont Tremblant,* 425–2153 or *Taxi St. Jovite,* 425–3212. The *Voyageur Bus* from Montreal to Mont Tremblant stops at several lodges and it is possible to hop a ride with them to St. Jovite for less than a taxi. This is done only when space is available. Inquire with your lodge or hotel.

SEASONAL EVENTS. Standard races are open to all every Sunday. The *Easter Bonnet Parade* takes place on that holiday. *Annual Shovel and Tap-Q* race is on the last day of the season. This race features area employees, mainly liftees, who at days' end usually come back down sitting on their shovel or on a ski-bob-like home-made single-ski device called a "tap-Q," roughly translated: "bum-bruiser!"

OTHER SPORTS AND ACTIVITIES. **Cross-country** skiing is very popular in the area with two particularly interesting trail networks. *Mont Tremblant Provincial Park* offers free skiing on 77 km or 16 trails for all abilities. It is located near the north side base of the alpine ski area. From the south side base take the Devil's River Road. to the north side. From there follow signs to Parc du Mont Tremblant. The St. Jovite–Mont Tremblant trail network runs from St. Jovite to Mont Tremblant and passes by most lodges and hotels. Trails are packed and track set by the *Club de Ski de Fond St. Jovite-Mont Tremblant,* 425–5278, and access is free. Inquire at your lodge for closest starting point. **Telemark** programs are also available from *SkiTour in St. Jovite;* 425–5278.

DAY-CARE FACILITIES. Located at the south side base next to the beginners' poma lift is the Mont Tremblant nursery and day-care facility, *Les Tout P'tits,* where children 3 years and over can be left for several hours or a complete day. Children are taken outdoors to play in the snow—weather permitting—and those who can ski are taken on the adjacent poma-slope. Cost is $2.50 an hour per child. Lunch is available for $3 and a nap or quiet-time is encouraged after lunch. Further information at Mont Tremblant Lodge front desk, 425–8711.

NIGHTLIFE. Most lodges and hotels have bars where you can relax and kick up your feet by the fire after a hard day on the slopes or cross-country skiing. Many feature after-dinner entertainment by either a solo musician or a live band. At **slope-side,** *Mont Tremblant Express* is a train-shaped disco located in the Mont Tremblant Lodge featuring disco dancing from 9 P.M. to 3 A.M.

After skiing a favorite spot is the *Octogone* in the Chalet des Voyageurs at the bottom of the south side. Disco music videos play on a giant screen all day until 6 P.M. A more relaxed place to kick up your heels after skiing is the *Catalogne Bar* located in the Mont Tremblant Lodge. Free appetizers from 4 to 7 P.M., giant screen TV for sporting events, and live music. Call 425–8711 for any of the above.

The *Thirsty Eagle Bar* (425–2771) is in the main lodge at Gray Rocks, 4 miles from Mont Tremblant. This is one of the most popular of local bars and since Gray Rocks always packs a full house of about 450 to 500 guests, the place rocks and rolls to a live band from 3 P.M. to 3 A.M. with a break for dinner between 6 and 9 P.M.

La Musicale (425–2734) is the disco at Villa Bellevue, 3 miles from the mountain at Lac Ouimet, next to Gray Rocks. Live band six days a week and disco music daily.

If blending in with the locals is a higher priority for you, try *Le Coin* at Hotel Mont Tremblant in Mont Tremblant Village (425–3232), a DJ-type disco operating every night from 10 P.M. to 3 A.M. It's currently the "in" spot.

Eastern Townships

Southeast of Montreal sits a region with a special heritage and some of the best skiing in Quebec. The Eastern Townships region is sandwiched between the St. Laurence Valley and the U.S. border, giving it a special cultural duality.

The region was settled jointly by French-speaking farmers and English United Empire Loyalists, who came from the United States after the American Revolution. Today the Townships, as they are called, are a patchwork of distinctive French and English towns and villages.

Reading a map of Quebec, you might think you're in heaven, with so many towns named after saints. But obviously the Eastern Townships were differently influenced. Names such as Abercorn, Knowlton, Mansonville, Eastman, and Ayer's Cliff underline an early English settlement. To this day, you're likely to hear mostly English spoken in the streets and shops of Knowlton and Mansonville. On the other hand, English and French are spoken equally by residents of Sherbrooke, Sutton, and Cowansville, while Bromont and Magog are more distinctively French. Although more international in scope, ski areas near those communities reflect the region's cultural heritage. Though all areas are bilingual, the flavor at Mont Orford and Bromont is distinctly French, at Owl's Head and Glen Mountain it is English, with Sutton providing an equal mix of both.

Compared to the Laurentians, skiing is a relatively new activity in the Eastern Townships. While there was skiing in the 1940s at Mont Orford, it was only in the early 1960s that it started to develop commercially with the opening of Mont Sutton with seven trails on a 1,000-foot vertical drop served by a double chair and a T-bar. From that point on, the region began to develop into one of the most important skiing regions of the province.

The topography of the Townships has its own peculiarities: 1,300-foot to 1,800-foot peaks that stand alone, separated by wide valleys. This has an effect on local weather, which often produces large quantities of snow on the mountains while the towns and villages often receive much less. And that suits almost everyone.

Southeast from Montreal, the region branches off Autoroute 10. The flatness of the St. Lawrence Valley extends to the foothills of the Townships region, which actually begins at Granby. Until that point, there is little sign of any of the great skiing that lies ahead. But at a point shortly past Granby, the peaks become visible and for a while all five mountains can be seen at once—Bromont, Sutton, Glen, and Owl's Head lining up on the right, Mont Orford standing dead ahead in the distance. Each area is located within a 25-mile radius of Knowlton, the center point of the region, with the farthest distance about 40 miles from Sutton to Mont Orford.

In the 1960s, an interchangeable ski-lift ticket was created by Ski East, the marketing arm of the region. Today skiers purchasing ski week packages can ski at all four Ski East centers—Bromont, Sutton, Owl's Head, and Mont Orford. At one time Jay Peak, VT, which is just across the border from Owl's Head, was also part of the arrangement, but not today. Jay Peak nonetheless is almost part of the Eastern Townships and considered by most Montrealers as a Montreal ski area. It is also an added skiing opportunity for someone vacationing in the Townships.

Unlike the Laurentians, which are purely a vacation and weekend chalet region, the Eastern Townships have more of a permanent population. There are farms from the minute you cross the St. Lawrence River at Montreal to the time you approach the ski areas. A few miles from the ski areas, you'll begin seeing sparsely scattered chalets with more and more condos near the slopes. There are few large hotels and resorts but charming inns abound.

The Big Four Ski East areas are the most attractive for ski vacationers, but two other areas of interest can provide an alternate on a busy weekend. Glen Mountain, located just southeast of Knowlton, is a good family area with 19 runs on a 1,050-foot vertical serviced by five lifts including two double chairs. Skiing is on natural snow but the lack of heavy skier traffic makes skiing on the heaven-sent more often pleasant than not.

Located just minutes east of Granby is Mont Shefford, another low-traffic, natural snow area with a 750-foot vertical and 12 runs served by three T-bars.

Alpine skiing has been the main star of the Eastern Townships' winter program, but in the past decade, four of the province's best cross-country centers have been developed in the immediate vicinity of the major alpine areas. Sutton-en-Haut is near Sutton, Farmer's Rest between Sutton and Glen Mountain, Parc de la Yamaska is just East of Granby, and Mont Orford Park is at the foot of Mont Orford. These centers offer another option to skiing in the East and the versatile skier should pack skinny skis as well when heading for the Eastern Townships on a skiing vacation.

Contrary to other regions, the Eastern Townships of Quebec are still country. And that's part of the unique charm of the region.

BROMONT

Box 29
Bromont PQ J0E 1L0
Tel: 514–534–2200; 800–363–8920 toll-free
from Montreal and area code 514;
800–361–8020 toll-free from the
Eastern United States

Snow Report: 514–534–2200
Area Vertical: 1,300 ft. (355 meters)
Number of Trails: 24
Lifts: 1 detachable quad chair, 3 doubles, 2
T-bars, 1 Pony lift
Snowmaking: 82 percent
Season: late November–mid-April

Developed in the early 1960s, Bromont has the highest vertical drop of any area close to Montreal: 1,300 feet. It is also one of the finest skiing mountains in the province for its size. The ratio of length of run per vertical foot of elevation is one of the best and could be compared to a smaller Stowe.

Bromont came of age in the early 1980s, when newly appointed general manager Robert Desourdy, then 28 years old, literally launched the area.

With all the natural elements in place to make the area successful—a good mountain and the proximity to a major market (Montreal, with a population of 2.5 million)—the area was not, however, in the best possible snow-belt. Snowmaking became the first priority for Desourdy, who was quick to realize that "without the raw material—snow—you can't run a success-ful ski area." Snowmaking now covers 18 of Bromont's 24 trails.

Night skiing at Bromont is almost as popular as day skiing. You can purchase a night skiing ticket as early as 3 P.M., and on weekends you can go skiing until midnight. At one time, night skiing at Bromont had been extended until 2 A.M., but that proved to be a little much. Not to say that it didn't work: in 1981 an all-night ski promotion called "La Grande Nuit Blanche" (the great white night) almost turned disastrously successful. Over 6,000 skiers managed to get to the area but an additional 4,000 had to be turned away. Although the management was somewhat embar-rassed, at least 10,000 skiers knew that Bromont had installed lights for night skiing.

Bromont is just that kind of area: a happening place. And when they do something, they do it big or they do it crazy. For example, don't be too frazzled if you're asked the right of way by a bed on skis. That'll be the day they have the annual Ski Bed Race. Every year local media mem-bers are teamed up with the various departments at Bromont (ski patrol, marketing, administration) for one of the wackiest, off-the-wall events of the winter in the Eastern Townships. The race is run under a different theme every year and the sleds—beds—are lavishly decorated to fit the theme. Bromont also successfully hosted the 1986 Ski World Cup Finals and plans to make the area a regular venue of the annual White Circus.

In 1986, the area acquired a high-speed quad that does wonders keeping lift lines moving. Three more double chairs, two on Mont Brome, the larg-er mountain, and one on Mont Soleil, provide enough uphill capacity to handle all but the busiest spring weekends.

From the top of the mountain on a clear day you can see Montreal. Beginners will delight in the 2½-mile Brome trail, a wide, gentle, and scenic run which winds its way around the mountain. Even a more advanced skier will find it a perfect warm-up run. It is also lit for night skiing.

Intermediate skiers as well as experts will delight in one of the area's best cruisers—the Knowlton, a medium-wide steady pitch that is sure to raise your confidence level.

An equally beautiful run for the more aggressive skier shoots from the top of the quad chair. The Waterloo is for advanced skiers and runs in a straight line with three or four good pitches along the way to wake you up.

One of Bromont's main qualities is the desire to please its skiers. Arriv-ing at the area, you get the feeling of being welcome; signs immediately say so! "Welcome to Bromont" written in a bubbly, fun style. There are few constraints at Bromont. Few signs saying "No poles," "No box lunch-es," "No checks," "No Fun!" Everything is planned to work. For example, lift-ticket prices vary with the hour of the day. You can choose from as many as 10 different price options, depending on when you arrive and how long you wish to stay.

Bromont is the first ski area in Quebec to have become a four-season resort offering in the summertime golf, swimming, alpine and water slides, chairlift rides and picnics to the summit, conditioning and mountain bike trails, and a number of other activities.

Anyone visiting Bromont for any period of time will certainly succumb to the desire to try the "Super Glissade"—The Super Slide, on the golf course just before entering the alpine parking lot. For a small daily fee you can rent a jumbo inner-tube and tackle the 350-foot slope with reckless abandon. Try it at the end of your ski week, however; Bromont's skiing is better than its tubing!

Bromont's proximity to Montreal makes a trip to the Canadian metropolis a short hour's drive on the toll-free Eastern Townships Autoroute 10. It takes you over the Champlain Bridge and right into Montreal's busy downtown. While your ski vacation may be a break from it all, if you've never visited the Paris of North America, dinner and an evening out in Montreal would certainly be a cultural plus to add to your stay in Quebec.

Practical Information for Bromont

HOW TO GET THERE. By air. Montreal is the gateway to the Eastern Townships and Bromont for travelers arriving by air or traveling in from the west. Montreal's Dorval Airport is conveniently located on the Island of Montreal and is the most convenient of the city's two airports for travelers going to the Eastern Townships. Dorval Airport is also the main gateway for flights originating within North America. Dorval offers a full slate of **car rental companies** including the big four: *Avis,* 800–331–1212; *Budget,* 800–527–0700; *Hertz,* 800–654–3131; and *Tilden,* the Canadian affiliate of *National,* 800–328–4567.

If you are particularly well-heeled, you can fly in with your private jet or prop plane. The *Aeroport Regional des Cantons de l'Est,* better known as Bromont Airport, is located only 6 km from the ski area. Full services, including UNICOM Radio, customs, regular and jet fuel, and maintenance are available between 6 A.M. and 9 P.M. as well as other hours by request. The 6,000-ft runway is equipped for night landings, is accessible around the clock, 12 months a year, and can handle aircrafts the size of a Challenger by *Canadair;* 514–534–2325.

By car. From Montreal, take Champlain Bridge across the St. Lawrence River. You will be heading east on Autoroute 10. At Exit 78 you have arrived; the mountain is right in front of you.

Coming from the United States, there are various routes, depending on your point of origin. From New York State and points west of Lake Champlain your best route is I–87 to Montreal, then Autoroute 10. From Connecticut, Massachusetts, Maine, New Hampshire, or Vermont, take I–91 which connects with Quebec Hwy. 33 and with Autoroute 10 at Magog, the easternmost point of the autoroute. From there, head west toward Montreal and take exit 78.

By bus. Regular daily bus service is also available from Montreal's Voyageur Terminal located at the intersection of Berri and DeMaisonneuve streets. Schedules may vary with time of year. For rates and schedules, call 514–842–2281.

TELEPHONES. The area code for Montreal and Bromont is 514.

ACCOMMODATIONS. Lodging prices in the Bromont area average about the same as at Mont Sutton, although there isn't as wide a selection. Rates are based on double occupancy. Categories, determined by price, are: *Expensive,* $75 and up; *Moderate,* $50–$75; *Inexpensive,* less than $50.

Auberge Bromont. *Moderate to Expensive.* 95 rue Montmorency, Box 29; 534–2200. The main lodge locally; it is less than a mile from the slopes. Located on the golf course adjacent to the mountain, this 55-room inn provides a peaceful get-away for both ski weekers and convention goers.

Le Chateau Bromont. *Moderate to Expensive.* 170 rue Champlain; 935–5161 or toll free from Eastern Canada 800–361–8020. Has 154 units with fireplaces and full kitchens that accommodate 2 to 6 persons, and is located right on the slopes. This complex includes a pool, exercise room, sauna, hot tubs, squash, racquetball, and golf-practice courts.

La Petite Auberge. *Inexpensive.* 360 Boulevard Pierre Laporte; 534–2707. A good lodging place, about 15 minutes from the ski center. It is small, however, with only 6 rooms, all with shower. The dining room features fine French cuisine, living-room type bar.

Outside the immediate Bromont region, the most convenient town is Granby, 12 miles east of the ski area. There you will find plenty of accommodations in the form of motels and hotels, including **Le Castel de l'Estrie**, 378–9071; **Motel le Granbyen**, 378–8406; and **Motel du Lac**, 372–5930.

Travel a little farther for a little more distinguished lodging in the central part of the Eastern Townships. About 20 minutes away from the mountain you'll find **Le Petit Hotel d'Eastman**, 297–2812, and **Auberge du Fenil**, 297–3362, in Eastman. Both are ideally located for you to take full benefit of the interchangeability of your Ski East lift ticket which lets you ski at Bromont, Sutton, Mont Orford, or Owl's Head.

RESTAURANTS. While the immediate Bromont area offers a limited number of eateries, within a half-hour's drive of the area can be found something to suit every taste, from Continental cuisine to nouvelle cuisine Quebecoise. In the sampling listed here, price classifications are based on the cost of an average dinner for one person, beverages and tip not included: *Expensive,* $20–$30; *Moderate,* $15–$20; *Inexpensive,* less than $15. All accept major credit cards.

La Jardinière. *Moderate to Expensive.* 95 rue Montmorency; 534–5200. Located in Auberge Bromont, a four-star dining room featuring game, Lake Brome duck, trout dishes, and Sunday brunch.

Le Castel de Brome. *Moderate.* 117 Boulevard Bromont; 534–3620. Specializes in fine Italian cuisine, including fettuccine Alfredo, mussels in a cream sauce, and seafood à l'Italienne.

La Maison de Chez Nous. *Moderate.* 847 Mountain Ave., in nearby Granby; 372–2991. Homey atmosphere; from 5 to 11 P.M. daily, except Mondays, it features all-you-can-eat frogs' legs and nouvelle cuisine Quebecoise, with duck, pheasant, rabbit, and other seasonal game dishes.

Two light-dining outlets that often suit families and children are the ever popular **Pizza Hut,** 550 Mont-Royal near the autoroute and adjacent to the drive-in (534–5577), and **Rotisserie St-Hubert** (534–0223), for barbecued chicken Montreal-style. Both are *Inexpensive.*

HOW TO GET AROUND. Bromont is a relatively isolated mountain and it is strongly recommended that you use a **car** to get around unless you are staying slopeside at Le Chateau Bromont. Getting to the village of Bromont and to the larger center of Granby requires wheels. **Car rental** companies are in Granby: *Hertz,* 378–8404; *Avis,* 378–9057; *Tilden,* 375–2818; and *Budget,* 378–4636. **Taxi** service is also available from *Taxi Bromont,* 534–3200.

OTHER SPORTS AND ACTIVITIES. Cross-country skiing is next after alpine skiing at Bromont, and if you're bunked in at the Auberge Bromont you can simply step out the front door onto the cross-country trails, which begin on the golf course and extend beyond into the forest for 16 km of track-set skiing. A full-service ski shop is available at the first tee.

Spa Bromont, 111 Boulevard Bromont, 534–2717, offers balnotherapy, algotherapy, masso-therapy, shiatsu, and reflexology—all you will ever need to relax your tired, aching muscles!

NIGHTLIFE. Luckily, Bromont's base lodge disco, *La Debarque,* 534–2200, is a humming place since there isn't much else around. However, you'll be kept on your toes with a good and steady turnover of people seven days a week from 3 P.M. to the small hours of the night. Bars mean people and La Debarque is sure to provide plenty of possibilities for encounters.

MONT ORFORD

Box 248
Magog PQ J1X 3W8
Tel: 819–843–6548
Reservations: 819–843–4200

Snow Report: 819–843–8822
Area Vertical: 1,772 ft. (540 meters)
Number of Trails: 33
Lifts: 1 quad, 1 triple chair, 3 double
  chairs, 1 T-bar, and 1 pony lift
Snowmaking: 80 percent of terrain
Season: early December–early April

Mont Orford is technically the oldest ski center in the Eastern Townships and yet, in many ways, it's the newest. While there was skiing by Sno-Cat in the 1930s and the first lift on Orford was erected in 1939, Mont Orford ski center would not be recognized by anyone who hadn't skied there since the mid-1970s. The '70s were difficult times for the fourth largest mountain in the province. Ownership and management uncertainty made it a no-growth sleeping giant. But the '80s have seen the giant awakening and at mid-decade the area was enjoying its greatest boom ever. Skiers are rediscovering the *new* Orford and as a visitor you'll certainly be pleased with the current version.

Mont Orford is the lone peak in the region, thus affording from the top a magnificent view from all sides. The best view is unquestionably to the south—shooting down majestic Lake Memphremagog stretching 30 miles from Magog to Newport in Vermont. Conversely, in a drive to the area from Montreal or from the U.S. border, the icy white summit of Orford appears and disappears for miles around as you make your way through the scenic Townships hills.

The base installations at Orford, newly upgraded and rebuilt in 1988, are neatly nestled at the bottom of the bowl-shaped skiing facilities in one of the best base set-ups any ski area could ever hope for. Everything converges toward a practical and attractive pavillion, which makes it most convenient for rendezvous, pit stops, and the like.

The color of the skiing changes from peak to peak. Orford is the main mountain with the most vertical, the most runs, the most lifts, and the most snowmaking. It also has the most black-diamond trails. As ski areas are modernized, many trails in the East lose some difficulty when they are widened. But not at Orford. The main mountain has enough pitch that even the widening process has not killed the kick. And one trail is so steep and twisty that no one has yet dared climb it with an axe. It's the Contour, a trail you must avoid if you're a newcomer who's been persuaded to take a learn-to-ski week. Modern teaching techniques cannot yet transform you into a mountain goat overnight.

Another good test for the advanced skier is the Maxi, which runs wide and mean right under the triple chair. It is unquestionably the area's best mogul run. Because of its width, it is also safe enough for a good intermediate to handle. It provides that extra challenge we all need occasionally to improve our skiing skills. And if you feel real hot one of those days, try the Super just to the left of the Maxi under the summit double chair. It's usually difficult to ski at even the best of times.

Orford also has more gentle terrain. Intermediates will love the *Trois Ruisseaux,* a trail which, in the old days, crossed three creeks—hence its name—and was one of the toughest on the mountain. This is one trail that lost some punch when it was widened, straightened, and rerouted, but it has provided intermediate and advanced skiers with the area's most popular cruiser. If you're into long, carved turns, you'll also enjoy the Grande Coulee, a run which begins like a cross-country trail but eventually opens up into a good steady pitch.

The Tele-7 is a 4-km road that runs top-to-bottom on Orford, providing the beginner with the longest novice run on the mountain.

Mont Giroux, the smallest of the three peaks, received a $4-million upgrade in 1987, when a new quad was installed and new trails were added. Further improvements to Mont Giroux were completed for the 1988–89 season, with another new quad servicing three new trails on a different face.

Mont Alfred Desrochers is the third peak at the area. It is named after a famous French Canadian poet who in the 1930s found much of his inspiration "in the shadow of Orford." Serviced by one double chair, it is the domain of the intermediate skier and an excellent shelter for anyone on those windy, cold days. Slopes are relatively narrow with the occasional dip forcing you to drive those knees a little more and carve that turn.

Because of Mont Orford's isolation, the very top of the mountain is often cold and windswept, so no matter what time of year, you should always come prepared with warm clothes.

Mont Orford's proximity to the town of Magog (5 miles) and to the popular summer attraction that is Lake Memphremagog gives it the best access to lodging and good restaurants of any ski resort in the Eastern Townships.

Practical Information for Mont Orford

HOW TO GET THERE. By air. Montreal is the gateway to the Eastern Townships and Mont Orford for travelers arriving by commercial airline or traveling in from the West. Montreal's Dorval Airport is conveniently located on the Island of Montreal and is the most convenient of the city's two airports for travelers going to the Eastern Townships. Dorval Airport is also the main gateway for flights originating within North America.

Dorval offers a full slate of **car rental companies,** including *Avis,* 800–331–1212; *Budget,* 800–527–0700; *Hertz,* 800–654–3131; and *Tilden,* 800–328–4567. The Sherbrooke Airport, located approximately 30 miles from Magog, has a 5,000-foot by 150-foot runway and can accommodate any type of private aircraft, prop or jet. Flight services are available 24 hours a day; 819–832–2560.

By car. From Montreal, take the Champlain Bridge across the St. Lawrence River. You will be heading east on Autoroute 10 to Exit 115, a straight and easy 80-mile drive. At this point you're on the west shoulder of Mont Orford. Exit 115 takes you right to the mountain's base installations.

Coming from the United States by car, there are various routes depending on your point of origin. Any connection to I–91 will have you connecting with Quebec Hwy. 55 north and from there to Autoroute 10 west. Once on the autoroute at Magog, look for Exits 118 or 115, either one of which will take you to the mountain.

By bus. Regular daily bus service is also available from Montreal's *Voyageur Terminal* located at the intersection of Berri and DeMaisonneuve streets. Schedules may vary with time of year. For rates and schedules call 514–842–2281.

TELEPHONES. The area code for the Mont Orford region is 819.

ACCOMMODATIONS. There is lodging for more than 4,000 people in the region and the *Mont Orford Reservation Bureau* can arrange your reservations or make suggestions. You can reach them by writing to *Mont Orford Reservation Bureau,* Box 248, Magog, PQ J1X 3W8; or calling 819–843–4200.

There are few *Expensive* ($65 and above) accommodations in the area although some suites at some of the *Moderate* ($40–$65) auberges can be considered relatively expensive. *Inexpensive* is less than $40.

Auberge Cheribourg. *Moderate to Expensive.* Box 337, Magog-Orford, QC J1X 3W9; 843–3308 or 800–567–6132 from Quebec, Ontario, and the Maritimes. One of the closest to the ski area, located on the mountain road—Cherry River Road— about 2 miles from the area. It offers 100 hotel rooms including 17 suites with fireplaces and 300 fully equipped condos. The auberge features a highly rated dining room, a disco—*La Cerise* (the Cherry)—and a piano bar. Recently added was a new convention center with all meeting amenities. Both the hotel and the surrounding condos have brightly colored orange metal roofs that make the place quite distinctive. In addition, the establishment is adjacent to Orford Provincial Park Cross-Country Center which features 42 km of meticulously maintained trails for all abilities. You can ski from the hotel to the park.

Auberge Estriemont. *Moderate to Expensive.* 44 Avenue de l'Auberge, Canton d'Orford, PQ J1X 3W7; 843–1616 or 800–567–7320 from Quebec, Ontario, and the Maritimes. A new complex that somewhat resembles the Cheribourg. It has 46 suite-type rooms, each equipped with a fireplace; 50 chalets with fireplace, fully equipped kitchen, dishwasher, color TVs, are also available. Estriemont is also one of the few local hotels to offer a fitness center, with an indoor swimming pool, squash and raquetball courts, weight room, sauna, and hot tub. There is also a 2-km cross-country trail right on the premises. The hotel has free mini-bus transport to and from the alpine or cross-country area.

O'Berge du Village. *Moderate to Expensive.* 261 Merry South, Magog; 843–6566 or 800–567–6089 from Quebec. Features fully equipped condos, including fireplace and balcony overlooking Lake Memphremagog. Located about 10 minutes from Mont Orford, it also has saunas, whirlpool, and squash courts.

Auberge l'Etoile sur le Lac. *Moderate.* 1150 Principale West, Magog; 843–6521 or toll-free in Canada, 800–567–7315. Has 26 motel-type rooms offering superior accommodations. All modern rooms have a view of Lake Memphremagog and cable color TV. There is also an excellent dining room featuring French cuisine.

Auberge Hatley. *Moderate.* 330 N. Hatley, PQ J0B 2C0; 842–2451. A romantic old country inn built in 1903, it has 22 rooms, some with fireplace and Jacuzzi and all furnished with old Quebec antiques. The dining room is rated Four Forks, the highest ranking of the Quebec Ministry of Tourism. It shares the same 100-km network of cross-country trails with Auberge Ripplecove, and is about 20 minutes from Mont Orford.

Auberge Orford. *Moderate.* 20 Merry South, Magog; 843–9361. A friendly inn with 12 spacious and comfortable rooms with private bath. The dining room, complete with fireplace and antique furniture, features regional specialty Italian cuisine. Every meal at the Auberge is said to be an experience in fine dining. There is also a good after-ski bar *Club Le Ski.*

Auberge Ripplecove. *Moderate.* Box 246, Ayer's Cliff, PQ J0B 1C0; 838–4296. On Lake Massawippi, equidistant from Mont Orford and the Vermont border, it offers a choice of 11 charming rooms furnished with antiques or 7 chalets and suites of 1, 2, or 3 bedrooms, many with fireplaces. The dining room boasts a gold medal at the Quebec Culinary Competition and is reputed for the excellence of its French menu. There are 35 km of cross-country skiing from the front door, sleigh rides, lighted skating rink, game rooms, ice fishing on the lake.

Auberge Sheraton-Orford. *Moderate.* C.P. 98, Magog-Orford, QC J1X 3W7; 843–1616. Part of the Sheraton chain, this new addition to the region's hotel network offers 117 rooms (many with fireplace), plus an indoor pool, exercise facilities, whirlpool, and sauna. Also 50 condo units that can accommodate 2–4 persons each. Located 4 km from Mont Orford.

Hovey Manor. *Moderate.* Box 60, North Hatley, PQ J0B 2C0; 842–2421. Formerly a private estate modeled on the Virginia home of George Washington, Hovey Manor is alive with antiques and offers a refined, modern cuisine. Most of the 36 bedrooms face Lake Massawippi; many with fireplaces, 4-poster beds and whirlpool baths. Hovey Manor is located 20 minutes from Mont Orford.

Auberge du Parc Orford. *Inexpensive.* 1259 Chemin de la Montagne, Cherry River, PQ J1X 3W3; 843–8887. Lodge located on the mountain road a little over a mile from the slopes; 42 rooms, each equipped with kitchenette, make it an affordable choice for a family. There is also transportation to and from the mountain available for a small fee.

RESTAURANTS. The Mont Orford-Magog region offers an excellent selection of restaurants and, within a 10-mile radius of the area, probably the best selection in the Eastern Townships. Restaurants are categorized on the basis of a full-course dinner for one, excluding drinks, tax, and tip: *Expensive,* $20–$30; *Moderate,* $15–$20; *Inexpensive,* less than $15. Restaurants accept most major credit cards unless indicated otherwise.

Moderate–Expensive

Auberge Cheribourg. On the mountain road about 2 miles from the area; 843–3313. Offers excellent French cuisine, with all major credit cards accepted.

Auberge Estrimont. 44 avenue de l'Auberge; 843–1616. Offers traditional French cuisine prepared by chef Guy, a native of the Auvergnes region of France. Table d'hôte is the main attraction with a selection of 4 main dishes nightly. Pianist every night in the dining room. Reservations suggested on weekends.

Chez Benito. 20 Merry South, Magog, across from McDonald's; 843–9361. Offers fine Italian cuisine and delicious wood-oven pizzas. Relaxed atmosphere, mostly moderate prices.

Chez Jean-Pierre. 112 rue Principale West, Magog; 843–8166. Features fine cuisine with a French touch. The table d'hôte menu is the main drawing card here offering appetizer, soup, and main course. Several dishes are flambéed at your table including desserts like crepes Suzette. Decor is warm and classic with white-and-pink tablecloths and lots of brass. Reservations are recommended.

Ristorante Di Leonardo. 20 Merry South in Magog; 843–9361. Fine Italian cuisine and homemade pasta. The restaurant is part of Auberge Orford.

Also found in this category are **Auberge de l'Etoile,** 1133 Principale West (843–6521), for fine French cuisine and **Le Moulin à Poivre** (843–4337), for fine Belgian cuisine.

Inexpensive–Moderate

Au Vieux Poêle. Located on Rte. 2 (the mountain road) at the intersection of Autoroute 10, at exit 118; 843–6442. Specialties include different types of fondues—onion, mushroom, regular—and a good selection of brochettes.

La Bonne Bouffe. 359 Principale, Eastman; 514–297–2420. A small, intimate restaurant featuring fine French cuisine. Reservations are recommended, since there are only 8 tables with a seating capacity of 30 people. House specialties include home-smoked trout, homemade pheasant paté, seafood platter au gratin and pepper steak, of which the owners are particularly proud.

Les Trois Marmites, 475 Principale, Magog; 843–4448. A family restaurant you should keep high on your list if your family includes teenage boys with bottomless appetites. On Wednesdays, Fridays, and Saturdays, it's all you can eat from a roast beef and salad bar, while on Thursdays and Sundays, you can indulge in your favorite Italian dishes—all you can eat Italian and salad bar.

OTHER SPORTS AND ACTIVITIES. The other major sporting activity in the area is **cross-country skiing.** Mont Orford Provincial Park (843–6233) is located on the mountain road about 1 mile before arriving at the alpine area. It is the finest cross-country skiing facility in all of the Eastern Townships and features 42 km of well-groomed, double-tracked trails for all abilities. Trail fee is $7 per person. A waxing room, warming huts, cafeteria, and ski patrol complete the center's offerings to the cross-country skier.

Skating is also available on Lake Memphremagog. A lighted skating oval is open whenever conditions permit through the winter months. It is operated by the Magog Chamber of Commerce at no fee. Access to the skating area is by Hwy. 112 right across from Auberge de l'Etoile.

On the backside of Mont Orford sits the town of Valcourt, known as the birthplace of the **snowmobile.** This is the site of the Bombardier plant, 1 de la Montagne St., makers of Ski-Doo, the first snowmobiles produced for mass consumption. Here you can visit the plant and see how snowmobiles are produced. For guided tour information and reservations call 514–532–2211, ext. 226. While in Valcourt, you must visit the J. Armand Bombardier Museum, 1000 J.A. Bombardier St. (514–532–2258), where you will discover that snowmobiles are almost as old as the automobile. Admission is free and the museum is open daily 1–4 P.M. You can also rent a snowmobile in the area from the Centre de la Motoneige de Valcour, 9058 rue de la Montagne, 514–532–2262.

Ice Fishing. Every winter as soon as the ice is thick enough on Lake Memphremagog a village of wood-heated cabins is erected about 2,000 feet off the north shore of the lake. Dress warmly and let yourself be taken to your rented cabin from which you can fish for trout, perch, bass, and pike. For information and reservations, call 819–843–8550 or 819–843–4322.

NIGHTLIFE. *La Grosse Pomme*—The Big Apple—270 Principale West, Magog (843–9365) is an entertainment complex of sorts with a cinema-bar featuring either two full-length movies, the Much Music Network, or sports on the giant screen. Disco with two dance floors, free admission, and free popcorn. You can also eat there between 11:30 A.M. and 9 P.M.—*bonne bouffe, pas cher* (good grub, cheap!), all in a bistro atmosphere. Clientele is generally 20–30 years of age. Good après-ski spot.

La Lanterne, 70 du Lac, Magog (843–7205), is a popular spot since it is a multipurpose après-ski bar, restaurant, and disco. Technically you could crawl into La Lanterne after the lifts close and leave there after the last call and all your needs would be taken care of. Clientele generally 25–45 years of age. The place is open Thursdays–Sundays only.

Culture. During the winter months the University of Sherbrooke Cultural Center offers a variety of quality entertainment including plays, jazz, and ballet. For information call 821–7744.

MONT SUTTON

Box 280
Sutton PQ J0E 2K0
Tel: 514–538–2338, 866–5156
Reservations: 514–538–2646 or
    514–538–2537

Snow Report: 514–866–7718, 866–7639
Area Vertical: 1500 ft. (460 meters)
Number of Trails: 53
Lifts: 1 high-speed quad, 2 fixed-grip quads,
    6 double chairs
Snowmaking: 60 percent of terrain
Season: late November–mid-April

The first commercial area in the Townships, Sutton was developed in 1960 by the Boulanger family, who still runs it today. Until recently, the popularity of Sutton was based strictly on skiing—very good skiing. When you skied at Sutton, you skied there for the slopes, the vertical, the snow. A sort of Alta of Eastern Canada.

The variety of trails at Sutton is unparalleled in the East. There are 53 runs cut on the 1,500-foot vertical, but the number of ways down is practically unlimited. What makes this possible is Sutton's *Sous-bois,* the French word for glades; about 40 percent of Sutton's skiable acreage is made up of glades.

The mountain is essentially divided into three sections. The main access to skiing is from the quadruple detachable chair that takes skiers to the main staging area, Top of Two. This refers to the lift number. There you'll also find a 120-seat chalet with sun deck where you can enjoy the scenic view, the sun, and special mid-mountain *Quebecois* lunches.

From this mid-mountain plateau, skiers can go three ways. Back down underneath and around the quad chair known as No. 2 area. This section provides mostly intermediate terrain. The lift-line run Sutton-ik is the toughest in the No. 2 area, a wide intermediate trail. No. 2 can also offer you your first *sous-bois* test on a gentle intermediate glade known as *Sous-bois 2* and is particularly enjoyable with a few inches of fresh powder.

Heading west from the mid-station, you head down toward beginner country also referred to as No. 1. Two double chairs serve another 10 trails for beginners and low intermediaters.

Heading east and down from the mid-station, skiers enter Sutton's most advanced and exciting terrain served by the Nos. 4, 5, 6, and 7 lifts, which consist of two quads and two double chairs. These lifts add another 500 vertical feet of skiing on mostly advanced terrain. And while there are easy ways down from this area, it is frequented mostly by the better skiers who can take advantage of superb glades and wild skiing to be found among the coniferous and twisted deciduous trees dwarfed by the altitude.

From the Top of Four, you can catch a glimpse of Roundtop, the highest point on Sutton's range located just behind chair No. 4's summit terminal. With a top elevation of 968 meters (almost 3,200 feet), it is the focus of future development plans for the area.

A firm believer in natural snow, Sutton has succumbed to a few bad snow years and embarked on a major snowmaking program that has now weatherproofed 60 percent of the area. And since 1985, a program of lift and grooming equipment improvement has been under way to round off the area where in the past skiing has been everything.

There is no better testimonial for Sutton's quality of skiing than the faithfulness of its clientele: *Les gens de Sutton* (the Sutton Crowd). It is a regular occurrence to meet skiers who have been there since the opening in 1960. Much of this following is due to the fact that through recent times Sutton was the area that offered the best skiing. However, a development push in the Eastern Townships lately has forced Sutton to refocus some of its development on the latest in ski-area technology and amenities.

Practical Information for Mont Sutton

HOW TO GET THERE. By air. Montreal is the gateway to the Eastern Townships and Sutton for travelers arriving by air or traveling in from the West. Montreal's Dorval Airport is conveniently located on the Island of Montreal and is the most convenient of the city's two airports for travelers going to the Eastern Townships. Dorval Airport is also the main gateway for flights originating within North America.

Dorval offers a full slate of **car rental** companies including the big four: *Avis,* 800–331–1212; *Budget,* 800–527–0700; *Hertz,* 800–654–3131; and *Tilden,* the Canadian affiliate of *National,* 800–328–4567.

By car. From Montreal, take Champlain Bridge across the St. Lawrence River. You will be heading east on Autoroute 10. At exit 68 take Hwy. 139 south to Sutton. Soon the northern edge of the Appalachian mountain range will appear before your eyes. Past Cowansville the road slaloms through magnificent vistas: you're almost there.

From the United States, there are various routes, depending on your point of origin. From New York and points west of Lake Champlain your best route is to travel to Montreal on I–87 which connects at Montreal's Champlain Bridge with Eastern Townships Autoroute 10. From Connecticut, Massachusetts, Maine, New Hampshire, or Vermont, take I–91 which connects with Eastern Townships Autoroute 10 at Magog, the easternmost point of the autoroute. From there, head west toward Montreal and take exit 68.

By bus. Regular daily bus service is also available from Montreal's Voyageur Terminal located at the intersection of Berri and DeMaisonneuve streets. Schedules may vary with time of year. For rates and schedules, call 514–842–2281.

TELEPHONES. The area code for this section of Quebec is 514.

ACCOMMODATIONS. Reservations and information on available accommodations can be obtained by contacting the *Sutton Tourist Association,* Sutton PQ, J0E 2K0; 514–538–2538 or 514–538–2646. Condominiums, both slopeside and away from the mountain, offer a wide variety of choices in prices, depending on the size of the units and the packages. A studio condo, for instance, can start at $450 for seven nights, while other units may cost $150 a night but can accommodate up to six people. In this listing, costs are estimated on what one person will pay per day. *Expensive,* $75 and up; *Moderate,* $50–$75; *Inexpensive,* less than $50.

At the Slopes

Village Archimede. *Inexpensive to Moderate.* Box 600, Mont Sutton; 538–3440. Sutton's slopeside condominium complex looks like it was conceived somewhere in outer space. Residence/hotel fully equipped; 40 units within walking distance of the lifts, 8 with full bathroom, 32 with shower only. Color TV in rooms; fireplace and/or sauna in some units; breakfast and dinner available at La Paimpolaise with a supplement.

La Paimpolaise. *Inexpensive.* Box 548, Mont Sutton; 538–3213. Located just below Sutton's chair No. 1. A small inn with plenty of atmosphere, it has 28 rooms with 2 double beds and 1 suite. All rooms with full bath and color TV. Because of its location, La Paimpolaise is also a very popular après-ski bar and has genuine French cuisine. Five-night package includes breakfast and dinner with wine.

In the Area

Loft Acres. *Moderate to Expensive.* Hwy. 139, West Brome; 263–3294. Although it is located farther from the hills, this modern condo-hotel complex is sure to delight the most discriminating traveler. Located on an old farm, the inn combines the ambience of a country inn with the comforts of more modern facilities. Sauna and hot tub, game room, bar, dining room, and 25 miles of cross-country skiing on a 200-acre farm. Accommodations in the inn are inexpensive while condos are moderate to expensive.

Auberge Santiago. *Moderate to Expensive.* 29 Principale, Sutton; 538–2660. Site of the excellent *Santiago* restaurant (see below), this New England–style inn has 10 new deluxe rooms with fireplaces and whirlpools.

Auberge De Sutton. *Moderate.* Box 340, Sutton; 538–2324. Rte. 139, about 6 miles from the mountain. Pleasant accommodations with good family atmosphere.

L'Estancia. *Moderate.* 164 Maple St., Sutton; 538–3501. Located 1 mile from the ski area, this modern apartment/hotel offers 11 units with full kitchen facilities. Fireplace in most units. Cross-country skiing on the premises.

Residences Val Sutton. *Moderate to Inexpensive.* Box 548, Sutton; 532–3212. This apartment complex is located on the mountain and offers 75 units of 1, 2, or 3 bedrooms, each equipped with kitchen, fireplace, and balcony. Every group of 15 apartments contains a sauna, whirlpool, and exercise, play, and meeting rooms. A shuttle bus service is available to the village of Sutton.

Hotel Horizon. *Inexpensive.* Mountain Rd., Sutton; 538–3212. Hotel-motel with spacious, modern rooms; has heated indoor swimming pool. Located about 1 mile from the alpine ski area, the Horizon can also offer cross-country skiing at adjacent Sutton-en-Haut center which has 55 km of well-groomed trails.

RESTAURANTS. The Sutton area has a number of excellent restaurants with a wide variety of menus, from French cuisine to Canadian standard. In this selection, *Expensive,* $20–$30; *Moderate,* $15–$20; *Inexpensive,* less than $15. These prices are for the average cost of a full-course meal for one person, excluding drinks, tip, and tax. Restaurants accept most major credit cards, but check ahead to be sure.

Auberge à la Fontaine. *Moderate to Expensive.* 30 Principale, Sutton; 538–3045. Located in a 150-year-old house with a renovated glassed-in section. Split-level dining room with lots of plants and an interesting French menu; open 7 days a week.

Santiago. *Moderate to Expensive.* 29 Principale, Sutton; 538–2660. Features French cuisine. Owners Jacques and Paule Conessa have a background that reflects what they serve. (Jacques is Spanish but was raised in Cuba, and Paule is half Swiss-half French and spent a good part of her life in Algeria). Thus you will find specials such as locally raised fresh lamb or veal prepared "à la française," with a touch of North African "spice."

Auberge Glen Sutton. *Moderate.* Glen Sutton; 538–2000. Mexican cuisine, with excellent tacos, enchiladas, nachos, and burritos, in a most unlikely spot, right behind Mont Sutton, equidistant from Owl's Head and Jay Peak and right on the Canada–U.S. border. It's the only Mexican restaurant in the region and well worth a 15-minute drive.

L'Auberge Le Refuge. *Moderate.* 33 Maple St., Sutton; 538–3802. Frenchman Patrice Falluel makes special crepes with seafood, snails, mushrooms Provençale, scampi flambé au Ricard, and a chicken and pork brochette served with fruit. Open 7 days a week.

Cafe Mocador. *Moderate.* 17 Principale, Sutton; 538–2426. French cuisine cooked by a French chef. Full lunches and dinners, 7 days a week. Ask about its fine cuisine section for extra delicate dining; daily specials. Sunday brunch is served, 11:30 A.M.–2:30 P.M.

The Loft. *Moderate.* Hwy. 139 south, 5 miles from Sutton; 263–3294. Can't be beat for barbecued spare ribs, beef on a spit, and steaks. The focal point of the dining room is an open barbecue where you can see your order being prepared. Every Friday and Saturday owners Rob and Dorthee Newcombe cook 100 lbs. of short hip of beef on an open pit outside for roast beef aficionados.

Camille's. *Inexpensive.* In Hotel Camille on Principale St., Sutton; 538–2456. Family oriented and offers a standard Canadian fare of chicken, pizzas, brochettes, steaks, and sandwiches.

HOW TO GET AROUND. The village of Sutton is 4 miles from the mountain. Most accommodations are either in the village or along the mountain road. Many lodges have their own **shuttle vans** to take skiers to and from the mountain. In addition, the colorful *Sutton Shuttle* ensures regular transportation from the village and the various inns and lodges to the mountain daily. Inquire at your lodge for schedule.

OTHER SPORTS AND ACTIVITIES. The Sutton area offers some excellent **cross-country skiing** facilities. Less than a mile before you reach the alpine area on the mountain road is *Pistes D & M* (538–2271), also known as Sutton-en-Haut. The area offers 55 km of double-tracked trails through scenic forests running off the west shoulder of the alpine area. There are two warming huts and a waxing room and the owner Daniel Dépelteau will do almost anything to make your visit enjoyable. Hit him on a klyster day and he will apply and remove the mucky stuff for you. His philosophy is that klyster works wonders *under* your skis but is deadly on your hands and clothes. Since he doesn't mind getting his hands dirty, you can better enjoy the good skiing.

An equally excellent facility is *The Farmer's Rest* located in Knowlton on the Mont Echo Rd.; 243–6843. There you'll find 55 km of track-set trails offering 11 different one-way runs for beginner and advanced skiers alike. A good base chalet with solid down-home cooking, a waxing room and a well-stocked ski and rental shop and two heated huts make it one of the favorite touring centers in the region.

The *Sutton Curling Club* (538–3226) is located at the corner of Pleasant and Academy in the village. It has two rinks and is open most nights and some afternoons.

The *Cowansville Cultural Center* (263–4311) and *Sports Pavilion* (263–4020) are located in the region's main town, Cowansville, which has a population of 12,000. They are at the Municipal Educational Complex, corner of Hwys. 139 and 104. The center has a 25-km indoor **swimming pool** and a large gym for **volleyball, basketball, badminton,** and **indoor running.** The adjacent Sports Pavilion has a **skating rink** that is open for free skating on weekends.

DAY-CARE SERVICES. Right at the ski area on the upper level of the base pavilion is *La Garderie de Tante Lucille,* founded when the area opened in 1960 by Lucille Boulanger, widow of the late prime mover of the area, Real Boulanger. Since loyalty is one of the trademarks of the Sutton skier, many having been season's pass holders since 1960, many of the young adults now patronizing Sutton spent many a diaper day there, raised, so to speak, by Tante Lucille. Open seven days a week from 9 A.M. to 4 P.M., La Garderie takes children 2 to 6 years old. You can check your child in by the hour, the half day, or the full day at rates comparable to regular baby-sitting. For information or reservations, call the main lodge at 538–2338 or 866–7639.

NIGHTLIFE. *La Pimpolaise,* just at the entrance to Mont Sutton ski area (538–3213), is a favorite après-ski spot along with the disco at *Hotel Horizon* (538–3212), 1 mile from the ski area on the mountain road where the action really steps up in the evening; DJ-operated disco with dancing. *The Loft* on Hwy. 139 (243–5755) has a couple of popular bars. At the Club Bar you can relax by the fireplace listening to a folksinger Wednesday, Friday, and Saturday nights. Downstairs the disco offers continuous DJ-operated dance music to help you work out those muscles unaffected by skiing. Another popular spot is *Bri's Disco,* 418 Maple St., Sutton (538–2845), where you can shake off a few extra calories after dining at its excellent steak house.

OTHER EASTERN TOWNSHIPS SKI AREAS

Your ski vacation in the Eastern Townships includes an interchangeable lift ticket valid at Bromont, Sutton, Mont Orford, and Owl's Head.

Owl's Head. Mansonville PQ J0E 1X0; 819–292–5592 or Montreal direct 514–878–1453.

In the past, the Owl's Head region was short on nearby accommodations, but the Owl's Head Apartment Hotel, built in 1987–88, has added 23 2- and 3-bedroom units right on the slopes. The Auberge Owl's Head, situated directly at the base of the ski area, has an additional 10 rooms. Notwithstanding, Owl's Head is worth experiencing on your Ski East interchangeable lift ticket. With a 1,770-foot rise, Owl's Head has the third highest vertical in Quebec. It has one high-speed quad, six double chairs, and 27 runs.

Access to Owl's Head is not easy. Eleven km out of Mansonville on roller-coaster roads is what keeps the area less busy than most other Townships centers. Eastern Townships' Highway 243 takes you to Mansonville and from there to Owl's Head.

It is more of a folksy area, where the owner sometimes hands you the chair and the staff will answer the business line with a simple but friendly "hello," which can often make you wonder if you dialed a wrong number.

The area is located at the southwestern extremity of Lake Memphremagog right alongside the Canadian–U.S. border. The original section of the mountain, developed in 1965–66, is on a fairly steep eastern exposure, giving on a clear day one of skiing's most spectacular views, along scenic Lake Memphremagog.

Many trails off the main peak have a difficulty level comparable to the Mont Tremblant of the early 1970s. Narrow trails snake their way down mostly advanced intermediate and expert terrain. Rough, steep liftlines, often barely covered, offer more "macho" skiing per acre than most other Townships areas.

The newer section, which includes Lake Chair and two others, is more contemporary in design with wider, gentler trails serving the less experienced skier.

Snowmaking covers about 80 percent of the skiing terrain, and the area was the recipient of the 1985 Award of Excellence for the best improvement in ski conditions that year. The award was given by The MRG Ski Network, one of Quebec's ski and snow reporting organization. In keeping with this spirit of improvement, in 1988 Owl's Head renovated its base chalet, doubling the size of the facility.

Glen Mountain. Box 248, Lac Brome PQ J0E 1V0; 514–243–6142.

Located off Hwy. 243, Glen Mountain is the family area of the Eastern Townships region, but with a 1,060-foot vertical it would be the envy of many other regions. Somewhat belittled by the larger Eastern Townships centers, it is not a member of the Ski East group and therefore not on the interchangeable ticket.

The area offers 19 trails for day skiing and four for night skiing, Fridays and Saturdays 6–11 P.M. The terrain, particularly on the upper mountain, is varied and interesting.

The area has one double chair and three T-bars but no snowmaking. However, skier traffic is very light most of the time and for that reason trails hold up reasonably well on natural snow alone. Since rates are considerably lower than at neighboring areas, Glen is an excellent choice when snowfall has been heavy and crowds are expected at other areas. "The Glen," as it is called by regulars, is located just outside the village of Knowlton, a great place to stay with lots of shops and activities.

Quebec City Region

Along with Salt Lake City, Utah, Quebec City rates as one of North America's two largest ski towns.

Indeed, all skiing in the Quebec City region is within 30–45 minutes of the city center. When Mont Ste-Anne opened in 1965, it was felt that the 30-mile drive would spell doom for the new resort.

Skiing in Quebec City started in the 1930s at Lac Beauport, just 15 minutes north of the city, and that's where all Quebecers learned to ski. Two ski areas, Mont St-Castin and Le Relais, are now well established on the perimeter of the popular lake that over the years has been one of the main year-round playgrounds for Quebec residents.

Just 20 minutes north of Quebec City and only about 5 minutes past Lac Beauport lies Quebec's mid-range ski area, Stoneham, a 1,250-foot vertical, 24-run, aggressively developed mountain that offers Mont Ste-Anne its only real competition.

So, well within an hour's drive, Quebecers have a choice of family skiing at Lac Beauport; big mountain, resort skiing at Mont Ste-Anne; or a happy compromise at Stoneham.

But more important than the proximity of skiing in Quebec is the flavor of the 350-year-old town that was founded in 1608 by Samuel de Champlain. It is unquestionably a jewel of North America, the cradle of French civilization in the New World, and the only true French city of its size on the continent—Montreal being much more cosmopolitan.

Although English is spoken here in most key areas when necessary, French, more than any other language and more than in any other city, is dominant. Ninety-six percent of the half-million people speak French. There is no second language in Quebec, and that's what makes it different from the rest of the continent. And while the province is generally French-speaking, nowhere is the flavor felt more intensely than in Quebec City. Quebecers even have their own accent.

The focal point of Quebec is the Old Town, which dates back to the 17th century and is the only walled city north of Mexico. Dominated by the Chateau Frontenac, a castlelike hotel built in 1892 by the Canadian Pacific Railway and still owned by the hotel arm of the company, CP Hotels, the Old Town is a treasury of history, with cobblestone streets, fine restaurants, guest houses, museums, and other attractions.

For many people, Quebec City is winter. This is one major city where snow has always been a fact of life and the population has learned to deal with it. It is indeed through the winter months that Quebec's *joie de vivre* reaches its climax as the city hosts its annual Winter Carnival. For 10 days each February the city—particularly the Old Town—becomes a sort of snowy Disneyland and all Quebecers are children again. Parades trumpet through the streets and some brave souls from all over North America show up for the annual International Canoe Race across the icy, 2-mile-wide St. Lawrence River, facing up to 6-knot tidal currents, while thousands watch in awe from the cold shoreline.

Skiing in the Quebec City region offers the visitor the choice of either staying "in town" and enjoying the excitement of a moderate-sized city to the fullest or staying at the areas with the option of an easy 15- to 45-minute drive to Quebec City for more excitement as desired. The choice is yours to make and to enjoy.

MONT STE-ANNE

Box 400
Beaupre PQ G0A 1E0
Tel: 418–827–4561

Snow Report: Quebec City, 418–827–4579
Montreal, 514–861–6670
Toronto, 416–597–1788
Area Vertical: 2,050 ft. (625 m)
Number of Trails: 50
Lifts: 1 eight-passenger high-speed gondola,
2 high-speed quads, 1 fixed-grip quad,
1 triple chair, 2 double chairs, 5
surface lifts (T-bars or pomas)
Snowmaking: 85 percent of area
Season: mid-November–late April

Ste-Anne-de-Beaupre, just 25 miles (40 km) east of Quebec City, has long been the "miracle capital" of North America, but since 1965, a new industry has been bringing more "manna" to the region: skiing.

With a 2,050-foot vertical drop, Mont Ste-Anne is the largest skiable mountain in eastern Canada and the second most popular ski area in the country, just behind the Whistler-Blackcomb complex in British Columbia in terms of skier-days.

Ste-Anne is somewhat of a late bloomer in terms of large destination ski resorts in Quebec. Although it has been in operation since 1965 and skiing on the mountain without lifts goes back to the mid-1940s, it is only since 1982 that it has started drawing more international attention.

While it has hosted several World Cup events since 1969, the area survived for 18 years with natural snow, abundant enough, particularly on the north slopes. But the snow drought that rocked Eastern ski areas in the early 1980s was to be the turning point for Mont Ste-Anne. Although Ste-Anne cured the sick and the injured, she unfortunately could not make it snow on the mountain. The area quickly realized the problem and a high-tech snowmaking system was installed to cover 82 percent of the mountain, now extended to 85 percent.

With 50 trails on three faces, eastern Canada's first and only eight-passenger gondola, six chairlifts, including two high-speed quads (one with a lexan bubble cover to protect skiers from the elements), and five other surface lifts, Mont Ste-Anne is the showcase of Quebec skiing.

Like Whiteface in upstate New York, Mont Ste-Anne is government owned and operated. Many a regular Ste-Anne skier feels that if the government would be as good at minding the provincial coffers as it has been at operating the ski area, Quebecers would be the fat cats of North America.

True, the area was long subsidized by the people, but it is now on its own feet. And while it certainly is not as lean in staff as private areas, with the government involved, many benefits filter down to the skier.

Prices at Mont Ste-Anne, for example, are no higher than at the other areas in the province, despite the fact that Ste-Anne is the biggest and the best. Signage and safety precautions are unparalleled in the province. Trails are seldom open prematurely and are often closed by midday if conditions deteriorate. Snow reports are dependable, which is a rare occurrence.

Grooming is also tops in the province in terms of large areas. Every night groomers tackle the mountain, leveling, resurfacing, and packing as many as 25 of the 50 runs. And while snowmaking is still a fairly recent art for Quebec's largest, it has already proven its will to produce and skills to make good snow. In 1986, the area closed in early May with south side trails still skiable in late April.

Recent improvements include a self-contained children's center and an eight-passenger high-speed gondola that takes skiers to the top of the south side in only 8 minutes.

The area continues to maintain its leadership role. In 1990–91 it became the first Canadian resort to implement the Ski Data lift-ticketing system. Ski Data uses electronically magnetized lift tickets you insert into a turnstile slot at the base of each lift. This allows you to purchase skiing "à la carte" according to your availability and/or budget: by the hour, or by points, in which a number of points is debited from your ticket as you use the lifts. Higher-vertical lifts use up more points than lower ones. The point system essentially charges you by the number of vertical feet that you ski. The philosophy behind the Ski Data system is that it offers skiers—particularly day skiers—more choices than the usual full-day or half-day tickets. If you have only 2 hours to ski, for example, you could pay by the hour and try to cram in as many runs as possible. Or, if you plan on spending the whole day at the mountain but are sore from the previous day of hard skiing, you can use a points ticket to ski a few cruising runs at your leisure, without feeling that you are wasting a full-day ticket.

Mont Ste-Anne is an oddly shaped mountain. It has the shape of a sleeping bear; flat-topped, a stand-alone mountain wider than it is high and skiable on 300 degrees. On approach, the area does not appear to have over 2,000 feet of vertical. But as you stare attentively at the two straight chutes on the left of the gondola line and see that those tiny black specks are skiers grinding their way down, you suddenly become a little more respectful of the mountain's size.

If your attention keeps drifting back to those monster tracks—they're not quite as mean as they look—keep in mind that there's more good cruising terrain for all abilities at Ste-Anne than straight gut-wrenching drops. In fact, the area's extensive grooming and snowmaking have opened up just about all trails to a good intermediate.

Mont Ste-Anne is easy enough to get around and to understand. On the south side everything left of the gondola is most difficult terrain with trails becoming easier and longer the farther right you go.

Intermediate skiers as well as those who like good cruising will find their best pickings on the north and west sides each with just over 1,000 feet of vertical. The latter for good intermediate skiers and up is, however, a bit short on uphill capacity serviced only by a T-bar. But it holds good future potential for expert skiers.

Beginner and novice country is mostly on the lower south and the upper right side shoulder of the mountain, which is well serviced by two comfortable quadruple chairs, one of which is high-speed.

In the morning, advanced skiers race to the south-side triple chair that services all of the south side's advanced runs. For openers, trails 1 *(La Crete)* and 1–B *(L'Espoir),* when they have been freshly groomed, are ideal warm-up runs. Although rated black, they are wide and usually kept smooth. If not groomed, however, look to something blue. The top of 1–B offers a breathtaking view of the surroundings, west to Quebec City and east down the wide and mighty St. Lawrence River to Ile-aux-Coudres, where fresh water turns to salt.

By the time you ski both those runs, each about a mile long, you'll probably have made enough turns to tackle your next challenge—the *"S"* and *"Super S"* trails, the area's toughest snowmaking serviced trails. Identical twins, the area differentiates them with grooming. And that separates the grown-ups from the kids. One is a rodeo trail with moguls that sometimes reach the size of a Volkswagen *Beetle;* the other, a steep but smooth drop that offers a tempting challenge to the strong intermediate skier and the challenge to ski it nonstop top to bottom for a good, strong expert.

Underneath the gondola lift is *La Gondoleuse,* another tough expert run made even tougher by the fact that it does not have snowmaking, which will remind you of what skiing was like "in the old days"!

For obvious reasons, the north side staring out at Quebec's wilderness is often colder but also more powdery. So when the shell begins to pop up on the south, head for the north and you'll often be surprised at the quality of the snow awaiting you.

Night skiing is the latest addition to Mont Ste-Anne's south side. Thirteen trails are lit, including the 2-mile Pichard, which provides skiers of all abilities with top-to-bottom skiing under the lights on the south side of the mountain.

Whatever your skiing ability, you'll find a lot of what you like at Mont Ste-Anne. And quite important in the successful operation of any ski area is a staff that has been there for a long time, knows the mountain and how to deal with it, and knows what skiers, regulars, and visitors want from their mountain. You'll find that at Mont Ste-Anne.

Practical Information for Mont Ste-Anne

HOW TO GET THERE. Quebec City is, of course, the gateway city to the Mont Ste-Anne region. **By air.** *Air Canada, Air Alliance, Air Quebec Metro, Air Nova, Intair* and *Northwest Airlink* (from Boston) fly into Quebec's Loretteville Airport several times a day connecting with Montreal International and from there to the rest of the world. Major **car rental** companies are on site at the airport and you can reserve a car from wherever you are through *Avis* (800–331–1212), *Budget* (800–527–0700), *Hertz* (800–654–3131), or *Tilden,* which is the Canadian agency for *National* (800–328–4567). Transfer from the airport otherwise by taxi or by bus, stopping at the major hotels.

By car. From points west of Quebec, you must first reach Montreal. From there, take either Hwy. 20 to Quebec on the south shore of the St. Lawrence or Hwy. 40 on the north shore. From the United States, both I–87 and I–89 will take you to Montreal. Coming from eastern New England on I–91, you can avoid Montreal by taking Hwy. 55 toward Sherbrooke and Drummondville and from there onto Hwy. 20 toward Quebec City.

From Quebec City, arriving from either the north or south shores, take *Autoroute de la Capitale*—the continuation of Hwy. 40 toward Beaupre. This autoroute bypasses Quebec City slightly to the north and will take you right to Beaupre. From there follow the signs to the area.

From the city center, you'll easily find Autoroute 440, which connects with Hwy. 40 and eventually reaches Beaupre.

The 25-mile drive to Beaupre from Quebec City is mostly on a four-lane undivided highway that passes several villages along the way. Traffic is fast, particularly on weekends. Beware of unmarked police patrols parked in commercial entrances along the way. Remember that the speed limit on that stretch of highway is 90 km/h (about 55 mph).

TELEPHONES. The area code for Mont Ste-Anne and the city of Quebec is 418.

ACCOMMODATIONS. As stated elsewhere, you have the choice of either staying in Quebec City and driving the 25 miles daily to Mont Ste-Anne or staying in the vicinity of the mountain. Of course, being the tourist attraction that it is, Quebec City has a wealth of accommodations of all types and for every purse. Listed here is but a selection. If you're going to stay in Quebec—as many skiers do—you'll be wise to stay in or near the Old Town for its accessibility to the mountain. Otherwise, Mont Ste-Anne should be your operating base.

Central Reservations Service. ReservOtel is Mont Ste-Anne region's central reservation service. It can be reached toll free from Quebec, Ontario, the Maritimes, and the eastern and central United States at 800–463–1568. It gives you a choice of more than 50 hotels, motels, inns, apartments, condominiums, and chalets, all selected for their comfort, location, and the quality of the services they offer. This is an ideal starting point for local reservations, since it can make helpful suggestions and mail informative brochures on different types of accommodations.

Hotel rates listed here are per person, based on double occupancy. Categories, determined by price, are: *Expensive,* $75 and up; *Moderate,* $50–$75; *Inexpensive,* less than $50. Most accept major credit cards. Those that do not are so indicated.

Mont Ste-Anne and Vicinity

Moderate to Expensive

Chalets Mont Ste-Anne. Box 288, Beaupre, PQ G0A 1E0; 418–827–5776 or 800–463–4395. Condominium rental complex nearest to the mountain. Offers completely furnished units with 3–5 bedrooms. All units have cable TV, fireplace, and kitchen; some have hot tub or sauna.

Le Chateau Mont Ste-Anne. 500 Blvd. Beau Pre, Beaupre, PQ G0A 1E0; 418–827–5211, 800–463–4467 from Ontario, Quebec, and the Maritimes, and 800–463–1568 from eastern and central United States. A 4-season conference resort center, it is the largest hotel at the foot of the mountain. Its 258 luxurious rooms are very large and have kitchenettes. Ski week and weekend packages available. An urban accommodation slopeside with piano bar, disco, and good après-ski action.

Hotel Val Des Neiges. Box 490, Beaupre, PQ G0A 1E0; 418–827–5711, 800–361–1155 from Ontario, Maritimes, and the United States; or 800–463–5250 from Quebec. Built in 1987, this modern, 4-season resort and convention center offers 86 luxurious rooms; a dining room; a piano bar; an indoor sports and fitness complex, including a swimming pool, hot tubs, a sauna, and exercise and game rooms, as well as a day-care center. Packages available for ski-weeks and weekends. Located ¼ mile east of Mont Ste-Anne.

Moderate

Auberge Le Refuge Du Parc. 186 Rang St-Julien, St-Fereol-les-Neiges, PQ G0A 3R0; 418–826–2363. Located about 4 miles east of the mountain at the main entrance to Mont Ste-Anne cross-country ski center. Its claim to fame is having been host to Ingemar Stenmark during World Cup events; a cozy and warm environment and excellent cuisine. Accommodation is available in either the lodge or in one of 12 chalets with full amenities and maid service. This is an attractive place not only to stay at but to visit, after skiing or for a delightful meal.

Chalets Hobec. 300 rue Dupont C.P. 265, Beaupre, PQ G0A 1E0; 418–827–3795 or 800–463–1594. At the foot of Mont Ste-Anne, only 2 km from the lifts. Two-story, 2-bedroom chalets sleeping a maximum of 6 people; all units have fireplace, cable TV, large living room, and complete kitchen. No credit cards accepted, deposit by check, balance by certified check or cash.

Chalets Montmorency. 1768 Royale, St-Fereol-les-Neiges, PQ G0A 3R0; 418–826–2600 or 800–463–2612 from Canada, 800–463–1568 from the United States. Less than 1 km from the lifts. Swiss-type chalets owned by former Mont Ste-Anne Ski School Director John Barclay, and his wife Gisele, it offers luxurious, clean, and spacious 1–3 bedroom apartments, all with fireplace, complete kitchen, dishwasher, and bathroom. Motel units with or without kitchenettes are also available, along with 11 new 1- and 3-bedroom condo units. In 1989, an indoor lap-pool and whirlpool bath were added to the amenities, which also include a recreation room sauna, and free shuttle to the lifts. Located near a bakery, restaurants, a grocery store, and right across from an access trail to the 200-km Parc du Mont Ste-Anne cross-country network. Prepayment by check.

Moderate to Inexpensive

Auberge La Becassine. 9341 Blvd. Ste-Anne, Ste-Anne-de-Beaupre PQ G0A 3C0; 418–827–4988 or 800–463–1568. A 5-minute drive from the lifts and one of the best in a strip of auberges and motels on the Quebec-Ste-Anne highway. Owners are friendly and accommodating, the food good, the hospitality warm, the bar lively, and accommodations clean and reasonable. Your choice of a room in the lodge or a convenient motel unit with full bathroom.

Others in the *inexpensive* category include **Motel Orleans,** 2941 Blvd. Ste-Anne, Beauport, G1E 3J2, 661–6916 or 800–463–5550; **Hotel Regent,** 1006 Blvd. Ste-Anne, Beauport, G1E 3M3, 667–1633, 800–463–1568 from the United States or 800–463–5291 from eastern Canada; **Auberge Café de la Paix,** 1930 Blvd. Les Neiges, St-Fereol-les-Neiges, G0A 3R0, 826–3366; **Refuge du Faubourg,** 1910 Blvd. Les Neiges, St-Fereol-les-Neiges, G0A 3R0, 826–2869 or 800–463–5752.

Quebec City

Of course, being the tourist attraction that it is, Quebec City has a wealth of accommodations of all types and for every purse. We won't attempt to list them all. If you're going to stay in Quebec—as many skiers do—you'll be wise to stay in or near the Old Town. Otherwise Mont Ste-Anne, only 30 minutes away, should be your operating base.

Expensive

Le Chateau Frontenac. 1 rue des Carrieres, G1R 4P5; 692–3861 or 800–268–9420. The provincial capital's most famous landmark. This 520-room hotel built in 1892 occupies the city's most strategic piece of real estate, on a point high atop Cap Diamand with a commanding view down the majestic St. Lawrence River toward Ile d'Orleans and Mont Ste-Anne, the south shore, the historic Plains of Abraham, and the Old Town. Wherever they put you, you'll have something interesting to look at. Ski packages, including lift ticket at Mont Ste-Anne, available for 2 nights double occupancy. If you don't stay here, drop in for a worthwhile visit.

Loews le Concorde. 1225 Place Montcalm (corner Grande Allee), G1R 4W6; 647–2222, 800–463–5256 from eastern Canada, or 800–223–0888 from eastern United States. One of Quebec's most modern and luxurious hotels. Bordering the Plains of Abraham, the 424-room hotel offers cross-country skiing at your doorstep or alpine skiing at any of the Quebec region's ski areas, including Mont Ste-Anne. The area is ideally located in the heart of Grande Allee's best discos and restaurants.

Hilton Quebec. 3 Place Quebec, G1K 7M9; 647–2411. Part of the international chain and located right behind the National Assembly, Quebec's government house, and within yards of the famous *Palais de Glace* (Ice Castle), built every year for the annual Winter Carnival in February. Ski Hilton packages include transportation to Mont Ste-Anne and lift ticket.

Moderate

Auberge des Gouverneurs. 690 East Blvd. St. Cyrille G1K 7M9; 647–1717, 800–463–2820 from eastern Canada, or 800–654–2000 from eastern United States. Similar to the Hilton next door, but somewhat less expensive. Ski packages available. Daily rate includes lift ticket to Mont Ste-Anne.

Holiday Inn Quebec City. 395 rue de la Couronne, G1K 6Z7; 647–2611, 800–465–4329 from Canada. Needs little introduction. It has 232 rooms. Ski packages with the hotel include lift tickets.

Hotel-Motel le Voyageur. 2250 Blvd. Ste-Anne, G1J 1Y2; 661–7701 or 800–463–5568 from Eastern Canada. Somewhat of a compromise between staying in town or at the area. Located on the outskirts of Quebec City on the road to Mont Ste-Anne, it has 64 rooms with lift ticket and breakfast included. Indoor pool.

Inexpensive

Centre International de Sejour de Quebec. 19 rue St. Ursule, G1R 4E1; 694–0755. Offers 40 rooms with breakfast and lift ticket included.

Hotel Clarendon. 57 Ste-Anne, G1K 7M9; 692–2480. In the heart of the Old Town; offers packages to Mont Ste-Anne.

RESTAURANTS. There are three main areas around Mont Ste-Anne in which to dine—in the adjacent village of St-Fereol-les-Neiges, in Beaupre where the mountain road joins the main highway, and at Ste-Anne-de-Beaupre, about 4 miles from the mountain. Restaurants are listed in order of price category. *Expensive:* $25 and up; *Moderate:* $13–$25; *Inexpensive:* less than $13. Restaurants accept most major credit cards unless otherwise noted.

Moderate to Expensive

Auberge le Refuge du Parc. At the entrance to Parc Mont Ste-Anne cross-country center, about 5 miles from the alpine base; 826–2363. Has always been an excellent choice for those who enjoy fine French and Canadian cuisine served in a relaxed, French-Canadian atmosphere. Excellent breakfasts, too.

Auberge Café de la Paix. 1930 Blvd. des Neiges in St-Fereol; 826–3366. Features French nouvelle cuisine and some of the best food available in the region. Three table d'hôte choices are offered every night, including such delights as frogs' legs, rabbit, and filet of pork in raspberry vinegar. There is also an 8-course gastronomical table offered and once a month the auberge prepares a *Gastronomie des Neiges* table featuring specialties from European ski countries such as Switzerland, Austria, Germany, Italy, and France. Reservations recommended on weekends.

La Camarine. 10947 Blvd. Ste-Anne, near the high school at the junction of the mountain road; 827–5566. This five-star restaurant, located in a 125-year-old Quebec farmhouse, is where locals bring guests they want to impress. The cuisine is inspired by French nouvelle cuisine and chef Francine, who studied in France, conjures up dishes such as salmon tartare, duck with raspberry vinegar sauce, scallops in pastry, and fresh Quebec lamb. The menu changes every day, with 6 to 7 different entrees offered. Downstairs, you'll find a wine bar where selections also change regularly. Here you can enjoy wine by the glass from $4 up to $25 for vintage selections. Reservations necessary. La Camarine is also a bed-and-breakfast.

Chateau Mont Ste-Anne. At the gondola lift base; 827–5211. Has 3 restaurants worth mentioning. *Le St Moritz* is the hotel's deluxe dining room offering a refined and select menu, including chateaubriand, seafood, rack of lamb, etc., and can be rated expensive. More moderately priced are *La Grive des Bois* facing the ski slopes and the more intimate, *Le Soleil Levant,* which essentially have the same menu including house special pizzas, Italian dishes, fish, and seafood as well as hot and cold sandwiches and special children's menus.

Chez Albert. 1805 Blvd. des Neiges in St-Fereol; 826–2184. Conveniently located just across the bridge on the left leaving the ski area—the one with the red roof. Features mostly Italian dishes including delicious open-hearth pizzas, the specialty of the house. The restaurant also serves meats, salads, and other pastas.

Chez Colette. 2190 Avenue Royale; 826–2944. One of the favorites of visitors to the region. Colette herself will be your hostess in this intimate (room for about 50), family-operated French-Canadian establishment. French onion soup au gratin, Caesar salads, beef Stroganoff, bouillabaisse, and several table d'hôte specials make up the enticing and diversified menu. Reservations recommended.

Restaurant Baker. 8790 Royale in Chateau Richer, just east of Ste-Anne-de-Beaupre, 824–4478 or 4852. A must dining experience for anyone visiting Mont Ste-Anne. The lovely 19th-century homestead converted into a cozy inn by Alvin Baker in 1935 is the region's finest eating establishment. Here you'll be offered anything from the most traditional of Quebec fare, Granny's pea soup, Aunt Gilberte's ragout of pig's feet and meatballs, Lac St Jean meat pie with beef, pork, veal, and potatoes, to more classical French-European dishes such as scallops on homemade puff pastry, onion soup au gratin, filet mignon with black peppercorns, and salmon with sorrel. Reservations recommended. Also a bed-and-breakfast.

Moderate to Inexpensive

Bistro Le Pétrin. 1806 Avenue Royale, across Chalets Montmorency in St-Fereol; 826–2699. This is a combination restaurant/bar/dance hall on the Hard Rock Café mode; same style of food with local and imported beers. Specialties include Paris-style steak-frites, Swiss and bourgignon fondues, chicken wings. The place is open for breakfast, lunch, and dinner and features stand-up comics and murder-mystery events in the evening.

Restaurant les Neiges. 3069 Avenue Royale; 826–2741. The local diner-type restaurant in the region. Good for a fast lunch or breakfast specialties include pizzas, cheese fondues, steaks, and barbecued chicken as well as the standard fare of hot and cold sandwiches, hot dogs, burgers, and fries. An advantage is that it delivers.

Restaurant Roma. 9450 Blvd. Ste-Anne (827–3681), and **Le Marie Antoinette** (827–3446) at the Carrefour, both in Ste-Anne-de-Beaupre. Family restaurants where there's something for everyone from spaghetti and pizzas to burgers, sandwiches, chicken, and grilled cheeses for your 3-year-old. Le Marie Antoinette is somewhat similar to Howard Johnson's.

Roulotte Bolduc. 10668 Blvd. Ste-Anne-Beaupre; 827–3226. For some typical Quebec greasies or a late-night burger the region's best. The best *frites* (french fries) around will accompany your steamie with *choux* (chopped cabbage), burger, or submarine. French fries, Quebec's national roadside dish, also comes *a la poutine*—only in Quebec—served with cheese curds and a brown sauce. If you've survived Austrian schnapps, this will be a snap! Cash only.

HOW TO GET AROUND. The past few years have seen the development of a base village with some accommodations in the form of condos. Shopping and restaurant facilities grow every year. Less than 1 km away from the mountain's south base is the village of St-Fereol-les-Neiges, where there are some accommodations that generally require your own, or rented, car. The village of Ste-Anne-de-Beaupre is less than 5 miles away from the mountain and has several motels. You'll be best served with your own transportation although a few motels can give you a free ride to the mountain. **Taxi** service is available from *Taxi Ste-Anne,* 827–2330, and *Taxi Tremblay,* 827–5160.

Many visitors to Mont Ste-Anne stay in Quebec City since it is only 25 miles away. Although car transportation is the best solution, a very efficient **ski bus** service takes skiers from many points in the city to the region's ski centers (Mont Ste-Anne, Stoneham, and Lac Beauport) every morning and returns them again in late afternoon. The ski bus has an extended route through the city but stops at the following hotels: Le Roussillon, Loews Le Concorde, Chateau Frontenac, Holiday Inn Mid-town, and Hotel des Gouverneurs Place Hauteville. For further information on service to Mont Ste-Anne, call 529–0616; for Lac Beauport and Stoneham, 627–2511.

A complete information packet on getting around in the Quebec City region can be obtained by contacting the Quebec City Region Tourism and Convention Bureau, 60 rue d'Auteuil, PQ G1R 4C4; 692–2471.

For **car rentals** contact the following:

Avis. Airport, 872–2861.

Hertz. Airport and Ste. Foy, 871–1571; 44 du Palais, 694–1224.

Budget. Airport and Ste. Foy, 872–9885; Cote du Palais, 692–3660; Place Quebec, 529–0966.

Rent-A-Wreck. 265 W. Blvd. Hamel, Vanier, 683–2333.

Tilden. Airport and Ste. Foy, 871–1224; 295 rue St. Paul, 694–1727; Sillery, 687–3322; and 5115 Blvd. Hamel, 872–5655.

SEASONAL EVENTS. Quebec Carnival. For 10 days in early **February** each year Quebec City becomes the capital of winter fun as the internationally famous Quebec Winter Carnival, led by *Bonhomme Carnaval,* opens its doors to the world.

Fantastic ice sculptures and castles pop up everywhere, parades trumpet through the streets, parties and balls are hosted by various groups and hotels, and everywhere the people of Quebec City celebrate winter with much gusto. Further information and the annual program of the Quebec Winter Carnaval can be obtained either from the Quebec City Region Tourism Bureau (692–2471) or by calling Tourism Quebec toll free, 800–361–6490 from eastern Canada, or 800–443–7000 from the United States.

OTHER SPORTS AND ACTIVITIES. Cross-country skiing is very big in the region and one need look no further than *Parc du Mont Ste-Anne* (827–4561), in St-Fereol-les-Neiges, 5 miles east of the alpine area, to find some of the best developed and maintained facilities in eastern Canada: 214 km (138 miles) of double-track trails for all abilities are maintained and patrolled throughout the winter. Rates in 1990 were $8 for adults, $6 for ages 14–20, $5 for 7–13 and over 65, and children under 6 ski free.

The trail network has been host to a number of prestigious events over the years, including several Canadian championships, and was also the back-up site for the 1980 Lake Placid Olympics. A restaurant, waxing facilities, and warming huts on the trails are open daily.

Dedicated cross-country skiers can stay at *l'Auberge du Fondeur* (827–4561), a ski-in, ski-out lodge right on the trail network. Private rooms and dorm-style accommodations are available; both are inexpensive.

Other cross-country centers in the region include *l'Eperon at Lac Beauport* (849–2778), 15 minutes north of the city with some 214 km of well-maintained trails; and *Camp Mercier* (848–2422), in Parc des Laurentides north of Mont Ste-Anne. With 192 km of maintained trails, it offers the longest cross-country skiing season in Quebec, often running into early May.

Should you be staying in Quebec City, the Plains of Abraham, which run along Cap Diamand from the Chateau Frontenac to the borough of Sillery, also offer several kilometers of easily accessible trails for urban skiing. You can reach the trail network from any entry point to the park from Grande Allee.

Hockey is Canada's national sport and should you be in Quebec City while the home team Nordiques play their archrivals the Montreal Canadiens, do try to get tickets. You'll witness a confrontation that often goes beyond the sport itself and possibly gain some insight into the French-Canadian way of thinking which makes Quebec so different in the North American context. For ticket information, call the Colisee, 691–7211.

NIGHTLIFE. Luckily Mont Ste-Anne is a good, tough, ski mountain and if the skiing doesn't tire you out then the midwinter cold and the wind certainly will. Good skiing and good eating, more than boogie, are the trademarks of the region, so if your main objective is to party then you'll be best served in Quebec City where discotheques and bars abound. Nonetheless, there are a few nearby spots worth noting.

For immediate après-ski, the "in" place is the *La Chouette Pub,* in the Mont Ste-Anne south-side base lodge. *Chateau Mont Ste-Anne,* also on the south side base of the area, is another choice spot for après-ski and nightlife. The après-ski crowd gathers from 4 to 8 P.M. in the *Piano Bar,* where live entertainment keeps the energy level high and free appetizers keep your appetite satisfied. The day's competition or other mountain activity is usually showed on a giant screen video. For more intimate situations the small *Cumulus Bar* just across from the Piano Bar is quieter and appropriate for more meaningful discussion. Later on, from about 9 P.M., the focus turns to *Le Crepuscule* (dusk) disco where you can spend your last daily bit of energy until 3 A.M., if it takes that long. All bars are part of the Chateau Mont Ste-Anne hotel, 500 Blvd. Beau-Pre (827–5211), and accept all major credit cards.

Bistro Le Pétrin (see restaurants, above) is also a good après-ski and night spot. Food, dancing, and live entertainment are featured.

In **Quebec City** the selection of discos, bars, and watering holes runs long and wide, of course.

Like everywhere else the focus of nightlife in larger towns has a way of shifting from area to area. Quebec is no exception and the hot spots these days are along the Grande Allee near the Old Town and the government buildings. Between the

Armory and the Loews Le Concorde Hotel you'll find three of the current top bars and disco: *Brandy, Vogue,* and *Dagobert,* with *Le Cabaret* at the Concorde Hotel said to be the top spot on the street. For a more mature atmosphere, head to Ste. Foy and Bogart's, 2590 Blvd. Laurier, between the two large shopping centers, Place Ste. Foy and Place Laurier.

OTHER ALPINE AREAS. There are three other areas worth visiting in the region: **Stoneham,** 848–2411, only 20 minutes north of the city, just past Lac Beauport. The area has a respectable 1,350 foot vertical and 24 runs off four mountains. Lifts include one high-speed quad, three quads (including one with a wind-protective bubble), two double chairs, and four surface lifts. Snowmaking covers all major trails with night skiing on 15 runs and breathtaking views of the Quebec City lights in the near distance from several. Stoneham is also one of the province's most attractive areas. A bowl-shaped dead end, it draws snow and offers something for everyone. Quality and service is the name of the game here. From the moment you enter the parking lot to the time you leave, the welcome signs are ever present. Attendants will help you unload your skis from your car in the arrival plaza, and you'll find three different types of restaurants, from standard-fare cafeteria to white-tablecloth fine dining. There is a lounge for teens where rock videos, ski films, and games are available after skiing. There are even tissue dispensers at lift lines. The most recent developments at Stoneham include a 60-room slopeside hotel complex with restaurants and shops. Another slopeside condo-hotel is scheduled to open in the winter of 1991–92. A "must" visit to write into your Quebec City agenda.

Lac Beauport is only about 15 minutes north of Quebec City via Highway 175, on the way to Stoneham. This is where skiing in the region began in the 1930s. Two smaller, family areas are found here: **Le Relais,** 849–1851, with 24 runs, and **Mont St-Castin-Les-Neiges,** 849–677, with 14 runs. Both areas are open for day and night skiing on a vertical of approximately 800 feet.

About 45 minutes east of Mont Ste-Anne lies a giant mountain with the only heated lifts in North America. **Le Massif** at Petite Riviere St-François is a 2,500-foot vertical slope on the shore of the 5-mile-wide St. Lawrence River. It can accommodate only about 300 skiers per day, since it is serviced only by buses that bring skiers to the top of the mountain. It is a mountain that, when fully developed, will be the size and scope of Killington, Vermont. For now though it is a sleeping giant. Skiing Le Massif's "off trail" type of skiing is by reservation only. Call 418–435–3593.

WESTERN
CANADA

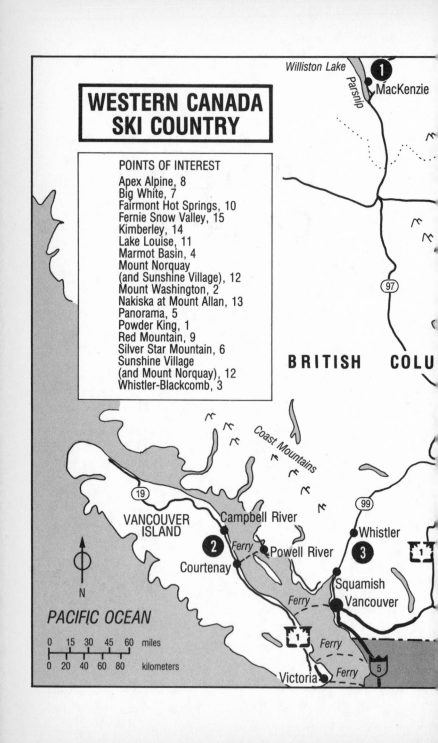

WESTERN CANADA SKI COUNTRY

POINTS OF INTEREST

Apex Alpine, 8
Big White, 7
Fairmont Hot Springs, 10
Fernie Snow Valley, 15
Kimberley, 14
Lake Louise, 11
Marmot Basin, 4
Mount Norquay
(and Sunshine Village), 12
Mount Washington, 2
Nakiska at Mount Allan, 13
Panorama, 5
Powder King, 1
Red Mountain, 9
Silver Star Mountain, 6
Sunshine Village
(and Mount Norquay), 12
Whistler-Blackcomb, 3

Williston Lake

Parsnip

MacKenzie

97

BRITISH COLU

Coast Mountains

19

VANCOUVER
ISLAND

Campbell River

Ferry

Powell River

Whistler

Courtenay

99

Squamish

Vancouver

N

Ferry

PACIFIC OCEAN

0   15   30   45   60   miles

0   20   40   60   80   kilometers

1

Ferry

Ferry

Victoria

Ferry

5

WESTERN CANADA

by
JOHN COLEBOURNE and DON BILODEAU
Updated by
GUY THIBAUDEAU

Big, bold, and rugged, the Canadian West has major-league skiing, yet has managed to keep its laid-back charm. The skiing is among the best anywhere, with an incredible variety of ski terrain. The abundant snowfall, spectacular scenery, untouched countryside, and friendly residents give this vast region a sense of a frontier waiting to be explored.

A western Canadian ski adventure takes place in two provinces: Alberta and British Columbia. Both are different in character and geography, yet they share the unique qualities that make western Canada's ski resorts so interesting.

Alberta, with its cowboy roots, is a combination of prairie scrubland, rolling foothills, and majestic mountain peaks. Oil wells, grazing horses, and huge cattle herds can be found throughout the province and bordering the Rocky Mountain range, which is being carefully preserved as part of the environmentally controlled Banff and Jasper National Parks. In the two parks lie four major ski resorts, all very different in size and character. Sunshine Village, Mt. Norquay, and Lake Louise all operate in Banff National Park. The drive through the range on the well-maintained road system is a treat in itself: Wild animals dot the roadside, and the parks' location in a valley floor showcases the imposing mountain peaks on both sides. The picturesque highway to Jasper is through an intimidating mountainous section dominated by huge glaciers, considered by many to be one of the most beautiful drives in the world. Just outside Jasper is Marmot Basin Ski Resort.

Alberta's neighbor to the west is British Columbia, a province of beautiful forested areas and abundant waterways. Its vast range of mountains stretch right to the ocean in Vancouver (and then over into Vancouver Island). In terms of size, the province spreads over an area larger than Washington, Oregon, and California combined. A European can measure it as being larger than Italy, France, Austria, and Switzerland all put together. There's an unlimited variety of skiing in British Columbia, everything from the small-town sleepy ski area to the international destination resort of Whistler. Because British Columbia gets so much snow, heli-ski operators in the province are finding more customers each season who seek the ultimate powder experience. Many heli-ski operators operate near the major ski areas.

Throughout the Canadian West, you'll find comfortable accommodations and a variety of dining spots. Most are at prices that won't take a big chunk out of your wallet. The region is accessible through three major gateways: Vancouver, British Columbia, and Calgary and Edmonton, Alberta. All are serviced by most major airlines from most North American cities.

Skiers who discover British Columbia's and Alberta's mountains return again and again. There's too much to experience in only one visit!

Note: Remember, all prices quoted in the western Canada section of this guide are in **Canadian dollars.**

Alberta

BANFF-LAKE LOUISE RESORTS

The town of Banff and the village of Lake Louise are located in Banff National Park, a 1½-hour drive west of Calgary International Airport. This first-class tri-resort area is famous for its spectacular scenery and wide variety of skiing terrain. Mount Norquay, Sunshine Village, and Lake Louise ski areas are located here.

The town of Banff is nestled at the junction of the valleys of the Bow and Spray rivers at an altitude of 4,538 feet. With a wide variety of hotels and restaurants, there is something for every taste and budget.

Banff was named after Banffshire, Scotland, the birthplace in 1883 of Lord Strathcona, then the president of the Canadian Pacific Railroad. The town has evolved from a Canadian Pacific Railroad (CPR) settlement called Siding 29, which serviced the railroad men, mines, and local trappers. By 1888, the area's hot springs and the 10 square miles around it had been made a natural reserve and several merchants had already established themselves on the main street, now called Banff Avenue. All the other streets in Banff are named for animals found in the park. Wildlife, especially elk, stroll through the town, often stopping in backyards and the local school, much to the amusement of passing tourists.

Lake Louise is spectacular country. You'll find Canada's largest ski area and across the valley one of the most beautiful lakes in the world situated at the base of Victoria Glacier. Back in 1882, an adventurer named Tom Wilson was guided up to the lake by a local Indian and was awestruck by its beauty. Word spread, and in 1890 a chalet for climbers and visitors was built. It later burned down and was replaced by a CPR hotel in 1924, later named Chateau Lake Louise.

Skiing in the Lake Louise region began in the 1920s and '30s with the building of Skoki Lodge in the back country behind Lake Louise Ski Area. Another lodge, called Mount Temple Chalet, was built in 1937 on the route to Skoki. Located 8 km from Lake Louise Station, it became the site of the first mechanical lift in the area. By 1967 it had grown into a major destination along with Sunshine Village, 60 km down the valley.

Mount Norquay is the smallest of the three ski areas and is conveniently situated overlooking the town of Banff. First developed in 1948 with the installation of the first single chairlift in western Canada, this ski area is noted for its super-steep terrain and pleasant view of the Bow Valley.

Banff National Park is under constant pressure from the ski-area opera-tors, who want to expand their facilities to remain competitive with other destination areas, and from environmentalists, who want to preserve the pristine nature of the park. This tension contributes to the maintenance of high-quality skiing conditions. Mother Nature, however, is a factor that cannot be discounted. The three ski areas are famous for the light cham-pagne-dry powder snow they get much of the winter. Because of the high altitude and dry mountain air, the snow stays light for a number of days after a snowfall. Winter conditions go into April and by May, spring skiing conditions prevail, but it is not unusual to get a snowstorm in this area in May.

Nordic skiing is equally spectacular in the Lake Louise region. Ski on 61 km of groomed trails in the immediate area or ski to the famous rustic Skoki Lodge 11 km from Temple Lodge.

LAKE LOUISE SKI AREA

Box 5
Lake Louise AB T0L 1E0
Tel: 403–522–3555

Snow Report: 403–244–6665
Area Vertical: 3,250 ft.
Number of Trails: 44 on 4,000 acres
Lifts: 2 high-speed quads, 2 triple chairs, 4
*   double chairs, 2 surface lifts, 1 high-*
*   speed poma*
Snowmaking: two-thirds of front face
Season: mid-November–May

Lake Louise is the largest ski area in Canada with the most skiable ter-rain. It has three faces: the front face, Larch area, and the back bowls. It takes several days truly to discover its variety of trails. There's plenty for every level of ability. Green or novice runs, 25 percent of the terrain, are available off every lift except the Summit poma. Since the winter of 1990 two new high-speed quad chairs have considerably improved uphill capacity on the front face and have provided easier access to the summit for skiers of all ability levels.

The scenery is spectacular and often considered one of the most majestic panoramas in the world. The long runs are great for cruising. Eagle Mead-ow and Juniper are the most popular intermediate trails on the front face while Saddleback, also intermediate, offers breathtaking scenery above treeline in the back bowls. Lynx, at Larch area, and Outer Limits down to Men's Downhill are favorites of the experts. On a clear day, the Summit poma, which serves the front face and back bowls, is a popular place. From it, there's a network of steep chutes and demanding trails that run into the base lodge.

Three main lodges—Whiskeyjack at the base, Whitehorn halfway up the front face, and Temple, on the other side at Larch area—offer skier services such as ski school and ski shop items. For the beginner, Lake Lou-ise offers a "Never Ever" ski package, which includes a beginner lift ticket, a 1½-hour lesson, and a coupon for another full-day lift ticket at half price for $29.95. Two-day lift passes during midweek are priced at $55. The Lake Louise Ski Friends, a volunteer free guide service, is available daily from the base of the front at 10 A.M. and 1 P.M.

MOUNT NORQUAY

Box 1258
Banff AB T0L 0C0
Tel: 403–762–4421

Snow Report: 403–221–8259 or 762–4421
Area Vertical: 1,650 ft.
Number of Trails: 25 on 161 acres
Lifts: 1 high-speed quad, 1 quad, 2 double
chairs, 1 T-bar, 1 platter pull, 1 rope
tow
Snowmaking: 90 percent of skiable terrain
Season: mid-November–early April

This is Banff's most convenient ski area, overlooking the Bow Valley and only a 10-minute drive from town. Norquay has long been known for its steep and challenging terrain, but in the past two years the area has expanded its gentle slopes, providing a better balance of terrain for all ability levels. Expert runs, which once accounted for more than half the trails, now cover 44 percent of the area; intermediate runs cover 45 percent; and novice runs make up 11 percent of the terrain. The beginner-novice trails are some of the region's best to learn on.

Experts will like the famous North American run off the upper chair. It's as steep and challenging as they come.

A bonus is the spectacular view here; at the 7,000-foot elevation you can see all the way across the valley.

Ski rentals and ski school lessons are available at the base day lodge, along with the ski-shop goods in an adjacent building. There is night skiing under the lights 4–9 P.M. each Wednesday, Thursday, Friday, and Saturday. The ski area also has snowboard rentals and lessons, and hosts a variety of snowboarding events throughout the winter. Wednesday night is adult race time at Mount Norquay.

SUNSHINE VILLAGE

Box 1510
Banff AB T0L 1C0
Tel: 403–762–6500

Snow Report: 403–762–6543
Area Vertical: 3,514 ft from gondola base
Number of Trails: 62 on 780 acres
Lifts: 1 six-passenger gondola, 1 triple chair,
4 double chairs, 1 high-speed quad, 3
T-bars,
2 rope tows
Snowmaking: none
Season: mid-November–early June

Sunshine is known for its abundance of fluffy powder and its cozy atmosphere high up in alpine meadows. The 14,084-foot-long gondola ride up to the actual ski area is spectacular in itself. Once you arrive at the village, it's just a quick chairlift ride up to terrain that varies from expert to notice.

Experts will enjoy the Tee-pee Town area, which has steep chutes and big bumps. The majority, 60 percent, of Sunshine's trails are intermediate. Brewster's Trail, off the Great Divide chair, is a favorite. You actually ride up the chair into the Province of British Columbia and ski back down into Alberta. Novices find runs off Strawberry lift a good place to learn and develop skills.

Sunshine Village was the first resort in the Banff–Lake Louise area to install a high-speed quad chairlift. The new Angel Express quad chair has virtually eliminated lines from the village base.

Sunshine boasts the longest ski season in Canada, running from November to early June. You'll find hundreds of sun worshipers each spring doing more tanning than skiing.

Rental equipment is available at the gondola base. The ski shop is found in the main day lodge up at the area, as is the repair shop. Nordic services are available with 20 km of track set trails in high alpine meadows. The nordic office is located adjacent to the upper gondola station.

Practical Information for Banff-Lake Louise

HOW TO GET THERE. Banff is located 128 km west of Calgary, on Trans-Canada Hwy. 1. Lake Louise is an additional 61 km northwest of Banff on Hwy. 1.

By air. Calgary, Edmonton, and Vancouver International airports are the gateways to the region. There are direct and connecting flights from all major North American cities. Calgary International Airport serves major airlines, including *Canadian Airlines, Air Canada, United, American, PWA,* and *Western Airlines.* Call (403) 250–0251 for general airport information.

Rental cars at the airport: *Avis,* (403) 250–0763 or toll-free 800–331–1212 in the U.S. and 800–268–2310 in Canada; *Budget,* (403) 250–0760 or toll-free 800–527–0700 in the U.S. and 800–268–8900 in Canada; *Hertz,* (403) 250–0746 or toll-free 800–654–3131 in the U.S. and 800–263–0600 in Canada; *Tilden,* the Canadian affiliate of *National,* (403) 250–0770 or toll-free 800–227–7368 in the U.S. and 800–387–4747 in Canada. You should rent a car at the airport; in Banff, it can cost up to 20 percent more per day.

By bus. *Brewster Transportation Tours,* (403) 260–0719, travels twice daily during ski season from the airport in Calgary to Banff. *Pacific Western Transportation,* (403) 243–4990, also makes the airport/Banff trip, three times daily, in season. The cost for both is $20 one way, $40 round-trip, plus tax. *Greyhound Bus Lines* travels three times daily from Calgary to Banff to Lake Louise; call toll-free from Canada 800–332–1016, or direct (403) 762–2286.

By car. From Calgary to Banff is an easy and enjoyable 2-hour drive on Hwy. 1. From Banff to Lake Louise is another hour.

TELEPHONES. The area code for all of Alberta is 403.

ACCOMMODATIONS. Banff has a wide variety of establishments. In the Lake Louise area you'll find a choice of several fine hotels and lodges. Sunshine has its own hotel right at the slopes. Based on double occupancy, per-night rates are *Expensive,* $80 and up; *Moderate,* $45–$80; and *Inexpensive,* below $45. Most have saunas and whirlpools. For additional information, call central reservations, (403) 762–5561, or write Ski Banff–Lake Louise, Banff AB T0L 1C0.

Banff

Expensive

Banff International Hotel. 333 Banff Ave.; 762–5666. Recently built luxury hotel with restaurant, lounge, Jacuzzi, and underground parking. Has 125 rooms.

Banff Park Lodge. 222 Lynx St.; 762–4433. With 210 rooms and pool, sauna, restaurant, TV.

Banff Springs Hotel. Spray Ave., Box 960; 762–2211. The most famous hotel in Banff celebrated its 100th birthday with renovations on 200 of its 834 rooms. The Banff Springs Hotel has been described as a magnificent castle in the mountains.

It overlooks the beautiful Bow Falls and has always been a favorite of honeymooners. It has all possible amenities on the premises: horseback riding, a golf course, indoor pool, outdoor pool, Jacuzzis, saunas, tennis courts, beauty salon, massage, cross-country skiing, shops, and its own ski rental shop.

Inns of Banff Park. 600 Banff Ave.; 762–4581. Deluxe accommodations with 180 rooms; pool, sauna, squash.

Moderate

Aspen Lodge. 501 Banff Ave.; 762–4418. Has 53 rooms, some with kitchens; whirlpool.

Banff Rocky Mountain Resort. Banff Ave. N.; 762–5531. Has 170 rooms condo-style and all facilities including pool, fireplaces.

Charlton's Cedar Court. 513 Banff Ave.; 762–4485. Has 63 rooms, outdoor heated pool, and kitchenettes.

Douglas Fir Resort. Tunnel Mtn. Road; 762–5591. Has 133 rooms overlooking Banff with a pool, racquetball and squash courts, and a weight room.

Ptarmigan Inn. Box 1840, Banff; 762–2207. Has 146 rooms, a sauna, and a whirlpool.

Rimrock Inn. Sulfur Mtn. Rd.; 762–3356. A 100-room hotel near the hot springs overlooking Banff with pool, Jacuzzi, and squash courts.

Voyager Inn. 555 Banff Ave.; 762–3301. Has 88 rooms, a pool, sauna, and whirlpool.

Inexpensive

Alpine Motel. 521 Banff Ave.; 762–2332. Has 22 rooms and some with kitchens and fireplaces.

King Edward Hotel. 137 Banff Ave.; 762–2251. Has 56 rooms in the center of Banff.

Mt. Royal Hotel. 138 Banff Ave.; 762–3331. Located in the center of Banff, this hotel has 95 rooms with a dining room and ski shop.

Traveler's Inn. 401 Banff Ave.; 762–4401. Has 90 rooms with a sauna, whirlpool, and ski rental shop.

Lake Louise

Chateau Lake Louise. *Expensive.* Box 96; 522–3511. A famous landmark hotel with 520 recently renovated rooms located minutes from the slopes on majestic Lake Louise. Amenities include pool, sauna, whirlpool, and restaurant.

Emerald Lake Lodge. *Expensive.* Box 10 Field, 800–663–6336. Located on picturesque Emerald Lake, named because of the beautiful color of the water. Excellent cross-country trails at your doorstep. Skiing at Lake Louise is a 20-minute drive.

Skoki Lodge. *Expensive.* At the Lake Louise Ski area; 522–3555. Owned and operated by the ski area, the Skoki Lodge, originally built in 1930, has 22 rooms in the lodge and cabins, 8 miles into the backcountry from the ski area. To get there, you gotta ski; perfect for cross-country tourers and downhillers who like to stay on the mountain.

Deer Lodge. *Moderate.* Box 100; 522–3747. Has 73 rooms near the Chateau Lake Louise and 5 minutes from the ski slopes.

Lake Louise Inn. *Moderate.* Box 209; 522–3791. Located in the valley floor near Hwy. 1, a few minutes from the ski slopes. Has a lounge, pool, 215 rooms and many amenities.

Post Hotel. *Inexpensive.* Box 69; 522–3989. Has 93 rooms and a famous Swiss dining room. Pool, hot tub, steam room, and lounge.

West Louise Lodge. *Inexpensive.* Box 5; 604–343–6311. Has 44 rooms located 20 km west on Hwy. 1, just across the British Columbia border. Owned and operated by Lake Louise Ski Area.

Sunshine Village. *Expensive.* At the slopes; 762–6555 or 800–661–1363 in the U.S. On-mountain is the best adjective for this place, since the only way you can get here is to take the gondola up. Has 84 rooms, hot tub, restaurant, and lounge with solarium.

RESTAURANTS. Slopeside at the ski mountains, you'll find a variety of eating places and cafeteria services. At **Lake Louise,** three main lodges—*Whiskeyjack* at the base, *Whitehorn,* halfway up the front face, and *Temple,* on the other side of the mountain at the Larch area—offer cafeteria food. Whiskeyjack also has a dining room. At **Mount Norquay,** the base *day lodge* has a cafeteria featuring great chili. At **Sunshine Village,** the 600-seat base *lodge dining room* features daily buffets as well as cafeteria and deli service.

In **Banff** there's a great choice for varied tastes and budgets. The selection of restaurants listed here is arranged by price category. Restaurant categories are *Expensive,* $15–$28; *Moderate,* $8–$15; *Inexpensive,* less than $8. These prices are for a meal for one person, exclusive of drinks or tip. All restaurants in this listing accept major credit cards unless otherwise noted.

Expensive

Giorgio's La Casa. 219 Banff Ave.; 762–5116. Sample the authentic cuisine of northern Italy: pasta, fish, meats. Excellent service. By reservation only.

Le Beaujolais. Corner of Buffalo St. and Banff Ave.; 762–2712. This is great Continental dining specializing in French cuisine, tableside service, and elegant decor. One of the most prestigious dining rooms in Canada. Reservations necessary.

Post Hotel Dining Room. Lake Louise Village; 522–3989. Warm country hospitality. Specializes in European dishes. Reserve for dinner. Serves breakfast, lunch, and dinner.

The Rob Roy Dining Room. Banff Springs Hotel, Spray Ave.; 762–2211. Fine dining featuring Alberta beef and seafood. By reservation.

Moderate

Bumpers, The Beef House. 603 Banff Ave.; 762–2622. Popular family restaurant specializing in Alberta beef, barbecued ribs, and salad bar. Serves dinner only.

Caboose. Located at the Banff railway depot; 762–3622. With interesting railroad history, decor, Alaska king crab and charcoal-broiled steaks are the specialties. Serves dinner only.

Cafe Louise. In Deer Lodge, Lake Louise; 522–3747. Serves braised chicken, salmon, Alberta beef. Serves breakfast, lunch, and dinner.

Eagle Nest Dining Room. In Rimrock Inn on Sulfur Mtn. Road; 762–3356. Offers spectacular view of Bow Valley and a balanced menu of beef, fish, veal, and poultry. Serves breakfast, lunch, and dinner. Reservations required for dinner.

Grizzly House. 207 Banff Ave.; 762–4055. Features fondue dishes and wild game such as Buffalo steak. The only place around where you can try rattlesnake fondue.

Guido's. 116 Banff Ave.; 762–4002. Features Italian specialties and fine desserts.

Heritage Restaurant. In the Lake Louise Inn; 522–3791. Family dining with great burgers and a fine dinner menu including filet mignon. Serves breakfast, lunch, and dinner. Dinner reservations welcome.

Joshua's. 204 Caribou St.; 762–2833. Has European specialties in addition to fish and beef plates. Turn-of-the-century atmosphere.

Magpie and Stump. 203 Caribou St.; 762–4067. With old west atmosphere, authentic Mexican dishes are a specialty. Serves dinner only.

Melissa's Missteak. 217 Lynx St.; 762–5511. Rustic log building constructed in 1928 offers pleasant atmosphere. Has great muffins, homemade soups, and deep-dish pizzas among other novel choices. Serves breakfast, lunch, and dinner.

Reflections. At Inns of Banff Park Hotel, 600 Banff Ave.; 762–4581. Serves fine Alberta beef, seafood, and poultry. Reservations appreciated. Serves breakfast, lunch, and dinner.

Suginoya Japanese Restaurant & Sushi Bar. Upstairs in Banff Ave. Mall; 762–4773. Wide variety of Japanese dishes or sushi bar, where you watch the chef make the food.

Ticino. 205 Wolf St.; 762–3848. You'll find fine Swiss-Italian dishes, cheese fondues, and steaks. Serves dinner only. Reservations recommended.

Victoria Dining Room. Chateau Lake Louise; 522–3511. Popular buffet breakfasts and lunches. À la carte dinner menu. Evenings by reservation.

West Louise Lodge. On Hwy. 1, 11 km west of Lake Louise; 604–343–6486. Homemade soups, beef, and poultry.

Inexpensive

A & W. 100 Caribou St.; 762–2562. Specializes in A & W root beer and burgers. Open 7 A.M. to 11 P.M.

Harvey's. 304 Caribou St.; 762–4951. Charbroiled burgers, hot dogs, and chicken sandwiches.

Joe Btfsplk's Diner. 221 Banff Ave.; 762–5529. Great diner food in a '50s atmosphere.

Phil's Restaurant. 109 Spray Ave.; 762–3655. Serves pancakes, waffles, burgers, and steaks; open 7 A.M.–10 P.M.

Picadilly Fare. 321 Banff Ave.; 762–3555. Daily lunch and dinner specials served in a quiet setting.

Smitty's. 227 Banff Ave.; 762–2533. Family prices on Canadian dishes; open 6:30 A.M.–10 P.M.

HOW TO GET AROUND. *Pacific Western Transportation* (762–4558) and *Brewster* (260–0719) run daily **shuttle buses** from Banff to each of the ski areas. In Lake Louise, *PWT* has a **shuttle bus** service running between Chateau Lake Louise, Deer Lodge, the Post, Lake Louise Inn, and the Mountaineer to the ski area from 8 A.M. to 4 P.M. daily, in season. For information contact *Skiing Louise,* 522–3555.

Car rentals are available in Banff: *Avis,* 762–3222; *Budget,* 762–4565; *Hertz,* 762–2027; or *Tilden,* 762–2688. For **taxi** service in Banff only, phone *Banff Taxi,* 762–4444; *Mountain Taxi,* 762–3351; *Lake Louise Taxi and Tours,* 522–2020; *Legion Taxi,* 762–3353 or *Taxi Taxi,* 762–3111.

SEASONAL EVENTS. The main skiing events in the Banff–Lake Louise area are the *World Cup ski races,* which take place in mid-**March.** Women run all three disciplines: downhill, giant slalom, and slalom. Men race downhill and super G. The Banff *Winter Festival* takes place each **February** with a parade down Banff Ave., torchlight demonstrations on Mount Norquay, sporting events, ice sculpture contest, costume party, and snow queen contest. The *Summit Cup* at Lake Louise in **March** and the Ken Read *Invitational* **in April** are popular races for locals and ex-national team members, respectively. An **annual** mogul skiing contest takes place in late April.

At **Sunshine** there's a special telemark weekend in early **February** and a recreational team downhill race called the "Over the Divide" in **March.** Also in **March** is the annual *Skiing Veterans Fun Race.* At the end of **May,** there's the *Slush Cup* when a giant jump is built and skiers try to go over a man-made pond of water. A comic way to wrap up the ski season.

Mount Norquay has the popular *Race for the Sun* series running weekly from mid-**January.**

Each **February,** nearby Canmore holds *Sled Dog races,* when some of the best sled-dog teams from all over North America compete. It always is an exciting event for spectators.

OTHER SPORTS AND ACTIVITIES. There's an **indoor water slide** at Douglas Fir Resort on Tunnel Mountain Road; 762–5591. **Sleigh rides** and **dog-sled** rides are available daily at Chateau Lake Louise; 522–3511. Many of the larger hotels have **swimming pools, saunas,** and Jacuzzis. The **skating rink** at the steps of Chateau Lake Louise (522–3511) is probably one of the most beautiful spots in the world to skate. The *Recreation Center* in Banff provides public ice time and the ice can be rented for private groups. Phone 762–4454 to reserve. **Curling** is popular in Banff; also at the Recreation Center.

The *Upper Hot Springs Pool* is open year round on Mountain Ave. The average temperature is 38°C (100°F) and it costs only $1.25. Phone 762–4454.

Nearby Vermillion Lakes and Twojack Lake are popular **skating** areas under good weather conditions.

The recently renovated *Lux Theatre* (229 Bear Street; 762–8595) now has 4 screens and operates daily.

The *Banff Centre for Performing Arts* has live theater, films, and musicals throughout the winter. Box office number is 762–6100. The center is on Julien Road, a short walk from town.

CHILDREN'S ACTIVITIES. All three ski areas provide children's programs. At **Lake Louise,** 552–3555, in *Chocolate Moose Playpark,* a nursery, is available for infants from 18 days to 18 months, daily from 8:30 A.M. to 4:30 P.M. Reservations are necessary. Day care for children 3–6 years is $3 per hour. A *Kinder-Ski* program for children 3–6 years is available with indoor/outdoor play and ski instruction daily at $19 for a full day. *Kid's Ski* for 7–12 years is $25 per day plus $8 for a lift ticket with instruction. Lunch is $5.

At **Sunshine,** 762–4000, the day-care program accepts children 19 months to 6 years at $3 per hour. One-hour lessons on the hill for 3–6-year-olds cost $10 per day. The *Kid's Day Program* offers advanced instruction for those 6–12 years old.

At **Norquay,** 764–4421, there is baby-sitting available. Kids under 8 years ski for free at each area.

NIGHTLIFE. There's a good choice of aprè-ski activities after dark in Banff. *The Works* nightclub at the Banff Springs Hotel is popular for disco dancing. For more hot dancing go to *Mr. C's* on Banff Ave. or to the *View Point Lounge* for easy listening music at the Rimrock Inn. The *Magpie and Stump* on Caribou St. has live entertainment, often in the form of folk music. The King Edward Hotel in the middle of town has top live bands throughout the winter and is a regular stop of the ski crowds.

Other popular bars include *Melissa's* on Lynx St., the *Royal Express* in the Mont Royal Hotel, and the *Chimney Corner* up at Sunshine Village. In Lake Louise, go to *Charlie II's* at Lake Louise Inn for casual disco atmosphere. Most other hotels have cozy lounges for drinks and quiet relaxation.

MARMOT BASIN SKI AREA

Box 1300
Jasper AB TOE 1EO
Tel: 403–852–3816

Snow Report: 403–488–5909
Area Vertical: 2,290 ft.
Number of Trails: 51 on 565 acres
Lifts: 1 high-speed quad, 1 triple chair, 2
*   double chairs and 2 T-bars*
Snowmaking: Some
Season: early December–early May

Located 3 hours north of Banff via the Icefields Parkway, which is considered to be one of the world's most scenic and spectacular highways, Jasper is both a summer and winter destination playground. A man named Jasper Hawes opened up a boarding house here about 160 years ago to accommodate local trappers, explorers, traders, and mountain men. The railway was also just being developed. In 1846, Hawes opened the Jasper House Hotel at the center of the fast-growing town that ultimately took his name.

It wasn't until the late 1920s, when a fellow named Joe Weiss explored the east face of Marmot Basin discovering ideal skiing slopes and conditions, that the area was opened for skiing. The first trail was blazed in the '30s, ending by the present upper chalet location. A road to the area was constructed from 1940 to 1945. In 1963 Parks Canada proposed an expansion of the ski area, resulting in the construction the following year of the upper yellow T-bar, new trails, and the rustic upper chalet.

Marmot Basin has since become a favorite ski destination for Albertans and an expanding American market. Jasper has comfortable accommodations and Marmot's skiing is great for the whole family. The park's untouched beauty is in every direction.

Only 22 km from the town of Jasper, the Marmot Basin ski slopes offer a broad range of terrain for all ability levels. The mountain is rated 35 percent "easiest," 35 percent "more difficult," and 30 percent "most difficult." The highest elevation is 8,517 feet, and there is a 158-inch annual snowfall. Lines are uncommon, so there's a lot of ski time from the top of the seven lifts. Marmot does not get the crowds of Banff, and the ski season runs from November often into early May. Marmot, like the Banff area, gets lots of fluffy dry powder snow, and with a lack of crowds, the area is regarded as one of the best-kept secrets of the Rockies.

Practical Information for Marmot Basin

HOW TO GET THERE. Marmot Basin is located 371 km west of Edmonton and 400 northwest of Calgary.

By air. Edmonton International Airport services major airlines, with connections from most North American cities. Contact *Air Canada or Canadian Airlines International,* among others. **Car rentals** available in Jasper are *Avis,* (403) 852–3970 or toll-free in Canada 800–268–2310, in the U.S. 800–331–1212; *Hertz,* (403) 852–3888 or toll-free in Canada 800–268–1311, in the U.S. 800–654–3131; and *Tilden,* (403) 852–3789. In Edmonton: *Avis,* (403) 955–7596 or toll-free numbers as given above; *Budget,* (403) 852–3330 or toll-free in Canada 800–268–8900, in the U.S. 800–527–0700; *Hertz,* (403) 955–8500 or toll-free as given above; and *Tilden,* (403) 955–7232.

By car. Jasper is about a 4½-hour drive from Edmonton, along windy, scenic Hwy. 16.

By bus. *Greyhound Bus Lines* provides daily service between Edmonton, Jasper, and Vancouver. Phone (403) 421–4211 for information and schedules.

By train. *Via Rail* has service between Edmonton and Jasper three days a week. Phone (403) 422–6032 or 800–665–8630 for information and schedules.

TELEPHONES. The area code for Jasper and all Alberta is 403.

ACCOMMODATIONS. Practically all accommodations at Marmot Basin can be arranged through *Ski World,* Box 1850, Jasper AB TOE 1E0; 852–4242. No accommodations are available on the hill at Marmot. It is about 15 minutes' drive from Marmot into nearby Jasper, where there is a wide selection of hotels and lodges, many with such amenities as saunas, whirlpools, and indoor swimming pools. Hotel rates are based on double occupancy. Categories, determined by price, are: *Expensive,* \$60–\$80; *Moderate,* \$45–\$60; *Inexpensive,* less than \$45.

Expensive

Chateau Jasper. 96 Giekie St.; 852–5644 and 800–661–9323 in Canada. Has 121 very comfortable rooms, pool, dining room. Kitchenettes available. Located about 20 minutes from Marmot Basin but definitely worth the drive.

Jasper Park Lodge. Hwy.16; 852–3301, 800–268–9420 in Ontario and Quebec, 800–268–9411 in other Canadian provinces, 800–828–7447 in the U.S. This hotel is the finest in the region and is located on Hwy. 16 approximately 5 miles from the Jasper town site. Features over 400 rooms, cedar chalets, and lakeside suites. On Lake Beauvert, the hotel has 8 restaurants and dining areas, an outdoor pool and health club, plus a 17-store shopping mall for incidentals and souvenirs.

Lobstick Lodge. 88 Giekie St.; 852–4431 and 800–661–9317 in Canada. Has 139 rooms, many with kitchenettes; indoor pool; dining services.

Marmot Lodge. 94 Connaught Dr.; 852–4471 and 800–661–6521 in Canada. Features swimming pool, kitchenettes, and fireplaces.

Sawridge Hotel. 82 Connaught Dr.; 852–5111 and 800–661–6427 in Canada. Has 154 rooms, with pool and sauna.

Moderate

Amethyst Lodge. 200 Connaught Dr.; 852–3394. Standard 100-room motor lodge with phones, TV, hot tub, and dining room.

Inexpensive

Astoria Hotel. 404 Connaught Dr.; 852–3351. In a convenient location, has 84 rooms, a pub and restaurant.

Athabasca Hotel. 510 Patricia St.; 852–3386. Located about 20 minutes from the slopes, here are 60 rooms for all budgets; dining room and pub with satellite TV.

Diamond Motel. 424 Connaught Dr.; 852–3143. Some rooms with kitchenettes; dining room, TV, and sauna.

Mt. Robson Motor Inn. 215 Connaught Dr.; 852–3327. Has 77 rooms, some with kitchenettes, dining room, TV.

Whistler Inn. 34 Miette St.; 852–3361. 40 rooms with phones, TV; dining room.

RESTAURANTS. There's a pleasant mix of eating places in Jasper, and most of them have reasonable prices: *Expensive,* $20 and up; *Moderate,* $10–$20; *Inexpensive,* less than $10. Prices are based on the average cost of a meal for one person, excluding drinks and tip. All but the inexpensive restaurants listed accept major credit cards, and no reservations are needed.

Moderate to Expensive

Amethyst Dining Room. 200 Connaught Dr.; 852–3394. Located in the Amethyst Lodge, you'll find dishes ranging from fruit and cheese platter to British Columbia salmon and prime Alberta beef.

Echoes Dining Room. In Marmot Lodge, 94 Connaught Dr.; 852–4544. Has Continental cuisine with original pasta dishes and homemade desserts.

Papa George's. In the Astoria Hotel, 404 Connaught Dr.; 852–3351. One of Jasper's better restaurants featuring T-bone steaks, a variety of pasta dishes, and home-baked breads.

Tokyo Tom's Place. 410 Connaught Dr.; 852–3780. Features complete sushi bar and intimate booths for eating fine Japanese dishes. Dinner only.

Walter's Dining Room. In Sawridge Hotel, 82 Connaught Dr.; 852–5111. A distinctive à la carte menu featuring seafood and Alberta beef.

Inexpensive

A & W. 624 Connaught Dr.; 852–4930. Home of the Papa burger, Teen burger, and A & W root beer. Fast service.

Jasper Pizza Place. 402 Connaught Dr.; 852–3225. Offers pizza, burgers, sandwiches, and barbecued chicken.

HOW TO GET AROUND. A ski **shuttle bus** departs from Jasper daily at 8:30 A.M. and 10:15 A.M. and returns at 4:15 P.M. For **taxi** service around town, phone *Jasper Taxi* and *Taxi of the Park* at their joint number, 852–3146 and 852–3600. Car rentals are available through *Avis,* 852–3970 in Jasper and 955–7596 in Edmonton; *Budget,* 852–3330 in Jasper or 800–268–8900 in Edmonton; *Hertz,* 852–3888 in Jasper and 955–8500 in Edmonton; and *Tilden,* 862–3798 in Jasper and 955–7232 in Edmonton.

SEASONAL EVENTS. The main event is *Labatt's St. Patrick's Recreational Downhill* in **March.** About 40 teams made up of at least one woman and one person over 35 years old compete in a race down the mountain. The big prizes are drawn and the atmosphere is friendly competition and socializing. The *Town and Country Weekend Fun Race* series runs in early **April** each year. It is the last big party on the ski hills before the season ends.

OTHER SPORTS AND ACTIVITIES. In Jasper there's **skating** and other sports activities nearby. **Ice fishing** is available at Talbot Lake close by and **ice fishing** is available on other local rivers. Licenses are available at Parks Canada office, 500 Connaught Dr.

Maligne Tours (852–3370) leads a **canyon crawl** that is described as a "scramble in the bottom of Maligne Canyon, a limestone gorge 50 meters deep." **Ice climbing** is also available for the experienced climber. The *Park Information Center* (852–

6161) can provide recommendations for guides and phone numbers for more information.

Most larger hotels have indoor **swimming pools, saunas,** and **whirlpools.** The *Jasper Activity Center,* 303 Pyramid Ave. (852–3381) has **raquetball courts, weight room,** and indoor **tennis** in the spring, and a skating rink operates in the winter. *Hoppy's Bowling* and *Billiard* is at 625 Patricia St.

CHILDREN'S ACTIVITIES. The *Little Rascal's Nursery* at the ski area, 852–3816, offers care to children 19 months through 5 years for $2.50 per hour plus $1.25 for each additional child in the same family. The nursery has a play-and-ski program in addition to structured activities. The *Kid's Camp* runs a morning and an afternoon program for ages 4–8 on Saturdays and Sundays. During Christmas, spring, and Easter breaks, the Kid's Camp is open daily. Ski lessons are available at Lower Ski Chalet.

NIGHTLIFE. At *Astoria Bar,* 404 Connaught Dr., you'll find a dance floor and imported beer. The *Night Club* in the Athabasca Hotel on Patricia St. features top-40 music, and the Athabasca hosts live bands during the winter months. More dancing can be found at *Champs* in the Sawridge Hotel. Most hotels have quiet lounges for relaxation. Go to *Echoes* in Marmot Lodge; *Whistle Stop Lounge* in Whistlers Motor Hotel, or *Le Bonhomme Lounge* in Chateau Jasper. (See *Accommodations* above.)

NAKISKA AT MOUNT ALLAN

Box 1988
Kananaskis AB T0L 2H0
Tel: 403–591–7777

Snow Report: 403–270–8680
Area Vertical: 2,493 feet
Number of Trails: 30
Lifts: 2 high-speed quads, 2 quads,
*   1 surface lift*
Snowmaking: 80 percent of terrain
Season: mid-November–April

About 55 miles southwest of Calgary in an area called Kananaskis Country sits Nakiska (the ski area) at Mount Allan (the mountain), the host site for the alpine skiing events of the 15th Olympic Winter Games in 1988. The Olympics spells controversy, and Nakiska was waist deep in it. It cost the government of Alberta $25.3 million to build and is state of the art in all respects. From rentals to racing runs to snowmaking, Nakiska is just about as high-tech as they come. The area, however, has been criticized by experts as an impractical place for a recreational ski resort because it is situated in a section of the Canadian Rockies that is affected by chinook winds. The chinooks are warm winds and have been known to heat the area to as high as 60 degrees Fahrenheit in the normally chilly winter months. As a result, the area has to rely on snowmaking.

The snowmaking facilities here are awesome. Two pumps draw water from the Kananaskis River, and seven others distribute it up to the mountain through a maze of compressors, 122,000 feet of piping, and 343 pairs of air and water hydrants. The $5 million system is capable of pumping 6 million gallons of water per day and is entirely computerized and run from a central operations room that rivals the screens and graphics of the main deck on *Star Trek.*

Snowmaking and controversy aside, the skiing at Nakiska is real downhill. The area's intermediate (70 percent) and expert (14 percent) runs are fast and well pitched. Almost all the terrain is straight fallaway mountainside, which makes for excellent high-speed cruising. At the top of the Gold chair, the intermediate runs are particularly interesting; seemingly easy flats pack some surprising steep pitches. Easy cruising intermediate runs are "Mighty Peace" off the Gold chair, and "Mapmaker" and "Eyeopener" off the Olympic chair.

Beginners need not worry. The Bronze chairlift, located below the main base area, takes them to a separate area (16 percent) where there are many smooth, easy, novice runs.

The area has a ski school, day-care facilities, a rental and repair shop, and two day lodges—one at mid-mountain and one at the base. Forty kilometers of cross-country trails connect with the base area. In addition, the area offers free tours of the mountain with guides who not only show the runs but who point out many interesting and amusing Olympic tidbits. A few miles away is Kananaskis Village, where you'll find lodging, dining, and all the recreation you could want.

Finally, if you want some skiing variety, Fortress Mountain, a day area quite popular with Calgarians that has yet to reach its full potential, is less than a half-hour bus ride away. Although Fortress does not have the high-caliber facilities or area vertical of Nakiska, it can offer some fun stuff. Skiers of all ability levels can ski on three different mountain faces, and better skiers can ski among the trees. Since Fortress has wide hills and is located in a heavy snowbelt, the area is becoming very popular with snowboarders. In all, Fortress offers a nice alternative and is worth the trip.

Practical Information for Nakiska at Mount Allan

HOW TO GET THERE. Nakiska is located about 55 miles southwest of Calgary.

By air. Calgary International Airport is the main gateway to the region. Most major airlines, including *Air Canada, United,* and *American* fly there. **Rental cars** available at the Calgary Airport include: *Avis,* (403) 250–0763 or toll-free 800–331–1212 in the U.S. and 800–268–2310 in Canada; *Budget,* (403) 250–0760 or toll-free 800–527–0700 in the U.S. and 800–268–8900 in Canada; *Hertz,* (403) 250–0746 or toll-free 800–654–3131 in the U.S. and 800–263–0600 in Canada; and *Tilden,* the Canadian affiliate of *National,* (403) 250–0770 or toll-free 800–227–7368 in the U.S. and 800–387–4747 in Canada.

By bus. *Brewster Transportation and Tours,* Box 1140, Banff, AB T0L 0C0 (403) 762–2241, has a **shuttle** that leaves the airport in Calgary and stops en route to Banff to meet another bus that will take you to the village. Make sure to check the schedule because times vary throughout the year. Brewster also operates a scheduled bus service to Nakiska and Fortress from Calgary.

By car. The village is roughly a 70-minute drive from Calgary. Take Hwy. 1 (the TransCanada Hwy.) to Hwy. 40, where you'll see signs for Nakiska and the village.

TELEPHONES. The area code for all Alberta is 403.

ACCOMMODATIONS. The lodgings nearest Nakiska are at Kananaskis Village, a few miles from the slopes. All accommodations in the village offer package deals and all have an array of different rooms in many price categories. Almost every room has a great view of the Canadian Rockies. You can make reservations through the *Kananaskis Village Center's* toll-free numbers: 800–661–1064 in the United States and Canada except in Alberta, where the number is 800–332–1013. The center will also send printed information: Box 100, Alberta T0L 2H0 Canada. You can also, of course, make direct reservations with the lodging of your choice.

Kananaskis Inn. 591–7500. Opened in June 1987, the inn is a family-oriented place with 96 rooms, ranging from $80 per night for a standard to $275 for a suite. The 32 loft rooms are a bargain; they have fireplaces, fully equipped kitchenettes, (save money by doing your own cooking), and some can sleep up to 10. They run from $100 to $120 per night, double occupancy, plus $10 for each additional person. The inn features a restaurant, a small indoor pool, Jacuzzi, and steam rooms, plus underground parking for 50 cars. *Woodies Pub* here is *the* party spot in the village.

The Lodge at Kananaskis. 591–7711. Also opened in June 1987, the Lodge is a full-service resort with a conference center, large indoor heated parking garage, 3 restaurants, 12 shops, and an extensive health club with tanning salon, beauty shop, aerobics rooms, Jacuzzis, steam rooms, Universal machines, and massage. The 255 rooms range from a standard (starting at $85) to a superior loft for 2 at $140. A deluxe loft with fireplace is $156 per night based on double occupancy. All rooms are decorated in soothing earth tones and have minibars.

Hotel Kananaskis. 591–7711. The newest of the 3 village hotels, the Hotel Kananaskis opened in December 1987. The hotel has the sense of detail one would expect from a 5-star resort. Each of the 69 rooms and suites has at least 1 kingsized bed and a minibar. All the doors have brass knockers (no more surprises by housekeeping), and the first-floor rooms have sliding glass doors, so you can walk right outside from your room. Rooms start at $92 per night and go as high $230 per night for a superior suite with your own private Jacuzzi. The hotel has a restaurant, bar, and a very small health club. Hotel guests, however, can use the lodge's club facilities free of charge. There is even an underground walkway between the 2 to take you there.

Both the lodge and the hotel are administered by Canadian Pacific Hotels; you can book your rooms directly through CP at 800–268–9411 in Canada except in Ontario and Quebec, where the number is 800–268–9420. In the United States, call 800–828–7447.

There are two other lodging possibilities in the area.

Mount Kidd Recreational Vehicle Park. Box 100, Edshaw, AB T0L 2C0; 591–7700. There are 229 hookups available; reservations required; $15–$25 per night, depending on type of hookup.

Ribbon Creek Hostel. General Delivery, Seebe AB TOL 0X1; 591–7333. Family accommodations and dorms; kitchens, showers; from $5 to $7 per night; reservations required.

At **Fortress Mountain,** 591–7108, there are accommodations in the lodge. Spartan double rooms cost $50 per night and there are also very inexpensive dorm rooms that attract school groups. The management hopes eventually to build condos at the base area (which would inevitably lead to improved facilities and begin to bring out the strong potential of the area), but at press time, plans were not approved.

RESTAURANTS. Slopeside at Nakiska, there are two restaurants. The bilevel base lodge has cafeteria-style service and, in the spring, weather permitting, you can have your food served on the outside deck. The mid-mountain lodge is a cafeteria. Fortress has a cafeteria and a restaurant/bar. All the restaurants listed below are located in the village and they all accept most major credit cards. Categories are based on the price of a full dinner for one, excluding tax, tip, and beverages: *Expensive,* over $40; *Moderate,* $15–$25; and *Inexpensive,* under $15.

L'Escapade. *Expensive.* In the Kananaskis Hotel; 591–7711. The most elegant restaurant in the village. the cuisine is Continental, the service is French, and the candlelight atmosphere is subdued. Harp or piano music accompanies dinner; reservations are necessary.

The Peaks Dining Room. *Moderate to Expensive.* In the Lodge at Kananaskis; 591–7711. Pleasant dining room overlooking the village courtyard and skating rink. The beef dishes are good. Also open for breakfast and lunch. The huge Sunday brunch brings in Calgarians just to eat (and maybe ski). Reservations are not required, but on busy weekends, you should make them in the morning unless you want to eat dinner at 10.

Rockies Supper Club. *Moderate.* In the Lodge at Kananaskis; 591–7711. Adjacent to the Peaks, here is a casual, relaxed dining room with entertainment. After 8 P.M. the menu lightens up with pasta specials, pizza, and light dinners.

Samurai Bar. *Moderate.* In the Lodge at Kananaskis; 591–7711. The only place around to get sushi and *shabu shabu*.

The Inn Restaurant. *Moderate to Inexpensive.* In the Kananaskis Inn; 591–7500. Casual dining in a lobby restaurant with a solarium deck and a fantastic view of the Canadian Rockies. The menu is basic and the wine list, although not extensive, is quite reasonably priced. A good spot for hearty skier breakfasts. Open all day and into the evening for dinner.

Big Horn Lobby Lounge. *Inexpensive.* In the Lodge at Kananaskis; 591–7711. Serves light snacks all day. Try the chicken wings—they are sure to clear your sinuses! Also has evening entertainment and a pleasant bar.

Woodies Pub. *Inexpensive.* In the Kananaskis Inn; 591–7500. Basic light dishes, pub grub, and snacks for lunch and dinner; things really get going here around 11 P.M., with nightly live entertainment during the winter.

HOW TO GET AROUND. *Brewster Transportation and Tours* runs a free **shuttle bus** from the village to Nakiska several times daily. It also has a bus going to Fortress and Banff. For details and schedules, visit Brewster's desk in the lobby of the Lodge, or call 591–7711, ext. 4027.

If you want to explore the area any further, you will need a **car.** Brewster rents cars in the village for 20 percent more than the regular price. If you need a car, rent it at the airport. (See *How to Get There,* above, for details.)

SEASONAL EVENTS. Nakiska continues its Olympic tradition by hosting *amateur races* throughout the winter. One of its expert runs, "Legacy," is maintained as a training run, and several Alberta racing clubs use the area to compete.

OTHER SPORTS AND ACTIVITIES. In addition to alpine skiing at Nakiska and Fortress there are hundreds of open acres that are perfect for **cross-country skiing** in the area.

The Village Center, 591–7555, can arrange just about any activity you want. The center was conceived as an information area and "lodge" for day trippers from Calgary. It has spa facilities, an infirmary, a post office, a lounge area, and an aerobics room with classes, and it houses the Ribbon Creek Grocery Store, a small convenience store. Ice skates are available to rent for use on the small rink in the village courtyard and cross-country skis to rent for use on the 30-plus km of groomed tracks and open fields. It also administers the six village tennis courts and has bike rentals and information on the Kananaskis Country Golf Course, one of the best in Alberta.

Boundery Stables offers sleigh rides and horseback riding; call 591–7171.

CHILDREN'S ACTIVITIES. At Nakiska, day care is available for children 19 months–6 years from 8:30 A.M. to 4 P.M. Children must be picked up between noon and 1 P.M. for lunch. Nakiska has a number of special programs for young children. Check with the area for further details.

At Fortress, the emphasis is on teaching the basics of skiing. In fact, the area caters to children and school groups. Contact the area at 591–7108 to get details on their ski programs.

NIGHTLIFE. *Woodies Pub* in the inn is the busiest night spot and a favorite of the many college-age people who work at the resort. Woodies features live entertainment, from country music to rock 'n' roll to blues. A pleasant alternative is the *Big Horn Lounge* in the Lodge, with a more sophisticated atmosphere and nightly entertainment. The *Fireside Lobby Bar* in the hotel is a quiet spot for a nightcap; it is also the only place in town that serves real cappuccino. The *Rockies Supper Club* in the Lodge offers entertainment and dining, and from 10 P.M. until 2 A.M., this little night spot plays contemporary recorded music.

British Columbia

APEX ALPINE SKI AREA

275 Rosetown Ave.
Penticton BC V2A 3J3
Tel: 604–292–8222

Snow Report: 604–493–3606
Area Vertical: 1,600 ft.
Number of Trails: 36
Lifts: 1 triple chair, 1 double chair, 1 T-bar,
*   1 poma*
Snowmaking: none
Season: November–mid-April

Situated 30 km west of Penticton in the mild Okanagan Valley of British Columbia, Apex Alpine is a rapidly developing ski center with lots of powder and challenging runs.

Apex Alpine was first developed in 1961 following regional intentions to develop a provincial park in the area. In prior years, a miner named C.L. Aikins had mining rights to the present ski area site and decided to give them up as long as his cabin would be made available for use by the local Penticton Boy Scouts. In 1960 plans for a road were realized along the Shatford Creek to Beaconsfield Mountain where the Apex Alpine slopes were cut. Mt. Apex is actually close by but the name seemed suitable and marketable, hence Apex Alpine. The first double chair was installed in 1971.

Apex claims to be British Columbia's sunniest resort. Somehow it still gets plenty of snow—up to 200 cm (80 in.) a year.

Apex Alpine is powder snow under warm, sunny skies. It has a good variety of trails suitable for the whole family. Since 50 percent of the runs are intermediate, it's also a nice cruising mountain. Runs like Juniper, Spruce Hollow, and Okanagan give you good value from any ski equipment. The Pet and the Bowls runs treat any expert to fine open meadows, usually with lots of powder. The area has recently completed some major terrain modifications, which will allow for better grooming on many runs.

Services at the mountain include condo-style accommodations, restaurants, and lounges, a grocery store, and recreational facilities. It's a family resort with plenty of kids' programs and services.

Mountain Magic Tours are available each day at 10 A.M. and 1 P.M. free of charge. There's a lot of "little extras" that make Apex Alpine more than just a good ski mountain: things like Sunday orientation evenings, farewell banquets, and a helpful guest services program.

Practical Information for Apex Alpine

HOW TO GET THERE. Apex Alpine is located in the Okanagan mountain range, 30 km from Penticton, BC, and some 490 km from Vancouver.

By air. There are regularly scheduled flights from Vancouver, Calgary, Edmonton, and Toronto via *Canadian Airlines International, Air Canada,* and *Time Air* into Kelowna Airport, some 60 km north, and Penticton Airport. Major **car rental** agencies at Kelowna Airport include *Budget,* (604) 860–2464 or 800–527–0700 in the United States, *Hertz,* (604) 860–7808 or 800–654–3131 in the United States and *Tilden,* (*National* in the United States) (604) 860–6000 or 800–328–4567 in the United States, *Avis,* (604) 493–8133; *Budget,* (604) 493–0212; and *Tilden,* (604) 493–7288 also operate out of Penticton.

By bus. *Greyhound Bus Lines.* (604) 860–3835, services Penticton from all western Canadian cities. From Vancouver or Calgary it is about 7–10 hours travel time.

By car. From Vancouver, take Hwy. 1 east, then Rte. 97 south to Penticton. Follow signs to the ski area; the trip takes about 5 hours. From Calgary, it is about a 9-hour drive along Hwy. 1 and Rte. 97.

TELEPHONES. The area code for all British Columbia is 604.

ACCOMMODATIONS. On-mountain lodging will handle up to 450 people and there's plenty more rooms available in Penticton 30 km away. There's an impressive new 1-, 2-, and 3-bedroom condominium complex with kitchens and fireplaces at the base of the slopes. For on-hill reservations, call 800–663–1900 or write *Apex Alpine Reservations,* Box 717, Penticton BC, V2A 6P1. Video or TV rentals are available. Hot tubs complement the comfortable lodging and evening relaxation. Apex midweek (Monday–Thursday) packages start as low as $43 per person, per day and the price includes accommodations and lift tickets. Weekend packages run $89 for 2-nights' stay and 2-days' skiing. Three-day midweek packages start at $99.

In Penticton at the **Coast Lakeside Resort,** 102 Lake Shore Rd. (493–8221), ski packages range from $65 for one day to $179 for three days (double occupancy) with lift tickets and lesson discount. Located about 45 minutes from the slopes, the hotel's facilities include a pool, sauna, weight room, Jacuzzi, and restaurant.

RESTAURANTS. Two restaurants, two lounges, and one cafeteria are situated at the ski village. The atmosphere is geared toward socializing with the help of organized theme nights and barbecues. Most major credit cards are accepted. Prices at all these restaurants range from $3 to $8 for entrees.

Longshot Bar & Grill 292–8633, a full-service restaurant at the base of the slopes, is open 8 A.M. to 10:30 P.M. The **Gun Barrel** (292–8515), near the upper parking lot, has a casual atmosphere and a good selection of home-style food. The building also has a saloon and happens to be an Apex Alpine historical landmark. You ski right to the front door.

In Penticton, go to **Granny Bogners** (493–2911) for fine dining and European dishes. **Theo's Greek Restaurant** (492–4019) has a variety of Greek specialties.

HOW TO GET AROUND. A bus runs up to Apex from Penticton each day at 9 A.M., returning at 4 P.M., and a limousine service is also available. Contact Apex Alpine (292–8211) for more information. For cabs, phone *Courtesy Taxi* at 492–7778 or *Peach City Taxi* at 492–4111.

SEASONAL EVENTS. The *Labatt's Annual Veteran's Race* is a modified giant slalom for older skiers and runs in the third week in **February.** The Shoot-the-Chute is Apex's zaniest event where some "crazy Canucks" race straight down the expert chute trail above the upper lodge. This wild race runs in **mid-March.**

OTHER SPORTS AND ACTIVITIES. Reservations for horse-drawn **sleigh rides** for groups or individuals can be made through the front desk (493–3606).

The **ice skating** rink is located adjacent to the day lodge. **Broomball** games for all take place regularly. **Hot tubs** are popular after a day's skiing.

CHILDREN'S ACTIVITIES. The *Apex Sunshine Kids Club* helps parents enjoy a carefree day while providing children with the care and instruction they need. *Kittycare* is a day-care facility for children ages 18 months to 6 years. *Kinder Kats* is for kids 3 to 6 who have never skied, and *Kinder Panthers* is for kids 4 to 8 who know how to ski and are ready to upgrade. For reservations, contact the ski area reception desk, 292–8221.

NIGHTLIFE. Practically all the après-ski activity at Apex Alpine centers around the bars at the lodges or the restaurants listed above.

BIG WHITE SKI RESORT LTD.

Box 2039, Station R
Kelowna BC V1X 4K5
Tel: 604–765–3101

Snow Report: 604–765–SNOW
Area Vertical: 2,050 ft.
Number of Trails: 47
Lifts: 2 high-speed quads, 1 quad, 1 triple
  chair, 1 platter pull, 1 T-bar
Snowmaking: none
Season: mid-November–mid-April

Located in the magnificent Monashee Mountain range, Big White is the highest skiable mountain in British Columbia. Known for its acres of deep, fluffy powder and mild temperatures, it is a self-contained ski village that caters to everyone.

As you drive into the village, probably the first impression will be of the snow banks along the narrow roads. They're massive and completely cover all road signs or anything 10 feet or shorter. Big White is without a doubt "snow country."

One of the most enticing qualities of Big White is the "ski-to-your-door" aspect. From every condominium, chalet, or hotel on the mountainside, you need only walk outside, slip on your skis, and head for the slopes.

With 79 percent of its skiable terrain rated novice or intermediate, Big White is a great family ski resort. However, the expert terrain can challenge even the most experienced skier. Lots of snow and good grooming make even the timid adventurer feel good on the skis. The longest run is a respectable 3 miles, and there's plenty of open and tree-line bowl skiing. Seven lifts and 47 runs cover the mountain's 2,050-foot vertical and offer plenty of variety during week-long vacations.

Skiing Big White is a pleasant experience, since mild weather and soft snow prevail. Cruising runs such as Poofter's Puff and Easy Out appeal to the slow and easy skiers, while Cliff and Dragon's Tongue keep the experts challenged during each ski turn.

Last season, Big White opened a new platter lift that rises over 1,000 feet up a 45-degree-plus slope. The lift takes skiers out of the infamous back basin and double-black-diamond skiing areas, known as the Cliff. It is skiing for the seasoned expert.

At Big White, the theme is "Ski a Village on a Mountain" and discover plenty of variety in accommodations and dining. The nightlife is good—it has to be when it is secluded up in the mountains. With an average snowfall of 223 inches (565 cms) and its great variety of slopes, Big White is the kind of place that makes you want to extend your vacation.

Practical Information for Big White

HOW TO GET THERE. Big White is situated 55 km east of Kelowna and 512 km from Vancouver on Rte. 33 in Central British Columbia. Major **rental car** agencies at Kelowna airport include *Budget,* (604) 860–2464, or 800–527–0700 in the United States; *Hertz,* (604) 860–7808, or 800–654–3131 in the United States; and *Tilden (National* in the United States), (604) 860–6000, or 800–328–4567 in the United States.

By air. There are regularly scheduled flights into Kelowna Airport from Vancouver, Calgary, Edmonton, and Toronto via *Canadian Airlines International* and *Air BC; Time Air* via Lethbridge, Alberta, and Vancouver; and *CP Holidays* from Vancouver. Prebooked transfers are available for individuals or groups from Kelowna to Big White Village.

By bus. *Greyhound Bus Lines* (604) 860–3835 services Kelowna from all western Canadian cities. From Vancouver or Calgary, it is approximately 7–10 hours travel time.

By car. From Vancouver, take Trans-Canada Hwy. 1 east, then south on Hwys. 97A and 97. The trip takes about 6 hours. Alternatively, take Hwy. 1 to Hwy. 3 east, and then north on Hwy. 97 to Kelowna; a scenic 7-hour drive. Calgary is 666 km east; take Hwy. 1, then Hwy. 97 south (about 8 hours). Seattle is 8 hours away and Spokane is only 6 hours.

TELEPHONES. The area code for all British Columbia is 604.

ACCOMMODATIONS. Phone *Central Reservation,* 765–8888 (it accepts collect calls) or 800–663–2772 from British Columbia to Thunder Bay, Ontario; or write to *Big White Central Reservations,* Box 2039, Station R, Kelowna V1X 4K5. Seven condominium complexes and a few chalets provide 2,400 beds all within walking or skiing distance of the slopes. Unit styles are hotel rooms, studios, and 1– 3-bedroom suites with fully equipped kitchens. Most have fireplaces and underground or covered parking. Amenities include saunas, hot tubs, racquetball courts, swimming pools, and laundry facilities. Accommodations are available for any number of days with a good choice of packages that can include lifts, lessons, and meals. A variety of dining rooms and lounges are within convenient walking distance. The Village Center also features a Mountain Mart (groceries), gift shop, day care, and shuttle bus system to main ski area day lodge, and liquor store.

All accommodations at Big White could be considered in the *Inexpensive– Moderate* price range. A hotel-style room for two persons, for instance, may cost $60, while a 2-bedroom for four people goes for $172, and a 4-bedroom suite accommodating eight persons goes for $249. A 2-person kitchenette and bedroom costs $89 and a studio $95. Each lodging place offers various combinations and each can be reached at the above listed Central Reservation address or phone number.

Listed below are the Big White Village lodges. A variety of motels and hotels is also available in Kelowna proper, but because of the distance, practically all skiers prefer to stay at the slopeside accommodations.

Das Hofbrauhaus. Features large 1- and 2-bedroom condominium units with kitchenettes, dining room, balcony, fireplace, and TV. This complex also has racquetball, indoor pool, hot tub, and sauna.

Greystoke Inn. Offers sauna, outdoor hot tub, satellite TV, and laundry. Most rooms have fireplace and balcony.

The Monashee. Closest to the ski day lodge, has large 1- to 3-bedroom units with large common area. Most rooms with fireplace and balcony.

The Ponderosa. Features large family condo units ranging from studio to 4 bedrooms. Each unit has full kitchen, satellite TV, and laundry.

Ptarmigan Inn. Situated close to center of village and activities. Offer sauna, dip pools, satellite TV, laundry, fireplaces, and balconies.

Tamarack Inn. Cozy surroundings in center of village; has 1- and 3-bedroom units, sauna, laundry, satellite TV, fireplaces, and balconies.

Whitefoot Lodge. All the amenities, including gift shop, food mart, rental shop, ski school, lift-ticket outlet, sauna, laundry, pools, and satellite TV; some units with fireplaces and balconies. The lodge has accommodations with up to 4 bedrooms. It is part of the main lodge where the ski school is located.

RESTAURANTS. This small mountain village features five restaurants and pubs in the *Moderate to Inexpensive* range ($5–$12 for entrees). The only *Expensive* restaurant is **The White Foot Dining Room** in the **T-Bar Bistro. Roses on the Ridge Pub** and restaurant has roadhouse-style food with fries; **Barclay's** in Das Hofbrauhaus has fine dining at moderate prices; the **Loose Moose Bar** in the Alpine Center, a good après-ski spot, offers bar and finger food, and **Snowshow Sam's** serves breakfast, lunch, and semiformal dinners.

HOW TO GET AROUND. All facilities and services at Big White are within walking distance. A **shuttle bus,** does the rounds from Kelowna to the Alpine Center, bringing skiers back and forth. Contact the base lodge for schedules and information; 765–3101.

SEASONAL EVENTS. The *Team Supreme Race,* a recreational series of races, takes place on the first weekends of **February, March,** and **April.** It's mainly for local restaurant people. In **April,** the *Ski to Sea* race entertains everyone. Designed as a relay, one team member skis downhill to a cross-country *skier,* who meets a *cyclist,* who rides down the road to Kelowna to a *runner* who goes to a *canoeist,* who then paddles to the city park in Kelowna. *Ski to Tee* is another fun event taking place in mid-**April.** This two-part race features a recreational ski race on Saturday followed by a golf tournament on Sunday.

OTHER SPORTS AND ACTIVITIES. Alpine skiing is the main activity, but not the only one up in these mountains. There are 25 km of cross-country trails accessible from the village and designed for all abilities. For information, call the main lodge, 765–3101.

Swimming and **racquetball** offer a nice change of pace and an opportunity to develop other muscles than those used in skiing. For court reservations, call 765–7578.

Children's activities include a *Kinderski* program for ages 3–8 for $21 a day; $25 if you need rental equipment. Day care is also available at the same price for children aged 18 months to 8 years. Call 765–3101 for reservations.

NIGHTLIFE. Après-ski activities at Big White center on the village restaurants. (See *Restaurants* above.)

FAIRMONT HOT SPRINGS

Box 10
Fairmont Hot Springs, BC V0B 1L0
Tel: 604–345–6311
Telex: 041–45108

Snow Report: 604–345–6311
Area Vertical: 1,000 ft. (300 meters)
Number of Trails: 12 on 60 acres
Lifts: 1 triple chair, 1 platter pull
Snowmaking: 70 percent of acreage (5 trails)
Season: mid-December–end of March

This family-owned luxury resort is nestled on the western slopes of the British Columbia Rockies overlooking the beautiful Columbia River Valley and Lake Windermere. Fairmont was homesteaded back in 1887, then grew into a rest stop for the valley stage coaches. Around the turn of the century, a wealthy visiting Englishman named W. H. Holland was so impressed by the quality of the mineral hot pools and the region's natural beauty that he settled in with his family to operate a resort ranch. Later, in 1956, some local businessmen, including Lloyd and Earl Wilder, purchased the resort. The Wilder brothers soon bought out the other partners and began the development toward today's grand resort.

Lloyd Wilder purchased his brother's share in 1965 and quickly stepped up expansion to include a ski area, an 18-hole par-70 championship golf course, time-share villas, and improved mineral hot pool facilities. In 1985 access to Fairmont increased significantly with the building of a new 6,200-foot airstrip capable of handling Boeing 737 aircraft.

Fairmont continues to grow and improve as a fabulous ski-and-swim family resort. Although their famous hot pools remain the main attraction, the moderate-sized ski area offers a pleasant experience for any level skier seeking a unique ski vacation.

Its respectable 1,000-foot vertical offers challenge on its 10 runs ranging from 2,000 to 6,000 feet in length. There's a great view of the Columbia River Valley and the Parcell Mountains beyond. The slopes sit at the base of majestic Rocky Mountain cliffs and peaks. Night skiing is available.

There are superb on-mountain facilities, including a large day-lodge and deck. There's a cafeteria and lounge with fireplace. The Ski School plays an active role in the ski packages. A pleasant mix of skiing, instruction, and social activities, such as a western barbecue and a fun race, enhance the snow vacation. Use of hot pools is also included as well as an optional ski day at nearby Panorama or Kimberley ski areas.

Practical Information for Fairmont Hot Springs

HOW TO GET THERE. Fairmont Hot Springs is located in the Columbia River Valley on Hwy. 93 near Ivermere, between Cranbrook and Golden, BC. Calgary, AB, is 270 km east and Cranbrook, a much smaller city, is 110 km to the south.

By air. Major airlines fly into Calgary International Airport with connections to Cranbrook via *Time Air* and *Air BC.* From the west, Vancouver is another gateway to the region, with connections to Cranbrook. For a list of **car rental** agencies at the Calgary airport, see the Banff/Lake Louise *How to Get There* section. **Car rentals** available in Cranbrook are *Hertz,* (604) 268–1311 or toll-free 800–654–3131 in the United States and 800–263–0600 in Canada; or *Tilden,* (604) 265–9111 or toll-free 800–227–7368 in the United States and 800–387–4747 in Canada.

By bus. *Greyhound Bus Lines* services are available from Calgary, Cranbrook, and Vancouver. For information on schedules and fares, phone (403) 762–2236.

By car. It takes approximately 3 hours to drive to Fairmont Hot Springs from Calgary, and 1½ hours from Cranbrook. From Calgary, take Hwy. 1 west, then Hwy. 93 south. From Cranbrook, drive north on Hwy. 93–95 to the resort. Vancouver is a 10-hour drive on scenic Hwy. 1 northward and eastward, then south on Hwy. 95 from Golden.

TELEPHONES. The area code for all British Columbia is 604, and for Alberta it is 403.

ACCOMMODATIONS. Fairmont has 700 pillows at the resort. For reservations at any of the lodgings contact Box 10, Fairmount Hot Springs, BC V0B 1L0; phone (604) 345–6311; (403) 264–0746 in Calgary; or 800–663–4979 in other parts of British Columbia, Alberta, or Saskatchewan.

Deluxe hotel accommodations are available in the Fairmont Lodge or the resort's new condominiums. The lodge features 140 rooms with full hotel services and access to its own mineral pool. There is a full-service dining room, a residents' lounge, and a selection of conference rooms for large or small groups. Prices per person, based on double occupancy, range from $60 to $100, depending on the season.

Lofts cost $100–$140 or a minimum of 4 people. Interval ownership is also available for **deluxe villas.**

A variety of packages, ranging from three to five days, is also available at the lodge, with special rates for children. Some packages offer ski instructions as well as passes for Fairmont and three other ski areas—Fernie, Kimberly, and Panorama.

RESTAURANTS. The **Fairmont Lodge Restaurant** has fine dining and reasonable prices. Entrees range from $7.95 to about $20. The town of Invermere is 25 km away and includes several restaurants and bars as well as daytime shopping. (See section on *Panorama* for more information on Invermere.)

HOW TO GET AROUND. For recreational vehicles, there are 30 year-round RV sites located near the main lodge and hot pools. A free **ski bus** service is available for guests to the ski slopes. Having your own car, however, is your best bet.

SEASONAL EVENTS. The resort runs the *Starlight Challenge* every Friday night throughout the winter. It is an adult race series and all abilities participate.

OTHER SPORTS AND ACTIVITIES. This is where Fairmont shines. There are more than enough things for the active guest to do. **Racquetball** and squash are available in the new recreational complex, the *Fairmont Sports Center,* which has a regular indoor **swimming pool,** saunas, Jacuzzi, and a gym. **Aerobics** classes are also scheduled.

No one can resist the 930 square meters of steaming hot mineral water in natural, odorless **hot pools.** Open year-round, the water temperatures vary between 34° and 45° C. There are small indoor soaking pools as well as a giant outdoor heated swimming pool, which is also open in winter. Soaking in the hot pools at the base of the Rockies surrounded by snow is an exhilarating experience. Pools are open 8 A.M. to 10 P.M. daily.

If you're lucky enough to be visiting in early spring, the valley's warm climate enables the 18-hole golf course to open early. Ski in the morning and golf in the afternoon. **Snowmobiling** and **fishing** are also offered nearby. For any activity, contact the resort's main office, 346–6341.

DAY-CARE FACILITIES. *Ski Chalet* baby-sitting services are available upon request. Phone 604–345–6311 for reservations. Baby-sitters are on duty 10 A.M.–4 P.M. daily for children 2–6 years old. Ski lessons are available for children aged 3–12 years. Skiing is free for kids under 8 years old and 4–8-year-olds can participate in the *Snow Bird* program of morning lessons and recreation.

NIGHTLIFE. The resort's lounge features nightly live entertainment for those with leftover energy. The town of Invermere, 25 km away, has several bars. (See section on *Panorama.*)

FERNIE SNOW VALLEY

Box 788
Fernie BC V0B 1M0
Tel: 604–423–4655

Snow Report: 604–423–9921
Area Vertical: 2,400 ft.
Number of Trails: 40 defined runs, 2 alpine bowls, and tree skiing
Lifts: 1 quad chair, 1 triple chair, 1 double chair, 2 T-bars, 1 platter pull, 1 rope tow
Snowmaking: for patching only
Season: mid-November–late April

Situated in the Crowsnest Pass area only a few minutes from the town of Fernie and a 3½-hour drive southwest of Calgary, Fernie Snow Valley is a paradise for skiers who want powder. With over 600 cm of snow annually, this quaint ski resort is considered (by *Ski Canada Magazine*) one of the best ski values in North America.

The community of Fernie was founded in the 19th century as a coal mining center. The lumber industry also contributed to its growth, and Fernie now has 7,500 or so people. In the winter, it becomes a real ski town nestled beneath the high peaks of Trinity Mountain, which is often called the Three Sisters because of its distinct triple-peak formation. The late Edwardian-style red brick buildings add to the town's charm with an awesome view of the ski area's peaks and bowls above.

Fernie credits its abundance of snow to a local legend named Griz, a century-old man of the mountains who hibernates in rock caves during the summers. He appears each fall ready to make more and more powder. He's worth visiting.

On average, the area gets over 15 feet of snow, adding to the quality of the upper-bowl skiing. The 2,100-foot vertical stretches out into a combination of wide bowls, ridges, and rolling tree runs, making it an interesting ski center for any level of skier. The novice will enjoy the Meadow run off the Deer T-bar, while the intermediate skier can test his skills off the mile-long Griz Chair on runs such as Lizard. The experts frolic in the deep stuff up in the Lizard or Cedar bowls or on Boomerang Ridge.

Fernie's longest run is about 5 km and its newest triple chair, called Boomerang, opened up great skiing terrain that was previously accessible only by long traverses in and out of the area. This is where the mountain's deeper and drier snow is found.

There is a CSIA-certified ski school open to teach both beginners and powderhounds. The rental shop offers complete equipment rentals. The day lodge facility answers all your skiing needs with licensed cafeteria, ski shop, and other facilities.

Practical Information for Fernie

HOW TO GET THERE. Fernie is 320 km from Calgary and 60 km from Cranbrook, BC.

By air. Fly to Calgary International or Vancouver airports via most major airlines such as *Air Canada* or *Canadian.* Connections can be made at either airport to *Time Air* or *Air BC* to the Kimberly/Cranbrook Airport, but it's probably cheaper to drive from Calgary. For a complete list of **rental cars** at the Calgary airport, see the Banff/Lake Louise *How To Get There* section.

By bus. *Greyhound Bus Lines,* (403) 265–9111, makes two trips to Fernie daily from Calgary.

By car. It takes 3½–4 hours to drive from Calgary, south on Hwy. 2, then west on Hwy. 3 to Fernie and the ski area. From Cranbrook, the trip is about 1½ hours east on Hwy. 3. The trip from Vancouver takes 10–11 hours, driving east on Hwy. 1, which connects with Hwy. 3 at Hope BC. From Spokane WA, 189 km away, drive north on Rte. 2 through the tip of Idaho onto Hwy. 3.

TELEPHONES. The area code for all British Columbia is 604, and for Alberta, it is 403.

ACCOMMODATIONS. At the ski resort itself the 36-unit **Griz Inn,** 423–9221, enables visitors to ski to their doors. Suites are self-contained condominiums with complete kitchens, microwave ovens, and dishwashers. Other facilities include Jacuzzi, sauna, game room, and dining room. **Wolfe's Den Mountain Lodge,** 423–9202, the other slopeside hotel, with 42 units, is located across from the day-lodge. It features outdoor hot tubs, games, and exercise rooms. Prices, considered *Expensive* in these parts, range from $56 per person, double occupancy, for a 1-bedroom unit to $109 for a 3-bedroom loft. Ski week packages are also available for five nights and include lift passes, lessons, and social activities.

Listed here are some accommodations in the town of Fernie, just a few miles away. Categories, determined by price, are *Moderate,* $35–$55; and *Inexpensive,* less than $35.

Cedar Lodge. *Moderate.* Box 1477; 423–4622. Has 48 rooms, with cable TV, swimming pool, whirlpool, and sauna.

Park Place Lodge. *Moderate.* Box 2199; 423–6871. Has 47 rooms, swimming pool, sauna, and lounge.

Anco Motel. *Inexpensive.* Box 1230; 423–4492. Features whirlpool, sauna, satellite TV with 36 rooms.

Inn Towner Motel. *Inexpensive.* 601 Second Ave.; 423–6308. Has 14 rooms with color TV, and some with kitchenettes.

Snow Valley Motel. *Inexpensive.* Box 1207; 423–4421. Pleasant facility with 21 units and cable TV.

Three Sisters Motel. *Inexpensive.* Box 280; 423–4438. Has a whirlpool and sauna for 38 comfortable units; 14 units have kitchens.

RESTAURANTS. As in the case of accommodations, the pocketbook can be spared either at the ski resort itself or in the small town of Fernie. For an *Expensive* meal in this area, expect to pay $10–$20; *Moderate* around $10; *Inexpensive* less than $10. Reservations are not required at any of the places listed, and all but the inexpensive places accept major credit cards.

Grizzly's Restaurant and Bar. *Expensive.* At the resort's Griz Inn on the slopes; 432–9221. Fine dining offers a wide choice of entrees; Continental cuisine.

Olde Elevator Steak House. *Expensive.* 291 First Ave., Fernie; 423–7115. Steaks done the way you like them.

Alpine Restaurant. *Moderate.* Hwy. 3, Fernie; 423–3211. Both Swiss and Chinese specialties.

Capone's Ristorante. *Moderate.* Hwy. 3; 423–7616. Italian cuisine.

Coal Valley Steak and Pancake House. *Moderate.* Hwy. 3, Fernie; 423–3118.

New Diamond Grill. *Moderate.* 551 2nd Ave.; 423–4611. As the name implies, grilled fare is available here.

Libby's. *Inexpensive.* Hwy. 3, Fernie; 423–7444. Pizza and lasagna.

HOW TO GET AROUND. It's best to have your own (or rented) car at this resort, but it will mostly stay put once you get here. There's taxi service available in the town of Fernie; call *Kootenay Taxi,* 423–4408.

SEASONAL EVENTS. Enjoy *Griz Days* in late **January.** In recognition of the legendary "Griz," Fernie's powdermaker, the townspeople hold a week-long festival, including sports events, competitions, and parades. *Powder 8* championships take place in **March** when teams attempt to make perfect figure eights in the powder. The *OKEE DOKEE Downhill* is a recreational downhill race in **late March.** The *Powder-Peddle-Paddle* is a fun-filled relay race each **April.** The *Spring Fiesta* in **May** is another annual party event held to mark the end of the ski season.

OTHER SPORTS AND ACTIVITIES. As noted, Fernie is a small town and **skiing** is the biggest activity. For relaxing the muscles, there's a hot tub at the ski center. In the village, the Cedar Lodge, 423–4622, and Park Place Lodge, 423–6871, both have swimming pools, and most other in-town hotels have saunas.

CHILDREN'S ACTIVITIES. Baby-sitting services are available upon reservation at the resort; 423–9221, ext. 119. The Nursery Ski School operates seven days per week for toddlers 3–5 years old from 10 A.M. to 3 P.M. The fee includes indoor play and outdoor skiing and instruction. Children under 6 ski free.

NIGHTLIFE. There's good entertainment here for such a small town. *Papa John's* at the corner of Second Ave. and 3rd St., 423–3343, is a popular pub with dancing and a big screen TV. *J.P.'s Place,* 691 First Ave. (423–6444), is where all the sports people meet. The *Sundown Nite Club* at 892 Sixth Ave. (423–7223) has lots of rock and roll for those looking for dancing. For a more sedate evening at the movies, there's the *Vogue Theater* at 321 Second Ave. (423–6665).

KIMBERLEY SKI RESORT

Box 40
Kimberley BC V1A 2Y5
Tel: 604–427–4881

Snow Report: 604–427–4881
Area Vertical: 2,300 ft.
Number of Trails: 34 on 425 skiable acres
Lifts: 2 triple chairs, 1 double chair, 1
    T-bar, 3 handle tows
Snowmaking: 15 percent of terrain
Season: December–mid-April

The small alpine city of Kimberley is situated in British Columbia's Purcell Mountains. Across the broad valley below is a great view of the Rockies. The site of one of the world's largest underground lead and zinc mines, Kimberley is also a year-round resort offering many events and sports activities.

Kimberley was transformed into a "Bavarian" city in 1972 as part of a major downtown beautification plan. Kimberley is actually a mix of Austrian, Swiss, and English Tudor styles. The Bavarian theme is appropriate to its alpine setting with its very own community ski area above the valley.

The Platzl, meaning "people's place," represents the two main commercial streets lined with Bavarian-style store fronts and home to the world's largest cuckoo clock. It's Kimberley's focal point, only minutes from the ski slopes. The Bavarian alpine architecture in this beautiful mountain setting, with cross-country and downhill facilities within city limits, evokes the feeling of a European ski village. These skiing facilities were built by volunteer labor in the 1950s as recreation for the local mine workers. The development of recreation was crucial to the Cominco Mines to retain miners in the region.

Today Kimberley ski resort is a leader in skiing for the disabled. The Canadian Association for Disabled Skiing is based here, and last spring the resort hosted the World Disabled Ski Championships.

You'll find an impressive 2,300-foot vertical with runs stretching out in all directions. The three major lifts service a mostly intermediate mountain for good cruising. Expert terrain represents 25 percent and novice is 15 percent of the total skiable area. The highest elevation is 6,500 feet, offering a pleasant view of the Kootenay River Valley lined with the Rockies to the east.

There's great night skiing, too. The Main, North America's largest illuminated run, is a unique ski experience with the lights of Kimberley town and the mountain village twinkling below. It presents yet another choice of activities for vacation evenings.

Practical Information for Kimberley

HOW TO GET THERE. Kimberley is 20 miles north of Cranbrook BC, on Hwy. 95A, and 55 miles from the U.S. border near the Montana and Idaho state line.

By air. Fly to Calgary International or Vancouver airports via most major airlines such as *Air Canada* and *Canadian Airlines International.* Connections can be made at either airport with *Time Air* and *Air BC,* which fly into Kimberley/Cranbrook Airport. **Car rentals** are available there from *Avis,* (604) 489–4710, or 800–331–1212 in the United States; *Budget,* (604) 489–4371 or 800–527–0700 in the United States; or *Tilden,* (604) 489–1335 or 800–387–4747 in Canada.

By bus. *Greyhound Bus Lines* serves Kimberley from most major western cities of Canada and the United States. From Calgary, the bus ride is about 5 hours; call (403) 265-9111.

By car. Driving distance from Vancouver is 870 km, east on Hwy. 1, which connects with Hwy. 3 at Hope BC, and onto 95A at Cranbrook. From Spokane WA, drive north on Rte. 2 through the tip of Idaho onto Hwy. 3. From any direction, it's a very scenic drive through various mountain ranges.

TELEPHONES. The area code for all British Columbia is 604, and for Alberta, it is 403.

ACCOMMODATIONS. The resort has condominium and chalet lodgings for 1,400 guests within walking distance of the ski lifts. Most lodgings have saunas, hot tubs, and recreation centers. Furthermore, all feature affordable prices. Reservations for on-mountain accommodations can be made either through *Kimberley Ski Resort,* Box 40, Kimberley BC V1A 2Y5 (427-4877), or by calling the number for each individual listing. Although most skiers prefer to stay at slopeside accommodations, a selection of hotels and motels is available in the city of Kimberley just a few minutes (7 km) away.

Hotel rates are per person, based on double occupancy. *Moderate,* $30-$50; *Inexpensive,* less than $30.

On-Mountain

Inn West/Kirkwood Inn. *Moderate.* 427-7616. Condominium units of 1-2 bedrooms, each with fireplace, kitchen, and balcony. Two-day packages include lift privileges and breakfast. Five-day packages also available. Children under 9 years stay free.

Mountain Edge Resort Inn. *Moderate.* 427-5381. The newest accommodation on the slopes with 42 1-bedroom condos with living room, kitchen, fireplace, balcony, satellite TV, and protected parking. Three-day packages available.

Purcell Condo Hotel. *Moderate.* 427-5385. Units of 1, 2 and 3 bedrooms, with kitchens, wood-burning stoves, and balconies. Two- and 5-day packages available, with breakfast and lift tickets.

Rocky Mountain Condo Hotel. *Moderate.* 427-5385. A short walk to the ski slopes. Amenities include breakfast with a 2-day package.

Silver Birch Chalets. *Moderate.* 427-5385. Located at the eastern end of Kimberley Village; 3 chalets are available, as are 2-day packages with breakfast and ski passes.

Kimberley

Inn of the Rockies. *Moderate.* 300 Wallington Ave.; 427-2266. Just 5 minutes from the lifts; 41 well-appointed rooms, satellite TV and disco; 2-day package available.

Kimberly Palace. *Inexpensive.* 2665 Warren Ave.; 427-4855. Offers 33 rooms with satellite TV, direct dial phones, dining room, and cocktail lounge.

CAMPING. The **Happy Hans Campgrounds** is located 2 km from Kimberley on Rte. 95A on the way to the ski resort; 427-3666. There are some 130 fully serviced wooded sites available for RVs. Fees are $10 for full service, including water and electrical hookups.

RESTAURANTS. On the mountains, there is a selection of eating places, from seated dining in the North Star Center, with burgers, club sandwiches, homemade soups, and full-course dinners, to cafeteria services in the main lodge. In Kimberley, there is a wider selection. The price categories are based on the cost of a three-course dinner for one person; beverages and tip not included. *Expensive,* $15-$25; *Moderate,* $8-$14; *Inexpensive,* less than $8. All the dining places at the resort are in the *Inexpensive-Moderate* range. Listed below is a selection of restaurants in Kimberley. All except the inexpensive places take most major credit cards.

Expensive

Gasthaus Am Platzl. 240 Spokane St.; 427–4851. Specializes in fine German dining. Lunch and dinner served; reservations suggested for dinner.

Moderate

Aikmans Restaurant. 175 Deer Park Rd.; 427–3626. Family dining. Canadian dishes, breakfast, lunch, and dinner.
Alpenrose. 136 Wallinger Ave.; 427–7461. Family dining for breakfast, lunch, and dinner.
Kimberley City Bakery. 287 Spokane St.; 427–2131. Swiss bakery, tea room, and sidewalk cafe. Lunches and take-out service.
Kimberly Palace. 2665 Warren Ave.; 427–5257. Serves breakfast, lunch, and dinner, Canadian dishes.
La Casa Amigos. 290 Spokane St.; 427–3739. Breakfast and lunches only. Features Mexican dishes. Takeout available.

Inexpensive

BJ's Breakfast. 340 Mark St.; 427–7618. Specializes in breakfasts, as name implies. Homemade food.
Dixie Lee Chicken and Seafood. 490 Wallinger Ave.; 427–7814. Lunches and dinner.
Mary's Kitchen. 324 Archibald St.; 427–3412. Breakfast, lunch, dinner, and takeouts.

HOW TO GET AROUND. Skiing guests are given a free shuttle pass that entitles them to use the **shuttle bus** service that runs several times daily between Kimberley Village and downtown. During the week, **taxi** service is available from *L & K Taxi Company,* 427–4442, at $4 for the 7-mile trip. If you wish to venture farther afield, it's best to have a **car.**

SEASONAL EVENTS. February brings disabled skiers from across the country for the *Disabled Skiers Challenge.* On the second weekend of **February,** the *Winterfest* kicks off with a beerfest. *Winter Carnival* takes place the end of **March.** The spectacular *Bavarian Iron Legs* competition is in mid- to late-**April.** Mid-April brings in the *Spring Splash.* You'll see crazy skiers in the true spring spirit attempting to ski through a pond of ice-cold snow-melt water at the base.

OTHER SPORTS AND ACTIVITIES. The lineup of slopeside activities include **indoor tennis, hot tubs, saunas,** and 26 km of groomed **cross-country ski trails.** A **tennis** bubble at the mountain is in operation throughout the winter. For information and reservations, contact the ski area, 427–4881. In the town of Kimberley, **curling** is available at the *Kimberley Curling Club,* 427–2591, and **bowling** is at *Head Pins Bowling,* 427–7514.

CHILDREN'S ACTIVITIES. *Kimbercare* day-care program is for children age 2–6. A learn-to-ski program run by *Ski Scamps,* is available on Monday, Wednesday, and Friday–Sunday, from 1 to 2 P.M. For information and reservations, contact the lodge office, 427–4881.

NIGHTLIFE. There are three hot spots in Kimberley. In the North Star Center at the ski hill, the *Disco Cabaret* (427–4881) has live entertainment and dancing. In town, visit the *Kimberly Palace,* 2665 Warren St. (427–4855), a disco and lounge. The *Inn of the Rockies Disco Cabaret,* at 300 Wallinger (427–2266), is another dance spot. Most hotels have quiet lounges for pleasant relaxation.

MOUNT WASHINGTON SKI RESORT LTD.

Box 3069
Courtenay BC V9N 5N3
Tel: 604–338–1386

Snow Report: 604–338–1515
Area Vertical: 1,600 ft.
Number of Trails: 28 trails on 172
skiable acres
Lifts: 2 triple chairs, 2 double chairs,
1 handletow
Snowmaking: none
Season: mid-November–end of April

To ski Mount Washington is to ski an island in the Pacific. With a yearly average snowfall of 1,200 cm (472 inches), this fairly remote ski center offers a unique experience and the opportunity to get away from it all.

The area was originally settled for the mining and lumber industries. Mount Washington Ski Area was begun in 1979 with the installation of two double chairlifts. Two businessmen from Campbell River foresaw the potential of the island resort and it hasn't stopped growing since.

Just 31 km (19 miles) from the Comox Valley, Mount Washington boasts scenic grandeur with ideal terrain for all levels of skiers. The highest elevation is 1,576 m (5,168 feet) above sea level, and the slopes vary from steep to easy. Beginners can conveniently reach the handletow just 50 meters from the rental shop. Maintained nordic trails and wilderness skiing are also available here.

There are extensive facilities at the base with rental shops, a CSIA-certified ski school, and a mountain village with 1-, 2-, 3-, and 4-bedroom units. Down in the Comox Valley and the town of Courtenay, you'll find plenty of shopping and entertainment.

Adventure ski weeks are popular at Mount Washington. With the ski pros as your hosts, the program includes a Monday evening greeting presentation and a Friday farewell dinner party. Also included in addition to accommodations are lifts, movies, evening entertainment in the lounge, and one other meal. With 260,000 skiers a season, some call Mount Washington the best-kept ski secret.

Practical Information for
Mount Washington

HOW TO GET THERE. Mount Washington is located 31 km west of Courtenay BC, 250 km from Victoria, and 135 km from Vancouver.

By air. Daily flights run via Dash 7 planes from Vancouver to Comox. *Canadian Airlines International* has several flights daily into Comox Airport on Vancouver Island. All connections to most North American cities can be made at Vancouver International Airport. **Car rentals** are available at the Comox Airport from *Budget,* (604) 338–7717 or toll-free 800–527–0700 in the United States and 800–268–8900 in Canada, and *Tilden,* (604) 339–63331 or toll-free 800–227–7368 in the United States and 800–387–4747 in Canada.

By bus. Buses run on various days from Victoria to Mount Washington. *Vancouver Islands Coachlines* provides bus service twice daily between Victoria and Courtenay. *Hilo Transportation* provides transport from Comox to Mount Washington. For information on any of these lines, call (604) 338–1386.

By ferry. Every 2 hours, from 7 A.M. to 9 P.M. the *BC Ferries* serve the Island between Vancouver and Nanaimo. Phone (604) 685–1021.

TELEPHONES. The area code for all British Columbia is 604.

ACCOMMODATIONS. For lodgings at the mountain, contact *Mount Washington Central Reservations,* Box 3069, Courtenay BC, V9N 5N3; 338–1386. Fully equipped 1–2-bedroom condominiums are available. In Courtenay there is a variety of hotels, lodges, inns, and motels. Hotel prices are based on double occupancy. Categories are: *Moderate,* $35–$50 and *Inexpensive,* less than $35. The mountain condo units fall in the moderate range. Listed below is a selection of accommodations in Courtenay, about a 45-minute drive from the mountain.

Arbutus TraveLodge. *Moderate.* 275 Eighth St.; 334–3121. Features sauna, lounge, restaurant, and satellite TV.

Collingwood Inn. *Moderate.* 1675 Cliffe Ave.; 338–1464. Cozy place with kitchenettes, lounge, restaurant, ski rentals, and laundromat.

Pacific Village. *Moderate.* Island Hwy. RR 1; 335–2333. Chalets with kitchenettes available; restaurant on property.

Port Augusta Motel. *Moderate.* 2082 Comox Ave.; 339–2277. Rooms with kitchenettes; pool, sauna, restaurant, laundromat.

Sleepy Hollow Inn. *Moderate.* 1190 Cliffe Ave.; 334–4476. Has kitchenettes, pool, sauna, and Jacuzzi.

Washington Inn. *Moderate.* 1001 Ryan Rd.; 338–5441. Features pool, sauna, Jacuzzi, lounge, restaurant, satellite TV, and ski rentals.

Anco Slumber Lodge. *Inexpensive.* 1885 Cliffe Ave.; 334–2451. Basic accommodations with kitchenettes, satellite TV.

RESTAURANTS. The Comox Village has several eating spots popular with skiers. *Expensive* prices for a full dinner for one without tax, tip, and beverages, range from $15 to $20; *Moderate,* $8–$15; *Inexpensive,* under $8. All major credit cards are accepted unless otherwise noted.

Cafeteria food is available in the Alpine Daylodge, breakfast and lunches. Moderately priced meals are served in the lodge's dining room. Reservations are welcome. Phone 338–1386.

The Gaff Rig Restaurant. *Expensive.* 1984 Buenavista Ave.; 339–7181. Fine European specialties, steaks, and seafood. Reservations required for dinner.

Mex Café. *Moderate.* 1001 Ryan Rd.; 338–5441. Specializes in Mexican cuisine but also offers a fine prime rib.

The Old House Restaurant. *Moderate.* 100 17th St.; 338–5406. Seafood and wild game.

The Pewter Room. *Moderate.* 498 North Island Hwy.; 334–4401. European atmosphere.

Bino's Restaurant. *Inexpensive.* 2601 South Island Hwy.; 334–3931. Canadian dishes.

Taco Time. *Inexpensive.* 450 Ryan Rd.; 338–1660. Has wide variety of Mexican dishes.

HOW TO GET AROUND. Once in the Comox Valley, the two options for traveling up to the mountain are driving your own—or rented—**car** or availing yourself of the convenient **shuttle bus** service between the mountain and Courtenay. For information and schedules, call the lodge office, 338–1386. For car rentals at Courtenay, contact *Budget,* 338–7717, or *Hertz,* 800–263–0600.

SEASONAL EVENTS. In **February,** the *Coca-Cola Classic* event is held, with proceeds going to the disabled skiers fund. Also in February is the lively *Winter Carnival.* In **March,** the *Canadian Armed Forces Championship* is held. These are recreational fun races with light competition. Also in March is the *Mount Washington Annual Cross-Country Marathon* and the *Canadian Masters Alpine Series.* The *Jester's Cup* takes place every **April** and features a beer garden, a breakfast barbecue, and a fun costume race.

OTHER SPORTS AND ACTIVITIES. In Courtenay, there are four **golf** courses and 13 public **tennis** courts that sometimes open in early April. With a choice of eight **fitness centers, tanning salons,** and **aerobics classes,** you're bound to leave healthier than you came. Phone 338–1386.

Other facilities in the Comox Valley include large indoor **pools, whirlpools,** and **saunas** at the Westerly Hotel (338–7741).

CHILDREN'S ACTIVITIES. The Mount Washington Ski School's *Kid's Brigade* is for 3–8-year-olds and includes a full day of skiing, building snowmen, and tobogganing. Lessons are also available on a half- or full-day basis. Children's ski-week packages include 2 hours of lessons daily.

Evening activities are scheduled daily for children 6–12 years of age. From 4 P.M. to 6 P.M. supervision is offered for the kids while the parents relax in the lounge. Formal activities, 7–10 P.M., include games, crafts, and movies. All evening programs are free of charge. Contact the Ski School for details, 338–1386.

NIGHTLIFE. The lounge at the *Alpine Daylodge* features après-ski and dancing each evening until 11. In Courtenay the *Courtenay House,* 334–4401, features Doc's Cabaret. The *Leeward Pub,* 339–5400, on Anderson Rd., has homemade country cooking for snacks. The *Whistle Stop,* 334–4500, on Mansfield St., is another relaxing neighborhood pub. *Jigger's Cabaret,* on Fifth St., 334–4455; features live entertainment Monday to Saturday.

PANORAMA RESORT

Box 7000
Invermere BC V0A 1K0
Tel: 604–342–6941

Snow Report: 604–342–6941
Area Vertical: 3,800 ft.
Trails: 33 on 260 acres of skiable terrain
Lifts: 1 high-speed quad, 1 triple chair,
*   2 double chairs, 2 T-bars, 1 poma,*
*   1 rope tow*
Snowmaking: 70 percent of acreage (10
*   trails)*
Season: December–mid-April

Panaroma has come a long way in the past several years. Once just a small community ski center on a winding dirt road used by miners on their way to nearby silver claims like Paradise Mines, this full-service resort has grown into a year-round luxury destination. Activities are abundant in any season and the accommodations can't be beat for convenience and comfort. Panorama calls itself "Canada's Alpine Family Resort."

By hosting the 1985 men's World Cup downhill race, it has established its ski slopes as world class. This winter, Panorama hosts a women's World Cup downhill and super-G, continuing its racing tradition. The skiing is exciting for any level and the scenery of the Purcell Mountains, including huge, jagged Mount Nelson, is spectacular.

Located only 20 minutes from the town of Invermere on Lake Windermere, it's the climax of a scenic drive up Toby Creek Road. All services are within walking distance, so if you're driving, just park your auto underground and enjoy your vacation. Choose from 350 comfortable hotel rooms, condos, or suites just a few steps from the slopes.

The very impressive 3,800-foot vertical splits up into 33 well-designed runs served by eight lifts. The state-of-the-art snowmaking system assures you of an extra snow base. Panorama boasts the highest-serviced vertical in the Rockies, complemented by great fall-line trails without the uneven side slopes common to many ski areas.

In 1989, Panorama installed Quadzilla, a high-speed detachable quad that starts at the base lodge. In just 4 minutes, the lift gets you to the top of the mountain.

A champagne T-bar at the top of the mountain takes you to the top of ski runs up to 5.5 km long. It's an ideal family ski area with 82 percent of the runs rated as novice and intermediate, leaving 18 percent for expert runs as a challenge to any ski adventurer.

One thing that makes Panorama even more unique is its heli-skiing package, which offers an easy-paced program with an on-hill prep course, heli-skiing in Purcell Mountains with the instructor and guide, and a hearty lunch. Intermediates are welcome. This is an extraordinary opportunity to try powder heli-skiing a bit at a time.

Panorama's (CSIA) qualified ski school will enhance your vacation with group, private, and multi-day lesson packages. The popular Ski Week program features video, 6 hours of group lessons, fun race, and social activities. Other packages without lessons are available and you can also enjoy cross-country skiing on 20 km of groomed trails. Equipment rentals and lessons are available.

Practical Information for Panorama

HOW TO GET THERE. Panorama is 120 km from Cranbrook and 297 km from Calgary.

By air. *Canadian Airlines International* and *Air Canada* fly to Cranbrook from Vancouver and Calgary. All connections to other airlines can be made in Vancouver and Calgary. For a complete list of **car rental** agencies in Calgary and Cranbrook, see *How To Get There* for Fairmont Hot Springs, above.

By bus. Originating from Cranbrook, Calgary, and Vancouver, *Greyhound Bus Lines,* 344–6172, stops in Invermere daily. Panorama has its own private pickup to take guests to and from the depot. Roundtrip from Cranbrook costs $13; from Calgary, $11; from Vancouver, $60.

By car. The routes are well maintained, paved, and easy to follow. Traveling from Calgary, follow Hwy. 1 to Hwy. 93 south. Hwy. 93 is a 2½-hour scenic drive to Invermere. From Vancouver, take Hwy. 1 to Golden and Hwy. 95 south to Inveremere. This route takes approximately 10 hours.

TELEPHONES. The area code for all British Columbia is 604.

ACCOMMODATIONS. A central reservation office at Panorama handles all the 350 condo and hotel units conveniently located at the base of the resort. Contact *Central Reservations,* Panorama Resort, Box 7000, Invermere BC V0A 1K0; 342–6941.

All rates can be considered *Moderate,* with prices ranging from $175 for a 3-day package to $275 for five days, based on double occupancy. Prices include accommodations, skiing, sleigh ride, and social programs.

Horsethief Lodge. This facility consists of 195 comfortable 1-, 2-, and 3-bedroom condominiums with fireplaces, full kitchens, and balconies or patios. Some units have lofts. Underground parking, outdoor hot tubs, and saunas are all featured.

Pine Inn. This establishment offers 102 varied rooms. Some have lofts and balconies. There are also executive suites, convention facilities, exercise room, and hot tub.

Toby Creek Lodge. There are 60 studios, 1-, and 2-bedroom condominiums, all of them spacious and some with lofts. Each offers a fireplace and full kitchen, balcony, or patio. In addition, Toby Creek has 24 hotel rooms with underground parking. The hot tubs are outdoor as well as indoor with sauna.

Vacation Villa Condominiums. This is a variety of luxurious "interval ownership" condos complete with quality furnishings and full kitchens. Available for purchase; phone Vacation Villa office, 343–6941, ext. 363.

RESTAURANTS. At the base of the mountain, you'll find two fine restaurants and five lounges and bars which also serve food. All can be contacted through the resort's main phone, 342–6941, and all accept major credit cards. No reservations are needed. In this area, consider an *Expensive* meal for one person to cost $15–$20; *Moderate,* $10–$15; *Inexpensive,* less than $10.

Paradise Dining Room and Lounge. *Expensive.* In Toby Creek Lodge. Fine cuisine served by a lovely stone fireplace in the lounge or by candlelight in the dining room.

Starbird Dining Room and Lounge. *Moderate.* In Pine Inn. Serves 3 meals from a location overlooking the ski hill.

Glacier Deck. *Inexpensive.* In Pine Inn. Outdoor service includes snacks and drinks.

Glacier Pub. *Inexpensive.* In Pine Inn. Standard pub fare, but gets hopping in the evenings.

Inn at the Beginning. *Inexpensive.* In day lodge at base of the lifts. Cafeteria-style service and drinks.

Strathcona Patio. *Inexpensive.* Located above Horsethief Lodge reception area. Full-service and self-service outdoor barbecues for private use and groups.

Strathcona Pub. *Inexpensive.* English-style atmosphere, down to the ales and dart games.

If the skier ventures to Invermere, 32 km away, some delightful dining facilities can be found. In the *Expensive* range are the *Black Forest,* 342–9417, which provides authentic Bavarian atmosphere and decor, and *Strands Restaurant,* 342–6344, a charming older village home setting with superb cuisine for dinners only. On the *Moderate* side are the *Greenery,* 342–9246, for standard fare, and *Lakeside Inn,* 342–6711, which specializes in fish and chips.

HOW TO GET AROUND. Once you arrive at Panorama, wheels won't be needed, for all services and ski lifts are within walking distance of accommodations. However, if you wish to travel to, say, Invermere, a **car** is necessary.

SEASONAL EVENTS. In **December** and **January,** the area hosts *Ski-Pro* and *Ski-Patrol workshops* for intense ski improvement enthusiasts. Each **February** Panorama hosts the *Women's Ski, Fitness, and Health Week* designed for women only. It includes lessons, fitness classes, manicure, pedicure, massage, and more. Panorama also hosts the *Citizen's Downhill,* a recreational race for amateurs.

OTHER SPORTS AND ACTIVITIES. **Horseback rides** are available through *Hopeful Creek Stables,* situated right at the resort. A nice relaxing ride through the Purcell Mountains on a crisp winter day is a unique and enjoyable experience. The **skating** rink invites you to try another alternative to skiing. Skate at day or at night under the lights. Lively games of **broomball** are common among guests. If you've never had a professional **massage,** here's your chance to ease those well-used muscles. A registered massage therapist is always on call. Another way to relax is by visiting nearby **hot pools** only 40 minutes away at *Radium Hot Springs* with temperatures of 27–41°C; open year-round. For information on these and other activities, contact the main office, 342–6941.

CHILDREN'S ACTIVITIES. The *Kiddies Korral Child Care* service is provided for $3.50 per hour with snacks. A hot lunch costs $3.50 extra. The services require an 18-month minimum age; however, baby-sitters can usually be arranged for younger ones. All skiing programs, which are set up for 3–5 year-olds, 6–9 year-olds, and 10 years and up, are priced $30 per day with lunch and snacks.

Teens will enjoy the *Activities Center and Arcade.* Children 8 and under ski free; juniors (9–14) ski for at a reduced rate.

NIGHTLIFE. Skiers at Panorama tend to spend their evenings at the resort, for the restaurants and pubs listed above offer pleasant après-ski activities. The *Glacier Pub* is of particular interest, since it features dancing either to live music or a "DJ extraordinaire." Otherwise, skiers spend the evening relaxing by a fireplace or playing darts or shuffleboard.

POWDER KING SKI VILLAGE

Box 2405
MacKenzie BC V0J 2C0
Tel: 604–561–1776

Snow Report: 604–561–1776
Area Vertical: 2,100 ft.
Number of Trails: 18 on 145 acres
Lifts: 1 triple chair, 2 T-bars, 1 handle-tow
Snowmaking: none
Season: November 15–April 30

Powder King was named Azu Mountain prior to its last face-lift. It is situated in big-time lumber and sawmill country midway between Dawson Creek and Prince George BC. Although the alpine mountain resort is only some 17 years old, skiers have been ski touring its flanks long before lifts were installed, attracted by the abundance of powder snow.

It's a fairly remote area where once the only real action was Tumbler Ridge Mining. Nowadays, Powder King even has its own on-site accommodations at the base of its slopes with a tavern, disco, and large video screen.

The base facilities provide a casual atmosphere, with a licensed cafeteria and tavern. There is a rental shop to outfit you in *Salomon* equipment. The retail gift shop offers accessories and souvenirs. Lessons are available through a CSIA-certified ski school.

The view is of the majestic Northern Rocky Mountain Range and their snowcapped peaks. And yes, there's plenty of snow. With an average annual snowfall of 495 inches, the Powder King name is indeed suitable. While experts frolic in the powder, groomed runs please both intermediate and novice skiers. The longest run is 8,690 feet stretching out the mountain's respectable 2100-foot vertical.

Seven of the 18 runs are easy cruising intermediate. The expert runs keep even the best working at each turn. Many of the runs are named after Beatles' songs—novice runs such as "Strawberry Fields," "Penny Lane," and "Ob-La-Di, Ob-La-Da." Try the intermediate "Let It Be" or "No. 9."

Practical Information for Powder King

HOW TO GET THERE. Powder King is located 203 km north of Prince George BC along John Hart River Highway (Hwy. 97).

By air. *Time Air* and *Air BC* fly into Prince George from Vancouver, where connections are made from major Canadian and American airlines. A **car** can be rented at Prince George Airport from *Tilden,* (604) 963–7474.

By bus. *Greyhound Bus Lines* has transportation to and from Powder King at Azu Village, near the base of the slopes. For information and schedules from Prince George, call (604) 564–5454.

By car. From Vancouver, take Hwy. 1 east and north, connecting with Hwy. 97 near Ashcroft into Prince George, which is 787 km from Vancouver. Continue northward on Hwy. 97 for 203 km to Dawson Creek and 203 km eastward to Powder King.

TELEPHONES. The area code for all British Columbia is 604.

ACCOMMODATIONS. Since Powder King is so remote, most visitors prefer to stay at the self-contained ski resort. Powder King recently built a 55-room modular complex at the base of the lift to complement its **Village Beds Resort Hotel.** For reservations at either, contact Powder King Resort, Box 2405, MacKenzie BC; 561–1776. Rates are considered *Inexpensive,* starting at $30 per person, double occupancy, on weekdays and $40 on weekends. Packages for multi-day or groups are also available. Children 12 years old and under are free, if staying with parents in their room.

RESTAURANTS. Because of its seclusion, the Powder King Resort offers only one dining area. It seems sufficient, however, to suit the demand. Prices are very reasonable for full meals, as low as $5–$6 per plate. It serves good steak. The base facilities include the renovated **Azu Mountain Cafe** and a bar. Both services offer a lovely view and friendly staff.

SEASONAL EVENTS. Powder King has an exciting lineup of activities that kick off with a *Challenge Santa Race* and *New Year's Eve Bash.* Every Sunday the *Pine Pass Ski Club* fun race is open to all abilities and ages. Every Wednesday is *Ladies Day.* **February** hosts a summer bash and boogie and a *Family Day.* The annual *Powder 8* contest is featured in February as well. Other events include triple slaloms, costume classics, Easter egg hunts, celebrity sweeps, and a suitcase race.

CHILDREN'S ACTIVITIES. The resort's *Powderpups Playroom* program offers daily babysitting for children 2 years old and up. Reservations are encouraged at the main office, 561–1776. For children old enough to ski, the program provides lessons and equipment as well as fun-in-the-snow. The age limit is 7 years. For older children, there are a number of green runs served by the resort's platter lift. Penny Lane is a run that is easy to get to off the base's triple chair.

RED MOUNTAIN SKI AREA

Box 939
Rossland BC V0G 1Y0
Tel: 604–362–7384

Snow Report: 604–362–5500
Area Vertical: 2,800 ft.
Number of Trails: 30 on over 600
  skiable acres
Lifts: 1 triple chair, 2 double chairs,
  1 T-bar
Snowmaking: none
Season: November 15–April 15

Red Mountain is known for its powder snow and challenging slopes. Located only 3 km from the heritage village of Rossland, "Big" Red is a low-profile world-class ski area waiting to be discovered.

The town of Rossland was settled in 1896 at one of the richest gold strikes in Canadian history. The hard-rock miners who flocked here were captivated by the region's ski terrain. Scandinavian ski champions set world records here in downhill, cross-country, and jumping half a century before modern ski lifts were installed.

The Rossland Ski Club, which developed skiing in the area, was founded in 1898 by a fellow named Olaus Jildness. As a means of keeping the miners around a little longer, skiing became a major recreational activity. A blend of Portuguese, Polish, Italian, and other nationalities matured into a down-to-earth community with some of the best "unknown" skiing in North America.

Alpine skiing began at Red Mountain with the installation of a single chair lift in 1947; since then, development has expanded skiing terrain to two mountains on three distinct slopes with plenty of tree skiing. Granite is the largest and most recently developed of the two mountains, and Red Mountain is as steep as they come.

Red Mountain is serviced by a high-capacity double chair and a T-bar. Its 1,420 vertical feet offers some of the most challenging skiing as well as wide-open intermediate and novice trails. A majority of these trails are lit for night skiing.

The adjacent Granite Mountain is a big-shouldered, two-faced hulk with 2,800 vertical feet of varied skiing. The longest run is 7 km, winding around the numerous meadows, glades, and powder fields. The Paradise side of this mountain is 1,200 vertical feet with a triple chair servicing mostly intermediate skiing in tree-lined, protected, rolling alpine meadows.

Cruising runs like Southern Comfort and Southern Belle are a treat on the Paradise side. Buffalo Ridge and Papoose Bowl take skiers down the other side of Granite into a void of bowls and bumps or in the direction of cruising runs like Mountain Chief. Ninety percent of Red Mountain Ski Area is intermediate or expert, which is a perfect match for the deep snow. And because Red Mountain does not get the major destination skiers, it always seems to have a powder run that's untouched.

Cross-country skiing is available by taking Granite lift to skiable terrain. Over 20 km of well-maintained trails are located nearby.

The Red Mountain Ski Shop located at the area provides equipment rentals or purchases. There's a cafeteria and a licensed lounge as well at the base. Lodging is located at the mountain and a few minutes away in Rossland.

Practical Information for Red Mountain

HOW TO GET THERE. Red Mountain is on Hwy. 38 in south-central British Columbia, about 630 km east of Vancouver and 210 km north of Spokane WA.

By air. Daily flights from Vancouver on *Canadian Airlines International,* make one stop on the way to Castlegar, taking about 1 hour and 45 minutes. Flights from Calgary on *Time Air* take about 30 minutes. At the Castlegar airport *Sandy's Bus Line,* (604) 368–5555, meets all flights and shuttles you to Trail, where you can taxi the last 8 km to the area. Many of the hotels have a pickup service; check when you make reservations. Calgary and Vancouver are served by major airlines including *Air Canada* from most Canadian and U.S. cities. Flying into Spokane is a good alternative for U.S. visitors.

Car rentals are available at Castlegar Airport from *Budget,* (604) 363–5733 or toll-free 800–527–0700 in the United States and 800–268–8900 in Canada.

By bus. *Spokane Trail Van Lines,* (509) 624–5251, provides service Monday through Friday from Spokane to Trail. *Greyhound,* (604) 368–5733, buses come through Rossland daily from Calgary or Vancouver regions.

By car. Driving time along Hwy. 38 is 8 hours from Calgary or Vancouver.

TELEPHONES. The area code for all British Columbia is 604. For Spokane it is 509.

ACCOMMODATIONS. A good variety of lodgings is available, including moderately priced motels (many with kitchen facilities), cabins, chalets, European-style inns, and modern full-service hotels. For central reservations call 362–7700 or write Box 939, Rossland BC, V0G 1Y0. Based on double occupancy, *Expensive* accommodations are over $70; *Moderate,* $40–$70; and *Inexpensive,* less than $40.

On-Mountain

Ram's Head Inn. *Expensive.* Box 636; 362–9577. This charming inn is right at the base of Red Mountain and has an outdoor hot tub nestled in a cedar woods. Also has telephones, sauna, and licensed facilities.

Red Mountain Resort Motel. *Moderate.* Box 816; 362–9000. Has cabins and approximately 30 rooms.

Red Shutter Inn. *Moderate.* Red Mountain Rd.; 362–5131. This is a quaint 8-room inn within walking distance of the mountain.

Rossland

Uplander Hotel. *Moderate.* 1919 Columbia Ave.; 362–7375. Telephones, television, kitchenettes, sauna/whirlpool, and licensed facilities.

Rossland Motel. *Inexpensive.* Cascade St.; 362–7218. Has 20 comfortable rooms with telephones.

Scotsman Motel. *Inexpensive.* Box 1527; 263–7364. Has 35 rooms with telephone. Kitchenettes available.

For a unique lodging experience try one of a number of low-cost bed-and-breakfasts in the area; call for directions and costs. *Angela's B&B,* 362–7790; *Carolyn's B&B,* 362–5590; *Happy Valley B&B,* 362–7104; *Heritage Hill B&B,* 362–9697; *Tinkers Hatch B&B,* 362–5905.

RESTAURANTS. Skiers at Red Mountain generally take their meals in the hotel or inn at which they are staying. The resort, however, sees to it that skiers don't go hungry. In the base lodge, 362–7384, the **Rafter Lounge and Cafeteria** provides breakfasts and lunches. In town, *Moderate* ($8–$13) homemade dinners are served at the **Red Mountain Resort Hotel** as well as in the **Louis Blue Room** and the **Powder Keg** Pub, both in the Uplander Hotel. Nearby on Columbia Ave., the **Sunshine Cafe,** 362–7630, serves *Inexpensive* ($8 and under) breakfasts, lunches, and dinners.

HOW TO GET AROUND. A **car** is a necessity at this small resort. Shuttle transportation is available to and from the mountain from the Uplander Hotel on special request; 362–7375. Check if your hotel provides shuttle service to and from the mountain.

OTHER SPORTS AND ACTIVITIES. There's **cross-country** skiing, at Red, 362–9611. **Ice skating** is at the *Rossland Civic Arena,* 362–5344. Other events include regularly scheduled amateur races and the regularly held Adult Racing League's competitions on weekends.

CHILDREN'S ACTIVITIES. Day care for children 18 months to 6 years old is located at the base of the mountain. The hours are 10 A.M. to 3:30 P.M. Contact ski school office, 362–7384.

NIGHTLIFE. Après-ski activities traditionally begin in the base lodge at the *Rafter Lounge and Cafeteria.* In town, it's generally a laid-back atmosphere at lounges or bars in the hotels. The *Powder Keg Pub,* however, in the Uplander Hotel, does swing a bit to live music.

SILVER STAR MOUNTAIN

Box 7000
Vernon BC V1T 8X5
Tel: 604–542–0224

Snow Report: 604–542–0224
Area Vertical: 1,600 ft.
Number of Trails: 35 on 300 acres
Lifts: 1 quad, 3 double chairs, 3 T-bars, 1
*   handle tow*
Snowmaking: none

Season: mid-November–late April

This Okanagan Mountain resort prides itself on its excellent snow conditions and its recent dramatic improvements in base facilities. When it comes to convenience and powder, Silver Star has got it all.

Named for a local turn-of-the-century silver mine, Silver Star presents old-fashioned quality and affordability. The on-mountain development is built in the tradition of the 1890s gaslight theme, including three hotels, a saloon, chapel, ski shop, and other facilities. It has come a long way since its first primitive poma back in 1959, which, although slow moving, opened up the silky smooth powder.

It's typical Okanagan feather-light snow that draws the still surprisingly small crowds. Short lift lines are another benefit.

Situated high on a southern plateau above the city of Vernon, 22 km down in the valley, the snow blankets Silver Star early in November and stays late, making a long, reliable season. The climate is ideal with lots of sunshine and an average winter temperature of -5°C. The Silver Star management even offers a money-back guarantee on their snow!

Silver Star, although predominantly an intermediate mountain, offers challenges even to experts. The eight lifts are accessible from each hotel with just a "click" into the skis.

You can choose from 35 well-groomed trails on moderately rolling slopes up to 2 miles in length. Steep verticals such as the Chute and Suicide are ideal for high performance skiing. The intermediate runs are great cruisers.

The ski school is good and specializes in ski week lessons. Rental equipment is available. The special instruction ski weeks offer something extra in après-ski activities such as wine and cheese reception, equipment workshops, movies, sleigh rides, and more.

Night skiing is a real bonus at Silver Star. If you haven't had enough during the day, go make some turns under the lights. Skiing at night feels different and is enjoyable.

The 500-seat Town Hall serves as the day lodge (evenings too) with full cafeteria services, snack bar, and playroom. The après-ski life is plentiful in the saloon, pubs, or the Wine Cellar.

Silver Star also features very well-developed nordic trails. Deep snow on well-groomed tracks makes for great gliding, November through April. A wide variety of trails are suited for all levels of nordic skiers ranging from short loops to all-day treks into the nearby Provincial Park. Night cross-country skiing is also available on a 4-km loop.

Practical Information for Silver Star

HOW TO GET THERE. Located in the mild Okanagen Valley region of British Columbia, Silver Star is relatively easy to reach. It's a scenic 22 km east of Vernon.

By air. *Canadian Airlines International* provides daily flights to Kelowna Airport from Calgary and Vancouver, which are both served by airlines from most major North American cities.

Car rentals are available at the Kelowna/Vernon Airport from *Budget,* (604) 860–2464, in the U.S. 800–527–0700, or in Canada, 800–268–8900; *Hertz,* (604) 860–7808, in the U.S. 800–654–3131, or in Canada 800–263–0600; *Tilden,* (604) 860–2464, in the U.S. 800–227–7368 (*National*), or in Canada 800–387–4747.

Time Air, 800–552–8007, flies in via Lethbridge AB, and Vancouver. Ground transportation to the mountain via airport bus is available at the airport.

By bus. *Greyhound Bus Lines,* provides transportation from both Vancouver and Calgary. Greyhound also provides service from Prince George BC and Edmonton AB.

By car. Silver Star is approached from both Calgary and Vancouver via Hwy. 1, from which Hwy. 97 leads into Vernon. From Seattle, US 5 leads directly into Vancouver, but, weather permitting, many miles can be lopped off the trip by turning off US 5 onto Rte. 542 at Bellingham, WA, then onto Rte. 9 north connecting with Hwy. 1 at Abbotsford BC.

TELEPHONES. The area code for all British Columbia is 604.

ACCOMMODATIONS. With the resort offering six lodging choices with over 650 beds most skiers stay at lodgings at the base. To make reservations, contact the *Silver Star Mountain Resorts,* Box 7000, Vernon BC, V1T 8X5; phone 542–0224 or 800–663–4431 in western Canada; Ski Can at 800–268–8880 in eastern Canada; Ski Pak at 800–562–2262 in Washington. Lodging rates are based on double occupancy. *Expensive,* $80 and up; *Moderate,* $45–$80; *Inexpensive,* $20–$45.

Silver Star

Putnam Station. *Moderate to Expensive;* 542–2459. Offers ski-week packages of 5 days and 5 nights as well as ski-weekend packages of 2 days. All the amenities of a resort hotel.

Kickwillie Inn. *Moderate;* 542–4548. Has a great view of the mountains, with 7 suites featuring full-size kitchens. Private entries, outside lockers, and some lofts for additional sleeping bags for more economical stay.

Silver Lode Inn. *Moderate;* 549–5105. Introduces a new flavor to the resort with 20 traditional European-style rooms, dining room, and lounge. The inn's home country Swiss cuisine is a delight. Package rates also available.

Vance Creek Hotel. *Moderate;* 549–5159. Located in the heart of the village, it offers 22 inn-style rooms and 8 fully contained suites; complete dining and lounge facilities, plus the Okanagan Valley Cellars with an array of local cheeses. Package rates also available.

Prospector Hotel. *Inexpensive to Moderate;* 542–2459. In center of the village, it features budget prices for 50 rooms with twin beds and shared washroom facilities.

The Pinnacles. *Inexpensive;* 542–4548. An alternative to conventional lodging, offers low-cost bed-and-breakfast accommodations.

Vernon

Village Green Inn. *Moderate to Expensive.* 4801 27th St.; 542–3321. Has 140 well-appointed rooms and suites; indoor swimming pool, Jacuzzi, sauna, and game rooms. Within 30 minutes of the slopes.

Sandman Motor Inn. *Moderate.* 4201 Third St.; 542–4325. Features color TV, sauna, whirlpool, and swimming pool. Has 70 rooms; less than 40 minutes' drive to the mountain.

Vernon Lodge Hotel. *Moderate.* 3914 Third St.; 545–3385. Neat place with 130 rooms, color TV, sauna, whirlpool, swimming pool. Thirty minutes from Silver Star.

RESTAURANTS. A visitor to this resort would be hard-pressed to spend more than $20 for a full-course dinner, exclusive of beverage and tips: *Expensive,* over $20; *Moderate,* $10–$20; *Inexpensive,* less than $10. All of the dining facilities in the compact Silver Star Mountain Village serves moderately priced meals, including the dining rooms at Prospector Hotel, Putnam Station, Silver Lode Inn, and Vance Creek Hotel. Prospector Hotel features Mexican specialties, and Silver Lode Inn has Swiss-style cuisine. All serve breakfast, lunch, and dinner, and all accept major credit cards. Phone 542–0224 for all. The lodgings also feature inexpensive cafeteria-style meals as well as coffee shops.

Two *Expensive* restaurants are located in lodges in Vernon: **Hy's Restaurant** at the Village Green Inn, 4801 27th St. (542–3321), and the dining room at **Vernon**

Lodge, 3914 Third St. (545–3385). Both serve lunch and dinner; reservations recommended for dinner.

HOW TO GET AROUND. Everything is within walking—or skiing—distance in this tiny mountain village, but to travel to Vernon or other nearby towns, it is necessary to have a **car.**

SEASONAL EVENTS. Recreational downhill racing is popular in western Canada and this is where it all started, with the *Over-The-Hill Downhill* every second weekend in **February.** Forty teams or so each with four racers, including one female and one person over 35, compete for the best combined time. The competition became secondary to the excitement of the event itself. The *Annual Vernon Winter Carnival* in **mid-February** is an active time in the area as a whole range of winter activities are highlighted. During the second weekend in **April,** the *Funner Daze* event takes place. It's a costume fun day with barbecue, race events, prizes, and decoration themes at each store, hotel, and restaurant.

CHILDREN'S ACTIVITIES. A program called *Kids Country* coordinates all youngsters' activities at the resort's main offices; call 542–0224. Baby-sitting services are available through reservations. For tots there's a playroom complete with expert child care. The *Stardusters* program combines ski instruction and playroom activities for children 3–8 years old. The ski slopes are wide and suitable for children. Special après-ski activities for kids include games, movies, and poolside fun.

NIGHTLIFE. With seating for 200, the *Vance Creek Saloon* in the mountain village provides live entertainment guaranteed to fill the dance floor. For a quieter, more intimate atmosphere, the *Okanagan Wine Cellar,* also in the village, offers rustic warmth by the fireplace. Each Mountain Village hotel features charming lounges with relaxing atmospheres. Even the *Bunkhouse* has its own 60-seat pub lounge. All are within walking (or skiing) distance of each other; 542–0224.

WHISTLER SKI AREA

Box 67
Whistler BC V0N 1B0
Tel: 604–932–3434

Snow Report: 604–932–4191
Area Vertical: 5,006 ft.
Number of Trails: 96 marked trails on more
    than 800 acres
Lifts: 1 four-passenger gondola, 1 ten-
    passenger gondola, 1 high-speed quad,
    3 triple chairs, 5 double chairs, 2
    T-bars, 1 platter pull, 2 handle tows
Snowmaking: 5 percent of area
Season: November–May

BLACKCOMB SKI AREA

Box 98
Whistler BC V0N 1B0
Tel: 604–932–3141

Snow Report: 604–932–4211
Area Vertical: 5,280 ft.
Number of Trails: 85 marked trails on
    1,100 acres
Lifts: 4 high-speed quads (one covered), 5
    triple chairs, 1 double chair, 2 T-bars,
    1 handle tow
Snowmaking: 28 percent of area
Season: November–May and year-round on
    summit glaciers

Just 120 km northeast of Vancouver is the town of Whistler, a four-season international resort area that has been ranked the number one resort in North America by several ski magazines. Located at the base of Whistler and Blackcomb mountains, Whistler Village is a unique European-style center featuring luxurious condominiums, gourmet restaurants, many shops, and an exciting nightlife. The lifts sit side-by-side, reaching out of the village and joining the two giant ski slopes and their 181 marked and groomed runs. Until recently, Whistler Mountain boasted the highest vertical drop in North America at 5,006 feet. Now Blackcomb, with the addition of its Seventh Heaven Express quad chair, has tripled its *own* ski terrain and raised its vertical to an incredible 5,280 feet. Small wonder that they call it the "mile-high mountain."

The Whistler-Blackcomb ski resort has a reputation for snow—lots of it. An incredible 1,140 cm (450 in.) falls annually. The ease of edging skis into this soft, thick pack makes even the novice look good. The two mountains have unique ski terrain. Blackcomb is wide-open fall-line skiing, while Whistler has a lot of narrow tree runs and chutes that wind around the mountain. What makes a Whistler experience so exciting is the fact that the two mountains have such different and varying terrain.

Whistler is called "Skier's Mountain" or "Big Old Softie." It's been a favorite of diehard skiers for many years. The top opens up into a wide choice of open bowls and exciting trails. Many keen skiers traverse across the upper snowfields in search of fresher powder routes. Mogul fields like "Chunky's Choice" seem to go on forever and challenge any steel-legged expert. Nicely groomed intermediate runs such as "Porcupine" and "Franz's Run" are old-time favorites for many loyalists. This giant mountain also has novice runs like "Fantastic" and "Foxy Hollow."

In 1988, Whistler Mountain installed an $18 million, 10-passenger gondola. The Whistler Express runs from the base of the village to the top of the mountain in 18 minutes, a ride that before took 45 minutes. The new lift also helps skiers keep dry in the snowy conditions that often hit the area for days at a time. Blackcomb Mountain represents super-long fall-line runs with an abundance of snow. Beginning at the top, the vast bowls above tree line served by the Seventh Heaven Express quad chair provide skiers with steep chutes or wide-open intermediate terrain. This terrain is named "Seventh Heaven" and adds 22 runs.

These trails feed down into the other well designed slopes like "Jersey Cream" and "Cougar's Milk." Most of the upper mountain below the bowls is well-groomed intermediate terrain with popular trails like "Springboard" and "Cruiser." Some of the expert runs like "Cat Skinner" and "Gear Jammer" test even the best of skiing skills. Novice runs on the lower double chair are easy to get to.

The Mountain Snow Hosts offer directions, general information, and free guided tours. They are found at the Skier Service Centers in the Carleton (lower) and Rendezvous lodges and the Summit restaurant. On-mountain picnics are also available for small groups served up by the Snow Hosts.

The village is a first-class resort with emphasis on quality. It has been called a "flowing" village because of its pedestrian orientation, light and shadowing, and view corridors. The architectural style maintains harmony with its natural environment, including the two flanking ski areas.

Practical Information for Whistler-Blackcomb

HOW TO GET THERE. By air. Fly to Vancouver International Airport via most major airlines including *Air Canada, Canadian Airlines,* and *United.* Connections with most other major airlines is through Seattle, a half-hour flight away.

Car rentals are available at Vancouver airport. Phone *Avis,* 604–273–4577 or toll-free 800–331–1212 in the U.S. and 800–268–2310 in Canada; *Budget,* 604–278–3994 or toll-free 800–527–0700 in the United States and 800–268–8900 in Canada; *Hertz,* 604–278–3051 or toll-free 800–654–3131 in the United States and 800–263–0600 in Canada; and *Tilden,* 604–273–3121 or toll-free 800–227–7638 in the United States and 800–387–4747 in Canada.

By bus. *Maverick Coach Lines,* (604) 255–1171, runs daily service from the main depot on Dunsmuir St. in Vancouver with transfers available from *Greyhound Bus Lines* servicing most Canadian cities. There are 3 departures daily to Whistler. *Perimeter Transportation,* (604) 273–0071, offers service directly from the airport to Whistler.

By train. *British Columbia Rail* has a weekend ski train from North Vancouver. Phone (604) 984–5213 for rates and schedule information.

By car. Driving into Whistler-Blackcomb is an adventure in itself. Hwy. 99 north from Vancouver, called the "Sea-to-Sky Highway," takes you on a dazzling 120-km ride along fjord-like Howe Sound along the west coast of British Columbia. It's breathtaking scenery on a clear day. The drive from Vancouver takes about 1½ hours. From Seattle, it's a 4½-hour drive along I–5, which leads into Hwy. 99 at Vancouver.

TELEPHONES. The area code for all British Columbia is 604.

ACCOMMODATIONS. Whistler-Blackcomb has all types of accommodations ranging from luxury condos to hotels and pensions. There are amenities of every kind: saunas, Jacuzzis, lounges and bars, conference center, shops, liquor store, pharmacy, and even a bank. Price ranges are: *Expensive,* $110 and up per night; *Moderate,* $75–$110; *Inexpensive,* $50–$75; based on double occupancy. For central reservations phone 932–4222, or write *Whistler Resort Association,* Box 1400, Whistler BC, VON 1BO. All hotels are located in the village or very close by in the valley.

Expensive

Blackcomb Lodge. 932–4155. Has 72 studios, some with lofts; saunas, Jacuzzi, fireplaces.

Chateau Whistler Resort. 938–8000 or 800–268–9420 in the U.S., 800–268–9411 in Canada. A true world-class hotel to match the world-class skiing. This 250-room hotel opened in 1990 and was built in the tradition of other grand resorts: the Empress in Victoria, the Banff Springs Hotel, and Chateau Lake Louise. Located slopeside in the new Village North Center, the hotel features a health club with an indoor-outdoor pool, indoor-outdoor whirlpools, massages, saunas, steam rooms, exercise room, and professionally trained attendants. Rooms have such amenities as 2-line telephones and in-house movie service, plus 3 restaurants and 2 bars (see *Restaurants*).

Delta Mountain Inn. 800–268–1133. A large 161-unit hotel. Sauna, Jacuzzi, fireplaces, and kitchenettes.

Mountainside Lodge. 932–4511. Has 89 studio rooms, sauna, Jacuzzi, fireplaces, and kitchenettes.

Moderate

Carleton Lodge. 932–4183. Has 31 units, 1–2 bedrooms with lofts, Jacuzzi, fireplaces, and kitchenettes.

The Fireplace Inn. 932–3200. Has 45 hotel rooms, saunas, fireplaces, and kitchenettes.

Highland Lodge. 932–5525. Has 55 hotel and studio units with sauna, Jacuzzi and kitchens.

Nancy Green's Lodge. 932–2221. Has 137 units with Jacuzzi.

Tantalus Lodge. 932–4146. Has 76 units as 1-bedroom studios or 4-person, 2 bedroom studios with sauna, Jacuzzi, fireplaces and kitchenettes.

Whistler Creek Lodge. 932–4111. Has 43 units, 2-person studios or studios with lofts. Sauna, Jacuzzi, fireplaces, and kitchenettes.

Whistler Village Inn. 932–4004. Has 88 hotel and studio units with saunas, Jacuzzi, fireplaces, and kitchenettes.

Inexpensive

Chalet Luise Pension. 932–4187. A small cozy place with only 4 hotel units, sauna, and fireplace.

Fitzsimmons Creek. 932–3338. Has 45 hotel rooms, saunas, fireplaces, and kitchenettes.

The Vale Inn. 932–5525. Has 62 hotel and studio units, fireplaces, and kitchenettes.

Whistler Resort and Club. 932–5756. Has 42 hotel and studio units, saunas, Jacuzzi, fireplaces, and kitchenettes.

RESTAURANTS. Whistler restaurants cater to a variety of tastes. You'll find steaks served in wood-finished rooms, classic European cuisine in elegant surroundings, charbroiled burgers, and pizza. *Expensive* entrees run from $15 to $24; *Moderate,* $8–$15; *Inexpensive,* $7 and under. All restaurants accept major credit cards unless otherwise noted, and all are in the village with no specific street address. Reserve at each unless specified.

Expensive

Black Forest. 932–4808. Features central European specialties prepared by German chefs—schnitzels, sauerkraut, and veal dishes.

Isabelle's. 932–6611. In the Nancy Greene Lodge. Serves fine Continental cuisine in luxurious decor. Features daily specials, buffet breakfasts, and children's menu. Live entertainment on weekends.

La Fiesta–The Hot Rock Café. 938–8000. In the Chateau Whistler. International restaurant featuring hot and cold tapas with hot rock cooking. Ideal for après-ski or to start off the evening. Seasonal specials and light musical entertainment.

Rim Rock Café and Oyster Bar. 932–5565. Locals call it the best restaurant in Whistler. Serves classic seafood, including lobster and fresh fish. Reservations recommended at this busy spot.

Sushi Village. 932–3330. Japanese and original terriyaki dishes. Intimate sushi bar.

Twigs. 932–1982. Located in the Delta Hotel and serving Canadian cuisine, breakfast, lunch, and dinner; table d'hôte and children's menu.

Wildflower Café. 938–8000. In the Chateau Whistler. Offers all-day dining from country kitchen breakfasts to light and quick lunch-time fare to intimate dining by the fireplace. A spectacular alpine market buffet with Pacific Northwest menu items such as fresh salmon.

Moderate

Araxis. 932–4540. Fresh seafood specialties along with great pasta and an extensive wine and champagne list.

Joël's. 932–2112. French dishes along with raclettes, fondues, and gluwein.

Nasty Jack's. 932–3531. Super breakfasts served early and quickly to get you to the slopes fast. Burgers, pizzas, pastas, and steak are featured for lunch and dinner. Busy après-ski spot as well.

Inexpensive

Keg at Mountain. 932–5151. Steaks, seafood, and pasta plus a great salad bar. Caters to groups. No reservations necessary.

HOW TO GET AROUND. There's a **shuttle bus** between the Whistler gondola, a few miles around the mountain, and the village several times daily beginning at

8 A.M. For schedules, call 932–3928. For those who insist on having wheels, *Budget,* 932–1236, is found in the village.

SEASONAL EVENTS. Recreational race camps are held throughout the season, and a *Women Only Program* takes place in **January** and **February.** The Whistler *Super "G" Top to Bottom Team* race is an exciting annual event each January.

In **February** there's the *Whistler Powder 8* contest, followed by the *McConkey Cup* in **March.** The annual *Saudan Couloir race,* a grueling 3-minute race down a steep chute at Blackcomb, known as one of the toughest extreme races around, is in late **March.**

OTHER SPORTS AND ACTIVITIES. In Whistler Village you'll find **ice skating** on Whistler Lake and hot tubs in most hotels. **Snowmobiling** (932–4086), and **sleigh rides** at *Whistler Outdoor Experience Co.* (932–3389) are also available. An indoor **swimming pool** is located in *Blackcomb Lodge* (932–4155). Go to *Blackcomb Physiotherapy* (932–2395) for a workout or a massage.

Cross-country ski on groomed trails in *Lost Lake Park* near the village. There is a daily user fee; phone 932–3327 for information. Free cross-country is available on other trails close by.

For exciting **heli-skiing** nearby, phone *Whistler Heli-Skiing,* 932–4105 or *Tyax Heli-Skiing,* 932–7007. Prices run $250–$340 per person for 10,000–12,000 vertical feet.

Ski **rentals** and CSIA-certified ski school lessons are available at the base. The Never-Ever ski package is a great deal and includes lift ticket, full equipment rental, and 2-hour lessons, all for $15. **Nordic skiing** is also available. Phone 932–6436.

HINTS TO THE HANDICAPPED. Whistler's program for the handicapped has been curtailed in recent seasons. The resort's racing department, however, still conducts coaching clinics for the disabled and hearing- and sight-impaired. For details, contact the main office at 932–3434 and ask for the racing department.

CHILDREN'S ACTIVITIES. At **Whistler,** the *7-Eleven Wee Patrol Day-Care Center* is located at the gondola base and operates 8 A.M.–5:30 P.M. daily. Lunch vouchers are available. The *Ski Scamps Program* for kids 2½–12 years is a supervision and ski instruction program with morning and afternoon lessons and playtime. Open 9 A.M. to 3:30 P.M. daily. Lunch vouchers are available. Phone 932–3434 to arrange participation in any of these programs.

At **Blackcomb,** the *Kid's Kamp* has as many as 25 instructors supervising and teaching kids to ski. *Kinder Kamp* is for those 3–6 years old and the *Black Busters* handles the 7- to 12-year category. Contact the main office, 932–3141.

NIGHTLIFE. There's an active nightlife in Whistler. For dancing and live bands go to the *Longhorn Pub, Garfinkel's,* or *Buffalo Bills* at the Timberline Lodge. Dancing also takes place in *The Umberto Cabaret* and *Shooters.* Other favorite spots for skiers are *The Brass Rail, Tapley's Pub, Brandy's Lounge,* and *Chez Joël,* where you'll find a mix of relaxing atmosphere and upbeat music. All are within walking distance in the village.

INDEX

Map pages are in **boldface.**

Fodor's Travel Guides

U.S. Guides

Alaska
Arizona
Boston
California
Cape Cod, Martha's
 Vineyard, Nantucket
The Carolinas & the
 Georgia Coast
The Chesapeake
 Region
Chicago
Colorado
Disney World & the
 Orlando Area
Florida
Hawaii

Las Vegas, Reno,
 Tahoe
Los Angeles
Maine, Vermont,
 New Hampshire
Maui
Miami & the
 Keys
National Parks
 of the West
New England
New Mexico
New Orleans
New York City
New York City
 (Pocket Guide)

Pacific North Coast
Philadelphia & the
 Pennsylvania
 Dutch Country
Puerto Rico
 (Pocket Guide)
The Rockies
San Diego
San Francisco
San Francisco
 (Pocket Guide)
The South
Santa Fe, Taos,
 Albuquerque
Seattle &
 Vancouver

Texas
USA
The U. S. & British
 Virgin Islands
The Upper Great
 Lakes Region
Vacations in
 New York State
Vacations on the
 Jersey Shore
Virginia & Maryland
Waikiki
Washington, D.C.
Washington, D.C.
 (Pocket Guide)

Foreign Guides

Acapulco
Amsterdam
Australia
Austria
he Bahamas
e Bahamas
 ocket Guide)
 & Mexico's Pacific
 st Resorts
 dos
 na, Madrid,
 &
 ourg

Cancun, Cozumel,
 Yucatan Peninsula
Caribbean
Central America
China
Czechoslovakia
Eastern Europe
Egypt
Europe
Europe's Great Cities
France
Germany
Great Britain
Greece
The Himalayan
 Countries
Holland
Hong Kong
India
Ireland
Israel
Italy

Italy 's Great Cities
Jamaica
Japan
Kenya, Tanzania,
 Seychelles
Korea
London
London
 (Pocket Guide)
London Companion
Mexico
Mexico City
Montreal &
 Quebec City
Morocco
New Zealand
Norway
Nova Scotia,
 New Brunswick,
 Prince Edward
 Island
Paris

Paris (Pocket Guide)
Portugal
Rome
Scandinavia
Scandinavian Cities
Scotland
Singapore
South America
South Pacific
Southeast Asia
Soviet Union
Spain
Sweden
Switzerland
Sydney
Thailand
Tokyo
Toronto
Turkey
Vienna & the Danube
 Valley
Yugoslavia

urnal Guides to Business Travel

International Cities   Pacific Rim   USA & Canada

Guides

Cruises and Ports
 of Call
Healthy Escapes
Fodor's Flashmaps
New York

Fodor's Flashmaps
 Washington, D.C.
Shopping in Europe
Skiing in the USA &
 Canada

Smart Shopper's
 Guide to London
Sunday in New York
Touring Europe
Touring USA